COMPUTER
ARITHMETIC

The Oxford Series in Electrical and Computer Engineering

Adel S. Sedra, Series Editor

Allen and Holberg, *CMOS Analog Circuit Design, 2nd Edition*
Bobrow, *Elementary Linear Circuit Analysis, 2nd Edition*
Bobrow, *Fundamentals of Electrical Engineering, 2nd Edition*
Burns and Roberts, *An Introduction to Mixed-Signal IC Test and Measurement*
Campbell, *The Science and Engineering of Microelectronic Fabrication, 2nd Edition*
Chen, *Analog & Digital Control System Design*
Chen, *Linear System Theory and Design, 3rd Edition*
Chen, *System and Signal Analysis, 2nd Edition*
Chen, *Digital Signal Processing*
Comer, *Digital Logic and State Machine Design, 3rd Edition*
Cooper and McGillem, *Probabilistic Methods of Signal and System Analysis, 3rd Edition*
DeCarlo and Lin, *Linear Circuit Analysis, 2nd Edition*
Dimitrijev, *Understanding Semiconductor Devices*
Fortney, *Principles of Electronics: Analog & Digital*
Franco, *Electric Circuits Fundamentals*
Granzow, *Digital Transmission Lines*
Guru and Hiziroglu, *Electric Machinery and Transformers, 3rd Edition*
Hoole and Hoole, *A Modern Short Course in Engineering Electromagnetics*
Jones, *Introduction to Optical Fiber Communication Systems*
Krein, *Elements of Power Electronics*
Kuo, *Digital Control Systems, 3rd Edition*
Lathi, *Modern Digital and Analog Communications Systems, 3rd Edition*
Lathi, *Signal Processing and Linear Systems*
Lathi, *Linear Systems and Signals*
Martin, *Digital Integrated Circuit Design*
McGillem and Cooper, *Continuous and Discrete Signal and System Analysis, 3rd Edition*
Miner, *Lines and Electromagnetic Fields for Engineers*
Parhami, *Computer Arithmetic*
Roberts and Sedra, *SPICE, 2nd Edition*
Roulston, *An Introduction to the Physics of Semiconductor Devices*
Sadiku, *Elements of Electromagnetics, 3rd Edition*
Santina, Stubberud and Hostetter, *Digital Control System Design, 2nd Edition*
Sarma, *Introduction to Electrical Engineering*
Schaumann and Van Valkenburg, *Design of Analog Filters*
Schwarz, *Electromagnetics for Engineers*
Schwarz and Oldham, *Electrical Engineering: An Introduction, 2nd Edition*
Sedra and Smith, *Microelectronic Circuits, 4th Edition*
Stefani, Savant, Shahian, and Hostetter, *Design of Feedback Control Systems, 4th Edition*
Van Valkenburg, *Analog Filter Design*
Warner and Grung, *Semiconductor Device Electronics*
Warner and Grung, *MOSFET Theory and Design*
Wolovich, *Automatic Control Systems*
Yariv, *Optical Electronics in Modern Communications, 5th Edition*

COMPUTER ARITHMETIC

Algorithms and Hardware Designs

Behrooz Parhami

Department of Electrical and Computer Engineering
University of California, Santa Barbara

New York   Oxford
OXFORD UNIVERSITY PRESS
2000

Oxford University Press

Oxford   New York
Athens   Auckland   Bangkok   Bogotá   Buenos Aires   Calcutta
Cape Town   Chennai   Dar es Salaam   Delhi   Florence   Hong Kong   Istanbul
Karachi   Kuala Lumpur   Madrid   Melbourne   Mexico City   Mumbai
Nairobi   Paris   São Paulo   Singapore   Taipei   Tokyo   Toronto   Warsaw

and associated companies in
Berlin   Ibadan

Published by Oxford University Press, Inc.
198 Madison Avenue, New York, New York 10016
http://www.oup-usa.org

Library of Congress Cataloging-in-Publication Data

Parhami, Behrooz.
   Computer arithmetic : algorithms and hardware designs / Behrooz Parhami.
     p.   cm.
   Includes bibliographical references and index.
   ISBN 0-19-512583-5 (cloth)
   1. Computer arithmetic.   2. Computer algorithms.   I. Title.
QA76.9.C62P37   1999
004'.01'513—dc21   98-44899
                                                       CIP

Printing (last digit): 9 8 7 6 5 4

Printed in the United States of America
on acid-free paper

To the memory of my father,
Salem Parhami (1922–1992),
and to all others on whom I can count
for added inspiration,
multiplied joy,
and divided anguish.

CONTENTS

PREFACE

THE CONTEXT OF COMPUTER ARITHMETIC

Advances in computer architecture over the past two decades have allowed the performance of digital computer hardware to continue its exponential growth, despite increasing technological difficulty in speed improvement at the circuit level. This phenomenal rate of growth, which is expected to continue in the near future, would not have been possible without theoretical insights, experimental research, and tool-building efforts that have helped transform computer architecture from an art into one of the most quantitative branches of computer science and engineering. Better understanding of the various forms of concurrency and the development of a reasonably efficient and user-friendly programming model have been key enablers of this success story.

The downside of exponentially rising processor performance is an unprecedented increase in hardware and software complexity. The trend toward greater complexity is not only at odds with testability and certifiability but also hampers adaptability, performance tuning, and evaluation of the various trade-offs, all of which contribute to soaring development costs. A key challenge facing current and future computer designers is to reverse this trend by removing layer after layer of complexity, opting instead for clean, robust, and easily certifiable designs, while continuing to try to devise novel methods for gaining performance and ease-of-use benefits from simpler circuits that can be readily adapted to application requirements.

In the computer designers' quest for user-friendliness, compactness, simplicity, high performance, low cost, and low power, computer arithmetic plays a key role. It is one of oldest subfields of computer architecture. The bulk of hardware in early digital computers resided in accumulator and other arithmetic/logic circuits. Thus, first-generation computer designers were motivated to simplify and share hardware to the extent possible and to carry out detailed cost–performance analyses before proposing a design. Many of the ingenious design methods that we use today have their roots in the bulky, power-hungry machines of 30–50 years ago.

In fact computer arithmetic has been so successful that it has, at times, become transparent. Arithmetic circuits are no longer dominant in terms of complexity; registers, memory and memory management, instruction issue logic, and pipeline control have become the dominant consumers of chip area in today's processors. Correctness and high performance of arithmetic circuits is routinely expected, and episodes such as the Intel Pentium division bug are indeed rare.

The preceding context is changing for several reasons. First, at very high clock rates, the interfaces between arithmetic circuits and the rest of the processor become critical. Arithmetic units can no longer be designed and verified in isolation. Rather, an integrated design optimization is required, which makes the development even more complex and costly. Second, optimizing arithmetic circuits to meet design goals by taking advantage of the strengths of new technologies, and making them tolerant to the weaknesses, requires a reexamination of existing design paradigms. Finally, incorporation of higher-level arithmetic primitives into hardware makes the design, optimization, and verification efforts highly complex and interrelated.

This is why computer arithmetic is alive and well today. Designers and researchers in this area produce novel structures with amazing regularity. Carry-lookahead adders comprise a case in point. We used to think, in the not so distant past, that we knew all there was to know about carry-lookahead fast adders. Yet, new designs, improvements, and optimizations are still appearing. The ANSI/IEEE standard floating-point format has removed many of the concerns with compatibility and error control in floating-point computations, thus resulting in new designs and products with mass-market appeal. Given the arithmetic-intensive nature of many novel application areas (such as encryption, error checking, and multimedia), computer arithmetic will continue to thrive for years to come.

THE GOALS AND STRUCTURE OF THIS BOOK

The field of computer arithmetic has matured to the point that a dozen or so texts and reference books have been published. Some of these books that cover computer arithmetic in general (as opposed to special aspects or advanced/unconventional methods) are listed at the end of the preface. Each of these books has its unique strengths and has contributed to the formation and fruition of the field. The current text, *Computer Arithmetic: Algorithms and Hardware Designs*, is an outgrowth of lecture notes the author developed and refined over many years. Here are the most important features of this text in comparison to the listed books:

Division of material into lecture-size chapters. In my approach to teaching, a lecture is a more or less self-contained module with links to past lectures and pointers to what will transpire in future. Each lecture must have a theme or title and must proceed from motivation, to details, to conclusion. In designing the text, I strived to divide the material into chapters, each of which is suitable for one lecture (1–2 hours). A short lecture can cover the first few subsections, while a longer lecture can deal with variations, peripheral ideas, or more advanced material near the end of the chapter. To make the structure hierarchical, as opposed to flat or linear, lectures are grouped into seven parts, each composed of four lectures and covering one aspect of the field (Fig. P.1).

Emphasis on both the underlying theory and actual hardware designs. The ability to cope with complexity requires both a deep knowledge of the theoretical underpinnings of computer arithmetic and examples of designs that help us understand the theory. Such designs also provide building blocks for synthesis as well as reference points for cost–performance comparisons. This viewpoint is reflected in, for example, the detailed coverage of redundant number representations and associated arithmetic algorithms (Chapter 3) that later lead to a better understanding of various multiplier designs and on-line arithmetic. Another example can be found in Chapter 22, where CORDIC algorithms are introduced from the more intuitive geometric viewpoint.

Linking computer arithmetic to other subfields of computing. Computer arithmetic is nourished by, and in turn nourishes, other subfields of computer architecture and technology. Examples of such links abound. The design of carry-lookahead adders became much more systematic once it was realized that the carry computation is a special case of parallel prefix computation that had been extensively studied by researchers in parallel computing. Arithmetic for and by neural networks is an area that is still being

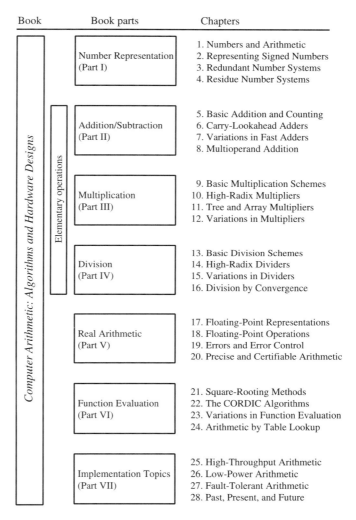

Fig. P.1   The structure of this book in parts and chapters.

explored. The residue number system has provided an invaluable tool for researchers interested in complexity theory and the limits of fast arithmetic, as well as to the designers of fault-tolerant digital systems.

Wide coverage of important topics. The text covers virtually all important algorithmic and hardware design topics in computer arithmetic, thus providing a balanced and complete view of the field. Coverage of unconventional number representation methods (Chapters 3 and 4), arithmetic by table lookup (Chapter 24), which is becoming increasingly important, multiplication and division by constants (Chapters 9 and 13), errors and certifiable arithmetic (Chapters 19 and 20), and the topics in Part VII (Chapters 25–28) do not all appear in other textbooks.

Unified and consistent notation and terminology throughout the text. Every effort is made to use consistent notation and terminology throughout the text. For example, r always stands for the number representation radix and s for the remainder in division or square-rooting. While other authors have done this in the basic parts of their texts, many tend to cover more advanced research topics by simply borrowing the notation and terminology from the reference source. Such an approach has the advantage of making the transition between reading the text and the original reference source easier, but it is utterly confusing to the majority of the students, who rely on the text and do not consult the original references except, perhaps, to write a research paper.

SUMMARY OF TOPICS

The seven parts of this book, each composed of four chapters, were written with the following goals.

Part I sets the stage, gives a taste of what is to come, and provides a detailed perspective on the various ways of representing fixed-point numbers. Included are detailed discussions of signed numbers, redundant representations, and residue number systems.

Part II covers addition and subtraction, which form the most basic arithmetic building blocks and are often used in implementing other arithmetic operations. Included in the discussions are addition of a constant (counting), various methods for designing fast adders, and multioperand addition.

Part III deals exclusively with multiplication, beginning with the basic shift/add algorithms and moving on to high-radix, tree, array, bit-serial, modular, and a variety of other multipliers. The special case of squaring is also discussed.

Part IV covers division algorithms and their hardware implementations, beginning with the basic shift/subtract algorithms and moving on to high-radix, prescaled, modular, array, and convergence dividers.

Part V deals with real number arithmetic, including various methods for representing real numbers, floating-point arithmetic, errors in representation and computation, and methods for high-precision and certifiable arithmetic.

Part VI covers function evaluation, beginning with the important special case of square-rooting and moving on to CORDIC algorithms, followed by general convergence and approximation methods, including the use of lookup tables.

Part VII deals with broad design and implementation topics, including pipelining, low-power arithmetic, and fault tolerance. This part concludes by providing historical perspective and examples of arithmetic units in real computers.

POINTERS ON HOW TO USE THE BOOK

For classroom use, the topics in each chapter of this text can be covered in a lecture lasting 1–2 hours. In my own teaching, I have used the chapters primarily for 1.5-hour lectures, twice a week, in a 10-week quarter, omitting or combining some chapters to fit the material into 18–20 lectures. But the modular structure of the text lends itself to other lecture formats, self-study, or review of the field by practitioners. In the latter two cases, readers can view each chapter as a study unit (for one week, say) rather than as a lecture. Ideally, all topics in each chapter should be covered before the reader moves to the next chapter. However, if fewer lecture hours are available, some of the subsections located at the end of chapters can be omitted or introduced only in terms of motivations and key results.

Problems of varying complexities, from straightforward numerical examples or exercises to more demanding studies or miniprojects, are supplied for each chapter. These problems form an integral part of the book: they were not added as afterthoughts to make the book more attractive for use as a text. A total of 464 problems are included (15–18 per chapter). Assuming that two lectures are given per week, either weekly or biweekly homework can be assigned, with each assignment having the specific coverage of the respective half-part (two chapters) or full-part (four chapters) as its "title."

An instructor's manual, with problem solutions and enlarged versions of the diagrams and tables, suitable for reproduction as transparencies, is planned. The author's detailed syllabus for the course ECE 252B at UCSB is available at:

http://www.ece.ucsb.edu/Faculty/Parhami/ece_252b.htm.

A simulator for numerical experimentation with various arithmetic algorithms is available at:

http://www.ecs.umass.edu/ece/koren/arith/simulator/

courtesy of Professor Israel Koren.

References to classical papers in computer arithmetic, key design ideas, and important state-of-the-art research contributions are listed at the end of each chapter. These references provide good starting points for in-depth studies or for term papers or projects. A large number of classical papers and important contributions in computer arithmetic have been reprinted in two volumes [Swar90].

New ideas in the field of computer arithmetic appear in papers presented at biannual conferences, known as ARITH-n, held in odd-numbered years [Arit]. Other conferences of interest include Asilomar Conference on Signals, Systems, and Computers [Asil], International Conference on Circuits and Systems [ICCS], Midwest Symposium on Circuits and Systems [MSCS], and International Conference on Computer Design [ICCD]. Relevant journals include *IEEE Transactions on Computers* [TrCo], particularly its special issues on computer arithmetic, *IEEE Transactions on Circuits and Systems* [TrCS], *Computers & Mathematics with Applications* [CoMa], *IEE Proceedings: Computers and Digital Techniques* [PrCD], *IEEE Transactions on VLSI Systems* [TrVL], and *Journal of VLSI Signal Processing* [JVSP].

ACKNOWLEDGMENTS

Computer Arithmetic: Algorithms and Hardware Designs is an outgrowth of lecture notes the author used for the graduate course "ECE 252B: Computer Arithmetic" at the University of California, Santa Barbara, and, in rudimentary forms, at several other institutions prior to 1988. The text has benefited greatly from keen observations, curiosity, and encouragement of my many students in these courses. A sincere thanks to all of them!

REFERENCES

[Arit]   International Symposium on Computer Arithmetic, sponsored by the IEEE Computer Society. This series began with a one-day workshop in 1969 and was subsequently held in 1972, 1975, 1978, and in odd-numbered years since 1981. The 15th symposium in the series, ARITH-15, was held on June 11–13, 2001, in Vail, Colorado. ARITH-16 was held June 15–18, 2003, in Santiago de Compostela, Spain.

[Asil]   Asilomar Conference on Signals Systems, and Computers, sponsored annually by IEÉE and held on the Asilomar Conference Grounds in Pacific Grove, California. The 32nd conference in this series was held on November 1–4, 1998.

[Cava84]   Cavanagh, J. J. F., *Digital Computer Arithmetic: Design and Implementation*, McGraw-Hill, 1984.

[CoMa]   *Computers & Mathematics with Applications*, journal published by Pergamon Press.

[Flor63]   Flores, I., *The Logic of Computer Arithmetic*, Prentice-Hall, 1963.

[Gosl80]   Gosling, J. B., *Design of Arithmetic Units for Digital Computers*, Macmillan, 1980.

[Hwan79]   Hwang, K., *Computer Arithmetic: Principles, Architecture, and Design*, Wiley, 1979.

[ICCD]   International Conference on Computer Design, sponsored annually by the IEEE Computer Society. ICCD-98 was held on October 4–7, 1998, in Austin, Texas.

[ICCS]   International Conference on Circuits and Systems, sponsored annually by the IEEE Circuits and Systems Society. The latest in this series was held on May 31–June 3, 1998, in Monterey, California.

[JVSP]   *J. VLSI Signal Processing*, published by Kluwer Academic Publishers.

[Knut97]   Knuth, D. E., *The Art of Computer Programming*, Vol. 2: *Seminumerical Algorithms*, 3rd ed., Addison-Wesley, 1997. (The widely used second edition, published in 1981, is cited in Parts V and VI.)

[Kore93]   Koren, I., *Computer Arithmetic Algorithms*, Prentice-Hall, 1993.

[Kuli81]   Kulisch, U. W., and W. L. Miranker, *Computer Arithmetic in Theory and Practice*, Academic Press, 1981.

[MSCS]   Midwest Symposium on Circuits and Systems, sponsored annually by the IEEE Circuits and Systems Society. This series of symposia began in 1955, with the 41st in the series held on August 9–12, 1998, in Notre Dame, Indiana.

[Omon94]   Omondi, A. R., *Computer Arithmetic Systems: Algorithms, Architecture and Implementations*, Prentice-Hall, 1994.

[PrCD]   *IEE Proc: Computers and Digital Techniques*, journal published by the Institution of Electrical Engineers, United Kingdom.

[Rich55]   Richards, R. K., *Arithmetic Operations in Digital Computers*, Van Nostrand, 1955.

[Scot85]   Scott, N. R., *Computer Number Systems and Arithmetic*, Prentice-Hall, 1985.

[Stei71]   Stein, M. L., and W. D. Munro, *Introduction to Machine Arithmetic*, Addison-Wesley, 1971.

[Swar90]   Swartzlander, E. E., Jr., *Computer Arithmetic*, Vols. I and II, IEEE Computer Society Press, 1990.

[TrCo]   *IEEE Trans. Computers*, journal published by the IEEE Computer Society. Occasionally entire special issues or sections are devoted to computer arithmetic (e.g.: Vol. 19, No. 8, August 1970; Vol. 22, No. 6, June 1973; Vol. 26, No. 7, July 1977; Vol. 32, No. 4, April 1983; Vol. 39, No. 8, August 1990; Vol. 41, No. 8, August 1992; Vol. 43, No. 8, August 1994; Vol. 47, No. 7, July 1998; Vol. 49, No. 7, July 2000).

[TrCS]   *IEEE Trans. Circuits and Systems—II: Analog and Digital Signal Processing*, journal published by IEEE.

[TrVL]   *IEEE Trans. Very Large Scale Integration (VLSI) Systems*, journal published jointly by the IEEE Circuits and Systems Society, Computer Society, and Solid-State Circuits Council.

[Wase82]   Waser, S., and M. J. Flynn, *Introduction to Arithmetic for Digital Systems Designers*, Holt, Rinehart, & Winston, 1982.

[Wino80]   Winograd, S., *Arithmetic Complexity of Computations*, SIAM, 1980.

COMPUTER ARITHMETIC

PART I

NUMBER REPRESENTATION

Number representation is arguably the most important topic in computer arithmetic. In justifying this claim, it suffices to note that several important classes of number representations were discovered, or rescued from obscurity, by computer designers in their quest for simpler and faster circuits. Furthermore, the choice of number representation affects the implementation cost and delay of all arithmetic operations. We thus begin our study of computer arithmetic by reviewing conventional and exotic representation methods for integers. Conventional methods are of course used extensively. Some of the unconventional methods have been applied to special-purpose digital systems or in the intermediate steps of arithmetic hardware implementations where they are often invisible to computer users. This part consists of the following four chapters:

Chapter 1 | NUMBERS AND ARITHMETIC

This chapter motivates the reader, sets the context in which the material in the rest of the book is presented, and reviews positional representations of fixed-point numbers. The chapter ends with a review of methods for number radix conversion and a preview of other number representation methods to be covered. Chapter topics include:

1.1 WHAT IS COMPUTER ARITHMETIC?

A sequence of events, begun in late 1994 and extending into 1995, embarrassed the world's largest computer chip manufacturer and put the normally dry subject of computer arithmetic on the front pages of major newspapers. The events were rooted in the work of Thomas Nicely, a mathematician at the Lynchburg College in Virginia, who is interested in twin primes (consecutive odd numbers such as 29 and 31 that are both prime). Nicely's work involves the distribution of twin primes and, particularly, the sum of their reciprocals $S = 1/5 + 1/7 + 1/11 + 1/13 + 1/17 + 1/19 + 1/29 + 1/31 + \cdots + 1/p + 1/(p+2) + \cdots$. While it is known that the infinite sum S has a finite value, no one knows what the value is.

Nicely was using several different computers for his work and in March 1994 added a machine based on the Intel Pentium processor to his collection. Soon he began noticing inconsistencies in his calculations and was able to trace them back to the values computed for $1/p$ and $1/(p+2)$ on the Pentium processor. At first, he suspected his own programs, the compiler, and the operating system, but by October, he became convinced that the Intel Pentium chip was at fault. This suspicion was confirmed by several other researchers following a barrage of e-mail exchanges and postings on the Internet.

The diagnosis finally came from Tim Coe, an engineer at Vitesse Semiconductor. Coe built a model of Pentium's floating-point division hardware based on the radix-4 SRT algorithm and came up with an example that produces the worst-case error. Using double-precision floating-point computation, the ratio $c = 4\,195\,835/3\,145\,727 = 1.333\,820\,44\cdots$ is computed as $1.333\,739\,06$ on the Pentium. This latter result is accurate to only 14 bits; the error is even larger than that of single-precision floating-point and more than 10 orders of magnitude worse than what is expected of double-precision computation [Mole95].

The rest, as they say, is history. Intel at first dismissed the severity of the problem and admitted only a "subtle flaw," with a probability of 1 in 9 billion, or once in 27,000 years for the average spreadsheet user, of leading to computational errors. It nevertheless published a "white paper" that described the bug and its potential consequences and announced a replacement policy for the defective chips based on "customer need"; that is, customers had to show that they were doing a lot of mathematical calculations to get a free replacement. Under heavy criticism from customers, manufacturers using the Pentium chip in their products, and the on-line community, Intel later revised its policy to no-questions-asked replacement.

Whereas supercomputing, microchips, computer networks, advanced applications (particularly chess-playing programs), and many other aspects of computer technology have made the news regularly in recent years, the Intel Pentium bug was the first instance of arithmetic (or anything inside the CPU for that matter) becoming front-page news. While this can be interpreted as a sign of pedantic dryness, it is more likely an indicator of stunning technological success. Glaring software failures have come to be routine events in our information-based society, but hardware bugs are rare and newsworthy.

Having read the foregoing account, you may wonder what the radix-4 SRT division algorithm is and how it can lead to such problems. Well, that's the whole point of this introduction! You need computer arithmetic to understand the rest of the story. Computer arithmetic is a subfield of digital computer organization. It deals with the hardware realization of arithmetic functions to support various computer architectures as well as with arithmetic algorithms for firmware or software implementation. A major thrust of digital computer arithmetic is the design of hardware algorithms and circuits to enhance the speed of numeric operations. Thus much of what is presented here complements the *architectural* and *algorithmic* speedup techniques studied in the context of high-performance computer architecture and parallel processing.

A majority of our discussions relate to the design of top-of-the-line CPUs with high-performance parallel arithmetic circuits. However, we will at times also deal with slow bit-serial designs for embedded applications, where implementation cost and I/O pin limitations are of prime concern. It would be a mistake, though, to conclude that computer arithmetic is useful only to computer designers. We will see shortly that you can use scientific calculators more effectively and write programs that are more accurate and/or more efficient after a study of computer arithmetic. You will be able to render informed judgment when faced with the problem of choosing a digital signal processor (DSP) chip for your project. And, of course, you will know what exactly went wrong in the Pentium.

Figure 1.1 depicts the scope of computer arithmetic. On the hardware side, the focus is on implementing the four basic arithmetic operations (five, if you count square-rooting), as well as commonly used computations such as exponentials, logarithms, and trigonometric functions. For this, we need to develop algorithms, translate them to hardware structures, and choose from among multiple implementations based on cost–performance criteria. Since the exact computations to be carried out by the general-purpose hardware are not known a priori, benchmarking is used to predict the overall system performance for typical operation mixes and to make various design decisions.

On the software side, the primitive functions are given (e.g., in the form of a hardware chip such as the Pentium processor or a software tool such as Mathematica), and the task is

Hardware (our focus in this book)	Software
Design of efficient digital circuits for primitive and other arithmetic operations such as $+, -, \times, \div, \sqrt{\ }$, log, sin, and cos	Numerical methods for solving systems of linear equations, partial differential equations and so on

Issues: Algorithms
Error analysis
Speed/cost trade-offs
Hardware implementation
Testing, verification

Issues: Algorithms
Error analysis
Computational complexity
Programming
Testing, verification

General-Purpose	Special-Purpose
Flexible data paths Fast primitive operations like $+, -, \times, \div, \sqrt{\ }$ Benchmarking	Tailored to application areas such as Digital filtering Image processing Radar tracking

Fig. 1.1   The scope of computer arithmetic.

to synthesize cost-effective algorithms, with desirable error characteristics, to solve various problems of interest. These topics are covered in numerical analysis and computational science courses and textbooks and are thus mostly outside the scope of this book.

Within the hardware realm, we will be dealing with both general-purpose arithmetic/logic units (ALUs), of the type found in many commercially available processors, and special-purpose structures for solving specific application problems. The differences in the two areas are minor as far as the arithmetic algorithms are concerned. However, in view of the specific technological constraints, production volumes, and performance criteria, hardware implementations tend to be quite different. General-purpose processor chips that are mass-produced have highly optimized custom designs. Implementations of low-volume, special-purpose systems, on the other hand, typically rely on semicustom and off-the-shelf components. However, when critical and strict requirements, such as extreme speed, very low power consumption, and miniature size, preclude the use of semicustom or off-the-shelf components, the much higher cost of a custom design may be justified even for a special-purpose system.

1.2 A MOTIVATING EXAMPLE

Use a calculator that has the square-root, square, and exponentiation (x^y) functions to perform the following computations. I have given the numerical results obtained with my (10+2)-digit scientific calculator. You may obtain slightly different values.

First, compute "the 1024th root of 2" in the following two ways:

$$u = \underbrace{\sqrt{\sqrt{\cdots\sqrt{2}}}}_{10 \text{ times}} = 1.000\ 677\ 131$$

$$v = 2^{1/1024} = 1.000\ 677\ 131$$

Save both u and v in memory, if possible. If you can't store u and v, simply recompute them when needed. Now, perform the following two equivalent computations based on u:

$$x = \left(\left((u^2)^2\right) \cdots\right)^{\overbrace{}^{\text{10 times}}2} = 1.999\,999\,963$$

$$x' = u^{1024} = 1.999\,999\,973$$

Similarly, perform the following two equivalent computations based on v:

$$y = \left(\left((v^2)^2\right) \cdots\right)^{\overbrace{}^{\text{10 times}}2} = 1.999\,999\,983$$

$$y' = v^{1024} = 1.999\,999\,994$$

The four different values obtained for x, x', y, and y', in lieu of 2, hint that perhaps v and u are not really the same value. Let's compute their difference:

$$w = v - u = 1 \times 10^{-11}$$

Why isn't w equal to zero? The reason is that even though u and v are displayed identically, they in fact have different internal representations. Most calculators have hidden or guard digits (mine has two) to provide a higher degree of accuracy and to reduce the effect of accumulated errors when long computation sequences are performed.

Let's see if we can determine the hidden digits for the u and v values above. Here is one way:

$$(u - 1) \times 1000 = 0.677\,130\,680 \qquad [\text{Hidden} \cdots (0)\,68]$$
$$(v - 1) \times 1000 = 0.677\,130\,690 \qquad [\text{Hidden} \cdots (0)\,69]$$

This explains why w is not zero, which in turn tells us why $u^{1024} \neq v^{1024}$. The following simple analysis might be helpful in this regard.

$$v^{1024} = (u + 10^{-11})^{1024}$$
$$\approx u^{1024} + 1024 \times 10^{-11} u^{1023} \approx u^{1024} + 2 \times 10^{-8}$$

The difference between v^{1024} and u^{1024} is in good agreement with the result of the preceding analysis. The difference between $\left(\left((u^2)^2\right) \cdots\right)^2$ and u^{1024} exists because the former is computed through repeated multiplications while the latter uses the built-in exponentiation routine of the calculator, which is likely to be less precise.

Despite the discrepancies, the results of the foregoing computations are remarkably precise. The values of u and v agree to 11 decimal digits, while those of x, x', y, y' are identical to eight digits. This is better than single-precision, floating-point arithmetic on the most elaborate and expensive computers. Do we have a right to expect more from a calculator that costs $20 or less? Ease of use is, of course, a different matter from speed or precision. For a detailed exposition of some deficiencies in current calculators, and a refreshingly new design approach, see [Thim95].

1.3 NUMBERS AND THEIR ENCODINGS

Number representation methods have advanced in parallel with the evolution of language. The oldest method for representing numbers consisted of the use of stones or sticks. Gradually, as larger numbers were needed, it became difficult to represent them or develop a feeling for their magnitudes. More importantly, comparing large numbers was quite cumbersome. Grouping the stones or sticks (e.g., representing the number 27 by 5 groups of 5 sticks plus 2 single sticks) was only a temporary cure. It was the use of different stones or sticks for representing groups of 5, 10, etc. that produced the first major breakthrough.

The latter method gradually evolved into a symbolic form whereby special symbols were used to denote larger units. A familiar example is the Roman numeral system. The units of this system are 1, 5, 10, 50, 100, 500, 1000, 10 000, and 100 000, denoted by the symbols I, V, X, L, C, D, M, ((I)), and (((I))), respectively. A number is represented by a string of these symbols, arranged in descending order of values from left to right. To shorten some of the cumbersome representations, allowance is made to count a symbol as representing a negative value if it is to the left of a larger symbol. For example, IX is used instead of VIIII to denote the number 9 and LD is used for CCCCL to represent the number 450.

Clearly, the Roman numeral system is not suitable for representing very large numbers. Furthermore, it is difficult to do arithmetic on numbers represented with this notation. The *positional* system of number representation was first used by the Chinese. In this method, the value represented by each symbol depends not only on its shape but also on its position relative to other symbols. Our conventional method of representing numbers is based on a positional system.

For example in the number 222, each of the "2" digits represents a different value. The leftmost 2 represents 200. The middle 2 represents 20. Finally, the rightmost 2 is worth 2 units. The representation of time intervals in terms of days, hours, minutes, and seconds (i.e., as four-element vectors) is another example of the positional system. For instance, in the vector $T = 5\ 5\ 5\ 5$, the leftmost element denotes 5 days, the second from the left represents 5 hours, the third element stands for 5 minutes, and the rightmost element denotes 5 seconds.

If in a positional number system, the unit corresponding to each position is a constant multiple of the unit for its right neighboring position, the conventional *fixed-radix* positional system is obtained. The decimal number system we use daily is a positional number system with 10 as its constant radix. The representation of time intervals, as just discussed, provides an example of a *mixed-radix* positional system for which the radix is the vector $R = 0\ 24\ 60\ 60$.

The method used to represent numbers affects not just the ease of reading and understanding numbers but also the complexity of arithmetic algorithms used for computing with numbers. The popularity of positional number systems is in part due to the availability of simple and elegant algorithms for performing arithmetic on such numbers. We will see in subsequent chapters that other representations provide advantages over the positional representation in terms of certain arithmetic operations or the needs of particular application areas. However, these systems are of limited use precisely because they do not support universally simple arithmetic.

In digital systems, numbers are encoded by means of binary digits or bits. Suppose you have 4 bits to represent numbers. There are 16 possible codes. You are free to assign the 16 codes to numbers as you please. However, since number representation has significant effects on algorithm and circuit complexity, only some of the wide range of possibilities have found applications.

To simplify arithmetic operations, including the required checking for singularities or special cases, the assignment of codes to numbers must be done in a logical and systematic manner. For example, if you assign codes to 2 and 3 but not to 5, then adding 2 and 3 will cause an "overflow" (yields an unrepresentable value) in your number system.

Figure 1.2 shows some examples of assignments of 4-bit codes to numbers. The first choice is to interpret the 4-bit patterns as 4-bit binary numbers, leading to the representation of natural numbers in the range $[0, 15]$. The signed-magnitude scheme results in integers in the range $[-7, 7]$ being represented, with 0 having two representations, (viz., ± 0). The 3-plus-1 fixed-point number system (3 whole bits, 1 fractional bit) gives us numbers from 0 to 7.5 in increments of 0.5. Viewing the 4-bit codes as signed fractions gives us a range of $[-0.875, +0.875]$ or $[-1, +0.875]$, depending on whether we use signed-magnitude or 2's-complement representation.

The 2-plus-2 unsigned floating-point number system in Fig. 1.2, with its 2-bit exponent e in the range $[-2, 1]$ and 2-bit integer significand s in $[0, 3]$, can represent certain values $s \times 2^e$ in $[0, 6]$. In this system, 0.00 has four representations, 0.50, 1.00, and 2.00 have two representations each, and 0.25, 0.75, 1.50, 3.00, 4.00, and 6.00 are uniquely represented. The 2-plus-2 logarithmic number system, which represents a number by approximating its 2-plus-2, fixed-point, base-2 logarithm, completes the choices shown in Fig. 1.2.

1.4 FIXED-RADIX POSITIONAL NUMBER SYSTEMS

A conventional fixed-radix, fixed-point positional number system is usually based on a positive integer *radix* (base) r and an implicit digit set $\{0, 1, \cdots, r - 1\}$. Each unsigned integer is represented by a digit vector of length $k + l$, with k digits for the whole part and l digits for the fractional part. By convention, the digit vector $x_{k-1}x_{k-2} \cdots x_1 x_0 . x_{-1} x_{-2} \cdots x_{-l}$ represents the value:

$$(x_{k-1}x_{k-2} \cdots x_1 x_0 . x_{-1} x_{-2} \cdots x_{-l})_r = \sum_{i=-l}^{k-1} x_i r^i$$

One can easily generalize to arbitrary radices (not necessarily integer or positive or constant) and digit sets of arbitrary size or composition. In what follows, we restrict our attention to digit sets composed of consecutive integers, since digit sets of other types complicate arithmetic and have no redeeming property. Thus, we denote our digit set by $\{-\alpha, -\alpha + 1, \cdots, \beta - 1, \beta\} = [-\alpha, \beta]$.

The following examples demonstrate the wide range of possibilities in selecting the radix and digit set.

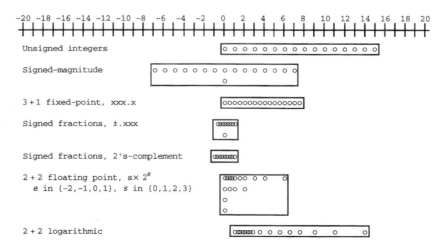

Fig. 1.2   Some of the possible ways of assigning 16 distinct codes to represent numbers.

■ **Example 1.1** Balanced ternary number system: $r = 3$, digit set $= [-1, 1]$.

■ **Example 1.2** Negative-radix number systems: radix $-r$, digit set $= [0, r - 1]$.

$$(\cdots x_5 x_4 x_3 x_2 x_1 x_0 . x_{-1} x_{-2} x_{-3} x_{-4} x_{-5} x_{-6} \cdots)_{-r} = \sum_i x_i (-r)^i$$

$$= \sum_{even\, i} d_i r^i - \sum_{odd\, i} d_i r^i$$

$$= (\cdots 0 x_4 0 x_2 0 x_0 . 0 x_{-2} 0 x_{-4} 0 x_{-6} \cdots)_r - (\cdots x_5 0 x_3 0 x_1 0 . x_{-1} 0 x_{-3} 0 x_{-5} 0 \cdots)_r$$

The special case with $r = -2$ and digit set of $[0, 1]$ is known as the negabinary number system.

■ **Example 1.3** Nonredundant signed-digit number systems: digit set $[-\alpha, r - 1 - \alpha]$ for radix r. As an example, one can use the digit set $[-4, 5]$ for $r = 10$. We denote a negative digit by preceding it with a minus sign, as usual, or by using a hyphen as a left superscript when the minus sign could be mistaken for subtraction. For example,

$$(3\ ^-1\ 5)_{ten} \quad \text{represents the decimal number} \quad 295 = 300 - 10 + 5$$

$$(^-3\ 1\ 5)_{ten} \quad \text{represents the decimal number} \quad -285 = -300 + 10 + 5$$

■ **Example 1.4** Redundant signed-digit number systems: digit set $[-\alpha, \beta]$, with $\alpha + \beta \geq r$ for radix r. One can use the digit set $[-7, 7]$, say, for $r = 10$. In such redundant number systems, certain values may have multiple representations. For example, here are some representations for the decimal number 295:

$$(3\ ^-1\ 5)_{ten} = (3\ 0\ ^-5)_{ten} = (1\ ^-7\ 0\ ^-5)_{ten}$$

We will study redundant representations in detail in Chapter 3.

■ **Example 1.5** Fractional radix number systems: $r = 0.1$ with digit set $[0, 9]$.

$$(x_{k-1} x_{k-2} \cdots x_1 x_0 . x_{-1} x_{-2} \cdots x_{-l})_{one\text{-}tenth} = \sum_i x_i 10^{-i}$$

$$= (x_{-l} \cdots x_{-2} x_{-1} x_0 . x_1 x_2 \cdots x_{k-2} x_{k-1})_{ten}$$

Example 1.6 Irrational radix number systems: $r = \sqrt{2}$ with digit set $[0, 1]$.

$$(\cdots x_5 x_4 x_3 x_2 x_1 x_0 . x_{-1} x_{-2} x_{-3} x_{-4} x_{-5} x_{-6} \cdots)_{\sqrt{2}} = \sum_i x_i (\sqrt{2})^i$$

$$= (\cdots x_4 x_2 x_0 . x_{-2} x_{-4} x_{-6} \cdots)_{\text{two}} + \sqrt{2} (\cdots x_5 x_3 x_1 . x_{-1} x_{-3} x_{-5} \cdots)_{\text{two}}$$

These examples illustrate the generality of our definition by introducing negative, fractional, and irrational radices and by using both nonredundant or minimal (r different digit values) and redundant ($> r$ digit values) digit sets in the common case of positive integer radices. We can go even further and make the radix an imaginary or complex number.

Example 1.7 Complex-radix number systems: the quater-imaginary number system uses $r = 2j$, where $j = \sqrt{-1}$, and the digit set $[0, 3]$.

$$(\cdots x_5 x_4 x_3 x_2 x_1 x_0 . x_{-1} x_{-2} x_{-3} x_{-4} x_{-5} x_{-6} \cdots)_{2j} = \sum_i x_i (2j)^i$$

$$= (\cdots x_4 x_2 x_0 . x_{-2} x_{-4} x_{-6} \cdots)_{-\text{four}} + 2j (\cdots x_5 x_3 x_1 . x_{-1} x_{-3} x_{-5} \cdots)_{-\text{four}}$$

It is easy to see that any complex number can be represented in the quater-imaginary number system of Example 1.7, with the advantage that ordinary addition (with a slightly modified carry rule) and multiplication can be used for complex-number computations. The modified carry rule is that a carry of -1 (a borrow actually) goes two positions to the left when the position sum, or digit total in a given position, exceeds 3.

In radix r, with the standard digit set $[0, r - 1]$, the number of digits needed to represents the natural numbers in $[0, max]$ is:

$$k = \lfloor \log_r max \rfloor + 1 = \lceil \log_r (max + 1) \rceil$$

Note that the number of different values represented is $max + 1$.

With fixed-point representation using k whole and l fractional digits, we have:

$$max = r^k - r^{-l} = r^k - ulp$$

We will find the term ulp, for unit in least (significant) position, quite useful in describing certain arithmetic concepts without distinguishing between integers and fixed-point representations that include fractional parts. For integers, $ulp = 1$.

Specification of time intervals in terms of weeks, days, hours, minutes, seconds, and milliseconds is an example of mixed-radix representation. Given the two-part radix vector $\cdots r_3 r_2 r_1 r_0; r_{-1} r_{-2} \cdots$ defining the mixed radix, the two-part digit vector $\cdots x_3 x_2 x_1 x_0; x_{-1} x_{-2} \cdots$ represents the value

$$\cdots x_3 r_2 r_1 r_0 + x_2 r_1 r_0 + x_1 r_0 + x_0 + \frac{x_{-1}}{r_{-1}} + \frac{x_{-2}}{r_{-1} r_{-2}} + \cdots$$

In the time interval example, the mixed radix is $\cdots 7, 24, 60, 60; 1000 \cdots$ and the digit vector 3, 2, 9, 22, 57; 492 (3 weeks, 2 days, 9 hours, 22 minutes, 57 seconds, and 492 milliseconds) represents

$$(3 \times 7 \times 24 \times 60 \times 60) + (2 \times 24 \times 60 \times 60) + (9 \times 60 \times 60) + (22 \times 60) + 57 + 492/1000$$
$$= 2\ 020\ 977.492 \text{ seconds}$$

In Chapter 4, we will see that mixed-radix representation plays an important role in dealing with values represented in residue number systems.

1.5 NUMBER RADIX CONVERSION

Assuming that the unsigned value u has exact representations in radices r and R, we can write:

$$u = w.v$$
$$= (x_{k-1}x_{k-2} \cdots x_1 x_0.x_{-1}x_{-2} \cdots x_{-l})_r$$
$$= (X_{K-1}X_{K-2} \cdots X_1 X_0.X_{-1}X_{-2} \cdots X_{-L})_R$$

If an exact representation does not exist in one or both of the radices, the foregoing equalities will be approximate.

The radix conversion problem is defined as follows:

Given	r	the old radix,
	R	the new radix, and the
	x_is	digits in the radix-r representation of u
find the	X_is	digits in the radix-R representation of u

In the rest of this section, we will describe two methods for radix conversion based on doing the arithmetic in the old radix r or in the new radix R. We will also present a shortcut method, involving very little computation, that is applicable when the old and new radices are powers of the same number (e.g., 8 and 16, which are both powers of 2).

Note that in converting u from radix r to radix R, where r and R are positive integers, we can convert the whole and fractional parts separately. This is because an integer (fraction) is an integer (fraction), independent of the number representation radix.

Doing the arithmetic in the old radix r

We use this method when radix-r arithmetic is more familiar or efficient. The method is useful, for example, when we do manual computations and the old radix is $r = 10$. The procedures for converting the whole and fractional parts, along with their justifications or proofs, are given below.

Converting the whole part w

Procedure: Repeatedly divide the integer $w = (x_{k-1}x_{k-2} \cdots x_1 x_0)_r$ by the radix-r representation of R. The remainders are the X_is, with X_0 generated first.

Justification: $(X_{K-1}X_{K-2} \cdots X_1 X_0)_R - (X_0)_R$ is divisible by R. Therefore, X_0 is the remainder of dividing the integer $w = (x_{k-1}x_{k-2} \cdots x_1 x_0)_r$ by the radix-r representation of R.

Example: $(105)_{ten} = (?)_{five}$
Repeatedly divide by 5:

	Quotient	Remainder
	105	0
	21	1
	4	4
	0	

From the above, we conclude that $(105)_{ten} = (410)_{five}$.

Converting the fractional part v

Procedure: Repeatedly multiply the fraction $v = (.x_{-1}x_{-2} \cdots x_{-l})_r$ by the radix-r representation of R. In each step, remove the whole part before multiplying again. The whole parts obtained are the X_is, with X_{-1} generated first.

Justification: $R \times (0.X_{-1}X_{-2} \cdots X_{-L})_R = (X_{-1}.X_{-2} \cdots X_{-L})_R$.

Example: $(105.486)_{ten} = (410.?)_{five}$
Repeatedly multiply by 5:

Whole part	Fraction
	.486
2	.430
2	.150
0	.750
3	.750
3	.750

From the above, we conclude that $(105.486)_{ten} \approx (410.22033)_{five}$.

Doing the arithmetic in the new radix R

We use this method when radix-R arithmetic is more familiar or efficient. The method is useful, for example, when we manually convert numbers to radix 10. Again, the whole and fractional parts are converted separately.

Converting the whole part w

Procedure: Use repeated multiplications by r followed by additions according to the formula $((\cdots ((x_{k-1}r + x_{k-2})r + x_{k-3})r + \cdots)r + x_1)r + x_0$.

Justification: The given formula is the well-known Horner's method (or rule), first presented in the early nineteenth century, for the evaluation of the $(k - 1)$th-degree polynomial $x_{k-1}r^{k-1} + x_{k-2}r^{k-2} + \cdots + x_1r + x_0$ [Knut97].

Example: $(410)_{\text{five}} = (?)_{\text{ten}}$

$$((4 \times 5) + 1) \times 5 + 0 = 105 \Rightarrow (410)_{\text{five}} = (105)_{\text{ten}}$$

Converting the fractional part v

Procedure: Convert the integer $r^l(0.v)$ and then divide by r^l in the new radix.

Justification: $r^l(0.v)/r^l = 0.v$

Example: $(410.220\ 33)_{\text{five}} = (105.?)_{\text{ten}}$

$$(0.220\ 33)_{\text{five}} \times 5^5 = (22\ 033)_{\text{five}} = (1518)_{\text{ten}}$$
$$1518/5^5 = 1518/3125 = 0.485\ 76$$

From the above, we conclude that $(410.22033)_{\text{five}} = (105.48576)_{\text{ten}}$.

Note: Horner's method works here as well but is generally less practical. The digits of the fractional part are processed from right to left and the multiplication operation is replaced with division. Figure 1.3 shows how Horner's method can be applied to the preceding example.

Shortcut method for $r = b^g$ and $R = b^G$

In the special case when the old and new radices are integral powers of a common base b, that is, $r = b^g$ and $R = b^G$, one can convert from radix r to radix b and then from radix b to radix R. Both these conversions are quite simple and require virtually no computation.

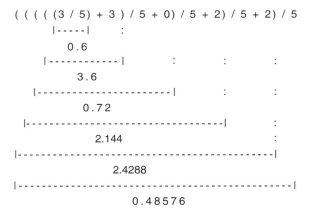

Fig. 1.3   Horner's rule used to convert $(.22033)_{\text{five}}$ to decimal.

To convert from the old radix $r = b^g$ to radix b, simply convert each radix-r digit individually into a g-digit radix-b number and then juxtapose the resulting g-digit numbers.

To convert from radix b to the new radix $R = b^G$, form G-digit groups of the radix-b digits starting from the radix point (to the left and to the right). Then convert the G-digit radix-b number of each group into a single radix-R digit and juxtapose the resulting digits.

■ **Example 1.8** $(2\,301.302)_{\text{four}} = (?)_{\text{eight}}$

We have $4 = 2^2$ and $8 = 2^3$. Thus, conversion through the intermediate radix 2 is used. Each radix-4 digit is independently replaced by a 2-bit radix-2 number. This is followed by 3-bit groupings of the resulting binary digits to find the radix-8 digits.

$$(2\,301.302)_{\text{four}} = (\underbrace{10}_{2}\,\underbrace{11}_{3}\,\underbrace{00}_{0}\,\underbrace{01}_{1}.\underbrace{11}_{3}\,\underbrace{00}_{0}\,\underbrace{10}_{2})_{\text{two}}$$

$$= (\underbrace{10}_{2}\,\underbrace{110}_{6}\,\underbrace{001}_{1}.\underbrace{110}_{6}\,\underbrace{010}_{2})_{\text{two}} = (261.62)_{\text{eight}}$$

Clearly, when $g = 1(G = 1)$, the first (second) step of the shortcut conversion procedure is eliminated. This corresponds to the special case of $R = r^G (r = R^g)$. For example, conversions between radix 2 and radix 8 or 16 belong to these special cases.

1.6 CLASSES OF NUMBER REPRESENTATIONS

In Sections 1.4 and 1.5, we considered the representation of unsigned fixed-point numbers using fixed-radix number systems, with standard and nonstandard digit sets, as well as methods for converting between such representations with standard digit sets. In digital computations, we also deal with signed fixed-point numbers as well as signed and unsigned real values. Additionally, we may use unconventional representations for the purpose of speeding up arithmetic operations or increasing their accuracy. Understanding different ways of representing numbers, including their relative cost–performance benefits and conversions between various representations, is an important prerequisite for designing efficient arithmetic algorithms or circuits.

In the next three chapters, we will review techniques for representing fixed-point numbers, beginning with conventional methods and then moving on to some unconventional representations.

Signed fixed-point numbers, including various ways of representing and handling the sign information, are covered in Chapter 2. Signed-magnitude, biased, and complement representations (including both 1's- and 2's-complement) are covered in some detail.

The signed-digit number systems of Chapter 3 can also be viewed as methods for representing signed numbers, although their primary significance lies in the redundancy that allows addition without carry propagation. The material in Chapter 3 is essential for understanding several speedup methods in multiplication, division, and function evaluation.

Chapter 4 introduces residue number systems (for representing unsigned or signed integers) that allow some arithmetic operations to be performed in a truly parallel fashion at very high speed. Unfortunately, the difficulty of division and certain other arithmetic operations renders these number systems unsuitable for general applications. In Chapter 4, we also use residue representations to explore the limits of fast arithmetic.

Representation of real numbers can take different forms. Examples include slash number systems (for representing rational numbers), logarithmic number systems (for representing real values), and of course, floating-point numbers that constitute the primary noninteger data format in modern digital systems. These representations are discussed in Chapter 17 (introductory chapter of Part V), immediately before we deal with algorithms, hardware implementations, and error analyses for real-number arithmetic.

By combining features from two or more of the aforementioned "pure" representations, we can obtain many hybrid schemes. Examples include hybrid binary/signed-digit (see Section 3.4), hybrid residue/binary (see Section 4.5), hybrid logarithmic/signed-digit (see Section 17.6), and hybrid floating-point/logarithmic (see Problem 17.16) representations.

PROBLEMS

1.1 **Arithmetic algorithms** Consider the integral $I_n = \int_0^1 x^n e^{-x} dx$ that has the exact solution $n![1 - (1/e)\sum_{r=0}^n 1/r!]$. The integral can also be computed based on the recurrence equation $I_n = nI_{n-1} - 1/e$ with $I_0 = 1 - 1/e$.

   a. Prove that the recurrence equation is correct.

   b. Use a calculator or write a program to compute the values of I_j for $1 \le j \le 20$.

   c. Repeat part b with a different calculator or with a different precision in your program.

   d. Compare your results to the exact value $I_{20} = 0.018\ 350\ 468$ and explain any difference.

1.2 **Arithmetic algorithms** Consider the sequence $\{u_i\}$ defined by the recurrence $u_{i+1} = iu_i - i$, with $u_1 = e$.

   a. Use a calculator or write a program to determine the values of u_i for $1 \le i \le 25$.

   b. Repeat part a with a different calculator or with a different precision in your program.

   c. Explain the results.

1.3 **Arithmetic algorithms** Consider the sequence $\{a_i\}$ defined by the recurrence $a_{i+2} = 111 - 1130/a_{i+1} + 3000/(a_{i+1}a_i)$, with $a_0 = 11/2$ and $a_1 = 61/11$. The exact limit of this sequence is 6; but on any real machine, a different limit is obtained. Use a calculator or write a program to determine the values of a_i for $2 \le i \le 25$. What limit do you seem to be getting? Explain the outcome.

1.4 **Positional representation of the integers**

   a. Prove that an unsigned nonzero binary integer x is a power of 2 if and only if the bitwise logical AND of x and $x - 1$ is 0.

   b. Prove that an unsigned radix-3 integer $x = (x_{k-1}x_{k-2}\cdots x_1x_0)_{three}$ is even if and only if $\sum_{i=0}^{k-1} x_i$ is even.

   c. Prove that an unsigned binary integer $x = (x_{k-1}x_{k-2}\cdots x_1x_0)_{two}$ is divisible by 3 if and only if $\sum_{even\ i} x_i - \sum_{odd\ i} x_i$ is a multiple of 3.

   d. Generalize the statements of parts b and c to obtain rules for divisibility of radix-r integers by $r - 1$ and $r + 1$.

1.5 Unconventional radices

a. Convert the negabinary number $(0001\ 1111\ 0010\ 1101)_{-two}$ to radix 16 (hexadecimal).

b. Repeat part a for radix -16 (negahexadecimal).

c. Derive a procedure for converting numbers from radix r to radix $-r$ and vice versa.

1.6 Unconventional radices Consider the number x whose representation in radix $-r$ (with r a positive integer) is the $(2k+1)$-element all-1s vector.

a. Find the value of x in terms of k and r.

b. Represent $-x$ in radix $-r$ (negation or sign change).

c. Represent x in the positive radix r.

d. Represent $-x$ in the positive radix r.

1.7 Unconventional radices Let θ be a number in the negative radix $-r$ whose digits are all $r-1$. Show that $-\theta$ is represented by a vector of all 2s, except for its most- and least-significant digits, which are 1s.

1.8 Unconventional radices Consider a fixed-radix positional number system with the digit set $[-2, 2]$ and the imaginary radix $r = 2j\,(j = \sqrt{-1})$.

a. Describe a simple procedure to determine whether a number thus represented is real.

b. Show that all integers are representable and that some integers have multiple representations.

c. Can this system represent any complex number with integral real and imaginary parts?

d. Describe simple procedures for finding the representations of $a - bj$ and $4(a + bj)$, given the representation of $a + bj$.

1.9 Unconventional radices Consider the radix $r = -1 + j\,(j = \sqrt{-1})$ with the digit set $[0, 1]$.

a. Express the complex number $-49 + j$ in this number system.

b. Devise a procedure for determining whether a given bit string represents a real number.

c. Show that any natural number is representable with this number system.

1.10 Number radix conversion

a. Convert the following octal (radix-8) numbers to hexadecimal (radix-16) notation: 12, 5 655, 2 550 276, 76 545 336, 3 726 755

b. Represent $(48A.C2)_{sixteen}$ and $(192.837)_{ten}$ in radices 2, 8, 10, 12, and 16.

c. Outline procedures for converting an unsigned radix-r number, using the standard digit set $[0, r-1]$, into radices $1/r$, $\sqrt{r}$ and $j\sqrt[4]{r}(j = \sqrt{-1})$, using the same digit set.

1.11 Number radix conversion Consider a fixed-point, radix-4 number system in which a number x is represented with k whole and l fractional digits.

    a. Assuming the use of standard radix-4 digit set [0, 3] and radix-8 digit set [0, 7], determine K and L, the numbers of whole and fractional digits in the radix-8 representation of x as functions of k and l.

    b. Repeat part a for the more general case in which the radix-4 and radix-8 digit sets are $[-\alpha, \beta]$ and $[-2\alpha, 2\beta]$, respectively, with $\alpha \geq 0$ and $\beta \geq 0$.

1.12 **Number radix conversion** Dr. N. E. Patent, a frequent contributor to scientific journals, claims to have invented a simple logic circuit for conversion of numbers from radix 2 to radix 10. The novelty of this circuit is that it can convert arbitrarily long numbers. The binary number is input one bit at a time. The decimal output will emerge one digit at a time after a fixed initial delay that is independent of the length of the input number. Evaluate this claim using only the information given.

1.13 **Fixed-point number representation** Consider a fixed-point, radix-3 number system, using the digit set $[-1, 1]$, in which numbers are represented with k integer digits and l fractional digits as: $d_{k-1}d_{k-2} \cdots d_1 d_0 . d_{-1} d_{-2} \cdots d_{-l}$

    a. Determine the range of numbers represented as a function of k and l.

    b. Given that each radix-3 digit needs a 2-bit encoding, compute the representation efficiency of this number system relative to the binary representation.

    c. Outline a carry-free procedure for converting one of the above radix-3 numbers to an equivalent radix-3 number using the redundant digit set [0, 3]. By a carry-free procedure, we mean a procedure that determines each digit of the new representation locally from a few neighboring digits of the original representation, so that the speed of the circuit is independent of the length of the original number.

1.14 **Number radix conversion** Discuss the design of a hardware number radix converter that receives its radix-r input digit-serially and produces the radix-R output ($R > r$) in the same manner. Multiple conversions are to be performed continuously; that is, once the last digit of one number has been input, the presentation of the second number can begin with no time gap [Parh92].

1.15 **Decimal-to-binary conversion** Consider a $2k$-bit register, the upper half of which holds a decimal number, with each digit encoded as a 4-bit binary number (binary-coded decimal or BCD). Show that repeating the following steps k times will yield the binary equivalent of the decimal number in the lower half of the $2k$-bit register: Shift the $2k$-bit register one bit to the right; independently subtract 3 units from each 4-bit segment of the upper half whose binary value equals or exceeds 8 (there are $k/4$ such 4-bit segments).

1.16 **Design of comparators** An h-bit comparator is a circuit with two h-bit unsigned binary inputs, x and y, and two binary outputs designating the conditions $x < y$ and $x > y$. Sometimes a third output corresponding to $x = y$ is also provided, but we do not need it for this problem.

    a. Present the design of a 4-bit comparator.

    b. Show how five 4-bit comparators can be cascaded to compare two 16-bit numbers.

    c. Show how a three-level tree of 4-bit comparators can be used to compare two 28-bit numbers. Try to use as few 4-bit comparator blocks as possible.

     d. Generalize the result of part b to derive a synthesis method for large comparators built from a cascaded chain of smaller comparators.

     e. Generalize the result of part c to derive a synthesis method for large comparators built from a tree of smaller comparators.

REFERENCES

[Knut97] Knuth, D. E., *The Art of Computer Programming*, 3rd ed., Vol. 2: *Seminumerical Algorithms*, Addison-Wesley, 1997.

[Mole95] Moler, C., "A Tale of Two Numbers," *SIAM News*, Vol. 28, No. 1, pp. 1, 16, 1995.

[Parh92] Parhami, B., "Systolic Number Radix Converters," *Computer J.*, Vol. 35, No. 4, pp. 405–409, August 1992.

[Scot85] Scott, N. R., *Computer Number Systems and Arithmetic*, Prentice-Hall, 1985.

[Thim95] Thimbleby, H., "A New Calculator and Why It Is Necessary," *Computer J.*, Vol. 38, No. 6, pp. 418–433, 1995.

Chapter 2

REPRESENTING SIGNED NUMBERS

This chapter deals with the representation of signed fixed-point numbers by providing an attached sign bit, adding a fixed bias to all numbers, complementing negative values, attaching signs to digit positions, or using signed digits. In view of its importance in the design of fast arithmetic algorithms and hardware, representing signed fixed-point numbers by means of signed digits is further explored in Chapter 3. Chapter topics include:

2.1 SIGNED-MAGNITUDE REPRESENTATION

The natural numbers $0, 1, 2, \cdots, max$ can be represented as fixed-point numbers without fractional parts (refer to Section 1.4). In radix r, the number k of digits needed for representing the natural numbers up to max is

$$k = \lfloor \log_r max \rfloor + 1 = \lceil \log_r (max + 1) \rceil$$

Conversely, with k digits, one can represent the values 0 through $r^k - 1$, inclusive; that is, the interval $[0, r^k - 1] = [0, r^k)$ of natural numbers.

Natural numbers are often referred to as "unsigned integers," which form a special data type in many programming languages and computer instruction sets. The advantage of using this data type as opposed to "integers" when the quantities of interest are known to be nonnegative is that a larger representation range can be obtained (e.g., maximum value of 255, rather than 127, with 8 bits).

One way to represent both positive and negative integers is to use "signed magnitudes," or the sign-and-magnitude format, in which one bit is devoted to sign. The common convention is to let 1 denote a negative sign and 0 a positive sign. In the case of radix-2 numbers with a total length of k bits, $k-1$ bits will be available to represent the magnitude or absolute value of the number. The range of k-bit signed-magnitude binary numbers is thus $[-(2^{k-1} - 1), 2^{k-1} - 1]$. Figure 2.1 depicts the assignment of values to bit patterns for a 4-bit signed-magnitude format.

Advantages of signed-magnitude representation include its intuitive appeal, conceptual simplicity, symmetric range, and simple negation (sign change) by flipping or inverting the sign bit. The primary disadvantage is that addition of numbers with unlike signs (subtraction) must be handled differently from that of same-sign operands.

The hardware implementation of an adder for signed-magnitude numbers either involves a magnitude comparator and a separate subtractor circuit or else is based on the use of complement representation (see Section 2.3) internally within the arithmetic/logic unit (ALU). In the latter approach, a negative operand is complemented at the ALU's input, the computation is done by means of complement representation, and the result is complemented, if necessary, to produce the signed-magnitude output. Because the pre- and postcomplementation steps add to the computation delay, it is better to use the complement representation throughout.

Besides the aforementioned extra delay in addition and subtraction, signed-magnitude representation allows two representations for 0, leading to the need for special care in number comparisons or added overhead for detecting -0 and changing it to $+0$. This drawback, however, is unavoidable in any radix-2 number representation system with symmetric range.

Figure 2.2 shows the hardware implementation of signed-magnitude addition using selective pre- and postcomplementation. The control circuit receives as inputs the operation to be performed (0 = add, 1 = subtract), the signs of the two operands x and y, the carry-out of the adder, and the sign of the addition result. It produces signals for the adder's carry-in, complementation of x, complementation of the addition result, and the sign of the result. Note that complementation hardware is provided only for the x operand. This is because $x - y$ can be obtained by first computing $y - x$ and then changing the sign of the result. You will understand this design much better after we have covered complement representations of negative numbers in Sections 2.3 and 2.4.

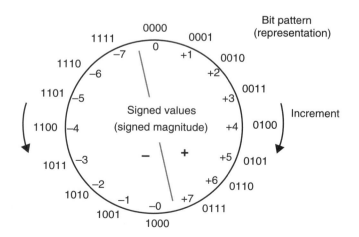

Fig. 2.1   A 4-bit signed-magnitude number representation system for integers.

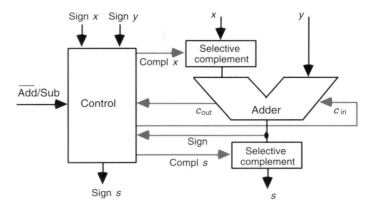

Fig. 2.2   Adding signed-magnitude numbers using precomplementation and postcomplementation.

2.2 BIASED REPRESENTATIONS

One way to deal with signed numbers is to devise a representation or coding scheme that converts signed numbers into unsigned numbers. For example, the biased representation is based on adding a positive value *bias* to all numbers, allowing us to represents the integers from *–bias* to *max – bias* using unsigned values from 0 to *max*. Such a representation is sometimes referred to as "excess-*bias*" (e.g., excess-3 or excess-128) coding. We will see in Chapter 17 that biased representation is used to encode the exponent part of a floating-point number.

Figure 2.3 shows how signed integers in the range $[-8, +7]$ can be encoded as unsigned values 0 through 15 by using a bias of 8. With k-bit representations and a bias of 2^{k-1}, the leftmost bit indicates the sign of the value represented (0 = negative, 1 = positive). Note that this is the opposite of the commonly used convention for number signs. With a bias of 2^k or $2^k - 1$, the range of represented integers is almost symmetric.

Biased representation does not lend itself to simple arithmetic algorithms. Addition and subtraction become somewhat more complicated because one must subtract or add the bias from/to the result of a normal add/subtract operation, since:

$$x + y + bias = (x + bias) + (y + bias) - bias$$
$$x - y + bias = (x + bias) - (y + bias) + bias$$

With k-bit numbers and a bias of 2^{k-1}, adding or subtracting the bias amounts to complementing the leftmost bit. Thus, the extra complexity in addition or subtraction is negligible.

Multiplication and division become significantly more difficult if these operations are to be performed directly on biased numbers. For this reason, the practical use of biased representation is limited to the exponent parts of floating-point numbers, which are never multiplied or divided.

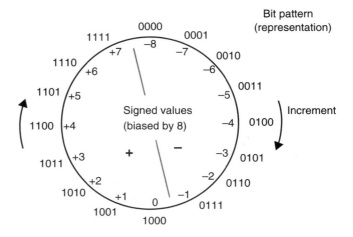

Fig. 2.3   A 4-bit biased integer number representation system with a bias of 8.

2.3 COMPLEMENT REPRESENTATIONS

In a complement number representation system, a suitably large complementation constant M is selected and the negative value $-x$ is represented as the unsigned value $M - x$. Figure 2.4 depicts the encodings used for positive and negative values and the arbitrary boundary between the two regions.

To represent integers in the range $[-N, +P]$ unambiguously, the complementation constant M must satisfy $M \geq N + P + 1$. This is justified by noting that to prevent overlap between the

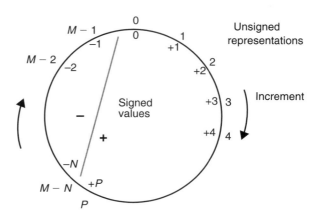

Fig. 2.4   Complement representation of signed integers.

representations of positive and negative values in Figure 2.4, we must have $M - N > P$. The choice of $M = N + P + 1$ yields maximum coding efficiency, since no code will go to waste.

In a complement system with the complementation constant M and the number representation range $[-N, +P]$, addition is done by adding the respective unsigned representations (modulo M). The addition process is thus always the same, independent of the number signs. This is easily understood if we note that in modulo-M arithmetic adding $M - 1$ (e.g.), is the same as subtracting 1. Table 2.1 shows the addition rules for complement representations, along with conditions that lead to overflow.

Subtraction can be performed by complementing the subtrahend and then performing addition. Thus, assuming that a selective complementer is available, addition and subtraction become essentially the same operation, and this is the primary advantage of complement representations.

Complement representation can be used for fixed-point numbers that have a fractional part. The only difference is that consecutive values in the circular representation of Fig. 2.4 will be separated by *ulp* instead of by 1. As a decimal example, given the complementation constant $M = 12.000$ and a fixed-point number range of $[-6.000, +5.999]$, the fixed-point number -3.258 has the complement representation $12.000 - 3.258 = 8.742$.

We note that two auxiliary operations are required for complement representations to be effective: complementation or change of sign (computing $M - x$) and computations of residues mod M. If finding $M - x$ requires subtraction and finding residues mod M implies division, then complement representation becomes quite inefficient. Thus M must be selected such that these two operations are simplified. Two choices allow just this for fixed-point radix-r arithmetic with k whole digits and l fractional digits:

$$\text{Radix complement} \qquad M = r^k$$
$$\text{Digit or diminished-radix complement} \quad M = r^k - ulp$$

For radix-complement representations, modulo-M reduction is done by ignoring the carry-out from digit position $k - 1$ in a $(k+l)$-digit radix-r addition. For digit-complement representations, computing the complement of x (i.e., $M - x$), is done by simply replacing each nonzero digit x_i by $r - 1 - x_i$. This is particularly easy if r is a power of 2. Complementation with $M = r^k$ and mod-M reduction with $M = r^k - ulp$ are similarly simple. You should be able to supply the details for radix r after reading Section 2.4, which deals with the important special case of $r = 2$.

TABLE 2.1
Addition in a complement number system with the complementation constant M and range $[-N, +P]$

Desired operation	Computation to be performed mod M	Correct result with no overflow	Overflow condition
$(+x) + (+y)$	$x + y$	$x + y$	$x + y > P$
$(+x) + (-y)$	$x + (M - y)$	$x - y$ if $y \leq x$ $M - (y - x)$ if $y > x$	N/A
$(-x) + (+y)$	$(M - x) + y$	$y - x$ if $x \leq y$ $M - (x - y)$ if $x > y$	N/A
$(-x) + (-y)$	$(M - x) + (M - y)$	$M - (x + y)$	$x + y > N$

2.4 TWO'S- AND 1'S-COMPLEMENT NUMBERS

In the special case of $r = 2$, the radix complement representation that corresponds to $M = 2^k$ is known as *two's complement*. Figure 2.5 shows the 4-bit, 2's-complement integer system ($k = 4, l = 0, M = 2^4 = 16$) and the meanings of the 16 representations allowed with 4 bits. The boundary between positive and negative values is drawn approximately in the middle to make the range roughly symmetric and to allow simple sign detection (the leftmost bit is the sign).

The 2's complement of a number x can be found via bitwise complementation of x and the addition of *ulp*:

$$2^k - x = [(2^k - ulp) - x] + ulp = x^{\text{compl}} + ulp$$

Note that the binary representation of $2^k - ulp$ consists of all 1s, making $(2^k - ulp) - x$ equivalent to the bitwise complement of x, denoted as x^{compl}. Whereas finding the bitwise complement of x is easy, adding *ulp* to the result is a slow process, since in the worst case it involves full carry propagation. We will see later how this addition of *ulp* can usually be avoided.

To add numbers modulo 2^k, we simply drop a carry-out of 1 produced by position $k - 1$. Since this carry is worth 2^k units, dropping it is equivalent to reducing the magnitude of the result by 2^k.

The range of representable numbers in a 2's-complement number system with k whole bits is:

$$\text{from} \qquad -2^{k-1} \qquad \text{to} \qquad 2^{k-1} - ulp$$

Because of this slightly asymmetric range, complementation can lead to overflow! Thus, if complementation is done as a separate sign change operation, it must include overflow detection.

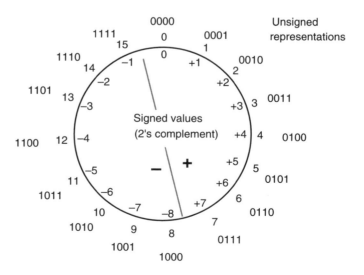

Fig. 2.5   A 4-bit, 2's-complement number representation system for integers.

However, we will see later that complementation needed to convert subtraction into addition requires no special provision.

The name "2's complement" actually comes from the special case of $k = 1$ that leads to the complementation constant $M = 2$. In this case, represented numbers have one whole bit, which acts as the sign, and l fractional bits. Thus, fractional values in the range $[-1, 1 - ulp]$ are represented in such a fractional 2's-complement number system.

The digit or diminished-radix complement representation is known as *one's complement* in the special case of $r = 2$. The complementation constant in this case is $M = 2^k - ulp$. For example, Fig. 2.6 shows the 4-bit, 1's-complement integer system ($k = 4, l = 0, M = 2^4 - 1 = 15$) and the meanings of the 16 representations allowed with 4 bits. The boundary between positive and negative values is again drawn approximately in the middle to make the range symmetric and to allow simple sign detection (the leftmost bit is the sign).

Note that compared to the 2's-complement representation of Fig. 2.5, the representation for -8 has been eliminated and instead an alternate code has been assigned to 0 (technically, -0). This may somewhat complicate 0 detection in that both the all-0s and the all-1s patterns represent 0. The arithmetic circuits can be designed such that the all-1s pattern is detected and automatically converted to the all-0s pattern. Keeping -0 intact does not cause problems in computations, however, since all computations are modulo 15. For example, adding $+1$ (0001) to -0 (1111) will yield the correct result of $+1$ (0001) when the addition is done modulo 15.

The 1's-complement of a number x can be found by bitwise complementation:

$$(2^k - ulp) - x = x^{compl}$$

To add numbers modulo $2^k - ulp$, we simply drop a carry-out of 1 produced by position $k - 1$ and simultaneously insert a carry-in of 1 into position $-l$. Since the dropped carry is worth 2^k units and the inserted carry is worth ulp, the combined effect is to reduce the magnitude of the result by $2^k - ulp$. In terms of hardware, the carry-out of our $(k + l)$-bit adder should be directly connected to its carry-in; this is known as *end-around carry*.

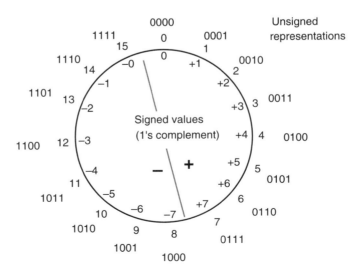

Fig. 2.6 A 4-bit, 1's-complement number representation system for integers.

The foregoing scheme properly handles any sum that equals or exceeds 2^k. When the sum is $2^k - ulp$, however, the carry-out will be zero and modular reduction is not accomplished. As suggested earlier, such an all-1s result can be interpreted as an alternate representation of 0 that is either kept intact (making 0 detection more difficult) or is automatically converted by hardware to $+0$.

The range of representable numbers in a 1's-complement number system with k whole bits is:

$$\text{from} \qquad -(2^{k-1} - ulp) \qquad \text{to} \qquad 2^{k-1} - ulp$$

This symmetric range is one of the advantages of 1's-complement number representation.

Table 2.2 presents a brief comparison of radix- and digit-complement number representation systems for radix r. We might conclude from Table 2.2 that each of the two complement representation schemes has some advantages and disadvantages with respect to the other, making them equally desirable. However, since complementation is often performed for converting subtraction to addition, the addition of ulp required in the case of 2's-complement numbers can be accomplished by providing a carry-in of 1 into the least significant, or $(-l)$th, position of the adder. Figure 2.7 shows the required elements for a 2's-complement adder/subtractor. With the complementation disadvantage mitigated in this way, 2's-complement representation has become the favored choice in virtually all modern digital systems.

Interestingly, the arrangement shown in Fig. 2.7 also removes the disadvantage of asymmetric range. If the operand y is -2^{k-1}, represented in 2's complement as 1 followed by all 0s, its complementation does not lead to overflow. This is because the two's complement of y is essentially represented in two parts: y^{compl}, which represents $2^{k-1} - 1$, and c_{in} which represents 1.

Occasionally we need to extend the number of digits in an operand to make it of the same length as another operand. For example, if a 16-bit number is to be added to a 32-bit number, the former is first converted to 32-bit format, with the two 32-bit numbers then added using a 32-bit adder. Unsigned or signed-magnitude fixed-point binary numbers can be extended from the left (whole part) or the right (fractional part) by simply padding them with 0s. This type of range or precision extension is only slightly more difficult for 2's- and 1's-complement numbers.

Given a 2's-complement number $x_{k-1}x_{k-2}\cdots x_1x_0.x_1x_2\cdots x_{-l}$, extension can be achieved from the left by replicating the sign bit (*sign extension*) and from the right by padding it with 0s.

$$\cdots x_{k-1}x_{k-1}x_{k-1}x_{k-1}x_{k-2}\cdots x_1x_0.x_{-1}x_{-2}\cdots x_{-l}000\cdots$$

TABLE 2.2
Comparing radix- and digit-complement number representation systems

Feature/Property	Radix complement	Digit complement
Symmetry ($P = N$?)	Possible for odd r (radices of practical interest are even)	Possible for even r
Unique zero?	Yes	No
Complementation	Complement all digits and add ulp	Complement all digits
Mod-M addition	Drop the carry-out	End-around carry

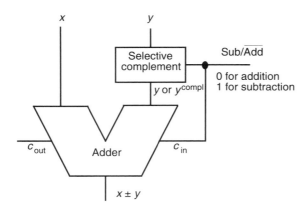

Fig. 2.7 Adder/subtractor architecture for 2's-complement numbers.

To justify the foregoing rule, note that when the number of whole (fractional) digits is increased from k (l) to k' (l'), the complementation constant increases from $M = 2^k$ to $M' = 2^{k'}$. Hence, the difference of the two complementation constants

$$M' - M = 2^{k'} - 2^k = 2^k(2^{k'-k} - 1)$$

must be added to the representation of any negative number. This difference is a binary integer consisting of $k' - k$ 1s followed by k 0s; hence the need for sign extension.

A 1's-complement number must be sign-extended from both ends:

$$\cdots x_{k-1} x_{k-1} x_{k-1} x_{k-1} x_{k-2} \cdots x_1 x_0 . x_1 x_2 \cdots x_{-l} x_{k-1} x_{k-1} x_{k-1} \cdots$$

Justifying the rule above for 1's-complement numbers is left as an exercise.

2.5 DIRECT AND INDIRECT SIGNED ARITHMETIC

In the preceding pages, we dealt with the addition and subtraction of signed numbers for a variety of number representation schemes (signed-magnitude, biased, complement). In all these cases, signed numbers were handled directly by the addition/subtraction hardware (*direct signed arithmetic*), consistent with our desire to avoid using separate addition and subtraction units.

For some arithmetic operations, it may be desirable to restrict the hardware to unsigned operands, thus necessitating *indirect signed arithmetic*. Basically, the operands are converted to unsigned values, a tentative result is obtained based on these unsigned values, and finally the necessary adjustments are made to find the result corresponding to the original signed operands. Figure 2.8 depicts the direct and indirect approaches to signed arithmetic.

Indirect signed arithmetic can be performed, for example, for multiplication or division of signed numbers, although we will see in Parts III and IV that direct algorithms are also available for this purpose. The process is trivial for signed-magnitude numbers. If x and y are biased

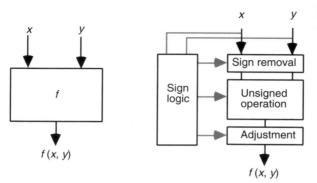

Fig. 2.8   Direct versus indirect operation on signed numbers.

numbers, then both the sign removal and adjustment steps involve addition/subtraction. If x and y are complement numbers, these steps involve selective complementation.

This type of preprocessing for operands, and postprocessing for computation results, is useful not only for dealing with signed values but also in the case of unacceptable or inconvenient operand values. For example, in computing $\sin x$, the operand can be brought to within $[0, \pi/2]$ by taking advantage of identities such as $\sin(-x) = -\sin x$ and $\sin(2\pi + x) = \sin(\pi - x) = \sin x$. Chapter 22 contains examples of such transformations. As a second example, some division algorithms become more efficient when the divisor is in a certain range (e.g., close to 1). In this case, the dividend and divisor can be scaled by the same factor in a preprocessing step to bring the divisor within the desired range (see Section 15.3).

2.6 USING SIGNED POSITIONS OR SIGNED DIGITS

The value of a 2's-complement number can be found by using the standard binary-to-decimal conversion process, except that the weight of the most significant bit (sign position) is taken to be negative. Figure 2.9 shows an example 8-bit, 2's-complement number converted to decimal by considering its sign bit to have the negative weight -2^7.

$$
\begin{array}{lcccccccc}
x \;=\; (& 1 & 0 & 1 & 0 & 0 & 1 & 1 & 0 \;)_{\text{two's-compl}} \\
& -2^7 & 2^6 & 2^5 & 2^4 & 2^3 & 2^2 & 2^1 & 2^0 \\[4pt]
& -128 & & +\,32 & & & +\,4 & +\,2 & & =\;\;-90
\end{array}
$$

Check:

$$
\begin{array}{lcccccccc}
x \;=\; (& 1 & 0 & 1 & 0 & 0 & 1 & 1 & 0 \;)_{\text{two's-compl}} \\
-x \;=\; (& 0 & 1 & 0 & 1 & 1 & 0 & 1 & 0 \;)_{\text{two}} \\
& 2^7 & 2^6 & 2^5 & 2^4 & 2^3 & 2^2 & 2^1 & 2^0 \\[4pt]
& & 64 & & +\,16 & +\,8 & & +\,2 & & =\;\;90
\end{array}
$$

Fig. 2.9   Interpreting a 2's-complement number as having a negatively weighted most significant digit.

This very important property of 2's-complement systems is used to advantage in many algorithms that deal directly with signed numbers. The property is formally expressed as follows:

$$x = (x_{k-1}x_{k-2} \cdots x_1 x_0 . x_{-1} x_{-2} \cdots x_{-l})_{\text{two's-compl}}$$

$$= -x_{k-1} 2^{k-1} + \sum_{i=-l}^{k-2} x_i \, 2^i$$

The proof is quite simple if we consider the two cases of $x_{k-1} = 0$ and $x_{k-1} = 1$ separately. For $x_{k-1} = 0$, we have:

$$x = (0x_{k-2} \cdots x_1 x_0 . x_{-1} x_{-2} \cdots x_{-l})_{\text{two's-compl}}$$

$$= (0x_{k-2} \cdots x_1 x_0 . x_{-1} x_{-2} \cdots x_{-1})_{\text{two}}$$

$$= \sum_{i=-l}^{k-2} x_i \, 2^i$$

For $x_{k-1} = 1$, we have:

$$x = (1x_{k-2} \cdots x_1 x_0 . x_{-1} x_{-2} \cdots x_{-l})_{\text{two's-compl}}$$

$$= -[2^k - (1x_{k-2} \cdots x_1 x_0 . x_{-1} x_{-2} \cdots x_{-l})_{\text{two}}]$$

$$= -2^{k-1} + \sum_{i=-l}^{k-2} x_i \, 2^i$$

Developing the corresponding interpretation for 1's-complement numbers is left as an exercise.

A simple generalization of the notion above immediately suggests itself [Kore81]. Let us assign negative weights to an arbitrary subset of the $k + l$ positions in a radix-r number and positive weights to the rest of the positions. A vector

$$\lambda = (\lambda_{k-1}\lambda_{k-2} \cdots \lambda_1 \lambda_0 . \lambda_{-1} \lambda_{-2} \cdots \lambda_{-l})$$

with elements λ_i in $\{-1, 1\}$, can be used to specify the signs associated with the various positions. With these conventions, the value represented by the digit vector x of length $k + l$ is:

$$(x_{k-1}x_{k-2} \cdots x_1 x_0 . x_{-1} x_{-2} \cdots x_{-l})_{r,\lambda} = \sum_{i=-l}^{k-1} \lambda_i x_i r^i$$

Note that the scheme above covers unsigned radix-r, 2's-complement, and negative-radix number systems as special cases:

$\lambda =$	1	1	1	$\cdots$	1	1	1	1	Positive radix
$\lambda = -1$		1	1	$\cdots$	1	1	1	1	Two's complement
$\lambda =$				$\cdots$	-1	1	-1	1	Negative radix

We can take one more step in the direction of generality and postulate that instead of a single sign vector λ being associated with the digit positions in the number system (i.e., with all numbers represented), a separate sign vector is defined for each number. Thus, the digits are viewed as having signed values:

$$x_i = \lambda_i |x_i|, \quad \text{with } \lambda_i \in \{-1, 1\}$$

Here, λ_i is the sign and $|x_i|$ is the magnitude of the ith digit. In fact once we begin to view the digits as signed values, there is no reason to limit ourselves to signed-magnitude representation of the digit values. Any type of coding, including biased or complement representation, can be used for the digits. Furthermore, the range of digit values need not be symmetric. We have already covered some examples of such signed-digit number systems in Section 1.4 (see Examples 1.1, 1.3, and 1.4).

Basically, any set $[-\alpha, \beta]$ of r or more consecutive integers that includes 0 can be used as the digit set for radix r. If exactly r digit values are used, then the number system is irredundant and offers a unique representation for each value within its range. On the other hand, if more than r digit values are used, $\rho = \alpha + \beta + 1 - r$ represents the *redundancy index* of the number system and some values will have multiple representations. In Chapter 3, we will see that such redundant representations can eliminate the propagation of carries in addition and thus allow us to implement truly parallel fast adders.

As an example of nonredundant signed-digit representations, consider a radix-4 number system with the digit set $[-1, 2]$. A k-digit number of this type can represent any integer from $-(4^k - 1)/3$ to $2(4^k - 1)/3$. Given a standard radix-4 integer using the digit set $[0, 3]$, it can be converted to the preceding representation by simply rewriting each digit of 3 as $-1 + 4$, where the second term becomes a carry of 1 that propagates leftward. Figure 2.10 shows a numerical example. Note that the result may require $k + 1$ digits.

The conversion process of Fig. 2.10 stops when there remains no digit with value 3 that needs to be rewritten. The reverse conversion is similarly done by rewriting any digit of -1 as 3 with a borrow of 1 (carry of -1).

More generally, to convert between digit sets, each old digit value is rewritten as a valid new digit value and an appropriate transfer (carry or borrow) into the next higher digit position. Because these transfers can propagate, the conversion process is essentially a digit-serial one, beginning with the least significant digit.

As an example of redundant signed-digit representations, consider a radix-4 number system with the digit set $[-2, 2]$. A k-digit number of this type can represent any integer from

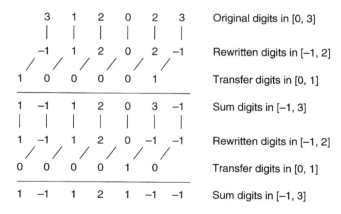

Fig. 2.10   Converting a standard radix-4 integer to a radix-4 integer with the nonstandard digit set $[-1, 2]$.

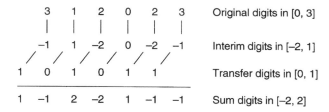

Fig. 2.11   Converting a standard radix-4 integer to a radix-4 integer with the nonstandard digit set [−2, 2].

$-2(4^k - 1)/3$ to $2(4^k - 1)/3$. Given a standard radix-4 number using the digit set [0, 3], it can be converted to the preceding representation by simply rewriting each digit of 3 as $-1 + 4$ and each digit of 2 as $-2 + 4$, where the second term in each case becomes a carry of 1 that propagates leftward. Figure 2.11 shows a numerical example.

In this case, the transfers do not propagate, since each transfer of 1 can be absorbed by the next higher position which has a digit value in [−2, 1], forming a final result digit in [−2, 2]. The conversion process from conventional radix-4 to the preceding redundant representation is thus carry-free. The reverse process, however, remains digit-serial.

PROBLEMS

2.1   **Signed-magnitude adder/subtractor**   Design the control circuit of Fig. 2.2 so that signed-magnitude inputs are added correctly regardless of their signs. Include in your design a provision for overflow detection in the form of a fifth control circuit output.

2.2   **Arithmetic on biased numbers**   Multiplication of biased numbers can be done in a direct or an indirect way.

   a.   Develop a direct multiplication algorithm for biased numbers. *Hint:* Use the identity $xy + bias = (x + bias)(y + bias) - bias[(x + bias) + (y + bias) - bias] + bias$.
   b.   Present an indirect multiplication algorithm for biased numbers.
   c.   Compare the algorithms of parts a and b with respect to delay and hardware implementation cost.
   d.   Repeat the comparison for part c in the special case of squaring a biased number.

2.3   **Representation formats and conversions**   Consider the following five ways for representing integers in the range [−127, 127] within an 8-bit format: (a) signed-magnitude, (b) 2's complement, (c) 1's complement, (d) excess-127 code (where an integer x is encoded using the binary representation of $x + 127$), (e) excess-128 code. Pick one of three more conventional and one of the two "excess" representations and describe conversion of numbers between the two formats in both directions.

2.4   **Representation formats and conversions**

   a.   Show conversion procedures from k-bit 2's-complement format to k-bit biased representation, with $bias = 2^{k-1}$, and vice versa. Pay attention to possible exceptions.
   b.   Repeat part a for $bias = 2^{k-1} - 1$.

c. Repeat part a for 1's-complement format.

d. Repeat part b for 1's-complement format.

2.5 **Complement representation of negative numbers** Consider a k-bit integer radix-2 complement number representation system with the complementation constant $M = 2^k$. The range of integers represented is taken to be from $-N$ to $+P$, with $N + P + 1 = M$. Determine all possible pairs of values for N and P (in terms of M) if the sign of the number is to be determined by:

a. Looking at the most significant bit only.

b. Inspecting the three most significant bits.

c. A single 4-input OR or AND gate.

d. A single 4-input NOR or NAND gate.

2.6 **Complement representation of negative numbers** Diminished radix complement was defined as being based on the complementation constant $r^k - ulp$. Study the implications of using an "augmented radix complement" system based on the complementation constant $r^k + ulp$.

2.7 **One's- and 2's-complement number systems** We discussed the procedures for extending the number of whole or fractional digits in a 1's- or 2's-complement number in Section 2.4. Discuss procedures for the reverse process of shrinking the number of digits (e.g., converting 32-bit numbers to 16 bits).

2.8 **Interpreting 1's-complement numbers** Prove that the value of the number $(x_{k-1}x_{k-2} \cdots x_1 x_0 . x_{-1} x_{-2} \cdots x_{-l})_{\text{1's-compl}}$ can be calculated from the formula $-x_{k-1}(2^{k-1} - ulp) + \sum_{i=-l}^{k-2} x_i 2^i$.

2.9 **One's- and 2's-complement number systems**

a. Prove that $x - y = (x^c + y)^c$, where the superscript "c" denotes any complementation scheme.

b. Find the difference between the two binary numbers 0010 and 0101 in two ways: First by adding the 2's complement of 0101 to 0010, and then by using the equality of part a, where "c" denotes bitwise complementation. Compare the two methods with regard to their possible advantages and drawbacks.

2.10 **Shifting of 1's- or 2's-complement numbers** Left/right shifting is used to double/halve the magnitude of unsigned binary integers. How can we use shifting to accomplish the same for 1's- or 2's-complement numbers?

2.11 **Arithmetic on 1's-complement numbers** Discuss the effect of the end-around carry needed for 1's-complement addition on the worst-case carry propagation delay and the total addition time.

2.12 **Range and precision extension for complement numbers** Prove that increasing the number of integer and fractional digits in one's-complement representation requires sign extension from both ends (i.e., positive numbers are extended with 0s and negative numbers with 1s at both ends).

2.13 Signed digits or digit positions

a. Present an algorithm for determining the sign of a number represented in a positional system with signed digit positions.

b. Repeat part a for signed-digit representations.

2.14 Signed digit positions
Consider a positional radix-r integer number system with the associated position sign vector $\lambda = (\lambda_{k-1}\lambda_{k-2}\cdots\lambda_1\lambda_0)$, $\lambda_i \in \{-1, 1\}$. The additive inverse of a number x is the number $-x$.

a. Find the additive inverse of the k-digit integer Q all of whose digits are $r - 1$.

b. Derive a procedure for finding the additive inverse of an arbitrary number x.

c. Specialize the algorithm of part b to the case of 2's-complement numbers.

2.15 Generalizing 2's complement: 2-adic numbers
Around the turn of the twentieth century, K. Hensel defined the class of p-adic numbers for a given prime p. Consider the class of 2-adic numbers with infinitely many digits to the left and a finite number of digits to the right of the binary point. An infinitely repeated pattern of digits is represented by writing down a single pattern (the period) within parentheses. Here are some example 2-adic representations using this notation:

$$7 = (0)111. = \cdots 00000000111. \qquad 1/7 = (110)111. = \cdots 110110110111.$$
$$-7 = (1)001. = \cdots 11111111001. \qquad -1/7 = (001). \quad = \cdots 001001001001.$$
$$7/4 = (0)1.11 \qquad\qquad\qquad 1/10 = (1100)110.1$$

We see that 7 and -7 have their standard 2's-complement forms, with infinitely many digits. The representations of $1/7$ and $-1/7$, when multiplied by 7 and -7, respectively, using standard rules for multiplication, yield the representation of 1. Prove the following for 2-adic numbers:

a. Sign change of a 2-adic number is similar to 2's complementation.

b. The representation of a 2-adic number x is ultimately periodic if and only if x is rational.

c. The 2-adic representation of $-1/(2n + 1)$ for $n \geq 0$ is (σ), for some bit string σ, where the standard binary representation of $1/(2n + 1)$ is $(0.\sigma\sigma\sigma\cdots)_{two}$.

REFERENCES

[Aviz61]   Avizienis, A., "Signed-Digit Number Representation for Fast Parallel Arithmetic," *IRE Trans. Electronic Computers*, Vol. 10, pp. 389-400, 1961.

[Gosl80]   Gosling, J. B., *Design of Arithmetic Units for Digital Computers*, Macmillan, 1980.

[Knut97]   Knuth, D. E., *The Art of Computer Programming*, 3rd ed., Vol. 2: *Seminumerical Algorithms*, Addison-Wesley, 1997.

[Kore81]   Koren, I., and Y. Maliniak, "On Classes of Positive, Negative, and Imaginary Radix Number Systems," *IEEE Trans. Computers*, No. 5, Vol. 30, pp. 312-317, 1981.

[Korn94]   Kornerup, P., "Digit-Set Conversions: Generalizations and Applications," *IEEE Trans. Computers*, Vol. 43, No. 8, pp. 622-629, 1994.

[Parh90]   Parhami, B., "Generalized Signed-Digit Number Systems: A Unifying Framework for Redundant Number Representations," *IEEE Trans. Computers*, Vol. 39, No. 1, pp. 89-98, 1990.

[Parh98]   Parhami, B., and S. Johansson, "A Number Representation Scheme with Carry-Free Rounding for Floating-Point Signal Processing Applications," *Proc. Int'l. Conf. Signal and Image Processing*, Las Vegas, Nevada, October 1998, pp. 90–92.

[Scot85]   Scott, N. R., *Computer Number Systems and Arithmetic*, Prentice-Hall, 1985.

Chapter 3
REDUNDANT NUMBER SYSTEMS

This chapter deals with the representation of signed fixed-point numbers using a positive integer radix r and a redundant digit set composed of more than r digit values. After showing that such representations eliminate carry propagation, we cover variations in digit sets, addition algorithms, input/output conversions, and arithmetic support functions. Chapter topics include:

3.1 Coping with the Carry Problem
3.2 Redundancy in Computer Arithmetic
3.3 Digit Sets and Digit-Set Conversions
3.4 Generalized Signed-Digit Numbers
3.5 Carry-Free Addition Algorithms
3.6 Conversions and Support Functions

3.1 COPING WITH THE CARRY PROBLEM

Addition is a primary building block in implementing arithmetic operations. If addition is slow or expensive, all other operations suffer in speed or cost. Addition can be slow and/or expensive because:

a. With k-digit operands, one has to allow for $O(k)$ worst-case carry-propagation stages in simple ripple-carry adder design.
b. The carry computation network is a major source of complexity and cost in the design of carry-lookahead and other fast adders.

The carry problem can be dealt with in several ways:

1. Limit carry propagation to within a small number of bits.
2. Detect the end of propagation rather than wait for worst-case time.
3. Speed up propagation via lookahead and other methods.
4. Ideal: Eliminate carry propagation altogether!

35

As examples of option 1, hybrid redundant and residue number system representations are covered in Section 3.4 and Chapter 4, respectively. Asynchronous adder design (option 2) is considered in Section 5.4. Speedup methods for carry propagation are covered in Chapters 6 and 7.

In the remainder of this chapter, we deal with option 4, focusing first on the question: Can numbers be represented in such a way that addition does not involve carry propagation? We will see shortly that this is indeed possible. The resulting number representations can be used as the primary encoding scheme in the design of high-performance systems and are also useful in representing intermediate results in machines that use conventional number representation.

We begin with a decimal example ($r = 10$), assuming the standard digit set [0, 9]. Consider the addition of the following two decimal numbers without carry propagation. For this, we simply compute "position sums" and write them down in the corresponding columns. We can use the symbols $A = 10, B = 11, C = 12$, etc. for the extended digit values or simply represent them with two standard digits.

$$
\begin{array}{ccccccl}
  & 5 & 7 & 8 & 2 & 4 & 9 \\
+ & 6 & 2 & 9 & 3 & 8 & 9 & \text{Operand digits in } [0, 9] \\
\hline
  & 11 & 9 & 17 & 5 & 12 & 18 & \text{Position sums in } [0, 18]
\end{array}
$$

So, if we allow the digit set [0, 18], the scheme works, but only for the first addition! Subsequent additions will cause problems.

Consider now adding two numbers in the radix-10 number system using the digit set [0, 18]. The sum of digits for each position is in [0, 36], which can be decomposed into an interim sum in [0, 16] and a transfer digit in [0, 2]. In other words:

$$[0, 36] = 10 \times [0, 2] + [0, 16]$$

Adding the interim sum and the incoming transfer digit yields a digit in [0, 18] and creates no new transfer. In interval notation, we have:

$$[0, 16] + [0, 2] = [0, 18]$$

Figure 3.1 shows an example addition.

So, even though we cannot do true carry-free addition (Fig. 3.2a), the next best thing, where carry propagates by only one position (Fig. 3.2b), is possible if we use the digit set [0, 18] in radix 10. We refer to this best possible scheme as "carry-free" addition. The key to the ability to do carry-free addition is the representational redundancy that provides multiple encodings for some numbers. Figure 3.2c shows that the single-stage propagation of transfers can be eliminated by a simple lookahead scheme; that is, instead of first computing the transfer into position i based on the digits x_{i-1} and y_{i-1} and then combining it with the interim sum, we can determine s_i directly from x_i, y_i, x_{i-1}, and y_{i-1}. This may make the adder logic somewhat more complex, but in general the result is higher speed.

In the decimal example of Fig. 3.1, the digit set [0, 18] was used to effect carry-free addition. The 9 "digit" values 10 through 18 are redundant. However, we really do not need this much redundancy in a decimal number system for carry-free addition; the digit set [0, 11] will do. Our example addition (after converting the numbers to the new digit set) is shown in Fig. 3.3.

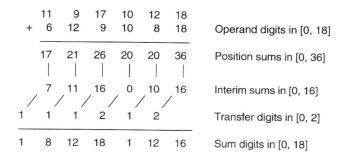

	11	9	17	10	12	18	
+	6	12	9	10	8	18	Operand digits in [0, 18]
	17	21	26	20	20	36	Position sums in [0, 36]
	7	11	16	0	10	16	Interim sums in [0, 16]
1	1	1	2	1	2		Transfer digits in [0, 2]
1	8	12	18	1	12	16	Sum digits in [0, 18]

Fig. 3.1   Adding radix-10 numbers with the digit set [0, 18].

A natural question at this point is: How much redundancy in the digit set is needed to enable carry-free addition? For example, will the example addition of Fig. 3.3 work with the digit set [0, 10]? (Try it and see.) We will answer this question in Section 3.5.

3.2 REDUNDANCY IN COMPUTER ARITHMETIC

Redundancy is used extensively for speeding up arithmetic operations. The oldest example, first suggested in 1959 [Metz59], pertains to carry-save or stored-carry numbers using the radix-2 digit set [0, 2] for fast addition of a sequence of binary operands. Figure 3.4 provides an example, showing how the intermediate sum is kept in stored-carry format, allowing each subsequent addition to be performed in a carry-free manner.

Why is this scheme called carry-save or stored-carry? Figure 3.5 provides an explanation. Let us use the 2-bit encoding

$$0 : (0, 0), \qquad 1 : (0, 1) \text{ or } (1, 0), \qquad 2 : (1, 1)$$

to represent the digit set [0, 2]. With this encoding, each stored-carry number is really composed of two binary numbers, one for each bit of the encoding. These two binary numbers can be added

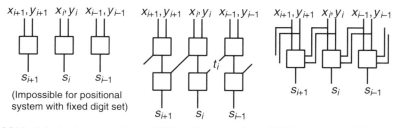

(a) Ideal single-stage carry-free.   **(b)** Two-stage carry-free.   **(c)** Single-stage with lookahead.

Fig. 3.2   Ideal and practical carry-free addition schemes.

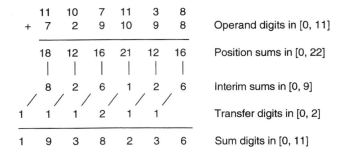

	11	10	7	11	3	8	
+	7	2	9	10	9	8	Operand digits in [0, 11]
	18	12	16	21	12	16	Position sums in [0, 22]
	8	2	6	1	2	6	Interim sums in [0, 9]
1	1	1	2	1	1		Transfer digits in [0, 2]
1	9	3	8	2	3	6	Sum digits in [0, 11]

Fig. 3.3   Adding radix-10 numbers with the digit set [0, 11].

to an incoming binary number, producing two binary numbers composed of the sum bits kept in place and the carry bits shifted one position to the left. These sum and carry bits form the partial sum and can be stored in two registers for the next addition. Thus, the carries are "saved" or "stored" instead of being allowed to propagate.

Figure 3.5 shows that one stored-carry number and one standard binary number can be added to form a stored-carry sum in a single full-adder delay (2–4 gate levels, depending on the full adder's logic implementation of the outputs $s = x \oplus y \oplus c_{in}$ and $c_{out} = xy + xc_{in} + yc_{in}$). This

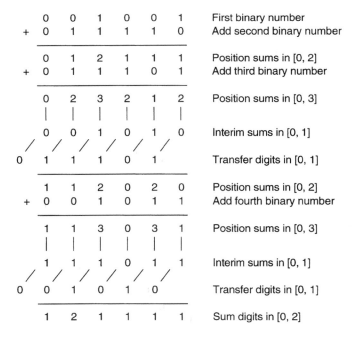

	0	0	1	0	0	1	First binary number
+	0	1	1	1	1	0	Add second binary number
	0	1	2	1	1	1	Position sums in [0, 2]
+	0	1	1	1	0	1	Add third binary number
	0	2	3	2	1	2	Position sums in [0, 3]
	0	0	1	0	1	0	Interim sums in [0, 1]
0	1	1	1	0	1		Transfer digits in [0, 1]
	1	1	2	0	2	0	Position sums in [0, 2]
+	0	0	1	0	1	1	Add fourth binary number
	1	1	3	0	3	1	Position sums in [0, 3]
	1	1	1	0	1	1	Interim sums in [0, 1]
0	0	1	0	1	0		Transfer digits in [0, 1]
	1	2	1	1	1	1	Sum digits in [0, 2]

Fig. 3.4   Addition of four binary numbers, with the sum obtained in stored-carry form.

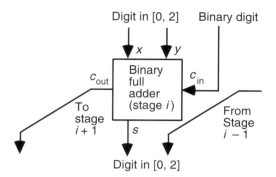

Fig. 3.5 Using an array of independent binary full adders to perform carry-save addition.

is significantly faster than standard carry-propagate addition to accumulate the sum of several binary numbers, even if a fast carry-lookahead adder is used for the latter. Of course once the final sum has been obtained in stored-carry form, it may have to be converted to standard binary by using a carry-propagate adder to add the two components of the stored-carry number. The key point is that the carry-propagation delay occurs only once, at the very end, rather than in each addition step.

Since the carry-save addition scheme of Fig. 3.5 converts three binary numbers to two binary numbers with the same sum, it is sometimes referred to as a 3/2 reduction circuit or (3; 2) counter. The latter name reflects the essential function of a full adder: it counts the number of 1s among its three input bits and outputs the result as a 2-bit binary number. More on this in Chapter 8.

Other examples of the use of redundant representations in computer arithmetic are found in fast multiplication and division schemes, where the multiplier or quotient is represented or produced in redundant form. More on these in Parts III and IV.

3.3 DIGIT SETS AND DIGIT-SET CONVERSIONS

Conventional radix-r numbers use the standard digit set $[0, r - 1]$. However, many other redundant and nonredundant digit sets are possible. A necessary condition is that the digit set contain at least r different digit values. If it contains more than r values, the number system is redundant.

Conversion of numbers between standard and other digit sets is quite simple and essentially entails a digit-serial process in which, beginning at the right end of the given number, each digit is rewritten as a valid digit in the new digit set and a transfer (carry or borrow) into the next higher digit position. This conversion process is essentially like carry propagation in that it must be done from right to left and, in the worst case, the most significant digit is affected by a "carry" coming from the least significant position. The following examples illustrate the process (see also the examples at the end of Section 2.6).

Example 3.1 Convert the following radix-10 number with the digit set [0, 18] to one using the conventional digit set [0, 9].

	11	9	17	10	12	18	Rewrite 18 as 10 (carry 1) + 8
	11	9	17	10	13	8	13 = 10 (carry 1) + 3
	11	9	17	11	3	8	11 = 10 (carry 1) + 1
	11	9	18	1	3	8	18 = 10 (carry 1) + 8
	11	10	8	1	3	8	10 = 10 (carry 1) + 0
	12	0	8	1	3	8	12 = 10 (carry 1) + 2
1	2	0	8	1	3	8	Answer: all digits in [0, 9]

Example 3.2 Convert the following radix-2 carry-save number to binary; that is, from digit set [0, 2] to digit set [0, 1].

	1	1	2	0	2	0	Rewrite 2 as 2 (carry 1) + 0
	1	1	2	1	0	0	2 = 2 (carry 1) + 0
	1	2	0	1	0	0	2 = 2 (carry 1) + 0
	2	0	0	1	0	0	2 = 2 (carry 1) + 0
1	0	0	0	1	0	0	Answer: all digits in [0, 1]

Another way to accomplish the preceding conversion is to decompose the carry-save number into two numbers, both of which have 1s where the original number has a digit of 2. The sum of these two numbers is then the desired binary number.

	1	1	1	0	1	0		First number: "sum" bits
+	0	0	1	0	1	0		Second number: "carry" bits
1	0	0	0	1	0	0		Sum of the two numbers

Example 3.3 Digit values do not have to be positive. We reconsider Example 3.1 using the asymmetric target digit set [−6, 5].

	11	9	17	10	12	18	Rewrite 18 as 20 (carry 2) − 2
	11	9	17	10	14	−2	14 = 10 (carry 1) + 4
	11	9	17	11	4	−2	11 = 10 (carry 1) + 1
	11	9	18	1	4	−2	18 = 20 (carry 2) − 2
	11	11	−2	1	4	−2	11 = 10 (carry 1) + 1
	12	1	−2	1	4	−2	12 = 10 (carry 1) + 2
1	2	1	−2	1	4	−2	Answer: all digits in [−6, 5]

On line 2 of this conversion, we could have rewritten 14 as 20 (carry 2) − 6, which would have led to a different, but equivalent, representation. In general, several representations may be possible with a redundant digit set.

■ **Example 3.4** If we change the target digit set of Example 3.2 from $[0, 1]$ to $[-1, 1]$, we can do the conversion digit-serially as before. However, carry-free conversion is possible for this example if we rewrite each 2 as 2 (carry 1) + 0 and each 1 as 2 (carry 1) −1. The resulting interim digits in $[-1, 0]$ can absorb an incoming carry of 1 with no further propagation.

	1	1	2	0	2	0	Given carry-save number
	−1	−1	0	0	0	0	Interim digits in $[-1, 0]$
1	1	1	0	1	0		Transfer digits in $[0, 1]$
1	0	0	0	1	0	0	Answer: all digits in $[-1, 1]$

3.4 GENERALIZED SIGNED-DIGIT NUMBERS

We have seen thus far that digit set of a radix-r positional number system need not be the standard set $[0, r - 1]$. Using the digit set $[-1, 1]$ for radix-2 numbers was proposed by E. Collignon as early as 1897 [Glas81]. Whether this was just a mathematical curiosity, or motivated by an application or advantage, is not known. In the early 1960s, Avizienis [Aviz61] defined the class of signed-digit number systems with symmetric digit sets $[-\alpha, \alpha]$ and radix $r > 2$, where α is any integer in the range $\lfloor r/2 \rfloor + 1 \leq \alpha \leq r - 1$. These number systems allow at least $2\lfloor r/2 \rfloor + 3$ digit values, instead of the minimum required r values, and are thus redundant.

More recently, redundant number systems with general, possibly asymmetric, digit sets of the form $[-\alpha, \beta]$ have been studied as tools for unifying all redundant number representations used in practice. This class is called "generalized signed-digit (GSD) representation" and differs from the ordinary signed-digit (OSD) representation of Avizienis in its more general digit set as well as the possibility of higher or lower redundancy.

Binary stored-carry numbers, with $r = 2$ and digit set $[0, 2]$, offer a good example for the usefulness of asymmetric digit sets. Higher redundancy is exemplified by the digit set $[-7, 7]$ in radix 4 or $[0, 3]$ in radix 2. An example for lower redundancy is the binary signed-digit representation with $r = 2$ and digit set $[-1, 1]$. None of these is covered by OSD.

An important parameter of a GSD number system is its *redundancy index*, defined as $\rho = \alpha + \beta + 1 - r$ (i.e., the amount by which the size of its digit set exceeds the size r of a nonredundant digit set for radix r). Figure 3.6 presents a taxonomy of redundant and nonredundant positional number systems showing the names of some useful subclasses and their various relationships.

Any hardware implementation of GSD arithmetic requires the choice of a binary encoding scheme for the $\alpha + \beta + 1$ digit values in the digit set $[-\alpha, \beta]$. Multivalued logic realizations have been considered, but we limit our discussion here to binary logic and proceed to show the importance and implications of the encoding scheme chosen through some examples.

Consider, for example, the binary signed-digit (BSD) number system with $r = 2$ and the digit set $[-1, 1]$. One needs at least 2 bits to encode these three digit values. Figure 3.7 shows four of the many possible encodings that can be used.

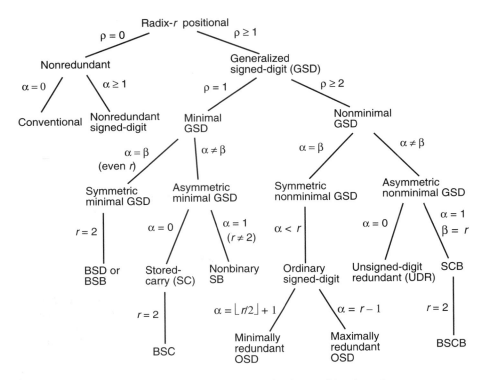

Fig. 3.6   A taxonomy of redundant and nonredundant positional number systems.

With the (n, p) encoding, the code $(1, 1)$ may be considered an alternate representation of 0 or else viewed as an invalid combination. Many implementations have shown that the (n, p) encoding tends to simplify the hardware and also increases the speed by reducing the number of gate levels [Parh88]. The 1-out-of-3 encoding requires more bits per number but allows the detection of some storage and processing errors.

Hybrid signed-digit representations [Phat94] came about from an attempt to strike a balance between algorithmic speed and implementation cost by introducing redundancy in selected positions only. For example, standard binary representation may be used with BSD digits allowed in every third position, as shown in the addition example of Fig. 3.8.

x_i	1	-1	0	-1	0	Representation of +6
(s, v)	01	11	00	11	00	Sign and value encoding
2's-compl	01	11	00	11	00	2-bit 2's-complement
(n, p)	01	10	00	10	00	Negative and positive flags
(n, z, p)	001	100	010	100	010	1-out-of-3 encoding

Fig. 3.7   Four encodings for the BSD digit set $[-1, 1]$.

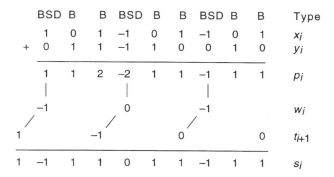

Fig. 3.8 Example of addition for hybrid signed-digit numbers.

The addition algorithm depicted in Fig. 3.8 proceeds as follows. First one completes the position sums p_i that are in $[0, 2]$ for standard binary and $[-2, 2]$ in BSD positions. The BSD position sums are then broken into an interim sum w_i and transfer t_{i+1}, both in $[-1, 1]$. For the interim sum digit, the value 1 (-1) is chosen only if it is certain that the incoming transfer cannot be 1 (-1); that is, when the two binary operand digits in position $i - 1$ are (not) both 0s. The worst-case carry propagation spans a single group, beginning with a BSD digit that produces a transfer digit in $[-1, 1]$ and ending with the next higher BSD position.

More generally, the group size can be g rather than 3. A larger group size reduces the hardware complexity (since the adder block in a BSD position is more complex than that in other positions) but adds to the carry-propagation delay in the worst case; hence, the hybrid scheme offers a trade-off between speed and cost.

Hybrid signed-digit representation with uniform spacing of BSD positions can be viewed as a special case of GSD systems. For the example of Fig. 3.8, arranging the numbers in 3-digit groups starting from the right end leads to a radix-8 GSD system with digit set $[-4, 7]$: that is, digit values from $(^-1\ 0\ 0)_{\text{two}}$ to $(1\ 1\ 1)_{\text{two}}$. So the hybrid scheme of Fig. 3.8 can be viewed as an implementation of (digit encoding for) this particular radix-8 GSD representation.

3.5 CARRY-FREE ADDITION ALGORITHMS

The GSD carry-free addition algorithm, corresponding to the scheme of Fig. 3.2b, is as follows:

Carry-free addition algorithm for GSD numbers

Compute the position sums $p_i = x_i + y_i$.

Divide each p_i into a transfer t_{i+1} and an interim sum $w_i = p_i - rt_{i+1}$.

Add the incoming transfers to obtain the sum digits $s_i = w_i + t_i$.

Let us assume that the transfer digits t_i are from the digit set $[-\lambda, \mu]$. To ensure that the last step leads to no new transfer, the following condition must be satisfied:

$$-\alpha + \lambda \quad \le \quad p_i - rt_{i+1} \quad \le \quad \beta - \mu$$

| interim sum |

Smallest interim sum   Largest interim sum
if a transfer of $-\lambda$ if a transfer of μ
is to be absorbable   is to be absorbable

From the preceding inequalities, we can easily derive the conditions $\lambda \ge \alpha/(r-1)$ and $\mu \ge \beta/(r-1)$. Once λ and μ are known, we choose the transfer digit value by comparing the position sum p_i against $\lambda + \mu + 2$ constants C_j, $-\lambda \le j \le \mu + 1$, with the transfer digit taken to be j if and only if $C_j \le p_i < C_{j+1}$. Figure 3.9 represents the decision process graphically. Formulas giving possible values for these constants can be found in [Parh90]. Here, we describe a simple intuitive method for deriving these constants.

■ **Example 3.5** For $r = 10$ and digit set $[-5, 9]$, we need $\lambda \ge 5/9$ and $\mu \ge 1$. Given minimal values for λ and μ that minimize the hardware complexity, we find by choosing the minimal values for λ and μ, we find:

$$\lambda_{\min} = \mu_{\min} = 1 \quad \text{(i.e., transfer digits are in } [-1, 1])$$
$$-\infty = C_{-1} \quad -4 \le C_0 \le -1 \quad 6 \le C_1 \le 9 \quad C_2 = +\infty$$

We next show how the allowable values for the comparison constant C_1, shown above, are derived. The position sum p_i is in $[-10, 18]$. We can set t_{i+1} to 1 for p_i values as low as 6; for $p_i = 6$, the resulting interim sum of -4 can absorb any incoming transfer in $[-1, 1]$ without falling outside $[-5, 9]$. On the other hand, we must transfer 1 for p_i values of 9 or more. Thus, for $p_i \ge C_1$, where $6 \le C_1 \le 9$, we choose an outgoing transfer of 1. Similarly, for $p_i < C_0$, we choose an outgoing transfer of -1, where $-4 \le C_0 \le -1$. In all other cases, the outgoing transfer is 0.

Assuming that the position sum p_i is represented as a 6-bit, 2's-complement number $abcdef$, good choices for the comparison constants in the above ranges are $C_0 = -4$ and $C_1 = 8$. The logic expressions for the signals g_1 and g_{-1} then become:

$$g_{-1} = a(\bar{c} + \bar{d}) \quad \text{Generate a transfer of } -1$$
$$g_1 = \bar{a}(b + c) \quad \text{Generate a transfer of } 1$$

An example addition is shown in Fig. 3.10.

It is proven in [Parh90] that the preceding carry-free addition algorithm is applicable to a redundant representation if and only if one of the following sets of conditions is satisfied:

a. $r > 2, \rho \ge 3$
b. $r > 2, \rho = 2, \alpha \ne 1, \beta \ne 1$

Constants	$C_{-\lambda}$	$C_{-\lambda+1}$	$C_{-\lambda+2}$	$\cdots$	C_0	C_1	$\cdots$	$C_{\mu-1}$	C_μ	$C_{\mu+1}$
	$-\infty$									$+\infty$
p_i range	[----)	[----)	[----)	$\cdots$	[----)	[----)	$\cdots$	[----)	[----)	
t_{i+1} chosen	$-\lambda$	$-\lambda+1$	$-\lambda+2$		0	1		$\mu-1$	μ	

Fig. 3.9 Choosing the transfer digit t_{i+1} based on comparing the interim sum p_i to the comparison constants C_j.

In other words, the carry-free algorithm is not applicable for $r = 2$, $\rho = 1$, or $\rho = 2$ with $\alpha = 1$ or $\beta = 1$. In such cases, a limited-carry addition algorithm is available:

Limited-carry addition algorithm for GSD numbers

Compute the position sums $p_i = x_i + y_i$.

Compare each p_i to a constant to determine whether $e_{i+1} =$ "low" or "high" (e_{i+1} is a binary range estimate for t_{i+1}).

Given e_i, divide each p_i into a transfer t_{i+1} and an interim sum $w_i = p_i - rt_{i+1}$.

Add the incoming transfers to obtain the sum digits $s_i = w_i + t_i$.

This "limited-carry" GSD addition algorithm is depicted in Fig. 3.11a; in an alternative implementation (Fig. 3.11b), the "transfer estimate" stage is replaced by another transfer generation/addition phase.

Even though Figs. 3.11a and 3.11b appear similar, they are quite different in terms of the internal designs of the square boxes in the top and middle rows. In both cases, however, the sum digit s_i depends on x_i, y_i, x_{i-1}, y_{i-1}, x_{i-2}, and y_{i-2}. Rather than wait for the limited transfer propagation from stage $i - 2$ to i, one can try to provide the necessary information directly from stage $i - 2$ to stage i. This leads to an implementation with parallel carries $t_{i+1}^{(1)}$ and $t_{i+2}^{(2)}$ from stage i, which is sometimes applicable (Fig. 3.11c).

■ **Example 3.6** Figure 3.12 depicts the use of carry estimates in limited-carry addition of radix-2 numbers with the digit set $[-1, 1]$. Here we have $\rho = 1$, $\lambda_{\min} = 1$, and $\mu_{\min} = 1$. The "low" and "high" subranges for transfer digits are $[-1, 0]$ and $[0, 1]$, respectively, with a transfer t_{i+1} in "high" indicated if $p_i \geq 0$.

	3	$^-4$	9	$^-2$	8		x_i in $[-5, 9]$
+	8	$^-4$	9	8	1		y_i in $[-5, 9]$
	11	-8	18	6	9		p_i in $[-10, 18]$
	|	|	|	|	|		
	1	2	8	6	-1		w_i in $[-4, 8]$
	/	/	/	/	/		
1	-1	1	0	1			t_{i+1} in $[-1, 1]$
1	0	3	8	7	$^-1$		s_i in $[-5, 9]$

Fig. 3.10 Adding radix-10 numbers with the digit set $[-5, 9]$.

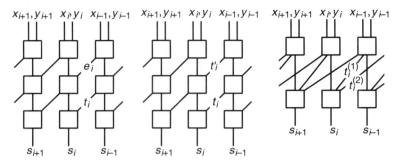

(a) Three-stage carry estimate.   (b) Three-stage repeated carry.   (c) Two-stage parallel carries.

Fig. 3.11   Some implementations for limited-carry addition.

■ **Example 3.7** Figure 3.13 shows another example of limited-carry addition with $r = 2$, digit set $[0, 3]$, $\rho = 2$, $\lambda_{\min} = 0$, and $\mu_{\min} = 3$, using carry estimates. The "low" and "high" subranges for transfer digits are $[0, 2]$ and $[1, 3]$, respectively, with a transfer t_{i+1} in "high" indicated if $p_i \geq 4$.

■ **Example 3.8** Figure 3.14 shows the same addition as in Example 3.7 ($r = 2$, digit set $[0, 3]$, $\rho = 2$, $\lambda_{\min} = 0$, $\mu_{\min} = 3$) using the repeated-carry scheme of Fig. 3.11b.

$$
\begin{array}{rrrrrll}
  & 1 & -1 & 0 & -1 & 0 & \quad x_i \text{ in } [-1, 1] \\
+ & 0 & -1 & -1 & 0 & 1 & \quad y_i \text{ in } [-1, 1] \\
\hline
  & 1 & -2 & -1 & -1 & 1 & \quad p_i \text{ in } [-2, 2] \\
\end{array}
$$

high low low low high high e_i in {low:$[-1, 0]$, high:$[0, 1]$}

$$
\begin{array}{rrrrrl}
  & 1 & 0 & 1 & -1 & -1 & \quad w_i \text{ in } [-1, 1] \\
0 & -1 & -1 & 0 & 1 & & \quad t_{i+1} \text{ in } [-1, 1] \\
\hline
0 & 0 & ^-1 & 1 & 0 & ^-1 & \quad s_i \text{ in } [-1, 1] \\
\end{array}
$$

Fig. 3.12   Limited-carry addition of radix-2 numbers with the digit set $[-1, 1]$ by means of carry estimates. A position sum of -1 is kept intact when the incoming transfer is in $[0, 1]$, whereas it is rewritten as 1 with a carry of -1 if the incoming transfer is in $[-1, 0]$. This scheme guarantees that $t_i \neq w_i$ and thus $-1 \leq s_i \leq 1$.

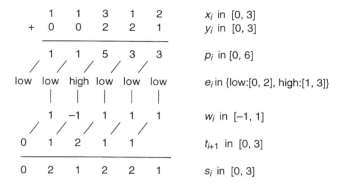

Fig. 3.13 Limited-carry addition of radix-2 numbers with the digit set [0, 3] by means of carry estimates. A position sum of 1 is kept intact when the incoming transfer is in [0, 2], whereas it is rewritten as -1 with a carry of 1 if the incoming transfer is in [1, 3].

■ **Example 3.9** Figure 3.15 shows the same addition as in Example 3.7 ($r = 2$, digit set [0, 3], $\rho = 2$, $\lambda_{min} = 0$, $\mu_{min} = 3$) using the parallel-carries scheme of Fig. 3.11c.

Subtraction of GSD numbers is very similar to addition. With a symmetric digit set, one can simply invert the signs of all digits in the subtractor y to obtain a representation of $-y$ and then perform the addition $x + (-y)$ using a carry-free or limited-carry algorithm as already discussed. Negation of a GSD number with an asymmetric digit set is somewhat more complicated, but can still be performed by means of a carry-free algorithm [Parh93]. This algorithm basically

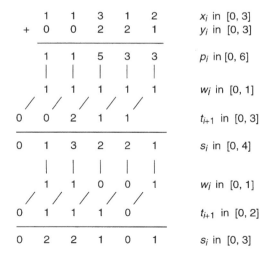

Fig. 3.14 Limited-carry addition of radix-2 numbers with the digit set [0, 3] by means of the repeated-carry scheme.

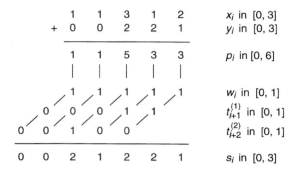

Fig. 3.15   Limited-carry addition of radix-2 numbers with the digit set [0, 3] by means of the parallel-carries scheme.

converts a radix-r number from the digit set $[-\beta, \alpha]$, which results from changing the signs of the individual digits of y, to the original digit set $[-\alpha, \beta]$. Alternatively, a direct subtraction algorithm can be applied by first computing position differences in $[-\alpha - \beta, \alpha + \beta]$, then forming interim differences and transfer digits. Details are omitted here.

3.6 CONVERSIONS AND SUPPORT FUNCTIONS

Since input numbers provided from the outside (machine or human interface) are in standard binary or decimal and outputs must be presented in the same way, conversions between binary or decimal and GSD representations are required.

■ **Example 3.10** Consider number conversions from or to standard binary to or from binary signed-digit representation. To convert from signed binary to BSD, we simply attach the common number sign to each digit, if the (s, v) code of Fig. 3.7 is to be used for the BSD digits. Otherwise, we need a simple digitwise converter from the (s, v) code to the desired code. To convert from BSD to signed binary, we separate the positive and negative digits into a positive and a negative binary number, respectively. A subtraction then yields the desired result. Here is an example:

1	−1	0	−1	0	BSD representation of +6
1	0	0	0	0	Positive part (1 digits)
0	1	0	1	0	Negative part (−1 digits)
0	0	1	1	0	Difference = conversion result

The positive and negative parts required above are particularly easy to obtain if the BSD number is represented using the (n, p) code of Fig. 3.7. The reader should be able to modify the process above for dealing with numbers, or deriving results, in 2's-complement format.

The conversion from redundant to nonredundant representation essentially involves carry propagation and is thus rather slow. Hopefully, however, we will not need conversions very often. Conversion is done at the input and output. Thus, if long sequences of computation are performed between input and output, the conversion overhead can become negligible.

Storage overhead (the larger number of bits that may be needed to represent a GSD digit compared to a standard digit in the same radix) used to be a major disadvantage of redundant representations. However, with advances in VLSI technology, this is no longer a major issue; though the increase in the number of pins for input and output may still be a factor.

In the rest of this section, we review some properties of GSD representations that are important for the implementation of arithmetic support functions: zero detection, sign test, and overflow handling [Parh93].

In a GSD number system, the integer 0 may have multiple representations. For example, the three-digit numbers 0 0 0 and $^-$1 4 0 both represent 0 in radix 4. However, in the special case of $\alpha < r$ and $\beta < r$, zero is uniquely represented by the all-0s vector. So despite redundancy and multiple representations, comparison of numbers for equality can be simple in this common special case, since it involves subtraction and detecting the all-0s pattern.

Sign test, and thus any relational comparison ($<$, $\leq$, etc.), is more difficult. The sign of a GSD number in general depends on all its digits. Thus sign test is slow if done through signal propagation (ripple design) or expensive if done by a fast lookahead circuit (contrast this with the trivial sign test for signed-magnitude and 2's-complement representations). In the special case of $\alpha < r$ and $\beta < r$, the sign of number is identical to the sign of its most significant nonzero digit. Even in this special case, determination of sign requires scanning of all digits in the worst case, a process that can be as slow as full carry propagation.

Overflow handling is also more difficult in GSD arithmetic. Consider the addition of two k-digit numbers, as shown in Fig. 3.16. Such an addition produces a transfer-out digit t_k. Since t_k is produced using the worst-case assumption about the as yet unknown t_{k-1}, we can get an overflow indication ($t_k \neq 0$) even when the result can be represented with k digits. It is possible to perform a test to see whether the overflow is real and, if it is not, to obtain a k-digit representation for the true result. However, this test and conversion are fairly slow.

The difficulties with sign test and overflow detection can nullify some or all of the speed advantages of GSD number representations. This is why applications of GSD are presently limited to special-purpose systems or to internal number representations, which are subsequently converted to standard representation.

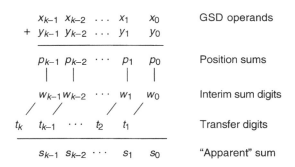

Fig. 3.16 Overflow and its detection in GSD arithmetic.

PROBLEMS

3.1   Stored-carry and stored-borrow representations The radix-2 number systems using the digit sets [0, 2] and [−1, 1] are known as binary stored-carry and stored-borrow representations, respectively. The general radix-r stored-carry and stored-borrow representations are based on the digit sets [0, r] and [−1, $r − 1$], respectively.

a. Show that carry-free addition is impossible for stored-carry/borrow numbers. Do not just refer to the results in [Parh90]; rather, provide your own proof.
b. Supply the details of limited-carry addition for radix-r stored-carry numbers.
c. Supply the details of limited-carry addition for radix-r stored-borrow numbers.
d. Compare the algorithms of parts b and c and discuss.

3.2   Stored-double-carry and stored-triple-carry representations The radix-4 number system using the digit set [0, 4] is a stored-carry representation. Use the digit sets [0, 5] and [0, 6] to form the radix-4 stored-double-carry and stored-triple-carry number systems, respectively.

a. Find the relevant parameters for carry-free addition in the two systems (i.e., the range of transfer digits and the comparison constants). Where there is a choice, select the best value and justify your choice.
b. State the advantages (if any) of one system over the other.

3.3   Stored-carry-or-borrow representations The general radix-r stored-carry-or-borrow representations use the digit set [−1, r].

a. Show that carry-free addition is impossible for stored-carry-or-borrow numbers.
b. Develop a limited-carry addition algorithm for such radix-r numbers.
c. Compare the stored-carry-or-borrow representation to the stored-double-carry representation based on the digit set [0, $r + 1$] and discuss.

3.4   Addition with parallel carries

a. The redundant radix-2 representation with the digit set [0, 3], used in several examples in Section 3.5, is known as the binary stored-double-carry number system [Parh96]. Design a digit slice of a binary stored-double-carry adder based on the addition scheme of Fig. 3.15.
b. Repeat part a with the addition scheme of Fig. 3.13.
c. Repeat part a with the addition scheme of Fig. 3.14.
d. Compare the implementations of parts a–c with respect to speed and cost.

3.5   Addition with parallel or repeated carries

a. Develop addition algorithms similar to those discussed in Section 3.5 for binary stored-triple-carry number system using the digit set [0, 4].
b. Repeat part a for the binary stored-carry-or-borrow number system based on the digit set [−1, 2].
c. Develop a sign detection scheme for binary stored-carry-or-borrow numbers.
d. Can one use digit sets other than [0, 3], [0, 4], and [−1, 2] in radix-2 addition with parallel carries?
e. Repeat parts a–d for addition with repeated carries.

3.6   **Nonredundant and redundant digit sets**   Consider a fixed-point, symmetric radix-3 number system, with k whole and l fractional digits, using the digit set $[-1, 1]$.

    a.   Determine the range of numbers represented as a function of k and l.

    b.   What is the representation efficiency relative to binary representation, given that each radix-3 digit needs a 2-bit code?

    c.   Devise a carry-free procedure for converting a symmetric radix-3 positive number to an unsigned radix-3 number with the redundant digit set $[0, 3]$, or show that such a procedure is impossible.

    d.   What is the representation efficiency of the redundant number system of part c?

3.7   **Digit-set and radix conversions**   Consider a fixed-point, radix-4 number system, with k whole and l fractional digits, using the digit set $[-3, 3]$.

    a.   Determine the range of numbers represented as a function of k and l.

    b.   Devise a procedure for converting such a radix-4 number to a radix-8 number that uses the digit set $[-7, 7]$.

    c.   Specify the numbers K and L of integer and fractional digits in the new radix of part b as functions of k and l.

    d.   Devise a procedure for converting such a radix-4 number to a radix-4 number that uses the digit set $[-2, 2]$.

3.8   **Hybrid signed-digit representation**   Consider a hybrid radix-2 number representation system with the repeating pattern of two standard binary positions followed by one BSD position. The addition algorithm for this system is similar to that in Fig. 3.8. Show that this algorithm can be formulated as carry-free radix-8 GSD addition and derive its relevant parameters (range of transfer digits and comparison constants for transfer digit selection).

3.9   **GSD representation of zero**

    a.   Obtain necessary and sufficient conditions for zero to have a unique representation in a GSD number system.

    b.   Devise a 0 detection algorithm for cases in which 0 has multiple representations.

    c.   Design a hardware circuit for detecting 0 in an 8-digit radix-4 GSD representation using the digit set $[-2, 4]$.

3.10   **Imaginary-radix GSD representation**   Show that the imaginary-radix number system with $r = 2j$, where $j = \sqrt{-1}$, and digit set $[-2, 2]$ lends itself to a limited-carry addition process. Define the process and derive its relevant parameters.

3.11   **Negative-radix GSD representation**   Do you see any advantage to extending the definition of GSD representations to include the possibility of a negative radix r? Explain.

3.12   **Mixed redundant–conventional arithmetic**   We have seen that BSD numbers cannot be added in a carry-free manner but that a limited-carry process can be applied to them.

    a.   Show that one can add a conventional binary number to a BSD number to obtain their BSD sum in a carry-free manner.

    b.   Supply the complete logic design for the carry-free adder of part a.

    c.   Compare your design to a carry-save adder and discuss.

3.13 Negation of GSD numbers One disadvantage of GSD representations with asymmetric digit sets is that negation (change of sign) becomes nontrivial. Show that negation of GSD numbers is always a carry-free process and derive a suitable algorithm for this purpose.

3.14 Digit-serial GSD arithmetic GSD representations allow fast carry-free or limited-carry parallel addition. GSD representations may seem less desirable for digit-serial addition because the simpler binary representation already allows very efficient bit-serial addition. Consider a radix-4 GSD representation using the digit set $[-3, 3]$.

    a. Show that two such GSD numbers can be added digit-serially beginning at the most significant end (MSD-first arithmetic).

    b. Present a complete logic design for your digit-serial adder and determine its latency.

    c. Do you see any advantage for MSD-first, as opposed to LSD-first, arithmetic?

3.15 BSD arithmetic Consider binary signed-digit numbers with digit set $[-1, 1]$ and the 2-bit (n, p) encoding of the digits (see Fig. 3.7). The code $(1, 1)$ never appears and can be used as don't-care.

    a. Design a fast sign detector for a 4-digit BSD input operand using full lookahead.

    b. How can the design of part a be used for 16-digit inputs?

    c. Design a single-digit BSD full adder producing the sum digit s_i and transfer t_{i+1}.

3.16 Unsigned-digit redundant representations Consider the hex-digit decimal (HDD) number system with $r = 10$ and digit set $[0, 15]$ for representing unsigned integers.

    a. Find the relevant parameters for carry-free addition in this system.

    b. Design an HDD adder using 4-bit binary adders and a simple postcorrection circuit.

3.17 Double-LSB 2's-complement numbers Consider k-bit 2's-complement numbers with an extra least significant bit attached to them [Parh98]. Show that such redundant numbers have symmetric range, allow for bitwise 2's-complementation, and can be added using a standard k-bit adder.

REFERENCES

[Aviz61]   Avizienis, A., "Signed-Digit Number Representation for Fast Parallel Arithmetic," *IRE Trans. Electronic Computers*, Vol. 10, pp. 389–400, 1961.

[Glas81]   Glaser, A., *History of Binary and Other Nondecimal Numeration*, rev. ed., Tomash Publishers, 1981.

[Korn94]   Kornerup, P., "Digit-Set Conversions: Generalizations and Applications," *IEEE Trans. Computers*, Vol. 43, No. 8, pp. 622–629, 1994.

[Metz59]   Metze, G., and J.E. Robertson, "Elimination of Carry Propagation in Digital Computers," *Information Processing '59* (Proceedings of a UNESCO Conference), 1960, pp. 389–396.

[Parh88]   Parhami, B., "Carry-Free Addition of Recoded Binary Signed-Digit Numbers," *IEEE Trans. Computers*, Vol. 37, No. 11, pp. 1470–1476, 1988.

[Parh90]   Parhami, B., "Generalized Signed-Digit Number Systems: A Unifying Framework for Redundant Number Representations," *IEEE Trans. Computers*, Vol. 39, No. 1, pp. 89–98, 1990.

[Parh93]   Parhami, B., "On the Implementation of Arithmetic Support Functions for Generalized Signed-Digit Number Systems," *IEEE Trans. Computers*, Vol. 42, No. 3, pp. 379–384, 1993.

[Parh96]   Parhami, B., "Comments on 'High-Speed Area-Efficient Multiplier Design Using Multiple-Valued Current Mode Circuits,'" *IEEE Trans. Computers*, Vol. 45, No. 5, pp. 637–638, 1996.

[Parh98]   Parhami, B., and S. Johansson, "A Number Representation Scheme with Carry-Free Rounding for Floating-Point Signal Processing Applications," *Proc. Int'l. Conf. Signal and Image Processing*, Las Vegas, Nevada, October 1998, pp. 90–92.

[Phat94]   Phatak, D. S., and I. Koren, "Hybrid Signed-Digit Number Systems: A Unified Framework for Redundant Number Representations with Bounded Carry Propagation Chains," *IEEE Trans. Computers*, Vol. 43, No. 8, pp. 880–891, 1994.

Chapter 4

RESIDUE NUMBER SYSTEMS

By converting arithmetic on large numbers to arithmetic on a collection of smaller numbers, residue number system (RNS) representations produce significant speedup for some classes of arithmetic-intensive algorithms in signal processing applications. Additionally, RNS arithmetic is a valuable tool for theoretical studies of the limits of fast arithmetic. In this chapter, we study RNS representations and arithmetic, along with their advantages and drawbacks. Chapter topics include:

4.1 RNS REPRESENTATION AND ARITHMETIC

What number has the remainders of 2, 3, and 2 when divided by the numbers 7, 5, and 3, respectively? This puzzle, written in the form of a verse by the Chinese scholar Sun Tsu more than 1500 years ago [Jenk93], is perhaps the first documented use of number representation using multiple residues. The puzzle essentially asks us to convert the coded representation (2 | 3 | 2) of a residue number system, based on the moduli (7 | 5 | 3), into standard decimal format.

In a residue number system (RNS), a number x is represented by the list of its residues with respect to k pairwise relatively prime moduli $m_{k-1} > \cdots > m_1 > m_0$. The residue x_i of x with respect to the ith modulus m_i is akin to a digit and the entire k-residue representation of x can be viewed as a k-digit number, where the digit set for the ith position is $[0, m_i - 1]$. Notationally, we write

$$x_i = x \bmod m_i = \langle x \rangle_{m_i}$$

and specify the RNS representation of x by enclosing the list of residues, or digits, in parentheses. For example,

$$x = (2|3|2)_{\text{RNS}(7|5|3)}$$

represents the puzzle given at the beginning of this section. The list of moduli can be deleted from the subscript when we have agreed on a default set. In many of the examples of this chapter, the following RNS is assumed:

$$\text{RNS}(8|7|5|3) \quad \text{Default RNS for Chapter 4}$$

The product M of the k pairwise relatively prime moduli is the number of different representable values in the RNS and is known as its *dynamic range*.

$$M = m_{k-1} \times \cdots \times m_1 \times m_0$$

For example, $M = 8 \times 7 \times 5 \times 3 = 840$ is the total number of distinct values that are representable in our chosen 4-modulus RNS. Because of the equality

$$\langle -x \rangle_{m_i} = \langle M - x \rangle_{m_i}$$

the 840 available values can be used to represent numbers 0 through 839, -420 through $+419$, or any other interval of 840 consecutive integers. In effect, negative numbers are represented using a complement system with the complementation constant M.

Here are some example numbers in $\text{RNS}(8|7|5|3)$:

$$
\begin{array}{ll}
(0 \mid 0 \mid 0 \mid 0)_{\text{RNS}} & \text{Represents 0 or 840 or} \cdots \\
(1 \mid 1 \mid 1 \mid 1)_{\text{RNS}} & \text{Represents 1 or 841 or} \cdots \\
(2 \mid 2 \mid 2 \mid 2)_{\text{RNS}} & \text{Represents 2 or 842 or} \cdots \\
(0 \mid 1 \mid 3 \mid 2)_{\text{RNS}} & \text{Represents 8 or 848 or} \cdots \\
(5 \mid 0 \mid 1 \mid 0)_{\text{RNS}} & \text{Represents 21 or 861 or} \cdots \\
(0 \mid 1 \mid 4 \mid 1)_{\text{RNS}} & \text{Represents 64 or 904 or} \cdots \\
(2 \mid 0 \mid 0 \mid 2)_{\text{RNS}} & \text{Represents } -70 \text{ or 770 or} \cdots \\
(7 \mid 6 \mid 4 \mid 2)_{\text{RNS}} & \text{Represents } -1 \text{ or 839 or} \cdots
\end{array}
$$

Given the RNS representation of x, the representation of $-x$ can be found by complementing each of the digits x_i with respect to its modules m_i (0 digits are left unchanged). Thus, given that $21 = (5 \mid 0 \mid 1 \mid 0)_{\text{RNS}}$, we find:

$$-21 = (8 - 5 \mid 0 \mid 5 - 1 \mid 0)_{\text{RNS}} = (3 \mid 0 \mid 4 \mid 0)_{\text{RNS}}$$

Any RNS can be viewed as a weighted representation. We will present a general method for determining the position weights (the Chinese remainder theorem) in Section 4.3. For $\text{RNS}(8|7|5|3)$, the weights associated with the four positions are:

$$105 \qquad 120 \qquad 336 \qquad 280$$

As an example, $(1 \mid 2 \mid 4 \mid 0)_{\text{RNS}}$ represents the number:

$$\langle (105 \times 1) + (120 \times 2) + (336 \times 4) + (280 \times 0) \rangle_{840} = \langle 1689 \rangle_{840} = 9$$

In practice, each residue must be represented or encoded in binary. For our example RNS, such a representation would require 11 bits (Fig. 4.1). To determine the number representation efficiency of our 4-modulus RNS, we note that 840 different values are being represented using 11 bits, compared to 2048 values possible with binary representation. Thus, the representational efficiency is

$$840/2048 = 41\%$$

Since $\log_2 840 = 9.714$, another way to quantify the representational efficiency is to note that in our example RNS, about 1.3 bits of the 11 bits goes to waste.

As noted earlier, the sign of an RNS number can be changed by independently complementing each of its digits with respect to its modulus. Similarly, addition, subtraction, and multiplication can be performed by independently operating on each digit. The following examples for RNS(8|7|5|3) illustrate the process:

$$(5 \mid 5 \mid 0 \mid 2)_{RNS} \quad \text{Represents } x = +5$$
$$(7 \mid 6 \mid 4 \mid 2)_{RNS} \quad \text{Represents } y = -1$$
$$(4 \mid 4 \mid 4 \mid 1)_{RNS} \quad x + y: \langle 5 + 7 \rangle_8 = 4, \langle 5 + 6 \rangle_7 = 4, \text{ etc.}$$
$$(6 \mid 6 \mid 1 \mid 0)_{RNS} \quad x - y: \langle 5 - 7 \rangle_8 = 6, \langle 5 - 6 \rangle_7 = 6, \text{ etc.}$$
$$\text{(alternatively, find } -y \text{ and add to } x)$$
$$(3 \mid 2 \mid 0 \mid 1)_{RNS} \quad x \times y: \langle 5 \times 7 \rangle_8 = 3, \langle 5 \times 6 \rangle_7 = 2, \text{ etc.}$$

Figure 4.2 depicts the structure of an adder, subtractor, or multiplier for RNS arithmetic. Since each digit is a relatively small number, these operations can be quite fast and simple in RNS. This speed and simplicity are the primary advantages of RNS arithmetic. In the case of addition, for example, carry propagation is limited to within a single residue (a few bits). Thus, RNS representation pretty much solves the carry propagation problem. As for multiplication, a 4×4 multiplier (e.g.), is considerably more than four times simpler than a 16×16 multiplier, besides being much faster. In fact, since the residues are small (say, 6 bits wide), it is quite feasible to implement addition, subtraction, and multiplication by direct table lookup. With 6-bit residues, say, each operation requires a $4K \times 6$ table. Thus, excluding division, a complete arithmetic unit module for one 6-bit residue can be implemented with 9 KB of memory.

Unfortunately, however, what we gain in terms of the speed and simplicity of addition, subtraction, and multiplication can be more than nullified by the complexity of division and the difficulty of certain auxiliary operations such as sign test, magnitude comparison, and overflow detection. Given the numbers

$$(7 \mid 2 \mid 2 \mid 1)_{RNS} \quad \text{and} \quad (2 \mid 5 \mid 0 \mid 1)_{RNS}$$

we cannot easily tell their signs, determine which of the two is larger, or find out whether $(1 \mid 0 \mid 2 \mid 2)_{RNS}$ represents their true sum as opposed to the residue of their sum modulo 840.

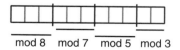

Fig. 4.1   Binary-coded number format for RNS(8|7|5|3).

mod 8   mod 7   mod 5   mod 3

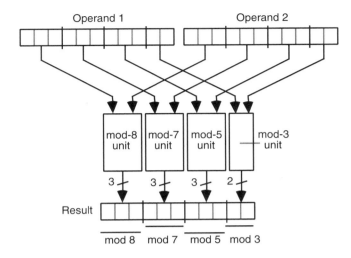

Fig. 4.2   The structure of an adder, subtractor, or multiplier for RNS(8|7|5|3).

These difficulties have thus far limited the application of RNS representations to certain signal processing problems in which additions and multiplications are used either exclusively or predominantly and the results are within known ranges (e.g., digital filters, Fourier transforms). Developments in recent years [Hung94] have greatly lessened the penalty for division and sign detection and may lead to more widespread applications for RNS in future. We discuss division and other "difficult" RNS operations in Section 4.4.

4.2 CHOOSING THE RNS MODULI

The set of the moduli chosen for RNS affects both the representational efficiency and the complexity of arithmetic algorithms. In general, we try to make the moduli as small as possible, since it is the magnitude of the largest modulus m_{k-1} that dictates the speed of arithmetic operations. We also often try to make all the moduli comparable in magnitude to the largest one, since with the computation speed already dictated by m_{k-1}, there is usually no advantage in fragmenting the design of Fig. 4.2 through the use of very small moduli at the right end.

We illustrate the process of selecting the RNS moduli through an example. Let us assume that we want to represent unsigned integers in the range 0 to $(100\,000)_{\text{ten}}$, requiring 17 bits with standard binary representation.

A simple strategy is to pick prime numbers in sequence until the dynamic range M becomes adequate. Thus, we pick $m_0 = 2, m_1 = 3, m_2 = 5$, etc. After we add $m_5 = 13$ to our list, the dynamic range becomes:

$$\text{RNS}(13 \mid 11 \mid 7 \mid 5 \mid 3 \mid 2) \qquad M = 30\,030$$

This range is not yet adequate, so we add $m_6 = 17$ to the list:

$$\text{RNS}(17 \mid 13 \mid 11 \mid 7 \mid 5 \mid 3 \mid 2) \qquad M = 510\,510$$

The dynamic range is now 5.1 times larger than needed, so we can remove the modulus 5 and still have adequate range:

$$\text{RNS}(17 \mid 13 \mid 11 \mid 7 \mid 3 \mid 2) \qquad M = 102\ 102$$

With binary encoding of the six residues, the number of bits needed for encoding each number is:

$$5 + 4 + 4 + 3 + 2 + 1 = 19 \text{ bits}$$

Now, since the speed of arithmetic operations is dictated by the 5-bit residues modulo m_5, we can combine the pairs of moduli 2 and 13, and 3 and 7, with no speed penalty. This leads to:

$$\text{RNS}(26 \mid 21 \mid 17 \mid 11) \qquad M = 102\ 102$$

This alternative RNS still needs $5 + 5 + 5 + 4 = 19$ bits per operand, but has two fewer modules in the arithmetic unit.

Better results can be obtained if we proceed as above, but include powers of smaller primes before moving to larger primes. The chosen moduli will still be pairwise relatively prime, since powers of any two prime numbers are relatively prime. For example, after including $m_0 = 2$ and $m_1 = 3$ in our list of moduli, we note that 2^2 is smaller than the next prime 5. So we modify m_0 and m_1 to get:

$$\text{RNS}(2^2 \mid 3) \qquad M = 12$$

This strategy is consistent with our desire to minimize the magnitude of the largest modulus. Similarly, after we have included $m_2 = 5$ and $m_3 = 7$, we note that both 2^3 and 3^2 are smaller than the next prime 11. So the next three steps lead to:

$$\text{RNS}(3^2 \mid 2^3 \mid 7 \mid 5) \qquad\qquad M = 2520$$
$$\text{RNS}(11 \mid 3^2 \mid 2^3 \mid 7 \mid 5) \qquad\ \, M = 27\ 720$$
$$\text{RNS}(13 \mid 11 \mid 3^2 \mid 2^3 \mid 7 \mid 5) \quad M = 360\ 360$$

The dynamic range is now 3.6 times larger than needed, so we can replace the modulus 9 with 3 and then combine the pair 5 and 3 to obtain:

$$\text{RNS}(15 \mid 13 \mid 11 \mid 2^3 \mid 7) \qquad M = 120\ 120$$

The number of bits needed by this last RNS is

$$4 + 4 + 4 + 3 + 3 = 18 \text{ bits}$$

which is better than our earlier result of 19 bits. The speed has also improved because the largest residue is now 4 bits wide instead of 5.

Other variations are possible. For example, given the simplicity of operations with power-of-2 moduli, we might want to backtrack and maximize the size of our even modulus within the 4-bit residue limit:

$$\text{RNS}(2^4 \mid 13 \mid 11 \mid 3^2 \mid 7 \mid 5) \qquad M = 720\ 720$$

We can now remove 5 or 7 from the list of moduli, but the resulting RNS is in fact inferior to RNS(15|13|11|2^3|7). This might not be the case with other examples; thus, once we have converged on a feasible set of moduli, we should experiment with other sets that can be derived from it by increasing the power of the even modulus at hand.

The preceding strategy for selecting the RNS moduli is guaranteed to lead to the smallest possible number of bits for the largest modulus, thus maximizing the speed of RNS arithmetic. However, speed and cost do not just depend on the widths of the residues but also on the moduli chosen. For example, we have already noted that power-of-2 moduli simplify the required arithmetic operations, so that the modulus 16 might be better than the smaller modulus 13 (except, perhaps, with table-lookup implementation). Moduli of the form $2^a - 1$ are also desirable and are referred to as *low-cost* moduli [Merr64], [Parh76]. From our discussion of addition of 1's-complement numbers in Section 2.4, we know that addition modulo $2^a - 1$ can be performed using a standard a-bit binary adder with end-around carry.

Hence, we are motivated to restrict the moduli to a power of 2 and odd numbers of the form $2^a - 1$. One can prove (left as exercise) that the numbers $2^a - 1$ and $2^b - 1$ are relatively prime if and only if a and b are relatively prime. Thus, any list of relatively prime numbers $a_{k-2} > \cdots > a_1 > a_0$ can be the basis of the following k-modulus RNS

$$\text{RNS}(2^{a_{k-2}} \mid 2^{a_{k-2}} - 1 \mid \cdots \mid 2^{a_1} - 1 \mid 2^{a_0} - 1)$$

for which the widest residues are a_{k-2}-bit numbers. Note that to maximize the dynamic range with a given residue width, the even modulus is chosen to be as large as possible.

Applying this strategy to our desired RNS with the target range [0, 100 000], leads to the following steps:

$$\text{RNS}(2^3 \mid 2^3 - 1 \mid 2^2 - 1) \qquad \text{Basis: 3, 2} \qquad M = 168$$
$$\text{RNS}(2^4 \mid 2^4 - 1 \mid 2^3 - 1) \qquad \text{Basis: 4, 3} \qquad M = 1680$$
$$\text{RNS}(2^5 \mid 2^5 - 1 \mid 2^3 - 1 \mid 2^2 - 1) \quad \text{Basis: 5, 3, 2} \quad M = 20\ 832$$
$$\text{RNS}(2^5 \mid 2^5 - 1 \mid 2^4 - 1 \mid 2^3 - 1) \quad \text{Basis: 5, 4, 3} \quad M = 104\ 160$$

This last system, RNS(32 | 31 | 15 | 7), possesses adequate range. Note that once the number 4 is included in the base list, 2 must be excluded because 4 and 2, and thus $2^4 - 1$ and $2^2 - 1$, are not relatively prime.

The derived RNS requires $5 + 5 + 4 + 3 = 17$ bits for representing each number, with the largest residues being 5 bits wide. In this case, the representational efficiency is close to 100% and no bit is wasted. In general, the representational efficiency of low-cost RNS is provably better than 50% (yet another exercise!), leading to the waste of no more than 1 bit in number representation.

To compare the RNS above to our best result with unrestricted moduli, we list the parameters of the two systems together:

$$\text{RNS}(15 \mid 13 \mid 11 \mid 2^3 \mid 7) \qquad \text{18 bits} \quad M = 120\ 120$$
$$\text{RNS}(2^5 \mid 2^5 - 1 \mid 2^4 - 1 \mid 2^3 - 1) \quad \text{17 bits} \quad M = 104\ 160$$

Both systems provide the desired range. The latter has wider, but fewer, residues. However, the simplicity of arithmetic with low-cost moduli makes the latter a more attractive choice. In general, restricting the moduli tends to increase the width of the largest residues and the optimal choice is dependent on both the application and the target implementation technology.

4.3 ENCODING AND DECODING OF NUMBERS

Since input numbers provided from the outside (machine or human interface) are in standard binary or decimal and outputs must be presented in the same way, conversions between binary/decimal and RNS representations are required.

Conversion from binary/decimal to RNS

The binary-to-RNS conversion problem is stated as follows: Given a number y, find its residues with respect to the moduli m_i, $0 \leq i \leq k - 1$. Let us assume that y is an unsigned binary number. Conversion of signed-magnitude or 2's-complement numbers can be accomplished by converting the magnitude and then complementing the RNS representation if needed.

To avoid time-consuming divisions, we take advantage of the following equality:

$$\langle (y_{k-1} \cdots y_1 y_0)_{\text{two}} \rangle_{m_i} = \langle \langle 2^{k-1} y_{k-1} \rangle_{m_i} + \cdots + \langle 2y_1 \rangle_{m_i} + \langle y_0 \rangle_{m_i} \rangle_{m_i}$$

If we precompute and store $\langle 2^j \rangle_{m_i}$ for each i and j, then the residue x_i of y (mod m_i) can be computed by modulo-m_i addition of some of these constants.

Table 4.1 shows the required lookup table for converting 10-bit binary numbers in the range [0, 839] to RNS(8 | 7 | 5 | 3). Only residues mod 7, mod 5, and mod 3 are given in the table, since the residue mod 8 is directly available as the 3 least significant bits of the binary number y.

■ Example 4.1 Represent $y = (1010\ 0100)_{\text{two}} = (164)_{\text{ten}}$ in RNS(8 | 7 | 5 | 3).

The residue of y mod 8 is $x_3 = (y_2 y_1 y_0)_{\text{two}} = (100)_{\text{two}} = 4$. Since $y = 2^7 + 2^5 + 2^2$, the required residues mod 7, mod 5, and mod 3 are obtained by simply adding the values stored in the three rows corresponding to $j = 7, 5, 2$ in Table 4.1:

$$x_2 = \langle y \rangle_7 = \langle 2 + 4 + 4 \rangle_7 = 3$$
$$x_1 = \langle y \rangle_5 = \langle 3 + 2 + 4 \rangle_5 = 4$$
$$x_0 = \langle y \rangle_3 = \langle 2 + 2 + 1 \rangle_3 = 2$$

Therefore, the RNS(8 | 7 | 5 | 3) representation of $(164)_{\text{ten}}$ is $(4 | 3 | 4 | 2)_{\text{RNS}}$.

In the worst case, k modular additions are required for computing each residue of a k-bit number. To reduce the number of operations, one can view the given input number as a number in a higher radix. For example, if we use radix 4, then storing the residues of 4^i, 2×4^i and 3×4^i in a table would allow us to compute each of the required residues using only $k/2$ modular additions.

The conversion for each modulus can be done by repeatedly using a single lookup table and modular adder or by several copies of each arranged into a pipeline. For a low-cost modulus $m = 2^a - 1$, the residue can be determined by dividing up y into a-bit segments and adding them modulo $2^a - 1$.

TABLE 4.1
Precomputed residues of the first 10 powers of 2

j	2^j	$\langle 2^j \rangle_7$	$\langle 2^j \rangle_5$	$\langle 2^j \rangle_3$
0	1	1	1	1
1	2	2	2	2
2	4	4	4	1
3	8	1	3	2
4	16	2	1	1
5	32	4	2	2
6	64	1	4	1
7	128	2	3	2
8	256	4	1	1
9	512	1	2	2

Conversion from RNS to mixed-radix form

Associated with any residue number system RNS($m_{k-1} \mid \cdots \mid m_2 \mid m_1 \mid m_0$) is a mixed-radix number system MRS($m_{k-1} \mid \cdots \mid m_2 \mid m_1 \mid m_0$), which is essentially a k-digit positional number system with position weights

$$m_{k-2}\cdots m_2 m_1 m_0 \quad \cdots \quad m_2 m_1 m_0 \quad m_1 m_0 \quad m_0 \quad 1$$

and digit sets $[0, m_{k-1}-1], \cdots, [0, m_2-1], [0, m_1-1]$, and $[0, m_0-1]$ in its k digit positions. Hence, the MRS digits are in the same ranges as the RNS digits (residues). For example, the mixed-radix system MRS(8 | 7 | 5 | 3) has position weights $7 \times 5 \times 3 = 105, 5 \times 3 = 15, 3$, and 1, leading to:

$$(0 \mid 3 \mid 1 \mid 0)_{\text{MRS}(8\mid7\mid5\mid3)} = (0 \times 105) + (3 \times 15) + (1 \times 3) + (0 \times 1) = 48$$

The RNS-to-MRS conversion problem is that of determining the z_i digits of MRS, given the x_i digits of RNS, so that:

$$y = (x_{k-1} \mid \cdots \mid x_2 \mid x_1 \mid x_0)_{\text{RNS}} = (z_{k-1} \mid \cdots \mid z_2 \mid z_1 \mid z_0)_{\text{MRS}}$$

From the definition of MRS, we have:

$$y = z_{k-1}(m_{k-2}\cdots m_2 m_1 m_0) + \cdots + z_2(m_1 m_0) + z_1(m_0) + z_0$$

It is thus immediately obvious that $z_0 = x_0$. Subtracting $z_0 = x_0$ from both the RNS and MRS representations, we get

$$y - x_0 = (x'_{k-1} \mid \cdots \mid x'_2 \mid x'_1 \mid 0)_{\text{RNS}} = (z_{k-1} \mid \cdots \mid z_2 \mid z_1 \mid 0)_{\text{MRS}}$$

where $x'_j = \langle x_j - x_0 \rangle_{m_j}$. If we now divide both representations by m_0, we get the following in the reduced RNS and MRS from which m_0 has been removed:

$$(x''_{k-1} \mid \cdots \mid x''_2 \mid x''_1)_{\text{RNS}} = (z_{k-1} \mid \cdots \mid z_2 \mid z_1)_{\text{MRS}}$$

Thus, if we demonstrate how to divide the number $y' = (x'_{k-1} \mid \cdots \mid x'_2 \mid x'_1 \mid 0)_{\text{RNS}}$ by m_0 to obtain $(x''_{k-1} \mid \cdots \mid x''_2 \mid x''_1)_{\text{RNS}}$, we have converted the original problem to a similar problem with one fewer modulus. Repeating the same process then leads to the determination of all the z_i digits in turn.

Dividing y', which is a multiple of m_0, by m_0 is known as *scaling* and is much simpler than general division in RNS. Division by m_0 can be accomplished by multiplying each residue by the *multiplicative inverse* of m_0 with respect to the associated modulus. For example, the multiplicative inverses of 3 relative to 8, 7, and 5 are 3, 5, and 2, respectively, because:

$$\langle 3 \times 3 \rangle_8 = \langle 3 \times 5 \rangle_7 = \langle 3 \times 2 \rangle_5 = 1$$

Thus, the number $y' = (0 \mid 6 \mid 3 \mid 0)_{\text{RNS}}$ can be divided by 3 through multiplication by $(3 \mid 5 \mid 2 \mid -)_{\text{RNS}}$:

$$\frac{(0 \mid 6 \mid 3 \mid 0)_{\text{RNS}}}{3} = (0 \mid 6 \mid 3 \mid 0)_{\text{RNS}} \times (3 \mid 5 \mid 2 \mid -)_{\text{RNS}} = (0 \mid 2 \mid 1 \mid -)_{\text{RNS}}$$

Multiplicative inverses of the moduli can be precomputed and stored in tables to facilitate RNS-to-MRS conversion.

Example 4.2 Convert $y = (0 \mid 6 \mid 3 \mid 0)_{\text{RNS}}$ to mixed-radix representation. We have $z_0 = x_0 = 0$. Based on the preceding discussion, dividing y by 3 yields:

$$\frac{(0 \mid 6 \mid 3 \mid 0)_{\text{RNS}}}{3} = (0 \mid 6 \mid 3 \mid 0)_{\text{RNS}} \times (3 \mid 5 \mid 2 \mid -)_{\text{RNS}} = (0 \mid 2 \mid 1 \mid -)_{\text{RNS}}$$

Thus we have $z_1 = 1$. Subtracting 1 and dividing by 5, we get:

$$\frac{(7 \mid 1 \mid 0 \mid -)_{\text{RNS}}}{5} = (7 \mid 1 \mid 0 \mid -)_{\text{RNS}} \times (5 \mid 3 \mid - \mid -)_{\text{RNS}} = (3 \mid 3 \mid - \mid -)_{\text{RNS}}$$

Next, we get $z_2 = 3$. Subtracting 3 and dividing by 7, we find:

$$\frac{(0 \mid 0 \mid - \mid -)_{\text{RNS}}}{7} = (0 \mid 0 \mid - \mid -)_{\text{RNS}} \times (7 \mid - \mid - \mid -)_{\text{RNS}}$$

$$= (0 \mid - \mid - \mid -)_{\text{RNS}}$$

We conclude by observing that $z_3 = 0$. The conversion is now complete:

$$y = (0 \mid 6 \mid 3 \mid 0)_{\text{RNS}} = (0 \mid 3 \mid 1 \mid 0)_{\text{MRS}} = 48$$

Mixed-radix representation allows us to compare the magnitudes of two RNS numbers or to detect the sign of a number. For example, the RNS representations $(0 \mid 6 \mid 3 \mid 0)_{\text{RNS}}$ and $(5 \mid 3 \mid 0 \mid 0)_{\text{RNS}}$ of 48 and 45 provide no clue to their relative magnitudes, whereas the equivalent mixed-radix representations $(0 \mid 3 \mid 1 \mid 0)_{\text{MRS}}$ and $(0 \mid 3 \mid 0 \mid 0)_{\text{MRS}}$, or $(000 \mid 011 \mid 001 \mid 00)_{\text{MRS}}$ and $(000 \mid 011 \mid 000 \mid 00)_{\text{MRS}}$, when coded in binary, can be compared as ordinary numbers.

Conversion from RNS to binary/decimal

One method for RNS-to-binary conversion is to first derive the mixed-radix representation of the RNS number and then use the weights of the mixed-radix positions to complete the conversion. We can also derive position weights for the RNS directly based on the Chinese remainder theorem (CRT), as discussed below.

Consider the conversion of $y = (3 \mid 2 \mid 4 \mid 2)_{RNS}$ from RNS($8 \mid 7 \mid 5 \mid 3$) to decimal. Based on RNS properties, we can write:

$$
\begin{aligned}
(3 \mid 2 \mid 4 \mid 2)_{RNS} &= (3 \mid 0 \mid 0 \mid 0)_{RNS} + (0 \mid 2 \mid 0 \mid 0)_{RNS} \\
&\quad + (0 \mid 0 \mid 4 \mid 0)_{RNS} + (0 \mid 0 \mid 0 \mid 2)_{RNS} \\
&= 3 \times (1 \mid 0 \mid 0 \mid 0)_{RNS} + 2 \times (0 \mid 1 \mid 0 \mid 0)_{RNS} \\
&\quad + 4 \times (0 \mid 0 \mid 1 \mid 0)_{RNS} + 2 \times (0 \mid 0 \mid 0 \mid 1)_{RNS}
\end{aligned}
$$

Thus, knowing the values of the following four constants (the RNS position weights) would allow us to convert any number from RNS($8|7|5|3$) to decimal using four multiplications and three additions.

$$
\begin{aligned}
(1 \mid 0 \mid 0 \mid 0)_{RNS} &= 105 \\
(0 \mid 1 \mid 0 \mid 0)_{RNS} &= 120 \\
(0 \mid 0 \mid 1 \mid 0)_{RNS} &= 336 \\
(0 \mid 0 \mid 0 \mid 1)_{RNS} &= 280
\end{aligned}
$$

Thus, we find:

$$
(3 \mid 2 \mid 4 \mid 2)_{RNS} = \langle (3 \times 105) + (2 \times 120) + (4 \times 336) + (2 \times 280) \rangle_{840} = 779
$$

It only remains to show how the preceding weights were derived. How, for example, did we determine that $w_3 = (1 \mid 0 \mid 0 \mid 0)_{RNS} = 105$?

To determine the value of w_3, we note that it is divisible by 3, 5, and 7, since its last three residues are 0s. Hence, w_3 must be a multiple of 105. We must then pick the right multiple of 105 such that its residue with respect to 8 is 1. This is done by multiplying 105 by its multiplicative inverse with respect to 8. Based on the preceding discussion, the conversion process can be formalized in the form of the Chinese remainder theorem.

THEOREM 4.1 (The Chinese remainder theorem)   The magnitude of an RNS number can be obtained from the CRT formula:

$$
x = (x_{k-1} \mid \cdots \mid x_2 \mid x_1 \mid x_0)_{RNS} = \left\langle \sum_{i=0}^{k-1} M_i \, \langle \alpha_i x_i \rangle_{m_i} \right\rangle_M
$$

where, by definition, $M_i = M/m_i$, and $\alpha_i = \langle M_i^{-1} \rangle_{m_i}$ is the multiplicative inverse of M_i with respect to m_i.

TABLE 4.2
Values needed in applying the Chinese remainder
theorem to RNS(8|7|5|3)

i	m_i	x_i	$\langle M_i \langle \alpha_i x_i \rangle_{m_i} \rangle_M$
3	8	0	0
		1	105
		2	210
		3	315
		4	420
		5	525
		6	630
		7	735
2	7	0	0
		1	120
		2	240
		3	360
		4	480
		5	600
		6	720
1	5	0	0
		1	336
		2	672
		3	168
		4	504
0	3	0	0
		1	280
		2	560

To avoid multiplications in the conversion process, we can store the values of $\langle M_i \langle \alpha_i x_i \rangle_{m_i} \rangle_M$ for all possible i and x_i in tables of total size $\sum_{i=0}^{k-1} m_i$ words. Table 4.2 shows the required values for RNS(8|7|5|3). Conversion is then performed exclusively by table lookups and modulo-M additions.

4.4 DIFFICULT RNS ARITHMETIC OPERATIONS

In this section, we discuss algorithms and hardware designs for sign test, magnitude comparison, overflow detection, and general division in RNS. The first three of these operations are essentially equivalent in that if an RNS with dynamic range M is used for representing signed numbers in the range $[-N, P]$, with $M = N + P + 1$, then sign test is the same as comparison with P and overflow detection can be performed based on the signs of the operands and that of the result. Thus, it suffices to discuss magnitude comparison and general division.

To compare the magnitudes of two RNS numbers, we can convert both to binary or mixed-radix form. However, this would involve a great deal of overhead. A more efficient approach is through approximate CRT decoding. Dividing the equality in the statement of Theorem 4.1 by M, we obtain the following expression for the scaled value of x in $[0, 1)$:

$$\frac{x}{M} = \frac{(x_{k-1} \mid \cdots \mid x_2 \mid x_1 \mid x_0)_{\text{RNS}}}{M} = \langle \sum_{i=0}^{k-1} m_i^{-1} \langle \alpha_i x_i \rangle_{m_i} \rangle_1$$

Here, the addition of terms is performed modulo 1, meaning that in adding the terms $m_i^{-1} \langle \alpha_i x_i \rangle_{m_i}$, each of which is in [0, 1), the whole part of the result is discarded and only the fractional part is kept; this is much simpler than the modulo-M addition needed in standard CRT decoding.

Again, the terms $m_i^{-1} \langle \alpha_i x_i \rangle_{m_i}$ can be precomputed for all possible i and x_i and stored in tables of total size $\sum_{i=0}^{k-1} m_i$ words. Table 4.3 shows the required lookup table for approximate CRT decoding in RNS(8|7|5|3). Conversion is then performed exclusively by table lookups and modulo-1 additions (i.e., fractional addition, with the carry-out simply ignored).

■ **Example 4.3** Use approximate CRT decoding to determine the larger of the two numbers $x = (0|6|3|0)_{\text{RNS}}$ and $y = (5|3|0|0)_{\text{RNS}}$.

Reading values from Table 4.3, we get:

$$\frac{x}{M} \approx \langle .0000 + .8571 + .2000 + .0000 \rangle_1 \approx .0571$$

$$\frac{y}{M} \approx \langle .6250 + .4286 + .0000 + .0000 \rangle_1 \approx .0536$$

Thus, we can conclude that $x > y$, subject to approximation errors to be discussed next.

If the maximum error in each table entry is ε, then approximate CRT decoding yields the scaled value of an RNS number with an error of no more than $k\varepsilon$. In the preceding example, assuming that the table entries have been rounded to four decimal digits, the maximum error in each entry is $\varepsilon = 0.00005$ and the maximum error in the scaled value is $4\varepsilon = 0.0002$. The conclusion $x > y$ is, therefore, safe.

Of course we can use highly precise table entries to avoid the possibility of erroneous conclusions altogether. But this would defeat the advantage of approximate CRT decoding in simplicity and speed. Thus, in practice, a two-stage process might be envisaged: a quick approximate decoding process is performed first, with the resulting scaled value(s) and error bound(s) used to decide whether a more precise or exact decoding is needed for arriving at a conclusion.

In many practical situations, an exact comparison of x and y might not be required and a ternary decision result $x < y, x \approx y$ (i.e., too close to call), or $x > y$ might do. In such cases, approximate CRT decoding is just the right tool. For example, in certain division algorithms (to be discussed in Chapter 14), the sign and the magnitude of the partial remainder s are used to choose the next quotient digit q_j from the redundant digit set $[-1, 1]$ according to the following:

$$s < 0 \quad \text{quotient digit} = -1$$
$$s \approx 0 \quad \text{quotient digit} = 0$$
$$s > 0 \quad \text{quotient digit} = 1$$

In this case, the algorithm's built-in tolerance to imprecision allows us to use it for RNS division. Once the quotient digit in $[-1, 1]$ has been chosen, the value $q_j d$, where d is the divisor, is subtracted from the partial remainder to obtain the new partial remainder for the next iteration.

TABLE 4.3
Values needed in applying approximate Chinese remainder theorem decoding to RNS(8|7|5|3)

i	m_i	x_i	$m_i^{-1}\langle\alpha_i x_i\rangle_{m_i}$
3	8	0	.0000
		1	.1250
		2	.2500
		3	.3750
		4	.5000
		5	.6250
		6	.7500
		7	.8750
2	7	0	.0000
		1	.1429
		2	.2857
		3	.4286
		4	.5714
		5	.7143
		6	.8571
1	5	0	.0000
		1	.4000
		2	.8000
		3	.2000
		4	.6000
0	3	0	.0000
		1	.3333
		2	.6667

Also, the quotient, derived in positional radix-2 format using the digit set $[-1, 1]$, is converted to RNS on the fly.

In other division algorithms, to be discussed in Chapters 14 and 15, approximate comparison of the partial remainder s and divisor d is used to choose a radix-r quotient digit in $[-\alpha, \beta]$. An example includes radix-4 division with the quotient digit set $[-2, 2]$. In these cases, too, approximate CRT decoding can be used to facilitate RNS division [Hung94].

4.5 REDUNDANT RNS REPRESENTATIONS

Just as the digits in a positional radix-r number system do not have to be restricted to the set $[0, r-1]$, we are not obliged to limit the residue digits for the modulus m_i to the set $[0, m_i - 1]$. Instead, we can agree to use the digit set $[0, \beta_i]$ for the mod-m_i residue, provided $\beta_i \geq m_i - 1$. If $\beta_i \geq m_i$, then the resulting RNS is redundant.

One reason to use redundant residues is to simplify the modular reduction step needed after each arithmetic operation. Consider, for example, the representation of mod-13 residues using 4-bit binary numbers. Instead of using residues in $[0, 12]$, we can use pseudoresidues in $[0, 15]$.

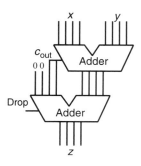

Figure 4.3   Adding a 4-bit ordinary mod-13 residue x to a 4-bit pseudoresidue y, producing a 4-bit mod-13 pseudoresidue z.

Residues 0, 1, and 2 will then have two representations, since $13 = 0$ mod 13, $14 = 1$ mod 13, and $15 = 2$ mod 13. Addition of such a pseudoresidue y to an ordinary residue x, producing a pseudoresidue z, can be performed by a 4-bit binary adder. If the carry-out is 0, the addition result is kept intact; otherwise, the carry-out, which is worth 16 units, is dropped and 3 is added to the result. Thus, the required mod-13 addition unit is as shown in Fig. 4.3. Addition of two pseudoresidues is possible in a similar way [Parh01].

One can go even further and make the pseudoresidues $2h$ bits wide, where normal mod-m residues would be only h bits wide. This simplifies a multiply-accumulate operation, which is done by adding the $2h$-bit product of two normal residues to a $2h$-bit running total, reducing the $(2h + 1)$-bit result to a $2h$-bit pseudoresidue for the next step by subtracting $2^h m$ from it if needed (Fig. 4.4). Reduction to a standard h-bit residue is then done only once at the end of accumulation.

4.6 LIMITS OF FAST ARITHMETIC IN RNS

How much faster is RNS arithmetic than conventional (say, binary) arithmetic? We will see later in Chapters 6 and 7 that addition of binary numbers in the range $[0, M - 1]$ can be done in

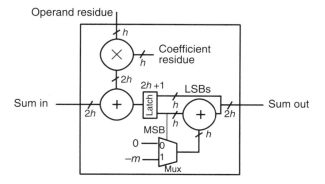

Fig. 4.4   A modulo-m multiply-add cell that accumulates the sum into a double-length redundant pseudoresidue.

$O(\log \log M)$ time and with $O(\log M)$ cost using a variety of methods such as carry-lookahead, conditional-sum, or multilevel carry-select. Both these are optimal to within constant factors, given the fixed-radix positional representation. For example, one can use the constant fan-in argument to establish that the circuit depth of an adder must be at least logarithmic in the number $k = \log_r M$ of digits. Redundant representations allow $O(1)$-time, $O(\log M)$-cost addition. What is the best one can do with RNS arithmetic?

Consider the residue number system RNS$(m_{k-1}|\cdots|m_1|m_0)$. Assume that the moduli are chosen as the smallest possible prime numbers to minimize the size of the moduli, and thus maximize computation speed. The following theorems from number theory help us in figuring out the complexity.

THEOREM 4.2   The ith prime p_i is asymptotically equal to $i \ln i$.

THEOREM 4.3   The number of primes in $[1, n]$ is asymptotically equal to $n/(\ln n)$.

THEOREM 4.4   The product of all primes in $[1, n]$ is asymptotically equal to e^n.

Table 4.4 lists some numerical values that can help us understand the asymptotic approximations given in Theorems 4.2 and 4.3.

Armed with these results from number theory, we can derive an interesting limit on the speed of RNS arithmetic.

TABLE 4.4
The ith-prime p_i and the number of primes in $[1, n]$ versus their asymptotic approximations

i	p_i	$i \ln i$	Error (%)	n	Number of primes in $[1, n]$	$n/(\ln n)$	Error (%)
1	2	0.000	100	5	2	3.107	55
2	3	1.386	54	10	4	4.343	9
3	5	3.296	34	15	6	5.539	8
4	7	5.545	21	20	8	6.676	17
5	11	8.047	27	25	9	7.767	14
10	29	23.03	21	30	10	8.820	12
15	47	40.62	14	40	12	10.84	10
20	71	59.91	16	50	15	12.78	15
30	113	102.0	10	100	25	21.71	13
40	173	147.6	15	200	46	37.75	18
50	229	195.6	15	500	95	80.46	15
100	521	460.5	12	1000	170	144.8	15

THEOREM 4.5   It is possible to represent all k-bit binary numbers in RNS with O(k/log k) moduli such that the largest modulus has O(log k) bits.

Proof: If the largest needed prime is n, by Theorem 4.4 we must have $e^n \approx 2^k$. This equality implies $n < k$. The number of moduli required is the number of primes less than n which by Theorem 4.3 is O(n/log n) = O(k/log k).

As a result, addition of such residue numbers can be performed in O(log log log M) time and with O(log M) cost. So, the cost of addition is comparable to that of binary representation whereas the delay is much smaller, though not constant.

If for implementation ease, we limit ourselves to moduli of the form 2^a or $2^a - 1$, the following results from number theory are applicable.

THEOREM 4.6   The numbers $2^a - 1$ and $2^b - 1$ are relatively prime if and only if a and b are relatively prime.

THEOREM 4.7   The sum of the first i primes is asymptotically O($i^2 \ln i$).

These theorems allow us to prove the following asymptotic result for low-cost residue number systems.

THEOREM 4.8   It is possible to represent all k-bit binary numbers in RNS with O($(k/\log k)^{1/2}$) low-cost moduli of the form $2^a - 1$ such that the largest modulus has O($(k \log k)^{1/2}$) bits.

Proof: If the largest modulus that we need is $2^l - 1$, by Theorem 4.7 we must have $l^2 \ln l \approx k$. This implies that $l = $ O($(k/\log k)^{1/2}$). By Theorem 4.2, the lth prime is approximately $p_l \approx l \ln l \approx$ O($(k \log k)^{1/2}$). The proof is complete upon noting that to minimize the size of the moduli, we pick the ith modulus to be $2^{p_i} - 1$.

As a result, addition of low-cost residue numbers can be performed in O(log log M) time with O(log M) cost and thus, asymptotically, offers little advantage over standard binary.

PROBLEMS

4.1   **RNS representation and arithmetic** Consider the RNS system RNS(15 | 13 | 11 | 8 | 7) derived in Section 4.2.

    a.   Represent the numbers $x = 168$ and $y = 23$ in this RNS.

    b.   Compute $x + y, x - y, x \times y$, checking the results via decimal arithmetic.

    c.   Knowing that x is a multiple of 56, divide it by 56 in the RNS. *Hint:* $56 = 7 \times 8$.

    d.   Compare the numbers $(5 | 4 | 3 | 2 | 1)_{RNS}$ and $(1 | 2 | 3 | 4 | 5)_{RNS}$ using mixed-radix conversion.

    e.   Convert the numbers $(5 | 4 | 3 | 2 | 1)_{RNS}$ and $(1 | 2 | 3 | 4 | 5)_{RNS}$ to decimal.

    f.   What is the representational efficiency of this RNS compared to standard binary?

4.2   **RNS representation and arithmetic** Consider the low-cost RNS system RNS(32 | 31 | 15 | 7) derived in Section 4.2.

    a.   Represent the numbers $x = 168$ and $y = -23$ in this RNS.

    b.   Compute $x + y, x - y, x \times y$, checking the results via decimal arithmetic.

    c.   Knowing that x is a multiple of 7, divide it by 7 in the RNS.

    d.   Compare the numbers $(4 | 3 | 2 | 1)_{RNS}$ and $(1 | 2 | 3 | 4)_{RNS}$ using mixed-radix conversion.

    e.   Convert the numbers $(4 | 3 | 2 | 1)_{RNS}$ and $(1 | 2 | 3 | 4)_{RNS}$ to decimal.

    f.   What is the representational efficiency of this RNS compared to standard binary?

4.3   **RNS representation** Find all numbers for which the RNS(8 | 7 | 5 | 3) representation is palindromic (i.e., the string of four "digits" reads the same forward and backward).

4.4   **RNS versus GSD representation** We are contemplating the use of 16-bit representations for fast integer arithmetic. One option, radix-8 GSD representation with the digit set $[-5, 4]$, can accommodate four-digit numbers. Another is RNS(16 | 15 | 13 | 11) with complement representation of negative values.

    a.   Compute and compare the range of representable integers in the two systems.

    b.   Represent the integers $+441$ and -228 and add them in the two systems.

    c.   Briefly discuss and compare the complexity of multiplication in the two systems.

4.5   **RNS representation and arithmetic** Consider a residue number system that can be used to represent the equivalent of 24-bit, 2's-complement numbers.

    a.   Select the set of moduli to maximize the speed of arithmetic operations.

    b.   Determine the representational efficiency of the resulting RNS.

    c.   Represent the numbers $x = +295$ and $y = -322$ in this number system.

    d.   Compute the representations of $x + y, x - y$, and $x \times y$; check the results.

4.6   **Binary-to-RNS conversion** In a residue number system, 11 is used as one of the moduli.

    a.   Design a mod-11 adder using two standard 4-bit binary adders and a few logic gates.

    b.   Using the adder of part a and a 10-word lookup table, show how the mod-11 residue of an arbitrarily long binary number can be computed by a serial-in, parallel-out circuit.

    c.   Repeat part a, assuming the use of mod-11 pseudoresidues in [0, 15].

    d.   Outline the changes needed in the design of part b if the adder of part c is used.

4.7   **Low-cost RNS** Consider residue number systems with moduli of the form 2^{a_i} or $2^{a_i} - 1$.

    a.   Prove that $m_i = 2^{a_i} - 1$ and $m_j = 2^{a_j} - 1$ are relatively prime if and only if a_i and a_j are relatively prime.

    b.   Show that such a system wastes at most one bit relative to binary representation.

    c.   Determine an efficient set of moduli to represent the equivalent of 32-bit unsigned integers. Discuss your efficiency criteria.

4.8   **Special RNS representations** It has been suggested that moduli of the form $2^{a_i} + 1$ also offer speed advantages. Evaluate this claim by devising a suitable representation for the $(a_i + 1)$-bit residues and dealing with arithmetic operations on such residues. Then, determine an efficient set of moduli of the form 2^{a_i} and $2^{a_i} \pm 1$ to represent the equivalent of 32-bit integers.

4.9   **Overflow in RNS arithmetic** Show that if $0 \leq x, y < m$, then $(x + y)$ mod m causes overflow if and only if the result is less than x (thus the problem of overflow detection in RNS arithmetic is equivalent to the magnitude comparison problem).

4.10   **Discrete logarithm** Consider a prime modulus p. From number theory, we know that there always exists an integer generator g such that the powers $g^0, g^1, g^2, g^3, \ldots$ (mod p) produce all the integers in $[1, p - 1]$. If $g^i = x$ mod p, then i is called the mod-p, base-g discrete logarithm of x. Outline a modular multiplication scheme using discrete log and $\log^{-1}$ tables and an adder.

4.11   **Halving even numbers in RNS** Given the representation of an even number in an RNS with only odd moduli, find an efficient algorithm for halving the given number.

4.12   **Symmetric RNS** In a symmetric RNS, the residues are signed integers, possessing the smallest possible absolute values, rather than unsigned integers. Thus, for an odd modulus m, symmetric residues range from $-(m - 1)/2$ to $(m - 1)/2$ instead of from 0 to $m - 1$. Discuss the possible advantages of a symmetric RNS over ordinary RNS.

4.13   **Approximate Chinese remainder theorem decoding** Consider the numbers $x = (0|6|3|0)_{RNS}$ and $y = (5|3|0|0)_{RNS}$ of Example 4.3 in Section 4.4.

    a.   Redo the example and its associated error analysis with table entries rounded to two decimal digits. How does the conclusion change?

    b.   Redo the example with table entries rounded to three decimal digits and discuss.

4.14   **Division of RNS numbers by the moduli**

    a.   Show how an RNS number can be divided by one of the moduli to find the quotient and the remainder, both in RNS form.

    b.   Repeat part a for division by the product of two or more moduli.

4.15   **RNS base extension** Consider a k-modulus RNS and the representation of a number x in that RNS. Develop an efficient algorithm for deriving the representation of x in a

$(k + 1)$-modulus RNS that includes all the moduli of the original RNS plus one more modulus that is relatively prime with respect to the preceding k. This process of finding a new residue given k existing residues is known as base extension.

4.16 **Automorphic numbers** An n-place *automorph* is an n-digit decimal number whose square ends in the same n digits. For example, 625 is a 3-place automorph, since $625^2 = 390\,625$.

    a. Prove that $x > 1$ is an n-place automorph if and only if $x \bmod 5^n = 0$ or 1 and $x \bmod 2^n = 1$ or 0, respectively.

    b. Relate n-place automorphs to a 2-residue RNS with $m_1 = 5^n$ and $m_0 = 2^n$.

    c. Prove that if x is an n-place automorph, then $(3x^2 - 2x^3) \bmod 10^{2n}$ is a $2n$-place automorph.

REFERENCES

[Garn59]   Garner, H. L., "The Residue Number System," *IRE Trans. Electronic Computers*, Vol. 8, pp. 140–147, June 1959.

[Jenk93]   Jenkins, W. K., "Finite Arithmetic Concepts," in *Handbook for Digital Signal Processing*, S. K. Mitra and J. F. Kaiser, (eds.), Wiley, 1993, pp. 611–675.

[Hung94]   Hung, C. Y., and B. Parhami, "An Approximate Sign Detection Method for Residue Numbers and Its Application to RNS Division," *Computers & Mathematics with Applications*, Vol. 27, No. 4, pp. 23–35, 1994.

[Hung95]   Hung, C. Y., and B. Parhami, "Error Analysis of Approximate Chinese-Remainder-Theorem Decoding," *IEEE Trans. Computers*, Vol. 44, No. 11, pp. 1344–1348, 1995.

[Merr64]   Merrill, R.D., "Improving Digital Computer Performance Using Residue Number Theory," *IEEE Trans. Electronic Computers*, Vol. 13, No. 2, pp. 93–101, April 1964.

[Parh76]   Parhami, B., "Low-Cost Residue Number Systems for Computer Arithmetic," *AFIPS Conf. Proc.*, Vol. 45 (1976 National Computer Conference), AFIPS Press, 1976, pp. 951–956.

[Parh93]   Parhami, B., and H.-F. Lai, "Alternate Memory Compression Schemes for Modular Multiplication," *IEEE Trans. Signal Processing*, Vol. 41, pp. 1378–1385, March 1993.

[Parh01]   Parhami, B., "RNS Representations with Redundant Residues," *Proc. 35th Asilomar Conf. Signals, Systems, and Computers*, Nov. 2001, pp. 1651–1655.

[Sode86]   Soderstrand, M. A., W. K. Jenkins, G. A. Jullien, and F. J. Taylor (eds.), *Residue Number System Arithmetic*, IEEE Press, 1986.

[Szab67]   Szabo, N. S., and R. I. Tanaka, *Residue Arithmetic and Its Applications to Computer Technology*, McGraw-Hill, 1967.

PART II | ADDITION/ SUBTRACTION

Addition is the most common arithmetic operation and also serves as a building block for synthesizing all other operations. Within digital computers, addition is performed extensively both in explicitly specified computation steps and as a part of implicit ones dictated by indexing and other forms of address arithmetic. In simple ALUs that lack dedicated hardware for fast multiplication and division, these latter operations are performed as sequences of additions. A review of fast addition schemes is thus an apt starting point in investigating arithmetic algorithms. Subtraction is normally performed by negating the subtrahend and adding the result to the minuend. This is quite natural, given that an adder must handle signed numbers anyway. Even when implemented directly, a subtractor is quite similar to an adder. Thus, in the following four chapters that constitute this part, we focus almost exclusively on addition:

Chapter 5 | BASIC ADDITION AND COUNTING

As stated in Section 3.1, propagation of carries is a major impediment to high-speed addition with fixed-radix positional number representations. Before exploring various ways of speeding up the carry propagation process, however, we need to examine simple ripple-carry adders, the building blocks used in their construction, the nature of the carry propagation process, and the special case of counting. Chapter topics include:

5.1 Bit-Serial and Ripple-Carry Adders
5.2 Conditions and Exceptions
5.3 Analysis of Carry Propagation
5.4 Carry Completion Detection
5.5 Addition of a Constant: Counters
5.6 Manchester Carry Chains and Adders

5.1 BIT-SERIAL AND RIPPLE-CARRY ADDERS

Single-bit half-adders and full adders are versatile building blocks that are used in synthesizing adders and many other types of arithmetic circuit. A half-adder (HA) receives two input bits x and y, producing a sum bit $s = x \oplus y = x\overline{y} + \overline{x}y$ and a carry bit $c = xy$. Figure 5.1 depicts three of the many possible logic realizations of a half-adder. A half-adder can be viewed as a single-bit binary adder that produces the 2-bit sum of its single-bit inputs, namely, $x + y = (c_{\text{out}}\ s)_{\text{two}}$, where the plus sign in this expression stands for arithmetic sum rather than logical OR.

A single-bit full adder (FA) is defined as follows:

$$
\begin{array}{lll}
\text{Inputs:} & \text{Operand bits } x, y \text{ and carry-in } c_{\text{in}} & \text{(or } x_i, y_i, c_i \text{ for stage } i) \\
\text{Outputs:} & \text{Sum bit } s \text{ and carry-out } c_{\text{out}} & \text{(or } s_i \text{ and } c_{i+1} \text{ for stage } i) \\
& s = x \oplus y \oplus c_{\text{in}} & \text{(odd parity function)} \\
& \quad = xyc_{\text{in}} + \overline{x}\,\overline{y}c_{\text{in}} + \overline{x}y\overline{c}_{\text{in}} + x\overline{y}\,\overline{c}_{\text{in}} & \\
& c_{\text{out}} = xy + xc_{\text{in}} + yc_{in} & \text{(majority function)}
\end{array}
$$

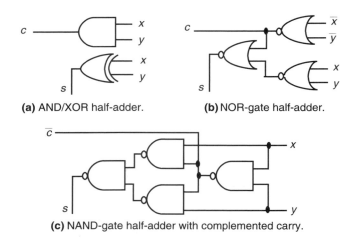

(a) AND/XOR half-adder.   (b) NOR-gate half-adder.

(c) NAND-gate half-adder with complemented carry.

Fig. 5.1   Three implementations of a half-adder.

A full adder can be implemented by using two half-adders and an OR gate as shown in Fig. 5.2a. The OR gate in Fig. 5.2a can be replaced with a NAND gate if the two HAs are NAND-gate half-adders with complemented carry outputs. Alternatively, one can implement a full adder as two-level AND-OR/NAND-NAND circuits according to the preceding logic equations for s and c_{out} (Fig. 5.2b). Because of the importance of the full adder as an arithmetic building block, many optimized FA designs exist for a variety of implementation technologies. Figure 5.2c shows a full adder, built of seven inverters and two 4-to-1 multiplexers (Mux), that is suitable for CMOS transmission-gate logic implementation.

Full and half-adders can be used for realizing a variety of arithmetic functions. We will see many examples in this and the following chapters. For instance, a bit-serial adder can be built from a full adder and a carry flip-flop, as shown in Fig. 5.3a. The operands are supplied to the FA one bit per clock cycle, beginning with the least significant bit, from a pair of shift registers, and the sum is shifted into a result register. Addition of k-bit numbers can thus be completed in k clock cycles. A k-bit ripple-carry binary adder requires k full adders, with the carry-out of the ith FA connected to the carry-in input of the $(i + 1)$th FA. The resulting k-bit adder produces a k-bit sum output and a carry-out; alternatively, c_{out} can be viewed as the most significant bit of a $(k + 1)$-bit sum. Figure 5.3b shows a ripple-carry adder for 4-bit operands, producing a 4-bit or 5-bit sum.

The ripple-carry adder shown in Fig. 5.3b leads directly to a CMOS implementation with transmission gate logic using the full adder design of Fig. 5.2c. A possible layout is depicted in Fig. 5.4, which also shows the approximate area requirements for the 4-bit ripple-carry adder in units of λ (half the minimum feature size). For details of this particular design, refer to [Puck94, pp. 213-223].

The latency of a k-bit ripple-carry adder can be derived by considering the worst-case signal propagation path. As shown in Fig. 5.5, the critical path usually begins at the x_0 or y_0 input, proceeds through the carry-propagation chain to the leftmost FA, and terminates at the s_{k-1} output. Of course, it is possible that for some FA implementations, the critical path

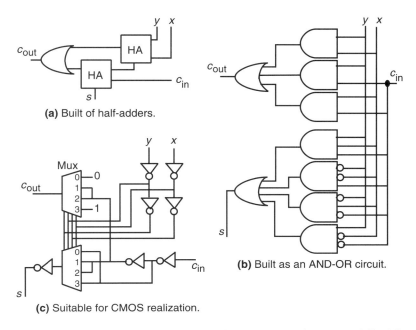

(a) Built of half-adders.

(b) Built as an AND-OR circuit.

(c) Suitable for CMOS realization.

Fig. 5.2   Possible designs for a full adder in terms of half-adders, logic gates, and CMOS transmission gates.

might begin at c_0 and/or terminate at c_k. However, given that the delay from carry-in to carry-out is more important than from x to carry-out or from carry-in to s, full-adder designs often minimize the delay from carry-in to carry-out, making the path shown in Fig. 5.5 the one with the largest delay. We can thus write the following expression for the latency of a k-bit ripple-carry adder:

$$T_{\text{ripple−add}} = T_{\text{FA}}(x, y \rightarrow c_{\text{out}}) + (k - 2) \times T_{\text{FA}}(c_{\text{in}} \rightarrow c_{\text{out}}) + T_{\text{FA}}(c_{\text{in}} \rightarrow s)$$

where $T_{\text{FA}}(\text{input} \rightarrow \text{output})$ represents the latency of a full adder on the path between its specified input and output. As an approximation to the foregoing, we can say that the latency of a ripple-carry adder is kT_{FA}.

We see that the latency grows linearly with k, making the ripple-carry design undesirable for large k or for high-performance arithmetic units. Note that the latency of a bit-serial adder is also $O(k)$, although the constant of proportionality is larger here because of the latching and clocking overheads.

Full and half-adders, as well as multibit binary adders, are powerful building blocks that can also be used in realizing nonarithmetic functions if the need arises. For example, a 4-bit binary adder with c_{in}, two 4-bit operand inputs, c_{out}, and a 4-bit sum output can be used to synthesize the four-variable logic function $w + xyz$ and its complement, as depicted and justified in Fig. 5.6. The logic expressions written next to the arrows in Fig. 5.6 represent the carries between various stages. Note, however, that the 4-bit adder need not be implemented as a ripple-carry adder for the results at the outputs to be valid.

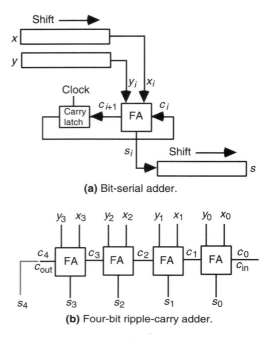

(a) Bit-serial adder.

(b) Four-bit ripple-carry adder.

Fig. 5.3   Using full adders in building bit-serial and ripple-carry adders.

5.2 CONDITIONS AND EXCEPTIONS

When a k-bit adder is used in an ALU, it is customary to provide the k-bit sum along with information about the following outcomes, which are associated with flag bits within a condition/exception register:

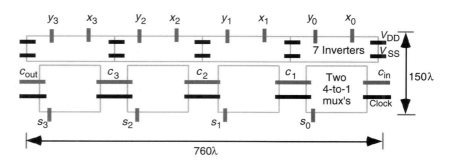

Fig. 5.4   Layout of a 4-bit ripple-carry adder in CMOS implementation [Puck94].

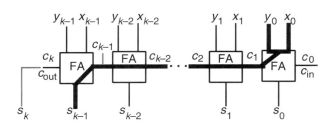

Fig. 5.5   Critical path in a k-bit ripple-carry adder.

c_{out}	Indicating that a carry-out of 1 is produced
Overflow	Indicating that the output is not the correct sum
Negative	Indicating that the addition result is negative
Zero	Indicating that the addition result is zero

When we are adding unsigned numbers, c_{out} and "overflow" are one and the same, and the "sign" condition is obviously irrelevant. For 2's-complement addition, overflow occurs when two numbers of like sign are added and a result of the opposite sign is produced. Thus:

$$\text{Overflow}_{2's-compl} = x_{k-1}y_{k-1}\overline{s}_{k-1} + \overline{x}_{k-1}\overline{y}_{k-1}s_{k-1}$$

It is fairly easy to show that overflow in 2's-complement addition can be detected from the leftmost two carries as follows:

$$\text{Overflow}_{2's-compl} = c_k \oplus c_{k-1} = c_k\overline{c}_{k-1} + \overline{c}_k c_{k-1}$$

In 2's-complement addition, c_{out} has no significance. However, since a single adder is frequently used to add both unsigned and 2's-complement numbers, c_{out} is useful as well. Figure 5.7 shows a ripple-carry implementation of an unsigned or 2's-complement adder with auxiliary outputs for conditions and exceptions. Because of the large number of inputs into the NOR gate that tests for zero, it must be implemented as an OR tree followed by an inverter.

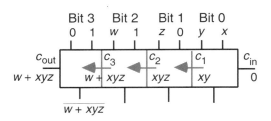

Fig. 5.6   Four-bit binary adder used to realize the logic function $f = w + xyz$ and its complement.

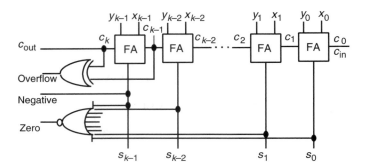

Fig. 5.7 Two's-complement adder with provisions for detecting conditions and exceptions.

5.3 ANALYSIS OF CARRY PROPAGATION

Various ways of dealing with the carry problem were enumerated in Section 3.1. Some of the methods already discussed include limiting the propagation of carries (hybrid signed-digit, RNS) or eliminating carry propagation altogether (GSD). The latter approach, when used for adding a set of numbers in carry-save form, can be viewed as a way of amortizing the propagation delay of the final conversion step over many additions, thus making the per-add contribution of the carry propagation delay quite small. What remains to be discussed, in this and the following chapter, is how one can speed up a single addition operation involving conventional (binary) operands.

We begin by analyzing how and to what extent carries propagate in adding two binary numbers. Consider the example addition of 16-bit binary numbers depicted in Fig. 5.8, where the carry chains of length 2, 3, 6, and 4 are shown. The length of a carry chain is the number of digit positions from where the carry is generated up to and including where it is finally absorbed or annihilated. A carry chain of length 0 thus means "no carry production," and a chain of length 1 means that the carry is absorbed in the next position. We are interested in the length of the longest propagation chain (6 in Fig. 5.8), which dictates the adder's latency.

Given binary numbers with random bit values, for each position i we have:

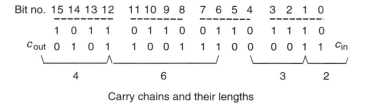

Carry chains and their lengths

Fig. 5.8 Example addition and its carry-propagation chains.

Probability of carry generation   = 1/4
Probability of carry annihilation   = 1/4
Probability of carry propagation   = 1/2

The probability that a carry generated at position i will propagate up to and including position $j - 1$ and stop at position $j (j > i)$ is $2^{-(j-1-i)} \times 1/2 = 2^{-(j-i)}$. The expected length of the carry chain that starts at bit position i is, therefore, given by

$$\sum_{j=i+1}^{k-1} (j - i)2^{-(j-i)} + (k - i)2^{-(k-1-i)} = \sum_{l=1}^{k-1-i} l2^{-l} + (k - i)2^{-(k-1-i)}$$

$$= 2 - (k - i + 1)\, 2^{-(k-1-i)} + (k - i)^{-(k-1-i)} = 2 - 2^{-(k-i-1)}$$

where the simplification is based on the identity $\sum_{l=1}^{p} l2^{-l} = 2 - (p+2)2^{-p}$. In the preceding derivation, the term $(k - i)\, 2^{-(k-1-i)}$ is added to the summation because carry definitely stops at position k; so we do not multiply the term $2^{-(k-1-i)}$ by 1/2, as was done for the terms within the summation.

The preceding result indicates that for $i << k$, the expected length of the carry chain that starts at position i is approximately 2. Note that the formula checks out for the extreme case of $i = k - 1$, since in this case, the exact carry chain length, and thus its expected value, is 1. We conclude that carry chains are usually quite short.

On the average, the longest carry chain in adding k-bit numbers is of length $\log_2 k$. This was first observed and proved by Burks, Goldstine, and von Neumann in their classic report defining the structure of a stored-program computer [Burk46]. An interesting analysis based on Kolmogorov complexity theory has been offered in [Beig98]. The latter paper also cites past attempts at providing alternate or more complete proofs of the proposition.

Here is one way to prove the logarithmic average length of the worst-case carry chain. Let $\eta_k(h)$ be the probability that the longest carry chain in a k-bit addition is of length h or more. Clearly, the probability of the longest carry chain being of length exactly h is $\eta_k(h) - \eta_k(h + 1)$. We can use a recursive formulation to find $\eta_k(h)$. The longest carry chain can be of length h or more in two mutually exclusive ways:

a. The least significant $k - 1$ bits have a carry chain of length h or more.
b. The least significant $k - 1$ bits do not have such a carry chain, but the most significant h bits, including the last bit, have a chain of the exact length h.

Thus, we have

$$\eta_k(h) \leq \eta_{k-1}(h) + 2^{-(h+1)}$$

where $2^{-(h+1)}$ is the product of 1/4 (representing the probability of carry generation) and $2^{-(h-1)}$ (probability that carry propagates across $h - 2$ intermediate positions and stops in the last one). The inequality occurs because the second term is not multiplied by a probability as discussed above. Hence, assuming $\eta_i(h) = 0$ for $i < h$:

$$\eta_k(h) = \sum_{i=h}^{k} [\eta_i(h) - \eta_{i-1}(h)] \leq (k - h + 1)\, 2^{-(h+1)} \leq 2^{-(h+1)}k$$

To complete our derivation of the expected length λ of the longest carry chain, we note that:

$$\lambda = \sum_{h=1}^{k} h[\eta_k(h) - \eta_k(h+1)]$$

$$= [\eta_k(1) - \eta_k(2)] + 2[\eta_k(2) - \eta_k(3)] + \cdots + k[\eta_k(k) - 0]$$

$$= \sum_{h=1}^{k} \eta_k(h)$$

We next break the final summation above into two parts: the first $\gamma = \lfloor \log_2 k \rfloor - 1$ terms and the remaining $k - \gamma$ terms. Using the upper bound 1 for the first part and $2^{-(h+1)}k$ for the second part, we get:

$$\lambda = \sum_{h=1}^{k} \eta_k(h) \le \sum_{h=1}^{\gamma} 1 + \sum_{h=\gamma+1}^{k} 2^{-(h+1)}k < \gamma + 2^{-(\gamma+1)}k$$

Now let $\varepsilon = \log_2 k - \lfloor \log_2 k \rfloor$ or $\gamma = \log_2 k - 1 - \varepsilon$, where $0 \le \varepsilon < 1$. Then, substituting the latter expression for γ in the preceding inequality and noting that $2^{\log_2 k} = k$ and $2^{\varepsilon} < 1 + \varepsilon$, we get:

$$\lambda < \log_2 k - 1 - \varepsilon + 2^{\varepsilon} < \log_2 k$$

This concludes our derivation of the result that the expected length of the worst-case carry chain in a k-bit addition with random operands is upper-bounded by $\log_2 k$. Experimental results verify the $\log_2 k$ approximation to the length of the worst-case carry chain and suggest that $\log_2(1.25k)$ is a better estimate [Hend61].

5.4 CARRY COMPLETION DETECTION

A ripple-carry adder is the simplest and slowest adder design. For k-bit operands, both the worst-case delay and the implementation cost of a ripple-carry adder are linear in k. However, based on the analysis in Section 5.3, the worst-case carry-propagation chain of length k almost never materializes.

A carry completion detection adder takes advantage of the $\log_2 k$ average length of the longest carry chain to add two k-bit binary numbers in O(log k) time on the average. It is essentially a ripple-carry adder in which a carry of 0 is also explicitly represented and allowed to propagate between stages. The carry into stage i is represented by the two-rail code:

$$
\begin{aligned}
(b_i, c_i) = (0, 0) &\quad \text{Carry not yet known} \\
(0, 1) &\quad \text{Carry known to be 1} \\
(1, 0) &\quad \text{Carry known to be 0}
\end{aligned}
$$

Thus, just as two 1s in the operands generate a carry of 1 that propagates to the left, two 0s would produce a carry of 0. Initially, all carries are $(0, 0)$ or unknown. After initialization, a bit position with $x_i = y_i$ makes the no-carry/carry determination and injects the appropriate carry $(b_{i+1}, c_{i+1}) = (\overline{x_i + y_i}, x_i y_i)$ into the carry propagation chain of Fig. 5.9 via the OR gates. The

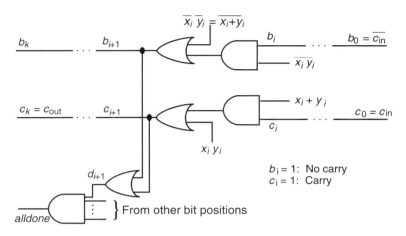

Fig. 5.9 The carry network of an adder with two-rail carries and carry completion detection logic.

carry ($\overline{c}_{\text{in}}$, c_{in}) is injected at the right end. When every carry has assumed one of the values (0, 1) or (1, 0), carry propagation is complete. The local "done" signals $d_i = b_i + c_i$ are combined by a global AND function into *alldone*, which indicates the end of carry propagation.

In designing carry completion adders, care must be taken to avoid hazards that might lead to a spurious *alldone* signal. Initialization of all carries to 0 through clearing of input bits and simultaneous application of all input data is one way of ensuring hazard-free operation.

Excluding the initialization and carry completion detection times, which must be considered and are the same in all cases, the latency of a k-bit carry completion adder ranges from 1 gate delay in the best case (no carry propagation at all: i.e., when adding a number to itself) to $2k + 1$ gate delays in the worst case (full carry propagation from c_{in} to c_{out}), with the average latency being about $2 \log_2 k + 1$ gate delays. Note that once the final carries have arrived in all bit positions, the derivation of the sum bits is overlapped with completion detection and is thus not accounted for in the preceding latencies.

Because the latency of the carry completion adder is data dependent, the design of Fig. 5.9 is suitable for use in asynchronous systems. Most modern computers, however, use synchronous logic and thus cannot take full advantage of the high average speed of a carry completion adder.

5.5 ADDITION OF A CONSTANT: COUNTERS

When one input of the addition operation is a constant number, the design can be simplified or optimized compared to that of a general two-operand adder. With binary arithmetic, we can assume that the constant y to be added to x is odd, since in the addition $s = x + y_{\text{even}} = x + (y_{\text{odd}} \times 2^h)$, one can ignore the h rightmost bits in x and add y_{odd} to the remaining bits. The special case of $y = 1$ corresponds to standard counters, while $y = \pm 1$ yields an up/down counter.

Let the constant to be added to $x = (x_{k-1} \cdots x_2 x_1 x_0)_{\text{two}}$ be $y = (y_{k-1} \cdots y_2 y_1 1)_{\text{two}}$. The least significant bit of the sum is $\overline{x}_0$. The remaining bits of s can be determined by a $(k - 1)$-bit

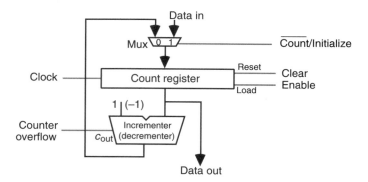

Fig. 5.10 An up (down) counter built of a register, an incrementer (decrementer), and a multiplexer.

ripple-carry adder, with $c_{in} = x_0$, each of its cells being a half-adder ($y_i = 0$) or a modified half-adder ($y_i = 1$). The fast adder designs to be covered later can similarly be optimized to take advantage of the known bits of y.

When $y = 1(-1)$, the resulting circuit is known as an *incrementer* (*decrementer*) and is used in the design of up (down) counters. Figure 5.10 depicts an up counter, with parallel load capability, built of a register, an incrementer, and a multiplexer. The design shown in Fig. 5.10 can be easily converted to an up/down counter by using an incrementer/decrementer and an extra control signal. Supplying the details is left as an exercise.

Many designs for fast counters are available [Ober81]. Conventional synchronous designs are based on full carry propagation in each increment/decrement cycle, thus limiting the counter's operating speed. In some cases, special features of the storage elements used can lead to simplifications. Figure 5.11 depicts an asynchronous counter built of cascaded negative-edge-triggered T (toggle) flip-flops. Each input pulse toggles the flip-flop at the least significant position, each 1-to-0 transition of the LSB flip-flop toggles the next flip-flop, and so on. The next input pulse can be accepted before the carry has propagated all the way to the left.

Certain applications require high-speed counting, with the count potentially becoming quite large. In such cases, a high-speed incrementer must be utilized. Methods used in the design of fast adders (Chapters 6 and 7) can all be adapted for building fast incrementers. When even the highest-speed incrementer cannot keep up with the input rate or when cost considerations preclude the use of an ultrafast incrementer, the frequency of the input can be reduced by applying it to a prescaler. The lower-frequency output of the prescaler can then be counted with less stringent speed requirements. In the latter case, the resulting count will be approximate.

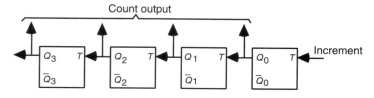

Fig. 5.11 Four-bit asynchronous up counter built only of negative-edge-triggered T flip-flops.

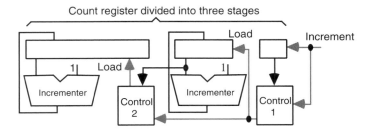

Fig. 5.12   Fast three-stage up counter.

Obviously, the count value can be represented in redundant format, allowing carry-free increment or decrement in constant time [Parh87]. However, with a redundant format, reading out the stored count involves some delay to allow for conversion of the internal representation to standard binary. Alternatively, one can design the counter as a cascade that begins with a very short, and thus fast, counter and continues with increasingly longer counters [Vuil91]. The longer counters on the left are incremented only occasionally and thus need not be very fast (their incremented counts can be precomputed by a slow incrementer and then simply loaded into the register when required). Figure 5.12 shows this principle applied to the design of a three-stage counter.

5.6 MANCHESTER CARRY CHAINS AND ADDERS

In the next three chapters, we will examine methods for speeding up the addition process for two operands (Chapters 6 and 7) and for multiple operands (Chapter 8). For two operands, the key to fast addition is a low-latency carry network, since once the carry into position i is known, the sum digit can be determined from the operand digits x_i and y_i and the incoming carry c_i in constant time through modular addtition:

$$s_i = (x_i + y_i + c_i) \bmod r$$

In the special case of radix 2, the relation above reduces to:

$$s_i = x_i \oplus y_i \oplus c_i$$

So, the primary problem in the design of two-operand adders is the computation of the k carries c_{i+1} based on the $2k$ operand digits x_i and y_i, $0 \leq i < k$.

From the point of view of carry propagation and the design of a carry network, the actual operand digits are not important. What matters is whether in a given position a carry is generated, propagated, or annihilated (absorbed). In the case of binary addition, the *generate*, *propagate*, and *annihilate* (*absorb*) signals are characterized by the following logic equations:

$$g_i = x_i y_i$$
$$p_i = x_i \oplus y_i$$
$$a_i = \overline{x}_i \overline{y}_i = \overline{x_i + y_i}$$

It is also helpful to define a *transfer* signal corresponding to the event that the carry-out will be 1, given that the carry-in is 1:

$$t_i = g_i + p_i = \overline{a}_i = x_i + y_i$$

More generally, for radix r, we have:

$$g_i = 1 \text{ iff } x_i + y_i \geq r$$
$$p_i = 1 \text{ iff } x_i + y_i = r - 1$$
$$a_i = 1 \text{ iff } x_i + y_i < r - 1$$

Thus, assuming that the signals above are produced and made available, the rest of the carry network design can be based on them and becomes completely independent of the operands or even the number representation radix.

Using the preceding signals, the *carry recurrence* can be written as follows:

$$c_{i+1} = g_i + c_i p_i$$

The carry recurrence essentially states that a carry will enter stage $i + 1$ if it is generated in stage i or it enters stage i and is propagated by that stage. Since

$$c_{i+1} = g_i + c_i p_i = g_i + c_i g_i + c_i p_i$$
$$= g_i + c_i(g_i + p_i) = g_i + c_i t_i$$

the carry recurrence can be written in terms of t_i instead of p_i. This latter version of the carry recurrence leads to slightly faster adders because in binary addition, t_i is easier to produce than p_i (OR instead of XOR).

In what follows, we always deal with the carry recurrence in its original form $c_{i+1} = g_i + c_i p_i$, since it is more intuitive, but we keep in mind that in most cases, p_i can be replaced by t_i if desired.

The carry recurrence forms the basis of a simple carry network known as *Manchester carry chain*. A *Manchester adder* is one that uses a Manchester carry chain as its carry network. Each stage of a Manchester carry chain can be viewed as consisting of three switches controlled by the signals p_i, g_i, and a_i, so that the switch closes (conducts electricity) when the corresponding control signal is 1. As shown in Fig. 5.13a, the carry-out signal c_{i+1} is connected to 0 if $a_i = 1$, to 1 if $g_i = 1$, and to c_i if $p_i = 1$, thus assuming the correct logical value $c_{i+1} = g_i + c_i p_i$. Note that one, and only one, of the signals p_i, g_i, and a_i is 1.

Figure 5.13b shows how a Manchester carry chain might be implemented in CMOS. When the clock is low, the c nodes precharge. Then, when the clock goes high, if g_i is high, c_{i+1} is asserted or drawn low. To prevent g_i from affecting c_i, the signal p_i must be computed as the XOR (rather than OR) of x_i and y_i. This is not a problem because we need the XOR of x_i and y_i for computing the sum anyway.

For a k-bit Manchester carry chain, the total delay consists of three components:

1. The time to form the switch control signals.
2. The setup time for the switches.
3. Signal propagation delay through k switches in the worst case.

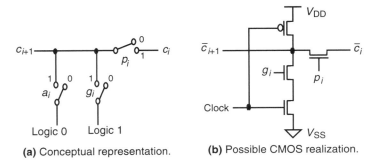

Fig. 5.13   One stage in a Manchester carry chain.

The first two components of delay are small, constant terms. The delay is thus dominated by the third component, which is at best linear in k. For modern CMOS technology, the delay is roughly proportional to k^2 (as k pass transistors are connected in series), making the method undesirable for direct realization of fast adders. However, when the delay is in fact linear in k, speed is gained over gate-based ripple-carry adders because we have one switch delay rather than two gate delays per stage. The linear or superlinear delay of a Manchester carry chain limits its usefulness for wide words or in high-performance designs. Its main application is in implementing short chains (say, up to 8 bits) as building blocks for use with a variety of fast addition schemes.

PROBLEMS

5.1   **Bit-serial 2's-complement adder**   Present the complete design of a bit-serial 2's-complement adder for 32-bit numbers. Include in your design the control details and provisions for overflow detection.

5.2   **Four-function ALU**   Extend the design of Fig. 5.2c into a bit-slice for a four-function ALU that produces any of the following functions of the inputs x and y based on the values of two control signals: Sum, OR, AND, XOR. *Hint:* What happens if c_{in} is forced to 0 or 1?

5.3   **Subtractive adder for 1's-complement numbers**   Show that the alternate representation of 0 in 1's complement, which is obtained only when x and $-x$ are added, can be avoided by using a "subtractive adder" that always complements y and performs subtraction to compute $x + y$.

5.4   **Digit-serial adders**

   a.   A radix-2^g digit-serial adder can be faster than a bit-serial adder. Show the detailed design of a radix-16 digit-serial adder for 32-bit unsigned numbers and compare it with respect to latency and cost to bit-serial and ripple-carry binary adders.

   b.   Design a digit-serial BCD (binary-coded decimal) adder to add decimal numbers whose digits are encoded as 4-bit binary numbers.

    c.   Combine the designs of parts a and b into an adder than can act as radix-16 or BCD adder according to the value of a control signal.

5.5   **Binary adders as versatile building blocks** A 4-bit binary adder can be used to implement many logic functions besides its intended function. An example appears in Fig. 5.6. Show how a 4-bit binary adder can be used to realize the following:

    a.   A 3-bit adder, with carry-in and carry-out.

    b.   Two independent single-bit full adders.

    c.   A single-bit full adder and a 2-bit binary adder operating independently.

    d.   A 4-bit odd parity generator (4-bit XOR).

    e.   A 4-bit even or odd parity generator under the control of an $\overline{\text{even/odd}}$ signal.

    f.   Two independent 3-bit odd parity generators.

    g.   A five-input AND circuit.

    h.   A five-input OR circuit.

    i.   A circuit to realize the four-variable logic function $wx + yz$.

    j.   A circuit to realize the four-variable logic function $wx\bar{y} + wx\bar{z} + \bar{w}yz + \bar{x}yz$.

    k.   A multiply-by-15 circuit for a 2-bit number x_1x_0, resulting in a 6-bit product.

    l.   A circuit to compute $x + 4y + 8z$, where x, y, and z are 3-bit unsigned numbers.

    m.   A five-input "parallel counter" producing the sum $s_2s_1s_0$ of five 1-bit numbers.

5.6   **Binary adders as versatile building blocks** Show how an 8-bit binary adder can be used to realize the following:

    a.   Three independent 2-bit binary adders, each with carry-in and carry-out.

    b.   A circuit to realize the six-variable logic function $uv + wx + yz$.

    c.   A circuit to compute $2w + x$ and $2y + z$, where w, x, y, z are 3-bit numbers.

    d.   A multiply-by-85 circuit for a number $x_3x_2x_1x_0$, resulting in an 11-bit product.

    e.   A circuit to compute the 5-bit sum of three 3-bit unsigned numbers.

    f.   A seven-input "parallel counter" producing the sum $s_2s_1s_0$ of seven 1-bit numbers.

5.7   **Decimal addition** Many microprocessors provide an 8-bit unsigned "add with carry" instruction that is defined as unsigned addition using the "carry flag" as c_{in} and producing two carries: carry-out or c_8, stored in the carry flag, and "middle carry" or c_4, stored in a special flag bit for subsequent use (e.g., as branch condition). Show how the "add with carry" instruction can be used to construct a routine for adding unsigned decimal numbers that are stored in memory with two BCD (binary-coded decimal) digits per byte.

5.8   **Two's-complement adder**

    a.   Prove that in adding k-bit 2's-complement numbers, overflow occurs if and only if $c_{k-1} \neq c_k$.

    b.   Show that in a 2's-complement adder that does not provide c_{out}, we can produce it externally using $c_{\text{out}} = x_{k-1}y_{k-1} + \bar{s}_{k-1}(x_{k-1} + y_{k-1})$.

5.9   **Carry completion adder** The computation of a k-input logic function requires $O(\log k)$ time if gates with constant fan-in are used. Thus, the AND gate in Fig. 5.9 that generates the *alldone* signal is really a tree of smaller AND gates that implies $O(\log k)$ delay. Wouldn't this imply that the addition time of the carry completion adder is $O(\log^2 k)$ rather than $O(\log k)$?

5.10   **Carry completion adder**

    a.   Design the sum logic for the carry completion adder of Fig. 5.9.

    b.   Design a carry completion adder using full and half-adders plus inverters as the only building blocks (besides the completion detection logic).

    c.   Repeat part a if the sum bits are to be obtained with two-rail (z, p) encoding whereby 0 and 1 are represented by $(1, 0)$ and $(0, 1)$, respectively. In this way, the sum bits are independently produced as soon as possible, allowing them to be processed by other circuits in an asynchronous fashion.

5.11   **Balanced ternary adder** Consider the balanced ternary number system with $r = 3$ and digit set $[-1, 1]$. Addition of such numbers involves carries in $\{-1, 0, 1\}$. Assuming that both the digit set and carries are represented using the (n, p) encoding of Fig. 3.7:

    a.   Design a ripple-carry adder cell for balanced ternary numbers.

    b.   Convert the adder cell of part a to an adder/subtractor with a control input.

    c.   Design and analyze a carry completion sensing adder for balanced ternary numbers.

5.12   **Synchronous binary counter** Design a synchronous counterpart for the asynchronous counter shown in Fig. 5.11.

5.13   **Negabinary up/down counter** Design an up/down counter based on the negabinary (radix -2) number representation in the count register. *Hint:* Consider the negabinary representation as a radix-4 number system with the digit set $[-2, 1]$.

5.14   **Design of fast counters** Design the two control circuits in Fig. 5.12 and determine optimal lengths for the three counter segments, as well as the overall counting latency (clock period), in each of the following cases. Assume the use of ripple-carry incrementers.

    a.   An overall counter length of 48 bits.

    b.   An overall counter length of 80 bits.

5.15   **Fast up/down counters** Extend the fast counter design of Fig. 5.12 to an up/down counter. *Hint:* Incorporate the sign logic in "Control 1," use a fast 0 detection mechanism, and save the old value when incrementing a counter stage.

5.16   **Manchester carry chains** Study the effects of inserting a pair of inverters after every g stages in a CMOS Manchester carry chain (Fig. 5.13b). In particular, discuss whether the carry propagation time can be made linear in k by suitable placement of the inverter pairs.

5.17   **Analysis of carry propagation** In deriving the average length of the worst-case carry propagation chain, we made substitutions and simplifications that led to the upper bound

$\log_2 k$. By deriving an O(log k) lower bound, show that the exact average is fairly close to this upper bound.

REFERENCES

[Beig98] Beigel, R., B. Gasarch, M. Li, and L. Zhang, "Addition in $\log_2 n + $O(1) Steps on Average: A Simple Analysis," *Theoretical Computer Science*, Vol. 191, Nos. 1–2, pp. 245–248, January 1998.

[Burk46] Burks, A. W., H. H. Goldstine, and J. von Neumann, "Preliminary Discussion of the Logical Design of an Electronic Computing Instrument," Institute for Advanced Study, Princeton, NJ, 1946.

[Gilc55] Gilchrist, B., J. H. Pomerene, and S. Y. Wong, "Fast Carry Logic for Digital Computers," *IRE Trans. Electronic Computers*, Vol. 4, pp. 133–136, 1955.

[Hend61] Hendrickson, H. C., "Fast High-Accuracy Binary Parallel Addition," *IRE Trans. Electronic Computers*, Vol. 10, pp. 465–468, 1961.

[Kilb60] Kilburn, T., D. B. G. Edwards, and D. Aspinall, "A Parallel Arithmetic Unit Using a Saturated Transistor Fast-Carry Circuit," *Proc. IEE*, Vol. 107B, pp. 573–584, 1960.

[Ober81] Oberman, R. M. M., *Counting and Counters*, Macmillan, London, 1981.

[Parh87] Parhami, B., "Systolic Up/Down Counters with Zero and Sign Detection," *Proc. Symp. Computer Arithmetic*, Como, Italy, May 1987, pp. 174–178.

[Puck94] Pucknell, D. A., and K. Eshraghian, *Basic VLSI Design*, 3rd ed., Prentice-Hall, 1994.

[Vuil91] Vuillemin, J. E., "Constant Time Arbitrary Length Synchronous Binary Counters," *Proc. Symp. Computer Arithmetic*, Grenoble, France, June 1991, pp. 180–183.

Chapter
6 CARRY-LOOKAHEAD ADDERS

Adder designs considered in Chapter 5 have worst-case delays that grow at least linearly with the word width k. Since the most significant bit of the sum is a function of all the $2k$ input bits, given that the gate fan-in is limited to d, a lower bound on addition latency is $\log_d(2k)$. An interesting question, therefore, is whether one can add two k-bit binary numbers in $O(\log k)$ worst-case time. Carry-lookahead adders, covered in this chapter, represent a commonly used scheme for logarithmic time addition. Other schemes are introduced in Chapter 7.

6.1 UNROLLING THE CARRY RECURRENCE

Recall the g_i (generate), p_i (propagate), a_i (annihilate or absorb), and t_i (transfer) auxiliary signals introduced in Section 5.6:

$$g_i = 1 \text{ iff } x_i + y_i \geq r \qquad \text{Carry is generated}$$
$$p_i = 1 \text{ iff } x_i + y_i = r - 1 \qquad \text{Carry is propagated}$$
$$t_i = \overline{a}_i = g_i + p_i \qquad \text{Carry is not annihilated}$$

These signals, along with the carry recurrence

$$c_{i+1} = g_i + p_i c_i = g_i + t_i c_i$$

allow us to decouple the problem of designing a fast carry network from details of the number system (radix, digit set). In fact it does not even matter whether we are adding or subtracting;

any carry network can be used as a borrow network if we simply redefine the preceding signals to correspond to borrow generation, borrow propagation, and so on.

The carry recurrence $c_{i+1} = g_i + p_i c_i$ states that a carry will enter stage $i + 1$ if it is generated in stage i or it enters stage i and is propagated by that stage. One can easily unroll this recurrence, eventually obtaining each carry c_i as a logical function of the operand bits and c_{in}. Here are three steps of the unrolling process for c_i:

$$c_i = g_{i-1} + c_{i-1} p_{i-1}$$
$$= g_{i-1} + (g_{i-2} + c_{i-2} p_{i-2}) p_{i-1} = g_{i-1} + g_{i-2} p_{i-1} + c_{i-2} p_{i-2} p_{i-1}$$
$$= g_{i-1} + g_{i-2} p_{i-1} + g_{i-3} p_{i-2} p_{i-1} + c_{i-3} p_{i-3} p_{i-2} p_{i-1}$$
$$= g_{i-1} + g_{i-2} p_{i-1} + g_{i-3} p_{i-2} p_{i-1} + g_{i-4} p_{i-3} p_{i-2} p_{i-1} + c_{i-4} p_{i-4} p_{i-3} p_{i-2} p_{i-1}$$

The unrolling can be continued until the last product term contains $c_0 = c_{in}$. The unrolled version of the carry recurrence has the following simple interpretation: carry enters into position i if and only if a carry is generated in position $i - 1 (g_{i-1})$, or a carry generated in position $i - 2$ is propagated by position $i - 1 (g_{i-2} p_{i-1})$, or a carry generated in position $i - 3$ is propagated at $i - 2$ and $i - 1 (g_{i-3} p_{i-2} p_{i-1})$, etc.

After full unrolling, we can compute all the carries in a k-bit adder directly from the auxiliary signals (g_i, p_i) and c_{in}, using two-level AND-OR logic circuits with maximum gate fan-in of $k + 1$. For $k = 4$, the logic expressions are as follows:

$$c_4 = g_3 + g_2 p_3 + g_1 p_2 p_3 + g_0 p_1 p_2 p_3 + c_0 p_0 p_1 p_2 p_3$$
$$c_3 = g_2 + g_1 p_2 + g_0 p_1 p_2 + c_0 p_0 p_1 p_2$$
$$c_2 = g_1 + g_0 p_1 + c_0 p_0 p_1$$
$$c_1 = g_0 + c_0 p_0$$

Here, c_0 and c_4 are the 4-bit adder's c_{in} and c_{out}, respectively. A carry network based on the preceding equations can be used in conjunction with 2-input ANDs, producing the g_i signals, and 2-input XORs, producing the p_i and sum bits, to build a 4-bit binary adder. Such an adder is said to have *full carry lookahead*.

Note that since c_4 does not affect the computation of the sum bits, it can be derived based on the simpler equation

$$c_4 = g_3 + c_3 p_3$$

with little or no speed penalty. The resulting carry network is depicted in Fig. 6.1.

Clearly, full carry lookahead is impractical for wide words. The fully unrolled carry equation for c_{31}, for example, consists of 32 product terms, the largest of which contains 32 literals. Thus, the required AND and OR functions must be realized by tree networks, leading to increased latency and cost. Two schemes for managing this complexity immediately suggest themselves:

high-radix addition (i.e., radix 2^g)

multilevel lookahead

High-radix addition increases the latency for generating the auxiliary signals and sum digits but simplifies the carry network. Depending on the implementation method and technology, an optimal radix might exist. Multilevel lookahead is the technique used in practice and is covered in Section 6.2.

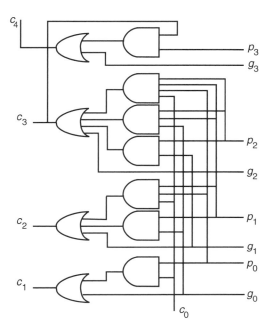

Fig. 6.1 Four-bit carry network with full lookahead.

6.2 CARRY-LOOKAHEAD ADDER DESIGN

Consider radix-16 addition of two binary numbers that are characterized by their g_i and p_i signals. For each radix-16 digit position, extending from bit position i to bit position $i + 3$ of the original binary numbers (where i is a multiple of 4), "block generate" and "block propagate" signals can be derived as follows:

$$g_{[i,i+3]} = g_{i+3} + g_{i+2}p_{i+3} + g_{i+1}p_{i+2}p_{i+3} + g_i p_{i+1}p_{i+2}p_{i+3}$$

$$p_{[i,i+3]} = p_i p_{i+1} p_{i+2} p_{i+3}$$

The preceding equations can be interpreted in the same way as unrolled carry equations: the four bit positions collectively propagate an incoming carry c_i if and only if each of the four positions propagates; they collectively generate a carry if a carry is produced in position $i + 3$, or it is produced in position $i + 2$ and propagated by position $i + 3$, etc.

If we replace the c_4 portion of the carry network of Fig. 6.1 with circuits that produce the block generate and propagate signals $g_{[i,i+3]}$ and $p_{[i,i+3]}$, the 4-bit *lookahead carry generator* of Fig. 6.2 is obtained. Figure 6.3 shows the 4-bit lookahead carry generator in schematic form. We will see shortly that such a block can be used in a multilevel structure to build a carry network of any desired width.

First, however, let us take a somewhat more general view of the block generate and propagate signals. Assuming $i_0 < i_1 < i_2$, we can write:

$$g_{[i_0,i_2-1]} = g_{[i_1,i_2-1]} + g_{[i_0,i_1-1]}p_{[i_1,i_2-1]}$$

This equation essentially says that a carry is generated by the block of positions from i_0 to $i_2 - 1$ if and only if a carry is generated by the $[i_1, i_2 - 1]$ block or a carry generated by the $[i_0, i_1 - 1]$ block is propagated by the $[i_1, i_2 - 1]$ block. Similarly:

$$p_{[i_0,i_2-1]} = p_{[i_0,i_1-1]}p_{[i_1,i_2-1]}$$

In fact the two blocks being merged into a larger block do not have to be contiguous; they can also be overlapping. In other words, for the possibly overlapping blocks $[i_1, j_1]$ and $[i_0, j_0]$, $i_0 \leq i_1 - 1 \leq j_0 < j_1$, we have:

$$g_{[i_0,j_1]} = g_{[i_1,j_1]} + g_{[i_0,j_0]}p_{[i_1,j_1]}$$

$$p_{[i_0,j_1]} = p_{[i_0,j_0]}p_{[i_1,j_1]}$$

Figure 6.4 shows that a 4-bit lookahead carry generator can be used to combine the g and p signals from adjacent or overlapping blocks into the p and g signals for the combined block.

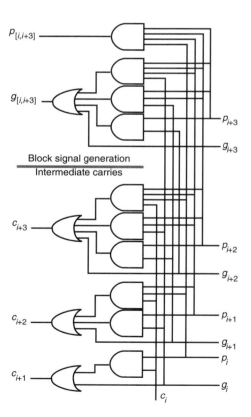

Fig. 6.2   Four-bit lookahead carry generator.

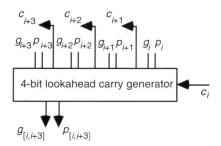

Fig. 6.3   Schematic diagram of a 4-bit lookahead carry generator.

Given the 4-bit lookahead carry generator of Fig. 6.3, it is an easy matter to synthesize wider adders based on a multilevel carry-lookahead scheme. For example, to construct a two-level 16-bit carry-lookahead adder, we need four 4-bit adders and a 4-bit lookahead carry generator, connected together as shown on the upper right quadrant of Fig. 6.5. The 4-bit lookahead carry generator in this case can be viewed as predicting the three intermediate carries in a 4-digit radix-16 addition. The latency through this 16-bit adder consists of the time required for:

Producing the g and p for individual bit positions (1 gate level).

Producing the g and p signals for 4-bit blocks (2 gate levels).

Predicting the carry-in signals c_4, c_8, and c_{12} for the blocks (2 gate levels).

Predicting the internal carries within each 4-bit block (2 gate levels).

Computing the sum bits (2 gate levels).

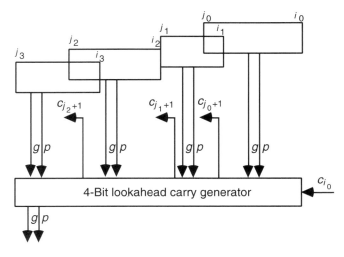

Fig. 6.4   Combining of g and p signals of four (contiguous or overlapping) blocks of arbitrary widths into the g and p signals for the overall block $[i_0, j_3]$.

Thus the total latency for the 16-bit adder is 9 gate levels, which is much better than the 32 gate levels required by a 16-bit ripple-carry adder.

Similarly, to construct a three-level 64-bit carry-lookahead adder, we can use four of the 16-bit adders above plus one 4-bit lookahead carry generator, connected together as shown in Fig. 6.5. The delay will increase by four gate levels with each additional level of lookahead: two levels in the downward movement of the g and p signals, and two levels for the upward propagation of carries through the extra level. Thus, the delay of a k-bit carry-lookahead adder based on 4-bit lookahead blocks is:

$$T_{\text{lookahead}-\text{add}} = 4 \log_4 k + 1 \text{ gate levels}$$

Hence, the 64-bit carry-lookahead adder of Fig. 6.5 has a latency of 13 gate levels.

One can of course use 6-bit or 8-bit lookahead blocks to reduce the number of lookahead levels for a given word width. But this may not be worthwhile in view of the longer delays introduced by gates with higher fan-in. When the word width is not a power of 4, some of the inputs and/or outputs of the lookahead carry generators remain unused, and the latency formula becomes $4 \lceil \log_4 k \rceil + 1$.

One final point about the design depicted in Fig. 6.5: this 64-bit adder does not produce a carry-out signal (c_{64}), which would be needed in many applications. There are two ways to remedy this problem in carry-lookahead adders. One is to generate c_{out} externally based on auxiliary signals or the operand and sum bits in position $k - 1$:

$$c_{\text{out}} = g_{[0,k-1]} + c_0 p_{[0,k-1]} = x_{k-1} y_{k-1} + \bar{s}_{k-1} (x_{k-1} + y_{k-1})$$

Another is to design the adder to be 1 bit wider than needed (e.g., 61 bits instead of 60), using the additional sum bit as c_{out}.

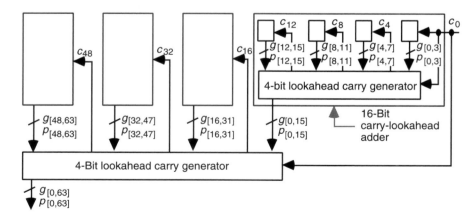

Fig. 6.5   Building a 64-bit carry-lookahead adder from 16 4-bit adders and 5 lookahead carry generators.

6.3 LING ADDER AND RELATED DESIGNS

The Ling adder is a type of carry-lookahead adder that achieves significant hardware savings. Consider the carry recurrence and its unrolling by four steps:

$$c_i = g_{i-1} + c_{i-1}p_{i-1} = g_{i-1} + c_{i-1}t_{i-1}$$

$$= g_{i-1} + g_{i-2}t_{i-1} + g_{i-3}t_{i-2}t_{i-1} + g_{i-4}t_{i-3}t_{i-2}t_{i-1} + c_{i-4}t_{i-4}t_{i-3}t_{i-2}t_{i-1}$$

Ling's modification consists of propagating $h_i = c_i + c_{i-1}$ instead of c_i. To understand the following derivations, we note that g_{i-1} implies c_i ($c_i = 1$ if $g_{i-1} = 1$), which in turn implies h_i.

$$c_{i-1}p_{i-1} = c_{i-1}p_{i-1} + g_{i-1}p_{i-1} \text{ \{zero\}} + p_{i-1}c_{i-1}p_{i-1} \text{ \{repeated term\}}$$

$$= c_{i-1}p_{i-1} + (g_{i-1} + p_{i-1}c_{i-1})p_{i-1}$$

$$= (c_{i-1} + c_i)p_{i-1} = h_i p_{i-1}$$

$$c_i = g_{i-1} + c_{i-1}p_{i-1}$$

$$= h_i g_{i-1} \text{\{since } g_{i-1} \text{ implies } h_i\} + h_i \ p_{i-1} \text{ \{from above\}}$$

$$= h_i(g_{i-1} + p_{i-1}) = h_i \ t_{i-1}$$

$$h_i = c_i + c_{i-1} = (g_{i-1} + c_{i-1}p_{i-1}) + c_{i-1}$$

$$= g_{i-1} + c_{i-1} = g_{i-1} + h_{i-1}t_{i-2} \text{ \{from above\}}$$

Unrolling the preceding recurrence for h_i, we get:

$$h_i = g_{i-1} + t_{i-2} \ h_{i-1} = g_{i-1} + t_{i-2}(g_{i-2} + h_{i-2} \ t_{i-3})$$

$$= g_{i-1} + g_{i-2} + h_{i-2} \ t_{i-2} \ t_{i-3} \text{ \{since } t_{i-2} \ g_{i-2} = g_{i-2}\}$$

$$= g_{i-1} + g_{i-2} + g_{i-3} \ t_{i-3} \ t_{i-2} + h_{i-3} \ t_{i-4} \ t_{i-3} \ t_{i-2}$$

$$= g_{i-1} + g_{i-2} + g_{i-3} \ t_{i-2} + g_{i-4} \ t_{i-3} \ t_{i-2} + h_{i-4} \ t_{i-4} \ t_{i-3} \ t_{i-2}$$

We see that expressing h_i in terms of h_{i-4} needs five product terms, with a maximum four-input AND gate, and a total of 14 gate inputs. By contrast, expressing c_i as

$$c_i = g_{i-1} + g_{i-2}t_{i-1} + g_{i-3}t_{i-2}t_{i-1} + g_{i-4}t_{i-3}t_{i-2}t_{i-1} + c_{i-4}t_{i-4}t_{i-3}t_{i-2}t_{i-1}$$

requires five terms, with a maximum five-input AND gate, and a total of 19 gate inputs. The advantage of h_i over c_i is even greater if we can use wired-OR (3 gates with 9 inputs vs. 4 gates with 14 inputs). Once h_i is known, however, the sum is obtained by a slightly more complex expression compared to $s_i = p_i \oplus c_i$:

$$s_i = p_i \oplus c_i$$

$$= p_i \oplus h_i t_{i-1} \quad \text{[and with straightforward manipulation]}$$

$$= (t_i \oplus h_{i+1}) + h_i \ g_i \ t_{i-1}$$

This concludes our presentation of Ling's improved carry-lookahead adder. As indicated, however, related designs have been developed. For example, Doran [Dora88] suggests that one can in general propagate η instead of c where:

$$\eta_{i+1} = f(x_i, y_i, c_i) = \psi(x_i, y_i)c_i + \phi(x_i, y_i)\bar{c}_i$$

The residual functions ψ and ϕ in the preceding Shannon expansion of f around c_i must be symmetric, and there are but eight symmetric functions of the two variables x_i and y_i. Doran [Dora88] shows that not all $8 \times 8 = 64$ possibilities are valid choices for ψ and ϕ, since in some cases the sum cannot be computed based on the η_i values. Dividing the eight symmetric functions of x_i and y_i into the two disjoint subsets $\{0, \bar{t}_i, g_i, \bar{p}_i\}$ and $\{1, t_i, \bar{g}_i, p_i\}$, Doran proves that ψ and ϕ cannot both belong to the same subset. Thus, there are only 32 possible adders. Four of these 32 possible adders have the desirable properties of Ling's adder, which represents the special case of $\psi(x_i, y_i) = 1$ and $\phi(x_i, y_i) = g_i = x_i y_i$.

6.4 CARRY DETERMINATION AS PREFIX COMPUTATION

Consider two contiguous or overlapping blocks B$'$ and B$''$ and their associated generate and propagate signal pairs (g', p') and (g'', p''), respectively. As shown in Fig. 6.6, the generate and propagate signals for the merged block B can be obtained from the equations:

$$g = g'' + g'p''$$
$$p = p'p''$$

That is, carry generation in the larger group takes place if the left group generates a carry or the right group generates a carry and the left one propagates it, while propagation occurs if both groups propagate the carry.

We note that in the discussion above, the indices i_0, j_0, i_1, and j_1 defining the two contiguous or overlapping blocks are in fact immaterial, and the same expressions can be written for any two adjacent groups of any length. Let us define the "carry" operator $\cent$ on (g, p) signal pairs as follows (right side of Fig. 6.6):

$$(g, p) = (g', p')\cent(g'', p'') \text{ means } g = g'' + g'p'', p = p'p''$$

The carry operator $\cent$ is *associative*, meaning that the order of evaluation does not affect the value of the expression $(g', p') \cent (g'', p'') \cent (g''', p''')$, but it is not *commutative*, since $g'' + g'p''$ is in general not equal to $g' + g''p'$.

Observe that in an adder with no c_{in}, we have $c_{i+1} = g_{[0,i]}$; that is, a carry enters position $i + 1$ if and only if one is generated by the block $[0, i]$. In an adder with c_{in}, a carry-in of 1 can be viewed as a carry generated by stage -1; we thus set $p_{-1} = 0$, $g_{-1} = c_{\text{in}}$ and compute $g_{[-1,i]}$ for all i. So, the problem remains the same, but with an extra stage ($k + 1$ rather than k). The problem of carry determination can, therefore, be formulated as follows:

Given
(g_0, p_0) (g_1, p_1) $\cdots$ (g_{k-2}, p_{k-2}) (g_{k-1}, p_{k-1})

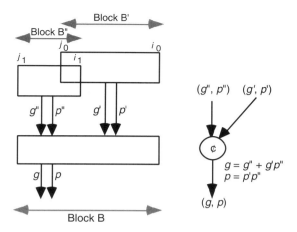

Fig. 6.6   Combining of g and p signals of two (contiguous or overlapping) blocks B' and B'' of arbitrary widths into the g and p signals for the overall block B.

Find
$$(g_{[0,0]}, p_{[0,0]}) \quad (g_{[0,1]}, p_{[0,1]}) \quad \cdots \quad (g_{[0,k-2]}, p_{[0,k-2]}) \quad (g_{[0,k-1]}, p_{[0,k-1]})$$

The desired signal pairs can be obtained by evaluating all the prefixes of

$$(g_0, p_0) \; ¢ \; (g_1, p_1) \; ¢ \; \cdots \; ¢ \; (g_{k-2}, p_{k-2}) \; ¢ \; (g_{k-1}, p_{k-1})$$

in parallel. In this way, the carry problem is converted to a parallel prefix computation, and any prefix computation scheme can be used to find all the carries.

A parallel prefix computation can be defined with any associative operator. In the following, we use the addition operator with integer operands, in view of its simplicity and familiarity, to illustrate the methods. The *parallel prefix sums* problem is defined as follows:

Given:	x_0	x_1	x_2	x_3	$\cdots$	x_{k-1}
Find:	x_0	$x_0 + x_1$	$x_0 + x_1 + x_2$	$x_0 + x_1 + x_2 + x_3$	$\cdots$	$x_0 + x_1 + \cdots + x_{k-1}$

Any design for this parallel prefix sums problem can be converted to a carry computation network by simply replacing each adder cell with the carry operator of Fig. 6.6. There is one difference worth mentioning, though. Addition is commutative. So if prefix sums are obtained by computing and combining the partial sums in an arbitrary manner, the resulting design may be unsuitable for a carry network. However, as long as blocks whose sums we combine are always contiguous, no problem arises.

Just as one can group numbers in any way to add them, (g, p) signal pairs can be grouped in any way for combining them into block signals. In fact, (g, p) signals give us an additional flexibility in that overlapping groups can be combined without affecting the outcome, whereas in addition, use of overlapping groups would lead to incorrect sums.

6.5 ALTERNATIVE PARALLEL PREFIX NETWORKS

Now, focusing on the problem of computing prefix sums, we can use several strategies to synthesize a parallel prefix sum network. Figure 6.7 is based on a divide-and-conquer approach. The low-order $k/2$ inputs are processed by the subnetwork at the right to compute the prefix sums $s_0, s_1, \cdots, s_{k/2-1}$. Partial prefix sums are computed for the high-order $k/2$ values (the left subnetwork) and $s_{k/2-1}$ (the leftmost output of the first subnetwork) is added to them to complete the computation. Such a network is characterized by the following recurrences for its delay (in terms of adder levels) and cost (number of adder cells):

$$\text{Delay recurrence:} \quad D(k) = D(k/2) + 1 = \log_2 k$$
$$\text{Cost recurrence:} \quad C(k) = 2C(k/2) + k/2 = (k/2) \, \log_2 k$$

A second design for computing prefix sums, again based on a divide-and-conquer approach, is depicted in Fig. 6.8. Here, the inputs are first combined pairwise to obtain the following sequence of length $k/2$:

$$x_0 + x_1 \qquad x_2 + x_3 \qquad x_4 + x_5 \qquad \cdots \qquad x_{k-4} + x_{k-3} \qquad x_{k-2} + x_{k-1}$$

Parallel prefix sum computation on this new sequence yields the odd-indexed prefix sums $s_1, s_3, s_5, \cdots$ for the original sequence. Even-indexed prefix sums are then computed by using $s_{2j} = s_{2j-1} + x_{2j}$. The cost and delay recurrences for the design of Fig. 6.8 are:

$$\text{Delay recurrence:} \quad D(k) = D(k/2) + 2 = 2 \, \log_2 k - 1$$
$$\text{actually we will see later that } D(k) = 2 \, \log_2 k - 2$$
$$\text{Cost recurrence:} \quad C(k) = C(k/2) + k - 1 = 2k - 2 - \log_2 k$$

So, the first design is faster ($\log_2 k$ as opposed to $2 \log_2 k - 2$ adder levels) but also much more expensive [$(k/2) \log_2 k$ as opposed to $2k - 2 - \log_2 k$ adder cells]. The first design also leads to large fan-out requirements if implemented directly in hardware. In other words, the output of one of the adders in the right part must feed the inputs of $k/2$ adders in the left part.

The design shown in Fig. 6.8 is known as the Brent–Kung parallel prefix graph. The 16-input instance of this graph is depicted in Fig. 6.9 [Bren82]. Note that even though the graph of

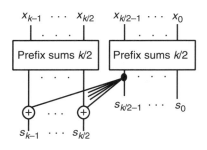

Fig. 6.7 Parallel prefix sums network built of two $k/2$-input networks and $k/2$ adders.

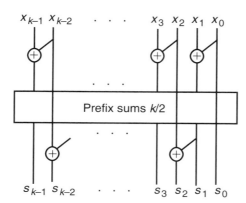

Fig. 6.8 Parallel prefix sums network built of one $k/2$-input network and $k-1$ adders.

Fig. 6.9 appears to have seven levels, two of the levels near the middle are independent, thus implying a single level of delay. In general, a k-input Brent–Kung parallel prefix graph will have a delay of $2 \log_2 k - 2$ levels and a cost of $2k - 2 - \log_2 k$ cells.

Figure 6.10 depicts a Kogge–Stone parallel prefix graph that has the same delay as the design shown in Fig. 6.7 but avoids its fan-out problem by distributing the computations. A k-input Kogge–Stone parallel prefix graph has a delay of $\log_2 k$ levels and a cost of $k \log_2 k - k + 1$ cells. The Kogge–Stone parallel prefix graph represents the fastest possible implementation of a parallel prefix computation if only two-input blocks are allowed. However, its cost can be prohibitive for large k, in terms of both the number of cells and the dense wiring between them.

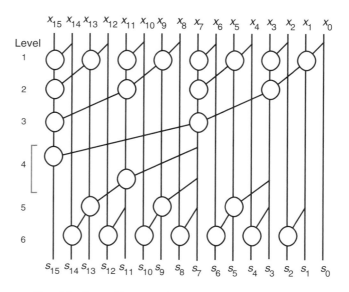

Fig. 6.9 Brent–Kung parallel prefix graph for 16 inputs.

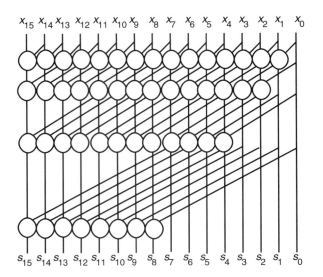

Fig. 6.10   Kogge–Stone parallel prefix graph for 16 inputs.

Many other parallel prefix network designs are possible. For example, it has been suggested that the Brent–Kung and Kogge–Stone approaches be combined to form hybrid designs [Sugl90]. In Fig. 6.11 the middle four of the six levels in the design of Fig. 6.9 (representing an eight-input parallel prefix computation) have been replaced by the eight-input Kogge–Stone network. The resulting design has five levels and 32 cells, placing it between the pure Brent–Kung (six levels, 26 cells) and pure Kogge–Stone (four levels, 49 cells) designs.

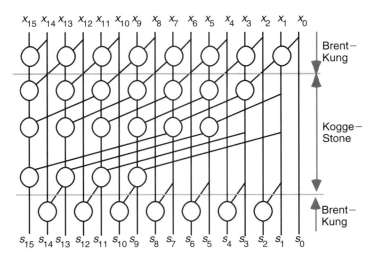

Fig. 6.11   A hybrid Brent–Kung/Kogge–Stone parallel prefix graph for 16 inputs.

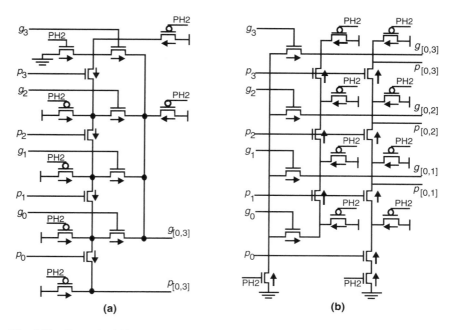

Fig. 6.12   Example 4-bit Manchester carry chain designs in CMOS technology [Lync92].

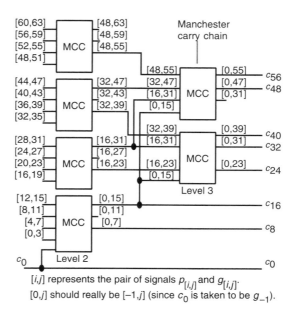

$[i,j]$ represents the pair of signals $p_{[i,j]}$ and $g_{[i,j]}$.

$[0,j]$ should really be $[-1,j]$ (since c_0 is taken to be g_{-1}).

Fig. 6.13   Spanning-tree carry-lookahead network [Lync92]. The 16 MCCs at level 1 that produce generate and propagate signals for 4-bit blocks are not shown.

More generally, if a single Brent–Kung level is used along with a $k/2$-input Kogge–Stone design, delay and cost of the hybrid network become $\log_2 k + 1$ and $(k/2)\log_2 k$, respectively. The resulting design is thus close to minimum in terms of delay (only one level more than Kogge–Stone) but costs roughly half as much.

The theory of parallel prefix graphs is quite rich and well developed. There exist both theoretical bounds and actual designs with different restrictions on fan-in/fan-out and with various optimality criteria in terms of cost and delay (see, e.g., Chapters 5–7, pp. 133–211, of [Laks94]).

In devising their design, Brent and Kung [Bren82] were motivated by the need to reduce the chip area in VLSI layout of the carry network. Other performance or hardware limitations may also be considered. The nice thing about formulating the problem of carry determination as a parallel prefix computation is that theoretical results and a wealth of design strategies carry over with virtually no effort. Not all such relationships between carry networks and parallel prefix networks, or the virtually unlimited hybrid combinations, have been explored in full.

6.6 VLSI IMPLEMENTATION ASPECTS

The carry network of Fig. 6.9 is quite suitable for VLSI implementation, but it might be deemed too slow for high-performance designs and/or wide words. Many designers have proposed alternate networks that offer reduced latency by using features of particular technologies and taking advantage of related optimizations. We review one example here that is based on radix-256 addition of 56-bit numbers as implemented in the Advanced Micro Devices Am29050 CMOS microprocessor. The following description is based on a 64-bit version of the adder.

In radix-256 addition of 64-bit numbers, only the carries $c_8, c_{16}, c_{24}, c_{32}, c_{40}, c_{48}$, and c_{56} need to be computed. First, 4-bit Manchester carry chains (MCCs) of the type shown in Fig. 6.12a are used to derive g and p signals for 4-bit blocks. These signals, denoted by [0, 3], [4, 7], [8, 11], etc. at the left edge of Fig. 6.13, then form the inputs to one 5-bit and three 4-bit MCCs that in turn feed two more MCCs in the third level. The MCCs in Fig. 6.13 are of the type shown in Fig. 6.12b; that is, they also produce intermediate g and p signals. For example, the MCC with inputs [16, 19], [20, 23], [24, 27], and [28, 31] yields the intermediate outputs [16, 23] and [16, 27], in addition to the signal pair [16, 31] for the entire group.

6.1   Borrow-lookahead subtractor We know that any carry network producing the carries c_i based on g_i and p_i signals can be used, with no modification, as a borrow propagation circuit to find the borrows b_i.

    a. Define the borrow-generate γ_i and borrow-propagate π_i signals in general and for the special case of binary operands.

    b. Present the design of a circuit to compute the difference digit d_i from γ_i, π_i, and the incoming borrow b_i.

6.2   One's-complement carry-lookahead adder Discuss how the requirement for end-around carry in 1's-complement addition affects the design and performance of a carry-lookahead adder.

6.3   **High-radix carry-lookahead adder** Consider radix-2^h addition of binary numbers and assume that the total time needed for producing the digit g and p signals, and determining the sum digits after all carries are known, equals δh, where δ is a constant. Carries are determined by a multilevel lookahead network using unit-time 2-bit lookahead carry generators. Derive the optimal radix that minimizes the addition latency as a function of δ and discuss.

6.4   **Unconventional carry-lookahead adder** Consider the following method for synthesizing a k-bit adder from four $k/4$-bit adders and a 4-bit lookahead carry generator. The $k/4$-bit adders have no group g or p output. Both the g_i and p_i inputs of the lookahead carry generator are connected to the carry-out of the ith $k/4$-bit adder, $0 \leq i \leq 3$. Intermediate carries of the lookahead carry generator and c_{in} are connected to the carry-in inputs of the $k/4$-bit adders. Will the suggested circuit add correctly? Find the adder's latency or justify your negative answer.

6.5   **Decimal carry-lookahead adder** Consider the design of a 15-digit decimal adder for unsigned numbers (width = 60 bits).

   a.   Design the required circuits for carry-generate and carry-propagate assuming binary-coded decimal digits.

   b.   Repeat part a with excess-3 encoding for the decimal digits, where digit value a is represented by the binary encoding of $a + 3$.

   c.   Complete the design of the decimal adder of part b by proposing a carry-lookahead circuit and the sum computation circuit.

6.6   **Carry lookahead with overlapped blocks**

   a.   Write down the indices for the g and p signals on Fig. 6.4. Then present expressions for these signals in terms of g and p signals of nonoverlapping subblocks such as $[i_0, i_1 - 1]$ and $[i_1, j_0]$.

   b.   Prove that the combining equations for the g and p signals for two contiguous blocks also apply to overlapping blocks (see Fig. 6.6).

6.7   **Latency of a carry-lookahead adder** Complete Fig. 6.5 by drawing boxes for the g and p logic and the sum computation logic. Then draw a critical path on the resulting diagram and indicate the number of gate levels of delay on each segment of the path.

6.8   **Ling adder or subtractor**

   a.   Show the complete design of a counterpart to the lookahead carry generator of Fig. 6.2 using Ling's method.

   b.   How does the design of a Ling subtractor differ from that of a Ling adder? Present complete designs for all the parts that are different.

6.9   **Ling-type adders** Based on the discussion at the end of Section 6.3, derive one the other three Ling-type adders proposed by Doran [Dora88]. Compare the derived adder to a Ling adder.

6.10   **Fixed-priority arbiters** A fixed-priority arbiter has k request inputs $R_{k-1}, \cdots, R_1, R_0$, and k grant outputs G_i. At each arbitration cycle, at most one of the grant signals is 1 and that corresponds to the highest-priority request signal (i.e., $G_i = 1$ iff $R_i = 1$ and $R_j = 0$ for $j < i$).

a. Design a synchronous arbiter using ripple-carry techniques. *Hint:* Consider $c_0 = 1$ along with carry propagate and annihilate rules; there is no carry generation.

b. Design the arbiter using carry-lookahead techniques. Determine the number of lookahead levels required with 64 inputs and estimate the total arbitration delay.

6.11   Carry-lookahead incrementer

a. Design a 16-bit incrementer using the carry-lookahead principle.

b. Repeat part a using Ling's approach.

c. Compare the designs of parts a and b with respect to delay and cost.

6.12   Parallel prefix networks Find delay and cost formulas for the Brent–Kung and Kogge–Stone designs when the word width k is not a power of 2.

6.13   Parallel prefix networks

a. Draw Brent–Kung, Kogge–Stone, and hybrid parallel prefix graphs for 12, 20, and 24 inputs.

b. Using the results of part a, plot the cost, delay, and cost–delay product for the five types of network for $k = 12, 16, 20, 24, 32$ bits and discuss.

6.14   Hybrid carry-lookahead adders

a. Find the depth and cost of a 64-bit hybrid carry network with two levels of the Brent–Kung scheme at each end and the rest built by the Kogge–Stone construction.

b. Compare the design of part a to pure Brent–Kung and Kogge–Stone schemes and discuss.

6.15   Parallel prefix networks

a. Obtain delay and cost formulas for a hybrid parallel prefix network that has l levels of Brent–Kung design at the top and bottom and a $k/2^l$-input Kogge–Stone network in the middle.

b. Use the delay–cost–product figure of merit to find the best combination of the two approaches for word lengths from 8 to 64 (powers of 2 only).

6.16   Speed and cost limits for carry computation Consider the computation of c_i, the carry into the ith stage of an adder, based on the g_j and t_j signals using only two-input AND and OR gates. Note that only the computation of c_i, independent of other carries, is being considered.

a. What is the minimum possible number of AND/OR gates required?

b. What is the minimum possible number of gate levels in the circuit?

c. Can one achieve the minima of parts a and b simultaneously? Explain.

6.17   Variable-block carry-lookahead adders Study the benefits of using nonuniform widths for the MCC blocks in a carry-lookahead adder of the type discussed in Section 6.6 [Kant93].

REFERENCES

[Bayo83]   Bayoumi, M. A., G. A. Jullien, and W. C. Miller, "An Area–Time Efficient NMOS Adder," *Integration: The VLSI Journal*, Vol. 1, pp. 317–334, 1983.

[Bren82]   Brent, R. P., and H. T. Kung, "A Regular Layout for Parallel Adders," *IEEE Trans. Computers*, Vol. 31, pp. 260–264, 1982.

[Dora88]   Doran, R. W., "Variants of an Improved Carry Look-Ahead Adder," *IEEE Trans. Computers*, Vol. 37, No. 9, pp. 1110–1113, 1988.

[Han87]   Han, T., and D. A. Carlson, "Fast Area-Efficient Adders," *Proc. 8th Symp. Computer Arithmetic*, pp. 49–56, 1987.

[Kant93]   Kantabutra, V., "A Recursive Carry-Lookahead/Carry-Select Hybrid Adder," *IEEE Trans. Computers*, Vol. 42, No. 12, pp. 1495–1499, 1993.

[Kogg73]   Kogge, P. M. and H. S. Stone, "A Parallel Algorithm for the Efficient Solution of a General Class of Recurrences," *IEEE Trans. Computers,* Vol. 22, pp. 786–793, 1973.

[Laks94]   Lakshmivarahan, S., and S. K. Dhall, *Parallel Computing Using the Prefix Problem*, Oxford University Press, 1994.

[Ling81]   Ling, H., "High-Speed Binary Adder," *IBM J. Research and Development*, Vol. 25, No. 3, pp. 156–166, 1981.

[Lync92]   Lynch, T., and E. Swartzlander, "A Spanning Tree Carry Lookahead Adder," *IEEE Trans. Computers*, Vol. 41, No. 8, pp. 931–939, 1992.

[Ngai84]   Ngai, T. F., M. J. Irwin, and S. Rawat, "Regular Area–Time Efficient Carry-Lookahead Adders," *J. Parallel and Distributed Computing*, Vol. 3, No. 3, pp. 92–105, 1984.

[Sugl90]   Sugla, B., and D. A. Carlson, "Extreme Area–Time Tradeoffs in VLSI," *IEEE Trans. Computers*, Vol. 39, No. 2, pp. 251–257, 1990.

[Wei90]   Wei, B. W. Y., and C. D. Thompson, "Area–Time Optimal Adder Design," *IEEE Trans. Computers*, Vol. 39, No. 5, pp. 666–675, 1990.

[Wein56]   Weinberger, A., and J. L. Smith, "A One-Microsecond Adder Using One-Megacycle Circuitry," *IRE Trans. Computers*, Vol. 5, pp. 65–73, 1956.

Chapter 7 | VARIATIONS IN FAST ADDERS

The carry-lookahead method of Chapter 6 represents the most widely used design for high-speed adders in modern computers. Certain alternative designs, however, either are quite competitive with carry-lookahead adders or offer advantages with particular hardware realizations or technology constraints. The most important of these alternative designs, and various hybrid combinations, are discussed in this chapter.

7.1 Simple Carry-Skip Adders

7.2 Multilevel Carry-Skip Adders

7.3 Carry-Select Adders

7.4 Conditional-Sum Adder

7.5 Hybrid Adder Designs

7.6 Optimizations in Fast Adders

7.1 SIMPLE CARRY-SKIP ADDERS

Consider a 4-bit group or block in a ripple-carry adder, from stage i to $i + 3$, where i is a multiple of 4 (Fig. 7.1a). A carry into stage i propagates through this group of 4 bits if and only if it propagates through all four of its stages. Thus, a "group propagate" signal is defined as $p_{[i,i+3]} = p_i p_{i+1} p_{i+2} p_{i+3}$, which is computable from individual propagate signals by a single four-input AND gate. To speed up carry propagation, one can establish bypass or skip paths around 4-bit blocks, as shown in Fig. 7.1b.

Let us assume that the delay of the two-level skip logic is equal to carry propagation delay through a single bit position. Then, the worst-case propagation delay through the carry-skip adder of Fig. 7.1b corresponds to a carry that is generated in stage 0, ripples through stages 1–3, goes through the OR gate, skips the middle two groups, and ripples in the last group from stage 12 to stage 15. This leads to 8.5 stages of propagation (17 gate levels) compared to 16 stages (32 gate levels) for a 16-bit ripple-carry adder.

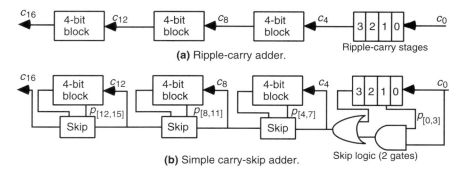

(a) Ripple-carry adder.

(b) Simple carry-skip adder.

Fig. 7.1 Converting a 16-bit ripple-carry adder into a simple carry-skip adder with 4-bit skip blocks.

Generalizing from the preceding example, the worst-case carry-propagation delay in a k-bit carry-skip adder with fixed block width b, assuming that one stage of ripple has the same delay as one skip, can be derived:

$$
T_{\text{fixed-skip-add}} = \underset{\text{in block 0}}{(b-1)} + \underset{\text{OR gate}}{0.5} + \underset{\text{skips}}{(k/b-2)} + \underset{\text{in last block}}{(b-1)}
$$

$$
\approx 2b + k/b \text{ - } 3.5 \ \text{ stages}
$$

The optimal fixed block size can be derived by equating $dT_{\text{fixed-skip-add}}/db$ with 0:

$$
\frac{dT_{\text{fixed-skip-add}}}{db} = 2 - k/b^2 = 0 \Rightarrow b^{\text{opt}} = \sqrt{k/2}
$$

The adder delay with the optimal block size above is:

$$
T^{\text{opt}}_{\text{fixed-skip-add}} = 2\sqrt{k/2} + \frac{k}{\sqrt{k/2}} - 3.5 = 2\sqrt{2k} - 3.5
$$

For example, to construct a 32-bit carry-skip adder with fixed-size blocks, we set $k = 32$ in the preceding equations to obtain $b^{\text{opt}} = 4$ bits and $T^{\text{opt}}_{\text{fixed-skip-add}} = 12.5$ stages (25 gate levels). By comparison, the propagation delay of a 32-bit ripple-carry adder is more than 2.5 times longer.

Clearly, a carry that is generated in, or absorbed by, one of the inner blocks travels a shorter distance through the skip blocks. We can thus afford to allow more ripple stages for such a carry without increasing the overall adder delay. This leads to the idea of variable skip-block sizes.

Let there be t blocks of widths $b_0, b_1, \cdots, b_{t-1}$ going from right to left (Fig. 7.2). Consider the two carry paths (1) and (2) in Fig. 7.2, both starting in block 0, one ending in block $t - 1$ and the other in block $t - 2$. Carry path (2) goes through one fewer skip than (1), so we can make block $t - 2$ one bit wider than block $t - 1$ without increasing the total adder delay. Similarly, by comparing carry paths (1) and (3), we conclude that block 1 can be one bit wider than block 0. So, assuming for ease of analysis that $b_0 = b_{t-1} = b$ and that the number t of blocks is even, the optimal block widths are:

$$b \qquad b+1 \qquad \cdots \qquad \frac{b+t}{2}-1 \qquad \frac{b+t}{2}-1 \qquad \cdots \qquad b+1 \qquad b$$

The first assumption ($b_0 = b_{t-1}$) is justified because the total delay is a function of $b_0 + b_{t-1}$ rather than their individual values and the second one (t even) does not affect the results significantly.

Based on the preceding block widths, the total number of bits in the t blocks is:

$$2[b + (b+1) + \cdots + (b+t/2-1)] = t(b+t/4-1/2)$$

Equating the total above with k yields:

$$b = k/t - t/4 + 1/2$$

The adder delay with the preceding assumptions is:

$$T_{\text{var}-\text{skip}-\text{add}} = 2(b-1) + 0.5 + t - 2$$
$$= \frac{2k}{t} + \frac{t}{2} - 2.5$$

The optimal number of blocks is thus obtained as follows:

$$\frac{dT_{\text{var}-\text{skip}-\text{add}}}{dt} = \frac{-2k}{t^2} + \frac{1}{2} = 0 \Rightarrow t^{\text{opt}} = 2\sqrt{k}$$

Note that the optimal number of blocks with variable-size blocks is $\sqrt{2}$ times larger than that obtained with fixed-size blocks. Note also that with the optimal number of blocks, b becomes $1/2$; thus we take it to be 1. The adder delay with t^{opt} blocks is

$$T^{\text{opt}}_{\text{var}-\text{skip}-\text{add}} \approx 2\sqrt{k} - 2.5$$

which is roughly a factor of $\sqrt{2}$ smaller than that obtained with optimal fixed-size skip-blocks.

The preceding analyses were based on a number of simplifying assumptions. For example, skip and ripple delays were assumed to be equal and ripple delay was assumed to be linearly proportional to the block width. These may not be true in practice. With CMOS implementation, for example, the ripple delay in a Manchester carry chain grows as the square of the block width. The analyses for obtaining the optimal fixed or variable block size carry-skip adder must be

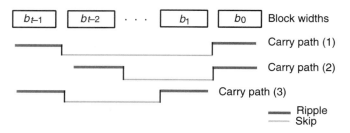

Fig. 7.2   Carry-skip adder with variable-size blocks and three sample carry paths.

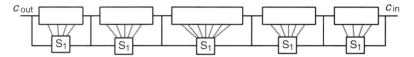

Fig. 7.3   Schematic diagram of a one-level carry-skip adder.

appropriately modified in such cases. A number of researchers have used various assumptions about technology-dependent parameters to deal with this optimization problem. Some of these variations are explored in the end-of-chapter problems.

7.2 MULTILEVEL CARRY-SKIP ADDERS

A (single-level) carry-skip adder of the types discussed in Section 7.1 can be represented schematically as in Fig. 7.3. The dotted lines between the various blocks and the first-level skip logic S_1 indicate that the control signal for the skip logic is derived from the propagate signals of the bit positions within the corresponding block. This relationship will be implicit in everything that follows, so the dotted lines are not shown hereafter.

In our subsequent discussions, we ignore the half-stage delay attributed to the single OR gate immediately preceding the first skip on the carry path (in contrast to the analyses of Section 7.1). This simplifies our discussions but has no significant effect on our procedures or conclusions. In addition, we continue to assume that the ripple and skip delays are equal, although the analyses can be easily modified to account for different ripple and skip delays. We thus equate the carry-skip adder delay with the worst-case sum, over all possible carry paths, of the number of ripple stages and the number of skip stages.

Multilevel carry-skip adders are obtained if we allow a carry to skip over several blocks at once. Figure 7.4 depicts a two-level carry-skip adder in which second-level skip logic has been provided for the leftmost three blocks. The signal controlling this second-level skip logic is derived as the logical AND of the first-level skip signals. A carry that would need 3 time units to skip these three blocks in a single-level carry-skip adder can now do so in a single time unit.

If the rightmost/leftmost block in a carry-skip adder is short, skipping it may not yield any advantage over allowing the carry to ripple through the block. In this case, the carry-skip adder of Fig. 7.4 can be simplified by removing such inefficient skip circuits. Figure 7.5 shows the resulting two-level carry-skip adder. With our simplifying assumption about ripple and skip delays being equal, the first-level skip circuit should be eliminated only for 1-bit, and possibly 2-bit, blocks (remember that generating the skip control signal also takes some time).

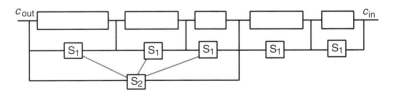

Fig. 7.4   Example of a two-level carry-skip adder.

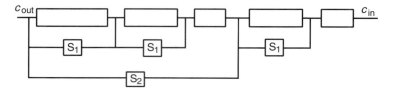

Fig. 7.5   Two-level carry-skip adder optimized by removing the short-block skip circuits.

■ **Example 7.1** Assume that each of the following operations takes 1 unit of time: generation of g_i and p_i signals, generation of a level-i skip signal from level-$(i-1)$ skip signals, ripple, skip, and computation of sum bit once the incoming carry is known. Build the widest possible single-level carry-skip adder with a total delay not exceeding 8 time units.

The numbers given on the adder diagram of Fig. 7.6 denote the time steps when the various signals stabilize, assuming that c_{in} is available at time 0. At the right end, block width is limited by the output timing requirement. For example, b_1 cannot be more than 3 bits if its output is to be available at time 3 (one time unit is taken by g_i, p_i generation at the rightmost bit, plus two time units for propagation across the other two bits). Block 0 is an exception, because to accommodate c_{in}, its width must be reduced by 1 bit. At the left end, block width is limited by input timing. For example, b_4 cannot be more than 3 bits, given that its input becomes available at time 5 and the total adder delay is to be 8 units. Based on this analysis, the maximum possible adder width is $1 + 3 + 4 + 4 + 3 + 2 + 1 = 18$ bits.

■ **Example 7.2** With the same assumptions as in Example 7.1, build the widest possible two-level carry-skip adder with a total delay not exceeding 8 time units.

We begin with an analysis of skip paths at level 2. In Fig. 7.7a, the notation $\{\beta, \alpha\}$ for a block means that the block's carry-out must become available no later than $T_{produce} = \beta$ and that the block's carry-in can take $T_{assimilate} = \alpha$ time units to propagate within the block without exceeding the overall time limit of 8 units. The remaining problem is to construct single-level carry-skip adders with the parameters $T_{produce} = \beta$ and $T_{assimilate} = \alpha$. Given the delay pair $\{\beta, \alpha\}$, the number of first-level blocks (subblocks) will be $\gamma = min(\beta - 1, \alpha)$, with the width of the ith subblock, $0 \le i \le \gamma - 1$, given by $b_i = min(\beta - \gamma + i + 1, \alpha - i)$; the only

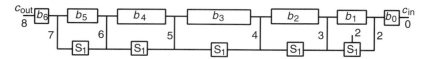

Fig. 7.6   Timing constraints of a single-level carry-skip adder with a delay of 8 units.

exception is subblock 0 in block A, which has one fewer bit (why?). So, the total width of such a block is $\sum_{i=0}^{\gamma-1} min(\beta - \gamma + i + 1, \alpha - i)$. Table 7.1 summarizes our analyses for the second-level blocks A–F. Note that the second skip level has increased the adder width from 18 bits (in Example 7.1) to 30 bits. Figure 7.7b shows the resulting two-level carry-skip adder.

The preceding analyses of one- and two-level carry-skip adders are based on many simplifying assumptions. If these assumptions are relaxed, the problem may no longer lend itself to analytical solution. Chan et al. [Chan92] use dynamic programming to obtain optimal configurations of carry-skip adders for which the various worst-case delays in a block of b full-adder units are characterized by arbitrary given functions (Fig. 7.8). These delays include:

$I(b)$ Internal carry-propagate delay for the block

$G(b)$ Carry-generate delay for the block

$A(b)$ Carry-assimilate delay for the block

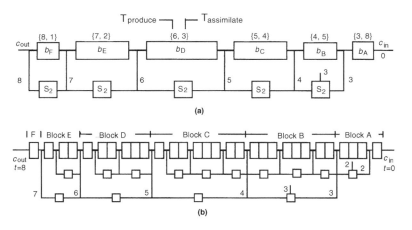

Fig. 7.7   Two-level carry-skip adder with a delay of 8 units: (a) Initial timing constraints, (b) Final design.

TABLE 7.1
Second-level constraints $T_{produce}$ and $T_{assimilate}$, with associated subblock and block widths, in a two-level carry-skip adder with a total delay of 8 time units (Fig. 7.7)

Block	$T_{produce}$	$T_{assimilate}$	Number of subblocks	Subblock widths (bits)	Block Width (bits)
A	3	8	2	1, 3	4
B	4	5	3	2, 3, 3	8
C	5	4	4	2, 3, 2, 1	8
D	6	3	3	3, 2, 1	6
E	7	2	2	2, 1	3
F	8	1	1	1	1

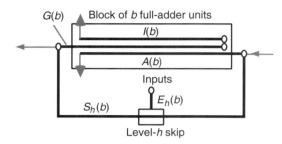

Fig. 7.8   Generalized delay model for carry-skip adders.

In addition, skip and enable delay functions, $S_h(b)$ and $E_h(b)$, are defined for each skip level h. In terms of this general model, our preceding analysis can be characterized as corresponding to $I(b) = b - 1$, $G(b) = b$, $A(b) = b$, $S_h(b) = 1$, and $E_h(b) = h + 1$. This is the model assumed by Turrini [Turr89]. Similar methods can be used to derive optimal block widths in variable-block carry-lookahead adders [Chan92].

7.3 CARRY-SELECT ADDERS

One of the earliest logarithmic time adder designs is based on the conditional-sum addition algorithm. In this scheme, blocks of bits are added in two ways: assuming an incoming carry of 0 or of 1, with the correct outputs selected later as the block's true carry-in becomes known. With each level of selection, the number of known output bits doubles, leading to a logarithmic number of levels and thus logarithmic time addition. Underlying the building of conditional-sum adders is the carry-select principle, described in this section.

A (single-level) carry-select adder is one that combines three $k/2$-bit adders of any design into a k-bit adder (Fig. 7.9). One $k/2$-bit adder is used to compute the lower half of the k-bit sum directly. Two $k/2$-bit adders are used to compute the upper $k/2$ bits of the sum and the carry-out under two different scenarios: $c_{k/2} = 0$ or $c_{k/2} = 1$. The correct values for the adder's carry-out signal and the sum bits in positions $k/2$ through $k - 1$ are selected when the value of $c_{k/2}$ becomes known. The delay of the resulting k-bit adder is two gate levels more than that of the $k/2$-bit adders that are used in its construction.

The following simple analysis demonstrates the cost-effectiveness of the carry-select method. Let us take the cost and delay of a single-bit 2-to-1 multiplexer as our units and assume that the cost and delay of a k-bit adder are $C_{\text{add}}(k)$ and $T_{\text{add}}(k)$, respectively. Then, the cost and delay of the carry-select adder of Fig. 7.9 are:

$$C_{\text{select}-\text{add}}(k) = 3C_{\text{add}}(k/2) + k/2 + 1$$

$$T_{\text{select}-\text{add}}(k) = T_{\text{add}}(k/2) + 1$$

If we take the product of cost and delay as our measure of cost effectiveness, the carry-select scheme of Fig. 7.9 is more cost-effective than the scheme used in synthesizing its component adders if and only if:

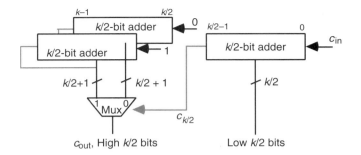

Fig. 7.9   Carry-select adder for k-bit numbers built from three $k/2$-bit adders.

$$[3C_{\text{add}}(k/2) + k/2 + 1][T_{\text{add}}(k/2) + 1] < C_{\text{add}}(k)T_{\text{add}}(k)$$

For ripple-carry adders, we have $C_{\text{add}}(k) = \alpha k$ and $T_{\text{add}}(k) = \tau k$. To simplify the analysis, assume $\tau = \alpha/2 > 1$. Then, it is easy to show that the carry-select method is more cost-effective that the ripple-carry scheme if $k > 16/(\alpha - 1)$. For $\alpha = 4$ and $\tau = 2$, say, the carry-select approach is almost always preferable to ripple-carry. Similar analyses can be carried out to compare the carry-select method against other addition schemes.

Note that in the preceding analysis, the use of three complete $k/2$-bit adders was assumed. With some adder types, the two $k/2$-bit adders at the left of Fig. 7.9 can share some hardware, thus leading to even greater cost effectiveness. For example, if the component adders used are of the carry lookahead variety, much of the carry network can be shared between the two adders computing the sum bits with $c_{k/2} = 0$ and $c_{k/2} = 1$ (how?).

Note that the carry-select method works just as well when the component adders have different widths. For example, Fig. 7.9 could have been drawn with one a-bit and two b-bit adders used to form an $(a + b)$-bit adder. Then c_a would be used to select the upper b bits of the sum through a $(b + 1)$-bit multiplexer. Unequal widths for the component adders is appropriate when the delay in deriving the selection signal c_a is different from that of the sum bits.

Figure 7.10 depicts how the carry-select idea can be carried one step further to obtain a two-level carry-select adder. Sum and carry-out bits are computed for each $k/4$-bit block (except for the rightmost one) under two scenarios. The three first-level multiplexers, each of which is $k/4 + 1$ bits wide, merge the results of $k/4$-bit blocks into those of $k/2$-bit blocks. Note how the carry-out signals of the adders spanning bit positions $k/2$ through $3k/4 - 1$ are used to select the most-significant $k/4$ bits of the sum under the two scenarios of $c_{k/2} = 0$ or $c_{k/2} = 1$. At this stage, $k/2$ bits of the final sum are known. The second-level multiplexer, which is $k/2 + 1$ bits wide, is used to select appropriate values for the upper $k/2$ bits of the sum (positions $k/2$ through $k - 1$) and the adder's carry-out.

Comparing the two-level carry-select adder of Fig. 7.10 to a similar two-level carry-lookahead adder (Fig. 6.5, but with 2-bit, rather than 4-bit, lookahead carry generators), we note that the one-directional top-to-bottom data flow in Fig. 7.10 makes pipelining easier and more efficient. Of course, from Section 6.5 and the example in Fig. 6.13, we know that carry-lookahead adders can also be implemented to possess one-directional data flow. In such cases, comparison is somewhat more difficult, insofar as carry-select adders have a more complex upper structure (the small adders) and simpler lower structure (the multiplexers).

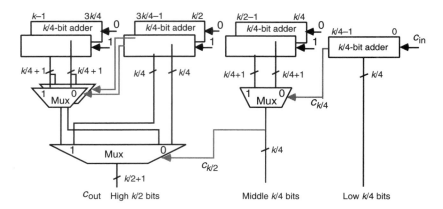

Fig. 7.10   Two-level carry-select adder built of $k/4$-bit adders.

Which design comes out ahead for a given word width depends on the implementation technology, performance requirements, and other design constraints. Very often, the best choice is a hybrid combination of carry-select and carry-lookahead (see Section 7.5).

7.4 CONDITIONAL-SUM ADDER

The process that led to the two-level carry-select adder of Fig. 7.10 can be continued to derive a three-level k-bit adder built of $k/8$-bit adders, a four-level adder composed of $k/16$-bit adders, and so on. A logarithmic time conditional-sum adder results if we proceed to the extreme of having single-bit adders at the very top. Thus, taking the cost and delay of a single-bit 2-to-1 multiplexer as our units, the cost and delay of a conditional-sum adder are characterized by the following recurrences:

$$C(k) \approx 2C(k/2) + k + 2 \approx k(\log_2 k + 2) + kC(1)$$
$$T(k) = T(k/2) + 1 = \log_2 k + T(1)$$

where $C(1)$ and $T(1)$ are the cost and delay of the circuit of Fig. 7.11 used at the top to derive the sum and carry bits with a carry-in of 0 and 1. The term $k + 2$ in the first recurrence represents an upper bound on the number of single-bit 2-to-1 multiplexers needed for combining two $k/2$-bit adders into a k-bit adder.

The recurrence for cost is approximate, since for simplicity, we have ignored the fact that the right half of Fig. 7.10 is less complex than its left half. In other words, we have assumed that two parallel $(b + 1)$-bit multiplexers are needed to combine the outputs from b-bit adders, although in some cases, one is enough.

An exact analysis leads to a comparable count for the number of single-bit multiplexers needed in a conditional-sum adder. Assuming that k is a power of 2, the required number of multiplexers for a k-bit adder is

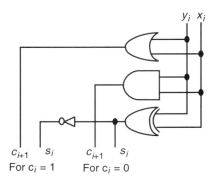

Fig. 7.11   Top-level block for one bit position of a conditional-sum adder.

$$(k/2 + 1) + 3(k/4 + 1) + 7(k/8 + 1) + \cdots + (k - 1)2 = (k - 1)(\log_2 k + 1)$$

leading to an overall cost of $(k - 1)(\log_2 k + 1) + kC(1)$.

The conditional-sum algorithm can be visualized by the 16-bit addition example shown in Table 7.2.

Given that a conditional-sum adder is actually a $(\log_2 k)$-level carry-select adder, the comparisons and trade-offs between carry-select adders and carry-lookahead adders, as discussed at the end of Section 7.3, are relevant here as well.

7.5 HYBRID ADDER DESIGNS

Hybrid adders are obtained by combining elements of two or more "pure" design methods to obtain adders with higher performance, greater cost-effectiveness, lower power consumption, and so on. Since any two or more pure design methods can be combined in a variety of ways, the space of possible designs for hybrid adders is immense. This leads to a great deal of flexibility in matching the design to given requirements and constraints. It also makes the designer's search for an optimal design nontrivial. In this section, we review several possible hybrid adders as representative examples.

The one- and two-level carry-select adders of Figs. 7.9 and 7.10 are essentially hybrid adders, since the top-level $k/2$- or $k/4$-bit adders can be of any type. In fact, a common use for the carry-select scheme is in building fast adders whose width would lead to inefficient implementations with certain pure designs. For example, when 4-bit lookahead carry blocks are used, both 16-bit and 64-bit carry-lookahead adders can be synthesized quite efficiently (Fig. 6.5). A 32-bit adder, on the other hand, would require two levels of lookahead and is thus not any faster than the 64-bit adder. Using 16-bit carry-lookahead adders, plus a single carry-select level to double the width, is likely to lead to a faster 32-bit adder. The resulting adder has a hybrid carry-select/carry-lookahead design.

The reverse combination (viz., hybrid carry-lookahead/carry-select) is also possible and is in fact used quite widely. An example hybrid carry-lookahead/carry-select adder is depicted in Fig. 7.12. The small adder blocks, shown in pairs, may be based on Manchester carry chains that supply the required g and p signals to the lookahead carry generator and compute the final intermediate carries as well as the sum bits once the block carry-in signals have become known.

TABLE 7.2
Conditional-sum addition of two 16-bit numbers: The width of the block for which the sum and carry bits are known doubles with each additional level, leading to an addition time that grows as the logarithm of the word width k

Block width	Block carry-in		15	14	13	12	11	10	9	8	7	6	5	4	3	2	1	0	c_{in}
		x	0	0	1	0	0	1	1	0	1	1	1	0	1	0	1	0	
		y	0	1	0	0	1	0	1	1	0	1	0	1	1	1	0	1	
1	0	s	0	1	1	0	1	1	0	1	1	0	1	1	0	1	1	1	
		c	0	0	0	0	0	0	1	0	0	1	0	0	1	0	0	0	0
	1	s	1	0	0	1	0	0	1	0	0	1	0	0	1	0	0		
		c	0	1	1	0	1	1	1	1	1	1	1	1	1	1	1		
2	0	s	0	1	1	0	1	1	0	1	0	0	1	1	0	1	1	1	
		c	0		0		0		1		1		0		1		0		
	1	s	1	0	1	1	0	0	1	0	0	1	0	0	1	0			
		c	0		0		1		1		1		1		1				
4	0	s	0	1	1	0	0	0	0	1	0	0	1	1	0	1	1	1	
		c	0				1				1				1				
	1	s	0	1	1	1	0	0	1	0	0	1	0	0					
		c	0				1				1								
8	0	s	0	1	1	1	0	0	0	1	0	1	0	0	0	1	1	1	
		c	0								1								
	1	s	0	1	1	1	0	0	1	0									
		c	0																
16	0	s	0	1	1	1	0	0	1	0	0	1	0	0	0	1	1	1	
		c	0																
	1	s																	
		c																	

c_{out}

A wider hybrid carry-lookahead/carry-select adder will likely have a multilevel carry-lookahead network rather than a single lookahead carry generator as depicted in Fig. 7.12. If the needed block g and p signals are produced quickly, the propagation of signals in the carry-lookahead network can be completely overlapped with carry propagation in the small carry-select adders. The carry-lookahead network of Fig. 6.13 was in fact developed for use in such a hybrid scheme, with 8-bit carry-select adders based on Manchester carry chains [Lync92]. The 8-bit adders complete their computation at about the same time that the carries c_{24}, c_{32}, c_{40}, c_{48}, and c_{56} become available (Fig. 6.13). Thus, the total adder delay is only two logic levels more than that of the carry-lookahead network.

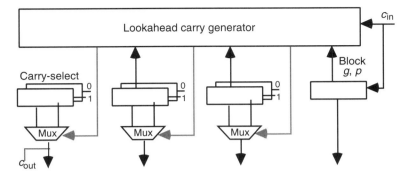

Fig. 7.12   A hybrid carry-lookahead/carry-select adder.

Another interesting hybrid design is the ripple-carry/carry-lookahead adder, an example of which is depicted in Fig. 7.13. This hybrid design is somewhat slower than pure carry-lookahead scheme, but its simplicity and greater modularity may compensate for this drawback. The analysis of cost and delay for this hybrid design relative to pure ripple-carry and carry-lookahead adders is left as an exercise, as is the development and analysis of the reverse carry-lookahead/ripple-carry hybrid combination.

Our final hybrid adder example uses the hybrid carry-lookahead/conditional-sum combination. One drawback of the conditional-sum adder for wide words is the requirement of large fan-out for the signals controlling the multiplexers at the lower levels (Fig. 7.10). This problem can be alleviated by, for example, using conditional-sum addition in smaller blocks, forming the interblock carries through carry-lookahead. For detailed description of one such adder, used in Manchester University's MU5 computer, see [Omon94, pp. 104-111].

Clearly, it is possible to combine ideas from various designs in many different ways, giving rise to a steady stream of new implementations and theoretical proposals for the design of fast adders. Different combinations become attractive with particular technologies in view of their specific cost factors and fundamental constraints [Kant93]. In addition, application requirements, such as low power consumption, may shift the balance in favor of a particular hybrid design.

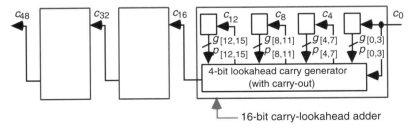

Fig. 7.13   Example 48-bit adder with hybrid ripple-carry/carry-lookahead design.

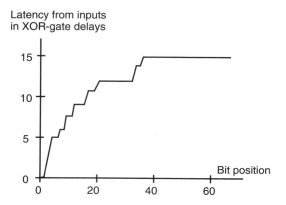

Fig. 7.14   Example arrival times for operand bits in the final fast adder of a tree multiplier [Oklo96].

7.6 OPTIMIZATIONS IN FAST ADDERS

Just as optimal carry-skip adders have variable block widths, it is often possible to reduce the delay of other (pure or hybrid) adders by optimizing the block widths. For example, depending on the implementation technology, a carry-lookahead adder with fixed blocks may not yield the lowest possible delay [Niga95]. Again, the exact optimal configuration is highly technology dependent. In fact, with modern VLSI technology, gate count alone is no longer a meaningful measure of implementation cost. Designs that minimize or regularize the interconnection may actually be more cost-effective despite using more gates. The ultimate test of cost-effectiveness for a particular hybrid design or "optimal" configuration is its actual speed and cost when implemented with the target technology.

So far our discussion of adder delay has been based on the tacit assumption that all input digits are available at the outset, or at time 0, and that all output digits are computed and taken out after worst-case carries have propagated. The other extreme, where input/output digits arrive and leave serially, leads to very simple digit-serial adder designs. In between the two extremes, there are practical situations in which different arrival times are associated with the input digits or certain output digits must be produced earlier than others.

We will later see, for example, that in multiplying two binary numbers, the partial products are reduced to two binary numbers, which are then added in a fast two-operand adder to produce the final product. The individual bits of these two numbers become available at different times in view of the differing logic path depths from primary inputs. Figure 7.14 shows a typical example for the input arrival times at various bit positions of this final fast adder. This information can be used in optimizing the adder design [Oklo96].

PROBLEMS

7.1   Optimal single-level carry-skip adders

   a.   Derive the optimal block width in a fixed-block carry-skip adder using the assumptions of Section 7.1, except that the carry production or assimilation delay in a block of width b is $b^2/2$ rather than b. Interpret the result.

b. Repeat part a with variable-width blocks. *Hint:* There will be several blocks of width b before the block width increases to $b + 1$.

7.2 **Optimal two-level carry-skip adders** For the two-level carry-skip adder of Example 7.2, Section 7.2, verify the block sizes given in Table 7.1 and draw a complete diagram for a 24-bit adder derived by pruning the design of Fig. 7.7.

7.3 **Optimal variable-block carry-skip adders**

    a. Build optimal single-level carry-skip adders for word widths $k = 24$ and $k = 80$.

    b. Repeat part a for two-level carry-skip adders.

    c. Repeat part a for three-level carry-skip adders.

7.4 **Carry-skip adders with given building blocks**

    a. Assume the availability of 4-bit and 8-bit adders with delays of 3 and 5 ns, respectively, and of 0.5-ns logic gates. Each of our building block adders provides a "propagate" signal in addition to the normal sum and carry-out signals. Design an optimal single-level carry-skip adder for 64-bit unsigned integers.

    b. Repeat part a for a two-level carry-skip adder.

    c. Would we gain any advantage by going to three levels of skip for the adder of part a?

    d. Outline a procedure for designing optimal single-level carry-skip adders from adders of widths $b_1 < b_2 < \cdots < b_h$ and delays $d_1 < d_2 < \cdots < d_h$, plus logic gates of delay δ.

7.5 **Fixed-block, two-level carry-skip adders** Using the assumptions in our analysis of single-level carry-skip adders in Section 7.1, present an analysis for a two-level carry-skip adder in which the block widths b_1 and b_2 in levels 1 and 2, respectively, are fixed. Hence, assuming that b_1 and b_2 divide k, there are k/b_2 second-level blocks and k/b_1 first-level blocks, with each second-level block encompassing b_2/b_1 first-level blocks. Determine the optimal block widths b_1 and b_2. Note that because of the fixed block widths, skip logic must be included even for the rightmost block at each level.

7.6 **Optimized multilevel carry-select adders** Consider the hierarchical synthesis of a k-bit multilevel carry-select adder where in each step of the process, an i-bit adder is subdivided into smaller j-bit and $(i - j)$-bit adders.

    a. At what value of i does it not make sense to further subdivide the block?

    b. When the width i of a block is odd, the two blocks derived from it will have to be of different widths. Is it better to make the right-hand or the left-hand block wider?

    c. Evaluate the suggestion that, just as in carry-skip adders, blocks of different widths be used to optimize the design of carry-select adders.

7.7 **Design of carry-select adders** Design 64-bit adders using ripple-carry blocks and 0, 1, 2, 3, or 4 levels of carry select.

    a. Draw schematic diagrams for the three- and four-level carry-select adders, showing all components and selection signals.

b. Obtain the exact delay and cost for each design in terms of the number of gates and gate levels using two-input NAND gates throughout. Construct the ripple-carry blocks using the full-adder design derived from Figs. 5.2a and 5.1c.

c. Compare the five designs with regard to delay, cost, and the composite delay–cost figure of merit and discuss.

7.8   The conditional-sum addition algorithm

a. Modify Table 7.2 to correspond to the same addition, but with $c_{in} = 1$.

b. Using a tabular representation as in Table 7.2, show the steps of deriving the sum of 24-bit numbers 0001 0110 1100 1011 0100 1111 and 0010 0111 0000 0111 1011 0111 by means of the conditional-sum method.

7.9   Design of conditional-sum adders Obtain the exact delay and cost for a 64-bit conditional-sum adder in terms of the number of gates and gate levels using two-input NAND gates throughout. For the topmost level, use the design given in Fig. 7.11.

7.10   Hybrid carry completion adder Suppose we want to design a carry completion adder to take advantage of its good average-case delay but would like to improve on its $O(k)$ worst-case delay. Discuss the suitability for this purpose of each of the following hybrid designs.

a. Completion-sensing blocks used in a single-level carry-skip arrangement.

b. Completion-sensing blocks used in a single-level carry-select arrangement.

c. Ripple-carry blocks with completion-sensing skip logic (separate skip circuits for 0 and 1 carries).

7.11   Hybrid ripple-carry/carry-lookahead adders Consider the hybrid ripple-carry/carry-lookahead adder design depicted in Fig. 7.13.

a. Present a design for the modified lookahead carry generator circuit that also produces the block's carry-out (e.g., c_{16} in Fig. 7.13).

b. Develop an expression for the total delay of such an adder. State your assumptions.

c. Under what conditions, if any, is the resulting adder faster than an adder with pure carry-lookahead design?

7.12   Hybrid carry-lookahead/ripple-carry adders Consider a hybrid adder based on ripple-carry blocks connected together with carry lookahead logic (i.e., the reverse combination compared to the design in Fig. 7.13). Present an analysis for the delay of such an adder and state under what conditions, if any, the resulting design is preferable to a pure carry-lookahead adder or to the hybrid design of Fig. 7.13.

7.13   Hybrid carry-select/carry-lookahead adders Show how carry-lookahead adders can be combined by a carry-select scheme to form a k-bit adder without duplicating the carry-lookahead logic in the upper $k/2$ bits.

7.14   Building fast adders from 4-bit adders Assume the availability of fast 4-bit adders with one (two) gate delay(s) to bit (block) g and p signals and two gate delays to sum and carry-out once the bit g and p and block carry-in signals are known. Derive the cost and delay of each of the following 16-bit adders:

   a.   Four 4-bit adders cascaded through their carry-in and carry-out signals.
   b.   Single-level carry-skip design with 4-bit skip blocks.
   c.   Single-level carry-skip design with 8-bit skip blocks.
   d.   Single-level carry-select, with each of the 8-bit adders constructed by cascading two 4-bit adders.

7.15   Carry-lookahead versus hybrid adders   We want to design a 32-bit fast adder from standard building blocks such as 4-bit binary full adders, 4-bit lookahead carry circuits, and multiplexers. Compare the following adders with respect to cost and delay:

   a.   Adder designed with two levels of lookahead.
   b.   Carry-select adder built of three 16-bit single-level carry-lookahead adders.

7.16   Comparing fast two-operand adders   Assume the availability of 1-bit full adders; 1-bit, two-input multiplexers, and 4-bit lookahead carry circuits as unit-delay building blocks. Draw diagrams for, and compare the speeds and costs of, the following 16-bit adder designs.

   a.   Optimal variable-block carry-skip adder using a multiplexer for each skip circuit.
   b.   Single-level carry-select adder with 8-bit ripple-carry blocks.
   c.   Two-level carry-select adder with 4-bit ripple-carry blocks.
   d.   Hybrid carry-lookahead/carry-select adder with duplicated 4-bit ripple-carry blocks in which the carry-outs with $c_{in} = 0$ and $c_{in} = 1$ are used as the group g and p signals.

7.17   Optimal adders with input timing information   For each fast adder type studied in Chapters 6 and 7, discuss how the availability of input bits at different times (Fig. 7.14) could be exploited to derive faster designs.

7.18   Fractional precision addition

   a.   We would like to design an adder that either adds two 32-bit numbers in their entirety or their lower and upper 16-bit halves independently. For each adder design discussed in Chapters 5–7, indicate how the design can be modified to allow such parallel half-precision arithmetic.
   b.   Propose a hybrid adder design that is particularly efficient for the design of part a.
   c.   Repeat part b, this time assuming two fractional precision modes: $4\times$ (8-bit) or $2\times$ (16-bit).

REFERENCES

[Bedr62]   Bedrij, O. J., "Carry-Select Adder," *IRE Trans. Electronic Computers*, Vol. 11, pp. 340–346, 1962.
[Chan90]   Chan, P. K., and M. D. F. Schlag, "Analysis and Design of CMOS Manchester Adders with Variable Carry Skip," *IEEE Trans. Computers*, Vol. 39, pp. 983–992, 1990.

[Chan92]   Chan, P. K., M. D. F. Schlag, C. D. Thomborson, and V. G. Oklobdzija, "Delay Optimization of Carry-Skip Adders and Block Carry-Lookahead Adders Using Multidimensional
Dynamic Programming," *IEEE Trans. Computers,* Vol. 41, No. 8, pp. 920–930, 1992.

[Guyo87]   Guyot, A., and J.-M. Muller, "A Way to Build Efficient Carry-Skip Adders," *IEEE Trans.
Computers*, Vol. 36, No. 10, pp. 1144–1152, 1987.

[Kant93]   Kantabutra, V., "Designing Optimum One-Level Carry-Skip Adders," *IEEE Trans. Computers*, Vol. 42, No. 6, pp. 759–764, 1993.

[Lehm61]   Lehman, M., and N. Burla, "Skip Techniques for High-Speed Carry Propagation in Binary
Arithmetic Units," *IRE Trans. Electronic Computers*, Vol. 10, pp. 691–698, December
1961.

[Lync92]   Lynch, T., and E. Swartzlander, "A Spanning Tree Carry Lookahead Adder," *IEEE Trans.
Computers*, Vol. 41, No. 8, pp. 931–939, 1992.

[Maje67]   Majerski, S., "On Determination of Optimal Distributions of Carry Skip in Adders," *IEEE
Trans. Electronic Computers*, Vol. 16, pp. 45–58, February 1967.

[Niga95]   Nigaglioni, R. H., and E. E. Swartzlander, "Variable Spanning Tree Adder," *Proc. Asilomar Conf. Signals, Systems, and Computers*, 1995, pp. 586–590.

[Oklo96]   Oklobdzija, V. G., D. Villeger, and S. S. Liu, "A Method for Speed Optimized Partial
Product Reduction and Generation of Fast Parallel Multipliers Using an Algorithmic
Approach," *IEEE Trans. Computers*, Vol. 45, No. 3, pp. 294–306, 1996.

[Omon94]   Omondi, A. R., *Computer Arithmetic Systems: Algorithms, Architecture and Implementation*, Prentice-Hall, 1994.

[Skla60]   Sklansky, J., "Conditional-Sum Addition Logic," *IRE Trans. Electronic Computers*, Vol.
9, No. 2, pp. 226–231, June 1960.

[Turr89]   Turrini, S., "Optimal Group Distribution in Carry-Skip Adders," *Proc. 9th Symp. Computer Arithmetic*, pp. 96–103, September 1989.

Chapter 8 | MULTIOPERAND ADDITION

In Chapters 6 and 7, we covered several speedup methods for adding two operands. Our primary motivation in dealing with multioperand addition in this chapter is that both multiplication and inner-product computation reduce to adding a set of numbers, namely, the partial products or the component products. The main idea used is that of *deferred carry assimilation* made possible by redundant representation of the intermediate results.

8.1 Using Two-Operand Adders

8.2 Carry-Save Adders

8.3 Wallace and Dadda Trees

8.4 Parallel Counters

8.5 Generalized Parallel Counters

8.6 Adding Multiple Signed Numbers

8.1 USING TWO-OPERAND ADDERS

Multioperand addition is implicit in both multiplication and computation of vector inner products (Fig. 8.1). In multiplying a multiplicand a by a k-digit multiplier x, the k partial products $x_i a$ must be formed and then added. For inner-product computation, the component product terms $p^{(j)} = x^{(j)} y^{(j)}$ obtained by multiplying the corresponding elements of the two operand vectors x and y, need to be added. Computing averages (e.g., in the design of a mean filter) is another application that requires multioperand addition.

Figure 8.1 uses what is known as "dot notation," a representation we will find quite useful when only the positioning or alignment of bits, rather than their values, is important. We will assume that the n operands are unsigned integers of the same width k and are aligned at the least significant end, as in the right side of Fig. 8.1. Extension of the methods to signed operands are discussed in Section 8.6. Application to multiplication is the subject of Part III.

Figure 8.2 depicts a serial solution to the multioperand addition problem using a single two-operand adder. The binary operands $x^{(i)}$, $i = 0, 1, \cdots, n - 1$, are applied, one per clock cycle,

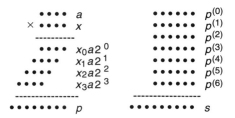

Fig. 8.1 Multioperand addition problems for multiplication or inner-product computation shown in dot notation.

to one input of the adder, with the other input fed back from a partial sum register. Since the final sum can be as large as $n(2^k - 1)$, the partial sum register must be $\log_2(n2^k - n + 1) \approx k + \log_2 n$ bits wide.

Assuming the use of a logarithmic time fast adder, the total latency of the scheme of Fig. 8.2 for adding n operands of width k is:

$$T_{serial-multi-add} = O(n \log(k + \log n))$$

Since $k + \log n$ is no less than $max(k, \log n)$ and no greater than $max(2k, 2 \log n)$, we have $\log(k + \log n) = O(\log k + \log \log n)$ and:

$$T_{serial-multi-add} = O(n \log k + n \log \log n)$$

Therefore, the addition time grows superlinearly with n when k is fixed and logarithmically with k for a given n.

One can pipeline this serial solution to get somewhat better performance. Figure 8.3 shows that if the adder is implemented as a four-stage pipeline, then three adders can be used to achieve the maximum possible throughput of one operand per clock cycle. Even though the clock cycle is now shorter because of pipelining, the latency from the first input to the last output remains asymptotically the same with h-stage pipelining for any fixed h.

Note that the schemes shown in Figs. 8.2 and 8.3 work for any prefix computation involving a binary operator $\otimes$, provided the adder is replaced by a hardware unit corresponding to the binary operator $\otimes$. For example, similar designs can be used to find the product of n numbers or the largest value among them.

For higher speed, a tree of two-operand adders might be used, as in Fig. 8.4. Such a binary tree of two-operand adders needs $n - 1$ adders and is thus quite costly if built of fast adders.

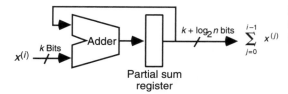

Fig. 8.2 Serial implementation of multioperand addition with a single two-operand adder.

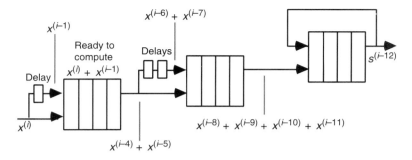

Fig. 8.3   Serial multioperand addition when each adder is a four-stage pipeline.

Strange as it may seem, the use of simple and slow ripple-carry (or even bit-serial) adders may be the best choice in this design. If we use fast logarithmic time adders, the latency will be:

$$T_{\text{tree}-\text{fast}-\text{multi}-\text{add}} = O(\log k + \log(k+1) + \cdots + \log(k + \lceil \log_2 n \rceil - 1))$$
$$= O(\log n \, \log k + \log n \log \log n)$$

The preceding equality can be proven by considering the two cases of $\log_2 n < k$ and $\log_2 n > k$ and bounding the right-hand side in each case. Supplying the needed details of the proof is left as an exercise. If we use ripple-carry adders in the tree of Fig. 8.4, the delay becomes

$$T_{\text{tree}-\text{ripple}-\text{multi}-\text{add}} = O(k + \log n)$$

which can be less than the delay with fast adders for large n. Comparing the costs of this and the preceding schemes for different ranges of values for the parameters k and n is left as an exercise.

Figure 8.5 shows why the delay with ripple-carry adders is $O(k + \log n)$. There are $\lceil \log_2 n \rceil$ levels in the tree. An adder in the $(i+1)$th level need not wait for full carry propagation in level i to occur, but rather can start its addition one full-adder delay after level i. In other words, carry propagation in each level lags one time unit behind the preceding level. Thus, we need to allow constant time for all but the last adder level, which needs $O(k + \log n)$ time.

Can we do better than the $O(k + \log n)$ delay offered by the tree of ripple-carry adders of Fig. 8.5? The absolute minimum time is $O(\log(kn)) = O(\log k + \log n)$, where kn is the total number of input bits to be processed by the multioperand adder, which is ultimately composed of constant-fan-in logic gates. This minimum is achievable with carry-save adders.

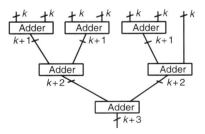

Fig. 8.4   Adding seven numbers in a binary tree of adders.

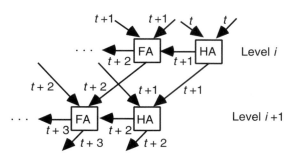

Fig. 8.5 Ripple-carry adders at levels i and $i + 1$ in the tree of full adders and half-adders (HA) used for multioperand addition.

8.2 CARRY-SAVE ADDERS

We can view a row of binary full adders as a mechanism to reduce three numbers to two numbers rather than as one to reduce two numbers to their sum. Figure 8.6 shows the relationship of a ripple-carry adder for the latter reduction and a carry-save adder for the former (see also Fig. 3.5).

Figure 8.7 presents, in dot notation, the relationship shown in Fig. 8.6. To specify more precisely how the various dots are related or obtained, we agree to enclose any three dots that form the inputs to a full adder in a dashed box and to connect the sum and carry outputs of a full-adder by a diagonal line (Fig. 8.8). Occasionally, only two dots are combined to form a sum bit and a carry bit. Then the two dots are enclosed in a dashed box and the use of a half-adder is signified by a cross line on the diagonal line connecting its outputs (Fig. 8.8).

Dot notation suggests another way to view the function of a carry-save adder: as converter of a radix-2 number with the digit set [0, 3] (three bits in one position) to one with the digit set [0, 2] (two bits in one position).

A carry-save adder tree (Fig. 8.9) can reduce n binary numbers to two numbers having the same sum in O(log n) levels. If a fast logarithmic time carry-propagate adder is then used to add

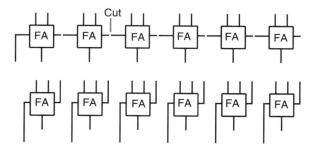

Fig. 8.6 A ripple-carry adder turns into a carry-save adder if the carries are saved (stored) rather than propagated.

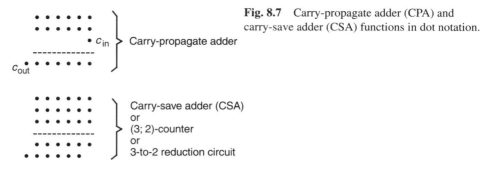

Fig. 8.7 Carry-propagate adder (CPA) and carry-save adder (CSA) functions in dot notation.

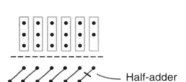

Fig. 8.8 Specifying full- and half-adder blocks, with their inputs and outputs, in dot notation.

the two resulting numbers, we have the following results for the cost and delay of n-operand addition:

$$C_{\text{carry-save-multi-add}} = (n - 2)C_{\text{CSA}} + C_{\text{CPA}}$$

$$T_{\text{carry-save-multi-add}} = \text{O(tree height} + T_{\text{CPA}}) = \text{O}(\log n + \log k)$$

The needed CSAs are of various widths, but generally the widths are close to k bits; the CPA is of width at most $k + \log_2 n$.

An example for adding seven 6-bit numbers is shown in Fig. 8.10. A more compact tabular representation of the same process is depicted in Fig. 8.11, where the entries represent the number of dots remaining in the respective columns or bit positions. We begin on the first row with seven dots in each of bit positions 0–5; these dots represent the seven 6-bit inputs. Two full-adders are used in each 7-dot column, with each FA converting 3 dots in its column to one dot in that column and one dot in the next higher column. This leads to the distribution of dots shown on the second row of Fig. 8.11. Next, one full adder is used in each of the bit positions 0–5 containing

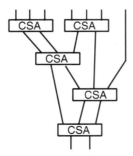

Fig. 8.9 Tree of carry-save adders reducing seven numbers to two.

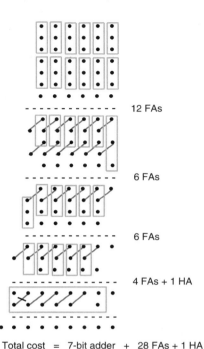

Fig. 8.10   Addition of seven 6-bit numbers in dot notation.

12 FAs

6 FAs

6 FAs

4 FAs + 1 HA

Total cost = 7-bit adder + 28 FAs + 1 HA

3 dots or more, and so on, until no column contains more than 2 dots (see below for details). At this point, a carry-propagate adder is used to reduce the resulting two numbers to the final 9-bit sum represented by a single dot in each of the bit positions 0–8.

In deriving the entries of a row from those of the preceding one, we begin with column 0 and proceed to the leftmost column. In each column, we cast out multiples of 3 and for each group of three that we cast out, we include 1 bit in the same column and 1 bit in the next column to the left. Columns at the right that have already been reduced to 1 need no further reduction. The rightmost column with a 2 can be either reduced using a half-adder or left intact, postponing its reduction to the final carry-propagate adder. The former strategy tends to make the width of the

8	7	6	5	4	3	2	1	0	Bit position
			7	7	7	7	7	7	$6 \times 2 = 12$ FAs
		2	5	5	5	5	5	3	6 FAs
		3	4	4	4	4	4	1	6 FAs
	1	2	3	3	3	3	2	1	4 FAs + 1 HA
	2	2	2	2	2	1	2	1	7-bit adder
		Carry-propagate adder							
1	1	1	1	1	1	1	1	1	

Fig. 8.11   Representing a seven-operand addition in tabular form.

final CPA smaller, while the latter strategy minimizes the number of full and half-adders at the expense of a wider CPA. In the example of Fig. 8.10, and its tabular form in Fig. 8.11, we could have reduced the width of the final CPA from 7 bits to 6 bits by applying an extra half-adder to the two dots remaining in bit position 1.

Figure 8.12 depicts a block diagram for the carry-save addition of seven k-bit numbers. By tagging each line in the diagram with the bit positions it carries, we see that even though the partial sums do grow in magnitude as more numbers are combined, the widths of the carry-save adders stay pretty much constant throughout the tree. Note that the lowermost CSA in Fig. 8.12 could have been made only $k - 1$ bits wide by letting the two lines in bit position 1 pass through. The carry-propagate adder would then have become $k + 1$ bits wide.

Of course carry-save addition can be implemented serially using a single CSA, as depicted in Fig. 8.13. This is the preferred method when the operands arrive serially or must be read out from memory one by one. Note, however, that in this case both the CSA and final CPA will have to be wider.

8.3 WALLACE AND DADDA TREES

The CSA tree of Fig. 8.12, which reduces seven k-bit operands to two $(k + 2)$-bit operands having the same sum, is known as a seven-input Wallace tree. More generally, an n-input Wallace tree reduces its k-bit inputs to two $(k + \log_2 n - 1)$-bit outputs. Since each CSA reduces the number of operands by a factor of 1.5, the smallest height $h(n)$ of an n-input Wallace tree satisfies the following recurrence:

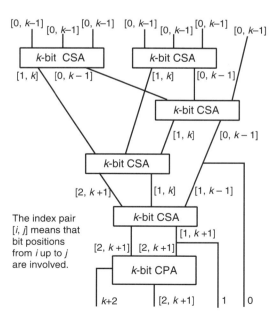

Fig. 8.12   Adding seven k-bit numbers and the CSA/CPA widths required.

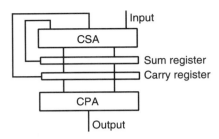

$$h(n) = 1 + h(\lceil 2n/3 \rceil)$$

Applying this recurrence provides an exact value for the height of an n-input Wallace tree. If we ignore the ceiling operator in the preceding equation and write it as $h(n) = 1 + h(2n/3)$, we obtain a lower bound for the height, $h(n) \geq \log_{1.5}(n/2)$, where equality occurs only for $n = 2, 3$. Another way to look at the above relationship between the number of inputs and the tree height is to find the maximum number of inputs $n(h)$ that can be reduced to two outputs by an h-level tree. The recurrence for $n(h)$ is:

$$n(h) = \lfloor 3n(h-1)/2 \rfloor$$

Again ignoring the floor operator, we obtain the upper bound $n(h) \leq 2(3/2)^h$. The lower bound $n(h) > 2(3/2)^{h-1}$ is also easily established. The exact value of $n(h)$ for $0 \leq h \leq 20$ is given in Table 8.1.

In Wallace trees, we reduce the number of operands at the earliest opportunity (see the example in Fig. 8.10). In other words, if there are m dots in a column, we immediately apply $\lfloor m/3 \rfloor$ full adders to that column. This tends to minimize the overall delay by making the final CPA as short as possible.

However, the delay of a fast adder is usually not a smoothly increasing function of the word width. A carry-lookahead adder, for example, may have essentially the same delay for word widths 17–32 bits. In Dadda trees, we reduce the number of operands to the next lower number in Table 8.1 using the fewest FAs and HAs possible. The justification is that 7, 8, or 9 operands, say, require four CSA levels; thus there is no point in reducing the number of operands below the next lower $n(h)$ value in the table, since this would not lead to a faster tree.

Let us redo the example of Fig. 8.10 by means of Dadda's strategy. Figure 8.14 shows the result. We start with seven rows of dots, so our first task is to reduce the number of rows to

TABLE 8.1
The maximum number $n(h)$ of inputs for an h-level carry-save-adder tree

h	$n(h)$	h	$n(h)$	h	$n(h)$
0	2	7	28	14	474
1	3	8	42	15	711
2	4	9	63	16	1066
3	6	10	94	17	1599
4	9	11	141	18	2398
5	13	12	211	19	3597
6	19	13	316	20	5395

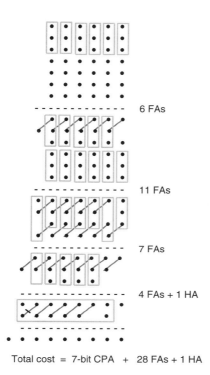

Fig. 8.14   Using Dadda's strategy to add seven 6-bit numbers

6 FAs

11 FAs

7 FAs

4 FAs + 1 HA

Total cost = 7-bit CPA + 28 FAs + 1 HA

the next lower $n(h)$ value (i.e., 6). This can be done by using 6 full adders; next, we aim for four rows, leading to the use of 11 FAs, and so on. In this particular example, the Wallace and Dadda approaches result in the same number of full and half-adders and the same width for the CPA. Again, the CPA width could have been reduced to 6 bits by using an extra half-adder in bit position 1.

Since a CPA has a carry-in signal that can be used to accommodate one of the dots, it is sometimes possible to reduce the complexity of the CSA tree by leaving three dots in the least significant position of the adder. Figure 8.15 shows the same example as in Figs. 8.10 and 8.14, but with two FAs replaced with HAs, leaving an extra dot in each of the bit positions 1 and 2.

8.4 PARALLEL COUNTERS

A single-bit full adder is sometimes referred to as a (3; 2)-counter, meaning that it counts the number of 1s among its three input bits and represents the result as a 2-bit number. This can be easily generalized: an $(n; \lceil \log_2(n+1) \rceil)$-counter has n inputs and produces a $\lceil \log_2(n+1) \rceil$-bit binary output representing the number of 1s among its n inputs. Such a circuit is also known as an n-input parallel counter.

A 10-input parallel counter, or a (10; 4)-counter, is depicted in Fig. 8.16 in terms of both dot notation and circuit diagram with full and half-adders. A row of such (10; 4)-counters, one per bit position, can reduce a set of 10 binary numbers to 4 binary numbers. The dot notation

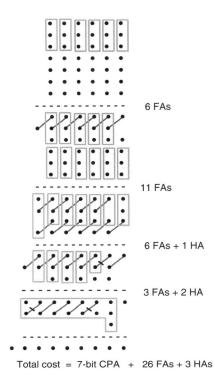

Fig. 8.15   Adding seven 6-bit numbers by taking advantage of the final adder's carry-in.

representation of this reduction is similar to that of (3; 2)-counters, except that each diagonal line connecting the outputs of a (10; 4) counter will go through four dots. A (7; 3)-counter can be similarly designed.

Even though a circuit that counts the number of 1s among n inputs is known as a parallel counter, we note that this does not constitute a true generalization of the notion of a sequential counter. A sequential counter receives a single bit (the count signal) and adds it to a stored count. A parallel counter, then, could have been defined as a circuit that receives n count signals and adds them to a stored count, thus in effect incrementing the count by the sum of the input count signals. Such a circuit has been called an "accumulative parallel counter" [Parh95]. An accumulative parallel counter can be built from a parallel incrementer (a combinational circuit receiving a number and producing the sum of the input number and n count signals at the output) along with a storage register. Both parallel and accumulative parallel counters can be extended by considering signed count signals. These would constitute generalizations of sequential up/down counters [Parh89].

8.5 GENERALIZED PARALLEL COUNTERS

A parallel counter reduces a number of dots in the same bit position into dots in different positions (one in each). This idea can be easily generalized to circuits that receive "dot patterns"

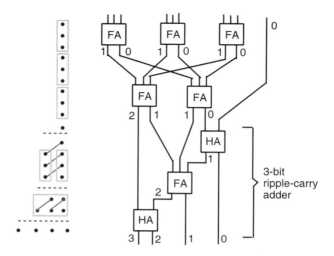

Fig. 8.16   A 10-input parallel counter also known as a (10; 4)-counter.

(not necessarily in a single column) and convert them to other dot patterns (not necessarily one in each column). If the output dot pattern has fewer dots that the input dot pattern, compression takes place; repeated use of such circuits can eventually lead to the reduction of n numbers to a small set of numbers (ideally two).

A generalized parallel counter (parallel compressor) is characterized by the number of dots in each input column and in each output column. We do not consider such circuits in their full generality but limit ourselves to those that output a single dot in each column. Thus, the output side of such parallel compressors is again characterized by a single integer representing the number of columns spanned by the output. The input side is characterized by a sequence of integers corresponding to the number of inputs in various columns.

For example, a (4, 4; 4)-counter receives 4 bits in each of two adjacent columns and produces a 4-bit number representing the sum of the four 2-bit numbers received. Similarly, a (5, 5; 4)-counter, depicted in Fig. 8.17, reduces five 2-bit numbers to a 4-bit number. The numbers of input dots in various columns do not have to be the same. For example, a (4, 6; 4)-counter receives 6 bits of weight 1 and 4 bits of weight 2 and delivers their weighted sum in the form of a 4-bit binary number. For a counter of this type to be feasible, the sum of the output weights must equal or exceed the sum of its input weights.

Fig. 8.17   Dot notation for a (5, 5; 4)-counter and the use of such counters for reducing five numbers to two numbers.

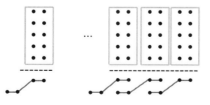

Generalized parallel counters are quite powerful. For example, a 4-bit binary full adder is really a (2, 2, 2, 3; 5)-counter.

Since our goal in multioperand carry-save addition is to reduce n numbers to two numbers, we sometimes talk of $(n; 2)$-counters, even though, with our preceding definition, this does not make sense for $n > 3$. By an $(n; 2)$-counter, $n > 3$, we usually mean a slice of a circuit that helps us reduce n numbers to two numbers when suitably replicated. Slice i of the circuit receives n input bits in position i, plus transfer or "carry" bits from one or more positions to the right $(i - 1, i - 2,$ etc.$)$, and produces output bits in the two positions i and $i + 1$ plus transfer bits into one or more higher positions $(i + 1, i + 2,$ etc.$)$. If ψ_j denotes the number of transfer bits from slice i to slice $i + j$, the fundamental inequality to be satisfied for this scheme to work is

$$n + \psi_1 + \psi_2 + \psi_3 + \cdots \le 3 + 2\psi_1 + 4\psi_2 + 8\psi_3 + \cdots$$

where 3 represents the maximum value of the 2 output bits. For example, a $(7; 2)$-counter can be built by allowing $\psi_1 = 1$ transfer bit from position i to position $i + 1$ and $\psi_2 = 1$ transfer bit into position $i + 2$. For maximum speed, the circuit slice must be designed in such a way that transfer signals are introduced as close to the circuit's outputs as possible, to prevent the transfers from rippling through many stages. Design of a $(7; 2)$-counter using these principles is left as an exercise.

8.6 ADDING MULTIPLE SIGNED NUMBERS

When the operands to be added are 2's-complement numbers, they must be sign-extended to the width of the final result if multiple-operand addition is to yield their correct sum. The example in Fig. 8.18 shows extension of the sign bits x_{k-1}, y_{k-1}, and z_{k-1} across five extra positions.

It appears, therefore, that sign extension may dramatically increase the complexity of the CSA tree used for n-operand addition when n is large. However, since the sign extension bits are identical, a single full adder can do the job of several full adders that would be receiving identical inputs if used. With this hardware-sharing scheme, the CSA widths are only marginally increased. For the three operands in Fig. 8.18a, a single $(3; 2)$-counter can be used in lieu of six that would be receiving the same input bits x_{k-1}, y_{k-1}, and z_{k-1}.

It is possible to avoid sign extension by taking advantage of the negative-weight interpretation of the sign bit in 2's-complement representation. A negative sign bit $-x_{k-1}$ can be replaced by $1 - x_{k-1} = \bar{x}_{k-1}$ (the complement of x_{k-1}), with the extra 1 canceled by inserting a -1 in that same column. Multiple -1s in a given column can be paired, with each pair replaced by a -1 in the next higher column. Finally, a solitary -1 in a given column is replaced by 1 in that column and -1 in the next higher column. Eventually, all the -1s disappear off the left end and at most a single extra 1 is left in some of the columns.

Figure 8.18b shows how this method is applied when adding three 2's-complement numbers. The three sign bits are complemented and three -1s are inserted in the sign position. These three -1s are then replaced by a 1 in the sign position and two -1s in the next higher position (k). These two -1s are then removed and, instead, a single -1 is inserted in position $k + 1$. The latter -1 is in turn replaced by a 1 in position $k + 1$ and a -1 in position $k + 2$, and so on. The -1 that moves out from the leftmost position is immaterial in view of $(k + 5)$-bit 2's-complement arithmetic being performed modulo-2^{k+5}.

Extended positions	Sign	Magnitude positions
$x_{k-1}\ x_{k-1}\ x_{k-1}\ x_{k-1}\ x_{k-1}$	x_{k-1}	$x_{k-2}\ x_{k-3}\ x_{k-4} \cdots$
$y_{k-1}\ y_{k-1}\ y_{k-1}\ y_{k-1}\ y_{k-1}$	y_{k-1}	$y_{k-2}\ y_{k-3}\ y_{k-4} \cdots$
$z_{k-1}\ z_{k-1}\ z_{k-1}\ z_{k-1}\ z_{k-1}$	z_{k-1}	$z_{k-2}\ z_{k-3}\ z_{k-4} \cdots$

(a)

Extended positions	Sign	Magnitude positions
1 1 1 1 0	$\overline{x}_{k-1}$	$x_{k-2}\ x_{k-3}\ x_{k-4} \cdots$
	$\overline{y}_{k-1}$	$y_{k-2}\ y_{k-3}\ y_{k-4} \cdots$
	$\overline{z}_{k-1}$	$z_{k-2}\ z_{k-3}\ z_{k-4} \cdots$
	1	

(b)

Fig. 8.18 Adding three 2's-complement numbers by means of sign extension (**a**) and by the method based on negatively weighted sign bits (**b**).

8.1 Pipelined multioperand addition

a. Present a design similar to Fig. 8.3 for adding a set of n input numbers, with a throughput of one input per clock cycle, if each adder block is a two-stage pipeline.

b. Repeat part a for a pipelined adder with eight stages.

c. Discuss methods for using the pipelined multi-operand addition scheme of Fig. 8.3 when the number of pipeline stages in an adder block is not a power of 2. Apply your method to the case of an adder with five pipeline stages.

8.2 Multioperand addition with two-operand adders Consider all the methods discussed in Section 8.1 for adding n unsigned integers of width k using two-operand adders.

a. Using reasonable assumptions, derive exact, as opposed to asymptotic, expressions for the delay and cost of each method.

b. On a two-dimensional coordinate system, with the axes representing n and k, identify the regions where each method is best in terms of speed.

c. Repeat part b, this time using delay $\times$ cost as the figure of merit for comparison.

8.3 Comparing multioperand addition schemes Consider the problem of adding n unsigned integers of width k.

a. Identify two methods whose delays are $O(\log k + n)$ and $O(k + \log n)$.

b. On a two-dimensional coordinate system, with logarithmic scales for both n and k, identify the regions in which one design is faster than the other. Describe your assumptions about implementations.

c. Repeat part b, this time comparing cost-effectiveness rather than just speed.

8.4 Building blocks for multioperand addition A carry-save adder reduces three binary numbers to two binary numbers. It costs c units and performs its function with a time delay d. An "alternative reduction adder" (ARA) reduces five binary numbers to two binary numbers. It costs $3c$ units and has a delay of $2d$.

a. Which of the two elements, CSA or ARA, is more cost-effective for designing a tree that reduces 32 operands to 2 operands if used as the only building block? Ignore the widths of the CSA and ARA blocks and focus only on their numbers.

b. Propose an efficient design for 32-to-2 reduction if both CSA and ARA building blocks are allowed.

8.5   Carry-save adder trees Consider the problem of adding eight 8-bit unsigned binary numbers.

a. Using tabular representation, show the design of a Wallace tree for reducing the 8 operands to two operands.

b. Repeat part a for a Dadda tree.

c. Compare the two designs with respect to speed and cost.

8.6   Carry-save adder trees We have seen that the maximum number of operands that can be combined using an h-level tree of CSAs is $n(h) = \lfloor 3n(h-1)/2 \rfloor$.

a. Prove the inequality $n(h) \geq 2n(h-2)$.

b. Prove the inequality $n(h) \geq 3n(h-3)$.

c. Show that both bounds of parts a and b are tight by providing one example in which equality holds.

d. Prove the inequality $n(h) \geq n(h-a)\lfloor n(a)/2 \rfloor$ for $a \geq 0$. *Hint:* Think of the h-level tree as the top $h-a$ levels followed by an a-level tree and consider the lines connecting the two parts.

8.7   A three-operand addition problem Effective 24-bit addresses in the IBM System 370 family of computers were computed by adding three unsigned values: two 24-bit numbers and a 12-bit number. Since address computation was needed for each instruction, speed was critical and using two addition steps wouldn't do, particularly for the faster computers in the family.

a. Suggest a fast addition scheme for this address computation. Your design should produce an "address invalid" signal when there is an overflow.

b. Extend your design so that it also indicates if the computed address is in the range $[0, u]$, where u is a given upper bound (an input to the circuit).

8.8   Parallel counters Design a 255-input parallel counter using (7; 3)-counters and 4-bit binary adders as the only building blocks.

8.9   Parallel counters Consider the synthesis of an n-input parallel counter.

a. Prove that $n - \log_2 n$ is a lower bound on the number of full adders needed.

b. Show that n full adders suffice for this task. *Hint:* Think in terms of how many full adders might be used as half-adders in the worst case.

c. Prove that $\log_2 n + \log_3 n - 1$ is a lower bound on the number of full-adder levels required. *Hint:* First consider the problem of determining the least significant output bit, or actually, that of reducing the weight-2^0 column to 3 bits.

8.10 **Generalized parallel counters** Consider a $(1, 4, 3; 4)$ generalized parallel counter.

    a. Design the generalized parallel counter using only full-adder blocks.

    b. Show how this generalized parallel counter can be used as a 3-bit binary adder.

    c. Use three such parallel counters to reduce five 5-bit unsigned binary numbers into three 6-bit numbers.

    d. Show how such counters can be used for 4-to-2 reduction.

8.11 **Generalized parallel counters**

    a. Is a $(3, 1; 3)$-counter useful? Why (not)?

    b. Design a $(3, 3; 4)$-counter using $(3; 2)$-counters as the only building blocks.

    c. Use the counters of part b, and a 12-bit adder, to build a 6×6 unsigned multiplier.

    d. Viewing a 4-bit binary adder as a $(2, 2, 2, 3; 5)$-counter and using dot notation, design a circuit to add five 6-bit binary numbers using only 4-bit adders as your building blocks.

8.12 **Generalized parallel counters** We want to design a slice of a $(7; 2)$-counter as discussed at the end of Section 8.5.

    a. Present a design for slice i based on $\psi_1 = 1$ transfer bit from position $i - 1$ along with $\psi_2 = 1$ transfer bit from position $i - 2$.

    b. Repeat part a with $\psi_1 = 4$ transfer bits from position $i - 1$ and $\psi_2 = 0$.

    c. Compare the designs of parts a and b with respect to speed and cost.

8.13 **Generalized parallel counters** We have seen that a set of $k/2$ $(5, 5; 4)$-counters can be used to reduce five k-bit operands to two operands. *Hint:* This is possible because the 4-bit outputs of adjacent counters overlap in 2 bits, making the height of the output dot matrix equal to 2.

    a. What kind of generalized parallel counter is needed to reduce seven operands to two operands?

    b. Repeat part a for reducing nine operands.

    c. Repeat part a for the general case of n operands, obtaining the relevant counter parameters as functions of n.

8.14 **Accumulative parallel counters** Design a 12-bit, 50-input accumulative parallel counter. The counter has a 12-bit register in which the accumulated count is kept. When the "count" signal goes high, the input count (a number between 0 and 50) is added to the stored count. Try to make your design as fast as possible. Ignore overflow (i.e., assume modulo-2^{12} operation). *Hint:* A 50-input parallel counter followed by a 12-bit adder isn't the best design.

8.15 **Unsigned versus signed multioperand addition** We want to add four 4-bit binary numbers.

    a. Construct the needed circuit, assuming unsigned operands.

    b. Repeat part a, assuming sign-extended 2's-complement operands.

    c. Repeat part a, using the negative-weight interpretation of the sign bits.

d. Compare the three designs with respect to speed and cost.

8.16   Adding multiple signed numbers

a. Present the design of a multioperand adder for computing the 9-bit sum of sixteen 6-bit, 2's-complement numbers based on the use of negatively weighted sign bits, as described at the end of Section 8.6.

b. Redo the design using straightforward sign extension.

c. Compare the designs of parts a and b with respect to speed and cost and discuss.

8.17   Ternary parallel counters   In balanced ternary representation (viz., $r = 3$ and digit set $[-1, 1]$), $(4; 2)$-counters can be designed [De94]. Choose a suitable encoding for the three digit values and present the complete logic design of such a $(4; 2)$-counter.

REFERENCES

[Dadd65] Dadda, L., "Some Schemes for Parallel Multipliers," *Alta Frequenza*, Vol. 34, pp. 349–356, 1965.

[Dadd76] Dadda, L., "On Parallel Digital Multipliers," *Alta Frequenza*, Vol. 45, pp. 574–580, 1976.

[De94]   De, M., and B. P. Sinha, "Fast Parallel Algorithm for Ternary Multiplication Using Multivalued I^{2}L Technology," *IEEE Trans. Computers*, Vol. 43, No. 5, pp. 603–607, 1994.

[Fost71] Foster, C. C., and F. D. Stockton, "Counting Responders in an Associative Memory," *IEEE Trans. Computers*, Vol. 20, pp. 1580–1583, 1971.

[Parh89] Parhami, B., "Parallel Counters for Signed Binary Signals," *Proc. 23rd Asilomar Conf. Signals, Systems, and Computers*, pp. 513–516, 1989.

[Parh95] Parhami, B., and C.-H. Yeh, "Accumulative Parallel Counters," *Proc. 29th Asilomar Conf. Signals, Systems, and Computers*, pp. 966–970, 1995.

[Swar73] Swartzlander, E. E., "Parallel Counters," *IEEE Trans. Computers*, Vol. 22, No. 11, pp. 1021–1024, 1973.

[Wall64] Wallace, C. S., "A Suggestion for a Fast Multiplier," *IEEE Trans. Electronic Computers*, Vol. 13, pp. 14–17, 1964.

PART III | MULTIPLICATION

Multiplication, often realized by k cycles of shifting and adding, is a heavily used arithmetic operation that figures prominently in signal processing and scientific applications. In this part, after examining shift/add multiplication schemes and their various implementations, we note that there are but two ways to speed up the underlying multioperand addition: reducing the number of operands to be added leads to high-radix multipliers, and devising hardware multioperand adders that minimize the latency and/or maximize the throughput leads to tree and array multipliers. Of course, speed is not the only criterion of interest. Cost, VLSI area, and pin limitations favor bit-serial designs, while the desire to use available building blocks leads to designs based on additive multiply modules. Finally, the special case of squaring is of interest as it leads to considerable simplification. This part consists of the following four chapters:

Chapter
9 | BASIC MULTIPLICATION SCHEMES

The multioperand addition process needed for multiplying two k-bit operands can be realized in k cycles of shifting and adding, with hardware, firmware, or software control of the loop. In this chapter, we review such economical, but slow, bit-at-a-time designs and set the stage for speedup methods and variations to be presented in Chapters 10–12. We also consider the special case of multiplication by a constant. Chapter topics include:

9.1 Shift/Add Multiplication Algorithms
9.2 Programmed Multiplication
9.3 Basic Hardware Multipliers
9.4 Multiplication of Signed Numbers
9.5 Multiplication by Constants
9.6 Preview of Fast Multipliers

9.1 SHIFT/ADD MULTIPLICATION ALGORITHMS

The following notation is used in our discussion of multiplication algorithms:

a Multiplicand $a_{k-1}a_{k-2}\cdots a_1 a_0$
x Multiplier $x_{k-1}x_{k-2}\cdots x_1 x_0$
p Product $(a \times x)$ $p_{2k-1}p_{2k-2}\cdots p_1 p_0$

Figure 9.1 shows the multiplication of two 4-bit unsigned binary numbers in dot notation. The two numbers a and x are shown at the top. Each of the following four rows of dots corresponds to the product of the multiplicand a and a single bit of the multiplier x, with each dot representing the product (logical AND) of two bits. Since x_j is in $\{0, 1\}$, each term $x_j a$ is either 0 or a. Thus, the problem of binary multiplication reduces to adding a set of numbers, each of which is 0 or a shifted version of the multiplicand a.

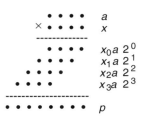

Fig. 9.1 Multiplication of two 4-bit unsigned binary numbers in dot notation.

Figure 9.1 also applies to nonbinary multiplication, except that with $r > 2$, computing the terms $x_j a$ becomes more difficult and the resulting numbers will be one digit wider than a. The rest of the process (multioperand addition), however, remains substantially the same.

Sequential or bit-at-a-time multiplication can be done by keeping a cumulative partial product (initialized to 0) and successively adding to it the properly shifted terms $x_j a$. Since each successive number to be added to the cumulative partial product is shifted by one bit with respect to the preceding one, a simpler approach is to shift the cumulative partial product by one bit in order to align its bits with those of the next partial product. Two versions of this algorithm can be devised, depending on whether the partial product terms $x_j a$ in Fig. 9.1 are processed from top to bottom or from bottom to top.

In multiplication with right shifts, the partial product terms $x_j a$ are accumulated from top to bottom:

$$p^{(j+1)} = (p^{(j)} + x_j a\, 2^k)2^{-1} \quad \text{with } p^{(0)} = 0 \text{ and } p^{(k)} = p$$
$$|\!\!-\!\!-\text{ add }-\!\!-\!\!|$$
$$|\!\!-\!\!-\text{ shift right }-\!\!|$$

Because the right shifts will cause the first partial product to be multiplied by 2^{-k} by the time we are done, we premultiply a by 2^k to offset the effect of the right shifts. This premultiplication is done simply by aligning a with the upper half of the $2k$-bit cumulative partial product in the addition steps (i.e., storing a in the left half of a double-length register).

After k iterations, the preceding recurrence leads to:

$$p^{(k)} = ax + p^{(0)}2^{-k}$$

Thus if instead of 0, $p^{(0)}$ is initialized to $y2^k$ the expression $ax + y$ will be evaluated. This multiply-add operation is quite useful for many applications and is performed at essentially no extra cost compared to plain shift/add multiplication.

In multiplication with left shifts, the terms $x_j a$ are added up from bottom to top:

$$p^{(j+1)} = 2p^{(j)} + x_{k-j-1}a \quad \text{with} \quad p^{(0)} = 0 \text{ and } p^{(k)} = p$$
$$\begin{vmatrix} \text{shift} \\ \text{left} \end{vmatrix}$$
$$|\!\!-\!\!-\text{ add }-\!\!-\!\!|$$

After k iterations, the preceding recurrence leads to:

$$p^{(k)} = ax + p^{(0)}2^k$$

In this case, the expression $ax + y$ will be evaluated if we initialize $p^{(0)}$ to $y2^{-k}$.

```
Right-shift algorithm                    Left-shift algorithm
============================             ============================
a        1 0 1 0                         a              1 0 1 0
x        1 0 1 1                         x              1 0 1 1
============================             ============================
p(0)     0 0 0 0                         p(0)           0 0 0 0
+x0a     1 0 1 0                         2p(0)        0 0 0 0 0
-------------------------                +x3a           1 0 1 0
2p(1)  0 1 0 1 0                         ----------------------------
p(1)     0 1 0 1 0                       p(1)         0 1 0 1 0
+x1a     1 0 1 0                         2p(1)      0 1 0 1 0 0
-------------------------                +x2a           0 0 0 0
2p(2)  0 1 1 1 1 0                       ----------------------------
p(2)     0 1 1 1 1 0                      p(2)       0 1 0 1 0 0
+x2a     0 0 0 0                         2p(2)    0 1 0 1 0 0 0
-------------------------                +x1a           1 0 1 0
2p(3)  0 0 1 1 1 1 0                      ----------------------------
p(3)     0 0 1 1 1 1 0                    p(3)     0 1 1 0 0 1 0
+x3a     1 0 1 0                         2p(3)  0 1 1 0 0 1 0 0
-------------------------                +x0a           1 0 1 0
2p(4)  0 1 1 0 1 1 1 0                    ----------------------------
p(4)     0 1 1 0 1 1 1 0                  p(4)   0 1 1 0 1 1 1 0
============================             ============================
```

Fig. 9.2   Examples of sequential multiplication with right and left shifts.

Figure 9.2 shows the multiplication of $a = (10)_{ten} = (1010)_{two}$ and $x = (11)_{ten} = (1011)_{two}$, to obtain their product $p = (110)_{ten} = (0110\ 1110)_{two}$, using both the right- and left-shift algorithms.

From the examples in Fig. 9.2, we see that the two algorithms are quite similar. Each algorithm entails k additions and k shifts; however, additions in the left-shift algorithm are $2k$ bits wide (the carry produced from the lower k bits may affect the upper k bits), whereas the right-shift algorithm requires k-bit additions. For this reason, multiplication with right shifts is preferable.

9.2 PROGRAMMED MULTIPLICATION

On a processor that does not have a multiply instruction, one can use shift and add instructions to perform integer multiplication. Figure 9.3 shows the structure of the needed program for the right-shift algorithm. The instructions used in this program fragment are typical of instructions available on many processors.

Ignoring operand load and result store instructions (which would be needed in any case), the function of a multiply instruction is accomplished by executing between $6k+3$ and $7k+3$ machine instructions, depending on the multiplier. For 32-bit operands, this means 200^+ instructions on the average. The situation improves somewhat if a special instruction that does some or all of the required functions within the multiplication loop is available. However, even then, no fewer than 32 instructions are executed in the multiplication loop. We thus see the importance of hardware multipliers for applications that involve a great deal of numerical computations.

Processors with microprogrammed control and no hardware multiplier essentially use a microroutine very similar to the program in Fig. 9.3 to effect multiplication. Since microinstructions typically contain some parallelism and built-in conditional branching, the number of microinstructions in the main loop is likely to be smaller than 6. This reduction, along with the

{Multiply, using right shifts, unsigned m_cand and m_ier,
storing the resultant 2k-bit product in p_high and p_low.
Registers: R0 holds 0   Rc for counter
                Ra for m_cand   Rx for m_ier
                Rp for p_high   Rq for p_low}

{Load operands into registers Ra and Rx}

```
mult:   load    Ra with m_cand
        load    Rx with m_ier
```

{Initialize partial product and counter}

```
        copy    R0 into Rp
        copy    R0 into Rq
        load    k  into Rc
```

{Begin multiplication loop}

```
m_loop:  shift   Rx right 1      {LSB moves to carry flag}
         branch  no_add if carry = 0
         add     Ra to Rp        {carry flag is set to c_out}
no_add:  rotate  Rp right 1      {carry to MSB, LSB to carry}
         rotate  Rq right 1      {carry to MSB, LSB to carry}
         decr    Rc              {decrement counter by 1}
         branch  m_loop if Rc ≠ 0
```

{Store the product}

```
        store   Rp into p_high
        store   Rq into p_low
m_done: ...
```

Fig. 9.3   Programmed multiplication using the right-shift algorithm.

savings in machine instruction fetching and decoding times, makes multiplication microroutines significantly faster than their machine-language counterparts, though still slower than hardwired implementations we examine next.

9.3 BASIC HARDWARE MULTIPLIERS

Hardware realization of the multiplication algorithm with right shifts is depicted in Fig. 9.4. The multiplier x and the cumulative partial product p are stored in shift registers. The next bit of the multiplier to be considered is always available at the right end of the x register and is used to select 0 or a for the addition. Addition and shifting can be performed in two separate cycles or in two subcycles within the same clock cycle. In either case, temporary storage for the adder's carry-out signal is needed. Alternatively, shifting can be performed by connecting the ith sum output of the adder to the $(k + i - 1)$th bit of the partial product register and the adder's carry-out to bit $2k - 1$, thus doing the addition and shifting in the same cycle.

     The control portion of the multiplier, which is not shown in Fig. 9.4, consists of a counter to keep track of the number of iterations and a simple circuit to effect initialization and detect

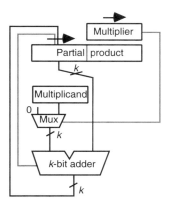

Fig. 9.4 Hardware realization of the sequential multiplication algorithm with additions and right-shifts.

termination. Note that the multiplier and the lower half of the cumulative partial product can share the same register, since as p expands into this register, bits of x are relaxed, keeping the total number of bits at $2k$.

Figure 9.5 shows the double-width register shared by the cumulative partial product and the unused part of the multiplier, along with connections needed to effect simultaneous loading and shifting. Since the register is loaded at the very end of each cycle, the change in its least significant bit, which is controlling the current cycle, will not cause any problem.

Hardware realization of the algorithm with left shifts is depicted in Fig. 9.6. Here too the multiplier x and the cumulative partial product p are stored in shift registers, but the registers shift to the left rather than to the right. The next bit of the multiplier to be considered is always available at the left end of the x register and is used to select 0 or a for the addition. Note that a $2k$-bit adder (actually, a k-bit adder in the lower part, augmented with a k-bit incrementer at the upper end) is needed in the hardware realization of multiplication with left shifts. Because the hardware in Fig. 9.6 is more complex than that in Fig. 9.4, multiplication with right shifts is the preferred method.

The control portion of the multiplier, which is not shown in Fig. 9.6, is similar to that for multiplication with right shifts. Here, register sharing is possible for the multiplier and the upper half of the cumulative partial product, since with each 1-bit expansion in p, one bit of x is relaxed. One difference with the right-shift scheme is that because the double-width register is shifted at the beginning of each cycle, temporary storage is required for keeping the multiplier bit that controls the rest of the cycle.

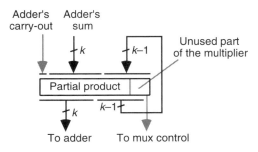

Fig. 9.5 Combining the loading and shifting of the double-width register holding the partial product and the partially used multiplier.

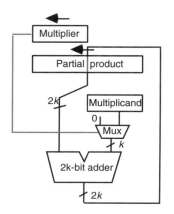

Fig. 9.6 Hardware realization of the sequential multiplication algorithm with left shifts and additions.

9.4 MULTIPLICATION OF SIGNED NUMBERS

The preceding discussions of multiplication algorithms and hardware realizations assume unsigned operands and result. Multiplication of signed-magnitude numbers needs little more, since the product's sign can be computed separately by XORing the operand signs.

One way to multiply signed values with complement representations is to complement the negative operand(s), multiply unsigned values, and then complement the result if only one operand was complemented at the outset. Such an indirect multiplication scheme is quite efficient for 1's-complement numbers but involves too much overhead for 2's-complement representation. It is preferable to use a direct multiplication algorithm for such numbers, as discussed in the remainder of this section.

We first note that the preceding bit-at-a-time algorithms can work directly with a negative 2's-complement multiplicand and a positive multiplier. In this case, each $x_j a$ term will be a 2's-complement number and the sum will be correctly accumulated if we use sign-extend values during the addition process. Figure 9.7 shows the multiplication of a negative multiplicand $a = (-10)_{ten} = (10110)_{2'\text{s-compl}}$ by a positive multiplier $x = (11)_{ten} = (01011)_{2'\text{s-compl}}$ using the right-shift algorithm. Note that the leftmost digit of the sum $p^{(i)} + x_i a$ is obtained assuming sign-extended operands.

In view of the negative-weight interpretation of the sign bit in 2's-complement numbers, a negative 2's-complement multiplier can be handled correctly if $x_{k-1} a$ is subtracted, rather than added, in the last cycle. In practice, the required subtraction is performed by adding the 2's-complement of the multiplicand or, actually, adding the 1's-complement of the multiplicand and inserting a carry-in of 1 into the adder (see Fig. 2.7). The required control logic becomes only slightly more complex. Figure 9.8 shows the multiplication of negative values $a = (-10)_{ten} = (10110)_{2'\text{s-compl}}$ and $x = (-11)_{ten} = (10101)_{two}$ by means of the right-shift algorithm.

Multiplication with left shifts becomes even less competitive when we are dealing with 2's-complement numbers directly. Referring to Fig. 9.6, we note that the multiplicand must be sign-extended by k bits. We thus have a more complex adder as well as slower additions. With right shifts, on the other hand, sign extension occurs incrementally; thus the adder needs to be only one bit wider. Alternatively, a k-bit adder can be augmented with special logic to handle the extra bit at the left.

```
=============================
a          1 0 1 1 0
x          0 1 0 1 1
=============================
p(0)       0 0 0 0 0
+x0a       1 0 1 1 0
-----------------------------
2p(1)    1 1 0 1 1 0
p(1)       1 1 0 1 1  0
+x1a       1 0 1 1 0
-----------------------------
2p(2)    1 1 0 0 0 1  0
p(2)       1 1 0 0 0  1 0
+x2a       0 0 0 0 0
-----------------------------
2p(3)    1 1 1 0 0 0  1 0
p(3)       1 1 1 0 0  0 1 0
+x3a       1 0 1 1 0
-----------------------------
2p(4)    1 1 0 0 1 0  0 1 0
p(4)       1 1 0 0 1  0 0 1 0
+x4a       0 0 0 0 0
-----------------------------
2p(5)    1 1 1 0 0 1  0 0 1 0
p(5)       1 1 1 0 0  1 0 0 1 0
=============================
```

Fig. 9.7 Sequential multiplication of 2's-complement numbers with right-shifts (positive multiplier).

An alternate way of dealing with 2's-complement numbers is to use Booth's recoding to represent the multiplier x in signed-digit format.

Booth's recoding (also known as Booth's encoding) was first proposed for speeding up radix-2 multiplication in early digital computers. Recall that radix-2 multiplication consists of a sequence of shifts and adds. When 0 is added to the cumulative partial product in a step,

```
=============================
a          1 0 1 1 0
x          1 0 1 0 1
=============================
p(0)       0 0 0 0 0
+x0a       1 0 1 1 0
-----------------------------
2p(1)    1 1 0 1 1 0
p(1)       1 1 0 1 1  0
+x1a       0 0 0 0 0
-----------------------------
2p(2)    1 1 1 0 1 1  0
p(2)       1 1 1 0 1  1 0
+x2a       1 0 1 1 0
-----------------------------
2p(3)    1 1 0 0 1 1  1 0
p(3)       1 1 0 0 1  1 1 0
+x3a       0 0 0 0 0
-----------------------------
2p(4)    1 1 1 0 0 1  1 1 0
p(4)       1 1 1 0 0  1 1 1 0
+(-x4a)    0 1 0 1 0
-----------------------------
2p(5)    0 0 0 1 1 0  1 1 1 0
p(5)       0 0 0 1 1  0 1 1 1 0
=============================
```

Fig. 9.8 Sequential multiplication of 2's-complement numbers with right-shifts (negative multiplier).

the addition operation can be skipped altogether. This does not make sense in the designs of Figs. 9.4 and 9.6, since the data paths go through the adder. But in an asynchronous implementation, or in developing a (micro)program for multiplication, shifting alone is faster than addition followed by shifting, and one may take advantage of this fact to reduce the multiplication time on the average. The resulting algorithm or its associated hardware implementation will have variable delay depending on the multiplier value: the more 1s there are in the binary representation of x, the slower the multiplication. Booth observed that whenever there are a large number of consecutive 1s in x, multiplication can be speeded up by replacing the corresponding sequence of additions with a subtraction at the least significant end and an addition in the position immediately to the left of its most significant end. In other words:

$$2^j + 2^{j-1} + \cdots + 2^{i+1} + 2^i = 2^{j+1} - 2^i$$

The longer the sequence of 1s, the larger the savings achieved. The effect of this transformation is to change the binary number x with digit set $[0, 1]$ to the binary signed-digit number y using the digit set $[-1, 1]$. Hence, Booth's recoding can be viewed as a kind of digit-set conversion. Table 9.1 shows how the digit y_i of the recoded number y can be obtained from the two digits x_i and x_{i-1} of x. Thus, as x is scanned from right to left, the digits y_i can be determined on the fly and used to choose add, subtract, or no-operation in each cycle.

For example, consider the following 16-bit binary number and its recoded version:

$$\begin{array}{lllll} & 1\ 0\ 0\ 1 & 1\ 1\ 0\ 1 & 1\ 0\ 1\ 0 & 1\ 1\ 1\ 0 & \text{Operand } x \\ (1)\ \text{-}1\ 0\ 1\ 0 & 0\ \text{-}1\ 1\ 0 & \text{-}1\ 1\ \text{-}1\ 1 & 0\ 0\ \text{-}1\ 0 & \text{Recoded version } y \end{array}$$

In this particular example, the recoding does not reduce the number of additions. However, the example serves to illustrate two points. First, the recoded number may have to be extended by one bit if the value of x as an unsigned number is to be preserved. Second, if x is a 2's-complement number, then not extending the length (ignoring the leftmost 1 in the recoded version above) leads to the proper handling of negative numbers. Note how in the example, the sign bit of the 2's-complement number has assumed a negative weight in the recoded version, as it should. A complete multiplication example is given in Fig. 9.9.

Radix-2 Booth recoding is not directly applied in modern arithmetic circuits, but it serves as a tool in understanding the radix-4 version of this recoding, to be discussed in Section 10.2.

TABLE 9.1
Radix-2 Booth's recoding

x_i	x_{i-1}	y_i	Explanation
0	0	0	No string of 1s in sight
0	1	1	End of string of 1s in x
1	0	-1	Beginning of string of 1s in x
1	1	0	Continuation of string of 1s in x

```
=============================
a          1  0  1  1  0
x          1  0  1  0  1     Multiplier
y         -1  1 -1  1 -1     Booth-recoded
=============================
p(0)       0  0  0  0  0
+y0a       0  1  0  1  0
-----------------------------
2p(1)   0  0  1  0  1  0
p(1)       0  0  1  0  1  0
+y1a       1  0  1  1  0
-----------------------------
2p(2)   1  1  1  0  1  1  0
p(2)       1  1  1  0  1  1  0
+y2a       0  1  0  1  0
-----------------------------
2p(3)   0  0  0  1  1  1  1  0
p(3)       0  0  0  1  1  1  1  0
+y3a       1  0  1  1  0
-----------------------------
2p(4)   1  1  1  0  0  1  1  1  0
p(4)       1  1  1  0  0  1  1  1  0
+y4a       0  1  0  1  0
-----------------------------
2p(5)   0  0  0  1  1  0  1  1  1  0
p(5)       0  0  0  1  1  0  1  1  1  0
=============================
```

Fig. 9.9 Sequential multiplication of 2's-complement numbers with right shifts by means of Booth's recoding.

9.5 MULTIPLICATION BY CONSTANTS

When a hardware multiplier, or a corresponding firmware routine, is unavailable, multiplication must be performed by a software routine similar to that in Fig. 9.3. In applications that are not arithmetic-intensive, loss of speed due to the use of such routines is infrequent, hence tolerable. However, many applications involve frequent use of multiplication; in these applications, indiscriminate use of such slow routines may be unacceptable.

Even for applications involving many multiplications, it is true that in a large fraction of cases, one of the operands is a constant that is known at compile time. We all know that multiplication and division by powers of 2 can be done through shifting. It is less obvious that multiplication by many other constants can be performed by short sequences of simple instructions without a need to invoke the complicated general multiplication routine or instruction.

Besides explicit multiplications appearing in arithmetic expressions within programs, there are many implicit multiplications to compute offsets into arrays. For example, if an $m \times n$ array A is stored in row-major order, the offset of the element $A_{i,j}$ (assuming 0-origin indexing) is obtained from the expression $ni + j$. In such implicit multiplications, as well as in a significant fraction of explicit ones, one of the operands is a constant. A multiply instruction takes much longer to execute than a shift or an add instruction even if a hardware multiplier is available. Thus, one might want to avoid the use of a multiply instruction even when it is supported by the hardware.

There are two aspects to multiplication by integer constants. First, one would like to produce optimal or near-optimal code using as few registers as possible. Second, one would like to find the best code by an algorithm that does not require an inordinate amount of time or space. In the examples that follow, R_1 denotes the register holding the multiplicand and R_i will denote an intermediate result that is i times the multiplicand (e.g., R_{65} denotes the result of multiplying the multiplicand a by 65).

A simple way to multiply the contents of a register by an integer constant multiplier is to write the multiplier in binary format and to use shifts and adds according to the 1s in the binary representation. For example to multiply R_1 by $113 = (1110001)_{two}$, one might use:

$$
\begin{array}{rcl}
R_2 & \leftarrow & R_1 \text{ shift-left } 1 \\
R_3 & \leftarrow & R_2 + R_1 \\
R_6 & \leftarrow & R_3 \text{ shift-left } 1 \\
R_7 & \leftarrow & R_6 + R_1 \\
R_{112} & \leftarrow & R_7 \text{ shift-left } 4 \\
R_{113} & \leftarrow & R_{112} + R_1
\end{array}
$$

Only two registers are required; one to store the multiplicand a and one to hold the partially computed result.

If a shift-and-add instruction is available, the sequence above becomes:

$$
\begin{array}{rcl}
R_3 & \leftarrow & R_1 \text{ shift-left } 1 + R_1 \\
R_7 & \leftarrow & R_3 \text{ shift-left } 1 + R_1 \\
R_{113} & \leftarrow & R_7 \text{ shift-left } 4 + R_1
\end{array}
$$

If only single-bit shifts are allowed, the last instruction in the preceding sequence must be replaced by three shifts followed by a shift-and-add. Note that the pattern of shift-and-adds and shifts (s&a, s&a, shift, shift, shift, s&a) in this latter version matches the bit pattern of the multiplier if its MSB is ignored (110001).

Many other instruction sequences are possible. For example, one could proceed by computing R_{16}, R_{32}, R_{64}, R_{65}, R_{97} ($R_{65} + R_{32}$), and R_{113} ($R_{97} + R_{16}$). However, this would use up more registers. If subtraction is allowed in the sequence, the number of instructions can be reduced in some cases. For example, by taking advantage of the equality $113 = 128-16+1 = 16(8-1)+1$, one can derive the following sequence of instructions for multiplication by 113:

$$
\begin{array}{rcl}
R_8 & \leftarrow & R_1 \text{ shift-left } 3 \\
R_7 & \leftarrow & R_8 - R_1 \\
R_{112} & \leftarrow & R_7 \text{ shift-left } 4 \\
R_{113} & \leftarrow & R_{112} + R_1
\end{array}
$$

In general, the use of subtraction helps if the binary representation of the integer has several consecutive 1s, since a sequence of j consecutive 1s can be replaced by $1\,0\,0\,0\cdots 0\,0\,{}^{\text{-}}1$, where there are $j-1$ zeros (Booth's recoding).

Factoring a number sometimes helps in obtaining efficient code. For example, to multiply R_1 by 119, one can use the fact that $119 = 7 \times 17 = (8-1) \times (16+1)$ to obtain the sequence:

$$
\begin{array}{rcl}
R_8 & \leftarrow & R_1 \text{ shift-left } 3 \\
R_7 & \leftarrow & R_8 - R_1 \\
R_{112} & \leftarrow & R_7 \text{ shift-left } 4 \\
R_{119} & \leftarrow & R_{112} + R_7
\end{array}
$$

With shift-and-add/subtract instructions, the preceding sequence reduces to only two instructions:

$$R_7 \quad \leftarrow \quad R_1 \text{ shift-left } 3 - R_1$$
$$R_{119} \quad \leftarrow \quad R_7 \text{ shift-left } 4 + R_7$$

In general, factors of the form $2^b \pm 1$ translate directly into a shift followed by an add or subtract and lead to a simplification of the computation sequence.

In a compiler that removes common subexpressions, moves invariant code out of loops, and performs a reduction of strength on multiplications inside loops (in particular changes multiplications to additions where possible), the effect of multiplication by constants is quite noticeable. It is not uncommon to obtain a 20% improvement in the resulting code, and some programs exhibit 60% improved performance [Bern86].

9.6 PREVIEW OF FAST MULTIPLIERS

If one views multiplication as a multioperand addition problem, there are but two ways to speed it up:

Reducing the number of operands to be added.

Adding the operands faster.

Reducing the number of operands to be added leads to high-radix multipliers in which several bits of the multiplier are multiplied by the multiplicand in one cycle. Speedup is achieved for radix 2^j as long as multiplying j bits of the multiplier by the multiplicand and adding the result to the cumulative partial product takes less than j times as long as multiplying one bit and adding the result. High-radix multipliers are covered in Chapter 10.

To add the partial products faster, one can design hardware multioperand adders that minimize the latency and/or maximize the throughput by using some of the ideas discussed in Chapter 8. These techniques lead to tree and array multipliers, which form the subjects of Chapter 11.

PROBLEMS

9.1   Multiplication in dot notation In Section 9.1, it was stated that for $r > 2$, Fig. 9.1 must be modified (since the partial product terms $x_i a$ will be wider than a). Is there an exception to this general statement?

9.2   Unsigned sequential multiplication Multiply the following 4-bit binary numbers using both the right-shift and left-shift multiplication algorithms. Present your work in the form of Fig. 9.2.

    a. $a = 1001$ and $x = 0101$

    b. $a = .1101$ and $x = .1001$

9.3   Unsigned sequential multiplication Multiply the following 4-digit decimal numbers using both the right-shift and left-shift multiplication algorithms. Present your work in the form of Fig. 9.2.

a. $a = 8765$ and $x = 4321$

b. $a = .8765$ and $x = .4321$

9.4   Two's-complement sequential multiplication   Represent the following signed-magnitude binary numbers in 5-bit, 2's-complement format and multiply them using the right-shift algorithm. Present your work in the form of Fig. 9.7. Then, redo each multiplication using Booth's recoding, presenting your work in the form of Fig. 9.9.

a. $a = +.1001$ and $x = +.0101$

b. $a = +.1001$ and $x = -.0101$

c. $a = -.1001$ and $x = +.0101$

d. $a = -.1001$ and $x = -.0101$

9.5   Programmed multiplication

a. Write the multiplication routine of Fig. 9.3 for a real processor of your choice.

b. Modify the routine of part a to correspond to multiplication with left shifts.

c. Compare the routines of parts a and b with respect to average speed.

d. Modify the routines of parts a and b so that they compute $ax + y$. Compare the resulting routines with respect to average speed.

9.6   Basic hardware multipliers

a. In a hardware multiplier with right shifts (Fig. 9.4), the adder's input multiplexer can be moved to its output side. Show the resulting multiplier design and compare it with respect to cost and speed to that in Fig. 9.4.

b. Repeat part a for the left-shift multiplier depicted in Fig. 9.6.

9.7   Multiplication with left shifts   Consider a hardware multiplier with left shifts as in Fig. 9.6, except that multiplier and the upper half of the cumulative partial product share the same register.

a. Draw a diagram similar to Fig. 9.5 for multiplication with left shifts.

b. Explain why carries from adding the multiplicand to the cumulative partial product do not move into, and change, the unused part of the multiplier.

9.8   Basic multiply-add units

a. Show how the multiplier with right shifts, depicted in Fig. 9.4, can be modified to perform a multiply-add step with unsigned operands (compute $ax + y$), where the additive operand y is stored in a special register.

b. Repeat part a for the left-shift multiplier depicted in Fig. 9.6.

c. Extend the design of part a to deal with signed operands.

d. Repeat part b for signed operands and compare the result to part c.

9.9   Direct 2's-complement multiplication

a. Show how the example multiplication depicted in Fig. 9.7 would be done with the left-shift multiplication algorithm.

b.   Repeat part a for Fig. 9.8.

c.   Repeat part a for Fig. 9.9.

9.10   **Booth's recoding**   Using the fact that we have $y_i = x_{i-1} - x_i$ in Table 9.1, prove the correctness of Booth's recoding algorithm for 2's-complement numbers.

9.11   **Direct 1's-complement multiplication**   Describe and justify a direct multiplication algorithm for 1's-complement numbers. *Hint:* Use initialization of the cumulative partial product and a modified last iteration.

9.12   **Multiplication of BSD numbers**

a.   Multiply the binary signed-digit numbers $(1\ 0\ \text{-}1\ 0\ 1)_{\text{BSD}}$ and $(0\ \text{-}1\ 1\ 0\ \text{-}1)_{\text{BSD}}$ using the right-shift algorithm.

b.   Repeat part a using the left-shift algorithm.

c.   Design the circuit required for obtaining the partial product $x_j a$ for a sequential BSD hardware multiplier.

9.13   **Fully serial multipliers**

a.   A fully serial multiplier with right shifts is obtained if the adder of Fig. 9.4 is replaced with a bit-serial adder. Show the block diagram of the fully serial multiplier based on the right-shift multiplication algorithm.

b.   Design the required control circuit for the fully serial multiplier of part a.

c.   Does a fully serial multiplier using the left-shift algorithm make sense?

9.14   **Multiplication by constants**   Using shift and add/subtract instructions only, devise efficient routines for multiplication by the following decimal constants. Assume 32-bit unsigned operands. Make sure that intermediate results do not lead to overflow.

a.   43

b.   129

c.   135

d.   189

e.   211

f.   867

g.   8.75 (the result is to be rounded down to an integer)

9.15   **Multiplication by constants**

a.   Devise a general method for multiplying an integer a by constant multipliers of the form $2^j + 2^i$, where $0 \le i < j$ (e.g., $36 = 2^5 + 2^2$, $66 = 2^6 + 2^1$).

b.   Repeat part a for constants of the form $2^j - 2^i$. Watch for possible overflow.

c.   Repeat part a for constants of the form $1 + 2^{-i} + 2^{-j} + 2^{-i-j}$, rounding the result down to an integer.

9.16   Multiplication by constants

a. Devise an efficient algorithm for multiplying an unsigned binary integer by the decimal constant 99. The complexity of your algorithm should be less than those obtained from the binary expansion of 99, with and without Booth's recoding.

b. What is the smallest integer whose binary or Booth-recoded representation does not yield the most efficient multiplication routine with additions and shifts?

REFERENCES

[Bern86]   Bernstein, R., "Multiplication by Integer Constants," *Software—Practice and Experience*, Vol. 16, No. 7, pp. 641–652, 1986.

[Boot51]   Booth, A. D., "A Signed Binary Multiplication Technique," *Quarterly J. Mechanics and Applied Mathematics*, Vol. 4, Pt. 2, pp. 236–240, June 1951.

[Kore93]   Koren, I., *Computer Arithmetic Algorithms*, Prentice-Hall, 1993.

[Omon94]   Omondi, A. R., *Computer Arithmetic Systems: Algorithms, Architecture and Implementations*, Prentice-Hall, 1994.

[Robe55]   Robertson, J. E., "Two's Complement Multiplication in Binary Parallel Computers," *IRE Trans. Electronic Computers*, Vol. 4, No. 3, pp. 118–119, September 1955.

[Shaw50]   Shaw, R. F., "Arithmetic Operations in a Binary Computer," *Rev. Scientific Instruments*, Vol. 21, pp. 687–693, 1950.

Chapter 10
HIGH-RADIX MULTIPLIERS

In this chapter, we review multiplication schemes that handle more than one bit of the multiplier in each cycle (2 bits per cycle in radix 4, 3 bits in radix 8, etc.). The reduction in the number of cycles, along with the use of recoding and carry-save addition to simplify the required computations in each cycle, leads to significant gains in speed over the basic multipliers of Chapter 9. Chapter topics include:

10.1 RADIX-4 MULTIPLICATION

For a given range of numbers to be represented, a higher representation radix leads to fewer digits. Thus, a digit-at-a-time multiplication algorithm requires fewer cycles as we move to higher radices. This motivates us to study high-radix multiplication algorithms and associated hardware implementations. Since a k-bit binary number can be interpreted as a $\lceil k/2 \rceil$-digit radix-4 number, a $\lceil k/3 \rceil$-digit radix-8 number, and so on, the use of high-radix multiplication essentially entails dealing with more than one bit of the multiplier in each cycle.

We begin by presenting the general radix-r versions of the multiplication recurrences given in Section 9.1:

$$p^{(j+1)} = (p^{(j)} + x_j a\, r^k)r^{-1} \text{ with } p^{(0)} = 0 \text{ and } p^{(k)} = p$$

$$|\text{---- add ----}|$$
$$|\text{---- shift right ----}|$$

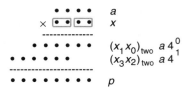

Fig. 10.1   Radix-4, or two-bit-at-a-time, multiplication in dot notation.

$$p^{(j+1)} = rp^{(j)} + x_{k-j-1}a \quad \text{with} \quad p^{(0)} = 0 \text{ and } p^{(k)} = p$$

$$\left|\begin{matrix}\text{shift}\\\text{left}\end{matrix}\right|$$

$$|\text{------ add ------}|$$

Since multiplication by r^{-1} or r still entails right or left shifting by one digit, the only difference between high-radix and radix-2 multiplication is in forming the terms $x_i a$, which now require more computation.

For example, if multiplication is done in radix 4, in each step, the partial product term $(x_{i+1}x_i)_{\text{two}}\, a$ needs to be formed and added to the cumulative partial product. Figure 10.1 shows the multiplication process in dot notation. Straightforward application of this method leads to the following problem. Whereas in radix-2 multiplication, each row of dots in the partial products matrix represents 0 or a shifted version of a, here we need the multiples $0a$, $1a$, $2a$, and $3a$. The first 3 of these present no problem ($2a$ is simply the shifted version of a). But computing $3a$ needs at least an addition operation ($3a = 2a + a$).

In the remainder of this section, and in Section 10.2, we review several solutions for the preceding problem in radix-4 multiplication.

The first option is to compute $3a$ once at the outset and store it in a register for future use. Then, the rest of the multiplier hardware will be very similar to that depicted in Fig. 9.4, except that the two-way multiplexer is replaced by a four-way multiplexer as shown in Fig. 10.2. An example multiplication is given in Fig. 10.3.

Another possible solution exists when $3a$ needs to be added: we add $-a$ and send a carry of 1 into the next radix-4 digit of the multiplier (Fig. 10.4). Including the incoming carry, the needed multiple in each cycle is in [0, 4]. The multiples 0, 1, and 2 are handled directly, while the multiples 3 and 4 are converted to -1 and 0, respectively, plus an outgoing carry of 1. An extra cycle may be needed at the end because of the carry.

The multiplication schemes depicted in Figs. 10.2 and 10.4 can be extended to radices 8, 16, etc., but the multiple generation hardware becomes more complex for higher radices, nullifying most, if not all, of the gain in speed due to fewer cycles. For example, in radix 8 one needs to precompute the multiples $3a$, $5a$, and $7a$, or else precompute only $3a$ and use a carry

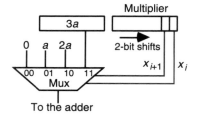

Fig. 10.2   The multiple generation part of a radix-4 multiplier with precomputation of $3a$.

```
====================================
a                    0 1 1 0
3a             0 1 0 0 1 0
x                    1 1 1 0
====================================
p(0)                 0 0 0 0
+(x1x0)two a   0 0 1 1 0 0
------------------------------------
4p(1)          0 0 1 1 0 0
p(1)                 0 0 1 1   0 0
+(x3x2)two a   0 1 0 0 1 0
------------------------------------
4p(2)          0 1 0 1 0 1   0 0
p(2)                 0 1 0 1  0 1 0 0
====================================
```

Fig. 10.3 Example of radix-4 multiplication using the 3a multiple.

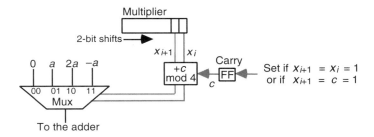

Fig. 10.4 The multiple generation part of a radix-4 multiplier based on replacing $3a$ with $4a$ (carry into the next higher radix-4 multiplier digit) and $-a$.

scheme similar to that in Fig. 10.4 to convert the multiples $5a$, $6a$, and $7a$ to $-3a$, $-2a$, and $-a$, respectively, plus a carry of 1. Supplying the details is left as an exercise.

We will see later in this chapter that with certain other hardware implementations, even higher radices become practical.

10.2 MODIFIED BOOTH'S RECODING

As stated near the end of Section 9.4, radix-2 Booth recoding is not directly applied in modern arithmetic circuits; however, it does serve as a tool in understanding the higher-radix versions of Booth's recoding. It is easy to see that when a binary number is recoded using Table 9.1, the result will not have consecutive 1s or ¯1s. Thus, if radix-4 multiplication is performed with the recoded multiplier, only the multiples $\pm a$ and $\pm 2a$ of the multiplicand will be required, all of which are easily obtained by shifting and/or complementation.

Now since y_{i+1} depends on x_{i+1} and x_i and y_i depends on x_i and x_{i-1}, the radix-4 digit $z_{i/2} = (y_{i+1}y_i)_{two}$, i even, can be obtained directly from x_{i+1}, x_i, and x_{i-1} without a need for first forming the radix-2 recoded number y (Table 10.1).

Like the radix-2 version, radix-4 Booth's recoding can be viewed as digit-set conversion: the recoding takes a radix-4 number with digits in [0, 3] and converts it to the digit set [−2, 2].

TABLE 10.1
Radix-4 Booth's recoding yielding $(z_{k/2} \cdots z_1 z_0)_{\text{four}}$

x_{i+1}	x_i	x_{i-1}	y_{i+1}	y_i	$z_{i/2}$	Explanation
0	0	0	0	0	0	No string of 1s in sight
0	0	1	0	1	1	End of a string of 1s in x
0	1	0	1	-1	1	Isolated 1 in x
0	1	1	1	0	2	End of a string of 1s in x
1	0	0	-1	0	-2	Beginning of a string of 1s in x
1	0	1	-1	1	-1	End one string, begin new string
1	1	0	0	-1	-1	Beginning of a string of 1s in x
1	1	1	0	0	0	Continuation of string of 1s in x

As an example, Table 10.1 can be used to perform the following conversion of an unsigned number into a signed-digit number:

$$(21\ 31\ 22\ 32)_{\text{four}} = (10\ 01\ 11\ 01\ 10\ 10\ 11\ 10)_{\text{two}}$$
$$= (1\ \text{-}2\ 2\ \text{-}1\ 2\ \text{-}1\ \text{-}1\ 0\ \text{-}2)_{\text{four}}$$

Note that the 16-bit unsigned number turns into a 9-digit radix-4 number. Generally, the radix-4 signed-digit representation of a k-bit unsigned binary number will need $\lfloor k/2 \rfloor + 1 = \lceil (k+1)/2 \rceil$ digits when its most-significant bit is 1. Note also that $x_{-1} = x_k = x_{k+1} = 0$ is assumed.

If the binary number in the preceding example is interpreted as being in 2's-complement format, then simply ignoring the extra radix-4 digit produced leads to correct encoding of the represented value:

$$(1001\ 1101\ 1010\ 1110)_{2'\text{s-compl}} = (\text{-}2\ 2\ \text{-}1\ 2\ \text{-}1\ \text{-}1\ 0\ \text{-}2)_{\text{four}}$$

Thus, for k-bit binary numbers in 2's-complement format, the Booth-encoded radix-4 version will have $\lceil k/2 \rceil$ digits. When k is odd, $x_k = x_{k-1}$ is assumed for proper recoding. In any case, $x_{-1} = 0$.

The digit-set conversion process defined by radix-4 Booth's recoding entails no carry propagation. Each radix-4 digit in $[-2, 2]$ is obtained, independently from all others, by examining 3 bits of the multiplier, with consecutive 3-bit segments overlapping in one bit. For this reason, radix-4 Booth's recoding is said to be based on overlapped 3-bit scanning of the multiplier. This can be extended to overlapped multiple-bit scanning schemes for higher radices (see Section 10.4).

An example radix-4 multiplication using Booth's recoding is shown in Fig. 10.5. The 4-bit 2's-complement multiplier $x = (1010)_{\text{two}}$ is recoded as a 2-digit radix-4 number $z = (\text{-}1\ \text{-}2)_{\text{four}}$, which then dictates the multiples $z_0 a = -2a$ and $z_1 a = -a$ to be added to the cumulative partial product in the two cycles. Note that in all intermediate steps, the upper half of the cumulative partial product is extended from 4 bits to 6 bits to accommodate the sign extension needed for proper handling of the negative values. Also, note the sign extension during the right shift to obtain $p^{(1)}$ from $4p^{(1)}$.

```
================================
a                0 1 1 0
x                1 0 1 0
z                 ⁻1  ⁻2    Radix-4 recoded version of x
================================
p(0)           0 0 0 0 0 0
+z₀a           1 1 0 1 0 0
                ─────────────
4p(1)          1 1 0 1 0 0
p(1)           1 1 1 1 0 1   0 0
+z₁a           1 1 1 0 1 0
                ─────────────
4p(2)          1 1 0 1 1 1   0 0
p(2)             1 1 0 1   1 1 0 0
================================
```

Fig. 10.5 Example radix-4 multiplication with modified Booth's recoding of the 2's-complement multiplier.

Figure 10.6 depicts a possible circuit implementation for multiple generation based on radix-4 Booth's recoding. Since five possible multiples of a or digits $(0, \pm1, \pm2)$ are involved, we need at least 3 bits to encode a desired multiple. A simple and efficient encoding is to devote one bit to distinguish 0 from nonzero digits, one bit to the sign of a nonzero digit, and one bit to the magnitude of a nonzero digit (2 encoded as 1 and 1 as 0). The recoding circuit thus has three inputs (x_{i+1}, x_i, x_{i-1}) and produces three outputs: "neg" indicates if the multiple should be added (0) or subtracted (1), "non0" indicates if the multiple is nonzero, and "two" indicates that a nonzero multiple is 2.

It is instructive to compare the recoding scheme implicit in the design of Fig. 10.4 to Booth's recoding of Fig. 10.6 in terms of cost and delay. This is left as an exercise. Note, in particular, that while the recoding produced in Fig. 10.4 is serial and must thus be done from right to left, Booth's recoding is fully parallel and carry-free. This latter property is of no avail in designing digit-at-a-time multipliers, since the recoded digits are used serially anyway. But we will see later that Booth's recoding can be applied to the design of tree and array multipliers, where all the multiples are needed at once.

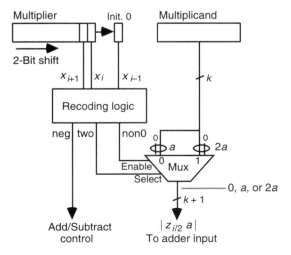

Fig. 10.6 The multiple generation part of a radix-4 multiplier based on Booth's recoding.

10.3 USING CARRY-SAVE ADDERS

Carry-save adders can be used to reduce the number of addition cycles as well as to make each cycle faster. For example, radix-4 multiplication without Booth's recoding can be implemented by using a CSA to handle the $3a$ multiple, as shown in Fig. 10.7. Here, the CSA helps us in doing radix-4 multiplication (generating the required multiples) without reducing the add time. In fact, one can say that the add time is slightly increased, since the CSA overhead is paid in every cycle, regardless of whether we actually need $3a$.

The CSA and multiplexers in the radix-4 multiplier of Fig. 10.7 can be put to better use for reducing the addition time in radix-2 multiplication by keeping the cumulative partial product in stored-carry form. In fact, only the upper half of the cumulative partial product needs to be kept in redundant form, since as we add the three values that form the next cumulative partial product, one bit of the final product is obtained in standard binary form and is shifted into the lower half of the double-width partial product register (Fig. 10.8). This eliminates the need for carry propagation in all but the final addition.

Each of the first $k - 1$ cycles can now be made much shorter, since in these cycles, signals pass through only a few gate levels corresponding to the multiplexers and the CSA. In particular, the delay in these cycles is independent of the word width k. Compared to a simple sequential multiplier (Fig. 9.4), the additional components needed to implement the CSA-based binary multiplier of Fig. 10.8 are a k-bit register, a k-bit CSA, and a k-bit multiplexer; only the extra k-bit register is missing in the design of Fig. 10.7.

The CSA-based design of Fig. 10.8 can be combined with radix-4 Booth's recoding to reduce the number of cycles by 50%, while also making each cycle considerably faster. The changes needed in the design of Fig. 10.8 to accomplish this are depicted in Fig. 10.9, where the small 2-bit adder is needed to combine two bits of the sum, one bit of the carry, and a carry from a preceding cycle into two bits that are shifted into the lower half of the cumulative partial product register and a carry that is kept for the next cycle. The use of the carry-in input of the 2-bit adder is explained shortly.

The Booth recoding and multiple selection logic of Fig. 10.9 is different from the arrangement in Fig. 10.6, since the sign of each multiple must be incorporated in the multiple itself, rather than as a signal that controls addition/subtraction. Figure 10.10 depicts Booth recoding and multiple selection circuits that can be used for high-radix and parallel multipliers.

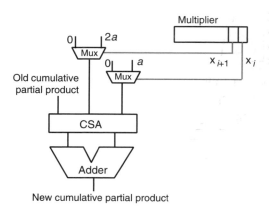

Fig. 10.7 Radix-4 multiplication with a carry-save adder used to combine the cumulative partial product, $x_i a$, and $2x_{i+1}a$ into two numbers.

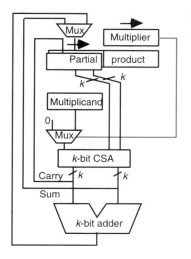

Fig. 10.8   Radix-2 multiplication with the upper half of the cumulative partial product kept in stored-carry form.

Note that in the circuit of Fig. 10.10, the negative multiples $-a$ and $-2a$ are produced in 2's-complement format. As usual, this is done by bitwise complementation of a or $2a$ and the addition of 1 in the LSB position. The multiple a or $2a$ produced from x_i and x_{i+1} is aligned at the right with bit position i and thus must be padded with i zeros at its right end when viewed as a $2k$-bit number. Bitwise complementation of these 0s, followed by the addition of 1 in the LSB position, converts them back to 0s and causes a carry to enter bit position i. For this reason, we can continue to ignore positions 0 through $i - 1$ in the negative multiples and insert the extra "dot" directly in bit position i (Fig. 10.10).

Alternatively, one can do away with Booth's recoding and use the scheme depicted in Fig. 10.7 to accommodate the required $3a$ multiple. Now, four numbers (the sum and carry components of the cumulative partial product, $x_i a$, and $2x_{i+1}a$) need to be combined, thus necessitating a two-level CSA tree (Fig. 10.11).

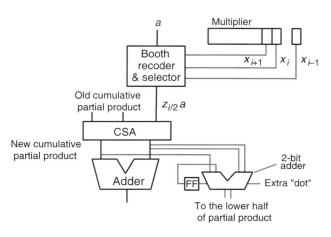

Fig. 10.9   Radix-4 multiplication with a carry-save adder used to combine the stored-carry cumulative partial product and $z_{i/2}a$ into two numbers.

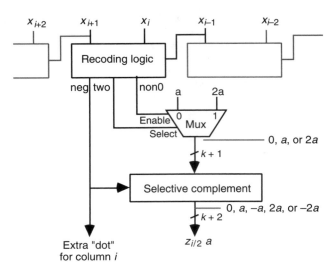

Fig. 10.10   Booth recoding and multiple selection logic for high-radix or parallel multiplication.

10.4 RADIX-8 AND RADIX-16 MULTIPLIERS

From the radix-4 multiplier in Fig. 10.11, it is an easy step to visualize higher-radix multipliers. A radix-8 multiplier, for example, might have a three-level CSA tree to combine the carry-save cumulative partial product with the three multiples $x_i a$, $2x_{i+1}a$, and $4x_{i+2}a$ into a new cumulative partial product in carry-save form. However, once we have gone to three levels

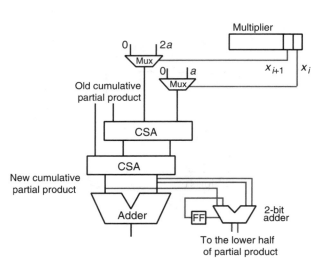

Fig. 10.11   Radix-4 multiplication, with the cumulative partial product, $x_i a$, and $2x_{i+1}a$ combined into two numbers by two carry-save adders

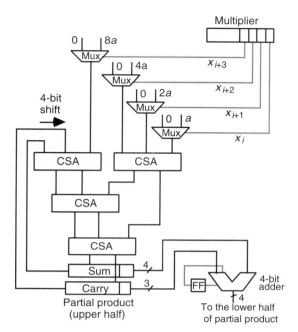

Fig. 10.12   Radix-16 multiplication with the upper half of the cumulative partial product in carry-save form.

of CSA, we might as well invest in one more CSA to implement a radix-16, or 4-bits-at-a-time, multiplier. The resulting design is depicted in Fig. 10.12.

An alternative radix-16 multiplier can be derived from Fig. 10.11 if we replace each of the multiplexers with Booth recoding and multiple selection circuits. Supplying the details of the multiplier design, including proper alignment and sign extension for the inputs to the CSA tree, is left as an exercise.

Which of the preceding radix-16 multipliers (Fig. 10.12, or Fig. 10.11 modified to include Booth's recoding) is faster or more cost-effective depends on the detailed circuit-level designs as well as technological parameters.

Note that in radix-2^b multiplication with Booth's recoding, we have to reduce $b/2$ multiples to 2 using a $(b/2 + 2)$-input CSA tree whose other two inputs are taken by the carry-save partial product. Without Booth's recoding, a $(b + 2)$-input CSA tree would be needed. Whether to use Booth's recoding is a fairly close call, since Booth recoding circuit and multiple selection logic is somewhat slower than a CSA but also has a larger reduction factor in the number of operands (2 vs. 1.5).

Varied as the preceding choices are, they do not exhaust the design space. Other alternatives include radix-8 and radix-16 Booth's recoding, which represent the multiplier using the digit sets $[-4, 4]$ and $[-8, 8]$, respectively. We will explore the recoding process and the associated multiplier design options in the end-of-chapter problems. Note, for example, that with radix-8 recoding, we have the $\pm 3a$ multiples to deal with. As before, we can precompute $3a$ or represent it as the pair of numbers $2a$ and a, leading to the requirement for an extra input into the CSA tree.

There is, of course, no compelling reason to stop at radix 16. A design similar to that in Fig. 10.12 can be used for radix-256 (8-bits-at-a-time) multiplication if Booth's recoding is applied first. This would require that the four multiplexers in Fig. 10.12 be replaced by the Booth recoding and selection logic. Again, whether this new arrangement will lead to a cost-effective

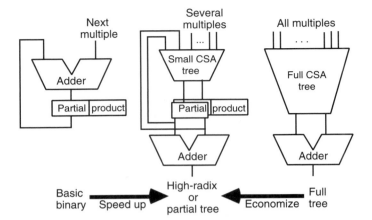

Fig. 10.13   High-radix multipliers as intermediate between sequential radix-2 and full-tree multipliers.

design (compared, e.g., to taking 7 bits of the multiplier and adding nine numbers in a four-level CSA tree) depends on the technology and cannot be discerned in general.

Designs such as the ones depicted in Figs. 10.11 and 10.12 can be viewed as intermediate between basic sequential (one-bit-at-a-time) multiplication and fully parallel tree multipliers to be discussed in Chapter 11. Thus, high-radix or partial-tree multipliers can be viewed as designs that offer speedup over sequential multiplication or economy over fully parallel tree multipliers (Fig. 10.13).

10.5 MULTIBEAT MULTIPLIERS

In the CSA-based binary multiplier shown in Fig. 10.8, CSA outputs are loaded into the same registers that supply its inputs. A common implementation method is to use master–slave flip-flops for the registers. In this method, each register has two sides: the master side accepts new data being written into the register while the slave side, which supplies the register's outputs, keeps the old data for the entire half-cycle when the clock is high. When the clock goes low, the new data in the master side is transferred to the slave side in preparation for the next cycle. In this case, one might be able to insert an extra CSA between the master and slave registers, with little or no effect on the clock's cycle time. This virtually doubles the speed of partial product accumulation.

Figure 10.14 shows a schematic representation of a 3-bit-at-a-time twin-beat multiplier that effectively retires 6 bits of the multiplier in each clock cycle. This multiplier, which uses radix-8 Booth's recoding, is similar to the twin-beat design used in Manchester University's MU5 computer [Gosl71].

Each clock cycle is divided into two phases or beats. In the first beat, the left multiplier register is used to determine the next multiple to be added, while in the second beat, the right multiplier register is used. After each cycle (two beats), the small adder at the lower right of Fig. 10.14 determines 6 bits of the product, which are shifted into the lower half of the cumulative

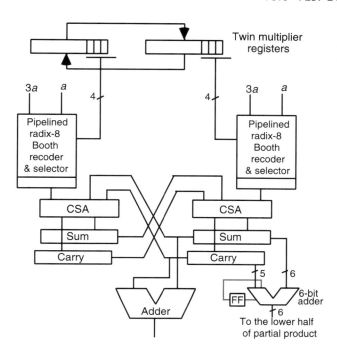

Fig. 10.14   Twin-beat multiplier with radix-8 Booth's recoding.

partial product register. This adder is in all likelihood slower than the CSAs; hence, to make each cycle as short as possible, the adder must be pipelined. Since the product bits, once produced, do not change, the latency in deriving these bits has no effect on the rest of the computation in the carry-save portion of the circuit.

The twin-beat concept can be easily extended to obtain a three-beat multiplier. Such a design can be visualized by putting the three CSAs and associated latches into a ring (Fig. 10.15), whose nodes are driven by a three-phase clock [deAn95]. Each node requires two beats before making its results available to the next node, thus leading to separate accumulation of odd- and even-indexed partial products. At the end, the four operands are reduced to two operands, which are then added to obtain the final product.

10.6 VLSI COMPLEXITY ISSUES

Implementation of sequential radix-2 and high-radix multipliers described thus far in Chapters 9 and 10 is straightforward. The components used are carry-save adders, registers, multiplexers, and a final fast carry-propagate adder, for which standard designs are available. A small amount of random control logic is also required. Note that each 2-to-1 multiplexer with one of the inputs tied to 0 can be simplified to a set of AND gates.

For the CSA tree of a radix-2^b multiplier, typically a bit slice is designed and then replicated. Since without Booth's recoding, the CSA tree receives $b + 2$ inputs, the required slice is a $(b + 2; 2)$-counter; see Section 8.5. For example, a set of $(7; 2)$-counter slices can be used to implement the CSA tree of a radix-32 multiplier without Booth's recoding. When radix-2^h Booth's recoding

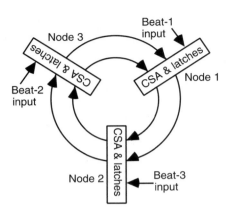

Fig. 10.15   Conceptual view of a three-beat multiplier.

is applied first, then the number of multiples per cycle is reduced by a factor of h and a $(b/h + 2; 2)$-counter slice will be needed.

In performing radix-2^b multiplication, bk two-input AND gates are required to form the b multiples for each cycle in parallel. The area complexity of the CSA tree that reduces these b multiples to 2 is O(bk). Since these complexities dominate that of the final fast adder, the overall area requirement is seen to be:

$$A = \mathrm{O}(bk)$$

In view of the logarithmic height of the CSA tree, as discussed in Section 8.3, multiplication is performed in k/b cycles of duration O($\log b$), plus a final addition requiring O($\log k$) time. The overall time complexity thus becomes:

$$T = \mathrm{O}((k/b)\log\, b + \log\, k)$$

It is well known that any VLSI circuit computing the product of two k-bit integers must satisfy the following constraints involving its layout area A and computational latency T: AT is at least proportional to $k\sqrt{k}$ and AT^2 grows at least as fast as k^2. For the preceding implementations, we have:

$$AT\ = \mathrm{O}(k^2 \log\, b + bk\, \log\, k)$$
$$AT^2\ = \mathrm{O}((k^3/b)\, \log^2 b)$$

At the lower end of the complexity scale, where b is a constant, the AT and AT^2 measures for our multipliers become O(k^2) and O(k^3), respectively. At the other extreme corresponding to $b = k$, where all the multiplier bits are considered at once, we have $AT = \mathrm{O}(k^2 \log\, k)$ and $AT^2 = \mathrm{O}(k^2 \log^2 k)$. Intermediate designs do not yield better values for AT and AT^2; thus, the multipliers remain asymptotically suboptimal for the entire range of the parameter b.

By the AT measure, which is often taken as an indicator of cost-effectiveness, the slower radix-2 multipliers are better than high-radix or tree multipliers. Therefore, in applications calling for a large number of independent multiplications, it may be appropriate to use the available chip area for a large number of slow multipliers as opposed to a small number of faster units.

We will see, in Chapter 11, that the time complexity of high-radix multipliers can actually be reduced from O($(k/b)\, \log\, b + \log\, k$) to O($k/b + \log\, k$) through a more effective pipelining scheme. Even though the resulting designs lead to somewhat better AT and AT^2 measures, the preceding conclusions do not change.

Despite these negative results pointing to the asymptotic suboptimality of high-radix and tree multipliers, such designs are quite practical for a wide range of the parameter b, given that the word width k is quite modest in practice.

PROBLEMS

10.1 **Radix-4 Booth's recoding** Prove that radix-4 Booth's recoding defined in Table 10.1 preserves the value of an unsigned or 2's-complement number. *Hint:* First show that the recoded radix-4 digit $z_{i/2}$ can be obtained from the arithmetic expression $-2x_{i+1} + x_i + x_{i-1}$.

10.2 **Sequential radix-4 multipliers**

 a. Consider the radix-4 multiplier depicted in Fig. 10.2. What provisions are needed if 2's-complement multipliers are to be handled appropriately?

 b. Repeat part a for the multiplier depicted in Fig. 10.4.

10.3 **Alternate radix-4 multiplication algorithms** Consider the example unsigned multiplication $(0\ 1\ 1\ 0)_{two} \times (1\ 1\ 1\ 0)_{two}$ depicted in Fig. 10.3.

 a. Redo the example multiplication using the scheme shown in Fig. 10.4.

 b. Redo the example multiplication using radix-4 Booth's recoding.

 c. Redo the example multiplication using the scheme shown in Fig. 10.7. Show the intermediate sum and carry values in each step.

10.4 **Sequential unsigned radix-4 multipliers**

 a. Design the recoding logic needed for the multiplier of Fig. 10.4.

 b. Give a complete design for the Booth recoding logic circuit shown in Fig. 10.6.

 c. Compare the circuits of parts a and b with respect to cost and delay. Which scheme is more cost-effective for sequential unsigned radix-4 multiplication?

 d. Compare the radix-4 multiplier shown in Fig. 10.2 against those in part c with respect to cost and delay. Summarize your conclusions.

10.5 **Alternate radix-4 recoding scheme**

 a. The design of the Booth recoder and multiple selection circuits in Fig. 10.6 assumes the use of a multiplexer with an enable control signal. How will the design change if such a multiplexer is not available?

 b. Repeat part a for the circuit of Fig. 10.10.

10.6 **Recoding for radix-8 multiplication**

 a. Construct a recoding table (like Table 10.1) to obtain radix-8 digits in $[-4, 4]$ based on overlapped 4-bit groups of binary digits in the multiplier.

 b. Show that your recoding scheme preserves the value of a number. *Hint:* Express the recoded radix-8 digit $z_{i/3}$ as a linear function of x_{i+2}, x_{i+1}, x_i, and x_{i-1}.

 c. Design the required recoding logic block.

 d. Draw a block diagram for the radix-8 multiplier and compare it to radix-4 design.

10.7   **Recoding for radix-16 multiplication**

    a.   Construct a recoding table (like Table 10.1) to obtain radix-16 digits in $[-8, 8]$ based on overlapped 5-bit groups of binary digits in the multiplier.

    b.   Show that your recoding scheme preserves the value of a number. *Hint:* Express the recoded radix-16 digit $z_{i/4}$ as a linear function of $x_{i+3}, x_{i+2}, x_{i+1}, x_i,$ and x_{i-1}.

    c.   Design the required recoding logic block.

    d.   Draw a block diagram for the radix-16 multiplier and compare it to radix-4 design.

10.8   **Alternate radix-4 recoding scheme**   The radix-4 Booth recoding scheme of Table 10.1 replaces the two bits x_{i+1} and x_i of the multiplier with a radix-4 digit 0, ± 1, or ± 2 by examining x_{i-1} as the recoding context. An alternative recoding scheme is to replace x_{i+1} and x_i with a radix-4 digit 0, ± 2, or ± 4 by using x_{i+2} as the context.

    a.   Construct the required radix-4 recoding table.

    b.   Design the needed recoding logic block.

    c.   Compare the resulting multiplier to that obtained from radix-4 Booth recoding with respect to possible advantages and drawbacks.

10.9   **Comparing radix-4 multipliers**   Compare the multipliers in Figs. 10.9 and 10.11 with regard to speed and hardware implementation cost. State and justify all your assumptions.

10.10   **Very-high-radix multipliers**   The 4-bit adder shown at the lower right of Fig. 10.12 may be slower than the CSA tree, thus lengthening the cycle time. The problem becomes worse for higher radices. Discuss how this problem can be mediated.

10.11   **Multibeat multipliers**   Study the design of the three-beat multiplier in [deAn95]. Based on your understanding of the design, discuss if anything can be gained by going to a four-beat multiplier.

10.12   **VLSI complexity of multipliers**

    a.   A proposed VLSI design for $k \times k$ multiplication requires chip area proportional to $k \log k$. What can you say about the asymptotic speed of this multiplier based on AT and AT^2 bounds?

    b.   What can you say about the VLSI area requirement of a multiplier that operates in optimal $O(\log k)$ time?

10.13   **VLSI multiplier realizations**   Design a slice of the (6; 2)-counter that is needed to implement the multiplier of Fig. 10.12.

10.14   **Multiply-add operation**

    a.   Show that the high-radix multipliers of this chapter can be easily adapted to compute $p = ax + y$ instead of $p = ax$.

    b.   Extend the result of part a to computing $p = ax + y + z$, where all input operands are k-bit unsigned integers. *Hint:* This is particularly easy with carry-save designs.

10.15 **Balanced ternary multiplication** Discuss the design of a radix-9 multiplier for balanced ternary operands that use the digit set $[-1, 1]$ in radix 3. Consider all the options presented in this chapter, including the possibility of recoding.

10.16 **Decimal multiplier** Consider the design of a decimal multiplier using a digit-at-a-time scheme. Assume BCD encoding for the digits.

  a. Using a design similar to that in Fig. 10.12, supply the hardware details and discuss how each part of the design differs from the radix-16 version. *Hint:* One approach is to design a special decimal divide-by-2 circuit for deriving the multiple $5a$ from $10a$, forming the required multiples by combining $10a$, $5a$, a, and $-a$.

  b. Using a suitable recoding scheme, convert the decimal number to digit set $[-5, 5]$. Does this recoding help make multiplication less complex than in part a?

10.17 **Signed-digit multiplier** Consider the multiplication of radix-3 integers using the redundant digit set $[-2, 2]$.

  a. Draw a block diagram for the requisite radix-3 multiplier using the encoding given in connection with radix-4 Booth's recoding (Fig. 10.6) to represent the digits.

  b. Show the detailed design of the circuit that provides the multiple $2a$.

  c. Present the design of a radix-9 multiplier that relaxes two multiplier digits per cycle.

REFERENCES

[Boot51]   Booth, A. D., "A Signed Binary Multiplication Technique," *Quarterly J. Mechanics and Applied Mathematics*, Vol. 4, Pt. 2, pp. 236–240, June 1951.

[deAn95]   de Angel, E., A. Chowdhury, and E.E. Swartzlander, "The Star Multiplier," *Proc. 29th Asilomar Conf. Signals, Systems, and Computers*, pp. 604–607, 1995.

[Gosl71]   Gosling, J. B., "Design of Large High-Speed Binary Multiplier Units," *Proc. IEE*, Vol. 118, Nos. 3/4, pp. 499–505, 1971.

[MacS61]   MacSorley, O. L., "High-Speed Arithmetic in Binary Computers," *Proc. IRE*, Vol. 49, pp. 67–91, 1961.

[Rubi75]   Rubinfield, L. P., "A Proof of the Modified Booth's Algorithm for Multiplication," *IEEE Trans. Computers*, Vol. 25, No. 10, pp. 1014–1015, 1975.

[Sam90]   Sam, H., and A. Gupta, "A Generalized Multibit Recoding of the Two's Complement Binary Numbers and Its Proof with Application in Multiplier Implementations," *IEEE Trans. Computers*, Vol. 39, No. 8, pp. 1006–1015, 1990.

[Vass89]   Vassiliadis, S., E. M. Schwartz, and D. J. Hanrahan, "A General Proof for Overlapped Multiple-Bit Scanning Multiplications," *IEEE Trans. Computers*, Vol. 38, No. 2, pp. 172–183, 1989.

[Wase82]   Waser, S., and M. J. Flynn, *Introduction to Arithmetic for Digital Systems Designers*, Holt, Rinehart, & Winston, 1982.

[Zura87]   Zurawski, J. H. P., and J. B. Gosling, "Design of a High-Speed Square-Root, Multiply, and Divide Unit," *IEEE Trans. Computers*, Vol. 36, No. 1, pp. 13–23, 1987.

Chapter 11 | TREE AND ARRAY MULTIPLIERS

Tree, or fully parallel, multipliers constitute limiting cases of high-radix multipliers (radix-2^k). With a high-performance CSA tree followed by a fast adder, logarithmic time multiplication becomes possible. The resulting multipliers are expensive but justifiable for applications in which multiplication speed is critical. One-sided CSA trees lead to much slower, but highly regular, structures known as array multipliers that offer higher pipelined throughput than tree multipliers and significantly lower chip area at the same time. Chapter topics include:

11.1 FULL-TREE MULTIPLIERS

In their simplest forms, parallel or full-tree multipliers can be viewed as extreme cases of the design in Fig. 10.12, where all the k multiples of the multiplicand are produced at once and a k-input CSA tree is used to reduce them to two operands for the final addition. Because all the multiples are combined in one pass, the tree does not require feedback links, making pipelining quite feasible.

Figure 11.1 shows the general structure of a full-tree multiplier. Various multiples of the multiplicand a, corresponding to binary or high-radix digits of the multiplier x or its recoded version, are formed at the top. The multiple-forming circuits may be a collection of AND gates (binary multiplier), radix-4 Booth's multiple generators (recoded multiplier), and so on. These multiples are added in a combinational partial products reduction tree, which produces their sum in redundant form. Finally, the redundant result is converted to standard binary output at the bottom.

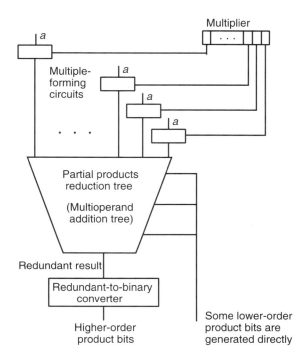

Fig. 11.1   General structure of a full-tree multiplier.

Many types of tree multiplier have been built or proposed. These are distinguished by the designs of the following three elements in Fig. 11.1:

multiple-forming circuits

partial products reduction tree

redundant-to-binary converter

In the remainder of this section, we focus on tree multiplier variations involving unsigned binary multiples and CSA reduction trees. With the redundant result in carry-save form, the final converter is simply a fast adder. Deviations from the foregoing multiple generation and reduction schemes are discussed in Section 11.2. Signed tree multipliers are covered in Section 11.3.

From our discussion of sequential multiplication in Chapters 9 and 10, we know how the partial products can be formed and how, through the use of high-radix methods, the number of partial products can be reduced. The trade-offs mentioned for high-radix multipliers exist here as well: more complex multiple-forming circuits can lead to simplification in the reduction tree. Again, we cannot say in general which combination will lead to greater cost-effectiveness because the exact nature of the trade-off is design- and technology-dependent.

Recall Wallace's and Dadda's strategies for constructing CSA trees discussed in Section 8.3. These give rise to Wallace and Dadda tree multipliers, respectively. Essentially, Wallace's strategy for building CSA trees is to combine the partial product bits at the earliest opportunity, while with Dadda's method, combining takes place as late as possible, consistent with keeping the critical path length of the CSA tree intact. Wallace's method leads to the fastest possible design and Dadda's strategy usually leads to a simpler CSA tree and a wider carry-propagate adder.

As a simple example, we derive Wallace and Dadda tree multipliers for 4×4 multiplication. Figure 11.2 shows the design process and results in tabular form, where the integers indicate the number of dots remaining in the various columns. Each design begins with 16 AND gates forming the $x_i a_j$ terms or dots, $0 \le i, j \le 3$. The resulting 16 dots are spread across seven columns in the pattern 1, 2, 3, 4, 3, 2, 1. The Wallace tree design requires 3 FAs and 1 HA in the first level, then 2 FAs and 2 HAs in the second level, and a 4-bit carry-propagate adder at the end. With the Dadda tree design, our first goal is to reduce the height of the partial products dot matrix from 4 to 3, thus necessitating 2 FAs in the first level. These are followed by 2 FAs and 2 HAs in the second level (reducing the height from 3 to 2) and a 6-bit carry-propagate adder at the end.

Intermediate approaches between those of Wallace and Dadda yield various designs that offer speed–cost trade-offs. For example, it may be that neither the Wallace tree nor the Dadda tree leads to a convenient width for the fast adder. In such cases a hybrid approach may yield the best results.

Note that the results introduced for carry-save multioperand addition in Chapter 8 apply to the design of partial products reduction trees with virtually no change. The only modifications required stem from the relative shifting of the operands to be added. For example, in Fig. 8.12, we see that in adding seven right-aligned k-bit operands, the CSAs are all k bits wide. In a seven-operand CSA tree of a 7×7 tree multiplier, the input operands appear with shifts of 0 to 6 bits, leading to the input configuration shown at the top of Fig. 11.3. We see that the shifted inputs necessitate somewhat wider blocks at the bottom of the tree. It is instructive to compare Figs. 11.3 and Fig. 8.12, noting all the differences.

Of course, there is no compelling reason to keep all the bits of the input or intermediate operands together and feed them to multibit CSAs, thus necessitating the use of many half-adders that simply rearrange the dots without contributing to their reduction. Doing the reduction with single-bit FAs and HAs, as in Fig. 11.2, leads to lower complexity and perhaps even greater speed. Deriving the Wallace and Dadda tree multipliers to perform the same function as the circuit of Fig. 11.3 is left as an exercise.

One point is quite clear from Fig. 11.3 or its Wallace tree and Dadda tree equivalents: a logarithmic depth reduction tree based on CSAs has an irregular structure that makes its design and layout quite difficult. Additionally, connections and signal paths of varying lengths lead to logic hazards and signal skew that have implications for both performance and power consumption. In VLSI design, we strive to build circuits from iterated or recursive structures that lend themselves to efficient automatic synthesis and layout. Alternative reduction trees that are more suitable for VLSI implementation are discussed next.

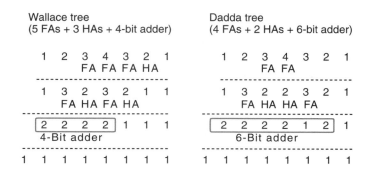

Fig. 11.2   Two different binary 4×4 tree multipliers.

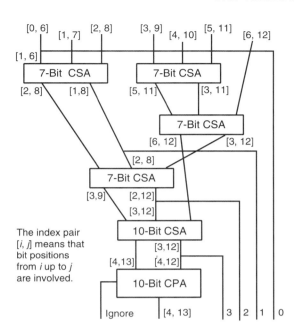

Fig. 11.3 Possible CSA tree for a 7 × 7 tree multiplier.

11.2 ALTERNATIVE REDUCTION TREES

Recall from our discussion in Section 8.5 that a (7; 2)-counter slice can be designed that takes 7 bits in the same column i as inputs and produces one bit in each of the columns i and $i + 1$ as outputs. Such a slice, when suitably replicated, can perform the function of the reduction tree part of Fig. 11.3. Of course, not all columns in Fig. 11.3 have seven inputs. The preceding iterative circuit can then be left intact and supplied with dummy 0 inputs in the interest of regularity, or it can be pruned by removing the redundant parts in each slice. Such optimizations are well within the power of automated design tools.

Based on Table 8.1, an (11; 2)-counter has at least five full-adder levels. Figure 11.4 shows a particular five-level arrangement of full adders for performing 11-to-2 reduction with the property that all outputs are produced after the same number of full-adder delays. Observe how all carries produced in level i enter FAs in level $i + 1$. The FAs of Fig. 11.4 can be laid out to occupy a narrow vertical slice that can then be replicated to form an 11-input reduction tree of desired width. Such balanced-delay trees are quite suitable for VLSI implementation of parallel multipliers.

The circuit of Fig. 11.4 is composed of three columns containing 1, 3, and 5 FAs, going from left to right. It is now easy to see that the number of inputs can be expanded from 11 to 18 by simply appending to the right of the circuit an additional column of 7 FAs. The top FA in the added column will accommodate three new inputs, while each of the others, except for the lowermost two, can accept one new input; these latter FAs must also accommodate a sum coming from above and a carry coming from the right. Note that the FAs in the various columns are more or less independent in that adjacent columns are linked by just one wire. This property

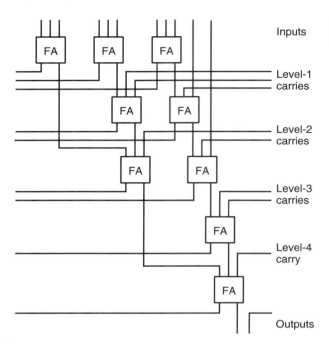

Inputs

Level-1 carries

Level-2 carries

Level-3 carries

Level-4 carry

Outputs

Fig. 11.4 A slice of a balanced-delay tree for 11 inputs.

makes it possible to lay out the circuit in a narrow slice without having to devote a lot of space to the interconnections.

Instead of building partial products reduction trees from CSAs, or (3; 2)-counters, one can use a module that reduces four numbers to two as the basic building block. Then, partial products reduction trees can be structured as binary trees that possess a recursive structure making them more regular and easier to lay out (Fig. 11.5). Figure 11.6 shows a possible way of laying out the seven-module tree of Fig. 11.5. Note that adding a level to the tree of Fig. 11.6 involves duplicating the tree and inserting a 4-to-2 reduction module between them.

In Fig. 11.6, the first, third, fifth, and seventh rectangular boxes correspond to top-level blocks of Fig. 11.5. These blocks receive four multiples of the multiplicand (two from above

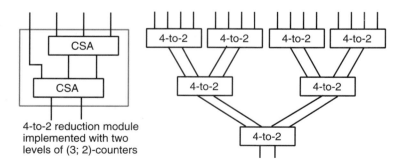

4-to-2 reduction module implemented with two levels of (3; 2)-counters

Fig. 11.5 Tree multiplier with a more regular structure based on 4-to-2 reduction modules.

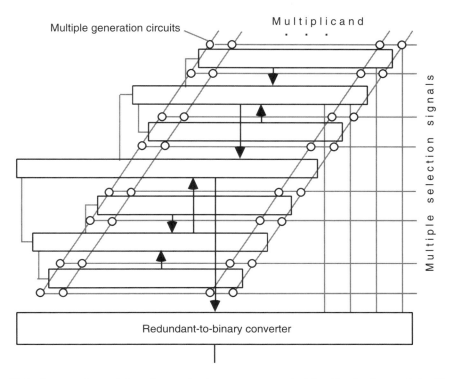

Fig. 11.6 Layout of a partial products reduction tree composed of 4-to-2 reduction modules. Each solid arrow represents two numbers.

and two from below) and reduce them to a pair of numbers for the second and sixth blocks. Each of the latter blocks in turn supplies two numbers to the fourth block, which feeds the redundant-to-binary converter.

If the 4-to-2 reduction modules are internally composed of two CSA levels, as suggested in Fig. 11.5, then there may be more CSA levels in the binary tree structure than in Wallace or Dadda trees. However, regularity of interconnections, and the resulting efficient layout, can more than compensate for the added logic delays due to the greater circuit depth.

Note that a 4-to-2 reduction circuit for binary operands can be viewed as a GSD adder for radix-2 numbers with the digit set $[0, 2]$, where the digits are encoded in the following 2-bit code:

$$\text{Zero: } (0, 0) \quad \text{One: } (0, 1) \text{ or } (1, 0) \quad \text{Two: } (1, 1)$$

A variant of this binary tree reduction scheme is based on binary-signed-digit, rather than carry-save, representation of the partial products [Taka85]. These partial products are combined by a tree of BSD adders to obtain the final product in BSD form. The standard binary result is then obtained via a BSD-to-binary converter, which is essentially a fast subtractor for subtracting the negative component of the BSD number from its positive part. One benefit of BSD partial products is that negative multiples resulting from the sign bit in 2's-complement numbers can be easily accommodated (see Section 11.3). Some inefficiency results from the extra bit used to accommodate the digit signs going to waste for most of the multiples that are positive.

Of course, carry-save and BSD numbers are not the only ones that allow fast reduction via limited-carry addition. Several other digit sets are possible that offer certain advantages depending on technological capabilities and constraints [Parh96]. For example, radix-2 partial products using the digit set [0, 3] lend themselves to an efficient parallel-carries addition process (Fig. 3.11c), while also accommodating three, rather than one or two, multiples of a binary multiplicand. Interestingly, the final conversion from the redundant digit set [0, 3] to [0, 1] is not any harder than conversion from [0, 2] to [0, 1].

Clearly, any method used for building the CSA tree can be combined with radix-2^b Booth's recoding to reduce the tree size. However, for modern VLSI technology, the use of Booth recoding in tree multipliers has been questioned [Vill93]; it seems that the additional CSAs needed for reducing k, rather than k/b, numbers could be less complex than the Booth recoding logic when wiring and the overhead due to irregularity and nonuniformity are taken into account.

11.3 TREE MULTIPLIERS FOR SIGNED NUMBERS

When one is multiplying 2's-complement numbers directly, each of the partial products to be added is a signed number. Thus, for the CSA tree to yield the correct sum of its inputs, each partial product must be sign-extended to the width of the final product. Recall our discussion of signed multioperand addition in Section 8.6, where the 2's-complement operands were assumed to be aligned at their LSBs. In particular, refer to Fig. 8.18 for two possible methods based on sign extension (with hardware sharing) and transforming negative bits into positive bits.

Considerations for adding 2's-complement partial products are similar, the only difference being the shifts. Figure 11.7 depicts an example with three sign-extended partial products. We see that here too a single full adder can produce the results needed in several different columns. If this procedure is applied to all rows in the partial products bit matrix, the resulting structure will be somewhat more complex than the one assuming unsigned operands. Note that because of the shifts, there are fewer repetitions in Fig. 11.7 than in Fig. 8.18, thus making the expansion in width to accommodate the signs slightly larger.

Another approach, due to Baugh and Wooley [Baug73], is even more efficient and is thus often preferred, in its original or modified form, for 2's-complement multiplication. To understand this method, we begin with unsigned multiplication in Fig. 11.8a and note that the negative weight of the sign bit in 2's-complement representation must be taken into account to obtain the correct product (Fig. 11.8b). To avoid having to deal with negatively weighted bits

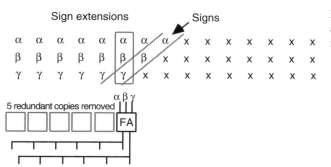

Fig. 11.7 Sharing of full adders to reduce the CSA width in a signed tree multiplier.

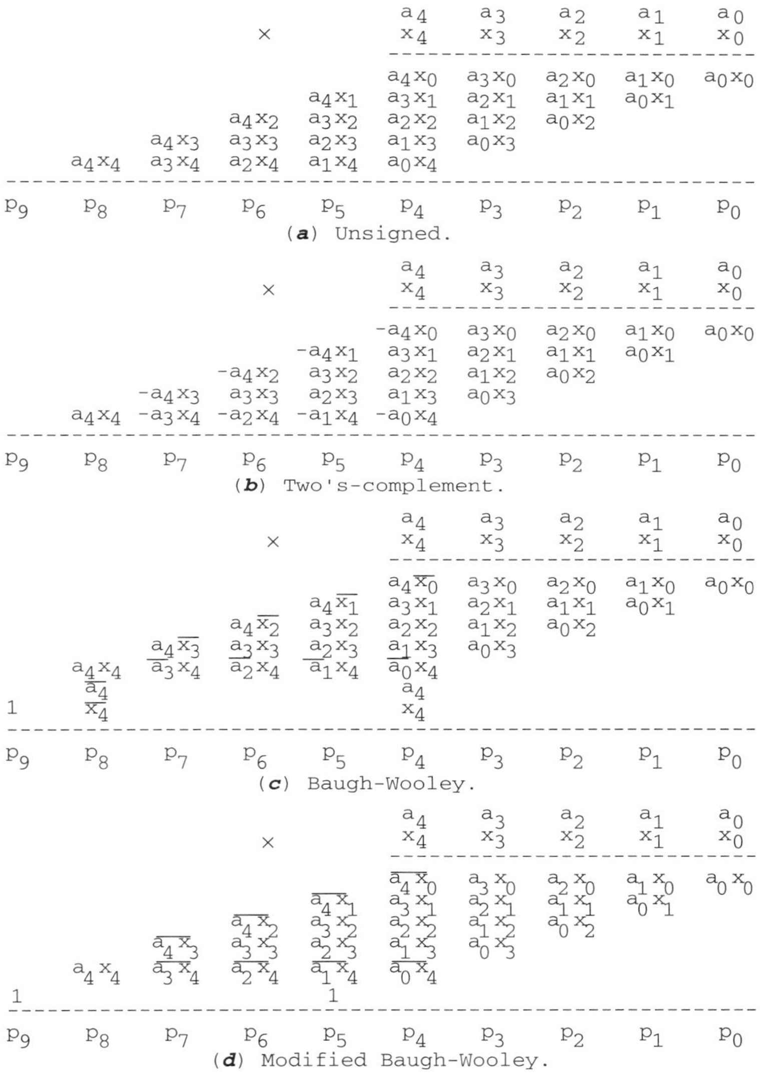

$$
\begin{array}{rccccccccc}
 & & & & & a_4 & a_3 & a_2 & a_1 & a_0 \\
\times & & & & & x_4 & x_3 & x_2 & x_1 & x_0 \\
\hline
 & & & & & a_4x_0 & a_3x_0 & a_2x_0 & a_1x_0 & a_0x_0 \\
 & & & & a_4x_1 & a_3x_1 & a_2x_1 & a_1x_1 & a_0x_1 & \\
 & & & a_4x_2 & a_3x_2 & a_2x_2 & a_1x_2 & a_0x_2 & & \\
 & & a_4x_3 & a_3x_3 & a_2x_3 & a_1x_3 & a_0x_3 & & & \\
 & a_4x_4 & a_3x_4 & a_2x_4 & a_1x_4 & a_0x_4 & & & & \\
\hline
p_9 & p_8 & p_7 & p_6 & p_5 & p_4 & p_3 & p_2 & p_1 & p_0
\end{array}
$$

(**a**) Unsigned.

$$
\begin{array}{rccccccccc}
 & & & & & a_4 & a_3 & a_2 & a_1 & a_0 \\
\times & & & & & x_4 & x_3 & x_2 & x_1 & x_0 \\
\hline
 & & & & & -a_4x_0 & a_3x_0 & a_2x_0 & a_1x_0 & a_0x_0 \\
 & & & & -a_4x_1 & a_3x_1 & a_2x_1 & a_1x_1 & a_0x_1 & \\
 & & & -a_4x_2 & a_3x_2 & a_2x_2 & a_1x_2 & a_0x_2 & & \\
 & & -a_4x_3 & a_3x_3 & a_2x_3 & a_1x_3 & a_0x_3 & & & \\
 & a_4x_4 & -a_3x_4 & -a_2x_4 & -a_1x_4 & -a_0x_4 & & & & \\
\hline
p_9 & p_8 & p_7 & p_6 & p_5 & p_4 & p_3 & p_2 & p_1 & p_0
\end{array}
$$

(**b**) Two's-complement.

$$
\begin{array}{rcccccccccc}
 & & & & & & a_4 & a_3 & a_2 & a_1 & a_0 \\
\times & & & & & & x_4 & x_3 & x_2 & x_1 & x_0 \\
\hline
 & & & & & & a_4\overline{x_0} & a_3x_0 & a_2x_0 & a_1x_0 & a_0x_0 \\
 & & & & & a_4\overline{x_1} & a_3x_1 & a_2x_1 & a_1x_1 & a_0x_1 & \\
 & & & & a_4\overline{x_2} & a_3x_2 & a_2x_2 & a_1x_2 & a_0x_2 & & \\
 & & & a_4\overline{x_3} & a_3x_3 & a_2x_3 & a_1x_3 & a_0x_3 & & & \\
 & & a_4x_4 & \overline{a_3}x_4 & \overline{a_2}x_4 & \overline{a_1}x_4 & \overline{a_0}x_4 & & & & \\
 & & \overline{a_4} & & & & a_4 & & & & \\
1 & & \overline{x_4} & & & & x_4 & & & & \\
\hline
p_9 & & p_8 & p_7 & p_6 & p_5 & p_4 & p_3 & p_2 & p_1 & p_0
\end{array}
$$

(**c**) Baugh-Wooley.

$$
\begin{array}{rccccccccc}
 & & & & & a_4 & a_3 & a_2 & a_1 & a_0 \\
\times & & & & & x_4 & x_3 & x_2 & x_1 & x_0 \\
\hline
 & & & & & \overline{a_4\,x}_0 & a_3\,x_0 & a_2\,x_0 & a_1\,x_0 & a_0\,x_0 \\
 & & & & \overline{a_4\,x}_1 & a_3\,x_1 & a_2\,x_1 & a_1\,x_1 & a_0\,x_1 & \\
 & & & \overline{a_4\,x}_2 & a_3\,x_2 & a_2\,x_2 & a_1\,x_2 & a_0\,x_2 & & \\
 & & \overline{a_4\,x}_3 & a_3\,x_3 & a_2\,x_3 & a_1\,x_3 & a_0\,x_3 & & & \\
 & a_4\,x_4 & \overline{a_3\,x}_4 & \overline{a_2\,x}_4 & \overline{a_1\,x}_4 & \overline{a_0\,x}_4 & & & & \\
1 & & & & 1 & & & & & \\
\hline
p_9 & p_8 & p_7 & p_6 & p_5 & p_4 & p_3 & p_2 & p_1 & p_0
\end{array}
$$

(**d**) Modified Baugh-Wooley.

Fig. 11.8 Baugh–Wooley 2's-complement multiplication.

in the partial products matrix, Baugh and Wooley suggest that we modify the bits in the way shown in Fig. 11.8c, adding a few entries to the bit matrix in the process.

Baugh and Wooley's strategy increases the maximum column height by 2, thus potentially leading to greater delay through the CSA tree. For example, in the 5×5 multiplication depicted in Fig. 11.8, column height is increased from 5 to 7, leading to an extra CSA level. In this particular example, however, the extra delay can be avoided by removing the x_4 entry from column 4 and placing two x_4 entries in column 3 which has only four entries. This reduces the height to 6, which can still be handled by a three-level CSA tree.

To prove the correctness of the Baugh–Wooley scheme, let us focus on the entry $a_4 \overline{x}_0$ in Fig. 11.8. Given that the sign bit in 2's-complement numbers has a negative weight, this entry should have been $-a_4 x_0$. We note that:

$$- a_4 x_0 = a_4(1 - x_0) - a_4 = a_4 \overline{x}_0 - a_4$$

Hence, we can replace $-a_4 x_0$ with the two entries $a_4 \overline{x}_0$ and $-a_4$. If instead of $-a_4$ we use an entry a_4, the column sum increases by $2a_4$. To compensate for this, we must insert $-a_4$ in the next higher column. The same argument can be repeated for $a_4 \overline{x}_1$, $a_4 \overline{x}_2$, and $a_4 \overline{x}_3$. Each column, other than the first, gets an a_4 and a $-a_4$, which cancel each other out. The p_8 column gets a $-a_4$ entry, which can be replaced with $\overline{a}_4 - 1$. The same argument can be repeated for the $\overline{a}_i x_4$ entries, leading to the insertion of x_4 in the p_4 column and $\overline{x}_4 - 1$ in the p_8 column. The two -1s thus produced in the eighth column are equivalent to a -1 entry in the p_9 column, which can in turn be replaced with a 1 and a borrow into the nonexistent (and inconsequential) tenth column.

Another way to justify the Baugh–Wooley method is to transfer all negatively weighted $a_4 x_i$ terms, $0 \leq i \leq 3$, to the bottom row, thus leading to two negative numbers (the preceding number and the one formed by the $a_i x_4$ bits, $0 \leq i \leq 3$) in the last two rows. Now, the two numbers $x_4 a$ and $a_4 x$ must be subtracted from the sum of all the positive elements. Instead of subtracting $x_4 \times a$, we add x_4 times the 2's complement of a, which consists of 1's complement of a plus x_4 (similarly for $a_4 x$). The reader should be able to supply the other details.

A modified form of the Baugh–Wooley method, (Fig. 11.8d) is preferable because it does not lead to an increase in the maximum column height. Justifying this modified form is left as an exercise.

11.4 PARTIAL-TREE MULTIPLIERS

If the cost of a full-tree multiplier is unacceptably high for a particular application, then a variety of mixed serial-parallel designs can be considered. Let h be a number smaller than k. One idea is to perform the k-operand addition needed for $k \times k$ multiplication via $\lceil k/h \rceil$ passes through a smaller CSA tree. Figure 11.9 shows the resulting design that includes an $(h + 2)$-input CSA tree for adding the cumulative partial product (in stored-carry form) and h new operands, feeding back the resulting sum and carry to be combined with the next batch of h operands.

Since the next batch of h operands will be shifted by h bits with respect to the current batch, h bits of the derived sum and $h - 1$ bits of the carry can be relaxed after each pass. These are combined using an h-bit adder to yield h bits of the final product, with the carry-out kept in a flip-flop to be combined with the next inputs. Alternatively, these relaxed bits can be kept in carry-save form by simply shifting them to the right in their respective registers and postponing the conversion to standard binary format to the very end. This is why parts of Fig. 11.9 are rendered in dotted form. The latter approach might be followed if a fast double-width adder is already available in the ALU for other reasons.

Note that the design depicted in Fig. 11.9 corresponds to radix-2^h multiplication. Thus, our discussions in Sections 10.3 and 10.4 are relevant here as well. In fact, the difference between high-radix and partial-tree multipliers is quantitative rather than qualitative (see Fig. 10.13). When h is relatively small, say up to 8 bits, we tend to view the multiplier of Fig. 11.9 as a high-radix multiplier. On the other hand, when h is a significant fraction of k, say $k/2$ or $k/4$, then we view the design as a partial-tree multiplier. In Section 11.6, we will see that a pipelined variant of the design in Fig. 11.9 can be considerably faster when h is large.

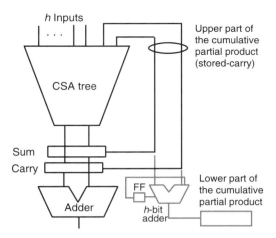

Fig. 11.9 General structure of a partial-tree multiplier.

Figure 11.9 has been drawn with the assumption of radix-2 multiplication. If radix-2^b Booth's recoding is applied first to produce one multiple for every b bits of the multiplier, then b times fewer passes are needed and bh bits can be relaxed after each pass. Thus, the small adder in Fig. 11.9 will be bh bits wide.

11.5 ARRAY MULTIPLIERS

Consider a full-tree multiplier (Fig. 11.1) in which the reduction tree is one-sided and the final adder has a ripple-carry design, as depicted in Fig. 11.10. Such a tree multiplier, which is composed of the slowest possible CSA tree and the slowest possible carry-propagate adder, is known as an array multiplier.

But why would anyone be interested in such a slow multiplier? The answer is that an array multiplier is very regular in its structure and uses only short wires that go from one full adder to horizontally, vertically, or diagonally adjacent full adders. Thus, it has a very simple and efficient layout in VLSI. Furthermore, it can be easily and efficiently pipelined by inserting latches after every CSA or after every few rows (the last row must be handled differently, as discussed in Section 11.6, because its latency is much larger than the others).

The free input of the topmost CSA in the array multiplier of Fig. 11.10 can be used to realize a multiply-add module yielding $p = ax + y$. This is useful in a variety of applications involving convolution or inner-product computation. When only the computation of ax is desired, the topmost CSA in the array multiplier of Fig. 11.10 can be removed, with x_0a and x_1a input to the second CSA directly.

Figure 11.11 shows the design of a 5×5 array multiplier in terms of full-adder cells and two-input AND gates. The sum outputs are connected diagonally, while the carry outputs are linked vertically, except in the last row, where they are chained from right to left. The design in Fig. 11.11 assumes unsigned numbers, but it can be easily converted to a 2's-complement array multiplier using the Baugh–Wooley method. This involves adding a full adder at the right end of the ripple-carry adder, to take in the a_4 and x_4 terms, and a couple of full adders at the lower left edge to accommodate the $\overline{a}_4$, $\overline{x}_4$, and 1 terms (see Fig. 11.12). Most of the connections between FA blocks in Fig. 11.12 have been removed to avoid clutter.

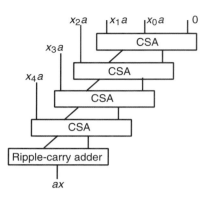

Fig. 11.10   A basic array multiplier uses a one-sided CSA tree and a ripple-carry adder.

In view of the simplicity of an array multiplier for 2's-complement numbers based on the Baugh–Wooley method (Fig. 11.12), we no longer use techniques proposed by Pezaris and others that required in some of the array positions variants of a full-adder cell capable of accommodating some negatively weighted input bits and producing one or both outputs with negative weight(s).

If we build a cell containing a full adder and an AND gate to internally form the term $a_j x_i$, the unsigned array multiplier of Fig. 11.11 turns into Fig. 11.13. Here, the x_i and a_j bits are broadcast to rows and columns of cells, with the row-i, column-j cell, forming the term $a_j x_i$ and using it as an input to its FA. If desired, one can make the design less complex by replacing the cells in the first row, or the first two rows, by AND gates.

The critical path through a $k \times k$ array multiplier, when the sum generation logic of a full-adder block has a longer delay than the carry-generation circuit, goes through the main (top left to bottom right) diagonal in Fig. 11.12 and proceeds horizontally in the last row to the p_9 output. The overall delay of the array multiplier can thus be reduced by rearranging the full-adder

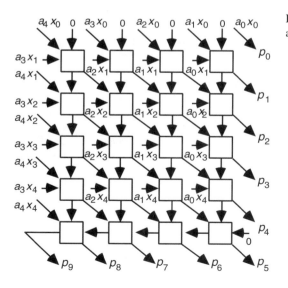

Fig. 11.11   Detailed design of a 5×5 array multiplier using full-adder blocks.

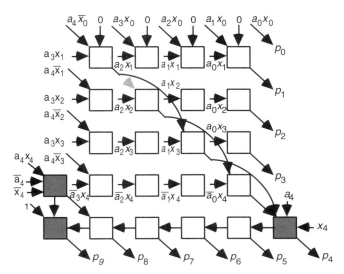

Fig. 11.12 Modifications in a 5×5 array multiplier to deal with 2's-complement inputs using the Baugh–Wooley method (inclusion of the three shaded FA blocks) or to shorten the critical path (the curved links).

inputs such that some of the sum signals skip rows (they go from row i to row $i + h$ for some $h > 1$). Figure 11.12 shows the modified connections on the main diagonal for $h = 2$. The lower right cell now has one too many inputs, but we can redirect one of them to the second cell on the main diagonal, which now has one free input. Note, however, that such skipping of levels makes for a less regular layout, which also requires longer wires, hence may not be a worthwhile modification in practice.

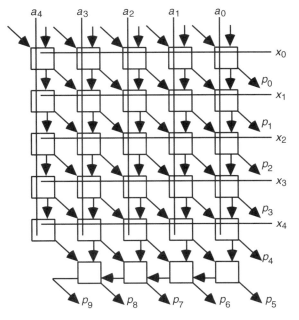

Fig. 11.13 Design of a 5×5 array multiplier with two additive inputs and full-adder blocks that include AND gates.

Since almost half the latency of an array multiplier is due to the cells in the last row, it is interesting to speculate about whether we can do the final addition faster. Obviously, it is possible to replace the last row of cells with a fast adder, but this would adversely affect the regularity of the design. Besides, even a fast adder is still much slower than the other rows, making pipelining more difficult.

To see how the ripple-carry portion of an array multiplier can be eliminated, let us arrange the k^2 terms $a_j x_i$ in a triangle, with bits distributed in $2k - 1$ columns according to the pattern:

$$1 \; 2 \; 3 \; \cdots \; k-1 \; \; k \; \; k-1 \; \cdots \; 3 \; 2 \; 1$$

The LSB of the product is output directly, and the other bits are reduced gradually by rows of full- and half-adders (rectangular boxes in Fig. 11.14). Let us focus on the ith level and assume that the first $i - 1$ levels have already yielded two versions of the final product bits past the B_i boundary, one assuming that the next carry-save addition will produce a carry across B_i and another assuming no carry (Fig. 11.15).

At the ith level, the shaded block in Fig. 11.14 produces two versions of its sum and carry, conditional upon a future carry or no carry across B_{i+1}. The conditional sum bits from the shaded block are simply appended to the i bits coming from above. So, two versions of the upper $i + 1$ bits of the product are obtained, conditional upon the future carry across the B_{i+1} boundary. The process is then repeated in the lower levels, with each level extending the length of the conditional portion by one bit and the final multiplexer providing the last k bits of the end product in nonredundant form.

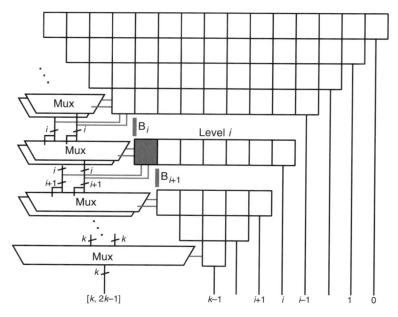

Fig. 11.14 Conceptual view of a modified array multiplier that does not need a final carry-propagate adder.

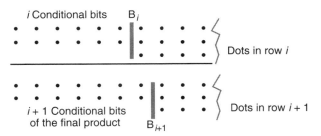

Fig. 11.15 Carry-save addition, performed in level i, extends the conditionally computed bits of the final product.

The conceptual design of Fig. 11.14 can be translated to an actual multiplier circuit after certain optimizations to remove redundant elements [Erce90], [Cimi96].

11.6 PIPELINED TREE AND ARRAY MULTIPLIERS

A full-tree multiplier can be easily pipelined. The partial products reduction tree of a full-tree multiplier is a combinational circuit that can be sliced into pipeline stages. A new set of inputs cannot be applied to the partial-tree multiplier of Fig. 11.9, however, until the sum and carry for the preceding set have been latched. Given that for large h, the depth of the tree can be significant, the rate of the application of inputs to the tree, and thus the speed of the multiplier, is limited.

Now, if instead of feeding back the tree outputs to its inputs, we feed them back into the middle of the $(h + 2)$-input tree, as shown in Fig. 11.16, the pipeline rate will be dictated by the delay through only two CSA levels rather than by the depth of the entire tree. This leads to much faster multiplication.

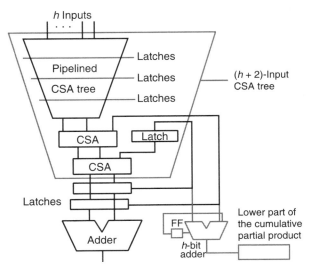

Fig. 11.16 Efficiently pipelined partial-tree multiplier.

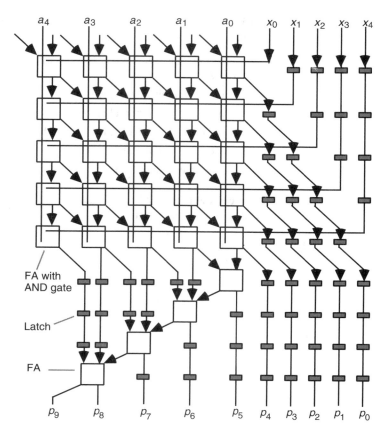

Fig. 11.17   Pipelined 5×5 array multiplier using latched FA blocks. The small shaded rectangles are latches.

Figure 11.17 shows one way to pipeline an array multiplier. Inputs are applied from above and the product emerges from below after nine clock cycles ($2k -1$ in general). These FA blocks used are assumed to have output latches for both sum and carry. Note how the x_i inputs needed for the various rows of the array multiplier are delayed through the insertion of latches in their paths and how the 4-bit ripple-carry adder at the bottom row of Fig. 11.13 has been pipelined in Fig. 11.17.

PROBLEMS

11.1   **Unsigned full-tree multipliers**   Consider the design of a 7×7 unsigned full-tree multiplier as depicted in Fig. 11.3.

   a.   Compare Figs. 11.3 and 8.12, discussing all the differences.
   b.   Design the required partial products reduction tree using Wallace's method.
   c.   Design the required partial products reduction tree using Dadda's method.
   d.   Compare the designs of parts a, b, and c with respect to speed and cost.

11.2 **Unsigned full-tree multipliers** Consider the design of an 8×8 unsigned full-tree multiplier.

    a. Draw a diagram similar to Fig. 11.3 to determine the number and widths of the carry-save adders required.

    b. Repeat part a, this time using 4-to-2 reduction circuits built of two CSAs.

    c. Design the required partial products reduction tree using Wallace's method.

    d. Design the required partial products reduction tree using Dadda's method.

    e. Produce one design with its final adder width between those in parts c and d.

    f. Compare the designs of parts a–e with respect to speed and cost.

11.3 **Balanced-delay trees** Find the relationship between the number n of inputs and circuit depth d of a balanced-delay tree (Fig. 11.4) and show that the depth grows as $\sqrt{n}$.

11.4 **Variations in full-tree multipliers** Tabulate the number of full-adder levels in a tree that reduces k multiples of the multiplicand to 2, for $4 \leq k \leq 1024$, using:

    a. Carry-save adders as the basic elements.

    b. Elements, internally built from two CSA levels, that reduce four operands to two.

    c. Same elements as in part b, except that in the first level of the tree only, the use of CSAs is allowed (this is helpful, e.g., for $k = 24$).

    d. Discuss the implications of the results of parts a–c in the design of full-tree multipliers.

11.5 **Tree multiplier with Booth's recoding** We need a 12×12 signed-magnitude binary multiplier. Design the required 11×11 unsigned multiplication circuit by first generating a recoded version of the multiplier having six radix-4 digits in $[-2, 2]$ and then adding the six partial products represented in 2's-complement form by a minimal network of FAs. *Hint:* 81 FAs should do.

11.6 **Modified Baugh–Wooley method** Prove that the modified Baugh–Wooley method for multiplying 2's-complement numbers, shown in Fig. 11.8d, is correct.

11.7 **Signed full-tree multipliers** Consider the design of an 8×8 full-tree multiplier for 2's-complement inputs.

    a. Draw a diagram similar to Fig. 11.3 to determine the number and widths of the carry-save adders required if the operands are to be sign-extended (Fig. 11.7).

    b. Design the 8×8 multiplier using the Baugh–Wooley method.

    c. Design the 8×8 multiplier using the modified Baugh–Wooley method.

    d. Compare the designs of parts a–c with respect to speed and cost.

11.8 **Partial-tree multipliers** In Fig. 11.9, the tree has been drawn with no intermediate output corresponding to the lower-order bits of the sum of its $h + 2$ inputs. If h is large, a few low-order bits of the sum will likely become available before the final sum and carry results. How does this affect the h-bit adder delineated by dotted lines?

11.9   **Pezaris array multiplier** Consider a 5×5 array multiplier, similar to that in Fig. 11.11 but with 2's-complement inputs, and view the AND terms $a_4 x_i$ and $a_j x_4$ as being negatively weighted. Consider also two modified forms of a full-adder cell: FA′ has one negatively weighted input, producing a negatively weighted sum and a positively weighted carry, while FA″ has two negatively weighted inputs, producing a negative carry and a positive sum. Design a 5×5 Pezaris array multiplier using FA, FA′, and FA″ cells as needed, making sure that any negatively weighted output is properly connected to a negatively weighted input (use small "bubbles" to mark negatively weighted inputs and outputs on the various blocks). Note that FA‴, with all three inputs and two outputs carrying negative weights, is the same as FA. Note also that the output must have only one negatively weighted bit at the sign position.

11.10   **Two's-complement array multipliers** Consider the design of an 5×5 2's-complement array multiplier. Assume that an FA block has latencies of T_c and T_s $(T_c < T_s < 2T_c)$ for its carry and sum outputs.

    a.   Find the overall latency for the 5×5 array multiplier with the Baugh–Wooley method (Fig. 11.12, regular design without row skipping).

    b.   Repeat part a with the modified Baugh–Wooley method.

    c.   Compare the designs in parts a and b and discuss.

    d.   Generalize the preceding results and comparison to the case of $k \times k$ array multipliers.

11.11   **Array multipliers** Design array multipliers for the following number representations.

    a.   Binary signed-digit numbers using the digit set $[-1, 1]$ in radix 2.

    b.   One's-complement numbers.

11.12   **Multiply-add modules** Consider the design of a module that performs the computation $p = ax + y + z$, where a and y are k-bit unsigned integers and x and z are l-bit unsigned integers.

    a.   Show that p is representable with $k + l$ bits.

    b.   Design a tree multiplier to compute p for $k = 8$ and $l = 4$ based on a Wallace tree and a CPA.

    c.   Repeat part b using a Dadda tree.

    d.   Show that an 8×4 array multiplier can be readily modified to compute p.

11.13   **Pipelined array multipliers** Consider the 5×5 pipelined array multiplier in Fig. 11.17.

    a.   Show how the four lowermost FAs and the latches immediately above them can be replaced by a number of latched HAs. *Hint:* Some HAs will have to be added in the leftmost column, corresponding to p_9, which currently contains no element.

    b.   Compare the design in part a with the original design in Fig. 11.17.

    c.   Redesign the pipelined multiplier in Fig. 11.17 so that the combinational delay in each pipeline stage is equal to two FA delays (ignore the difference in delays between the sum and carry outputs).

    d.   Repeat part c for the array multiplier derived in part a.

e. Compare the array multiplier designs of parts c and d with respect to throughput and throughput/cost. State your assumptions clearly.

11.14 Effectiveness of Booth's recoding As mentioned at the end of Section 11.2, the effectiveness of Booth recoding in tree multipliers has been questioned [Vill93]. Booth's recoding essentially reduces the number of partial products by a factor of 2. A (4, 2) reduction circuit built (e.g.) from two CSAs offers the same reduction. Show through a simple approximate analysis of the delay and cost of a $k \times k$ unsigned multiplier based on Booth's recoding and (4, 2) initial reduction that Booth's recoding has the edge in terms of gate count but that it may lose on other counts. Assume, for simplicity, that k is even.

11.15 VLSI implementation of tree multipliers Wallace and Dadda trees tend to be quite irregular and thus ill-suited to compact VLSI implementation. Study the bit-slice implementation method for tree multipliers suggested in [Mou92] and apply it to the design of a 12×12 multiplier.

11.16 Faster array multipliers Present the complete design of an 8×8 array multiplier built without a final carry-propagate adder (Fig. 11.14). Compare the resulting design to a simple 8×8 array multiplier with respect to speed, cost, and cost-effectiveness.

11.17 Pipelined partial-tree multipliers

a. Would it be cost-effective to implement an 8×8 unsigned multiplier using the pipelined design of Fig. 11.16 with $h = 4$?

b. With reference to the VLSI complexity discussions in Section 10.6, show that the multiplication time in a pipelined partial-tree multiplier is $O(k/h + \log k)$.

REFERENCES

[Baug73] Baugh, C. R., and B. A. Wooley, "A Two's Complement Parallel Array Multiplication Algorithm," *IEEE Trans. Computers*, Vol. 22, pp. 1045–1047, December 1973.
[Cimi96] Ciminiera, L., and P. Montuschi, "Carry-Save Multiplication Schemes Without Final Addition," *IEEE Trans. Computers*, Vol. 45, No. 9, pp. 1050–1055, 1996.
[Dadd65] Dadda, L., "Some Schemes for Parallel Multipliers," *Alta Frequenza*, Vol. 34, pp. 349–356, 1965.
[Erce90] Ercegovac, M. D., and T. Lang, "Fast Multiplication Without Carry-Propagate Addition," *IEEE Trans. Computers*, Vol. 39, No. 11, pp. 1385–1390, 1990.
[Mou92] Mou, Z.-J., and F. Jutand, " 'Overturned-Stairs' Adder Trees and Multiplier Design," *IEEE Trans. Computers*, Vol. 41, No. 8, pp. 940–948, 1992.
[Parh96] Parhami, B., "Comments on 'High-Speed Area-Efficient Multiplier Design Using Multiple-Valued Current Mode Circuits'," *IEEE Trans. Computers*, Vol. 45, No. 5, pp. 637–638, 1996.
[Peza71] Pezaris, S. D., "A 40-ns 17-Bit by 17-Bit Array Multiplier," *IEEE Trans. Computers*, Vol. 20, pp. 442–447, April 1971.
[Taka85] Takagi, N., H. Yasuura, and S. Yajima, "High-Speed VLSI Multiplication Algorithm with a Redundant Binary Addition Tree," *IEEE Trans. Computers*, Vol. 34, No. 9, pp. 789–796, 1985.

[Vill93]   Villager, D., and V. G. Oklobdzija, "Analysis of Booth Encoding Efficiency in Parallel Multipliers Using Compressors for Reduction of Partial Products," *Proc. Asilomar Conf. Signals, Systems, and Computers*, pp. 781–784, 1993.

[Vuil83]   Vuillemin, J., "A Very Fast Multiplication Algorithm for VLSI Implementation," *Integration: The VLSI Journal*, Vol. 1, pp. 39–52, 1983.

[Wall64]   Wallace, C. S., "A Suggestion for a Fast Multiplier," *IEEE Trans. Electronic Computers*, Vol. 13, pp. 14–17, 1964.

[Zura86]   Zuras, D., and W. H. McAllister, "Balanced Delay Trees and Combinatorial Division in VLSI," *IEEE J. Solid-State Circuits*, Vol. 21, pp. 814–819, October 1986.

Chapter
12 | VARIATIONS IN MULTIPLIERS

We do not always synthesize our multipliers from scratch but may desire, or be required, to use building blocks such as adders, small multipliers, or lookup tables. Furthermore, limited chip area and/or pin availability may dictate the use of bit-serial designs. In this chapter, we discuss such variations and also deal with modular multipliers, the special case of squaring, and multiply-accumulators. Chapter topics include:

12.1 DIVIDE-AND-CONQUER DESIGNS

Suppose you have $b \times b$ multipliers and would like to use them to synthesize a $2b \times 2b$ multiplier. Denoting the high and low halves of the multiplicand (multiplier) by a_H and a_L (x_H and x_L), we can use four $b \times b$ multipliers to compute the four partial products $a_L x_L$, $a_L x_H$, $a_H x_L$, and $a_H x_H$ as shown in Fig. 12.1. These four values must then be added to obtain the final product. Actually, as shown on the right side of Fig. 12.1, only three values need to be added, since the nonoverlapping partial products $a_H x_H$ and $a_L x_L$ can be viewed as a single $4b$-bit number.

We see that our original $2b \times 2b$ multiplication problem has been reduced to four $b \times b$ multiplications and a three-operand addition problem. The $b \times b$ multiplications can be performed by smaller hardware multipliers or via table lookup. Then, we can compute the $4b$-bit product by means of a single level of carry-save addition, followed by a $3b$-bit carry-propagate addition. Note that b bits of the product are directly available following the $b \times b$ multiplications.

Larger multipliers, such as $3b \times 3b$ or $4b \times 4b$, can be similarly synthesized from $b \times b$-multiplier building blocks. Figure 12.2 shows that $3b \times 3b$ multiplication leads to five numbers, while $4b \times 4b$ multiplication produces seven numbers. Hence, we can complete the multiplication

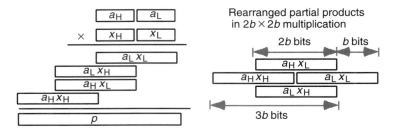

Fig. 12.1 Divide-and-conquer strategy for synthesizing a $2b \times 2b$ multiplier from $b \times b$ multipliers.

process in these two cases by using a row of (5; 2)- or (7; 2)-counters, followed by a $5b$- or $7b$-bit fast adder, respectively. Note that b bits of the product are obtained directly from a small multiplier.

For example, given 4×4 multipliers as building blocks, we can synthesize a 16×16 multiplier using 16 of the small multipliers, along with 24 (7; 2)-counters and a 28-bit fast adder. The structure of a 32×32 multiplier built of 8×8-multiplier building blocks is identical to the device above.

One can view the preceding divide-and-conquer scheme, depicted in Figs. 12.1 and 12.2, as radix-2^b multiplication, except that each radix-2^b digit of the multiplier produces several partial products, one for each radix-2^b digit of the multiplicand, instead just one.

For $2b \times 2b$ multiplication, one can use b-bit adders exclusively to accumulate the partial products, as shown in Fig. 12.3 for $b = 4$. The pair $[i, j]$ of numbers shown next to a solid line in Fig. 12.3 indicate that the 4-bit bundle of wires represented by that line spans bit positions i through j. A dotted line represents one bit, with its positions given by a single integer. We need five b-bit adder blocks, arranged in a circuit of depth 4, to perform the accumulation. This is attractive if b-bit adders are available as economical, off-the-shelf components. The resulting design is not much slower than the design based on CSA reduction if the latter design uses a cascade of three b-bit adders for the final $3b$-bit addition.

Instead of $b \times b$ multipliers, one can use $b_1 \times b_2$ multipliers. For example, with 8×4 multipliers as building blocks, a 16×16 multiplier can be synthesized from eight such units, followed by a 5-to-2 reduction circuit and a 28-bit adder.

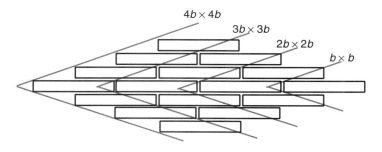

Fig. 12.2 Using $b \times b$ multipliers to synthesize $2b \times 2b$, $3b \times 3b$, and $4b \times 4b$ multipliers.

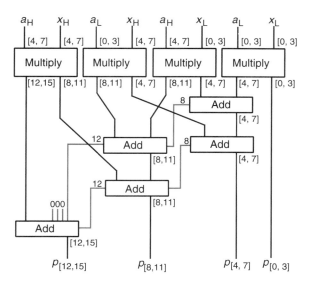

Fig. 12.3 Using 4×4 multipliers and 4-bit adders to synthesize an 8×8 multiplier.

12.2 ADDITIVE MULTIPLY MODULES

We note from the discussion in Section 12.1, and Fig. 12.3 in particular, that synthesizing large multipliers from smaller ones requires both multiplier and adder units. If we can combine the multiplication and addition functions into one unit, then perhaps a single module type will suffice for implementing such multipliers. This is the idea behind additive multiply modules (AMMs).

The additive multiply module in Fig. 12.4a, performs the computation $p = ax + y + z$, where a and y are 4-bit numbers and x and z are 2-bit numbers. The maximum value of the result p is $(15 \times 3) + 15 + 3 = 63$, which can be represented with 6 bits. Figure 12.4b shows an implementation of this AMM using four full adders (boxes enclosing three dots) and a 4-bit adder in dot notation.

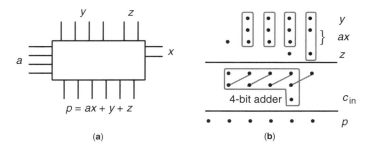

Fig. 12.4 Additive multiply module with 4×2 multiplier (ax) plus 4-bit and 2-bit additive inputs (y and z).

Figure 12.5 shows how the 8×8 multiplier example of Fig. 12.3 can be built from eight AMMs of the type depicted in Fig. 12.4. Note that eight 4×2 multipliers would have been needed for this design; so the number of modules is kept to a minimum. Each AMM is slower than a 4×2 multiplier by at most one full-adder level. So, the delay in Fig. 12.5 that is attributable to the addition function is no more than six FA delays (the critical path goes through six AMM modules). Thus, given that the cost of a 4×2 AMM is less than the combined costs of a 4×2 multiplier and a 4-bit adder, the design shown in Fig. 12.5 is very cost-effective.

Figure 12.6 depicts an alternate design for an 8×8 multiplier using the same number and type of 4×2 AMMs as in Fig. 12.5 (as well as the same notational conventions). This latter design is slower that the design of Fig. 12.5 because its critical path goes through all eight modules. However, it is more regular and, thus, readily generalizable to any $4h_2 \times 2h_1$ multiplier with compact VLSI layout.

In general, a $b \times c$ AMM will have a pair of b-bit and c-bit multiplicative inputs, two b-bit and c-bit additive inputs, and a $(b+c)$-bit output. The number of bits in the output is just adequate to represent the largest possible output value, as evident from the following identity:

$$(2^b - 1)(2^c - 1) + (2^b - 1) + (2^c - 1) = 2^{b+c} - 1$$

In designing larger multipliers based on $b \times c$ AMMs, the $(b + c)$-bit output of each AMM is divided into a b-bit upper part and a c-bit lower part that are supplied as additive inputs to other AMMs or serve as primary outputs. An AMM that receives $a_{[j,j+b-1]}$ and $x_{[i,i+c-1]}$ as its multiplicative inputs should have values spanning the bit positions $[i + j, i + j + b - 1]$ and $[i + j, i + j + c - 1]$ as its additive inputs (why?). To design a $k \times l$ multiplier, where b and

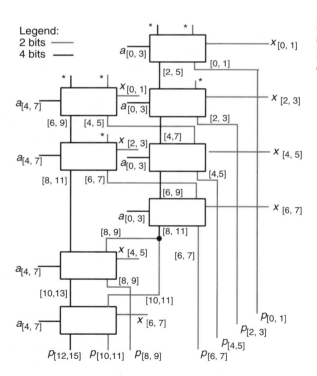

Fig. 12.5   An 8×8 multiplier built of 4×2 additive multiply modules. Inputs marked with an asterisk carry 0s.

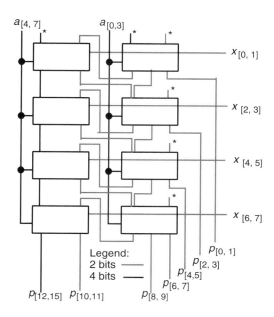

Fig. 12.6 Alternate 8×8 multiplier design based on 4×2 AMMs. Inputs marked with an asterisk carry 0s.

c divide both k and l, one can organize the $kl/(bc)$ AMMs as a $(k/b) \times (l/c)$ or a $(k/c) \times (l/b)$ array. This provides some flexibility in fitting the design to the available chip area. However, the choice may have nontrivial implications for speed.

12.3 BIT-SERIAL MULTIPLIERS

Bit-serial arithmetic is attractive in view of its smaller pin count, reduced wire length, and lower floor space requirements in VLSI. In fact, the compactness of the design may allow us to run a bit-serial multiplier at a clock rate high enough to make the unit almost competitive with much more complex designs with regard to speed. In addition, in certain application contexts inputs are supplied bit-serially anyway. In such a case, using a parallel multiplier would be quite wasteful, since the parallelism may not lead to any speed benefit. Furthermore, in applications that call for a large number of independent multiplications, multiple bit-serial multipliers may be more cost-effective than a complex highly pipelined unit.

Bit-serial multipliers can be designed as systolic arrays: synchronous arrays of processing elements that are interconnected by only short, local wires thus allowing very high clock rates. Let us begin by introducing a semisystolic multiplier, so named because its design involves broadcasting a single bit of the multiplier x to a number of circuit elements, thus violating the "short, local wires" requirement of pure systolic design [Kung82].

Figure 12.7 shows a semisystolic 4×4 multiplier. The multiplicand a is supplied in parallel from above and the multiplier x is supplied bit-serially from the right, with its least significant bit arriving first. Each bit x_i of the multiplier is multiplied by a and the result added to the cumulative partial product, kept in carry-save form in the carry and sum latches. The carry bit stays in its current position, while the sum bit is passed on to the neighboring cell on the

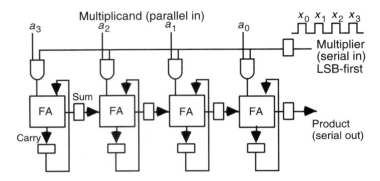

Fig. 12.7   Semisystolic circuit for 4×4 multiplication in eight clock cycles.

right. This corresponds to shifting the partial product to the right before the next addition step (normally the sum bit would stay put and the carry bit would be shifted to the left). Bits of the result emerge serially from the right as they become available.

A k-bit unsigned multiplier x must be padded with k zeros to allow the carries to propagate to the output, yielding the correct $2k$-bit product. Thus, the semisystolic multiplier of Fig. 12.7 can perform one $k \times k$ unsigned integer multiplication every $2k$ clock cycles. If k-bit fractions need to be multiplied, the first k output bits are discarded or used to properly round the most significant k bits.

To make the multiplier of Fig. 12.7 fully systolic, we must remove the broadcasting of the multiplier bits. This can be accomplished by a process known as systolic retiming, which is briefly explained below.

Consider a synchronous (clocked) circuit, with each line between two functional parts having an integral number of unit delays (possibly 0). Then, if we cut the circuit into two parts c_L and c_R, we can delay (advance) all the signals going in one direction and advance (delay) the ones going in the opposite direction by the same amount without affecting the correct functioning or external timing relations of the circuit. Of course, the primary inputs and outputs to the two parts c_L and c_R must be correspondingly advanced or delayed, too (see Fig. 12.8).

For the retiming shown in Fig. 12.8 to be possible, all the signals that are advanced by d must have had original delays of d or more (negative delays are not allowed). Note that all the

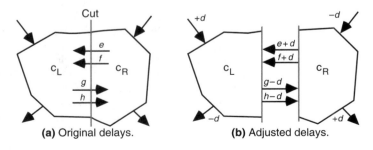

Fig. 12.8   Example of retiming by delaying the inputs to c_L and advancing the outputs from c_L by d units.

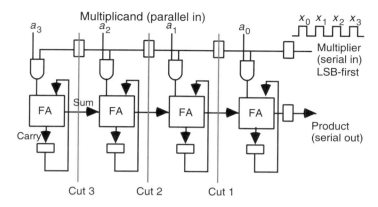

Fig. 12.9 A retimed version of our semisystolic multiplier.

signals going into c_L have been delayed by d time units. Thus, c_L will work as before, except that everything, including output production, occurs d time units later than before retiming. Advancing the outputs by d time units will keep the external view of the circuit unchanged.

We apply the preceding process to the multiplier circuit of Fig. 12.7 in three successive steps corresponding to cuts 1, 2, and 3 in Fig. 12.9, each time delaying the left-moving signal by one unit and advancing the right-moving signal by one unit. Verifying that the multiplier in Fig. 12.9 works correctly is left as an exercise. This new version of our multiplier does not have the fan-out problem of the design in Fig. 12.7 but it suffers from long signal propagation delay through the four FAs in each clock cycle, leading to inferior operating speed. Note that the culprits are zero-delay lines that lead to signal propagation through multiple circuit elements.

One way of avoiding zero-delay lines in our design is to begin by doubling all the delays in Fig. 12.7. This is done by simply replacing each of the sum and carry flip-flops with two cascaded flip-flops before retiming is applied. Since the circuit is now operating at half its original speed, the multiplier x must also be applied on alternate clock cycles. The resulting design in Fig. 12.10 is fully systolic, inasmuch as signals move only between adjacent cells in each clock cycle. However, twice as many cycles are needed.

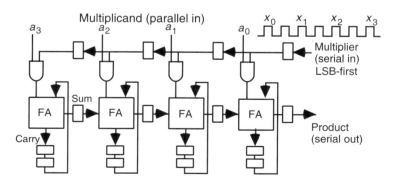

Fig. 12.10 Systolic circuit for 4×4 multiplication in 15 cycles.

The easiest way to derive a multiplier with both inputs entering bit-serially is to allow k clock ticks for the multiplicand bits to be put into place in a shift register and then use the design of Fig. 12.7 (or its fully systolic counterpart in Fig. 12.10) to compute the product. This increases the total delay by k cycles.

An alternative bit-serial input/output design is obtained by writing the relationship between the output and inputs in the form of a recurrence and then implementing it in hardware. Let $a^{(i)}$ and $x^{(i)}$ denote the values of a and x up to bit position i ($a^{(0)} = a_0$, $a^{(1)} = (a_1 a_0)_{\text{two}}$, etc.). Assume that the k-bit, 2's-complement inputs are sign-extended to $2k$ bits. Define the partial product $p^{(i)}$ as follows:

$$p^{(i)} = 2^{-(i+1)} a^{(i)} x^{(i)}$$

Then, given that $a^{(i)} = 2^i a_i + a^{(i-1)}$ and $x^{(i)} = 2^i x_i + x^{(i-1)}$, we have:

$$2p^{(i)} = 2^{-i}(2^i a_i + a^{(i-1)})(2^i x_i + x^{(i-1)})$$
$$= p^{(i-1)} + a_i x^{(i-1)} + x_i a^{(i-1)} + 2^i a_i x_i$$

Thus, if $p^{(i-1)}$ is stored in double-carry-save form (three rows of dots in dot notation, as opposed to two for ordinary carry-save), it can be combined with the terms $a_i x^{(i-1)}$ and $x_i a^{(i-1)}$ using a (5; 3)-counter to yield a double-carry-save result for the next step. The final term $2^i a_i x_i$ has a single 1 in the ith position where all the other terms have 0s. Thus it can be handled by using a multiplexer (Fig. 12.11). In cycle i, a_i and x_i are input and stored in the ith cell (the correct timing is achieved by a "token" t, which is provided to cell 0 at time 0 and is then shifted leftward with each clock tick). The terms $a^{(i-1)}$ and $x^{(i-1)}$, which are already available in registers, are ANDed with x_i and a_i, respectively, and supplied along with the three bits of $p^{(i-1)}$ as inputs to the (5; 3)-counter. Figures 12.11 and 12.12 show the complete cell design and cell interconnection [Ienn94]. The AND gate computing $a_i x_i$ is replicated in each cell for the sake of uniformity. A single copy of this gate could be placed outside the cells, with its output broadcast to all cells.

Note that the 3-bit sum of the five inputs to the (5; 3)-counter is shifted rightward before being stored in latches by connecting its LSB to the right neighboring cell, keeping its middle

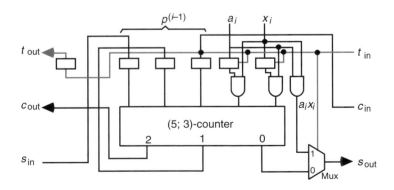

Fig. 12.11   Building block for a latency-free, bit-serial multiplier.

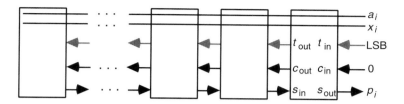

Fig. 12.12   The cellular structure of the bit-serial multiplier based on the cell in Fig. 12.11.

bit in place, and shifting its MSB to the left. The product becomes available bit-serially at the s_{out} output of the rightmost cell. Only $k - 1$ such cells are needed to compute the full $2k$-bit product of two k-bit numbers. The reason is that the largest intermediate partial product is $2k - 1$ bits wide, but by the time we get to this partial product, k bits of the product have already been produced and shifted out.

Figure 12.13 uses dot notation to show the justification for the bit-serial multiplier design above. Figure 12.13a depicts the meanings of the various partial operands and results, while Fig. 12.13b represents the operation of the (5; 3)-counters. Note, in particular, how the dot representing $a_i x_i$ is transferred to the s_{out} output by the cell holding the token (refer to the lower right corner of Fig. 12.11).

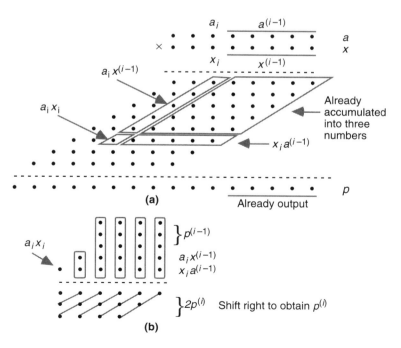

Fig. 12.13   Bit-serial multiplier design in dot notation.

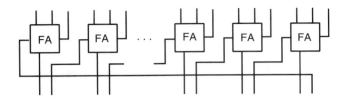

Fig. 12.14   Modulo-$(2^b - 1)$ carry-save adder.

12.4 MODULAR MULTIPLIERS

A modular multiplier is one that produces the product of two (unsigned) integers modulo some fixed constant m. It is useful, for example, for implementing the multiplication operation for residue number systems. A modular multiplier could be implemented by attaching a modular reduction circuit to the output of a standard binary multiplier. However, simpler designs are often possible if the modular reduction is combined with the accumulation of partial products. In particular, this approach obviates the need for keeping longer intermediate values.

The two special cases of $m = 2^b$ and $m = 2^b - 1$ are, as usual, simpler to deal with. For example, if the partial products are accumulated through carry-save addition, then for $m = 2^b$, the modular version simply ignores the carry output of the full adder in position $b - 1$ and for $m = 2^b - 1$, the carry out of position $b - 1$ is combined with bits in column 0 (Fig. 12.14).

As an example, consider the design of a modulo-15 multiplier for 4-bit operands. Since $16 = 1 \bmod 15$, the six heavy dots in the dotted triangle in the upper left corner of Fig. 12.15 can be moved as shown, leading to the square partial products matrix on the lower left. The four 4-bit values can then be reduced by two levels of CSA (with wraparound links, as in Fig. 12.14) followed by a 4-bit adder (again with end-around carry). We see that this particular modular multiplier is in fact simpler than a standard 4×4 binary multiplier.

Similar techniques can be used to handle modular multiplication in the general case. For example, a modulo-13 multiplier can be designed by using the identities $16 = 3 \bmod 13$, $32 = 6 \bmod 13$, and $64 = 12 \bmod 13$. Each dot inside the triangle in Fig. 12.15 must now be replaced with two dots in the four lower-order columns (Fig. 12.16). Thus, some complexity is added

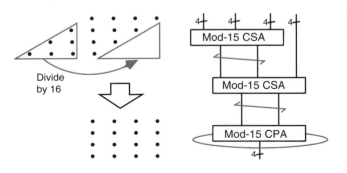

Fig. 12.15   Design of a 4×4 modulo-15 multiplier.

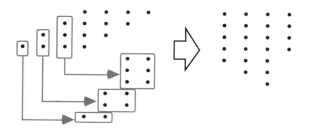

Fig. 12.16   One way to design of a 4 × 4 modulo-13 multiplier.

in view of the larger number of dots to be reduced and the need for the final adjustment of the result to be in [0, 12].

To complete the design of our 4 × 4 modulo-13 multiplier, the values shown on the right-hand side of Fig. 12.16 must be added modulo 13. After a minor simplification, consisting of removing one dot from column 1 and replacing it with two dots in column 0, a variety of methods can be used for the required modular multioperand addition [Pies94].

For example, one can use a CSA tree in which carries into column 4 are reinserted into columns 0 and 1. However, this scheme will not work toward the end of the process and must thus be supplemented with a different modular reduction scheme. Another approach is to keep some of the bits emerging from the left end (e.g., those that cannot be accommodated in the dot matrix without increasing its height) and reduce them modulo 13 by means of a lookup table or specially designed logic circuit. Supplying the details is left as an exercise. Figure 12.17 shows a general method for converting an n-input modulo-m addition problem to a three-input problem.

12.5 THE SPECIAL CASE OF SQUARING

Any standard or modular multiplier can be used for computing $p = x^2$ if both its inputs are connected to x. However, a special-purpose k-bit squarer, if built in hardware, will be significantly lower in cost and delay than a $k \times k$ multiplier.

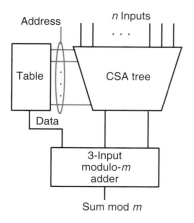

Fig. 12.17   A general method for modular multioperand addition.

To see why, consider the problem of squaring a 5-bit unsigned binary integer $(x_4x_3x_2x_1x_0)_{two}$. As shown in Fig. 12.18a, the partial products matrix can be considerably simplified before performing multioperand addition. A term $x_i x_i$ reduces to x_i and a pair of terms $x_i x_j$ and $x_j x_i$ in any given column can be replaced by $x_i x_j$ in the next higher column. The resulting simplified partial products matrix for our 5-bit example is shown in Fig. 12.18b. We see that the two least significant bits of the square are obtained with no effort and that computing the remaining bits involves a three-operand addition as opposed to a five-operand addition needed for 5×5 multiplication.

Further simplifications and fine-tuning are often possible. For example, based on the identities

$$
\begin{aligned}
x_1 x_0 + x_1 &= 2x_1 x_0 + x_1 - x_1 x_0 \\
&= 2x_1 x_0 + x_1(1 - x_0) \\
&= 2x_1 x_0 + x_1 \overline{x}_0
\end{aligned}
$$

we can remove the two terms $x_1 x_0$ and x_1 from column 2, replacing them by $x_1 \overline{x}_0$ in column 2 and $x_1 x_0$ in column 3. This transformation reduces the width of the final carry-propagate adder from 7 to 6 bits. Similar substitutions can be made for the terms in columns 4 and 6, but they do not lead to any simplification or speedup in this particular example.

For a short word width k, the square of a k-bit number can be easily obtained from a $2^k \times (2k - 2)$ lookup table, whereas a much larger table would be needed for multiplying two k-bit numbers. In fact, two numbers can be multiplied based on two table-lookup evaluations of the square function, and three additions, using the identity $ax = [(a + x)^2 - (a - x)^2]/4$.

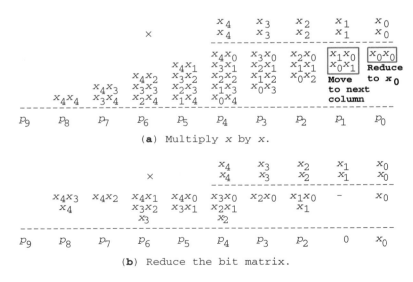

Fig. 12.18   Design of a 5-bit squarer.

Chapter 24 contains a comprehensive discussion of table-lookup methods for performing, or facilitating, arithmetic computations.

Finally, exponentiation can be performed by a sequence of squaring or square-multiply steps. For example, based on the identity

$$x^{13} = x((x(x^2))^2)^2$$

we can compute x^{13} by squaring x, multiplying the result by x, squaring twice, and finally multiplying the result by x. We discuss exponentiation for both real and integer operands in greater detail in Section 23.3.

12.6 COMBINED MULTIPLY-ADD UNITS

In certain computations, such as vector inner-product, convolution, or fast Fourier transform, multiplications are commonly followed by additions. In such cases, implementing a multiply-add unit in hardware to compute $p = ax + y$ might be cost-effective. Since the preceding computations are commonplace in signal processing applications, most modern digital signal processors (DSPs) have built-in hardware capability for multiply-add, or multiply-accumulate, operations. An example of this capability in DSP chips is presented in the last chapter (see Section 28.4).

We have already discussed additive multiply modules (Section 12.2) that add one or two numbers to the product of their multiplicative inputs. Similarly, at several points in this and the preceding three chapters we have hinted at a means of incorporating an additive input into the multiplication process (e.g., by initializing the cumulative partial product to a nonzero value or by entering a nonzero value to the top row of an array multiplier). In all cases, however, the additive inputs are comparable in width to the multiplicative inputs.

The type of multiply-add operation of interest to us here involves an additive input that is significantly wider than the multiplicative inputs (perhaps even wider than their product). For example, we might have 24-bit multiplicative inputs, yielding a 48-bit product, that is then added to a 64-bit running sum. The wider running sum may be required to avoid overflow in the intermediate computation steps or to provide greater precision to counter the accumulation of errors.

Figure 12.19 depicts several methods for incorporating a wide additive input into the multiplication process. First, we might use a CSA tree to find the product of the multiplicative inputs in carry-save form and then add the result to the additive input using a CSA followed by a fast adder (Fig. 12.19a). To avoid a carry-propagate addition in every step, the running sum may itself be kept in carry-save form, leading to the requirement for two CSA levels (Fig. 12.19b). The resulting hardware implementation for this latter scheme is quite similar to the partial-tree multiplier of Fig. 11.9.

Alternatively, the two-step process of computing the product in carry-save form and adding it to the running sum can be replaced by a merged multiply-add operation that directly operates on the dots from the additive input(s) and the partial products dot matrix (Figs. 12.19c and 12.19d). We will revisit this notion of merged arithmetic in Section 23.6.

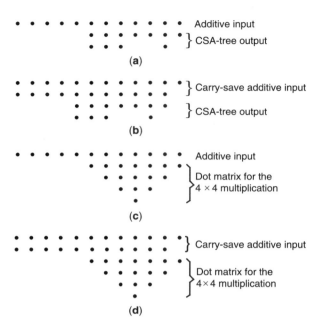

Fig. 12.19   Dot notation representations of various methods for performing a multiply-add operation in hardware.

12.1   **Multipliers built of smaller modules**

    a.   Draw a schematic diagram of the 16×4 multiplier for unsigned numbers using only 4×4 multipliers and 4-bit adders.

    b.   Using dot notation, show an implementation for summing the four partial products of part a using only 4-bit CSA modules and 4-bit carry-propagate adders.

    c.   Repeat part a with the 16-bit number in 2's-complement format.

    d.   Repeat part b for the multiplier of part c.

12.2   **Multipliers built of smaller modules**   Consider Fig. 12.2 depicting the construction of $gb \times gb$ multipliers from $b \times b$ units.

    a.   Express the height of the partial products matrix of Fig. 12.2 as a function of g.

    b.   Generalize the result of part a to $gb \times hb$ multiplier built of $b \times b$ modules.

    c.   Repeat part a for the case of $b \times c$ multipliers being used to synthesize a $gb \times gc$ multiplier.

    d.   Generalize the result of part c to $gb \times hc$ multiplier synthesized from $b \times c$ units.

12.3   **Multipliers built of AMMs**   Compare the 8×8 multiplier designs in Figs. 12.5 and 12.6 with respect to speed, assuming the following implementations for the 2×4 AMM of Fig. 12.4.

    a.   Four-bit CSA followed by 4-bit ripple-carry adder.

    b.   Four-bit CSA followed by 4-bit carry-lookahead adder.

12.4   **Multipliers built of AMMs**

a.   Design a 2×2 AMM, with two 2-bit additive inputs, using only four single-bit full adders and four AND gates.

b.   Show how to connect four AMMs of part a to form a 4×4 unsigned multiplier.

c.   Estimate the delay of the 4×4 multiplier of part b, in units of FA delay, by drawing and justifying the critical path on the circuit diagram.

d.   Can one use the multiplier of part b as a 4×4 AMM? How or why not?

12.5   **Building larger AMMs**

a.   We have an unlimited supply of 2×4 AMMs of the type depicted in Fig. 12.4. Using a minimal number of these AMMs, and no other component, synthesize a 4×4 AMM (with two 4-bit additive inputs).

b.   Repeat part a for a 2×8 AMM (additive inputs are 2 and 8 bits wide).

c.   Repeat part a for a 6×6 AMM (additive inputs are both 6 bits wide).

d.   Repeat part a for a 4×8 AMM (additive inputs are 4 and 8 bits wide).

e.   Build the 4×8 AMM of part d using two of the 4×4 AMMs designed in part a.

f.   Compare the designs of parts d and e with respect to speed and cost.

12.6   **Multipliers built of AMMs**

a.   Design a 16×8 multiplier using 4×2 AMMs arranged in a 4×4 array.

b.   Repeat part a, this time arranging the modules in an 8×2 array.

c.   Compare the designs of parts a and b with respect to speed.

d.   Convert the designs of parts a and b into 16×8 AMMs.

12.7   **AMMs for 2's-complement multiplication**

a.   Design a 2×4 AMM, similar to that in Fig. 12.4, but with the following changes. The x input is internally recoded using the digit set $[-2, 2]$, so a third x bit, x_{-1}, is needed as context and a fifth a input, a_{-1}, in case of left shifting. The 2-bit additive input is replaced by a 1-bit input c_i and a 1-bit output c_{i+4} that completes the 5-bit sum of the two 4-bit values. A 6-bit result is needed at the most significant end, so the AMM should also produce the two most significant bits of the result, to be used in lieu of c_{i+4} when needed.

b.   Build a 4×4 2's-complement multiplier using the AMMs of part a.

c.   Repeat part b for an 8×8 2's-complement multiplier.

12.8   **Systolic multipliers**

a.   Present an argument for the correctness of the systolic multiplier in Fig. 12.10.

b.   Trace the steps of the unsigned binary multiplication $(1101)_{two} \times (0101)_{two}$ to verify your conclusion in part a.

c.   Propose a cell design such that the multiplicand is stored internally and can be modified when needed (this is useful when the multiplicand is a coefficient that seldom changes). There are two operation modes. In "load" mode, the serial input pin is used to shift the multiplicand into internal latches (LSB-first). In "multiply" mode, the multiplier is supplied as input and the product emerges as output.

12.9   Systolic multipliers   A fully bit-serial $k \times k$ systolic multiplier can be designed on the basis of a linear array of $2k$ cells, numbered 0 through $2k - 1$ from right to left, which at the end will hold the $2k$-bit product. The multiplier x is input from the left on even-numbered clock ticks, with x_i arriving at time $2i$. The multiplicand a is input from the right, MSB first, on odd numbered clock ticks, with a_j input at time $2k - 2j + 1$.

    a.   Show that x_i and a_j meet at cell h if and only if $i + j = h$.

    b.   Use the result of part a to derive a suitable cell design and intercell connections.

12.10   Modular multipliers   Discuss the design of modulo-$(2^b + 1)$ multipliers using a suitable $(b + 1)$-bit encoding of the inputs and intermediate results. *Hint:* Consider using one bit to represent 0 and reducing all nonzero values by 1 for representation with the remaining b bits.

12.11   Modular multipliers

    a.   Present a complete design for the modulo-13 multiplier discussed at the end of Section 12.4.

    b.   Compare the design of part a to a standard 4×4 multiplier with respect to speed and cost.

    c.   Design a 5×5 modulo-29 multiplier. *Hint:* Work with partial results in $[0, 31]$ rather than $[0, 28]$. When a partial result exceeds 31, subtract 29 from it by discarding the carry-out (worth 32 units) and adding 3. Thus, a wraparound connection similar to that in Fig. 12.14 must be established from the carry-out to the two least significant positions. The final sum in $[0, 31]$ may need adjustment.

12.12   Modular squarers

    a.   Simplify the reduced partial products matrix of Fig. 12.18 to the extent possible if the square of the 5-bit number x is to be obtained modulo 31.

    b.   Repeat part a for modulo-29 squaring of a 5-bit number.

    c.   Discuss how modular multiplication $ax \bmod m$ can be performed based on modular squaring tables that hold $z^2 \bmod m$.

12.13   Design of squarers

    a.   Show that a 4-bit unsigned squarer can be designed using only two-input AND gates, one full-adder, and a 5-bit binary adder.

    b.   Using the identity $x_1 x_0 + x_1 = 2x_1 x_0 + x_1 \overline{x}_0$, as discussed near the end of Section 12.5, reduce the complexity of the 4-bit squarer of part a to a 4-bit adder plus a few logic gates.

    c.   Design a circuit to compute the square of a 4-bit 2's-complement input integer. *Hint:* Use the identity $-x_j x_i = -2x_j + x_j \overline{x}_i + x_j$ and note that the final product is representable in only 7 bits.

12.14   Bit-serial squarers   Present a simplified version of the bit-serial multiplier design in Fig. 12.11 for squaring a number x [Ienn94]. *Hint:* The two terms $a_i x^{(i-1)}$ and $x_i a^{(i-1)}$

are the same. So a single value needs to be added to the accumulated result. Because of this, the accumulated result can be kept in carry-save form, rather than as three numbers, allowing the use of a (3; 2)-counter.

12.15 Bit-serial inner-product computation Consider replacing the (5; 3)-counter in Fig. 12.11 by a (7; 3)-counter and using the two extra inputs to accommodate serial inputs b and y, so that the value of $ax + by$ is computed bit-serially [Hayn96].

    a. How should the part of the circuit producing s_{out} be modified?

    b. Show that the resulting cells can in fact be used to compute $ax + by + z$.

12.16 Multiplication of complex numbers The quater-imaginary number system of Example 1.7 in Section 1.4 can be easily generalized to radix $j\sqrt{r}$ and digit set $[0, r-1]$. Show that any complex number is representable in such a number system and discuss whether this representation leads to faster multiplication for complex numbers.

12.17 Multipliers with narrower products Our discussions in Chapters 9–12 were based on the assumption that in multiplying two k-bit operands, the full $2k$-bit product must be produced.

    a. Present a thorough discussion of how the various multiplier designs are affected if the k-bit product of two k-bit integers, plus an overflow indication, are sufficient.

    b. Repeat part a, assuming that the input operands are k-bit fractions yielding a k-bit product by truncating all bits of p beyond p_{-k}.

12.18 Fractional precision multiplication

    a. Consider a 6×6 multiplier that uses a Wallace tree to reduce the six partial products to two numbers and then adds them in a fast adder to obtain the product. Suggest modifications in the design such that under the control of a "fractional precision" signal, the multiplier acts as two independent 3×3 multipliers operating on the low and high halves of the 6-bit inputs.

    b. Repeat part a, this time assuming that the 6×6 multiplier is built of 3×3 AMMs.

    c. Compare the incremental cost of adding the fractional precision arithmetic capability to the multipliers of parts a and b and discuss.

    d. Many modern microprocessors have a capability for fractional precision arithmetic that allows them to handle multimedia data efficiently. How would you go about designing a 32×32 multiplier so that it can also view its 32-bit inputs as two pairs of 16-bit values or four pairs of 8-bit values?

REFERENCES

[Alia91] Alia, G., and E. Martinelli, "A VLSI Modulo m Multiplier," *IEEE Trans. Computers*, Vol. 40, No. 7, pp. 873–878, 1991.

[Chen79] Chen, I.-N., and R. Willowner, "An O(n) Parallel Multiplier with Bit-Sequential Input and Output," *IEEE Trans. Computers*, Vol. 28, No. 10, pp. 721–727, 1979.

[Ghes71] Ghest, C., "Multiplying Made Easy for Digital Assemblies," *Electronics*, Vol. 44, pp. 56–61, November 22, 1971.

[Hayn96]   Haynal, S., and B. Parhami, "Arithmetic Structures for Inner-Product and Other Computations Based on a Latency-Free Bit-Serial Multiplier Design," *Proc. 30th Asilomar Conf. Signals, Systems, and Computers*, November 1996.

[Hwan79]   Hwang, K., *Computer Arithmetic: Principles, Architecture, and Design*, Wiley, 1979.

[Ienn94]   Ienne, P., and M. A. Viredaz, "Bit-Serial Multipliers and Squarers," *IEEE Trans. Computers*, Vol. 43, No. 12, pp. 1445–1450, 1994.

[Kung82]   Kung, H. T., "Why Systolic Architectures?" *Computer*, Vol. 15, No. 1, pp. 37–46, 1982.

[Parh93]   Parhami, B., and H.-F. Lai, "Alternate Memory Compression Schemes for Modular Multiplication," *IEEE Trans. Signal Processing*, Vol. 41, No. 3, pp. 1378–1385, 1993.

[Pies94]   Piestrak, S. J., "Design of Residue Generators and Multioperand Modular Adders Using Carry-Save Adders," *IEEE Trans. Computers*, Vol. 43, No. 1, pp. 68–77, 1994.

PART IV | DIVISION

Division is the most complex of the four basic arithmetic operations and the hardest one to speed up. Thus, dividers are more expensive and/or slower than multipliers. Fortunately, division operations are also less common than multiplications. Two classes of dividers are discussed here. In digit-recurrence schemes, the quotient is generated one digit at a time, beginning at the most significant end. Binary versions of digit-recurrence division can be implemented through shifting and addition, in much the same way as shift/add multiplication schemes. Determining the digits of the quotient from the most significant end allows us to "converge" to a k-digit quotient in k cycles. Speeding up of division via reducing the number of shift/add cycles leads to high-radix dividers. Array dividers as well as convergence methods that require far fewer than k iterations, with each iteration being more complex, are also discussed. This part is composed of the following four chapters:

Chapter
13 | BASIC DIVISION SCHEMES

Like sequential multiplication of k-bit operands, yielding a $2k$-bit product, the division of a $2k$-bit dividend by a k-bit divisor can be realized in k cycles of shifting and adding (actually subtracting), with hardware, firmware, or software control of the loop. In this chapter, we review such economical, but slow, bit-at-a-time designs and set the stage for speedup methods and variations to be presented in Chapters 14–16. We also consider the special case of division by a constant. Chapter topics include:

13.1 Shift/Subtract Division Algorithms
13.2 Programmed Division
13.3 Restoring Hardware Dividers
13.4 Nonrestoring and Signed Division
13.5 Division by Constants
13.6 Preview of Fast Dividers

13.1 SHIFT/SUBTRACT DIVISION ALGORITHMS

The following notation is used in our discussion of division algorithms:

z	Dividend	$z_{2k-1}z_{2k-2}\cdots z_1 z_0$
d	Divisor	$d_{k-1}d_{k-2}\cdots d_1 d_0$
q	Quotient	$q_{k-1}q_{k-2}\cdots q_1 q_0$
s	Remainder $[z-(d\times q)]$	$s_{k-1}s_{k-2}\cdots s_1 s_0$

The expression $z-(d\times q)$ for the remainder s is derived from the basic division equation $z=(d\times q)+s$. This equation, along with the condition $s<d$, completely defines unsigned integer division.

Figure 13.1 shows a $2k$-bit by k-bit unsigned integer division in dot notation. The dividend z and divisor d are shown near the top. Each of the following four rows of dots corresponds to the product of the divisor d and one bit of the quotient q, with each dot representing the product

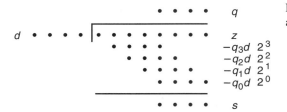

Fig. 13.1 Division of an 8-bit number by a 4-bit number in dot notation.

(logical AND) of two bits. Since q_{k-j} is in $\{0, 1\}$, each term $q_{k-j}d$ is either 0 or d. Thus, the problem of binary division reduces to subtracting a set of numbers, each being 0 or a shifted version of the divisor d, from the dividend z.

Figure 13.1 also applies to nonbinary division, except that with $r > 2$, both the selection of the next quotient digit q_{k-j} and the computation of the terms $q_{k-j}d$ become more difficult and the resulting products are one digit wider than d. The rest of the process, however, remains substantially the same.

Just as sequential multiplication was done by repeated additions, sequential division is performed by repeated subtractions. The partial remainder is initialized to $s^{(0)} = z$. In step j, the next quotient digit q_{k-j} is selected. Then, the product $q_{k-j}d$ (which is either 0 or d) is shifted and the result subtracted from the partial remainder. So, compared to multiplication, division has the added complication of requiring quotient digit selection or estimation.

Another aspect of division that is different from multiplication is that whereas the product of two k-bit numbers is always representable in $2k$ bits, the quotient of a $2k$-bit number divided by a k-bit number may have a width of more than k bits. Thus, an overflow check is needed before division algorithm is applied. Since, for unsigned division, we have $q < 2^k$ and $s < d$, to avoid overflow, we must have:

$$z < (2^k - 1)d + d = 2^k d$$

Hence, the high-order k bits of z must be strictly less than d. Note that this overflow check also detects the divide-by-0 condition.

Fractional division can be reformulated as integer division, and vice versa. In an integer division characterized by $z = (d \times q) + s$, we multiply both sides by 2^{-2k}:

$$2^{-2k}z = \left[(2^{-k}d) \times (2^{-k}q)\right] + 2^{-2k}s$$

Now, letting the $2k$-bit and k-bit inputs be fractions, we see that their fractional values are related by:

$$z_{\text{frac}} = (d_{\text{frac}} \times q_{\text{frac}}) + 2^{-k}s_{\text{frac}}$$

Therefore, we can divide fractions just as we divide integers, except that the final remainder must be shifted to the right by k bits. In effect, this means that k zeros are to be inserted after the radix point to make the k-bit (fractional) remainder into a $2k$-bit fractional number with k leading 0s. This makes sense because when we divide z_{frac} by a number d_{frac} that is less than 1, the remainder should be less than ulp in the quotient (otherwise, the quotient could be increased without the remainder going negative). The condition for no overflow in this case is $z_{\text{frac}} < d_{\text{frac}}$, which is checked in exactly the same way as for integer division.

Sequential or bit-at-a-time division can be performed by keeping a partial remainder, initialized to $s^{(0)} = z$, and successively subtracting from it the properly shifted terms $q_{k-j}d$ (Fig. 13.1). Since each successive number to be subtracted from the partial remainder is shifted by one bit with respect to the preceding one, a simpler approach is to shift the partial remainder by one bit, to align its bits with those of the next term to be subtracted. This leads to the well-known sequential division algorithm with left shifts:

$$s^{(j)} = 2s^{(j-1)} - q_{k-j}(2^k d) \quad \text{with} \quad s^{(0)} = z \quad \text{and} \quad s^{(k)} = 2^k s$$
$$\underset{\begin{vmatrix} \text{shift} \\ \text{left} \end{vmatrix}}{}$$
$$|\!\!-\!\!-\!\!- \text{subtract} -\!\!-\!\!-\!|$$

The factor 2^k by which d is premultiplied ensures proper alignment of the values. After k iterations, the preceding recurrence leads to:

$$s^{(k)} = 2^k s^{(0)} - q(2^k d) = 2^k[z - (q \times d)] = 2^k s$$

The fractional version of the division recurrence is:

$$s_{\text{frac}}^{(j)} = 2s_{\text{frac}}^{(j-1)} - q_{-j}d_{\text{frac}} \quad \text{with} \quad s_{\text{frac}}^{(0)} = z_{\text{frac}} \quad \text{and} \quad s_{\text{frac}}^{(k)} = 2^k s_{\text{frac}}$$

Note that unlike multiplication, where the partial products can be produced and processed from top to bottom or bottom to top, in the case of division, the terms to be subtracted from the initial partial remainder must be produced from top to bottom. The reason is that the quotient bits become known sequentially, beginning with the most significant one, whereas in multiplication all the multiplier bits are known at the outset. This is why we do not have a division algorithm with right shifts (corresponding to multiplication with left shifts).

The division of $z = (117)_{\text{ten}} = (0111\ 0101)_{\text{two}}$ by $d = (10)_{\text{ten}} = (1010)_{\text{two}}$ to obtain the quotient $q = (11)_{\text{ten}} = (1011)_{\text{two}}$ and the remainder $s = (7)_{\text{ten}} = (0111)_{\text{two}}$ is depicted on the left-hand side of Fig. 13.2. Figure 13.2 (right) shows the fractional version of the same division, with the operands $z = (117/256)_{\text{ten}} = (.0111\ 0101)_{\text{two}}$, $d = (10/16)_{\text{ten}} = (.1010)_{\text{two}}$ and the results $q = (11/16)_{\text{ten}} = (.1011)_{\text{two}}$, $s = (7/256)_{\text{ten}} = (.0000\ 0111)_{\text{two}}$.

In practice, the required subtraction is performed by adding the 2's complement of $2^k d$ or d to the partial remainder (more on this later). Note that there are but two choices for the value of the next quotient digit q_{k-j} or q_{-j} in radix 2, with the value 1 selected whenever the shifted partial remainder $2s^{(j-1)}$ is greater than $2^k d$ or d. Sections 13.3 and 14.4 contain more detailed discussions on quotient digit selection.

13.2 PROGRAMMED DIVISION

On a processor that does not have a divide instruction, one can use shift and add instructions to perform integer division. Since one quotient digit is produced after each left shift of the partial remainder, we need only two k-bit registers to store the partial remainder and the quotient: Rz for the most significant k bits of the partial remainder, and Rq for the rest of the partial remainder plus the partial quotient produced thus far (Fig. 13.3). In each cycle, the double-width register Rz|Rq is shifted left and the new quotient digit is inserted in the just-vacated LSB of Rq. This insertion is accomplished by incrementing Rq by 1 if the next quotient digit is 1.

```
Integer division                        Fractional division
=====================================   =====================================
z       0 1 1 1  0 1 0 1                 z_frac    . 0 1 1 1  0 1 0 1
2⁴d     1 0 1 0                          d_frac    . 1 0 1 0
=====================================   =====================================
s⁽⁰⁾      0 1 1 1  0 1 0 1              s⁽⁰⁾      . 0 1 1 1  0 1 0 1
2s⁽⁰⁾   0 1 1 1 0  1 0 1                2s⁽⁰⁾    0 . 1 1 1 0  1 0 1
-q₃2⁴d    1 0 1 0  {q₃ = 1}            -q₋₁d      . 1 0 1 0  {q₋₁ = 1}

s⁽¹⁾      0 1 0 0  1 0 1                s⁽¹⁾      . 0 1 0 0  1 0 1
2s⁽¹⁾   0 1 0 0 1  0 1                  2s⁽¹⁾    0 . 1 0 0 1  0 1
-q₂2⁴d    0 0 0 0  {q₂ = 0}            -q₋₂d      . 0 0 0 0  {q₋₂ = 0}

s⁽²⁾      1 0 0 1  0 1                  s⁽²⁾      . 1 0 0 1  0 1
2s⁽²⁾   1 0 0 1 0  1                    2s⁽²⁾    1 . 0 0 1 0  1
-q₁2⁴d    1 0 1 0  {q₁ = 1}            -q₋₃d      . 1 0 1 0  {q₋₃ = 1}

s⁽³⁾      1 0 0 0  1                    s⁽³⁾      . 1 0 0 0  1
2s⁽³⁾   1 0 0 0 1                       2s⁽³⁾    1 . 0 0 0 1
-q₀2⁴d    1 0 1 0  {q₀ = 1}            -q₋₄d      . 1 0 1 0  {q₋₄ = 1}

s⁽⁴⁾      0 1 1 1                       s⁽⁴⁾      . 0 1 1 1
s                  0 1 1 1              s_frac    . 0 0 0 0  0 1 1 1
q                  1 0 1 1              q_frac    . 1 0 1 1
=====================================   =====================================
```

Fig. 13.2   Examples of sequential division with integer and fractional operands.

Figure 13.4 shows the structure of the needed program for sequential division. The instructions used in this program fragment are typical of instructions available on many processors.

The subtract instruction in the program fragment of Fig. 13.4 needs some elaboration. If we reach the subtract instruction by falling through its preceding branch instruction, then Rs $\geq$ Rd, and the desired effect of leaving Rs $-$ Rd in Rs is achieved through subtraction. However, if we reach the subtract instruction from the skip instruction, then the carry flag is 1 and Rs $<$ Rd. In this case, the proper result is to leave $(2^k + \text{Rs}) - \text{Rd}$ in Rs, where 2^k represents the MSB of the shifted partial remainder held in the carry flag. But we have:

$$(2^k + \text{Rs}) - \text{Rd} = \text{Rs} + (2^k - \text{Rd})$$

$$= \text{Rs} + 2\text{'s-complement of Rd}$$

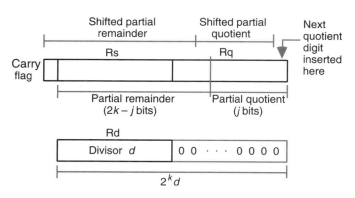

Fig. 13.3   Register usage for programmed division.

```
{Using left shifts, divide unsigned 2k-bit dividend,
z_highlz_low, storing the k-bit quotient and remainder.
Registers:    R0 holds 0              Rc for counter
              Rd for divisor          Rs for z_high & remainder
              Rq for z_low & quotient}

{Load operands into registers Rd, Rs, and Rq}

      div:    load      Rd with divisor
              load      Rs with z_high
              load      Rq with z_low

{Check for exceptions}

              branch    d_by_0 if Rd = R0
              branch    d_ovfl if Rs > Rd

{Initialize counter}

              load      k  into Rc

{Begin division loop}

      d_loop: shift     Rq left 1        {zero to LSB, MSB to carry}
              rotate    Rs left 1        {carry to LSB, MSB to carry}
              skip      if carry = 1
              branch    no_sub if Rs < Rd
              sub       Rd from Rs
              incr      Rq               {set quotient digit to 1}
      no_sub: decr      Rc               {decrement counter by 1}
              branch    d_loop if Rc ≠ 0

{Store the quotient and remainder}

              store     Rq into quotient
              store     Rs into remainder
      d_done: . . .
      d_by_0: . . .
      d_ovfl: . . .
```

Fig. 13.4 Programmed division using left shifts.

Thus, even though we are performing unsigned division, a 2's-complement subtract instruction produces the proper result in either case.

Ignoring operand load and result store instructions (which would be needed in any implementation), the function of a divide instruction is accomplished by executing between $6k+3$ and $8k+3$ machine instructions, depending on the operands. For 32-bit operands, this means well over 200 instructions on the average. The situation improves somewhat if a special instruction that does some or all of the required functions within the division loop is available. However, even then, no fewer than 32 instructions would be executed in the division loop. We thus see the importance of hardware dividers for applications that involve a great deal of numerical computations.

Microprogrammed processors with no hardware divider use a microroutine very similar to the program in Fig. 13.4 to perform division. For the same reasons given near the end of Section 9.2 in connection with programmed multiplication, division microroutines are significantly faster than their machine-language counterparts, though still slower than the hardwired implementations we examine next.

13.3 RESTORING HARDWARE DIVIDERS

Figure 13.5 shows a hardware realization of the sequential division algorithm for unsigned integers. At the start of each cycle j, the partial remainder $s^{(j-1)}$ is shifted to the left, with its MSB moving into a special flip-flop. Then the trial difference $2s^{(j-1)} - q_{k-j}(2^k d)$ is computed. Because of the 2^k factor in the preceding expression, the divisor is aligned with the upper k bits of the partial remainder for the trial subtraction and the lower part of the partial remainder is not affected.

As stated in connection with programmed division in Section 13.2, the next quotient digit should be 1 if the MSB of $2s^{(j-1)}$, held in the special flip-flop, is 1 or if the trial difference is positive ($c_{out} = 1$). In either case, $q_{k-j} = 1$ becomes the shift input for the quotient register and also causes the trial difference to be loaded into the upper half of the partial remainder register to form the new partial remainder for the next cycle. Otherwise, $q_{k-j} = 0$, and the partial remainder does not change.

We refer to the division scheme of Fig. 13.5 as restoring division. The quotient digit in radix 2 is in {0, 1}. The trial subtraction corresponds to assuming $q_{k-j} = 1$. If the trial difference is positive, then the next quotient digit is indeed 1. Otherwise, $q_{k-j} = 1$ is too large and the quotient digit must be 0. The term "restoring division" means that the remainder is restored to its correct value if the trial subtraction indicates that 1 was not the right choice for q_{k-j}. Note that we could have chosen to load the trial difference in the partial remainder register in all cases, restoring the remainder to its correct value by a compensating addition step when needed. However, this would have led to slower hardware.

Just as the multiplier could be stored in the lower half of the partial product register (Fig. 9.4), the quotient and the lower part of the partial remainder can share the same space, since quotient bits are derived as bits of the partial remainder move left, freeing the required space for them. Excluding the control logic, the hardware requirements of multiplication and division are quite similar, so the two algorithms can share much hardware components (compare Figs. 9.4 and 13.5).

As a numerical example, we use the restoring algorithm to redo the integer division given in Fig. 13.2. The result is shown in Fig. 13.6; note the restoration step corresponding

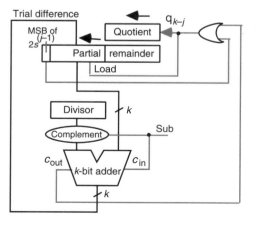

Fig. 13.5 Shift/subtract sequential restoring divider.

to $q_2 = 0$ and the extra bit devoted to sign in intermediate operands. A shifted partial remainder does not need an extra sign bit, since its magnitude is immediately reduced by a trial subtraction.

Thus far, we have assumed unsigned operands and results. For signed operands, the basic division equation $(d \times q) + s$, along with

$$\text{sign}(s) = \text{sign}(z) \quad \text{and} \quad |s| < |d|$$

uniquely define the quotient q and remainder s.

Consider the following examples of integer division with all possible combinations of signs for z and d:

$$
\begin{aligned}
z = 5 \quad & d = 3 \quad && \Rightarrow \quad q = 1 \quad && s = 2 \\
z = 5 \quad & d = -3 \quad && \Rightarrow \quad q = -1 \quad && s = 2 \\
z = -5 \quad & d = 3 \quad && \Rightarrow \quad q = -1 \quad && s = -2 \\
z = -5 \quad & d = -3 \quad && \Rightarrow \quad q = 1 \quad && s = -2
\end{aligned}
$$

We see from the preceding examples that the magnitudes of q and s are unaffected by the input signs and that the signs of q and s are easily derivable from the signs of z and d. Hence, one way to do signed division is through an indirect algorithm that converts the operands into unsigned values and, at the end, accounts for the signs by adjusting the sign bits or via complementation. This is the method of choice with the restoring division algorithm.

```
===============================
z                0 1 1 1  0 1 0 1        No overflow, since:
2⁴d            0  1 0 1 0                (0111)₂wo < (1010)₂wo
-2⁴d           1  0 1 1 0
===============================
s(0)           0  0 1 1 1  0 1 0 1
2s(0)          0  1 1 1 0  1 0 1
+(-2⁴d)        1  0 1 1 0
                 ─────────────
s(1)           0  0 1 0 0  1 0 1        Positive, so set q₃ = 1
2s(1)          0  1 0 0 1  0 1
+(-2⁴d)        1  0 1 1 0
                 ─────────────
s(2)           1  1 1 1 1  0 1          Negative, so set q₂ = 0
s(2) = 2s(1)   0  1 0 0 1  0 1          and restore
2s(2)          1  0 0 1 0  1
+(-2⁴d)        1  0 1 1 0
                 ─────────────
s(3)           0  1 0 0 0  1            Positive, so set q₁ = 1
2s(3)          1  0 0 0 1
+(-2⁴d)        1  0 1 1 0
                 ─────────────
s(4)           0  0 1 1 1                Positive, so set q₀ = 1
s                         0 1 1 1
q                         1 0 1 1
===============================
```

Fig. 13.6 Example of restoring unsigned division.

13.4 NONRESTORING AND SIGNED DIVISION

Implementation of restoring division requires paying attention to the timing of various events. Each of the k cycles must be long enough to allow the following events in sequence:

Shifting of the registers.

Propagation of signals through the adder.

Storing of the quotient digit.

Thus, the sign of the trial difference must be sampled near the end of the cycle (say at the negative edge of the clock). To avoid such timing issues, which tend to lengthen the clock cycle, one can use the nonrestoring division algorithm. As before, we assume $q_{k-j} = 1$ and perform a subtraction. However, we always store the difference in the partial remainder register. This leads to the partial remainder being temporarily incorrect (hence the name "nonrestoring").

Let us see why it is acceptable to store an incorrect value in the partial remainder register. Suppose that the shifted partial remainder at the start of the cycle was u. If we had restored the partial remainder $u - 2^k d$ to its correct value u, we would proceed with the next shift and trial subtraction, getting the result $2u - 2^k d$. Instead, because we used the incorrect partial remainder, a shift and trial subtraction would yield $2(u - 2^k d) - 2^k d = 2u - (3 \times 2^k d)$, which is not the intended result. However, an addition would do the trick, resulting in $2(u - 2^k d) + 2^k d = 2u - 2^k d$, which is the same value obtained after restoration and trial subtraction. Thus, in nonrestoring division, when the partial remainder becomes negative, we keep the incorrect partial remainder, but note the correct quotient digit and also remember to add, rather than subtract, in the next cycle.

Before discussing the adaptation of nonrestoring algorithm for use with signed operands, let us use the nonrestoring algorithm to redo the example division of Fig. 13.6. The result is shown in Fig. 13.7. We still need just one extra bit for the sign of $s^{(j)}$, which doubles as a magnitude bit for $2s^{(j)}$.

Figure 13.8 depicts the relationship between restoring division and nonrestoring division for the preceding example division, namely, $(117)_{\text{ten}}/(10)_{\text{ten}}$. In each cycle, the value $2^k d = (160)_{\text{ten}}$ is added to or subtracted from the shifted partial remainder.

Recall that in restoring division, the quotient digit values of 0 and 1 corresponded to "no subtraction" (or subtraction of 0) and "subtraction of d," respectively. In nonrestoring division, we always subtract or add. Thus, it is as if the quotient digits are selected from the set $\{1, \text{-}1\}$, with 1 corresponding to subtraction and -1 to addition. Our goal is to end up with a remainder that matches the sign of the dividend (positive in unsigned division). Well, this viewpoint (of trying to match the sign of the partial remainder s with the sign of the dividend z) leads to the idea of dividing signed numbers directly. The rule for quotient digit selection becomes:

$$\text{If } \text{sign}(s) = \text{sign}(d) \text{ then } q_{k-j} = 1 \text{ else } q_{k-j} = \text{-}1$$

Two problems must be dealt with at the end:

1. The quotient with digits 1 and -1 must be converted to standard binary.
2. If the final remainder s has a sign opposite that of z, a correction step, involving the addition of $\pm d$ to the remainder and subtraction of ± 1 from the quotient, is needed (since there is no next step to compensate for the nonrestoration of the correct remainder).

Note that the correction step might be required even in unsigned division (when the final remainder is negative). We deal with the preceding two problems in turn.

```
===============================
z                0 1 1 1   0 1 0 1          No overflow, since:
2⁴d            0 1 0 1 0                      (0111)_two< (1010)_two
−2⁴d          1 0 1 1 0
===============================
s(0)             0 0 1 1 1   0 1 0 1
2s(0)          0 1 1 1 0   1 0 1          Positive,
+(−2⁴d)       1 0 1 1 0                      so subtract
              ─────────────────
s(1)             0 0 1 0 0   1 0 1
2s(1)          0 1 0 0 1   0 1          Positive, so set q₃ = 1
+(−2⁴d)       1 0 1 1 0                      and subtract
              ─────────────────
s(2)             1 1 1 1 1   0 1
2s(2)          1 1 1 1 0   1          Negative, so set q₂ = 0
+2⁴d          0 1 0 1 0                      and add
              ─────────────────
s(3)             0 1 0 0 0   1
2s(3)          1 0 0 0 1          Positive, so set q₁ = 1
+(−2⁴d)       1 0 1 1 0                      and subtract
              ─────────────────
s(4)             0 0 1 1 1          Positive, so set q₀ = 1
s                                0 1 1 1
q                                1 0 1 1
===============================
```

Fig. 13.7   Example of nonrestoring unsigned division.

To convert a k-digit BSD quotient $q = (q_{k-1}q_{k-2} \cdots q_0)_{BSD}$ with $q_i \in \{\text{-}1, 1\}$ to a k-bit, 2's-complement number, do as follows:

a. Replace all -1 digits with 0s to get the k-bit number $p = p_{k-1}p_{k-2} \cdots p_0$, with $p_i \in \{0, 1\}$. Note that the p_is and q_is are related by $q_i = 2p_i - 1$.

b. Complement p_{k-1} and then shift p left by 1 bit, inserting 1 into the LSB, to get the 2's-complement quotient $q = (\overline{p}_{k-1}p_{k-2} \cdots p_0 1)_{2's-compl}$.

The proof of correctness for the preceding conversion process is straightforward (note that we have made use of the identity $\sum_{i=0}^{k-1} 2^i = 2^k - 1$):

$$(\overline{p}_{k-1}p_{k-2} \cdots p_0 1)_{2's-compl} = -(1 - p_{k-1})2^k + 1 + \sum_{i=0}^{k-2} p_i 2^{i+1}$$

$$= -(2^k - 1) + 2\sum_{i=0}^{k-1} p_i 2^i$$

$$= \sum_{i=0}^{k-1} (2p_i - 1)2^i$$

$$= \sum_{i=0}^{k-1} q_i 2^i = q$$

From the preceding algorithm, we see that the conversion is quite simple and can be done on the fly as the digits of the quotient are obtained. If the quotient is to be representable as a k-bit,

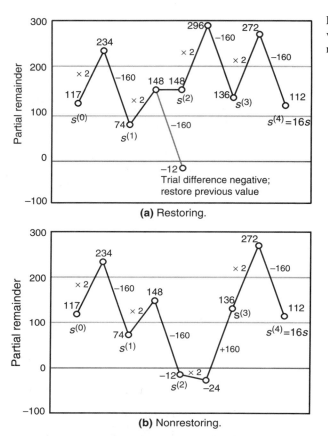

Fig. 13.8 Partial remainder variations for restoring and nonrestoring division.

2's-complement number, then we must have $\overline{p}_{k-1} = p_{k-2}$, leading to the requirement that the BSD digits q_{k-1} and q_{k-2} be different. Thus, overflow is avoided if and only if:

$$\text{sign}(z) \neq \text{sign}(s^{(1)})$$

Hence, on-the-fly conversion consists of setting the quotient sign bit in the initial cycle, producing a 1 (0) for each subtract (add) thereafter, and producing a 1 for the last digit before proceeding to the correction step.

The final correction, needed when $\text{sign}(s^{(k)}) \neq \text{sign}(z)$, is also quite simple. It involves adding/subtracting 1 to/from q and subtracting/adding $2^k d$ from/to the remainder. Note that the aim of the correction step is to change the sign of the remainder. Thus if $\text{sign}(s^{(k)}) = \text{sign}(d)$, we subtract from s and increment q; otherwise, we add to s and decrement q.

In retrospect, the need for a correction cycle is easy to see: with the digit set {-1, 1} we can represent only odd integers. So, if the quotient happens to be even, a correction is inevitable.

Figure 13.9 shows an example nonrestoring division with 2's-complement operands. The example illustrates all aspects of the nonrestoring division algorithm, including remainder correction and quotient conversion/correction. The reader is urged to examine Fig. 13.9 closely and to construct other examples for practice.

```
===============================
z              0 0 1 0  0 0 0 1      Dividend = (33)ten
2⁴d          1 1 0 0 1              Divisor = (−7)ten
−2⁴d         0 0 1 1 1
===============================
s(0)           0 0 0 1 0  0 0 0 1
2s(0)          0 0 1 0 0  0 0 1      sign(s(0)) ≠ sign(d),
+2⁴d         1 1 0 0 1              so set q3 = ⁻1 and add
             ───────────────
s(1)         1 1 1 0 1  0 0 1
2s(1)        1 1 0 1 0  0 1        sign(s(1)) = sign(d),
+(−2⁴d)      0 0 1 1 1              so set q2 = 1 and subtract
             ───────────────
s(2)           0 0 0 0 1  0 1
2s(2)          0 0 1 0  1          sign(s(2)) ≠ sign(d),
+2⁴d         1 1 0 0 1              so set q1 = ⁻1 and add
             ───────────────
s(3)         1 1 0 1 1  1
2s(3)        1 0 1 1 1             sign(s(3)) = sign(d),
+(−2⁴d)      0 0 1 1 1              so set q0 = 1 and subtract
             ───────────────
s(4)         1 1 1 1 0              sign(s(4)) ≠ sign(z)
+(−2⁴d)      0 0 1 1 1              Corrective subtraction
             ───────────────
s(4)           0 0 1 0 1
s                        0 1 0 1    Remainder = (5)ten
q                       ⁻1 1 ⁻1 1   Uncorrected BSD quotient
             ───────────────
p                        0 1 0 1    ⁻1s replaced by 0s
                         / / / /
Shifted p              1 1 0 1 1    Add 1 to correct
q2's-compl             1 1 0 0     Quotient = (−4)ten
===============================
```

Fig. 13.9   Example of nonrestoring signed division.

Figure 13.10 shows a hardware realization of the sequential nonrestoring division algorithm. At the start of each cycle j, the partial remainder $s^{(j-1)}$ is shifted to the left, with its MSB moving into a special flip-flop. Except for the first cycle, the quotient digit is derived by XORing the sign of the divisor and the complement of the sign of the partial remainder. The latter is the same as c_{out} (since the two terms added to form the new partial remainder always are opposite in sign).

Once all the digits of q have been derived in k cycles, two to four additional cycles may be needed to correct the quotient q and the final remainder s. Implementation details depend on various hardware issues such as whether q in the quotient register (or lower half of the partial remainder register) can be directly input to the adder for correction or it should be moved to a different register to gain access to the adder. Practical implementation details, including a complete microprogram for nonrestoring division can be found elsewhere [Wase82, pp. 181-192].

13.5 DIVISION BY CONSTANTS

Justification for our discussion of division by constants is similar to that given for multiplication by constants in Section 9.5. The performance benefits of these methods is even more noticeable here, given that division is generally a slower operation than multiplication. In what follows, we

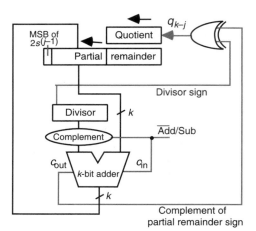

Fig. 13.10 Shift/subtract sequential nonrestoring divider.

consider only division by odd integers, since division by an even integer can be performed by first dividing by an odd integer and then shifting the result. For example, to divide by 20, one can divide by 5 and then shift the result right by two bit positions.

If only a limited number of constant divisors are of interest, their reciprocals can be precomputed with an appropriate precision and stored in a table. Then, the problem of division by any of these constants can be converted to that of multiplication by its constant reciprocal, using the methods discussed in Section 9.5.

Faster constant division routines can be obtained for many small odd divisors by using the mathematical property that for each odd integer d there exists an odd integer m such that $d \times m = 2^n - 1$. Thus:

$$\frac{1}{d} = \frac{m}{2^n - 1} = \frac{m}{2^n(1 - 2^{-n})}$$

$$= \frac{m}{2^n}(1 + 2^{-n})(1 + 2^{-2n})(1 + 2^{-4n}) \cdots$$

Note that the expansion of $1/(1 - 2^{-n})$ involves an infinite number of product terms of the form $1 + 2^{-2^i n}$. Thus to divide z by d, we need to multiply it by $m/2^n$ (which is itself a constant that can be precomputed for integer divisors of interest) and then by several factors of the form $1 + 2^{-j}$. The number of such factors is proportional to the logarithm of the word width and multiplication by each one involves a shift followed by an addition.

Consider as an example division by the constant $d = 5$. We find $m = 3$ and $n = 4$ by inspection. Thus, for 24 bits of precision, we have:

$$\frac{z}{5} = \frac{3z}{2^4 - 1} = \frac{3z}{16(1 - 2^{-4})}$$

$$= \frac{3z}{16}(1 + 2^{-4})(1 + 2^{-8})(1 + 2^{-16})$$

Note that the next term $(1 + 2^{-32})$ would shift out the entire operand and thus does not contribute anything to a result with 24 bits of precision. Based on the preceding expansion, we obtain the following procedure, consisting of shift and add operations, to effect division by 5:

$$q \leftarrow z + z \text{ shift-left 1} \qquad \{3z \text{ computed}\}$$
$$q \leftarrow q + q \text{ shift-right 4} \qquad \{3z(1 + 2^{-4})\}$$
$$q \leftarrow q + q \text{ shift-right 8} \qquad \{3z(1 + 2^{-4})(1 + 2^{-8})\}$$
$$q \leftarrow q + q \text{ shift-right 16} \qquad \{3z(1 + 2^{-4})(1 + 2^{-8})(1 + 2^{16})\}$$
$$q \leftarrow q \text{ shift-right 4} \qquad \{3z(1 + 2^{-4})(1 + 2^{-8})(1 + 2^{-16})/16\}$$

The preceding algorithm uses five shifts and four additions to divide z by 5.

In an application reported over a decade ago [Li85], division by odd constants of up to 55 was frequently required. So the corresponding routines were obtained, fine-tuned, and stored in the system. An aspect of the fine-tuning involved compensating for truncation errors in the course of computations. For example, it was found, through experimentation, that replacing the first statement in the preceding algorithm (division by 5) by $q \leftarrow z + 3 + z$ shift-left 1 would minimize the truncation error on the average. Similar modifications were introduced elsewhere.

Simple hardware structures can be devised for division by certain constants [Scho97]. For example, one way to divide a number z by 3 is to multiply it by 4/3, shifting the result to the right by 2 bits to cancel the factor of 4. Multiplication by 4/3 can in turn be implemented by noting that the following recurrence has the solution $q = 4z/3$:

$$q^{(i)} = q^{(i-1)}/4 + z \quad \text{with} \quad q^{(0)} = 0$$

An alternative to computing q sequentially is to use the fact that q is the output of an adder with inputs $y = q/4$ (right-shifted version of the adder's output) and z. The problem with this implementation strategy is that feeding back the output q_i to the input y_{i-2} creates a feedback loop, given carry propagation between the positions $i - 2$ and i. However, the feedback loop can be eliminated by using a carry-save adder instead of a carry-propagate adder. Working out the implementation details is left as an exercise.

13.6 PREVIEW OF FAST DIVIDERS

Like multiplication, sequential division can be viewed as a multioperand addition problem (Fig. 13.11). Thus, there are but two ways to speed it up:

Reducing the number of operands to be added.

Adding the operands faster.

Reducing the number of operands leads to high-radix division. Adding them faster leads to the use of carry-save representation of the partial remainder. One complication makes division more difficult and thus slower than multiplication: the terms to be subtracted from (added to) the dividend z are not known a priori but become known as the quotient digits are computed. The quotient digits are in turn dependent on the relative magnitudes of the intermediate partial remainders and the divisor (or at least the sign of the partial remainder in the radix-2 nonrestoring algorithm). With carry-save representation of the partial remainder, the magnitude or sign information is no longer readily available; rather, it requires full carry propagation in the worst case.

High-radix dividers, introduced in Chapter 14 and further developed in Chapter 15, produce several bits of the quotient, and multiply them by the divisor, at once. Speedup is achieved for

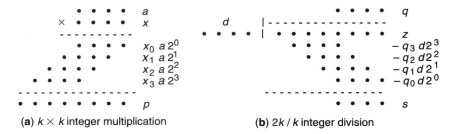

Fig. 13.11   (a) Multiplication and (b) division as multioperand addition problems.

radix 2^j as long as each radix-2^j division cycle is less than j times as long as a radix-2 division cycle. A key issue in the design of high-radix dividers is the selection of the next quotient digit directly from a few bits of the carry-save partial remainder, thus postponing full carry propagation to the very end.

Because of the sequential nature of quotient digit production, there is no counterpart to tree multipliers in the design of dividers. However, array dividers do exist and are discussed in Chapter 15, along with some variations in the design of dividers and combined multiplier/divider units.

Of course there is no reason to limit ourselves to the use of shift and add/subtract operations for implementing dividers. We will see, in Chapter 15, that division by repeated multiplications can be quite cost-effective and competitive in speed, especially when one or more fast parallel multipliers are available.

PROBLEMS

13.1   **Unsigned decimal division** Perform the division z/d for the following dividend/divisor pairs, obtaining the quotient q and the remainder s. Present your work in tabular form, as in Fig. 13.2.

    a. $a = 1234\ 5678$ and $x = 4321$

    b. $a = .1234\ 5678$ and $x = .4321$

13.2   **Programmed nonrestoring division** Write a program similar to the one in Fig. 13.4 for nonrestoring division. Compare the running time of your program to the restoring version and discuss.

13.3   **Programmed restoring division**

    a.   Modify the division program of Fig. 13.4 for the case in which both the dividend and the divisor are k bits wide. Analyze the running time of the new program.

    b.   Modify the division program of Fig. 13.4 to correspond to true restoring division, where subtraction is always performed, but the partial remainder is restored to its original value via addition if it becomes negative. Compare the running time of your modified program to the original one and discuss.

13.4   **Fixed-time programmed division** We would like to modify the division program of Fig. 13.4 so that it always takes the same number of machine cycles to execute, provided a divide-by-zero or overflow exception does not occur. We do not know the number of machine cycles taken by each instruction, but any particular instruction always takes the same number of cycles. Suggest the required modifications in the program and compare the running time of the resulting program to the original one.

13.5 **Unsigned sequential restoring division** Perform the division z/d for the following dividend/divisor pairs, obtaining the quotient q and the remainder s. Use the restoring algorithm and present your work in tabular form, as in Fig. 13.6.

    a. $z = 0101$ and $d = 1001$

    b. $z = .0101$ and $d = .1001$

    c. $z = 1001\ 0100$ and $d = 1101$

    d. $z = .1001\ 0100$ and $d = .1101$

13.6 **Sequential nonrestoring division**

    a.   After complementing z, redo the division example of Fig. 13.7.

    b.   After complementing both z and d, redo the division example of Fig. 13.7.

13.7 **Sequential nonrestoring division** Represent the following signed-magnitude dividends and divisors in 5-bit, 2's-complement format and then perform the division using the nonrestoring algorithm. In each case, convert the quotient to 2's-complement format.

    a. $z = +.1001$ and $d = +.0101$

    b. $z = +.1001$ and $d = -.0101$

    c. $z = -.1001$ and $d = +.0101$

    d. $z = -.1001$ and $d = -.0101$

13.8 **Sequential multiplication/division** Assuming 2's-complement binary operands:

    a.   Perform the division $z/d = 1.100/0.110$ and obtain the 4-bit, 2's-complement quotient q and remainder s using the nonrestoring method.

    b.   Check your answer to part a by doing the 2's-complement multiplication $d \times q$, with q as the multiplier, and adding the remainder s to the resulting product.

    c.   Use the restoring method to perform the division of part a.

13.9 **Radix-2 unsigned integer division** Given the binary dividend $z = 0110\ 1101\ 1110\ 0111$ and the divisor $d = 1010\ 0111$, perform the unsigned division z/d to determine the 8-bit quotient q and remainder s using both the restoring and nonrestoring algorithms.

13.10 **Radix-2 signed division** Given the binary 2's-complement operands $z = 1.1010\ 0010\ 11$ and $d = 0.10110$, use both the restoring and nonrestoring algorithms to perform the division z/d to find the 2's-complement quotient $q = q_0.q_{-1}q_{-2}q_{-3}q_{-4}q_{-5}$ and remainder $1.11111s_{-6}s_{-7}s_{-8}s_{-9}s_{-10}$. Present your work in tabular form as in Fig. 13.9.

13.11 **Nonrestoring hardware dividers** By analyzing all eight possible combinations of signs for the dividend, divisor, and final remainder, along with the corrective actions required in each case, propose an efficient hardware design for a nonrestoring divider. *Hint:* Based on the sign of the final remainder, produce an extra bit q_{-1} of the quotient, which becomes the LSB of the left-shifted p in converting to 2's-complement. Then, only negative quotients will need correction [Wase82, pp. 183–186].

13.12 Division by constants Using shift and add/subtract instructions only, devise efficient routines for division by the following constants. Assume 32-bit unsigned operands.

  a. 19
  b. 43
  c. 88
  d. 129 (*Hint:* $2^{14} - 1 = 127 \times 129$.)

13.13 Division by special constants

  a. Discuss the division of unsigned binary numbers by constants of the form $2^b \pm 1$.
  b. Extend the procedure of part a to the case of a divisor that can be factored into a product of terms, each of which is of the form $2^b \pm 1$ [e.g., $45 = (2^2 + 1)(2^3 + 1)$].
  c. Apply the method of part b to division by 99, with 32 bits of precision.
  d. Compare the result of part c to that obtained from the method discussed in Section 13.5.

13.14 Division by special constants

  a. Devise general strategies for dividing z by positive constants of the form $2^j - 2^i$, where $0 < i < j$ (e.g., $62 = 2^6 - 2^1$, $28 = 2^5 - 2^2$).
  b. Repeat part a for constants of the form $2^j + 2^i$.

13.15 Fully serial dividers

  a. A fully serial, nonrestoring divider is obtained if the adder of Fig. 13.10 is replaced with a bit-serial adder. Show the block diagram of the fully serial divider based on the nonrestoring division algorithm.
  b. Design the required control circuit for the fully serial divider of part a.
  c. Does it make sense to build a fully serial divider based on the restoring algorithm?

13.16 Hardware for division by constants A simple hardware scheme for dividing z by certain constants was discussed at the end of Section 13.5 [Scho97].

  a. Supply the details of the required circuit for computing $z/3$.
  b. Outline the algorithm and hardware requirements for dividing z by 5.
  c. Characterize the class of constants for which this scheme can be used.

REFERENCES

[Kore93] Koren, I., *Computer Arithmetic Algorithms*, Prentice-Hall, 1993.
[Li85]   Li, R. S.-Y., "Fast Constant Division Routines," *IEEE Trans. Computers*, Vol. 34, No. 9, pp. 866–869, 1985.

[Omon94]   Omondi, A. R., *Computer Arithmetic Systems: Algorithms, Architecture and Implementation*, Prentice-Hall, 1994.

[Scho97]   Schoner, B., and S. Molloy, "A New Architecture for Area-Efficient Multiplication by a Class of Rational Coefficients," *Proc. Midwest Symp. Circuits and Systems*, August 1997, Vol. 1, pp. 373–376.

[Wase82]   Waser, S., and M. J. Flynn, *Introduction to Arithmetic for Digital Systems Designers*, Holt, Rinehart, & Winston, 1982.

Chapter 14 | HIGH-RADIX DIVIDERS

In this chapter, we review division schemes that produce more than one bit of the quotient in each cycle (2 bits per cycle in radix 4, 3 bits in radix 8, etc.). The reduction in the number of cycles, along with the use of carry-save addition to simplify the required computations in each cycle, leads to significant speed gain over the basic restoring and nonrestoring dividers discussed in Chapter 13. Chapter topics include:

14.1 BASICS OF HIGH-RADIX DIVISION

Recall, from Chapter 13, that the equation $z = (d \times q) + s$, along with the two conditions $\text{sign}(s) = \text{sign}(z)$ and $|s| < |d|$, completely defines the results q (quotient) and s (remainder) of fixed-point division.

The radix-r counterpart of the binary division recurrence, derived in Section 13.1, can be written as follows:

$$s^{(j)} = rs^{(j-1)} - q_{k-j}(r^k d) \quad \text{with} \quad s^{(0)} = z \quad \text{and} \quad s^{(k)} = r^k s$$

where the radix-r division parameters are:

z	Dividend	$z_{2k-1}z_{2k-2}\cdots z_1 z_0$
d	Divisor	$d_{k-1}d_{k-2}\cdots d_1 d_0$
q	Quotient	$q_{k-1}q_{k-2}\cdots q_1 q_0$
s	Remainder $[z - (d \times q)]$	$s_{k-1}s_{k-2}\cdots s_1 s_0$

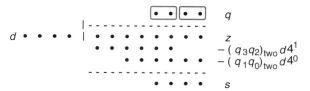

Fig. 14.1 Radix-4 division in dot notation.

High-radix dividers of practical interest have $r = 2^b$ (and, occasionally, $r = 10$). Consider, for example, radix-4 division. Each radix-4 quotient digit, obtained in one division cycle, represents two radix-2 digits. So, radix-4 division can be viewed as radix-2 division with 2 bits of the quotient obtained in each cycle. In an 8-by-4 binary division performed in radix 4, for example, q_3 and q_2 are determined first, with $(q_3q_2)_{\text{two}}(4^2d)$ subtracted from $4z$ to obtain the first partial remainder. This partial remainder is then used for determining q_1 and q_0 in the second and final cycle. Figure 14.1 shows the preceding radix-4 division in dot notation.

Figure 14.2 depicts examples of radix-4 and radix-10 division. The radix-4 division example shown has $z = (7003)_{\text{ten}} = (0123\ 1123)_{\text{four}}$ and $d = (99)_{\text{ten}} = (1203)_{\text{four}}$, yielding the quotient $q = (70)_{\text{ten}} = (1012)_{\text{four}}$ and the remainder $s = (73)_{\text{ten}} = (1021)_{\text{four}}$. The radix-10 example corresponds to the division $(.7003)_{\text{ten}}/(.99)_{\text{ten}}$, yielding $q = (.70)_{\text{ten}}$ and $s = (.0073)_{\text{ten}}$.

Dividing binary numbers in radix 2^b reduces the number of cycles required by a factor of b, but each cycle is more difficult to implement because:

Radix-4 integer division
```
===============================
z         0 1 2 3   1 1 2 3
4⁴d       1 2 0 3
===============================
s⁽⁰⁾      0 1 2 3   1 1 2 3
4s⁽⁰⁾   0 1 2 3 1   1 2 3
-q₃4⁴d  0 1 2 0 3           {q₃ = 1}

s⁽¹⁾      0 0 2 2   1 2 3
4s⁽¹⁾   0 0 2 2 1   2 3
-q₂4⁴d  0 0 0 0 0           {q₂ = 0}

s⁽²⁾      0 2 2 1   2 3
4s⁽²⁾   0 2 2 1 2   3
-q₁4⁴d  0 1 2 0 3           {q₁ = 1}

s⁽³⁾      1 0 0 3   3
4s⁽³⁾   1 0 0 3 3
-q₀4⁴d  0 3 0 1 2           {q₀ = 2}

s⁽⁴⁾      1 0 2 1
s                   1 0 2 1
q                   1 0 1 2
===============================
```

Radix-10 fractional division
```
===================
z_frac    . 7 0 0 3
d_frac    . 9 9
===================
s⁽⁰⁾      . 7 0 0 3
10s⁽⁰⁾   7 . 0 0 3
-q₋₁d    6 . 9 3    {q₋₁ = 7}

s⁽¹⁾      . 0 7 3
10s⁽¹⁾   0 . 7 3
-q₋₂d    0 . 0 0    {q₋₂ = 0}

s⁽²⁾      . 7 3
s_frac    . 0 0 7 3
q_frac    . 7 0
===================
```

Fig. 14.2 Examples of high-radix division with integer and fractional operands.

a. The higher radix makes the guessing of the correct quotient digit more difficult; we certainly do not want to try subtracting $2^k d$, $2(2^k d)$, $3(2^k d)$, etc., and noting the sign of the partial remainder in each case, until the correct quotient digit has been determined—this would nullify all the speed gain (in radix 4, two trial subtractions of d and $2d$ would be needed, thus making each cycle almost twice as long with one adder).

b. Unlike multiplication, where all the partial products can be computed initially and then subjected to parallel processing by multiple carry-save adders, the values to be subtracted from (added to) z in division are determined sequentially, one per cycle. Furthermore, the determination of the quotient digits depends on the magnitude and/or sign of the partial remainder; information that is not readily available from the stored-carry representation.

Thus before discussing high-radix division in depth, we try to solve the more pressing problem of using carry-save techniques to speed up the iterations in binary division [Nadl56]. Once we have learned how to use a carry-save representation for the partial remainder, we will revisit the problem of high-radix division. The reason we attach greater importance to the use of carry-save partial remainders than to high-radix division is that in going from radix 2 to radix 4, say, the division is at best speeded up by a factor of 2. The use of carry-save partial remainders, on the other hand, can lead to a larger performance improvement via replacing the delay of a carry-propagate adder by the delay of a single full adder.

The key to being able to keep the partial remainder in carry-save form is introducing redundancy in the representation of the quotient. With a nonredundant quotient, there is no room for error. If the binary quotient is $(0110 \cdots)_{\text{two}}$, say, subsequent recovery from an incorrect guess setting the MSB of q to 1 will be impossible. However, if we allow the digit set $[-1, 1]$ for the radix-2 quotient, the partial quotient $(1 \cdots)_{\text{two}}$ can be modified to $(1 \ ^{-}1 \cdots)_{\text{two}}$ in the next cycle if we discover that 1 was too large a guess for the MSB. The aforementioned margin for error allows us to guess the next quotient digit based on the approximate magnitude of the partial remainder. The greater the margin for error, the less precision (fewer bits of the carry-save partial remainder) we need in determining the quotient digits.

14.2 RADIX-2 SRT DIVISION

Let us reconsider the radix-2 nonrestoring division algorithm for fractional operands characterized by the recurrence

$$s^{(j)} = 2s^{(j-1)} - q_{-j}d \quad \text{with} \quad s^{(0)} = z \quad \text{and} \quad s^{(k)} = 2^k s$$

with $q_{-j} \in \{-1, 1\}$. Note that the same algorithm can be applied to integer operands if d is viewed as standing for $2^k d$.

The quotient is obtained with the digit set $\{-1, 1\}$ and is then converted (on the fly) to standard digit set $\{0, 1\}$. Figure 14.3 plots the new partial remainder, $s^{(j)}$, as a function of the shifted old partial remainder, $2s^{(j-1)}$. For $2s^{(j-1)} \geq 0$, we subtract the divisor d from $2s^{(j-1)}$ to obtain $s^{(j)}$, while for $2s^{(j-1)} < 0$, we add d to obtain $s^{(j)}$. These actions are represented by the two oblique lines in Fig. 14.3. The heavy dot in Fig. 14.3 indicates the action taken for $2s^{(j-1)} = 0$.

Nonrestoring division with shifting over 0s is a method that avoids addition or subtraction when the partial remainder is "small." More specifically, when $2s^{(j-1)}$ is in the range $[-d, d)$,

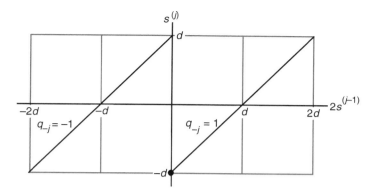

Fig. 14.3   The new partial remainder, $s^{(j)}$, as a function of the shifted old partial remainder, $2s^{(j-1)}$, in radix-2 nonrestoring division.

we know that the addition/subtraction prescribed by the algorithm will change its sign. Thus, we can choose $q_{-j} = 0$ and only shift the partial remainder. This will not cause a problem because the shifted partial remainder will still be in the valid range $[-2d, 2d)$ for the next step. With this method, the quotient is obtained using the digit set $\{-1, 0, 1\}$, corresponding to "add," "no operation," and "subtract," respectively. Figure 14.4 plots the new partial remainder $s^{(j)}$ as a function of the shifted old partial remainder $2s^{(j-1)}$ for such a modified nonrestoring division algorithm that selects $q_{-j} = 0$ for $-d \leq 2s^{(j-1)} < d$.

Since, with the preceding method, some iterations are reduced to just shifting, one might think that the average division speed will improve in an asynchronous design in which the adder can be selectively bypassed. But how can you tell if the shifted partial remainder is in $[-d, d)$? The answer is that you can't, unless you perform trial subtractions. But the trial subtractions would take more time than they save! An ingenious solution to this problem was independently suggested by Sweeney, Robertson, and Tocher. The resulting algorithm is known as SRT division in their honor.

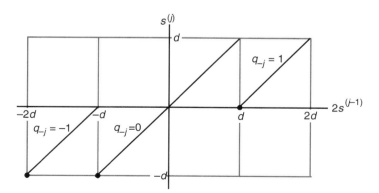

Fig. 14.4   The new partial remainder, $s^{(j)}$, as a function of the shifted old partial remainder, $2s^{(j-1)}$, with q_{-j} in $\{-1, 0, 1\}$.

Let us assume $d \geq 1/2$ (positive bit-normalized divisor) and restrict the partial remainder to the range $[-1/2, 1/2)$ rather than $[-d, d)$. Initially this latter condition might not hold, so we may have to shift the dividend z (which is assumed to be in the range $-d \leq z < d$ if overflow is to be avoided) to the right by one bit. To compensate for this initial right shift, we double the quotient and remainder obtained after $k + 1$ cycles.

Once the initial partial remainder $s^{(0)}$ is adjusted to be in the range $[-1/2, 1/2)$, all subsequent partial remainders can be kept in that range, as evident from the solid rectangle in Fig. 14.5.

The quotient digit selection rule associated with Fig. 14.5 to guarantee that $s^{(j)}$ remains in the range $[-1/2, 1/2)$ is:

$$\text{if } 2s^{(j-1)} < -1/2$$
$$\text{then } q_{-j} = -1$$
$$\text{else } \quad \text{if } 2s^{(j-1)} \geq 1/2$$
$$\text{then } q_{-j} = 1$$
$$\text{else } q_{-j} = 0$$
$$\text{endif}$$
$$\text{endif}$$

Two comparisons are still needed to select the appropriate quotient digit, but the comparisons are with the constants $-1/2$ and $1/2$ rather than with $-d$ and d. Comparison with $1/2$ or $-1/2$ is quite simple. When the partial remainder $s^{(j-1)}$ is in $[-1/2, 1/2)$, the shifted partial remainder $2s^{(j-1)}$ will be in $[-1, 1)$, thus requiring 1 bit before the radix point (the sign bit) for its 2's-complement representation.

$$2s^{(j-1)} \geq +1/2 = (0.1)_{2's-compl} \quad \text{implies} \quad 2s^{(j-1)} = (0.1u_{-2}u_{-3}\cdots)_{2's-compl}$$
$$2s^{(j-1)} < -1/2 = (1.1)_{2's-compl} \quad \text{implies} \quad 2s^{(j-1)} = (1.0u_{-2}u_{-3}\cdots)_{2's-compl}$$

We see that the condition $2s^{(j-1)} \geq 1/2$ is given by the logical AND term $\overline{u}_0 u_{-1}$ and that of $2s^{(j-1)} < -1/2$ by $u_0 \overline{u}_{-1}$. Thus, the required comparisons are preformed by two 2-input AND gates. What could be simpler?

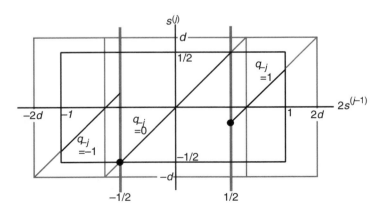

Fig. 14.5   The relationship between new and old partial remainders in radix-2 SRT division.

The nonrestoring divider of Fig. 13.10 is also valid for the SRT algorithm (only the control state machine will change). Everything in the data path portion, including the quotient digit selection logic and the conversion process, remains the same. What the SRT algorithm does is similar to Booth's recoding: it changes an addition (subtraction) followed by a sequence of subtractions (additions) to a number of no-ops followed by a single addition (subtraction); that is, it takes advantage of the equality $\pm(2^j - 2^{j-1} - 2^{j-2} - \cdots - 2^i) = \pm 2^i$.

Figure 14.6 shows an example division performed with the SRT algorithm. The rules for the final correction, if required, are exactly the same as for nonrestoring division, but the quotient conversion algorithm given in Section 13.4 in inapplicable here in view of the presence of 0s in the quotient. One can use an on-the-fly conversion algorithm to convert the BSD quotient to binary [Erce87]. Alternatively, one can have two quotient registers into which the positive and negative digits of q are shifted. The binary version of q, before correction, can then be obtained by a subtraction after all digits have been shifted in.

To further speed up the division process, we can skip over any number of identical leading bits in $s^{(j-1)}$ by shifting. A combinational logic circuit can detect the number of identical leading bits, resulting in significant speedup if a variable shifter is available. Here are two examples:

$$s^{(j-1)} = 0.0000110\cdots \quad \text{Shift left by 4 bits and subtract}$$
$$s^{(j-1)} = 1.1110100\cdots \quad \text{Shift left by 3 bits and add}$$

```
===============================
z              . 0 1 0 0   0 1 0 1    In [−1/2, 1/2), so OK
d              . 1 0 1 0               In [1/2, 1), so OK
−d           1 . 0 1 1 0
===============================
s(0)         0 . 0 1 0 0   0 1 0 1
2s(0)        0 . 1 0 0 0   1 0 1      ≥ 1/2, so set q−1 = 1
+(−d)        1 . 0 1 1 0               and subtract
            ─────────────────────
s(1)         1 . 1 1 1 0   1 0 1
2s(1)        1 . 1 1 0 1   0 1        In [−1/2, 1/2), so set q−2 = 0
            ─────────────────────
s(2) = 2s(1) 1 . 1 1 0 1   0 1
2s(2)        1 . 1 0 1 0   1          In [−1/2, 1/2) so set q−3 = 0
            ─────────────────────
s(3) = 2s(2) 0 . 1 0 1 0   1
2s(3)        1 . 0 1 0 1             < −1/2, so set q−4 = −1
+d           0 . 1 0 1 0               and add
            ─────────────────────
s(4)         1 . 1 1 1 1              Negative,
+d           0 . 1 0 1 0               so add to correct
            ─────────────────────
s(4)         0 . 1 0 0 1
s            0 . 0 0 0 0   1 0 0 1
q            0 . 1 0 0 -1             Uncorrected BSD quotient
q            0 . 0 1 1 0             Convert and subtract ulp
===============================
```

Fig. 14.6   Example of unsigned radix-2 SRT division.

When we shift the partial remainder to the left by h bits, the quotient is extended by $h-1$ zeros and one nonzero digit in $\{-1, 1\}$. In the first example above, the digits 0 0 0 1 must be appended to q, while in the second example, the quotient is extended using the digits 0 0·1.

Through statistical analysis, the average skipping distance in variable-shift SRT division has been determined to be 2.67 bits. This means that on the average, one add/subtract is performed per 2.67 bits, compared to one per bit in simple nonrestoring division. The result above assumes random bit values in the numbers. However, numbers encountered in practice are not uniformly distributed. This leads to a slight increase in the average shift distance.

Speedup of division by means of standard or variable-shift SRT algorithm is no longer applied in practice. One reason is that modern digital systems are predominantly synchronous. Another, equally important, reason is that in fast dividers, we do not really perform a carry-propagate addition in every cycle. Rather, we keep the partial remainder in stored-carry form, which needs only a carry-save addition in each cycle (see Section 14.3). Now, carry-save addition is so fast that skipping it does not buy us anything; in fact the logic needed to decide whether to skip will have delay comparable to the carry-save addition itself.

14.3 USING CARRY-SAVE ADDERS

Let us set aside SRT division and go back to the radix-2 division scheme with the partial remainders in $[-d, d)$, as represented by Fig. 14.4. However, instead of forcing the selection of $q_{-j} = 0$ whenever $2s^{(j-1)}$ falls in the range $[-d, d)$, we allow the choice of either valid digit in the two overlap areas where the quotient digit can be -1 or 0 and 0 or $+1$ (see Fig. 14.7).

Now, if we want to choose the quotient digits based on comparing the shifted partial remainder to constants, the two constants can fall anywhere in the overlap regions. In particular, we can use the thresholds $-1/2$ and 0 for our decision, choosing $q_{-j} = -1$, 0, or 1 when $2s^{(j-1)}$ falls in the intervals $[-2d, -1/2)$, $[-1/2, 0)$, or $[0, 2d)$, respectively. The advantages of these particular comparison constants will become clear shortly.

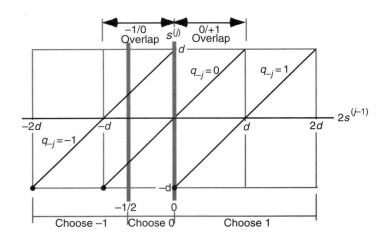

Fig. 14.7 Constant thresholds used for quotient digit selection in radix-2 division with q_{k-j} in $\{-1, 0, 1\}$.

Suppose that the partial remainder is kept in stored-carry form: that is, as two numbers whose sum is equal to the true partial remainder. To perform exact magnitude comparison with such carry-save numbers would require full carry propagation since, in the worst case, the least significant bit values can affect the most significant end of the sum. However, the overlaps in valid ranges of $2s^{(j-1)}$ for selecting $q_{-j} = -1$, 0, or 1 in Fig. 14.7 allow us to perform approximate comparisons without risk of choosing a wrong quotient digit.

Let $u = (u_1 u_0.u_{-1} u_{-2} \cdots)_{2'\text{s-compl}}$ and $v = (v_1 v_0.v_{-1} v_{-2} \cdots)_{2'\text{s-compl}}$ be the sum and carry components of the stored-carry representation of $2s^{(j-1)}$. Like $2s^{(j-1)}$ itself, each of these components is a 2's-complement number in the range $[-2d, 2d)$. Then the following quotient digit selection algorithm can be devised based on Fig. 14.7:

$$t = u_{[-2,1]} + v_{[-2,1]} \quad \{\text{Add the most significant 4 bits of } u \text{ and } v\}$$
if $t < -1/2$
then $q_{-j} = -1$
else   if $t \geq 0$
        then $q_{-j} = 1$
        else $q_{-j} = 0$
        endif
endif

The 4-bit number $t = (t_1 t_0.t_{-1} t_{-2})_{2'\text{s-compl}}$ obtained by adding the most significant 4 bits of u and v [i.e., $(u_1 u_0.u_{-1} u_{-2})_{2'\text{s-compl}}$ and $(v_1 v_0.v_{-1} v_{-2})_{2'\text{s-compl}}$] can be compared to the constants $-1/2$ and 0 based only on the three bit values t_1, t_0, and t_{-1}. If $t < -1/2$, the true value of $2s^{(j-1)}$ is guaranteed to be less than 0, since the error in truncating each component was less than 1/4. Similarly, if $t < 0$, we are guaranteed to have $2s^{(j-1)} < 1/2 \leq d$. Note that when we truncate a 2's-complement number, we always reduce its value independent of the number's sign. This is true because the discarded bits are positively weighted.

The preceding division algorithm requires the use of a 4-bit fast adder to propagate the carries in the high-order 4 bits of the stored-carry shifted partial remainder. Then, the high-order 3 bits of the 4-bit result can be supplied to a logic circuit or an eight-entry table to obtain the next quotient digit. Figure 14.8 is a block diagram for the resulting divider. The 4-bit fast adder to compute t and the subsequent logic circuit or table to obtain q_{-j} are lumped together into the box labeled "Select q_{-j}." Each cycle for this divider entails quotient digit selection, as discussed above, plus only a few logic gate levels of delay through the multiplexer and CSA.

Even though a 4-bit adder is quite simple and fast, we can obtain even better performance by using a 256×2 table in which the 2-bit encoding of the quotient digit is stored for all possible combinations of $4 + 4$ bits from the two components u and v of the shifted partial remainder. Equivalently, an eight-input programmable logic array (PLA) can be used to derive the two output bits using two-level AND-OR logic. This does not affect the block diagram of Fig. 14.8, since only the internal design of the "Select q_{-j}" box will change. The delay per iteration now consists of a table lookup (PLA) plus a few logic levels.

Can we use stored-carry partial remainders with SRT division? Unless we modify the algorithm in some way, the answer is "no." Figure 14.9, derived from Fig. 14.5 by extending the lines corresponding to $q_{-j} = -1$ and $q_{-j} = 1$ inside the solid rectangle, tells us why. The width of each overlap region in Fig. 14.9 is $1 - d$. Thus, the overlaps can become arbitrarily small as d approaches 1, leaving no margin for error and making approximate comparisons impossible.

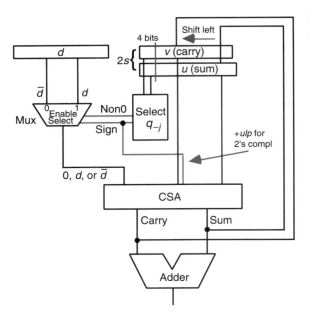

Fig. 14.8 Block diagram of a radix-2 divider with partial remainder in stored-carry form.

14.4 CHOOSING THE QUOTIENT DIGITS

We can use a *p-d* plot (shifted partial remainder vs. divisor) as a graphical tool for understanding the quotient digit selection process and deriving the needed precision (number of bits to look at) for various division algorithms. Figure 14.10 shows the *p-d* plot for the radix-2 division, with quotient digits in $[-1, 1]$, depicted in Fig. 14.7. The area between lines $p = -d$ and $p = d$

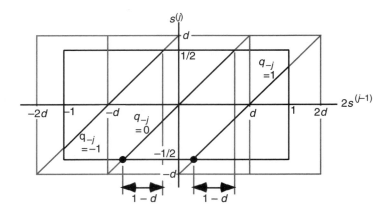

Fig. 14.9 Overlap regions in radix-2 SRT division.

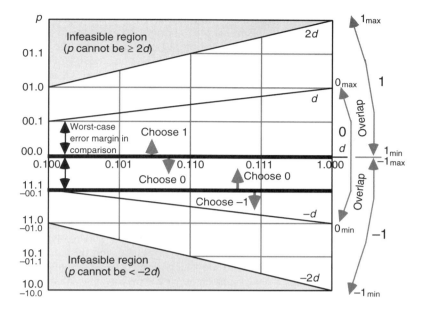

Fig. 14.10 A p-d plot for radix-2 division with $d \in [1/2, 1)$, partial remainder in $[-d, d)$, and quotient digits in $[-1, 1]$.

is the region in which 0 is a valid choice for the quotient digit q_{-j}. Similar observations apply to -1 and 1, whose associated areas overlap with that of $q_{-j} = 0$.

In the overlap regions between $p = 0$ and $p = \pm d$, two valid choices for the quotient digit exist. As noted earlier, placing the decision lines at $p = 0$ and $p = -1/2$ would allow us to choose the quotient digit by inspecting the sign, one integer, and two fractional bits in the sum and carry parts of p. This is because the error margins of $1/2$ in the partial remainder depicted in Fig. 14.10 allow us to allocate an error margin of $1/4$ in each of its two components. We use an approximate shifted partial remainder $t = (t_1 t_0 . t_{-1} t_{-2})_{2\text{'s-compl}}$, obtained by adding 4 bits of the sum and carry components, to select the quotient digit value of 1 when $t_1 = 0$ and -1 when $t_1 = 1$ and t_0 and t_{-1} are not both 1s. Thus the logic equations for the "Non0" and "Sign" signals in Fig. 14.8 become:

$$\text{Non0} = \bar{t}_1 + \bar{t}_0 + \bar{t}_{-1} = \overline{t_1 t_0 t_{-1}}$$

$$\text{Sign} = t_1 (\bar{t}_0 + \bar{t}_{-1})$$

Because decision boundaries in the p-d plot of Fig. 14.10 are horizontal lines, the value of d does not affect the choice of q_{-j}. We will see later that using horizontal decision lines is not always possible in high-radix division. In such cases, we embed staircaselike boundaries in the overlap regions that allow us to choose the quotient digit value by inspecting a few bits of both p and d.

Note that the decision process for quotient digit selection is asymmetric about the d axis. This is due to the asymmetric effect of truncation on positive and negative values represented in 2's-complement format.

In our discussions thus far, we have assumed that the divisor d is positive. For a 2's-complement divisor, the p-d plot must be extended to the left to cover negative divisors. If Fig. 14.10 is thus extended for negative values of d, the two straight lines can still be used as decision boundaries, as the value of d is immaterial. However, for staircaselike boundaries just alluded to, the asymmetry observed about the d axis is also present about the p axis. Thus, all four quadrants of the p-d plot must be used to derive the rules for quotient digit selection. Very often, though, we draw only one quadrant of the p-d plot, corresponding to positive values for d and p, with the understanding that the reader can fill in the details for the other three quadrants if necessary.

14.5 RADIX-4 SRT DIVISION

We are now ready to present our first high-radix division algorithm with the partial remainder kept in stored-carry form. We begin by looking at radix-4 division with quotient digit set $[-3, 3]$. Figure 14.11 shows the relationship of new and shifted old partial remainders along with the overlapping regions within which various quotient digit values can be selected.

The p-d plot corresponding to the division algorithm above is shown in Fig. 14.12. For the sake of simplicity, the decision boundaries (heaviest lines) are drawn with the assumption that the exact partial remainder is used in the comparisons. In this example, we see, for the first time, a decision boundary that is not a straight horizontal line. What this means is that the choice between $q_{-j} = 3$ or $q_{-j} = 2$ depends not only on the value of p but also on one bit, d_{-2}, of d (to tell us whether d is in $[1/2, 3/4)$ or in $[3/4, 1)$. If p is only known to us approximately, the selection boundaries must be redrawn to allow for correct selection with the worst-case error in p. More on this later.

When the quotient digit value of ± 3 is selected, one needs to add/subtract the multiple $3d$ of the divisor to/from the partial remainder. One possibility is to precompute and store $3d$ in a register at the outset. Recall that we faced the same problem of needing the multiple $3a$ in radix-4 multiplication. This reminds us of Booth's recoding and the possibility of restricting the quotient digits to $[-2, 2]$, since this restriction would facilitate quotient digit selection (fewer comparisons) and the subsequent multiple generation.

Figure 14.13 shows that we can indeed do this if the partial remainder range is suitably restricted. To find the allowed range, let the restricted range be $[-hd, hd)$ for some $h < 1$. Then, $4s^{(j-1)}$ will be in the range $[-4hd, 4hd)$. We should be able to bring the worst-case values to within the original range by adding $\pm 2d$ to it. Thus, we must have $4hd - 2d \leq hd$ or $h \leq 2/3$. Let us choose $h = 2/3$. As in SRT division, since z may not be in this range, an initial shift and final adjustment of the results may be needed.

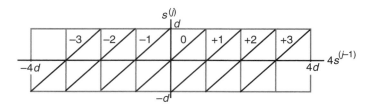

Fig. 14.11   New versus shifted old partial remainder in radix-4 division with q_{-j} in $[-3, 3]$.

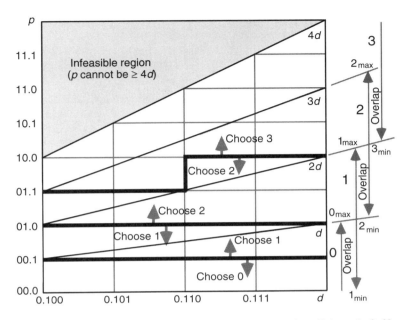

Fig. 14.12   A p-d plot for radix-4 SRT division with quotient digit set $[-3, 3]$.

The p-d plot corresponding to the preceding division scheme is given in Fig. 14.14. Upon comparing Figs. 14.14 and 14.12, we see that restricting the digit set to $[-2, 2]$ has made the overlap regions narrower, forcing us to examine p and d with greater accuracy to correctly choose the quotient digit. On the positive side, we have gotten rid of the $3d$ multiple, which would be hard to generate. Based on staircaselike boundaries in the p-d plot of Fig. 14.14, we see that 5 bits of p (plus its sign) and 4 bits of d must be inspected (d_{-1} also provides the sign information).

The block diagram of a radix-4 divider based on the preceding algorithm is quite similar to the radix-2 divider in Fig. 14.8 except for the following changes:

Four bits of d are also input to the quotient digit selection box.

We need a four-input multiplexer, with "enable" and two select control lines, the inputs to which are d and $2d$, as well as their complements. Alternatively, a two-input multiplexer

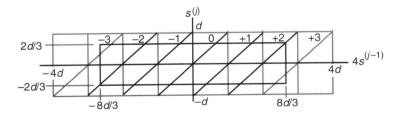

Fig. 14.13   New versus shifted old partial remainder in radix-4 division with q_{-j} in $[-2, 2]$.

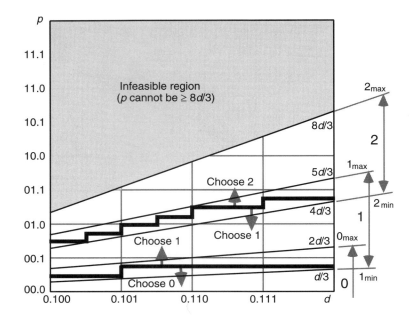

Fig. 14.14   A p-d plot for radix-4 SRT division with quotient digit set $[-2, 2]$.

with "enable" line can be used to choose between 0, d, and $2d$, followed by a selective complementer to produce $-d$ or $-2d$ if needed.

The final conversion of the quotient from radix-4 signed-digit form, with the digit set $[-2, 2]$, to 2's-complement form, is more involved.

Radix-4 SRT division is the division algorithm used in the Intel Pentium processor. The quotient selection box in Pentium's hardware is implemented by a programmable logic array. According to Intel's explanation of the division bug in early Pentium chips, after the p-d plot was numerically generated, a script was written to download the entries into a hardware PLA. An error in this script resulted in the inadvertent removal of a few table entries from the lookup table. These missing entries, when hit, would result in the digit 0, instead of $+2$, being read out from the PLA [Gepp95].

Unfortunately for Intel, these entries are consulted very rarely, and thus the problem was not caught during the testing of the chip. Fuller explanations of the mathematics behind the Intel Pentium division flaw, and why it was very subtle and difficult to detect, are offered in [Coe95] and [Edel97].

14.6 GENERAL HIGH-RADIX DIVIDERS

Now that we know how to construct a fast radix-4 divider, it is quite easy to generalize the idea to higher radices. For example, a radix-8 divider can be built by restricting the partial remainder in the range $[-4d/7, 4d/7)$ and using the minimal quotient digit set $[-4, 4]$. The required

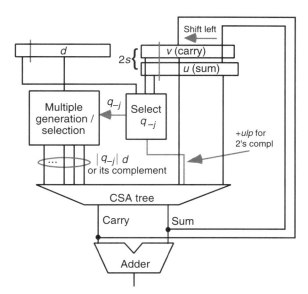

Fig. 14.15 Block diagram of radix-r divider with partial remainder in stored-carry form.

$3d$ multiple can either be precomputed and stored in a register or dynamically produced by selectively supplying $2d$ and d as inputs to a CSA tree that receives the two numbers representing the partial remainder as its other two inputs. Determining the required precision in inspecting the partial remainder and the divisor to select the next quotient digit is left as an exercise.

Digit sets with greater redundancy, such as $[-7, 7]$ in radix 8, are possible and lead to wider overlap regions and, thus, lower precision in the comparisons needed for selecting the quotient digit. However, they also lead to more comparisons and the need to generate other difficult multiples (e.g., ± 5 and ± 7) of the divisor.

The block diagram of a radix-r hardware divider is shown in Fig. 14.15. Note that this radix-r divider is similar to the radix-2 divider in Fig. 14.8, except that its more general multiple generation/selection circuit may produce the required multiple as a set of numbers, and several bits of d are also examined by the quotient digit selection logic. For further details and design issues for high-radix dividers, see Sections 15.1 and 15.2.

PROBLEMS

14.1   Nonrestoring unsigned integer division Given the binary dividend $z = 0110\ 1101\ 1110\ 0111$ and the divisor $d = 1010\ 0111$, perform the unsigned radix-2 division z/d to determine the 8-bit quotient q and 16-bit remainder s, selecting the quotient digits according to

   a. Fig. 14.3
   b. Fig. 14.4
   c. Fig. 14.5
   d. Fig. 14.10

14.2   Nonrestoring signed integer division Given the binary 2's-complement operands $z = 1.1010\ 0010\ 11$ and $d = 0.10110$, perform the signed radix-2 division z/d to determine the 2's-complement quotient $q = q_0.q_{-1}q_{-2}q_{-3}q_{-4}q_{-5}$ and remainder $1.11111s_{-6}s_{-7}s_{-8}s_{-9}s_{-10}$, selecting the quotient digits according to:

  a. Fig. 14.3
  b. Fig. 14.4
  c. Fig. 14.5
  d. Fig. 14.10

14.3 **Carry-save and high-radix division** Perform the division z/d, with $z = 1.1010\ 0010\ 11$ and $d = 0.10110$, using:

  a. Radix-2 division, with the partial remainder kept in carry-save form (Fig. 14.7).
  b. The radix-4 division scheme depicted in Fig. 14.12.
  c. The radix-4 division scheme depicted in Fig. 14.14.

14.4 **Robertson diagram for division** A Robertson diagram for division is constructed as follows. We take the $s^{(j)}$-versus-$2s^{(j-1)}$ plot of the division algorithm, exemplified by Figs. 14.3–14.5, and mark off the dividend $z = s^{(0)}$ on the vertical axis. We then draw a curved arrow from this point to the point representing $2s^{(0)}$ on the horizontal axis, a vertical arrow from there to the diagonal line representing the quotient digit value, followed by a horizontal arrow to the $s^{(1)}$ point on the vertical axis. If we continue in this manner, the arrows will trace a path showing the variations in the partial remainders and the accompanying quotient digits selected. Construct Robertson diagrams corresponding to the following divisions using the nonrestoring algorithm.

  a. $z = +.1001$ and $d = +.1010$
  b. $z = +.1001$ and $d = -.1010$
  c. $z = -.1001$ and $d = +.1010$
  d. $z = -.1001$ and $d = -.1010$

14.5 **Restoring binary division**

  a. Construct a diagram similar to Figs. 14.3–14.5 for restoring division.
  b. Draw a Robertson diagram (see Problem 14.4) for the unsigned binary division $.101001/.110$.

14.6 **Radix-4 SRT division**

  a. Complete Fig. 14.14 by drawing all four quadrants on graph paper.
  b. Use rectangular tiles to tile the diagram of part a with dimensions determined by smallest step size in each direction. On each tile, write the quotient digit value(s).
  c. If the quotient digit is to be selected by a PLA, rather than a ROM table, adjacent tiles of part b that have identical labels can be merged into a single product term. Combine the tiles to minimize the number of product terms required.

14.7 **Radix-4 SRT division** Present a complete logic design for the quotient digit selection box of Fig. 14.8, trying to maximize the speed.

14.8   Radix-8 SRT division

    a.   Draw a *p-d* plot, similar to Fig. 14.14, for radix-8 division using the quotient digit set $[-4, 4]$.

    b.   Estimate the size of the ROM table needed for quotient digit selection with and without a small fast adder to add a few bits of the stored-carry partial remainder.

14.9   Pentium's division flaw The Intel Pentium division flaw was due to five incorrect entries in the quotient digit lookup table for its radix-4 SRT division algorithm with carry-save partial remainder and quotient digits in $[-2, 2]$. The bad entries should have contained ± 2 but instead contained 0. Because of redundancy, it is conceivable that on later iterations, the algorithm could recover from a bad quotient digit. Show that recovery is impossible for the Pentium flaw.

14.10   Division with shifting over 0s and 1s

    a.   Assuming uniform distribution of 0 and 1 digits in the dividend, divisor, and all intermediate partial remainders, determine the expected shift amount if division is performed by shifting over 0s and 1s, as discussed at the end of Section 14.2.

    b.   Arbitrarily long shifts require the use of a complex shifter. What would be the expected shift amount in part a if the maximum shift is limited to 4 bits?

    c.   Repeat part b with maximum shift limited to 8 bits and discuss whether increasing the maximum shift to 8 bits would be cost-effective.

    d.   Explain the difference between the result of part a and the 2.67-bit average shift mentioned near the end of Section 14.2.

14.11   Conversion of redundant quotients A redundant radix-*r* quotient resulting from high-radix division needs to be converted to standard representation at the end of the division process.

    a.   Show how to convert the BSD quotient of SRT division to 2's-complement.

    b.   To avoid a long conversion delay on the critical path of the divider, one can use on-the-fly conversion [Erce87]. Show that by keeping two standard binary versions of the quotient and updating them appropriately as each quotient digit is chosen in $[-1, 1]$, one can obtain the final 2's-complement quotient by simple selection from one of the two registers.

    c.   Repeat part a for radix-4 SRT algorithm with the digit set $[-2, 2]$.

    d.   Repeat part b for radix-4 SRT algorithm with the digit set $[-2, 2]$.

14.12   Radix-3 division

    a.   Develop an algorithm for unsigned radix-3 division with standard operands (i.e., digit set $[0, 2]$) and the quotient obtained with the redundant digit set $[-2, 2]$.

    b.   Repeat part a when the inputs are signed radix-3 numbers using the symmetric digit set $[-1, 1]$.

14.13   SRT division with 2*d* and *d*/2 multiples The following method has been suggested to increase the average shift amount, and thus the speed, of SRT division. Suppose we shift over 0s in a positive partial remainder. In the next step, corresponding to a 1 digit in the partial remainder, we choose the quotient digit 1 and subtract d. If the partial remainder is much larger than the divisor, the 1 in the quotient will be followed by other 1s, as in $\cdots 0000111 \cdots$, necessitating several subtractions. In this case, we can subtract $2d$ instead of d, which is akin to going back and "correcting" the previous 0 digit in the quotient to 1 and setting the current digit to 0 in order to produce a small negative partial remainder and thus a larger shift. On the other hand, if the partial remainder is much smaller than the divisor, the 1 in the quotient will be followed by -1s, and thus one or more additions. In this case, it is advantageous to subtract $d/2$ rather than d, which corresponds to picking the current and next quotient digits to be 01.

   a. Construct an 8×8 table in which, for the various combination of values in the upper 4 bits of d and s, you indicate whether $d/2$, d, or $2d$ should be subtracted. Assume that d is of the form .1xxx and s is positive.

   b. Extend the table in part a to negative partial remainders.

   c. Use the table of part b to perform the example division z/d with 2's-complement operands $z = 1.1010\ 0010\ 11$ and $d = 0.10110$.

14.14   **Radix-2 division with over-redundant quotient** Consider radix-2 division with the "over-redundant" [Srin97] quotient digit set $[-2, 2]$.

   a. Draw a *p-d* plot for this radix-2 division.

   b. Show that inspecting the sign and two digits of the partial remainder (three if in carry-save form) is sufficient for determining the next quotient digit.

   c. Devise a method for converting the over-redundant quotient to binary signed-digit using the digit set $[-1, 1]$ as the first step of converting it to standard binary. *Hint:* When a quotient digit is ± 2, the next digit must be 0 or of the opposite sign. Rewrite a digit ± 2 as ± 1, with a right-moving "carry" of ± 2.

14.15   **Decimal division** The quotient digit set $[-\alpha, \alpha]$ can be used to perform radix-10 division.

   a. Determine the minimally redundant quotient digit set if the next quotient digit is to be determined based on 1 decimal digit each from the partial remainder and divisor.

   b. Present a design for the decimal divider, including its quotient digit selection box.

   c. Assume that the decimal partial remainder is kept in carry-save form (i.e., using the digit set $[0, 10]$). How does this change affect the quotient digit selection logic?

REFERENCES

[Atki68]   Atkins, D. E., "Higher-Radix Division Using Estimates of the Divisor and Partial Remainders," *IEEE Trans. Computers*, Vol. 17, No. 10, pp. 925–934, 1968.

[Coe95]   Coe, T., and P. T. P. Tang, "It Takes Six Ones to Reach a Flaw," *Proc. 12th Symp. Computer Arithmetic*, July 1995, pp. 140–146.

[Edel97]   Edelman, A., "The Mathematics of the Pentium Division Bug," *SIAM Rev.*, Vol. 39, No. 1, pp. 54–67, March 1997.

[Erce87]   Ercegovac, M. D., and T. Lang, "On-the-Fly Conversion of Redundant into Conventional Representations," *IEEE Trans. Computers*, Vol. 36, No. 7, pp. 895–897, 1987.

[Frei61]   Freiman, C. V., "Statistical Analysis of Certain Binary Division Algorithms," *Proc. IRE*, Vol. 49, No. 1, pp. 91–103, 1961.

[Gepp95]   Geppert, L., "Biology 101 on the Internet: Dissecting the Pentium Bug," *IEEE Spectrum*, pp. 16–17, 1995.

[Nadl56]   Nadler, M., "A High-Speed Electronic Arithmetic Unit for Automatic Computing Machines," *Acta Technica* (Prague), No. 6, pp. 464–478, 1956.

[Robe58]   Robertson, J. E., "A New Class of Digital Division Methods," *IRE Trans. Electronic Computers*, Vol. 7, pp. 218–222, September 1958.

[Srin97]   Srinivas, H. R., K. K. Parhi, and L. A. Montalvo, "Radix 2 Division with Over-Redundant Quotient Selection," *IEEE Trans. Computers*, Vol. 46, No. 1, pp. 85–92, 1997.

[Tayl85]   Taylor, G. S., "Radix-16 SRT Dividers with Overlapped Quotient Selection Stages," *Proc. 7th Symp. Computer Arithmetic*, pp. 64–71, 1985.

[Toch58]   Tocher, K. D., "Techniques of Multiplication and Division for Automatic Binary Computers," *Quarterly J. Mechanics and Applied Mathematics*, Vol. 11, Pt. 3, pp. 364–384, 1958.

Chapter 15 | VARIATIONS IN DIVIDERS

In this chapter, we cover some practical aspects in implementing high-radix dividers. We also deal with prescaling methods, modular dividers, and array dividers. Chapter 12, entitled "Variations in Multipliers," covered the special case of squaring. It may appear, therefore, that a discussion of square-rooting belongs in this chapter. However, square-rooting, though quite similar to division, is not its special case. We will deal with square-rooting methods in Chapter 21. Chapter topics include:

15.1 QUOTIENT DIGIT SELECTION REVISITED

In the first two sections of this chapter, we elaborate on the quotient digit selection process and the practical use of *p-d* plots for high-radix division.

The dotted portion of Fig. 15.1 defines radix-r SRT division where the partial remainder s is in $[-d, d)$, the shifted partial remainder is in $[-rd, rd)$, and quotient digits are in $[-(r-1), r-1]$. Radix-4 division with the quotient digit set $[-3, 3]$, discussed in Section 14.5, is an example of this general scheme.

Consider now radix-r division with the symmetric quotient digit set $[-\alpha, \alpha]$, where $\alpha < r - 1$. Because of the restriction on quotient digit values, we need to restrict the partial remainder range, say to $[-hd, hd)$, to ensure that a valid quotient digit value always exists. From the solid rectangle in Fig. 15.1, we can easily derive the condition $rhd - \alpha d \leq hd$ or, equivalently, $h \leq \alpha/(r-1)$. To minimize the restriction on range, we usually choose:

$$h = \frac{\alpha}{r - 1}$$

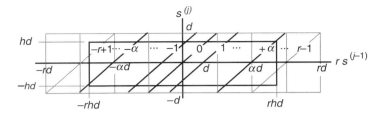

Fig. 15.1   The relationship between new and shifted old partial remainders in radix-r division with quotient digits in $[-\alpha, +\alpha]$.

As a special case, $r = 4$ and $\alpha = 2$ lead to $h = 2/3$ and the range $[-2d/3, 2d/3)$ for the partial remainder (see Fig. 14.13). Note that since $\alpha \geq r/2$, we have $h > 1/2$. Thus, a 1-bit right shift is always enough to ensure that $s^{(0)}$ is brought to within the required range at the outset.

The p-d plot is a very general and useful tool. Even though thus far we have assumed that d is in the range $[1/2, 1)$, this does not have to hold, and we can easily draw a p-d plot in which d ranges from any $d^{\min}$ to any $d^{\max}$ (e.g., from 1 to 2 for IEEE floating-point significands, introduced in Chapter 17). Figure 15.2 shows a portion of a p-d plot with this more general view of d.

With reference to the partial p-d plot depicted in Fig. 15.2, let us assume that inspecting 4 bits of p and 3 bits of d places us at point A. Because of truncation, the point representing the actual values of p and d can be anywhere inside the rectangle attached to point A. As long as the entire area of this "uncertainty rectangle" falls within the region associated with β or $\beta + 1$, there is no problem. So, at point A, we can confidently choose $q_{-j} = \beta + 1$ despite the uncertainty.

Now consider point B in Fig. 15.2 and assume that 3 bits of p and 4 bits of d are inspected. The new uncertainty rectangle drawn next to point B is twice as tall and half as wide and contains points for which each of the values β or $\beta + 1$ is the only correct choice. In this case, the ambiguity cannot be resolved and a choice for q_{-j} that is valid within the entire rectangle does not exist.

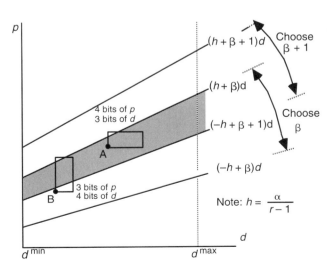

Fig. 15.2   A part of p-d plot showing the overlap region for choosing the quotient digit value β or $\beta + 1$ in radix-r division with quotient digit set $[-\alpha, \alpha]$.

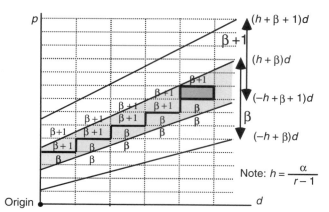

Fig. 15.3 A part of *p-d* plot showing an overlap region and its staircaselike selection boundary.

In practice, we want to make the uncertainty rectangle as large as possible, to minimize the number of bits in p and d needed for choosing the quotient digits. To determine whether uncertainty rectangles of a given size (say the one shown at point A in Fig. 15.2) are admissible, we tile the entire *p-d* plot with the given rectangle beginning at the origin (see Fig. 15.3). Next we verify that no tile intersects both boundaries of an overlap region (touching one boundary, while intersecting another one, is allowed). This condition is equivalent to being able to embed a staircaselike path, following the tile boundaries, in each overlap region (Fig. 15.3).

If the tiling is successful, we complete the process by associating a quotient digit value with each tile. This value is the table entry corresponding to the lower left corner point of the tile. When there is a choice, as is the case for the dark tile in Fig. 15.3, we use implementation- and technology-dependent criteria to pick one value over the other. More on this later.

In the preceding discussion, the partial remainder was assumed to be in standard binary form. If p is in carry-save form, then to get l bits of accuracy for p, we need to inspect $l + 1$ bits in each of its two components. Hence to simplify the selection logic (or size of the lookup table), we try to maximize the height of the uncertainty rectangle. For example, if both rectangles shown in Fig. 15.2 represented viable choices for the precision required of p and d, then the one associated with point B would be preferable (the quotient digit is selected based on $4+4+4 = 12$ bits, rather than $5 + 5 + 3 = 13$ bits, of information).

15.2 USING *p-d* PLOTS IN PRACTICE

Based on the preceding discussion, the goal of the designer of a high-radix divider is to find the coarsest possible grid (the dotted lines in Fig. 15.3) such that staircaselike boundaries, entirely contained within each of the overlap areas, can be built. Unfortunately, there is no closed-form formula for the required precisions, given the parameters r and α and the range of d. Thus, the process involves some trial and error, with the following analytical results used to limit the search space.

Consider the staircase embedded in the narrowest overlap area corresponding to the overlap between the digit values α and $\alpha - 1$. The minimum horizontal and vertical distances between the lines $(-h + \alpha)d$ and $(h + \alpha - 1)d$ place upper bounds on the dimensions of uncertainty rectangles (why?). From Fig. 15.4, these bounds, Δd and Δp, can be found:

$$\Delta d = d^{\min}\frac{2h-1}{-h+\alpha}$$

$$\Delta p = d^{\min}(2h-1)$$

For example, in radix-4 division with the divisor range $[1/2, 1)$ and the quotient digit set $[-2, 2]$, we have $\alpha = 2$, $d^{\min} = 1/2$, and $h = \alpha/(r-1) = 2/3$. Therefore:

$$\Delta d = (1/2)\frac{4/3-1}{-2/3+2} = 1/8$$

$$\Delta p = (1/2)(4/3-1) = 1/6$$

Since $1/8 = 2^{-3}$ and $2^{-3} \le 1/6 < 2^{-2}$, at least 3 bits of d (2, excluding its leading 1) and 3 bits of p must be inspected. These are lower bounds, and they may turn out to be inadequate. However, they help us limit the search to larger values only. Constructing a detailed p-d plot on graph paper for the preceding example shows that in fact 3 bits of p and 4 (3) bits of d are required. If p is kept in carry-save form, then 4 bits of each component must be inspected (or first added in a small fast adder to give the high-order 3 bits).

The entire process discussed thus far, from determining lower bounds on the precisions required to finding the actual precisions along with table contents or PLA structure, can be easily automated. However, the Intel Pentium bug teaches us that the results of such an automated design process must be rigorously verified.

So far, our p-d plots have been mostly limited to the upper right quadrant of the plane (nonnegative p and d). Note that even if we divide unsigned numbers, p can become negative in the course of division. So, we must consider at least one other quadrant of the p-d plot. We emphasize that the asymmetric effect of truncation of positive and negative values in 2's-complement format prevents us from using the same table entries, but with opposite signs, for the lower right quadrant.

To justify the preceding observation, consider point A, with coordinates d and p, along with its mirror image B, having coordinates d and $-p$ (Fig. 15.5). We see, from Fig. 15.5, that the quotient digit value associated with point B is not the negative of that for point A. So the table size must be expanded to include both (all four) quadrants of the p-d plot. To account for the sign information, one bit must be added to the number of bits inspected in both d and p.

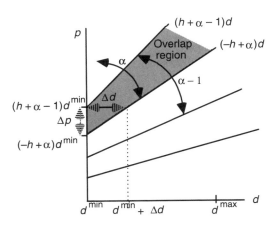

Fig. 15.4 Establishing upper bounds on the dimensions of uncertainty rectangles.

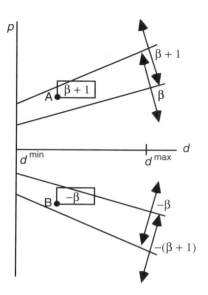

Fig. 15.5 The asymmetry of quotient digit selection process.

Occasionally, we have a choice of two different quotient digit values for a given tile in the p-d plot (dark tiles in Figs. 15.3 and 15.6). In a full table-lookup implementation of the quotient digit selection box, the choice has no implication for cost or delay. With a PLA implementation, however, such entries constitute partial don't-cares and can lead to logic simplification. The extent of simplification is of course dependent on the encoding used for the quotient digit.

In practice, one might select a lower precision that is "almost" good enough in the sense that only a few uncertainty rectangles are not totally contained within the region of a single quotient digit. These exceptions are then handled by including more inputs in their corresponding product terms. For the portion of the p-d plot shown in Fig. 15.6, the required precision can be reduced by one bit for each component (combining four small tiles into a larger tile), except for the four small tiles marked with asterisks.

For instance, if 3 bits of p in carry-save form ($u_{-1}, u_{-2}, u_{-3}, v_{-1}, v_{-2}, v_{-3}$) and 2 bits of d (d_{-2}, d_{-3}) are adequate in most cases, with d_{-4} also needed occasionally, the logical expression for each of the PLA outputs will consist of the sum of product terms involving eight variables in true or complement form. The ninth variable is needed in only a few of the product terms; thus its effect on the complexity of the required PLA is small.

15.3 DIVISION WITH PRESCALING

By inspecting Fig. 15.6 (or any of the other p-d plots that we have encountered thus far), one may observe that the overlap regions are wider toward the high end of the divisor range. Thus, if we can restrict the magnitude of the divisor to an interval close to $d^{\max}$ (say $1 - \varepsilon < d < 1 + \delta$, when $d^{\max} = 1$), the selection of quotient digits may become simpler; that is, it may be based on inspecting fewer bits of p and d or perhaps even made independent of d altogether.

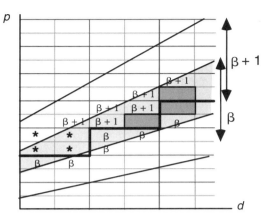

Fig. 15.6 Example of p-d plot allowing larger uncertainty rectangles, if the four cases marked with asterisks are handled as exceptions.

The preceding goal can be accomplished by performing the division $(zm)/(dm)$, instead of z/d, for a suitably chosen scale factor m ($m > 1$). Multiplying both the dividend and the divisor by a factor m to put the divisor in the restricted range $(1 - \varepsilon, 1 + \delta)$ is called "prescaling."

Of course for an arbitrary scaling factor, two multiplications would be required to find the scaled dividend and divisor. The trick is to accomplish the scaling through addition. A reasonable restriction, to keep the time and hardware overhead of prescaling to a minimum, is to require that only one pass through the hardware circuit that performs the division iterations be used for scaling each operand. In this way, we essentially use two additional cycles in the division process (one for scaling each operand). Since simpler quotient selection logic makes each iteration simpler and thus faster, a net gain in speed may result despite the extra cycles.

For example, in radix-8 division of 60-bit fractions, the number of iterations required is increased by 10% (from 20 to 22). A reduction of 20%, say, in the delay of each iteration would lead to a net gain of 12% in division time.

A main issue in the design of division algorithms with prescaling is the choice of the scaling factors. Consider the high-radix divider shown in Fig. 14.15: except that the partial remainder is kept as a single number rather than in stored-carry form. In the new arrangement, the carry-propagate adder is used in each cycle, with its output loaded into the partial remainder register. If the multiple generation/selection circuit provides h inputs to the CSA tree, then each division cycle essentially consists of an $(h + 1)$-operand addition. Let the scaling factor m be represented in radix 4 as $m = (m_0.m_{-1}m_{-2} \cdots m_{-h})_{\text{four}}$ using the digit set $[-1, 2]$; in fact, m_0 can be further restricted to $[1, 2]$. Then, the scaled divisor $m \times d$ can be computed by the $(h + 1)$-operand summation

$$m_0 d + 4^{-1} m_{-1} d + 4^{-2} m_{-2} d + \cdots + 4^{-h} m_{-h} d$$

Each of the $h + 1$ terms is easily obtained from d by shifting. The m_j values can be read out from a table based on a few most significant bits of d.

Consider an example with $h = 3$. If we inspect only 4 bits of d (beyond the mandatory 1) and they happen to be 0110, then $d = (0.10110 \cdots)_{\text{two}}$ is in the range $[11/16, 23/32]$. To put the scaled divisor as close to 1 as possible, we can pick the scale factor to be $m = (1. 2 \text{ }^{-}1 \text{ }^{-}1)_{four} = 91/64$. The scaled divisor will thus be in $[1001/1024, 2093/2048)$ or $[1 - 23/1024, 1 + 45/2048)$. For more detail and implementation considerations, see [Erce94].

15.4 MODULAR DIVIDERS AND REDUCERS

Given a dividend z and divisor d, with $d \geq 0$, a modular divider computes

$$q = \lfloor z/d \rfloor \quad \text{and} \quad s = z \bmod d = \langle z \rangle_d$$

Note that the quotient q is, by definition, an integer, but the inputs z and d do not have to be integers. For example, we have:

$$\lfloor -3.76/1.23 \rfloor = -4 \quad \text{and} \quad \langle -3.76 \rangle_{1.23} = 1.16$$

When z is positive, modular division is the same as ordinary integer division. Even when z and d are fixed-point numbers with fractional parts, we can apply an integer division algorithm to find q and s (how?). For a negative dividend z, however, ordinary division yields a negative remainder s, whereas the remainder (residue) in modular division is always positive. Thus, in this case, we must follow the division iterations with a correction step (adding d to the remainder and subtracting 1 from the integer quotient) whenever the final remainder is negative.

Often the aim of modular division is determining only the quotient q, or only the remainder s, with no need to obtain the other result. When only q is needed, we still have to perform a normal division; the remainder is obtained as a by-product of computing q. However, the computation of $\langle z \rangle_d$, which is referred to as modular reduction, might be faster or need less work than a full-blown division.

We have already discussed modular reduction for a constant divisor d in connection with obtaining the RNS representation of binary or decimal numbers (Section 4.3). Consider now the computation of $\langle z \rangle_d$ for arbitrary $2k$-bit dividend z and k-bit divisor d (both unsigned integers). The $2k$-bit dividend z can be decomposed into k-bit parts z_H and z_L, leading to:

$$\langle z \rangle_d = \langle z_H 2^k + z_L \rangle_d = \langle z_H (2^k - 1) + z_H + z_L \rangle_d$$

Thus, modular reduction can be converted to mod-d multiplication of z_H by $2^k - 1$ (see Section 12.4) and a couple of modular additions. This might be an attractive option if a fast modular multiplier is already available. One of the two additive terms, z_H or z_L, can be accommodated by using it as the initial value of the cumulative partial product. Both additive terms can be accommodated initially if the modular multiplier uses a stored-carry cumulative partial product.

If d is bit-normalized (its MSB is 1), then:

$$\langle 2^k \rangle_d = 2^k - d = \text{ 2's-complement of } d$$

Thus, in this case, $\langle z \rangle_d$ can be computed by mod-d multiplication of z_H and $2^k - d$, with the cumulative partial product initialized to z_L.

Of course, the preceding methods are relevant only if we do not have, or need, a fast hardware divider.

15.5 ARRAY DIVIDERS

Cells and structure very similar to those of array multipliers, discussed in Section 11.5, can be used to build an array divider. Figure 15.7 shows a restoring array divider built of controlled subtractor cells. Each cell has a full subtractor (FS) and a two-input multiplexer. When the control input broadcast to the multiplexers in a row of cells is 0, the cells' vertical inputs (bits of the partial remainder) are passed down unchanged. Otherwise, the diagonal input (divisor) is subtracted from the partial remainder and the difference is passed down. Note that the layout of the cells in Fig. 15.7 resembles the layout of dots in the dot notation view of division, exemplified by Fig. 13.1.

Effectively, each row of cells performs a trial subtraction, with the sign of the result determining the next quotient digit as well as whether the original partial remainder or the trial difference is to be forwarded to the next row. For practical hardware implementation, a faster cell can be built by merging the function of the multiplexer with that of the full subtractor.

The similarity of the array divider of Fig. 15.7 to an array multiplier is somewhat deceiving. The same number of cells is involved in both designs, and the cells have comparable complexities. However, the critical path in a $k \times k$ array multiplier contains $O(k)$ cells, whereas in Fig. 15.7 the critical path passes through all k^2 cells. This is because the borrow signal ripples in each row. Thus, an array divider is quite slow, and, given its high cost, not very cost-effective.

If many divisions are to be performed, pipelining can be applied to improve the throughput of the array divider. For example, if latches are inserted on the output lines for each row of cells in Fig. 15.7, the input data rate will be dictated by the delay associated with borrow propagation in a single row. Thus, with pipelining, the array divider of Fig. 15.7 becomes much more cost-effective, though it will still be slower than its pipelined array multiplier counterpart.

Figure 15.8 depicts a nonrestoring array divider. The cells have roughly the same complexity as the controlled subtractor cells of Fig. 15.7, but more of them are used to handle the extra sign

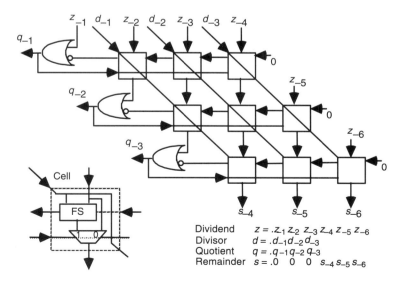

Dividend $\quad z = .z_{-1} z_{-2} z_{-3} z_{-4} z_{-5} z_{-6}$
Divisor $\quad d = .d_{-1} d_{-2} d_{-3}$
Quotient $\quad q = .q_{-1} q_{-2} q_{-3}$
Remainder $\quad s = .0 \quad 0 \quad 0 \quad s_{-4} s_{-5} s_{-6}$

Fig. 15.7 Restoring array divider composed of controlled subtractor cells.

position and the final correction of the partial remainder (last row of cells). The XOR gate in the cells of Fig. 15.7 acts as a selective complementer that passes the divisor or its complement to the full adder, thus leading to addition or subtraction being performed, depending on the sign of the previous partial remainder. The delay is still $O(k^2)$, and considerations for pipelining remain the same as for the restoring design.

Several techniques are available for reducing the delay of an array divider, but in each case additional complexity is introduced into the design. Therefore, none of these methods has found significant practical applications.

To obviate the need for carry/borrow propagation in each row, the partial remainder can be passed between rows in carry-save form. However, we still need to know the carry-out or borrow-out resulting from each row in order to determine the action to be performed in the following row (subtract vs. do not subtract in Fig. 15.7 or subtract vs. add in Fig. 15.8). This can be accomplished by using a carry- (borrow-) lookahead circuit laid out between successive rows of the array divider. However, in view of their need for long wires, the tree-structured lookahead circuits add considerably to the layout area and nullify some of the speed advantages of the original regular layout with localized connections.

Alternatively, a radix-2 or high-radix SRT algorithm can be used to estimate the quotient digit from a redundant digit set, using only a few of the most significant bits of the partial remainder and divisor. This latter approach may simplify the logic to be inserted between rows, but necessitates a more complex conversion of the redundant quotient to standard binary. Even though the wires required for this scheme are shorter than those for a lookahead circuit, they tend to make the layout irregular and thus less efficient.

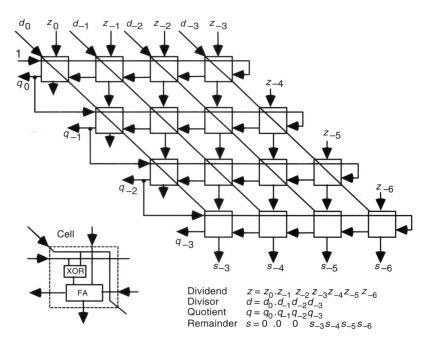

Dividend $z = z_0.z_{-1}\,z_{-2}\,z_{-3}z_{-4}z_{-5}\,z_{-6}$
Divisor $d = d_0.d_{-1}d_{-2}d_{-3}$
Quotient $q = q_0.q_{-1}q_{-2}q_{-3}$
Remainder $s = 0\ .0\quad 0\quad s_{-3}s_{-4}s_{-5}s_{-6}$

Fig. 15.8   Nonrestoring array divider built of controlled add/subtract cells.

15.6 COMBINED MULTIPLY/DIVIDE UNITS

Except for the quotient digit selection logic in dividers, which has no counterpart in multipliers, the required hardware elements for multipliers and dividers are quite similar. This similarity, which extends from basic radix-2 units, through high-radix designs, to array implementations, stems from the fact that both multiplication and division are essentially multioperand addition problems.

It is thus quite natural to combine multiplication and division capabilities into a single unit. Often, a capability for square-rooting is also included in the unit, since it too requires the same hardware elements (see Chapter 21). Such combined designs are desirable when the volume of numerical computations in expected applications does not warrant the inclusion of separate dedicated multiply and divide units. Even in a high-performance CPU optimized for applications with heavy use of multiplications and divisions, the use of two combined multiply/divide units, say, provides more opportunities for concurrent execution than separate multiply and divide units.

Figure 15.9 shows a radix-2 multiply/divide unit obtained by merging the multiplier of Fig. 9.4 with the nonrestoring divider of Fig. 13.10. The reader should be able to understand all elements in Fig. 15.9 by referring to the aforementioned figures and their accompanying descriptions. Note that the multiplier (quotient) register has been merged with the partial product (remainder) register, with their shifting boundary shown by a dotted line. Another difference is that the extra flip-flop in Fig. 13.10, used to hold the MSB of $2s^{(j-1)}$ has been incorporated into the multiply/divide control unit logic.

A similar merging of high-radix multipliers and dividers leads to combined high-radix multiply/divide units. For example, a radix-4 multiplier with Booth's recoding (Fig. 10.9) can be merged with a radix-4 SRT divider based on the quotient digit set $[-2, 2]$ (Fig. 14.8, modified for radix-4 division, as suggested near the end of Section 14.5) to yield a radix-4 multiply/divide unit. Since the recoded multiplier and the redundant quotient use the same digit set $[-2, 2]$, much of the multiple selection circuitry for the multiplicand and divisor can be shared. Supplying the block diagram and design details is left as an exercise.

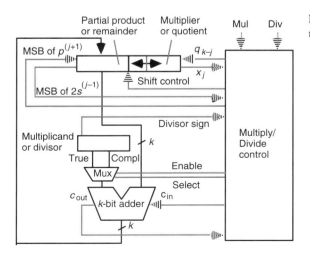

Fig. 15.9 Sequential radix-2 multiply/divide unit.

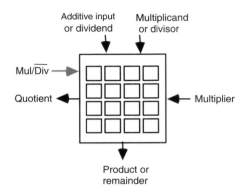

Additive input   Multiplicand
or dividend   or divisor

Mul/$\overline{\text{Div}}$ ——→

Quotient ◄——   ◄—— Multiplier

Product or
remainder

Fig. 15.10   I/O specification of a universal circuit that can act as an array multiplier or array divider.

Merging of partial- or full-tree multipliers with very-high-radix dividers is also possible. One way is to use the multioperand addition capability of the multiplier's partial or full tree to generate a reasonably accurate estimate for the divisor reciprocal $1/d$. This initial step is then followed by a small number of multiplications to produce the quotient q. Division algorithms based on multiplication are discussed in depth in Chapter 16.

Because of the similarity of a nonrestoring array divider (Fig. 15.8) to an array multiplier (Fig. 11.13), it is possible to design a universal circuit that can act as an array multiplier or divider depending on the value of a control input. Figure 15.10 shows a high-level view of such a circuit that also accepts an additive input for multiplication. The cells now become more complex than their array multiplier or divider counterparts, but the universality of the design obviates the need for separate circuits for multiplication and division. In an early universal pipelined array design of this type [Kama74], squaring and square-rooting were also included among the functions that could be performed. The array consisted of identical computational cells, plus special control cells in a column on its left edge.

PROBLEMS

15.1   Decimal division   Consider radix-10 division using the quotient digit set $[-6, 6]$.

    a.   Construct the upper right quadrant of the $p\text{-}d$ plot and determine the number of decimal digits that need to be examined in p and d for selecting the quotient digit.

    b.   Can the quotient digit selection logic or ROM be simplified if we are not restricted to inspect whole decimal digits (e.g., we can, if necessary, inspect the most significant 2 bits in the binary encoding of a decimal digit)?

    c.   Present a hardware design for the decimal divider assuming that the multiples $2d$, $3d$, $4d$, $5d$, and $6d$ are precomputed through five additions and stored in registers.

15.2   Quotient digit selection logic   Formulate a lower bound on the size of the lookup table for quotient digit selection as a function of Δd and Δp, introduced in Section 15.2. State all your assumptions. Does your lower bound apply to the number of product terms in a PLA implementation?

15.3   Radix-8 division

    a.   Draw the complete $p\text{-}d$ plot (both quadrants) for radix-8 division, with quotient digits in $[-4, 4]$ and the divisor in the range $[1, 2)$, on graph paper.

b. Using Δd and Δp, as discussed in Section 15.2, determine lower bounds on the precisions required of d and p in order to correctly select the quotient digit.

c. Assuming that p is in stored-carry form, determine the needed precision for d and p to minimize the number of input bits to the quotient digit selection logic or table.

d. Can you reduce the precisions obtained in part c for common cases by allowing a few special cases with higher precision?

15.4   Theory of high-radix division Prove or disprove the following assertions.

a. Once lower bounds on the number of bits of precision in p and d have been obtained through the analysis presented in Section 15.2 (i.e., from Δd and Δp), the use of one extra bit of precision for each is always adequate.

b. It is always possible to trade off one extra bit of precision in d for one less bit of precision in p in quotient digit selection.

15.5   Bit-serial division Prove that bit-serial division is infeasible for standard binary numbers, regardless of whether the inputs are supplied LSB-first or MSB-first. We are, of course, excluding any scheme in which all input bits are shifted in serially before division begins.

15.6   High-radix division with over-redundant quotient Study the effect of changing the radix from r to $r/2$, while keeping the same digit set as in radix r, on the overlap regions in Fig. 15.4 and the precision required of p and d in selecting the quotient digit. Relate your discussion to radix-2 division with over-redundant quotient introduced in Problem 14.14.

15.7   Significand divider with no remainder In dividing the significands of two floating-point numbers, both the dividend and divisor are k bits wide and computing the remainder is not needed. Discuss if and how this can lead to simplified hardware for the significand divider. Note that the divider can have various designs (restoring or nonrestoring binary, high-radix, array, etc.).

15.8   One's-complement binary dividers

a. Draw the block diagram of a restoring signed divider for 1's-complement numbers. Discuss any complication due to the use of 1's-complement operands and differences with a 2's-complement divider.

b. Repeat part a for a nonrestoring 1's-complement binary divider.

15.9   RNS dividers Sketch the design of an RNS divider that uses approximate magnitude comparison between RNS partial remainder and divisor, as discussed in Section 4.4, to produce a BSD quotient. Include on-the-fly conversion hardware to generate an RNS quotient from the BSD quotient and an analysis of the precision required in the comparisons.

15.10   Division with prescaling Suppose that prescaling is used to limit the range of the divisor d to $(0.9, 1.1)$.

     a. Construct a *p-d* plot similar to that in Fig. 14.14 for radix-4 division with the digit set [−2, 2].

     b. Derive the required precision in p and d for quotient digit selection.

     c. Compare the results of part b to those obtained from Fig. 14.14 and discuss.

15.11 **Division with prescaling** Discuss whether it is possible to apply prescaling to a divider that keeps its partial remainder in stored-carry form.

15.12 **Restoring array divider** For the restoring array divider of Fig. 15.7:

     a. Explain the function of the OR gates at the left edge of the array.

     b. Can the OR gates be replaced by controlled subtractor cells in the interest of uniformity? How or why not?

     c. Verify that the array divider works correctly by tracing through the signal values for the division .011111/.110.

     d. Explain how the array can be modified to perform signed division.

15.13 **Nonrestoring array divider** For the nonrestoring array divider of Fig. 15.8:

     a. Explain the wraparound links for the four cells located at the right edge of the array.

     b. Explain the dangling or unused outputs in three of the four cells located at the left edge of the array.

     c. Verify that the array divider works correctly by tracing through the signal values for the division 0.011111/0.110.

     d. Present modifications in the design such that partial remainders are passed downward in carry-save form and lookahead circuits are used between rows to derive the carry-out q_{-i}.

     e. Estimate the improvement in speed as a result of the modifications presented in part e and discuss the cost-effectiveness of the new design.

     f. Show how the array can be used for signed division. *Hint:* Modify the input at the upper left corner, which is now connected to the constant 1.

     g. Test your proposed solution to part g by tracing the division 1.10001/0.110.

     h. Show how the array can be modified to perform modular division, as discussed in Section 15.4.

15.14 **BSD array divider** We would like to construct an array divider for binary signed-digit (BSD) numbers using the digit set [−1, 1], encoded as 10, 00, and 01, for −1, 0, and 1, respectively.

     a. Present the design of a controlled subtractor cell for BSD numbers.

     b. Show how the structure of a nonrestoring array divider must be modified to deal with BSD numbers.

     c. Compare the resulting design with a nonrestoring array divider with respect to speed and cost.

15.15   Combined multiply/divide units

    a.   Draw a complete block diagram for a radix-4 multiply/divide unit, as discussed in Section 15.6.

    b.   Supply the detailed design of the array multiplier/divider shown in Fig. 15.10, assuming unsigned inputs.

    c.   Discuss modifications required to the design of part b for 2's-complement inputs.

15.16   Divider with a multiplicative input Consider the design of a unit to compute $y = az/d$, where y, a, z, and d are k-bit fractions. A radix-4 algorithm is to be used for computing $q = z/d$. As digits of $q = z/d$ in $[-2, 2]$ are obtained, they are multiplied by a and the product aq is accumulated using radix-4 multiplication with left shifts.

    a.   Present a block diagram for the design of this divider with multiplicative input.

    b.   Evaluate the speed advantage of the unit compared to cascaded multiply and divide units.

    c.   Evaluate the speed penalty of the unit when used to perform simple multiplication or division.

15.17   Division with quotient digit prediction In a divider, whether using a carry-propagate or a carry-save adder in each cycle, the quotient digit selection logic is on the critical path that determines the cycle time. Since the delay for quotient digit selection can be significant for higher radices, one idea is to select the following cycle's quotient digit q_{-j-1} as the current cycle's quotient digit q_{-j} is used to produce the new partial remainder $s^{(j)}$. The trick is to overcome the dependence of q_{-j-1} on $s^{(j)}$ by generating an approximation to $s^{(j)}$ that is then used to predict q_{-j-1} in time for the start of the next cycle. Discuss the issues involved in the design of dividers with quotient digit prediction. Include in your discussion the two cases of carry-propagate and carry-save division cycles [Erce94].

REFERENCES

[Agra79]   Agrawal, D. P., "High-Speed Arithmetic Arrays," *IEEE Trans. Computers*, Vol. 28, No. 3, pp. 215–224, 1979.

[Atki68]   Atkins, D. E., "Higher-Radix Division Using Estimates of the Divisor and Partial Remainders," *IEEE Trans. Computers*, Vol. 17, No. 10, pp. 925–934, 1968.

[Capp73]   Cappa, M., and V. C. Hamacher, "An Augmented Iterative Array for High-Speed Binary Division," *IEEE Trans. Computers*, Vol. 22, pp. 172–175, February 1973.

[Erce94]   Ercegovac, M. D., and T. Lang, *Division and Square Root: Digit-Recurrence Algorithms and Implementations*, Kluwer, 1994.

[Kama74]   Kamal, A. K., et al., "A Generalized Pipeline Array," *IEEE Trans. Computers*, Vol. 23, No. 5, pp. 533–536, 1974.

[Lo86]   Lo, H.-Y., "An Improvement of Nonrestoring Array Divider with Carry-Save and Carry-Lookahead Techniques," in *VLSI '85*, E. Horbst, (ed.), Elsevier, 1986, pp. 249–257.

[Ober97]   Oberman, S. F., and M. J. Flynn, "Division Algorithms and Implementations," *IEEE Trans. Computers*, Vol. 46, No. 8, pp. 833–854, 1997.

[Robe58]   Robertson, J. E., "A New Class of Digital Division Methods," *IRE Trans. Electronic Computers*, Vol. 7, pp. 218–222, September 1958.

[Schw93]   Schwarz, E. M., and M. J. Flynn, "Parallel High-Radix Nonrestoring Division," *IEEE Trans. Computers*, Vol. 42, No. 10, pp. 1234–1246, 1993.

[Stef72]   Stefanelli, R., "A Suggestion for a High-Speed Parallel Divider," *IEEE Trans. Computers*, Vol. 21, No. 1, pp. 42–55, 1972.

[Tayl85]   Taylor, G. S., "Radix-16 SRT Dividers with Overlapped Quotient Selection Stages," *Proc. 7th Symp. Computer Arithmetic*, pp. 64–71, 1985.

[Zura87]   Zurawski, J. H. P., and J. B. Gosling, "Design of a High-Speed Square Root, Multiply, and Divide Unit," *IEEE Trans. Computers*, Vol. 36, No. 1, pp. 13–23, 1987.

Chapter 16 | DIVISION BY CONVERGENCE

Digit-recurrence division schemes discussed in Chapters 13-15 can be viewed as manipulation of s (initially z) and q (initially 0) in k cycles such that s tends to 0 as q converges to the quotient. One digit of convergence is obtained per cycle. In this chapter, we will see that through the use of multiplication as the basic step, instead of addition, convergence of q to its final value can occur in $O(\log k)$ rather than $O(k)$ cycles, albeit with each cycle being more complex than in digit-recurrence division.

16.1 GENERAL CONVERGENCE METHODS

Convergence computation methods are characterized by two or three recurrence equations that are used to iteratively adjust/update the values of the variables u and v (and w). The two- and three-variable versions of such convergence methods are written as follows:

$$u^{(i+1)} = f(u^{(i)}, v^{(i)}) \qquad u^{(i+1)} = f(u^{(i)}, v^{(i)}, w^{(i)})$$
$$v^{(i+1)} = g(u^{(i)}, v^{(i)}) \qquad v^{(i+1)} = g(u^{(i)}, v^{(i)}, w^{(i)})$$
$$w^{(i+1)} = h(u^{(i)}, v^{(i)}, w^{(i)})$$

The functions f and g (and h) specify the computations to be performed in each updating cycle. Beginning with the initial values $u^{(0)}$ and $v^{(0)}$ (and $w^{(0)}$), we go through a number of iterations, each time computing $u^{(i+1)}$ and $v^{(i+1)}$ (and $w^{(i+1)}$) based on $u^{(i)}$ and $v^{(i)}$ (and $w^{(i)}$). We direct the iterations such that one value, say u, converges to some constant. The value of v (and/or w) then converges to the desired function(s).

The complexity of this method obviously depends on two factors:

ease of evaluating f and g (and h)

rate of convergence (or number of iterations needed)

Many specific instances of the preceding general method are available and can be used to compute a variety of useful functions. A number of examples are discussed in this chapter and in Chapters 21–23.

Digit-recurrence division methods, discussed in Chapters 13–15, can in fact be formulated as convergence computations. Given the fractional dividend z and divisor d, the quotient q and remainder s can be computed by a recurrence scheme of the general form

$$s^{(j)} = s^{(j-1)} - \gamma^{(j)}d \qquad \text{Set } s^{(0)} = z; \text{ make } s \text{ converge to } 0$$
$$q^{(j)} = q^{(j-1)} + \gamma^{(j)} \qquad \text{Set } q^{(0)} = 0; \text{ obtain } q \approx q^{(k)}$$

where the $\gamma^{(j)}$ can be any sequence of values that make the residual (partial remainder) s converge to 0. The invariant of the iterative computation above is

$$s^{(j)} + q^{(j)}d = z$$

which leads to $q^{(k)} \approx z/d$ when $s^{(k)} \approx 0$.

In digit-recurrence division with fractional operands, $\gamma^{(j)}$ is taken to be $q_{-j}r^{-j}$ (i.e., the contribution of the jth digit of the quotient q to its value). We can rewrite the preceding recurrences by dealing with $r^j s^{(j)}$ and $r^j q^{(j)}$ as the scaled residual and quotient, respectively:

$$s^{(j)} = rs^{(j-1)} - q_{-j}d \qquad \text{Set } s^{(0)} = z; \text{ keep } s \text{ bounded}$$
$$q^{(j)} = rq^{(j-1)} + q_{-j} \qquad \text{Set } q^{(0)} = 0; \text{ obtain } q \approx q^{(k)}r^{-k}$$

The original residual s can be made to converge to 0 by keeping the magnitude of the scaled residual in check. For example, if the scaled residual $s^{(j)}$ is in $[-d, d)$, the unscaled residual would be in $[-d2^{-j}, d2^{-j})$; thus convergence of s to 0 is readily accomplished.

The many digit-recurrence division schemes considered in Chapters 13–15 simply correspond to variations in the radix r, the scaled residual bound, and quotient digit selection rule. The functions f and g of digit-recurrence division are quite simple. The function f, for updating the scaled residual, is computed by shifting and (multioperand) addition. The function g, for updating the scaled quotient, corresponds to the insertion of the next quotient digit into a register via a one-digit left shift.

Even though high-radix schemes can reduce the number of iterations in digit-recurrence division, we still need O(k) iterations with any small fixed radix $r = 2^b$. The rest of this chapter deals with division by other convergence methods that require far fewer [i.e. O(log k)] iterations. Note that as we go to digit-recurrence division schemes entailing very high radices, quotient digit selection and the computation of the subtractive term $q_{-j}d$ become more difficult. Computation of $q_{-j}d$ involves a multiplication in which one of the operands is much narrower than the other one. So, in a sense, high-radix digit-recurrence division also involves multiplication.

16.2 DIVISION BY REPEATED MULTIPLICATIONS

To compute the ratio $q = z/d$, one can repeatedly multiply z and d by a sequence of m multipliers $x^{(0)}, x^{(1)}, \ldots, x^{(m-1)}$:

$$q = \frac{z}{d} = \frac{zx^{(0)}x^{(1)}\cdots x^{(m-1)}}{dx^{(0)}x^{(1)}\cdots x^{(m-1)}}$$

If this is done in such a way that the denominator $dx^{(0)}x^{(1)}\cdots x^{(m-1)}$ converges to 1, the numerator $zx^{(0)}x^{(1)}\cdots x^{(m-1)}$ will converge to q. This process does not yield a remainder, but the remainder s (if needed) can be computed, via an additional multiplication and a subtraction, using $s = z - qd$.

To perform division based on the preceding idea, we face three questions:

1. How should we select the multipliers $x^{(i)}$ such that the denominator does in fact converge to 1?
2. Given a selection rule for the multipliers $x^{(i)}$ how many iterations (pairs of multiplications) are needed?
3. How are the required computation steps implemented in hardware?

In what follows, we will answer these three questions in turn. But first, let us formulate this process as a convergence computation.

Assume a bit-normalized fractional divisor d in $[1/2, 1)$. If this condition is not satisfied initially, it can be made to hold by appropriately shifting both z and d. The corresponding convergence computation is formulated as follows:

$$d^{(i+1)} = d^{(i)}x^{(i)} \qquad \text{Set } d^{(0)} = d; \text{ make } d^{(m)} \text{ converge to 1}$$
$$z^{(i+1)} = z^{(i)}x^{(i)} \qquad \text{Set } z^{(0)} = z; \text{ obtain } z/d = q \approx z^{(m)}$$

We now answer the first question posed above by selecting:

$$x^{(i)} = 2 - d^{(i)}$$

This choice transforms the recurrence equations into:

$$d^{(i+1)} = d^{(i)}(2 - d^{(i)}) \qquad \text{Set } d^{(0)} = d; \text{ iterate until } d^{(m)} \approx 1$$
$$z^{(i+1)} = z^{(i)}(2 - d^{(i)}) \qquad \text{Set } z^{(0)} = z; \text{ obtain } z/d = q \approx z^{(m)}$$

Thus, computing the functions f and g consists of determining the 2's-complement of $d^{(i)}$ and two multiplications by the result $2 - d^{(i)}$.

Now on to the second question: How quickly does $d^{(i)}$ converge to 1? In other words, how many multiplications are required to perform division? Noting that

$$d^{(i+1)} = d^{(i)}(2 - d^{(i)}) = 1 - (1 - d^{(i)})^2$$

we conclude that:

$$1 - d^{(i+1)} = (1 - d^{(i)})^2$$

Thus, if $d^{(i)}$ is already close to 1 (i.e., $1 - d^{(i)} \leq \varepsilon$), $d^{(i+1)}$ will be even closer to 1 (i.e., $1 - d^{(i+1)} \leq \varepsilon^2$). This property is known as *quadratic convergence* and leads to a logarithmic number m of iterations to complete the process. To see why, note that because d is in [1/2, 1), we begin with $1 - d^{(0)} \leq 2^{-1}$. Then, in successive iterations, we have $1 - d^{(1)} \leq 2^{-2}$, $1 - d^{(2)} \leq 2^{-4}, \cdots, 1 - d^{(m)} \leq 2^{-2^m}$. If the machine word is k bits wide, we can get no closer to 1 than $1 - 2^{-k}$. Thus, the iterations can stop when 2^m equals or exceeds k. This gives us the required number of iterations:

$$m = \lceil \log_2 k \rceil$$

Table 16.1 shows the progress of computation, and the pattern of convergence, in the four cycles required with 16-bit operands. For a 16-by-16 division, the preceding convergence method requires 7 multiplications (two per cycle, except in the last cycle, where only $z^{(4)}$ is computed); with 64-bit operands, we need 11 multiplications and 6 complementation steps. In general, for k-bit operands, we need

$$2m - 1 \text{ multiplications} \qquad \text{and} \qquad m \text{ 2's-complementations}$$

where $m = \lceil \log_2 k \rceil$.

Figure 16.1 shows a graphical representation of the convergence process in division by repeated multiplications. Clearly, convergence of $d^{(i)}$ to 1 and $z^{(i)}$ to q occurs from below; that is, in all intermediate steps, $d^{(i)} < 1$ and $z^{(i)} < q$. After the required number m of iterations, $d^{(m)}$ equals $1 - ulp$, which is the closest it can get to 1. At this point, $z^{(m)}$ is the required quotient q.

Answering the third, and final, question regarding hardware implementation is postponed until after the discussion of a related algorithm in Section 16.3.

Let us now say a few words about computation errors. Note that even if machine arithmetic is completely error-free, $z(m)$ can be off from q by up to ulp (when $z = d$, both $d^{(i)}$ and $z^{(i)}$ converge to $1 - ulp$). The maximum error in this case can be reduced to $ulp/2$ by simply adding ulp to any quotient with $q_{-1} = 1$.

The following approximate analysis captures the effect of errors in machine arithmetic. We present a more detailed discussion of computation errors in Chapter 19 in connection with real-number arithmetic.

TABLE 16.1
Quadratic convergence in computing z/d by repeated multiplications, where $1/2 \leq d = 1 - y < 1$

i	$d^{(i)} = d^{(i-1)} x^{(i-1)}$, with $d^{(0)} = d$	$x^{(i)} = 2 - d^{(i)}$
0	$1 - y \quad = (.1xxx\ xxxx\ xxxx\ xxxx)_{two} \geq 1/2$	$1 + y$
1	$1 - y^2 \quad = (.11xx\ xxxx\ xxxx\ xxxx)_{two} \geq 3/4$	$1 + y^2$
2	$1 - y^4 \quad = (.1111\ xxxx\ xxxx\ xxxx)_{two} \geq 15/16$	$1 + y^4$
3	$1 - y^8 \quad = (.1111\ 1111\ xxxx\ xxxx)_{two} \geq 255/256$	$1 + y^8$
4	$1 - y^{16} = (.1111\ 1111\ 1111\ 1111)_{two} = 1 - ulp$	

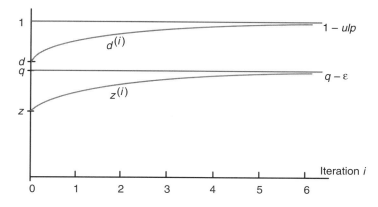

Fig. 16.1 Graphical representation of convergence in division by repeated multiplications.

Suppose that $k \times k$ multiplication is performed by simply truncating the exact $2k$-bit product to k bits, thus introducing a negative error that is upper-bounded by ulp. Note that computing $2 - d^{(i)}$ can be error-free, provided we can represent, and compute with, numbers that are in $[0, 2)$, or else we scale down such numbers by shifting them to the right and keeping an extra bit or two of precision beyond position $-k$. We can also ignore any error in computing $d^{(i+1)}$, since such errors affect both recurrence equations and thus do not change the ratio z/d.

The worst-case error of ulp, introduced by the multiplication used to compute z in each iteration, leads to an accumulated error that is bounded by $m\,ulp$ after m iterations. If we want to keep this error bound below 2^{-k}, we must perform all intermediate computations with at least $\log_2 m$ extra bits of precision. Since in practice m is quite small (say, $m \le 5$), this requirement can be easily satisfied.

16.3 DIVISION BY RECIPROCATION

Another way to compute $q = z/d$ is to first find $1/d$ and then multiply the result by z. If several divisions by the same divisor d need to be performed, this method is particularly efficient, since once $1/d$ is found for the first division, each subsequent division involves just one additional multiplication.

The method we use for computing $1/d$ is based on Newton–Raphson iteration to determine a root of $f(x) = 0$. We start with some initial estimate $x^{(0)}$ for the root and then iteratively refine the estimate using the recurrence

$$ x^{(i+1)} = x^{(i)} - \frac{f(x^{(i)})}{f'(x^{(i)})} $$

where $f'(x)$ is the derivative of $f(x)$. Figure 16.2 provides a graphical representation of the refinement process. Let $\tan \alpha^{(i)}$ be the slope of the tangent to $f(x)$ at $x = x^{(i)}$. Then, referring to Fig. 16.2, the preceding iterative process is easily justified by noting that:

$$\tan \alpha^{(i)} = f'(x^{(i)}) = \frac{f(x^{(i)})}{x^{(i)} - x^{(i+1)}}$$

To apply the Newton–Raphson method to reciprocation, we use $f(x) = 1/x - d$ which has a root at $x = 1/d$. Then, $f'(x) = -1/x^2$, leading to the recurrence:

$$x^{(i+1)} = x^{(i)}(2 - x^{(i)}d) \quad \text{See below for the initial value } x^{(0)}$$

Computationally, two multiplications and a 2's-complementation step are required per iteration. Let $\delta^{(i)} = 1/d - x^{(i)}$ be the error at the ith iteration. Then:

$$\delta^{(i+1)} = 1/d - x^{(i+1)} = 1/d - x^{(i)}(2 - x^{(i)}d)$$
$$= d(1/d - x^{(i)})^2 = d(\delta^{(i)})^2$$

Since $d < 1$, we have $\delta^{(i+1)} < (\delta^{(i)})^2$, proving quadratic convergence. If the initial value $x^{(0)}$ is chosen such that $0 < x^{(0)} < 2/d$, leading to $|\delta^{(0)}| < 1/d$, convergence is guaranteed.

At this point, we are interested only in simple schemes for selecting $x^{(0)}$, with more elaborate, and correspondingly more accurate, methods to be discussed later. For d in [1/2, 1), picking

$$x^{(0)} = 1.5$$

is quite simple and adequate, since it limits $|\delta^{(0)}|$ to the maximum of 0.5. A better approximation, with a maximum error of about 0.1, is

$$x^{(0)} = 4(\sqrt{3} - 1) - 2d = 2.9282 - 2d$$

which can be obtained easily and quickly from d by shifting and adding.

The effect of inexact multiplications on the final error $\delta^{(m)} = 1/d - x^{(m)}$ can be determined by an analysis similar to that offered at the end of Section 16.2. Here, each iteration involves two back-to-back multiplications, thus leading to the bound $2m$ ulp for the accumulated error and the requirement for an additional bit of precision in the intermediate computations.

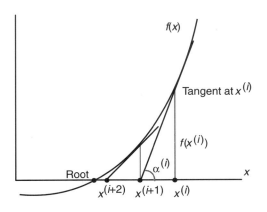

Fig. 16.2   Convergence to a root of $f(x) = 0$ in the Newton–Raphson method.

16.4 SPEEDUP OF CONVERGENCE DIVISION

Thus far, we have shown that division can be performed via $2\lceil \log_2 k \rceil - 1$ multiplications. This is not yet very impressive, since with 64-bit numbers and a 5-ns multiplier, division would need at least 55 ns. Three types of speedup are possible in division by repeated multiplications or by reciprocation:

reducing the number of multiplications

using narrower multiplications

performing the multiplications faster

Note that convergence is slow in the beginning. For example, in division by repeated multiplications, it takes six multiplications to get 8 bits of convergence and another five to go from 8 bits to 64 bits. The role of the first four multiplications is to provide a number $x^{(2)} = 2 - dx^{(0)}x^{(1)}$ such that when $x^{(2)}$ is multiplied by $z^{(2)}$ and $d^{(2)} = dx^{(0)}x^{(1)}$, we have 8 bits of convergence in the latter.

$$d = (0.1\text{xxx xxxx} \cdots)_{\text{two}}$$
$$dx^{(0)} = (0.11\text{xx xxxx} \cdots)_{\text{two}}$$
$$dx^{(0)}x^{(1)} = (0.1111 \text{ xxxx} \cdots)_{\text{two}}$$
$$dx^{(0)}x^{(1)}x^{(2)} = (0.1111 \text{ } 1111 \cdots)_{\text{two}}$$

Since $x^{(0)}x^{(1)}x^{(2)}$ is essentially an approximation to $1/d$, these four initial multiplications can be replaced by a table-lookup step that directly supplies $x^{(0+)}$, an approximation to $x^{(0)}x^{(1)}x^{(2)}$ obtained based on a few high-order bits of d, provided the same convergence is achieved. Similarly, in division by reciprocation, a better starting approximation can be obtained via table lookup.

The remaining question is: How many bits of d must be inspected to achieve w bits of convergence after the first iteration? This is important because it dictates the size of the lookup table. In fact, we will see that $x^{(0+)}$ need not be a full-width number. If $x^{(0+)}$ is 8 bits rather than 64 bits wide, say, the lookup table will be eight times smaller and the first iteration can become much faster, since it involves multiplying an 8-bit multiplier by two 64-bit multiplicands.

We will prove, in Section 16.6, that a $2^w \times w$ lookup table is necessary and sufficient for achieving w bits of convergence after the first pair of multiplications. Here, we make a useful observation. For division by repeated multiplications, we saw that convergence to 1 and q occurred from below (Fig. 16.1). This does not have to be the case. If at some point in our iterations, $d^{(i)}$ overshoots 1 (e.g., becomes $1 + \varepsilon$), the next multiplicative factor $2 - d^{(i)} = 1 - \varepsilon$ will lead to a value smaller than 1, but still closer to 1, for $d^{(i+1)}$ (Fig. 16.3).

So, in fact, what is important is that $|d^{(i)} - 1|$ decrease quadratically. It does not matter if $x^{(0+)}$ obtained from the table causes $dx^{(0+)}$ to become greater than 1; all we need to guarantee that $1 - 2^{-16} \le dx^{(0+)}x^{(3)} < 1$ is to have $1 - 2^{-8} \le dx^{(0+)} \le 1 + 2^{-8}$. This added flexibility helps us in reducing the table size (both the number of words and the width).

We noted earlier that the first pair of multiplications following the table-lookup involve a narrow multiplier and may thus be faster than a full-width multiplication. The same applies to subsequent multiplications if the multiplier is suitably truncated. The result is that convergence occurs from above or below (Fig. 16.4).

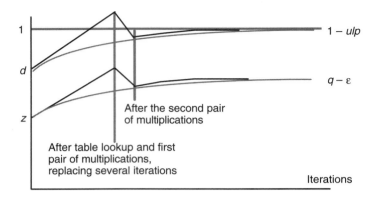

Fig. 16.3   Convergence in division by repeated multiplications with initial table lookup.

Here is an analysis for the effect of truncating the multiplicative factors to speed up the multiplications. We begin by noting that:

$$dx^{(0)}x^{(1)}\cdots x^{(i)} = 1 - y^{(i)}$$
$$x^{(i+1)} = 2 - (1 - y^{(i)}) = 1 + y^{(i)}$$

Assume that we truncate $1 - y^{(i)}$ to an a-bit fraction, thus obtaining $(1 - y^{(i)})_T$ with an error of $\alpha < 2^{-a}$. With this truncated multiplicative factor, we get

$$(x^{(i+1)})_T = 2 - (1 - y^{(i)})_T \quad \text{where} \quad 0 \le (x^{(i+1)})_T - x^{(i+1)} < 2^{-a}$$

Thus:

$$dx^{(0)}x^{(1)}\cdots x^{(i)}(x^{(i+1)})_T = (1 - y^{(i)})(1 + y^{(i)} + \alpha) = 1 - (y^{(i)})^2 + \alpha(1 - y^{(i)})$$
$$= dx^{(0)}x^{(1)}\cdots x^{(i)}x^{(i+1)} + \alpha(1 - y^{(i)})$$

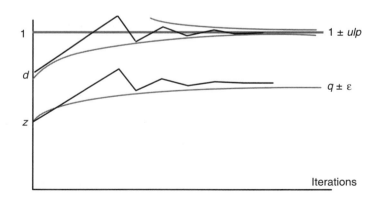

Fig. 16.4   Convergence in division by repeated multiplications with initial table lookup and the use of truncated multiplicative factors.

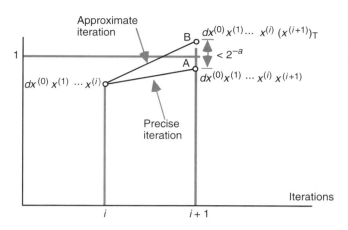

Fig. 16.5 One step in convergence division with truncated multiplicative factors.

Since $(1 - y^{(i)})$ is less than 1, the last term above is less than α and we have:

$$0 \le \alpha(1 - y^{(i)}) < 2^{-a}$$

Hence, if we are aiming to go from l bits to $2l$ bits of convergence, we can truncate the next multiplicative factor to $2l$ bits. To justify this claim, consider Fig. 16.5. Point A, which is the result of precise iteration, is no more than 2^{-2l} below 1. Thus, with $a = 2l$, point B, arrived at by the approximate iteration, will be no more than 2^{-2l} above 1.

Now, putting things together for an example 64-bit multiplication, we need a table of size $256 \times 8 = 2\text{K}$ bits for the lookup step. Then we need pairs of multiplications, with the multiplier being 9 bits, 17 bits, and 33 bits wide. The final step involves a single 64×64 multiplication.

16.5 HARDWARE IMPLEMENTATION

The hardware implementation of basic schemes for division by repeated multiplications or by reciprocation is straightforward. Both methods need two multiplications per iteration and both can use an initial table lookup step and truncation of the intermediate results to reduce the number of iterations and to speed up the multiplications.

If the hardware multiplier used is based on a digit-recurrence (binary or high-radix) algorithm, then narrower operands translate directly into fewer steps and correspondingly higher speed. For the 64-bit example at the end of Section 16.4, the total number of bit-level iterations to perform the seven multiplications required would be $2(9 + 17 + 33) + 64 = 182$. This is roughly equivalent to the number of bit-level iterations in three full 64×64 multiplications.

Convergence division methods are more likely to be implemented when a fast parallel (tree) multiplier is available. In the case of a full-tree multiplier, the narrower multiplicative factors may not offer any speed advantage. However, if a partial CSA tree, of the type depicted in Fig. 11.9 is used, a narrower multiplier leads to higher speed. For example, if the tree can handle $h = 9$ new inputs at once, the first pair of multiplications in our 64-bit example would require just one pass through the tree, the second pair would need two passes each (one pass if Booth's recoding is applied), and so on.

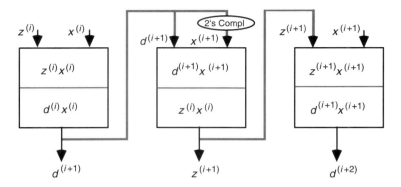

Fig. 16.6   Two multiplications fully overlapped in a two-stage pipelined multiplier.

Finally, since two independent multiplications by the same multiplier are performed in each step of division by repeated multiplications, the two can be pipelined (in both the full-tree and partial-tree implementations), thus requiring less time than two back-to-back multiplications. In such a case, the multiplication for $d^{(i)}$ is scheduled first, to get the result needed for the next iteration quickly and to keep the pipeline as full as possible. This is best understood for a multiplier that is implemented as a two-stage pipeline (Fig. 16.6). As the computation of $z^{(i)}x^{(i)}$ moves from the top to the bottom pipeline stage, the next iteration begins by computing the top stage of $d^{(i+1)}x^{(i+1)}$. We thus see that with a pipelined multiplier, the two multiplications needed in each iterations can be fully overlapped.

The pipelining scheme shown in Fig. 16.6 is not applicable to convergence division through divisor reciprocation, since in the recurrence $x^{(i+1)} = x^{(i)}(2 - x^{(i)}d)$, the second multiplication by $x^{(i)}$ needs the result of the first one. The most promising speedup method in this case relies on deriving a better starting approximation to $1/d$. For example, if the starting approximation is obtained with an error bound of 2^{-16}, then only three multiplications would be needed for a 32-bit quotient and five for a 64-bit result. But 16 bits of precision in the starting approximation would imply a large lookup table. The required lookup table can be made smaller, or totally eliminated, by a variety of methods:

1. Store the reciprocal values for fewer points and use linear (one multiply-add operation) or higher-order interpolation to compute the starting approximation (see Section 24.4).
2. Formulate the starting approximation as a multioperand addition problem and use one pass through the multiplier's CSA tree, suitably augmented, to compute it [Schw96].

With all the speedup methods discussed so far, the total division time can often be reduced to that of two to five ordinary multiplications. This has made convergence division a common choice for high-performance CPUs.

16.6 ANALYSIS OF LOOKUP TABLE SIZE

The required table size, for radix 2 with the goal of w bits of convergence after the first iteration (i.e., $1 - 2^{-w} \le dx^{(0+)} \le 1 + 2^{-w}$), is given in the following theorem.

THEOREM 16.1   To get $w \geq 5$ bits of convergence in the first iteration of division by repeated multiplications, w bits of d (beyond the mandatory 1) must be inspected. The factor $x^{(0+)}$ read out from the table is of the form $(1. \text{xxxx} \cdots \text{xxxx})_{\text{two}}$, with w bits after the radix point [Parh87].

Based on the Theorem 16.1, the required table size is $2^w \times w$ and the first pair of multiplications involve a $(w + 1)$-bit multiplier $x^{(0+)}$.

A proof sketch for Theorem 16.1 begins as follows. A general analysis for an arbitrary radix r as well as a complete derivation of special cases that allow smaller tables (in number of words and/or width) can be found elsewhere [Parh87]. These special cases ($r = 3$ and $w = 1$, or $r = 2$ with $w \leq 4$) almost never arise in practice, and we can safely ignore them here.

Recall that our objective is to have $1 - 2^{-w} \leq dx^{(0+)} \leq 1 + 2^{-w}$. Let

$$d = (0.1\underline{d_{-2}d_{-3} \cdots d_{-(w+1)}}d_{-(w+2)} \cdots d_{-l})_{\text{two}}$$
$$\underbrace{\phantom{0.1 d_{-2}d_{-3} \cdots d_{-(w+1)}}}_{w \text{ bits to be inspected}}$$

Theorem 16.1 postulates the existence of $x^{(0+)} = (1.x_{-1}^{+}x_{-2}^{+} \cdots x_{-w}^{+})_{\text{two}}$ satisfying the objective inequality. Let $u = (1d_{-2}d_{-3} \cdots d_{-(w+1)})_{\text{two}}$, satisfying $2^w \leq u < 2^{w+1}$, be the integer composed of the first $w + 1$ bits of d. We have:

$$2^{-(w+1)}u \leq d < 2^{-(w+1)}(u + 1)$$

Similarly, let $v = (1x_{-1}^{+}x_{2}^{+} \cdots x_{-w}^{+})_{\text{two}}$ be obtained from $x^{(0+)}$ by removing its radix point (multiplying it by 2^w). From the preceding inequalities for d and because the objective inequality can be rewritten as $2^w - 1 \leq dv \leq 2^w + 1$, we derive the following sufficient conditions:

$$2^w - 1 \leq 2^{-(w+1)}uv \qquad \text{and} \qquad 2^{-(w+1)}(u + 1)v \leq 2^w + 1$$

These conditions lead to the following restrictions on v:

$$\frac{2^{w+1}(2^w - 1)}{u} \leq v \leq \frac{2^{w+1}(2^w + 1)}{u + 1}$$

The existence of $x^{(0+)}$, as postulated, is thus contingent upon the preceding inequalities yielding an integer solution for v. This latter condition is equivalent to:

$$\left\lceil \frac{2^{w+1}(2^w - 1)}{u} \right\rceil \leq \left\lfloor \frac{2^{w+1}(2^w + 1)}{u + 1} \right\rfloor$$

Showing that this last inequality always holds is left as an exercise and completes the "sufficiency" part of the proof. The "necessity" part—namely, that at least w bits of d must be inspected and that $x^{(0+)}$ must have at least w bits after the radix point—is also left as an exercise.

Thus, to achieve 8 bits of convergence after the initial pair of multiplications, we need to look at 8 bits of d (beyond the mandatory 1) and read out an 8-bit fractional part f for $x^{(0+)} = 1 + .f$. Table 16.2 shows two sample entries in the required lookup table. The first entry in this table

TABLE 16.2
Sample entries in the lookup table replacing the first four multiplications in division by repeated multiplications

Address	$d = 0.1$ xxxx xxxx	$x^{(0+)} = 1.$xxxx xxxx
55	0011 0111	1010 0101
64	0100 0000	1001 1001

has been determined as follows. Since d begins with the bit pattern 0.1001 1011 1, its value is in the range

$$311/512 \le d < 312/512$$

Given the requirement for 8 bits of convergence after the first pair of multiplications, the table entry f must be chosen such that

$$311/512(1 + .f) \ge 1 - 2^{-8}$$
$$312/512(1 + .f) \le 1 + 2^{-8}$$

From the preceding restrictions, we conclude that $199/311 \le .f \le 101/156$, or for the integer $f = 256 \times .f$, $163.81 \le f \le 165.74$. Hence, the table entry f can be either of the integers $164 = (1010\,0100)_{two}$ or $165 = (1010\,0101)_{two}$.

PROBLEMS

16.1   Division by repeated multiplications

  a. Perform the division z/d, with unsigned fractional dividend $z = (.0101\,0110)_{two}$ and divisor $d = (.1011\,1001)_{two}$, through repeated multiplications.

  b. Construct a table that provides the initial factor leading to 4 bits of convergence after the first multiplication. Note that $w = 4$ is a special case that leads to a smaller table compared to the one suggested by Theorem 16.1.

  c. Perform the division of part a using the table of part b at the outset.

16.2   Division by repeated multiplications

  a. Perform the division z/d, with unsigned fractional dividend $z = (.4321)_{ten}$ and divisor $d = (.4456)_{ten}$, through repeated multiplications.

  b. Suggest a simple final correction to improve the accuracy of the result in part a.

  c. Construct a table that provides the initial multiplicative factor leading to 1 decimal digit of convergence after the first multiplication.

  d. Perform the division of part a using the table of part b at the outset.

16.3   Iterative reciprocation Using Newton–Raphson iterations and decimal arithmetic with six digits of precision after the radix point throughout:

  a. Compute the reciprocal of $d = (.823\,456)_{ten}$.

b. Compute the reciprocal of $d = (.512\ 345)_{\text{ten}}$.

c. Construct a segment of the initial lookup table with 10 two-digit entries (corresponding to $d = .50, .51, \cdots, .59$, with an entry ij representing $1.ij$) to provide the best possible initial approximation to $1/d$.

d. Repeat part b, this time using the table of part c at the outset.

16.4 Iterative reciprocation

a. Compute the reciprocal of $d = (.318\ 310)_{\text{ten}} \approx 1/\pi$ using $x^{(i+1)} = x^{(i)}(2 - x^{(i)}d)$ and arithmetic with six digits after the decimal point throughout. Keep track of the difference between $x^{(i)}$ and π to determine the number of iterations needed.

b. Repeat part a, using the expansion $1/d = 1/(1 - y) \approx (1+y)(1+y^2)(1+y^4)\cdots$, where $y = 1 - d$, instead of the Newton–Raphson iteration. Each term $1 + y^{2^{i+1}}$ is computed by squaring y^{2^i} and adding 1.

c. Compare the methods of parts a and b and discuss.

16.5 Division by reciprocation

a. Perform the division z/d, with unsigned fractional dividend $z = (.0101\ 0110)_{\text{two}}$ and divisor $d = (.1010\ 1100)_{\text{two}}$, through reciprocation.

b. Construct a table of approximate reciprocals providing 4 bits of convergence (i.e., the product of the approximate reciprocal and d should have four leading 0s or 1s).

c. Perform the division of part a using the table of part b at the outset.

d. Based on the example of part b, formulate and prove a theorem, similar to Theorem 16.1, for the initial reciprocal approximation.

16.6 Division by reciprocation An alternative Newton–Raphson iterative method for computing the reciprocal of d uses $f(x) = (x - 1 + 1/d)/(x - 1)$, which has a root at the complement of $1/d$.

a. Find the alternative iteration formula.

b. Compute the error term and prove quadratic convergence.

c. Use this alternative method to compute the reciprocal of $d = (.823\ 456)_{\text{ten}}$.

d. Use this alternative method to compute the reciprocal of $d = (.512\ 345)_{\text{ten}}$.

e. Comment on this new algorithm compared to the original one.

16.7 Division by reciprocation

a. Derive the maximum error for the starting approximation $x^{(0)} = 4(\sqrt{3} - 1) - 2d$ in division by reciprocation.

b. Find the best linear approximation involving a multiply-add operation and compare its worst-case error to the error of part a.

16.8 Table lookup for convergence division

a. Complete the "sufficiency" proof of Theorem 16.1 by showing that the inequality $\lceil 2^{w+1}(2^w - 1)/u \rceil \le \lfloor 2^{w+1}(2^w + 1)/(u + 1) \rfloor$ always holds. *Hint:* Let q and s

($s \leq u$) be the quotient and remainder of dividing $2^{w+1}(2^w + 1)$ by $u + 1$. The right-hand side of the inequality is thus q. Try simplifying the left-hand side.

b. Construct the "necessity" part of the proof of Theorem 16.1 by showing that $x^{(0+)}$ satisfying $1 - 2^{-w} \leq dx^{(0+)} \leq 1 + 2^{-w}$ cannot have fewer than w bits after the radix point and cannot be obtained by inspecting fewer than w bits of d.

16.9   Convergence division with truncated multipliers

a. Prove that in division through repeated multiplications, a truncated denominator $d^{(i)}$, with a identical leading bits and b extra bits ($b \leq a$), will lead to a new denominator $d^{(i+1)}$ with at least $a + b$ identical leading bits.

b. Briefly discuss the implications of the result of part a for an arithmetic unit that uses an initial table lookup to obtain 8 bits of convergence and can perform 18×64 multiplications about 2.5 times as fast as full 64×64 multiplications.

16.10   Cubic convergence method Consider the following iterative formula for finding an approximate root of a nonlinear function f [Pozr98]: $x^{(i+1)} = x^{(i)} - [f(x^{(i)})/f'(x^{(i)})][1 + f(x^{(i)})f''(x^{(i)})/(2f'^2(x^{(i)}))]$.

a. Show that this iterative scheme exhibits cubic convergence.

b. Discuss the practical use of this method for function evaluation.

16.11   Cubic convergence method Consider the following iterative formula for finding an approximate root of a nonlinear function f: $x^{(i+1)} = x^{(i)} - 2f(x^{(i)})f'(x^{(i)})/[2(f'(x^{(i)}))^2 - f(x^{(i)})f''(x^{(i)})]$.

a. Show that this iterative scheme exhibits cubic convergence.

b. Try out the iterative formula for a nonlinear function of your choosing.

c. Discuss the practicality of the formula for function evaluation in digital computers.

16.12   Table lookup for convergence division Justify the second entry in Table 16.2 in the same manner as was done for the first entry in Section 16.6. Then, supply the entries for the addresses 5, 158, and 236.

16.13   Mystery convergence method The following two iterative formulas are applied to a bit-normalized binary fraction z in [1/2, 1): $u^{(i+1)} = u^{(i)}(x^{(i)})^2$ with $u^{(0)} = z$ and $v^{(i+1)} = v^{(i)}x^{(i)}$ with $v^{(0)} = z$.

a. Determine the function $v = g(z)$ that is computed if $x^{(i)} = 1 + (1 - u^{(i)})/2$.

b. Discuss the number of iterations that are needed and the operations that are executed in each iteration.

c. Suggest how the multiplicative term $x^{(i)}$ might be calculated.

d. Estimate the error in the final result.

e. Suggest ways to speed up the calculation.

f. Calculate the 8-bit result $v = g(z)$ using the procedure above and compare it to the correct result, given $z = (.1110\ 0001)_{two}$.

16.14   Table lookup for reciprocal approximation Inspecting w bits of the divisor in the initial table lookup for division by reciprocation divides the divisor range into 2^w equal-width intervals $[a^{(i)}, b^{(i)})$.

a. Show that a table entry equal to the average of $1/a^{(i)}$ and $1/b^{(i)}$ minimizes the worst-case error.

b. Show that a table entry equal to $2/(a^{(i)}+b^{(i)})$, that is, the reciprocal of the midpoint of the interval, minimizes the average-case error, assuming uniform distribution of divisor values.

16.15 **Table lookup for reciprocal approximation** Inspecting w bits of the divisor in the initial table lookup for division by reciprocation divides the divisor range into 2^w equal-width intervals. Prove that rounding the reciprocals of the midpoints of these intervals provides minimal worst-case relative errors in a w-bits-in, $(w+b)$-bits-out table [DasS94].

16.16 **Division by convergence** Consider the recurrences $s^{(j)} = rs^{(j-1)} - q_{-j}d$ and $q^{(j)} = rq^{(j-1)} + q_{-j}$, discussed in Section 16.1. We can take a somewhat more general view of these recurrences by rewriting q_{-j} as γ_j, an estimate for the rest of the quotient rather than its next digit. The estimate is obtained by table lookup based on a few high-order bits in $rs^{(j-1)}$. With this more general view, the second recurrence must be evaluated through addition rather than by concatenation (shifting the next digit into a register). Evaluate the suitability of this method for division via repeated multiplications [Wong92].

REFERENCES

[Ande67] Anderson, S. F., J. G. Earle, R. E. Goldschmidt, and D. M. Powers, "The IBM System/360 Model 91: Floating-Point Execution Unit," *IBM J. Research and Development*, Vol. 11, No. 1, pp. 34–53, 1967.
[DasS94] DasSarma, D., and D. W. Matula, "Measuring the Accuracy of ROM Reciprocal Tables," *IEEE Trans. Computers*, Vol. 43, No. 8, pp. 932–940, 1994.
[Ferr67] Ferrari, D., "A Division Method Using a Parallel Multiplier," *IEEE Trans. Electronic Computers*, Vol. 16, pp. 224–226, April 1967
[Flyn70] Flynn, M. J., "On Division by Functional Iteration," *IEEE Trans. Computers*, Vol. 19, pp. 702–706, August 1970.
[Kris70] Krishnamurthy, E. V., "On Optimal Iterative Schemes for High Speed Division," *IEEE Trans. Computers*, Vol. 19, No. 3, pp. 227–231, 1970.
[Ober97] Oberman, S. F., and M. J. Flynn, "Division Algorithms and Implementations," *IEEE Trans. Computers*, Vol. 46, No. 8, pp. 833–854, 1997.
[Omon94] Omondi, A. R., *Computer Arithmetic Systems: Algorithms, Architecture and Implementation*, Prentice-Hall, 1994.
[Parh87] Parhami, B., "On the Complexity of Table Look-Up for Iterative Division," *IEEE Trans. Computers*, Vol. 36, No. 10, pp. 1233–1236, 1987.
[Pozr98] Pozrikidis, C., *Numerical Computation in Science and Engineering*, Oxford, 1998, p. 203.
[Schw96] Schwarz, E. M., and M. J. Flynn, "Hardware Starting Approximation Method and Its Application to the Square Root Operation," *IEEE Trans. Computers*, Vol. 45, No. 12, pp. 1356–1369, 1996.
[Wong92] Wong, D., and M. Flynn, "Fast Division Using Accurate Quotient Approximations to Reduce the Number of Iterations," *IEEE Trans. Computers*, Vol. 41, No. 8, pp. 981–995, 1992.

PART V | REAL ARITHMETIC

In many scientific and engineering computations, numbers in a wide range, from very small to extremely large, are processed. Fixed-point number representations and arithmetic are ill-suited to such applications. For example, a fixed-point decimal number system capable of representing both 10^{-20} and 10^{20} would require at least 40 decimal digits and even then, would not offer much precision with numbers close to 10^{-20}. Thus, we need special number representations that possess both a wide range and acceptable precision. Floating-point numbers constitute the primary mode of real arithmetic in most digital systems. In this part, we discuss key topics in floating-point number representation, arithmetic, and computational errors. Additionally, we cover alternative representations, such as logarithmic and rational number systems, that can offer certain advantages in range and/or accuracy. This part is composed of the following four chapters:

Chapter
17 | FLOATING-POINT REPRESENTATIONS

In Chapters 1–3, we dealt with various methods for representing fixed-point numbers. Such representations suffer from limited range and/or precision, in the sense that they can provide high precision only by sacrificing the dynamic range, and vice versa. By contrast, a floating-point number system offers both a wide dynamic range for accommodating extremely large numbers (e.g., astronomical distances) and high precision for very small numbers (e.g., atomic distances). Chapter topics include:

17.1 FLOATING-POINT NUMBERS

Clearly, no finite representation method is capable of representing all real numbers, even within a small range. Thus, most real values will have to be represented in an approximate manner. Various methods of representation can be used:

Fixed-point number systems: offer limited range and/or precision. Computations must be "scaled" to ensure that values remain representable and that they do not lose too much precision.

Rational number systems: approximate a real value by the ratio of two integers. Lead to difficult arithmetic operations (see Section 20.2).

Floating-point number systems: the most common approach; discussed in Chapters 17–20.

Logarithmic number systems: represent numbers by their signs and logarithms. Attractive for applications needing low precision and wide dynamic range. Can be viewed as a limiting special case of floating-point representation (see Section 17.6).

Fixed-point representation leads to equal spacing in the set of representable numbers. Thus the maximum absolute error is the same throughout (*ulp* with truncation and *ulp*/2 with rounding). The problem with fixed-point representation is illustrated by the following examples:

$$x = (0000\ 0000.\ 0000\ 1001)_{two} \qquad \text{Small number}$$
$$y = (1001\ 0000.\ 0000\ 0000)_{two} \qquad \text{Large number}$$

The relative representation error due to truncation or rounding is quite significant for x while it is much less severe for y. On the other hand, both x^2 and y^2 are unrepresentable, because their computations lead to underflow (number too small) and overflow (too large), respectively.

The other three representation methods listed above lead to denser codes for smaller values and sparser codes for larger values. However, the code assignment patterns are different, leading to different ranges and error characteristics. For the same range of representable values, these representations tend to be better than fixed-point systems in terms of average relative representation error, even though the absolute representation error increases as the values get larger.

The numbers x and y in the preceding examples can be represented as $(1.001)_{two} \times 2^{-5}$ and $(1.001)_{two} \times 2^{+7}$, respectively. The exponent -5 or $+7$ essentially indicates the direction and amount by which the radix-point must be moved to produce the corresponding fixed-point representation shown above. Hence the designation "floating-point numbers."

A floating-point number has four components: the sign, the significand s, the exponent base b, and the exponent e. The exponent base b is usually implied (not explicitly represented) and is usually a power of 2, except, of course, for decimal arithmetic, where it is 10. Together, these four components represent the number:

$$x = \pm s \times b^e \quad \text{or} \quad \pm\ \text{significand} \times \text{base}^{\text{exponent}}$$

A typical floating-point representation format is shown in Fig. 17.1. A key point to observe is that two signs are involved in a floating-point number.

1. The significand or number sign, which indicates a positive or negative floating-point number and is usually represented by a separate sign bit (signed-magnitude convention).
2. The exponent sign which, roughly speaking, indicates a large or small number and is usually embedded in the biased exponent (Section 2.2). When the bias is a power of 2 (e.g., 128 with an 8-bit exponent), the exponent sign is the complement of its most significant bit.

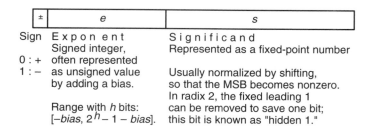

Fig. 17.1   Typical floating-point number format.

The use of a biased exponent format has virtually no effect on the speed or cost of exponent arithmetic (addition/subtraction), given the small number of bits involved. It does, however, facilitate zero detection (zero can be represented with the smallest biased exponent of 0 and an all-zero significand) and magnitude comparison (we can compare normalized floating-point numbers as if they were integers).

The range of values in a floating-point number representation format is composed of the intervals $[-max, -min]$ and $[min, max]$, where:

$$max = \text{largest significand} \times b^{\text{largest exponent}}$$

$$min = \text{smallest significand} \times b^{\text{smallest exponent}}$$

Figure 17.2 shows the number distribution pattern and the various subranges in floating-point representations. In particular, it includes the three special or singular values $-\infty$, 0, and $+\infty$ (0 is special because it cannot be represented with a normalized significand) and depicts the meanings of overflow and underflow. Overflow occurs when a result is less than $-max$ or greater than max. Underflow, on the other hand, occurs for results in the range $(-min, 0)$ or $(0, min)$.

Within the preceding framework, many alternative floating-point representation formats can be devised. In fact, before the IEEE standard format (see Section 17.2) was adopted, numerous competing, and incompatible, floating-point formats existed in digital computers. Even now that the IEEE standard format is dominant, on certain (rare) occasions in the design of special-purpose systems, the designer might choose a different format for performance or cost reasons.

The equation $x = \pm s \times b^e$ for the value of a floating-point number suggests that the range $[-max, max]$ increases if we choose a larger exponent base b. A larger b also simplifies arithmetic operations on the exponents, since for a given range, smaller exponents must be dealt with. However, if the significand is to be kept in normalized form, effective precision decreases for larger b. In the past, machines with $b = 2, 8, 16$, or 256 were built. But the modern trend is to use $b = 2$ to maximize the precision with normalized significands.

The exponent sign is almost always encoded in a biased format, for reasons given earlier in this section. As for the sign of a floating-point number, alternatives to the currently dominant signed-magnitude format include the use of 1's- or 2's-complement representation. Several variations have been tried in the past, including the complementation of the significand part only and the complementation of the entire number (including the exponent part) when the number to be represented is negative.

Once we have fixed b and assigned one bit to the number sign, the next question is the allocation of the remaining bits to the exponent and significand parts. Devoting more bits to the exponent part widens the number representation range but reduces the precision. So, the designer's choice is dictated by the range and precision requirements of the application(s) at hand.

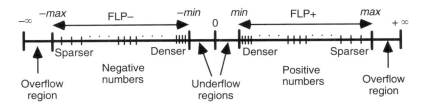

Fig. 17.2 Subranges and special values in floating-point number representations.

The final question, given the allocation of a total of m bits for the binary fixed-point significand s, is the choice of k, the number of whole bits to the left of the radix point in s. Again, many variations appeared in the past. The choice $k = 0$ leads to a fractional significand in the range $[0, 1)$, sometimes referred to as the *mantissa*. At the other extreme, choosing $k = m$ leads to an integer significand that increases both *max* and *min* (see Fig. 17.2), thus narrowing the overflow region and widening the underflow region. The same effect can be achieved by choosing an off-center bias for the exponent.

The only other common choice for the number of whole bits in the significand of a floating-point number, and the one used in the IEEE standard, is $k = 1$, leading to significands in the range $[1, 2)$. With normalized binary significands, this single whole bit, which is always 1, can be dropped and the significand represented by its fractional part alone.

Virtually all digital computers have separate formats for integers and floating-point numbers, even though, in principle, k-digit integers can be represented in a floating-point format that has a k-digit significand. One reason is that integer arithmetic is both simpler and faster; thus there is no point in subjecting integers to unnecessary complications. Another reason is that with a separate integer format, that has no exponent part, larger numbers can be represented exactly.

If one chooses to have a common format for integers and floating-point numbers, it is a good idea to include an "inexact flag" in the representation. For numbers that have exact representations in the floating-point format, the inexact flag may be set to 0. When the result of a computation with exact operands is too small or too large to be represented exactly, the inexact flag of the result can be set to 1. Note that dealing with this inexact flag is another source of complexity.

17.2 THE ANSI/IEEE FLOATING-POINT STANDARD

In the early days of digital computers, it was quite common for machines from various vendors to have different word widths and unique floating-point formats. Word widths were standardized at powers of 2 early on, with nonconforming word widths such as 24, 36, 48, and 60 bits all but disappearing. However, even after 32- and 64-bit words became the norm, different floating-point formats persisted. A main objective in developing a standard floating-point representation is to make numerical programs predictable and completely portable, in the sense of producing the same results when run on different machines.

The two representation formats in IEEE standard for binary floating-point numbers, formally known as "ANSI/IEEE Std 754-1985," are depicted in Fig. 17.3. The short, or single-precision, format is 32 bits wide, whereas the long, or double-precision, version requires 64 bits. The two formats have 8- and 11-bit exponent fields and use exponent biases of 127 and 1023, respectively. The significand is in the range $[1, 2)$, with its single whole bit, which is always 1, removed and only the fractional part shown. The notation "$23 + 1$" or "$52 + 1$" for the width of the significand is meant to explicate the role of the hidden bit, which does contribute to the precision without taking up space.

Table 17.1 summarizes the most important features of the IEEE standard floating-point representation format.

Since 0 cannot be represented with a normalized significand, a special code must be assigned to it. In the IEEE standard format, zero has the all-0s representation, with positive or negative sign. Special codes are also needed for representing $\pm\infty$ and NaN (not-a-number). The NaN special value is useful for representing undefined results such as 0/0. When one of these special

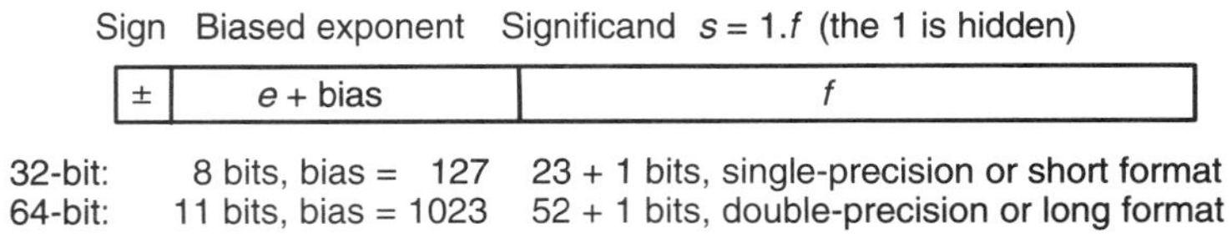

Sign   Biased exponent   Significand $s = 1.f$ (the 1 is hidden)

±	e + bias	f

32-bit: 8 bits, bias =   127   23 + 1 bits, single-precision or short format
64-bit: 11 bits, bias = 1023   52 + 1 bits, double-precision or long format

Fig. 17.3   The ANSI/IEEE standard floating-point number representation formats.

values appears as an operand in an arithmetic operation, the result of the operation is specified according to defined rules that are part of the standard. For example:

$$\text{Ordinary number } \div (+\infty) = \pm 0$$

$$(+\infty) \times \text{Ordinary number} = \pm\infty$$

$$\text{NaN} + \text{Ordinary number} = \text{NaN}$$

The special codes thus allow exceptions to be propagated to the end of a computation rather than bringing it to a halt. More on this later.

Denormals, or denormalized values, are defined as numbers without a hidden 1 and with the smallest possible exponent. They are provided to make the effect of underflow less abrupt. In other words, certain small values that are not representable as normalized numbers, hence must be rounded to 0 if encountered in the course of computations, can be represented more precisely as denormals. For example, $(0.0001)_{\text{two}} \times 2^{-126}$ is a denormal that does not have a normalized representation in the IEEE single/short format. Because this "graceful underflow" provision can lead to cost and speed overhead in hardware, many implementations of the standard do not support denormals, opting instead for the faster "flush to zero" mode. Figure 17.4 shows the role of denormals in providing representation points in the otherwise empty interval (0, *min*).

TABLE 17.1
Some features of the ANSI/IEEE standard floating-point number representation formats

Feature	Single/Short	Double/Long
Word width, bits	32	64
Significand bits	23 + 1 hidden	52 + 1 hidden
Significand range	$[1, 2 - 2^{-23}]$	$[1, 2 - 2^{-52}]$
Exponent bits	8	11
Exponent bias	127	1023
Zero (± 0)	$e + bias = 0, f = 0$	$e + bias = 0, f = 0$
Denormal	$e + bias = 0, f \neq 0$ represents $\pm 0.f \times 2^{-126}$	$e + bias = 0, f \neq 0$ represents $\pm 0.f \times 2^{-1022}$
Infinity ($\pm\infty$)	$e + bias = 255, f = 0$	$e + bias = 2047, f = 0$
Not-a-number (NaN)	$e + bias = 255, f \neq 0$	$e + bias = 2047, f \neq 0$
Ordinary number	$e + bias \in [1, 254]$ $e \in [-126, 127]$ represents $1.f \times 2^e$	$e + bias \in [1, 2046]$ $e \in [-1022, 1023]$ represents $1.f \times 2^e$
min	$2^{-126} \approx 1.2 \times 10^{-38}$	$2^{-1022} \approx 2.2 \times 10^{-308}$
max	$\approx 2^{128} \approx 3.4 \times 10^{38}$	$\approx 2^{1024} \approx 1.8 \times 10^{308}$

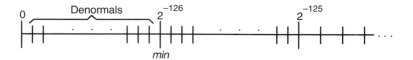

Fig. 17.4   Denormals in the IEEE single-precision format.

The IEEE floating-point standard also defines the four basic arithmetic operations (add, subtract, multiply, divide), as well as square-root, with regard to the expected precision in their results. Basically, the results of these operations must match the results that would be obtained if all intermediate computations were carried out with infinite precision. Thus, it is up to the designers of floating-point hardware units adhering to the IEEE standard to carry sufficient precision in intermediate results to satisfy this requirement.

Finally, the IEEE standard defines extended formats that allow implementations to carry higher precisions internally to reduce the effect of accumulated errors. Two extended formats are defined:

Single-extended: ≥ 11 bits for exponent, ≥ 32 bits for significand
(Bias unspecified, but exponent range must include $[-1022, 1023]$.)

Double-extended: ≥ 15 bits for exponent, ≥ 64 bits for significand
(Bias unspecified, but exponent range must include $[-16382, 16383]$.)

The use of an extended format does not, in and of itself, guarantee that the precision requirements of floating-point operations will be satisfied. Rather, extended formats are useful for controlling error propagation in a sequence of arithmetic operations. For example, when adding a list of floating-point numbers, a more precise result is obtained if positive and negative values are added separately, with the two subtotals combined in a final addition (we discuss computation errors in Chapter 19). Now if the list of numbers has thousands of elements, it is quite possible that computing one or both subtotals will lead to overflow. If an extended format is used (single-extended with single-precision operands, double-extended for double-precision operands), overflow becomes much less likely.

17.3   BASIC FLOATING-POINT ALGORITHMS

Basic arithmetic on floating-point numbers is conceptually simple. However, care must be taken in hardware implementations for ensuring correctness and avoiding undue loss of precision; in addition, it must be possible to handle any exceptions.

Addition and subtraction are the most difficult of the elementary operations for floating-point operands. Here, we deal only with addition, since subtraction can be converted to addition by flipping the sign of the subtrahend. Consider the addition:

$$(\pm s1 \times b^{e1}) + (\pm s2 \times b^{e2}) = \pm s \times b^e$$

Assuming $e1 \geq e2$, we begin by aligning the two operands through right-shifting of the significand $s2$ of the number with the smaller exponent:

$$\pm s2 \times b^{e2} = \frac{\pm s2}{b^{e1-e2}} \times b^{e1}$$

If the exponent base b and the number representation radix r are the same, we simply shift $s2$ to the right by $e1 - e2$ digits. When $b = r^a$ the shift amount, which is computed through direct subtraction of the biased exponents, is multiplied by a. In either case, this step is referred to as *alignment shift*, or *preshift* (in contrast to *normalization shift* or *postshift*, which is needed when the resulting significand s is unnormalized). We then perform the addition as follows:

$$(\pm s1 \times b^{e1}) + (\pm s2 \times b^{e2}) = (\pm s1 \times b^{e1}) + \left(\frac{\pm s2}{b^{e1-e2}} \times b^{e1} \right)$$

$$= \left(\pm s1 \pm \frac{s2}{b^{e1-e2}} \right) \times b^{e1} = \pm s \times b^e$$

When the operand signs are alike, a single-digit normalizing shift is always enough. For example, with the IEEE format, we have $1 \le s < 4$, which may have to be reduced by a factor of 2 through a single-bit right shift (and adding 1 to the exponent to compensate). However, when the operands have different signs, the resulting significand may be very close to 0 and left shifting by many positions may be needed for normalization. Overflow/underflow can occur during the addition step as well as due to normalization.

Floating-point multiplication is simpler than floating-point addition; it is performed by multiplying the significands and adding the exponents:

$$(\pm s1 \times b^{e1}) \times (\pm s2 \times b^{e2}) = \pm (s1 \times s2) \times b^{e1+e2}$$

Postshifting may be needed, since the product $s1 \times s2$ of the two significands can be unnormalized. For example, with the IEEE format, we have $1 \le s1 \times s2 < 4$, leading to the possible need for a single-bit right shift. Also, the computed exponent needs adjustment if the exponents are biased or if a normalization shift is performed. Overflow/underflow is possible during multiplication if $e1$ and $e2$ have like signs; overflow is also possible due to normalization.

Similarly, floating-point division is performed by dividing the significands and subtracting the exponents:

$$\frac{\pm s1 \times b^{e1}}{\pm s2 \times b^{e2}} = \pm \frac{s1}{s2} \times b^{e1-e2}$$

Here, problems to be dealt with are similar to those of multiplication. The ratio $s1/s2$ of the significands may have to be normalized. With the IEEE format, we have $1/2 < s1/s2 < 2$ and a single-bit left shift is always adequate. The computed exponent needs adjustment if the exponents are biased or if a normalizing shift is performed. Overflow/underflow is possible during division if $e1$ and $e2$ have unlike signs; underflow due to normalization is also possible.

To extract the square root of a positive floating-point number, we first make its exponent even. This may require subtracting 1 from the exponent and multiplying the significand by b. We then use the following:

$$\sqrt{s \times b^e} = \sqrt{s} \times b^{e/2}$$

In the case of IEEE floating-point numbers, the adjusted significand will be in the range $1 \le s < 4$, which leads directly to a normalized significand for the result. Square-rooting never produces overflow or underflow.

In the preceding discussion, we ignored the need for rounding. The product $s1 \times s2$ of two significands, for example, may have more digits than can be accommodated. When such a value is rounded so that it is representable with the available number of digits, the result may have to be normalized and the exponent adjusted again. Thus, though the event is quite unlikely, rounding can potentially lead to overflow as well.

17.4 CONVERSIONS AND EXCEPTIONS

An important requirement for the utility of a floating-point system is the ability to convert decimal or binary numbers from/to the format for input/output purposes. Also, at times we need to convert numbers from one floating-point format to another (say from double- to single-precision, or from single-precision to extended-single). These conversions, and their error characteristics, are also spelled out as part of the ANSI/IEEE standard.

Whenever a number with higher precision is to be converted to a format offering lower precision (e.g., double-precision or extended-single to single-precision), rounding is required as part of the conversion process. The same applies to conversions between integer and floating-point formats. Because of their importance, rounding methods, are discussed separately in Section 17.5. Here, we just mention that the ANSI/IEEE standard includes four rounding modes:

Round to nearest even.

Round toward zero (inward).

Round toward $+\infty$ (upward).

Round toward $-\infty$ (downward).

The first of these is the default rounding mode. The latter two rounding modes find applications in performing interval arithmetic (see Section 19.5).

Another important requirement for any number representation system is defining the order of values in comparisons that yield true/false results. Such comparisons are needed for conditional computations such as "if $x > y$ then $\cdots$". The ANSI/IEEE standard defines comparison results in a manner that is consistent with mathematical laws and intuition. Clearly comparisons of ordered values (ordinary floating-point numbers, ± 0, and $\pm\infty$) should yield the expected results (e.g., $-\infty < +0$ should yield "true"). The two representations of 0 are considered to be the same number, so $+0 > -0$ yields "false." It is somewhat less clear what the results of comparisons such as NaN $\neq$ NaN (true) or NaN $\leq +\infty$ (false) should be. The general rule is that NaN is considered unordered with everything, including itself. Thus, comparisons such as NaN $\leq +\infty$ also produce an "invalid operation" exception.

When the values being compared have different formats (e.g., single vs. single-extended or single vs. double), the result of comparison is defined based on infinitely precise versions of the two numbers being compared.

Besides the exception signaled when certain comparisons between unordered values are performed, the ANSI/IEEE standard also defines exceptions associated with divide by zero, overflow, underflow, inexact result, and invalid operation. The first three conditions are obvious. The "inexact exception" is signaled when the rounded result of an operation or conversion is not exactly representable. The "invalid operation" exception occurs in the following situations, among others:

Addition:	$(+\infty) + (-\infty)$
Multiplication:	$0 \times \infty$
Division:	$0/0$ or ∞/∞
Square-root:	Operand < 0

For a more complete description, refer to the ANSI/IEEE standard document [IEEE85].

17.5 ROUNDING SCHEMES

Rounding is needed to convert higher-precision values, or intermediate computation results with additional digits, to lower-precision formats for storage and/or output. In the discussion that follows, we assume that an unsigned number with integer and fractional digits is to be rounded to an integer.

$$x_{k-1}x_{k-2} \cdots x_1 x_0 . x_{-1} x_{-2} \cdots x_{-l} \xrightarrow{\text{round}} y_{k-1} y_{k-2} \cdots y_1 y_0.$$

The simplest rounding method is truncation or chopping, which is accomplished by dropping the extra bits:

$$x_{k-1}x_{k-2} \cdots x_1 x_0 . x_{-1} x_{-2} \cdots x_{-l} \xrightarrow{\text{chop}} x_{k-1} x_{k-2} \cdots x_1 x_0.$$

The effect of chopping is different for signed-magnitude and 2's-complement numbers. Figure 17.5 shows the effect of chopping on a signed-magnitude number. The magnitude of the result $y = \text{chop}(x)$ is always smaller than the magnitude of x. Thus, this is sometimes referred to as "round toward 0." Figure 17.6 shows that chopping a 2's-complement number always reduces its value. This is known as "downward-directed rounding" or "rounding toward $-\infty$".

With the "round to nearest" (rtn) scheme, depicted in Fig. 17.7 for signed-magnitude numbers, a fractional part of less than 1/2 is dropped, while a fractional part of 1/2 or more (.1xxx $\cdots$ in binary) leads to rounding to the next higher integer. The only difference when

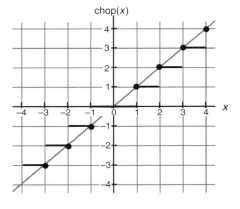

Fig. 17.5 Truncation or chopping of a signed-magnitude number (same as round toward 0).

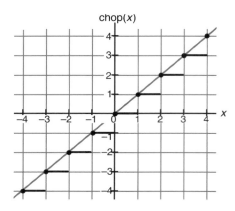

Fig. 17.6 Truncation or chopping of a 2's-complement number (same as downward-directed rounding, or rounding toward $-\infty$).

this rule is applied to 2's-complement numbers is that in Fig. 17.7, the heavy dots for negative values of x move to the left end of the respective heavy lines. Thus, a slight upward bias is created. Such a bias exists for signed-magnitude numbers as well if we consider only positive or negative values.

To understand the effect of this slight bias on computations, assume that a number $(x_{k-1} \cdots x_1 x_0 . x_{-1} x_{-2})_{\text{two}}$ is to be rounded to an integer $y_{k-1} \cdots y_1 y_0$. The four possible cases, and their representation errors are:

$$x_{-1}x_{-2} = 00 \qquad \text{Round down} \qquad \text{error} = 0$$
$$x_{-1}x_{-2} = 01 \qquad \text{Round down} \qquad \text{error} = -0.25$$
$$x_{-1}x_{-2} = 10 \qquad \text{Round up} \qquad \text{error} = 0.5$$
$$x_{-1}x_{-2} = 11 \qquad \text{Round up} \qquad \text{error} = 0.25$$

If these four cases occur with equal probability, the average error is 0.125. The resulting bias may create problems owing to error accumulation. In practice, the situation may be somewhat

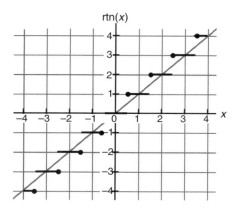

Fig. 17.7 Rounding of a signed-magnitude value to the nearest number.

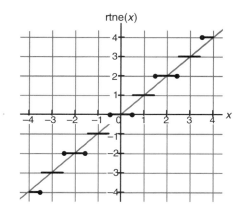

Fig. 17.8 Rounding to the nearest even number.

worse in that for certain calculations, the probability of getting a midpoint value can be much higher than 2^{-l}.

One way to deal with the preceding problem is to always round to an even (or odd) integer, thus causing the "midpoint" values ($x_{-1}x_{-2} = 10$ in our example) to be rounded up or down with equal probabilities. Rounding to the nearest even (rather than odd) value has the additional benefit that it leads to "rounder" values and, thus, lesser errors downstream in the computation. Figure 17.8 shows the effect of the "round to nearest even" (rtne) scheme on signed-magnitude numbers. The diagram for 2's-complement numbers is the same (since, e.g., -1.5 will be rounded to -2 in either case). Round-to-nearest-even is the default rounding scheme of the IEEE floating-point standard.

Another scheme, known as R* rounding, is similar to the preceding methods except that for midpoint values (e.g., when $x_{-1}x_{-2} = 10$), the fractional part is chopped and the least significant bit of the rounded result is forced to 1. Thus, in midpoint cases, we round up if the least significant bit happens to be 0 and round down when it is 1. This is clearly the same as the "round to nearest odd" scheme. Figure 17.9 contains a graphical representation of R* rounding.

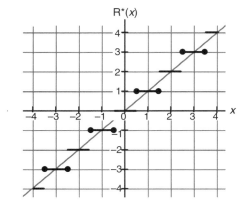

Fig. 17.9 R* rounding or rounding to the nearest odd number.

In all the rounding schemes discussed thus far, full carry-propagation over the k integer positions is needed in the worst case. This imposes an undesirable overhead on floating-point arithmetic operations, especially since the final rounding is always on the critical path. The next two methods, which eliminate this overhead, are not used in practice because they are accompanied by other problems.

Jamming, or von Neumann rounding, is simply truncation with the least significant bit forced to 1. As shown in Fig. 17.10, this method combines the simplicity of chopping with the symmetrical error characteristics of ordinary rounding (not rounding to nearest even). However, its worst-case error is twice as large as that of rounding to the nearest integer.

ROM rounding is based on directly reading a few of the least significant bits of the rounded result from a table, using the affected bits, plus the most significant (leftmost) dropped bit, as the address. For example, if the 4 bits $y_3 y_2 y_1 y_0$ of the rounded result are to be determined, a 32×4 ROM table can be used that takes $x_3 x_2 x_1 x_0 x_{-1}$ as the address and supplies 4 bits of data:

$$x_{k-1} \cdots x_4 x_3 x_2 x_1 x_0 . x_{-1} \cdots x_{-l} \xrightarrow{\;32 \times 4 - \text{ROM} - \text{round}\;} x_{k-1} \cdots x_4 y_3 y_2 y_1 y_0 .$$

$$\underbrace{\qquad\qquad}_{\text{ROM address}} \qquad\qquad\qquad \underbrace{\qquad\qquad}_{\text{ROM data}}$$

Thus, in the preceding example, the fractional bits of x are dropped, the 4 bits read out from the table replace the 4 least significant integral bits of x, and the higher-order bits of x do not change. The ROM output bits $y_3 y_2 y_1 y_0$ are related to the address bits $x_3 x_2 x_1 x_0 x_{-1}$ as follows:

$$(y_3 y_2 y_1 y_0)_{\text{two}} = (x_3 x_2 x_1 x_0)_{\text{two}} \qquad \text{when } x_{-1} = 0 \text{ or } x_3 = x_2 = x_1 = x_0 = 1$$
$$(y_3 y_2 y_1 y_0)_{\text{two}} = (x_3 x_2 x_1 x_0)_{\text{two}} + 1 \qquad \text{otherwise}$$

Thus, the rounding result is the same as that of the round to nearest scheme in 15 of the 16 possible cases, but a larger error is introduced when $x_3 = x_2 = x_1 = x_0 = 1$. Figure 17.11 depicts the results of ROM rounding for a smaller 8×2 table.

Finally, we sometimes need to force computational errors to be in a certain known direction. For example, if we are computing an upper bound for some quantity, larger results are acceptable, since the derived upper bound will still be valid, but results that are smaller than correct values

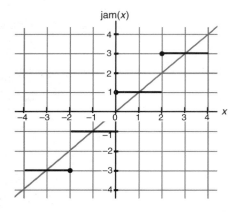

Fig. 17.10   Jamming or von Neumann rounding.

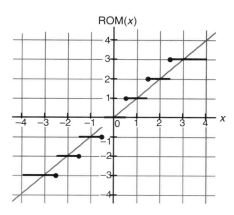

ROM(x)

Fig. 17.11   ROM rounding with an 8×2 table.

could invalidate the upper bound. This leads to the definition of upward-directed rounding (round toward $+\infty$) and downward-directed rounding (round toward $-\infty$) schemes depicted in Figs. 17.12 and 17.6, respectively. Upward- and downward-directed rounding schemes are required features of the IEEE floating-point standard.

17.6 LOGARITHMIC NUMBER SYSTEMS

Fixed-point representations can be viewed as extreme special cases of floating-point numbers with the exponent equal to 0, thus making the exponent field unnecessary. The other extreme of removing the significand field, and assuming that the significand is always 1, is known as logarithmic number representation. With the IEEE floating-point standard terminology, the significand of a logarithmic number system consists only of the hidden 1 and has no fractional part.

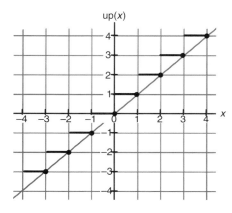

up(x)

Fig. 17.12   Upward-directed rounding, or rounding toward $+\infty$ (see Fig. 17.6 for downward-directed rounding, or rounding toward $-\infty$).

The components of a logarithmic number are its sign, exponent base b (not explicitly shown), and exponent e, together representing the number $x = \pm b^e$. Since the relationship between x and e can be written as

$$e = \log_b |x|$$

we often refer to b as the logarithm base, rather than the exponent base, and to the number system as the sign-and-logarithm representation. Of course, if e were an integer, as is the case in floating-point representations, only powers of b would be representable. So we allow e to have a fractional part (Fig. 17.13). Since numbers between 0 and 1 have negative logarithms, the logarithm must be viewed as a signed number or all numbers scaled up by a constant factor (the logarithm part biased by the logarithm of that constant) if numbers less than 1 are to be representable. The base b of the logarithm is usually taken to be 2.

In what follows, we will assume that the logarithm part is a 2's-complement number. A number x is thus represented by a pair:

$$(Sx, Lx) = (\operatorname{sign}(x), \log_2 |x|)$$

■ **Example 17.1** Consider a 12-bit, base-2, logarithmic number system in which the 2's-complement logarithm field contains 5 whole and 6 fractional bits. The exponent range is thus $[-16, 16 - 2^{-6}]$, leading to a number representation range of approximately $[-2^{16}, 2^{16}]$, with $min = 2^{-16}$. The bit pattern

$$\begin{array}{cccccccccccc} 1 & 1 & 0 & 1 & 1 & 0 & 0 & 0 & 1 & 0 & 1 & 1 \end{array}$$

$$\underset{\text{Sign}}{} \qquad \underset{\text{Radix point}}{\triangle}$$

represents the number $-2^{-9.828125} \approx -(0.0011)_{\text{ten}}$.

Multiplication and division of logarithmic numbers are quite simple, and this constitutes the main advantage of logarithmic representations. To multiply, we XOR the signs and add the logarithms:

$$(\pm 2^{e1}) \times (\pm 2^{e2}) = \pm 2^{e1+e2}$$

To divide, we XOR the signs and subtract the logarithms:

$$\frac{\pm 2^{e1}}{\pm 2^{e2}} = \pm 2^{e1-e2}$$

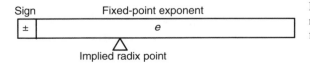

Fig. 17.13 Logarithmic number representation with sign and fixed-point exponent.

Addition/subtraction of logarithmic numbers is equivalent to solving the following problem: given $\log x$ and $\log y$, find $\log(x \pm y)$. This is somewhat more difficult than multiplication or division. Straightforward table lookup requires a table of size $2^{2k} \times k$ with k-bit representations (including the sign bit), so it is impractical unless the word width k is fairly small (say, 8–12 bits). A more practical hardware realization scheme is presented in Section 18.6.

Number conversions from binary to logarithmic, and from logarithmic to binary, representation involve computing the logarithm and inverse logarithm (exponential) functions. These are covered in Chapters 22 and 23, which deal with methods of function evaluation.

PROBLEMS

17.1 **Unnormalized floating-point numbers** In an unnormalized floating-point representation format, a significand of 0 with any exponent can be used to represent 0, since $0 \times 2^e = 0$. Argue that even in this case, it is beneficial to represent 0 with the smallest possible exponent. *Hint:* Consider floating-point addition.

17.2 **Spacing of floating-point numbers**

    a. In Fig. 17.4, three of the vertical tick marks have been labeled with the numbers 0, 2^{-126}, and 2^{-125}. Supply the labels for the remaining 13 tick marks shown.

    b. Draw a similar diagram for the double-precision format and label its tick marks.

17.3 **Floating-point puzzle** You are given a bit string $x_{k-1}x_{k-2} \cdots x_1 x_0$ and told that it is a floating-point number. You can make no assumption about the format except that it consists of a sign bit, an exponent field, and a significand field with their usual meanings (i.e., you cannot assume that the sign is the leftmost bit, that 1 means negative, or that the exponent is to the left of the significand). Your goal is to decode the format and find the number being represented by asking a *minimal* number of questions in the worst case. Questions must be about the format, not the number itself, and must be posed so that they can be answered yes/no or with an integer (e.g., How many bits are there in the exponent field?). Present your strategy in the form of a decision tree.

17.4 **Floating-point representations** Consider the IEEE 32-bit standard floating-point format.

    a. Ignoring $\pm\infty$, denormals, etc., how many distinct real numbers are representable?

    b. What is the smallest number of bits needed to represent this many distinct values? What is the encoding or representation efficiency of this format?

    c. Discuss the consequences (in terms of range and precision) of shortening the exponent field by 2 bits, adding 2 bits to the significand field, and using the exponent base of 16 instead of 2.

17.5 **Fixed- and floating-point representations** Find the largest value of n for which $n!$ can be represented exactly in the following two formats. Explain the results.

    a. 32-bit, 2's-complement integer format.

    b. 32-bit IEEE standard floating-point format.

17.6 **Fixed- versus floating-point systems** Digital signal processor chips are special-purpose processors that have been tailored to the need of signal processing applications. They come in both fixed-point and floating-point versions. Discuss the issues involved in choosing a fixed- versus floating-point DSP chip for such applications [Inac96].

17.7   **Floating-point arithmetic operations** Represent each of the following floating-point operands in 32-bit IEEE standard format. Then perform the specified operations, normalizing the results if necessary.

   a. $(+41 \times 2^{+0}) \times (+0.875 \times 2^{-16})$

   b. $(-4.5 \times 2^{-1}) \div (+0.0625 \times 2^{+12})$

   c. $\sqrt{+1.125 \times 2^{+11}}$

   d. $(+1.25 \times 2^{-10}) + (+0.5 \times 2^{+11})$

   e. $(-1.5 \times 2^{-11}) + (+0.625 \times 2^{-10})$

17.8   **Floating-point exceptions** Give examples of IEEE 32-bit standard floating-point numbers x and y such that they produce overflow in the rounding stage of computing $x + y$. Repeat for computing the product $x \times y$. Then show that rounding overflow is impossible in the normalization phase of floating-point division.

17.9   **Conversion of floating-point numbers** The conversion problem for floating-point numbers involves changing representations from radix r with exponent base b to radix R with exponent base B.

   a.   Describe the conversion process for the special case of $r = b$ and $R = B$.

   b.   Apply the method of part a to convert $(0.2313\ 0130)_{four} \times 4^{(-0211)_{four}}$ from $r = 4$ to $R = 10$.

   c.   Describe a shortcut method for the conversion when $r = \beta^g$ and $R = \beta^G$ for some β.

   d.   Apply the shortcut method of part c to convert the radix-4 floating-point number of part b to radix $R = 8$.

17.10   **Denormalized floating-point numbers** The ANSI/IEEE floating-point standard allows denormalized numbers to be used when the results obtained are too small for normalized representation.

   a.   Can floating-point numbers be compared as integers even when denormals are considered?

   b.   Is it possible for an operation involving one or two denormals to yield a normalized result?

   c.   Prove or disprove: the sum of two denormals is always exactly representable.

17.11   **Errors in floating-point representations** Only some real numbers are exactly representable in the ANSI/IEEE standard floating-point format (or any finite number representation method for that matter).

   a.   Plot the absolute representation error of the IEEE single format for a number x in $[1, 16)$, as a function of x, using logarithmic scales for both x and the error value.

   b.   Repeat part a for the relative representation error in $[1, 16)$.

   c.   What are the worst-case relative and absolute representation errors in $[1,16)$?

d. Does the relative (absolute) error get better or worse for numbers greater than 16? What about for numbers less than 1?

17.12 Round-to-nearest-even The following example shows the advantage of rounding to nearest even over ordinary rounding. All numbers are decimal. Consider the floating-point numbers $u = .100 \times 10^0$ and $v = -.555 \times 10^{-1}$. Let $u^{(0)} = u$ and use the recurrence $u^{(i+1)} = (u^{(i)} -_{fp} v) +_{fp} v$ to compute $u^{(1)}, u^{(2)}, \cdots$. With ordinary rounding, we get the sequence of values .101, .102, $\cdots$, an occurrence known as *drift* [Knut81, p. 222]. Verify that drift does not occur in the preceding example if round to nearest even is used. Then prove the general result $(((u +_{fp} v) -_{fp} v) +_{fp} v) -_{fp} v = (u +_{fp} v) -_{fp} v$ when floating-point operations are exactly rounded using the round-to-nearest-even rule.

17.13 ROM rounding

a. In ROM rounding, only the most significant one of the bits to be dropped is used as part of the ROM address. Is there any benefit to using the other dropped bits as part of the address?

b. Discuss the feasibility of compensating for the downward bias of ROM rounding (because of using truncation in the one special case) through the introduction of upward bias in some cases.

17.14 Logarithmic number systems Consider a 16-bit sign-and-logarithm number system, using $k = 6$ whole and $l = 9$ fractional bits for the logarithm. Assume that the logarithm base is 2 and that 2's-complement representation is used for negative logarithms.

a. Find the smallest and largest positive numbers that can be represented.

b. Calculate the maximum relative representation error.

c. Find the representations of $x = 2.5$ and $y = 3.7$ in this number system.

d. Perform the operations $x \times y, x/y, 1/x, x^2$, and $\sqrt{x}$, in this number system.

e. Find the representations of $x + y, x - y$, and x^y, using a calculator where needed.

f. Repeat part b, this time assuming that the logarithm base is 10.

17.15 Logarithmic number systems Compare a sign-and-logarithm number system with 8 whole bits, 23 fractional bits, and a bias of 127, to the 32-bit IEEE standard floating-point format with regard to range and precision. Devise methods for converting numbers between the two formats.

17.16 Semilogarithmic number systems Consider a floating-point system in which the exponent is a multiple of 2^{-h} (i.e., it is a fixed-point number with h fractional bits) and the k-bit significand is in $[1, 1 + 2^{-h})$ with $h + 1$ hidden bits $1.00 \cdots 0$. The extremes of $h = 0$ and $h = k$ in such a semilogarithmic number system [Mull98] correspond to floating-point and logarithmic number systems.

a. What are possible advantages of such a number system?

b. Describe basic arithmetic algorithms for semilogarithmic numbers.

c. Develop algorithms for conversion of such numbers to/from floating-point.

d. Compare a semilogarithmic number system to floating-point and logarithmic number systems with regard to representation error.

REFERENCES

[Camp62] Campbell, S. G., "Floating-Point Operation," in *Planning a Computer System: Project Stretch*, W. Buchholz, (ed.), McGraw-Hill, 1992, pp. 92–121.

[Holm97] Holmes, W. N., "Composite Arithmetic: Proposal for a New Standard," *IEEE Computer*, Vol. 30, No. 3, pp. 65–73, 1997.

[IEEE85] *IEEE Standard for Binary Floating-Point Arithmetic* (ANSI/IEEE Std 754-1985), IEEE Press, 1985.

[Inac96] Inacio, C., and D. Ombres, "The DSP Decision: Fixed Point or Floating?" *IEEE Spectrum*, Vol. 33, No. 9, pp. 72–74, 1996.

[Knut81] Knuth, D. E., *The Art of Computer Programming*, 2nd ed., *Vol. 2: Seminumerical Algorithms*, Addison-Wesley, 1981.

[Kuck77] Kuck, D. J., D. S. Parker, and A. H. Sameh, "Analysis of Rounding Methods in Floating-Point Arithmetic," *IEEE Trans. Computers*, Vol. 26, No. 7, pp. 643–650, 1977.

[Mull98] Muller, J.-M., A. Scherbyna, and A. Tisserand, "Semi-Logarithmic Number Systems," *IEEE Trans. Computers*, Vol. 47, No. 2, pp. 145–151, 1998.

[Swar75] Swartzlander, E. E., and A. G. Alexopoulos, "The Sign/Logarithm Number System," *IEEE Trans. Computers*, Vol. 24, No. 12, pp. 1238–1242, 1975.

[Yohe73] Yohe, J. M., "Roundings in Floating-Point Arithmetic," *IEEE Trans. Computers*, Vol. 22, No. 6, pp. 577–586, 1973.

[Yoko92] Yokoo, H., "Overflow/Underflow-Free Floating-Point Number Representations with Self-Delimiting Variable-Length Exponent Field," *IEEE Trans. Computers*, Vol. 41, No. 8, pp. 1033–1039, 1992.

Chapter
18

FLOATING-POINT OPERATIONS

In this chapter, we examine hardware implementation issues for the four basic floating-point arithmetic operations of addition, subtraction, multiplication, and division. Consideration of square-rooting is postponed to Section 21.6. The bulk of our discussions concern the handling of exponents, alignment of significands, and normalization and rounding of the results. Arithmetic operations on significands, which are fixed-point numbers, have already been covered. Chapter topics include:

18.1 Floating-Point Adders/Subtractors

18.2 Pre- and Postshifting

18.3 Rounding and Exceptions

18.4 Floating-Point Multipliers

18.5 Floating-Point Dividers

18.6 Logarithmic Arithmetic Unit

18.1 FLOATING-POINT ADDERS/SUBTRACTORS

A floating-point adder/subtractor consists of a fixed-point adder for the aligned significands, plus support circuitry to deal with the signs, exponents, alignment preshift, normalization postshift, and special values (0, $\pm\infty$, etc.). Figure 18.1 is the block diagram of a floating-point adder. The major components of this adder are described in Sections 18.1–18.3. Floating-point multipliers and dividers, which are relatively simpler, are covered in Sections 18.4 and 18.5, respectively.

As shown in Fig. 18.1, the two operands entering the floating-point adder are first unpacked. Unpacking involves:

Separating the sign, exponent, and significand for each operand and reinstating the hidden 1.

Converting the operands to the internal format, if different (e.g., single-extended or double-extended).

Testing for special operands and exceptions (e.g., recognizing NaN inputs and bypassing the adder).

The difference of the two exponents is used to determine the amount of alignment right shift and the operand to which it should be applied. To economize on hardware, preshifting capability is often provided for only one of the two operands, with the operands swapped if the other one needs to be shifted. Since the computed sum or difference may have to be shifted to the left in the post normalization step, several bits of the right-shifted operand, which normally would be discarded as they moved off the right end, may be kept for the addition. Thus, the significand adder is typically wider than the significands of the input numbers. More on this in Section 18.3.

Similarly, complementation logic may be provided for only one of the two operands (typically the one that is not preshifted, to shorten the critical path). If both operands have the same sign, the common sign can be ignored in the addition process and later attached to the result. If $-x$ is the negative operand and complementation logic is provided only for y, which is positive, y is complemented and the negative sign of $-x$ ignored, leading to the result $x - y$ instead of $-x + y$. This negation is taken into account by the sign logic in determining the correct sign of the result.

Selective complementation, and the determination of the sign of the result, are also affected by the $+/-$ control input of the floating-point adder/subtractor, which specifies the operation to be performed.

With IEEE standard floating-point format, the sum/difference of the aligned significands has a magnitude in the range $[0, 4)$. If the result is in $[2, 4)$, then it is too large and must be normalized by shifting it one bit to the right and incrementing the tentative exponent to compensate for the shift. If the result is in $[0, 1)$, it is too small. In this case, a multibit left shift may be required, along with a compensatory reduction of the exponent.

Note that a positive (negative) 2's-complement number $(x_1 x_0 . x_{-1} x_{-2} \cdots)_{2\text{'s-compl}}$ whose magnitude is less than 1 will begin with two or more 0s (1s). Hence, the amount of left shift needed is determined by a special circuit known as *leading zeros/ones counter*. It is also possible, with a somewhat more complex circuit, to *predict* the number of leading zeros/ones in parallel with the addition process rather than detecting them after the addition result becomes known. This removes the leading zeros/ones detector from the critical path and improves the overall speed. Details are given in Section 18.2.

Rounding the result may necessitate another normalizing shift and exponent adjustment. To improve the speed, adjusted exponent values can be precomputed and the proper value selected once the normalization results become known. To obtain a properly rounded floating-point sum or difference, a binary floating-point adder must maintain at least three extra bits beyond the *ulp*; these are called *guard bit*, *round bit*, and *sticky bit*. The roles of these bits, along with the hardware implementation of rounding, are discussed in Sections 18.3.

The significand adder is almost always a fast logarithmic time 2's-complement adder, usually with carry-lookahead design. Two's-complement addition is the preferred choice because with 1's-complement addition, the end-around carry can cause speed degradation in fast adders. Two's-complementation does not cause any difficulty because at most one of the operands is complemented and the addition of *ulp* can be performed by setting the carry-in of the significand adder to 1 (see problem 18.4). When the resulting significand is negative, it must be complemented to form the signed-magnitude output. As usual, this is done by 1's-complementation and addition of *ulp*. The latter addition can be merged with the addition of *ulp*, which may be needed for rounding. Thus, 0, *ulp* or 2*ulp* will be added to the true or complemented output of the significand adder during the rounding process.

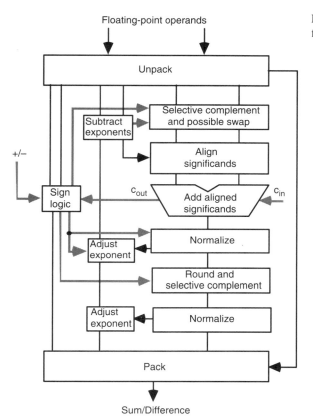

Floating-point operands

Fig. 18.1 Block diagram of a floating-point adder/subtractor.

Unpack

Selective complement
and possible swap

Subtract
exponents

Align
significands

+/–

Sign
logic

c_{out} Add aligned
significands c_{in}

Adjust
exponent

Normalize

Round and
selective complement

Adjust
exponent

Normalize

Pack

Sum/Difference

If an equally fast adder can be designed for 1's-complement numbers, then 1's-complementation becomes the preferred choice, especially when results are to be rounded by chopping.

Finally, packing the result involves:

Combining the sign, exponent, and significand for the result and removing the hidden 1.

Testing for special outcomes and exceptions (e.g., zero result, overflow, or underflow).

Note that unlike the unpacking step, conversion between the internal and external formats is not included in the packing process. This is because converting a wider significand to a narrower one requires rounding and is best accomplished in the rounding stage, which produces the result with the desired output precision.

Floating-point adders found in various processors may differ in details from the generic design depicted in Fig. 18.1. However, the basic principles are the same, and the differences in implementation relate to clever schemes for speeding up the various subcomputations or for economizing on hardware cost. Some of these techniques are covered in Sections 18.2 and 18.3.

18.2 PRE- AND POSTSHIFTING

The preshifter always shifts to the right by an amount equal to the difference of the two exponents. Note that with the IEEE single-precision floating-point format, the difference of the two exponents can be as large as $127 - (-126) = 253$. However, even with extra bits of precision maintained during addition, the operands and results are much narrower. This allows us to simplify and speed up the exponent subtractor and preshift logic in Fig. 18.1.

For example, if the adder is 32 bits wide, then any preshift of 32 bits or more will result in the preshifted input becoming 0. Thus, only the least significant 5 bits of the exponent difference needs to be computed, with the preshifted input forced to 0 when the difference is 32 or more.

Let us continue with the assumption that right shifts of 0 to 31 bits must be implemented. In principle, this can be done by a set of 32-to-1 multiplexers, as shown in Fig. 18.2. The multiplexer producing the bit y_i of the shifted operand selects one of the bits x_i through x_{i+31} of the (sign-extended) 32-bit input that is being aligned based on the 5-bit shift amount. Such a design, however, would lead to fan-in and fan-out problems, especially for the sign bit, which will have to feed multiple inputs of several multiplexers.

As usual, a multistage design can be used to mitigate the fan-in and fan-out problems. Figure 18.3 shows a portion of a combinational shifter that can preshift an input operand x by any amount from 0 to 15 bits. Each circular node is a 2-to-1 multiplexer, with its output fanned out to two nodes in the level below. The four levels, from top to bottom, correspond to shifting by 1, 2, 4, and 8 bits, respectively.

In practice, designs that fall between the two extremes shown in Figs. 18.2 and 18.3 are used. For example, preshifts of up to 31 bits might be implemented in two stages, one performing any shift from 0 to 7 bits and the other performing shifts of 0, 8, 16, and 24 bits. The first stage is then controlled by the three least significant bits, and the second stage by the two most significant bits, of the binary shift amount.

Note that the difference $e1 - e2$ of the two (biased) exponents may be negative. The sign of the difference indicates which operand is to be preshifted, while the magnitude provides the shift amount. One way to obtain the shift amount in case of a negative difference is to complement it. However, this introduces additional delay due to carry propagation. A second way is to use a ROM table or PLA that receives the signed difference as input and produces the shift amount as output. A third way is to compute both $e1 - e2$ and $e2 - e1$, choosing the positive value as the shift amount. Given that only a few bits of the difference need to be computed, duplicating the exponent subtractor does not have significant cost implications.

The postshifter is similar to the preshifter, with one difference: it should be able to perform either a right shift of 0–1 bit or a left shift of 0–31 bits, say. One hardware implementation option is to use two separate shifters for right- and left-shifting. Another option is to combine the two functions into one multistage combinational shifter. Supplying the details in the latter case is left as an exercise.

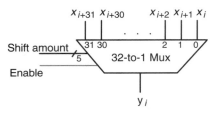

Fig. 18.2   One bit slice of a single-stage preshifter.

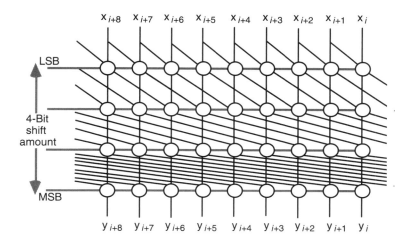

Fig. 18.3   Four-stage combinational shifter for preshifting an operand by 0 to 15 bits.

For IEEE floating-point operands, the need for right-shifting by 1 bit during normalization is indicated by the magnitude of the adder output equaling or exceeding 2. The adder output is a 2's-complement number in the range $(-4, 4)$, represented as $z = (c_{\text{out}} z_1 z_0 . z_{-1} z_{-2} \cdots)_{2'\text{s-compl}}$. The condition for right-shifting is thus easily determined as $c_{\text{out}} \neq z_1$. Assuming that right-shifting is not needed for normalization, we must have $c_{\text{out}} = z_1$, with the left-shift amount then determined by the number of consecutive bits in z that are identical to z_1. So, if $z_1 = 0$ (1), we need to detect the number of consecutive 0s (1s) in z, beginning with z_0. As mentioned in Section 18.1, this is done either by applying a leading zeros/ones counter to the adder output or by predicting the number of leading zeros/ones concurrently with the addition process (to shorten the critical path). The two schemes are depicted in Fig. 18.4.

Leading zeros/ones counting is quite simple and is thus left as an exercise. Predicting the number of leading zeros/ones can be accomplished as follows. Note that when the inputs to a floating-point adder are normalized, normalization left shift is needed only when the operands, and thus the inputs to the significand adder, have unlike signs. Leading zeros/ones prediction for unnormalized inputs is somewhat more involved, but not more difficult conceptually.

Let the inputs to the significand adder be 2's-complement positive and negative values $(0x_0.x_{-1}x_{-2}\cdots)_{2'\text{s-compl}}$ and $(1y_0.y_{-1}y_{-2}\cdots)_{2'\text{s-compl}}$. Let there be exactly i consecutive positions, beginning with position 0, that propagate the carry during addition. Borrowing the carry "generate," "propagate," and "annihilate" notation from our discussions of adders, we have the following:

$$p_0 = p_{-1} = p_{-2} = \cdots = p_{-i+1} = 1$$
$$p_{-i} = 0 \quad (\text{i.e., } g_{-i} = 1 \text{ or } a_{-i} = 1)$$

In case $g_{-i} = 1$, let j be the smallest index such that:

$$g_{-i} = a_{-i-1} = a_{-i-2} = \cdots = a_{-j+1} = 1$$
$$a_{-j} = 0 \quad (\text{i.e., } g_{-j} = 1 \text{ or } p_{-j} = 1)$$

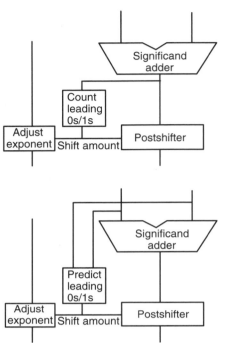

Fig. 18.4   Leading zeros/ones counting versus prediction.

Then, we will have j or $j - 1$ leading 0s depending on whether the carry leaving position j is 0 or 1, respectively.

In case $a_{-i} = 1$, let j be the smallest index such that:

$$a_{-i} = g_{-i-1} = g_{-i-2} = \cdots = g_{-j+1} = 1$$
$$g_{-j} = 0 \quad \text{(i.e., } p_{-j} = 1 \text{ or } a_{-j} = 1)$$

Then, we will have $j - 1$ or j leading 1s, depending on whether the carry-out of position j is 0 or 1, respectively.

Note that the g, p, a, and carry signals needed for leading zeros/ones prediction can be extracted from the significand adder to save on hardware. Based on the preceding discussion, given the required signals, the circuit needed to predict the number of leading zeros/ones can be designed with two stages. The first stage, which is similar to a carry-lookahead circuit, produces a 1 in the jth position and 0s in all positions to its left (this can be formulated as a parallel prefix computation, since we are essentially interested in detecting one of the four patterns $pp \cdots ppgaa \cdots aag$, $pp \cdots ppgaa \cdots aap$, $pp \cdots ppgagg \cdots gga$, or $pp \cdots ppgagg \cdots ggp$). The second stage is an encoder or priority encoder (depending on the design of the first stage) that yields the index of the leading 1.

Finally, in the preceding discussion, we assumed separate hardware for pre- and postshifting. This is a desirable choice for higher-speed or pipelined operation. If the two shifters are to be combined for economy, the unit must be capable of shifting both to the right and to the left by an arbitrary amount. Modifying the design of Fig. 18.3 to derive a bidirectional shifter is straightforward.

18.3 ROUNDING AND EXCEPTIONS

If an alignment preshift is performed, the bits that are shifted out should not all be discarded, since they can potentially affect the rounding of the result. Recall that proper floating-point addition/subtraction requires that the result match what would be obtained if the computation were performed with infinite precision and the result rounded. In may thus appear that we have to keep all bits that are shifted out in case left-shifting is later needed for normalization. Keeping all the bits that are shifted out effectively doubles the width of the significand adder.

We know from earlier discussions that the significand adder must be widened by one bit at the left to accommodate the sign bit of its 2's-complement inputs. It turns out that widening the adder by 3 bits at the right is adequate for obtaining properly rounded results. Calling the three extra bits at the right G, R, and S, for reasons to become apparent shortly, the output of the significand adder can be represented as follows:

$$\text{Adder output } = (c_{\text{out}} z_1 z_0 . z_{-1} z_{-2} \cdots z_{-l} G R S)_{2\text{'s-compl}}$$

In the preceding equation, z_1 is the sign indicator, c_{out} represents significand overflow, and the extra bits at the right are:

G: Guard bit

R: Round bit

S: Sticky bit

We next explain the roles of the G, R, and S bits and why they are adequate for proper rounding. The explanation is in terms of the IEEE floating-point format, but it is valid in general.

When an alignment right-shift of 1 bit is performed, G will hold the bit that is shifted out and no precision is lost (so, G "guards" against loss of precision). For alignment right shifts of 2 bits or more, the shifted significand will have a magnitude in [0, 1/2). Since the magnitude of the unshifted significand is in [1, 2), the difference of the aligned significands will have a magnitude in [1/2, 2). Thus, in this latter case, the normalization left shift will be by at most one bit, and G is still adequate to protect us against loss of precision.

In case a normalization left shift actually takes place, the "round bit" is needed for determining whether to round the resulting significand down ($R = 0$, discarded part $< ulp/2$) or up ($R = 1$, discarded part $\geq ulp/2$). All that remains is to establish whether the discarded part is exactly equal to $ulp/2$. This information is needed in some rounding schemes, and providing it is the role of the "sticky bit," which is set to the logical OR of all the bits that are shifted through it. Thus, following an alignment right shift of 7 bits, say, the sticky bit will be set to the logical OR of the 5 bits that move past G and R. This logical ORing operation can be accommodated in the design of the preshifter (how?).

The effect of 1-bit normalization shifts on the rightmost few bits of the significand adder output is as follows

Before postshifting (z)	$\cdots$	z_{-l+1}	z_{-l} |	G	R	S
1-bit normalizing right-shift	$\cdots$	z_{-l+2}	z_{-l+1} |	z_{-l}	G	$R \vee S$
1-bit normalizing left-shift	$\cdots$	z_{-l}	G |	R	S	0
After normalization (Z)	$\cdots$	Z_{-l+1}	Z_{-l} |	Z_{-l-1}	Z_{-l-2}	Z_{-l-3}

where the Z_h are the final digit values in the various positions, after any normalizing shift has been applied. Note that during a normalization right shift, the new value of the sticky bit is set to the logical OR of its old value and the value of R. Given a positive normalized result Z, we can round it to nearest even by simply dropping the extra 3 bits and:

Doing nothing	if $Z_{-l-1} = 0$ or $Z_{-l} = Z_{-l-2} = Z_{-l-3} = 0$
Adding $ulp = 2^{-l}$	otherwise

Note than no rounding is necessary in case of a multibit normalizing left shift, since full precision is preserved in this case. Other rounding modes can be implemented similarly.

Overflow and underflow exceptions are easily detected by the exponent adjustment blocks in Fig. 18.1. Overflow can occur only when we have a normalizing right shift, while underflow is possible only with normalizing left shifts. Exceptions involving NaNs and invalid operations are handled by the unpacking and packing blocks in Fig. 18.1. One remaining issue is the detection of a zero result and encoding it as the all-zeros word. Note that detection of a zero result is essentially a by-product of the leading zeros/ones detection discussed earlier. Determining when the "inexact" exception must be signaled is left as an exercise.

18.4 FLOATING-POINT MULTIPLIERS

A floating-point multiplier consists of a fixed-point multiplier for the significands, plus peripheral and support circuitry to deal with the exponents and special values (0, $\pm\infty$, etc.). Figure 18.5 depicts a generic block diagram for a floating-point multiplier. The role of unpacking is exactly as discussed for floating-point adders at the beginning of Section 18.1. Similarly, the final packing of the result is done as for floating-point adders. The sign of the product is obtained by XORing the signs of the two operands.

A tentative exponent is computed by adding the two biased exponents and subtracting the bias from the sum. With the ANSI/IEEE short floating-point format, subtracting the bias of 127 can be easily accomplished by providing a carry-in of 1 into the exponent adder and subtracting 128 from the sum. This latter subtraction amounts to simply flipping the most significant bit of the result.

The significand multiplier is the slowest and most complex part of the unit shown in Fig. 18.5. With the IEEE floating-point format, the product of the two unsigned significands, each in the range [1, 2), will be in the range [1, 4). Thus, the result may have to be normalized by shifting it one position to the right and incrementing the tentative exponent. Rounding the result may necessitate another normalizing shift and exponent adjustment. When each significand has a hidden 1 and l fractional bits, the significand multiplier is an unsigned $(l + 1) \times (l + 1)$

multiplier that would normally yield a $(2l + 2)$-bit product. Since this full product must be rounded to $l + 1$ bits at the output, it may be possible to discard the extra bits gradually as they are produced, rather than in a single step at the end. All that is needed is to keep an extra round bit and a sticky bit to be able to round the final result properly. Keeping a guard bit is not needed here (why?).

To improve the speed, the incremented exponent can be precomputed and the proper value selected once it is known whether a normalization postshift is required. Since multiplying the significands is the most complex part of floating-point multiplication, there is ample time for such computations. Also, rounding need not be a separate step at the end. With proper design, it may be possible to incorporate the bulk of the rounding process in the multiplication hardware.

To see how, note that most multipliers produce the least significant half of the product earlier than the rest of the bits. So, the bits that will be used for rounding are produced early in the multiplication cycle. However, the need for normalization right shift becomes known at or near the end. Since there are only two possibilities (no postshift or a right shift of 1 bit), we can devise a stepwise rounding scheme by developing two versions of the rounded product and selecting the correct version in the final step. Alternatively, rounding can be converted to truncation through the injection of corrective terms during multiplication [Even00].

Because floating-point multiplication consists of several sequential stages or subcomputations, it is quite simple and natural to pipeline it for increased throughput. Pipeline latches can be inserted across the natural block boundaries in Fig. 18.5 as well as within the significand multiplier if the latter is of the full-tree or array variety. Chapter 25 presents a detailed discussion of pipelining considerations and design methods.

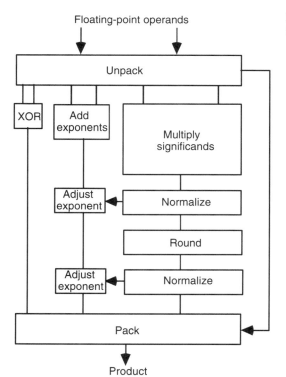

Fig. 18.5   Block diagram of a floating-point multiplier.

18.5 FLOATING-POINT DIVIDERS

A floating-point divider has the same overall structure as a floating-point multiplier. Figure 18.6 is a generic block diagram for a floating-point divider. The two operands of floating-point division are unpacked, the resulting components pass through several computation steps, and the final result is packed into the appropriate format for output. Unpacking and packing have the same roles here as those discussed for floating-point adders in Section 18.1 (the divide-by-0 exception is detected during unpacking). The sign of the quotient is obtained by XORing the operand signs.

A tentative exponent is computed by subtracting the divisor's biased exponent from the dividend's biased exponent and adding the bias to the difference. With the ANSI/IEEE short floating-point format, the bias of 127 must be added to the difference of the two exponents. Since adding 128 is simpler than adding 127, we can compute the difference less one by holding c_{in} to 0 in a 2's-complement subtraction (normally, in 2's-complement subtraction, $c_{in} = 1$) and then flipping the most significant bit of the result.

The significand divider is the slowest and the most complex part of the unit shown in Fig. 18.6. With ANSI/IEEE floating-point format, the ratio of two significands in [1, 2) is in the range (1/2, 2). Thus, the result may have to be normalized by shifting it one position to the left and decrementing the tentative exponent. Rounding the result may necessitate another normalizing shift and exponent adjustment.

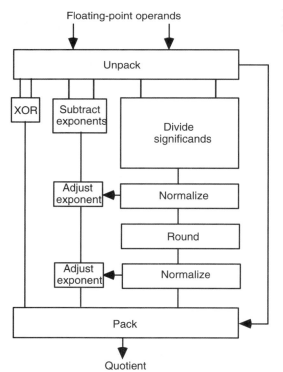

Fig. 18.6 Block diagram of a floating-point divider.

As in the case of multiplication, speed can be gained by precomputing the adjusted exponent and selecting the proper value when the need for normalization becomes known. Since dividing the significands is the most complex part of floating-point division, there is ample time for such computations. Considerations for pipelining of the computations are also quite similar to those of floating-point multiplication (see Section 18.4).

One main difference between floating-point division and multiplication is in rounding. Since the significand divider's output may have to be left-shifted by 1 bit for normalization, the quotient must be developed with two extra bits that serve as the guard and round bits (see the discussion of rounding for floating-point addition in Section 18.3). In division schemes that produce a remainder, the final remainder is used to derive the value of the sticky bit (how?). Then, the rounding process discussed at the end of Section 18.3 is applied. Convergence division creates some difficulty for rounding in view of the absence of a remainder.

As was the case for fixed-point multipliers and dividers, floating-point multipliers and dividers can share much hardware. In particular, when the significand division is performed by one of the convergence methods discussed in Chapter 16, little additional hardware is required to convert a floating-point multiplier into a floating-point multiply/divide unit.

18.6 LOGARITHMIC ARITHMETIC UNIT

As discussed in Section 17.6, representing numbers by their signs and base-b logarithms offers the advantage of simple multiplication and division, inasmuch as these operations are converted to addition and subtraction of the logarithms, respectively. In this section, we demonstrate the algorithms and hardware needed for adding and subtracting logarithmic numbers and present the design of a complete logarithmic arithmetic unit.

We noted, in Section 17.6, that addition and subtraction of logarithmic numbers can, in principle, be performed by table lookup. One method of reducing the size of the required table is via converting the two-operand (binary) operation of interest to a single-operand (unary) operation that needs a smaller table. Consider the add/subtract operation

$$(Sx, Lx) \pm (Sy, Ly) = (Sz, Lz)$$

for logarithmic operands and assume $x > y > 0$ (other cases are similar). Then:

$$Lz = \log z = \log(x \pm y) = \log(x(1 \pm y/x))$$
$$= \log x + \log(1 \pm y/x)$$

Note that $\log x$ is known and $\log(y/x)$ is easily computed as $\Delta = -(\log x - \log y)$. Given Δ, the term

$$\log(1 \pm y/x) = \log(1 \pm \log^{-1} \Delta)$$

is easily obtained by table lookup (two tables, φ^+ and φ^-, are needed). Hence, addition and subtraction of logarithmic numbers can be based on the following computations:

$$\log(x + y) = \log x + \varphi^+(\Delta)$$
$$\log(x - y) = \log x + \varphi^-(\Delta)$$

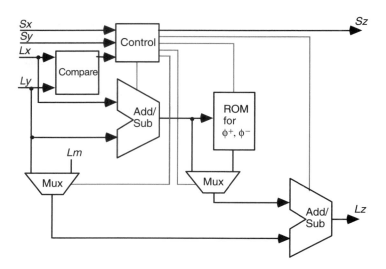

Fig. 18.7   Arithmetic unit for a logarithmic number system.

Figure 18.7 depicts a complete arithmetic unit for logarithmic numbers. For addition and subtraction, Lx and Ly are compared to determine which one is larger. This information is used by the control box for properly interpreting the result of the subtraction $Lx - Ly$. The reader should be able to supply the details.

The design of Fig. 18.7 assumes the use of scaling of all values by a multiplicative factor m so that numbers between 0 and 1 are also represented with unsigned logarithms. Because of this scaling, the logarithm of the scale factor m (or the bias Lm) must be subtracted in multiplication and added in division.

PROBLEMS

18.1   Exponent arithmetic in floating-point adder

    a. Design the "Subtract exponents" block of the floating-point adder in Fig. 18.1 for the IEEE standard 64-bit floating-point format. Assume that a 6-bit difference, plus a "force to zero" output, is to be provided.

    b. Repeat part a, this time assuming that the output difference is to be forced to 63 if the real difference exceeds 63.

    c. Compare the designs of parts a and b and discuss.

18.2   Sign logic in floating-point adder Consider the "Sign logic" block in the floating-point adder of Fig. 18.1.

    a. Explain the role of the output from this block that is fed to the "Normalize" and "Adjust exponent" blocks.

    b. Supply a complete logic design for this block, assuming the use of a 2's-complement significand adder.

18.3   Alignment preshifter Design an alignment preshifter for IEEE single-precision floating-point numbers that produces a shifted output with guard, round, and sticky bits.

18.4   **Precision in floating-point adders**   Referring to the discussion at the beginning of Section 18.3, why would the width of the significand adder double if we were to keep all the bits that are shifted out during the alignment preshift? In other words, doesn't the presence of 0s in those extra positions of the unshifted operand mean that the addition width will not change? Of course, the same question applies when we keep only three extra bits of precision. Do we really have to extend the adder width by 3 bits? *Hint:* The answer depends on which operand is complemented.

18.5   **Leading zeros/ones counter**

    a.   Design a ripple-type leading zeros/ones counter for the normalization stage of floating-point addition and derive its worst-case delay. Is this a viable design?

    b.   Show that the problem of leading zeros/ones detection can be converted to parallel prefix logical AND.

    c.   Using the result of part b, design a logarithmic time, leading zeros/ones counter.

18.6   **Leading zeros/ones counter**

    a.   Use a PLA to design an 8-input leading zeros/ones counter with the following specifications: eight data inputs, two control inputs, three address (index) outputs, and one "all-zeros/ones" output. One of the control inputs specifies whether leading 0s or leading 1s should be counted. The other control input turns the tristate drivers of the address outputs on or off, thus allowing the address outputs of several modules to be tied together. The tristate drivers are also turned off when the "all-zeros/ones" output is asserted.

    b.   Show how two leading zeros/ones counters of the type described in part a can be cascaded to form a 16-bit leading zeros/ones counter.

    c.   Can the cascading scheme of part b be extended to wider inputs (say 24 or 32 bits)?

18.7   **Leading zeros/ones prediction**   Extend the results concerning leading zeros/ones prediction, presented at the end of Section 18.2, to unnormalized inputs. *Hint:* Consider three separate cases of positive inputs, negative inputs, and inputs with unlike signs.

18.8   **Rounding in floating-point operations**

    a.   Extend the round-to-nearest-even procedure for a positive value, given near the end of Section 18.3, to a 2's-complement result Z.

    b.   Occasionally, when performing double-precision arithmetic, we would like to be able to specify that the result be rounded as if it were a single-precision number, with the single-rounded result then output in double-precision format. Why might such an option be useful, and how can it be implemented?

    c.   Show how the guard, round, and sticky bits can be used when an "inexact" exception is to be indicated following the rounding process.

18.9   **Rounding in floating-point operations**   Given that an intermediate 2's-complement result for a floating-point operation with guard, round, and sticky bits is at hand, describe how each of the following rounding schemes can be implemented:

    a.   Round toward 0.

     b. Round toward $+\infty$.

     c. Round toward $-\infty$.

     d. R* rounding (see Fig. 17.9).

18.10 **Floating-point multipliers** In multiplying the significands of two floating-point numbers, the lower half of the fractional part is not needed, except to properly round the upper half. Discuss whether, and if so, how, this can lead to simplified hardware for the significand multiplier. Note that the significand multiplier can have various designs (tree, array, built of AMMs, etc.).

18.11 **Floating-point multiply-add unit** In many computation-intensive applications, a significant fraction of floating-point multiplications are immediately followed by a floating-point addition. This justifies additional investment in hardware to build a floating-point multiply-add unit.

     a. Sketch the design of such a unit. Then, enumerate, and discuss, the main sources of speedup over cascaded multiply and add operations.

     b. Extend your discussion to a multiply-add unit that is optimized for inner-product computations. The unit allows several products to be computed in sequence, while maintaining a running sum of greater precision. This approach allows the rounding step to be postponed to the very end of the inner product computation.

18.12 **Rounding in floating-point division**

     a. Explain how the sticky bit needed for properly rounding the quotient of floating-point division is derived from the final remainder.

     b. Explain how a properly rounded result might be derived with convergence division.

18.13 **On-the-fly rounding in division** To avoid a carry-propagate addition in rounding the quotient of floating-point division, one can combine the rounding process with the on-the-fly conversion of the quotient digits from redundant to conventional binary format [Erce92]. Outline the algorithm and hardware requirements for such an on-the-fly rounding scheme.

18.14 **Floating-point operations on denormals** Based on what you have learned about floating-point add/subtract, multiply, and divide units in this chapter, briefly discuss design complications if denormalized numbers of the IEEE floating-point format were to be accepted as inputs and produced as output.

18.15 **Logarithmic arithmetic** Consider a 16-bit sign-and-logarithm number system, using $k = 6$ whole and $l = 9$ fractional bits for the logarithm. Assume that the logarithm base is 2 and that 2's-complement representation is used for negative logarithms.

     a. Find the representations of $x = 2.5$ and $y = 3.7$ in this number system.

     b. What is the required ROM size for the arithmetic unit of Fig. 18.7?

     c. Do the operations $x + y$ and $x - y$, supplying the needed table entries φ^+ and φ^-.

18.16 **Flexible floating-point processor** Consider a 64-bit floating-point number representation format where the sign bit is followed by a 5-bit "exponent width" field. This field specifies the exponent field as being 0–31 bits wide, the remaining 27–58 bits being a fractional significand with no hidden 1. Do not worry about special values such as $\pm\infty$ or NaN.

   a. Enumerate the advantages and possible drawbacks of this format.

   b. Outline the design of a floating-point adder to add two numbers in this format.

   c. Draw a block diagram of a multiplier for flexible floating-point numbers.

   d. Briefly discuss any complication in the design of a divider for flexible floating-point numbers.

18.17 **Double rounding** Consider the multiplication of two-digit, single-precision decimal values .34 and .78, yielding .2652. If we round this exact result to an internal three-digit, extended-precision format, we get .265, which when subsequently rounded to single precision by means of round-to-nearest-even, yields .26. However, if the exact result were directly rounded to single precision, it would yield .27.

   a. Can double rounding lead to a similar problem if we always round up the halfway cases instead of applying round-to-nearest-even?

   b. Prove that for floating-point operands x and y with p-bit significands, if $x + y$ is rounded to p' bits of precision ($p' \geq 2p + 2$), a second rounding to p bits of precision will yield the same result as direct rounding of the exact sum to p bits.

   c. Show that the claim of part b also holds for multiplication, division, and square-rooting.

   d. Discuss the implications of the preceding results for converting the results of double-precision IEEE floating-point arithmetic to single precision.

18.18 **Rounding in ternary arithmetic** If we had ternary as opposed to binary computers, radix-3 arithmetic would be in common use today. Discuss the effects of this change on rounding in floating-point arithmetic.

REFERENCES

[Ande67] Anderson, S. F., J. G. Earle, R. E. Goldschmidt, and D. M. Powers, "The IBM System/360 Model 91: Floating-Point Execution Unit," *IBM J. Research and Development*, Vol. 11, No. 1, pp. 34–53, 1967.

[Bose87] Bose, B. K., L. Pei, G. S. Taylor, and D. A. Patterson, "Fast Multiply and Divide for a VLSI Floating-Point Unit," *Proc. 8th Symp. Computer Arithmetic*, pp. 87–94, 1987.

[Coon80] Coonen, J. T., "An Implementation Guide to a Proposed Standard for Floating-Point Arithmetic," *IEEE Computer*, Vol. 13, pp. 69–79, January 1980.

[Davi74] Davis, R. L., "Uniform Shift Networks," *IEEE Computer*, Vol. 7, pp. 60–71, September 1974.

[Erce92] Ercegovac, M. D., and T. Lang, "On-the-Fly Rounding," *IEEE Trans. Computers*, Vol. 41, No. 12, pp. 1497–1503, 1992.

[Even00] Even, G. and P.-M. Seidel, "A Comparison of Three Rounding Algorithms for IEEE Floating-Point Multiplication," *IEEE Trans. Computers*, Vol. 49, No. 7, pp. 638–650, July 2000.

[Gosl71] Gosling, J. B., "Design of Large High-Speed Floating-Point Arithmetic Units," *Proc. IEE*, Vol. 118, pp. 493–498.

[Mont90] Montoye, R. K., E. Hokonek, and S. L. Runyan, "Design of the Floating-Point Execution Unit in the IBM RISC System/6000," *IBM J. Research and Development*, Vol. 34, No. 1, pp. 59–70, 1990.

[Ober97] Oberman, S. F., and M. J. Flynn, "Design Issues in Division and Other Floating-Point Operations," *IEEE Trans. Computers*, Vol. 46, No. 2, pp. 154–161, 1997.

[Omon94] Omondi, A. R., *Computer Arithmetic Systems: Algorithms, Architecture and Implementation*, Prentice-Hall, 1994.

[Wase82] Waser, S., and M. J. Flynn, *Introduction to Arithmetic for Digital Systems Designers*, Holt, Rinehart, & Winston, 1982.

Chapter
19 | ERRORS AND ERROR CONTROL

Machine arithmetic is inexact in two ways. First, many numbers of interest, such as $\sqrt{2}$ or π, do not have exact representations. Second, floating-point operations, even when performed on exactly representable numbers, may lead to errors in the results. It is essential for arithemetic designers and serious computer users to understand the nature and extent of such errors, as well as how they can lead to results that are counterintuitive and, occasionally, totally invalid. Chapter topics include:

19.1 SOURCES OF COMPUTATIONAL ERRORS

Integer arithmetic is exact and all integer results can be trusted to be correct as long as overflow does not occur (assuming, of course, that the hardware was designed and built correctly and has not since failed; flaw- and fault-induced errors are dealt with in Chapter 27). Floating-point arithmetic, on the other hand, only approximates exact computations with real numbers. There are two sources of errors: (1) representation errors and (2) arithmetic errors.

Representation errors occur because many real numbers do not have exact machine representations. Examples include 1/3, $\sqrt{2}$, and π. Arithmetic errors, on the other hand, occur because some results are inherently inexact or need more bits for exact representation than are available. For example, a given exact operand may not have a finitely representable square root and multiplication produces a double-width result that must be rounded to single-width format.

Thus, familiarity with representation and arithmetic errors, as well as their propagation and accumulation in the course of computations, is important for the design of arithmetic algorithms and their realizations in hardware, firmware, or software. Example 19.1 illustrates the effect of representation and computation errors in floating-point arithmetic.

■ **Example 19.1** Consider the decimal computation 1/99 −1/100, using a decimal floating-point format with a four-digit significand in [1, 10) and a single-digit signed exponent. Given that both 99 and 100 have exact representations in the given format, the floating-point divider will compute 1/99 and 1/100 accurately to within the machine precision:

$$x = 1/99 \approx 1.010 \times 10^{-2} \qquad \text{error} \approx 10^{-6} \text{ or } 0.01\%$$
$$y = 1/100 = 1.000 \times 10^{-2} \qquad \text{error} = 0$$

The precise result is 1/9900, with its floating-point representation 1.010×10^{-4} containing an approximate error of 10^{-8} or 0.01%. However, the floating-point subtraction $z = x -_{\text{fp}} y$ yields the result

$$z = 1.010 \times 10^{-2} - 1.000 \times 10^{-2} = 1.000 \times 10^{-4}$$

which has a much larger error of around 10^{-6} or 1%.

A floating-point number representation system may be characterized by a radix r (which we assume to be the same as the exponent base b), a precision p in terms of radix-r digits, and an approximation or "rounding" scheme A. We symbolize such a floating-point system as

$$\text{FLP}(r, p, A)$$

where $A \in \{\text{chop, round, rtne, chop}(g), \dots\}$; "rtne" stands for "round to nearest even" and chop(g) for a chopping method with g guard digits kept in all intermediate steps. Rounding schemes were discussed in Section 17.5.

Let $x = r^e s$ be an unsigned real number, normalized such that $1/r \le s < 1$, and x_{fp} be its representation in FLP(r, p, A). Then

$$x_{\text{fp}} = r^e s_{\text{fp}} = (1 + \eta)x$$

where

$$\eta = \frac{x_{\text{fp}} - x}{x} = \frac{s_{\text{fp}} - s}{s}$$

is the relative representation error. One can establish bounds on the value of η:

A = chop	$-ulp < s_{\text{fp}} - s \le 0$	$r \times ulp < \eta \le 0$
A = round	$-ulp/2 < s_{\text{fp}} - s \le ulp/2$	$\|\eta\| \le r \times ulp/2$

where $ulp = r^{-p}$. We note that the worst-case relative representation error increases linearly with r; the larger the value of r, the larger the worst-case relative error η and the greater its variations. As an example, for FLP($r = 16, p = 6$, chop), we have $|\eta| \le 16^{-5} = 2^{-20}$. Such a floating-point system uses a 24-bit fractional significand. To achieve the same bound for $|\eta|$ in FLP($r = 2, p$, chop), we need $p = 21$.

Arithmetic in FLP(r, p, A) assumes that an infinite precision result is obtained and then chopped, rounded, . . . , to the available precision. Some real machines approximate this process by keeping $g > 0$ guard digits, thus doing arithmetic in FLP(r, p, chop(g)). In either case, the result of a floating-point arithmetic operation is obtained with a relative error that is bounded by some constant η, which depends on the parameters r and p and the approximation scheme A. Consider multiplication, division, addition, and subtraction of the positive operands

$$x_{\mathrm{fp}} = (1 + \sigma)x \text{ and } y_{\mathrm{fp}} = (1 + \tau)y$$

with relative representation errors σ and τ, respectively, in FLP(r, p, A). Note that the relative errors σ and τ can be positive or negative.

For the multiplication operation $x \times y$, we can write

$$
\begin{aligned}
x_{\mathrm{fp}} \times_{\mathrm{fp}} y_{\mathrm{fp}} &= (1 + \eta)x_{\mathrm{fp}}y_{\mathrm{fp}} = (1 + \eta)(1 + \sigma)(1 + \tau)xy \\
&= (1 + \eta + \sigma + \tau + \eta\sigma + \eta\tau + \sigma\tau + \eta\sigma\tau)xy \\
&\approx (1 + \eta + \sigma + \tau)xy
\end{aligned}
$$

where the last expression is obtained by ignoring second- and third-order error terms. We see that in multiplication, relative errors add up in the worst case.

Similarly, for the division operation x/y, we have:

$$
\begin{aligned}
x_{\mathrm{fp}} /_{\mathrm{fp}} y_{\mathrm{fp}} &= \frac{(1 + \eta)x_{\mathrm{fp}}}{y_{\mathrm{fp}}} = \frac{(1 + \eta)(1 + \sigma)x}{(1 + \tau)y} \\
&= (1 + \eta)(1 + \sigma)(1 - \tau)(1 + \tau^2)(1 + \tau^4)(\cdots)\frac{x}{y} \\
&\approx (1 + \eta + \sigma - \tau)\frac{x}{y}
\end{aligned}
$$

So, relative errors add up in division just as they do in multiplication.

Now, let's consider the addition operation $x + y$:

$$
\begin{aligned}
x_{\mathrm{fp}} +_{\mathrm{fp}} y_{\mathrm{fp}} &= (1 + \eta)(x_{\mathrm{fp}} + y_{\mathrm{fp}}) = (1 + \eta)(x + \sigma x + y + \tau y) \\
&= \left[(1 + \eta)\left(1 + \frac{\sigma x + \tau y}{x + y}\right)\right](x + y)
\end{aligned}
$$

Since $|\sigma x + \tau y| \le max(|\sigma|, |\tau|)(x + y)$, the magnitude of the worst-case relative error in the computed sum is upper-bounded by $|\eta| + max(|\sigma|, |\tau|)$.

Finally, for the subtraction operation $x - y$, we have:

$$
\begin{aligned}
x_{\mathrm{fp}} -_{\mathrm{fp}} y_{\mathrm{fp}} &= (1 + \eta)(x_{\mathrm{fp}} - y_{\mathrm{fp}}) = (1 + \eta)(x + \sigma x - y - \tau y) \\
&= \left[(1 + \eta)\left(1 + \frac{\sigma x - \tau y}{x - y}\right)\right](x - y)
\end{aligned}
$$

Unfortunately, $(\sigma x - \tau y)/(x - y)$ can be very large if x and y are both large but $x - y$ is relatively small (recall that τ can be negative). The arithmetic error η is also unbounded for subtraction without guard digits, as we will see shortly. Thus, unlike the three preceding operations, no bound can be placed on the relative error when numbers with like signs are being subtracted (or numbers with different signs are added). This situation is known as cancellation or loss of significance.

The part of the problem that is due to η being large can be fixed by using guard digits, as suggested by the following result.

THEOREM 19.1   In FLP(r, p, chop(g)) with $g \geq 1$ and $-x < y < 0 < x$, we have:

$$x +_{\text{fp}} y = (1 + \eta)(x + y) \text{ with } -r^{-p+1} < \eta < r^{-p-g+2}$$

COROLLARY: In FLP(r, p, chop(1))

$$x +_{\text{fp}} y = (1 + \eta)(x + y) \text{ with } |\eta| < r^{-p+1}$$

So, a single guard digit is sufficient to make the relative arithmetic error in floating-point addition or subtraction comparable to the representation error with truncation.

■ **Example 19.2** Consider a decimal floating-point number system ($r = 10$) with $p = 6$ and no guard digit. The exact operands x and y are shown below along with their floating-point representations in the given system:

$$\begin{array}{ll} x = \quad 0.100\,000\,000 \times 10^3 & x_{\text{fp}} = \quad .100\,000 \times 10^3 \\ y = -0.999\,999\,456 \times 10^2 & y_{\text{fp}} = -.999\,999 \times 10^2 \end{array}$$

Then, $x + y = 0.544 \times 10^{-4}$ and $x_{\text{fp}} + y_{\text{fp}} = 10^{-4}$, but:

$$x_{\text{fp}} +_{\text{fp}} y_{\text{fp}} = .100\,000 \times 10^3 -_{\text{fp}} .099\,999 \times 10^3 = .100\,000 \times 10^{-2}$$

The relative error of the result is thus $[10^{-3} - (0.544 \times 10^{-4})]/(0.544 \times 10^{-4}) \approx 17.38$; that is, the result is 1738% larger than the correct sum! With 1 guard digit, we get:

$$x_{\text{fp}} +_{\text{fp}} y_{\text{fp}} = .100\,000\,0 \times 10^3 -_{\text{fp}} .099\,999\,9 \times 10^3 = .100\,000 \times 10^{-3}$$

The result still has a large relative error of 80.5% compared to the exact sum $x + y$; but the error is 0% with respect to the correct sum of x_{fp} and y_{fp} (i.e., what we were given to work with).

19.2 INVALIDATED LAWS OF ALGEBRA

Many laws of algebra do not hold for floating-point arithmetic (some don't even hold approximately). Such areas of inapplicability can be a source of confusion and incompatibility. For example, take the associative law of addition:

$$a + (b + c) = (a + b) + c$$

If the associative law of addition does not hold, as we will see shortly, then an optimizing compiler that changes the order of operations in an attempt to reduce the delays resulting from data dependencies may inadvertently change the result of the computation.

The following example shows that the associative law of addition does not hold for floating-point computations, even in an approximate sense:

$$a = 0.123\,41 \times 10^5 \quad b = -0.123\,40 \times 10^5 \quad c = 0.143\,21 \times 10^1$$

$$
\begin{aligned}
a +_{\text{fp}} (b +_{\text{fp}} c) &= (0.123\,41 \times 10^5) +_{\text{fp}} \left[(-0.123\,40 \times 10^5) +_{\text{fp}} (0.143\,21 \times 10^1)\right] \\
&= (0.123\,41 \times 10^5) -_{\text{fp}} (0.123\,39 \times 10^5) = 0.200\,00 \times 10^1 \\
(a +_{\text{fp}} b) +_{\text{fp}} c &= \left[(0.123\,41 \times 10^5) -_{\text{fp}} (0.123\,40 \times 10^5)\right] +_{\text{fp}} (0.143\,21 \times 10^1) \\
&= (0.100\,00 \times 10^1) +_{\text{fp}} (0.143\,21 \times 10^1) = 0.243\,21 \times 10^1
\end{aligned}
$$

The two results $0.200\,00 \times 10^1$ and $0.243\,21 \times 10^1$ differ by about 20%. So the associative law of addition does not hold.

One way of dealing with the preceding problem is to use unnormalized arithmetic. With unnormalized arithmetic, intermediate results are kept in their original form (except as needed to avoid overflow). So normalizing left shifts are not performed. Let us redo the two computations using unnormalized arithmetic:

$$
\begin{aligned}
a +_{\text{fp}} (b +_{\text{fp}} c) &= (0.123\,41 \times 10^5) +_{\text{fp}} \left[(-0.123\,40 \times 10^5) +_{\text{fp}} (0.143\,21 \times 10^1)\right] \\
&= (0.123\,41 \times 10^5) -_{\text{fp}} (0.123\,39 \times 10^5) = 0.000\,02 \times 10^5 \\
(a +_{\text{fp}} b) +_{\text{fp}} c &= \left[(0.123\,41 \times 10^5) -_{\text{fp}} (0.123\,40 \times 10^5)\right] +_{\text{fp}} (0.143\,21 \times 10^1) \\
&= (0.000\,01 \times 10^5) +_{\text{fp}} (0.143\,21 \times 10^1) = 0.000\,02 \times 10^5
\end{aligned}
$$

Not only are the two results the same but they carry with them a kind of warning about the extent of potential error in the result. In other words, here we know that our result is correct to only one significant digit, whereas the earlier result (0.24321×10^1) conveys five digits of accuracy without actually possessing it. Of course the results will not be identical in all cases (i.e., the associative law still does not hold), but the user is warned about potential loss of significance.

The preceding example, with normalized arithmetic and two guard digits, becomes:

$$
\begin{aligned}
a +_{\text{fp}} (b +_{\text{fp}} c) &= (0.123\,41 \times 10^5) +_{\text{fp}} \left[(-0.123\,40 \times 10^5) +_{\text{fp}} (0.143\,21 \times 10^1)\right] \\
&= (0.123\,41 \times 10^5) -_{\text{fp}} (0.123\,385\,7 \times 10^5) = 0.243\,00 \times 10^1 \\
(a +_{\text{fp}} b) +_{\text{fp}} c &= \left[(0.123\,41 \times 10^5) -_{\text{fp}} 0.123\,40 \times 10^5)\right] +_{\text{fp}} (0.143\,21 \times 10^1) \\
&= (0.100\,00 \times 10^1) +_{\text{fp}} (0.143\,21 \times 10^1) = 0.243\,21 \times 10^1
\end{aligned}
$$

The difference has now been reduced to about 0.1%; the error is much better but still too high to be acceptable in practice.

Using more guard digits will improve the situation but the laws of algebra still cannot be assumed to hold in floating-point arithmetic. Here are some other laws of algebra that do not hold in floating-point arithmetic:

Associative law of multiplication $a \times (b \times c) = (a \times b) \times c$

Cancellation law (for $a > 0$) $a \times b = a \times c$ implies $b = c$

Distributive law $a \times (b + c) = (a \times b) + (a \times c)$

Multiplication canceling division $a \times (b/a) = b$

Before the ANSI/IEEE floating-point standard became available and widely adopted, the preceding problem was exacerbated by different ranges and precisions in the floating-point representation formats of various computers. Now, with standard representation, one of the sources of difficulties has been removed, but the fundamental problems persist.

Because laws of algebra do not hold for floating-point computations, it is desirable to determine, if possible, which of several algebraically equivalent computations yields the most accurate result. Even though no general procedure exists for selecting the best alternative, numerous empirical and theoretical results have been developed over the years that help us in organizing or rearranging the computation steps to improve the accuracy of the results. We present two examples that are indicative of the methods used. Additional examples can be found in the problems at the end of the chapter.

■ **Example 19.3** The formula $x = -b \pm d$, with $d = \sqrt{b^2 - c}$, yields the two roots of the quadratic equation $x^2 + 2bx + c = 0$. The formula can be rewritten as $x = -c/(b \pm d)$. When $b^2 >> c$, the value of d is close to $|b|$. Thus, if $b > 0$, the first formula results in cancellation or loss of significance in computing the first root $(-b + d)$, whereas no such cancellation occurs with the second formula. The second root $(-b - d)$, however, is more accurately computed based on the first formula. The roles of the two formulas are reversed for $b < 0$.

■ **Example 19.4** The area of a triangle with sides of length a, b, and c is given by the formula $A = \sqrt{s(s - a)(s - b)(s - c)}$, where $s = (a + b + c)/2$. For ease of discussion, let $a \geq b \geq c$. When the triangle is very flat, such that $a \approx b + c$, we have $s \approx a$ and the term $s - a$ in the preceding formula causes precision loss. The following version of the formula, attributed to W. Kahan [Gold91], returns accurate results, even for flat triangles:

$$A = \frac{1}{4}\sqrt{(a + (b + c))(c - (a - b))(c + (a - b))(a + (b - c))}$$

Kahan offers a thorough discussion in "Miscalculating Area and Angles of a Needle-like Triangle" (http://www.cs.berkeley.edu/~wkahan/Triangle.pdf).

19.3 WORST-CASE ERROR ACCUMULATION

In a sequence of computations, arithmetic or round-off errors may accumulate. The larger the number of cascaded computation steps (that depend on results from earlier steps), the greater the chance for, and the magnitude of, accumulated errors. With rounding, errors of opposite signs tend to cancel each other out in the long run, thus leading to smaller average error in the final result. Yet one cannot count on such cancellations.

For example, in computing the inner product

$$z = \sum_{i=0}^{1023} x^{(i)} y^{(i)}$$

if each multiply-add step introduces an absolute error of $ulp/2 + ulp/2 = ulp$, the total absolute error will be 1024 ulp in the worst case. This is equivalent to losing 10 bits of precision. As for the relative error, the situation may be worse. This is because in computing the sum of signed values, cancellations, or loss of precision, can occur in one or more intermediate steps.

The kind of worst-case analysis carried out for the preceding example is very rough, and its results are expressed in terms of the number of *significant digits* in the computation results. When cascading of computations lead to the worst-case accumulation of an absolute error of m ulp, the effect is equivalent to losing $\log_2 m$ bits of precision.

For our inner-product example, if we begin with 24 bits of precision, say, the result is only guaranteed to have $24 - 10 = 14$ significant digits. For more complicated computations, the worth of such a worst-case estimate decreases (the analysis might indicate that the result has no significant digit remaining).

An obvious cure for our inner-product example is to keep the double-width products in their entirety and add them to compute a double-width result, which is then rounded to single-width at the very last step. Now, the multiplications do not introduce any round-off error and each addition introduces a worst-case absolute error of $ulp^2/2$. Thus, the total error is bounded by $1024 \times ulp^2/2$ (or $n \times ulp^2/2$ when n product terms are involved). Therefore, provided overflow is not a problem, a highly accurate result is obtained. In fact, if n is smaller than $r^p = 1/ulp$, the result can be guaranteed accurate to within ulp (error of $n \times ulp^2/2 < ulp/2$ as described above, plus $ulp/2$ for the final rounding). This is as good as one would get with infinitely precise computation and final truncation.

The preceding discussion explains the need for performing the intermediate computations with a higher precision than is required in the final result. Carrying more precision in intermediate results is in fact very common in practice; even inexpensive calculators use several "guard digits" to protect against serious error accumulation (see Section 1.2). The IEEE floating-point standard defines extended formats associated with single- and double-precision numbers (see Section 17.2) for precisely this reason. Virtually all digital signal processors, which are essentially microprocessor chips designed with the goal of efficiently performing the computations commonly required in signal processing applications, have the built-in capability to compute inner products with very high precision (see Section 28.4).

Clearly, reducing the number of cascaded arithmetic operations counteracts the effect of error accumulation. So, using computationally more efficient algorithms has the double benefit of reducing both execution time and accumulated errors. However, in some cases, simplifying the arithmetic leads to problems elsewhere. A good example is found in numerical computations whose inherent accuracy is a function of a step size or grid resolution (numerical integration is a case in point). Since a smaller step size or finer grid leads to more computation steps, and thus greater accumulation of round-off errors, there may be an optimal choice that yields the best result with regard to the worst-case total error.

Since summation of a large number of terms is a frequent cause of error accumulation in software floating-point computations, Kahan's summation algorithm or formula is worth mentioning here. To compute $s = \sum_{i=0}^{n-1} x^{(i)}$, proceed as follows (justifying this algorithm is left as an exercise):

$$s \leftarrow x^{(0)}$$

$$c \leftarrow 0 \qquad \{c \text{ is a correction term}\}$$

for $i = 1$ to $n - 1$ do

$\qquad y \leftarrow x^{(i)} - c \qquad \{\text{subtract correction term}\}$

$\qquad z \leftarrow s + y$

$\qquad c \leftarrow (z - s) - y \qquad \{\text{find next correction term}\}$

$\qquad s \leftarrow z$

endfor

19.4 ERROR DISTRIBUTION AND EXPECTED ERRORS

Analyzing worst-case errors and their accumulation (as was done in Section 19.3) is an overly pessimistic approach, but it is necessary if guarantees are to be provided for the precision of the results. From a practical standpoint, however, the distribution of errors and their expected values may be more important. In this section, we review some results concerning average representation errors with chopping and rounding.

Denoting the magnitude of the worst-case or maximum relative representation error by MRRE, we recall that in Section 19.1 we established:

$$\text{MRRE(FLP}(r, p, \text{chop})) = r^{-p+1}$$

$$\text{MRRE(FLP}(r, p, \text{round})) = \frac{r^{-p+1}}{2}$$

In the analysis of the magnitude of average relative representation error (ARRE), we limit our attention to positive significands and begin by defining:

$$\text{ARRE(FLP}(r, p, \text{A})) = \int_{1/r}^{1} \frac{|x_{\text{fp}} - x|}{x} \frac{dx}{x \ln r}$$

where "ln" stands for the natural logarithm ($\log_e$) and $|x_{\text{fp}} - x|/x$ is the magnitude of the relative representation error for x. Multiplying this relative error by the probability density function $1/(x \ln r)$ is a consequence of the logarithmic law for the distribution of normalized significands [Tsao74]. Recall that a density function must be integrated to obtain the cumulative distribution function, prob($\varepsilon \leq z$), and that the area underneath it is 1.

Figure 19.1 plots the probability density function $1/(x \ln r)$ for $r = 2$. The density function $1/(x \ln r)$ essentially tells us that the probability of having a significand value in the range $[x, x + dx]$ is $dx/(x \ln r)$, thus leading to the integral above for the average relative representation error. Note that smaller significand values are more probable than larger values.

For a first-cut approximate analysis, we can take $|x_{\text{fp}} - x|$ to be equal to $r^{-p}/2$ for FLP(r, p, chop) and $r^{-p}/4$ for FLP(r, p, round): that is, half of the respective maximum absolute errors. Then the definite integral defining ARRE can be evaluated to yield the expected errors in the two cases:

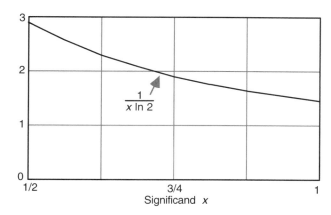

Fig. 19.1 Probability density function for the distribution of normalized significands in FLP($r = 2, p,$ A).

$$\text{ARRE}(\text{FLP}(r, p, \text{chop})) \approx \int_{1/r}^{1} \frac{r^{-p}}{2x} \frac{dx}{x \ln r} = \frac{(r - 1)r^{-p}}{2 \ln r}$$

$$\text{ARRE}(\text{FLP}(r, p, \text{round})) \approx \frac{(r - 1)r^{-p}}{4 \ln r}$$

More detailed analyses can be carried out to derive probability density functions for the relative error $|x_{\text{fp}} - x|/x$ with various rounding schemes, which are then integrated to provide accurate estimates for the expected errors.

One such study [Tsao74] has yielded the following probability density functions for the relative error ε being equal to z with chopping and rounding:

$$\text{pdf}_{\text{chop}}(z) = \begin{cases} \dfrac{r^{p-1}(r - 1)}{\ln r} & \text{for } 0 \leq z < r^{-p} \\[3mm] \dfrac{1/z - r^{p-1}}{\ln r} & \text{for } r^{-p} \leq z < r^{-p+1} \end{cases}$$

$$\text{pdf}_{\text{round}}(z) = \begin{cases} \dfrac{r^{p-1}(r - 1)}{\ln r} & \text{for } |z| \leq \dfrac{r^{-p}}{2} \\[3mm] \dfrac{1/(2z) - r^{p-1}}{\ln r} & \text{for } \dfrac{r^{-p}}{2} \leq |z| < \dfrac{r^{-p+1}}{2} \end{cases}$$

Note the uniform distribution of the relative error at the low end and the reciprocal distribution for larger values of the relative error z. From the preceding probability density functions, the expected error can be easily derived:

$$\text{ARRE}(\text{FLP}(r, p, \text{chop})) = \int_{0}^{r^{-p+1}} [\text{pdf}_{\text{chop}}(z)]z \, dz = \frac{(r - 1)r^{-p}}{2 \ln r}$$

$$\text{ARRE}(\text{FLP}(r, p, \text{round})) = \int_{-r^{-p+1}/2}^{r^{-p+1}/2} [\text{pdf}_{\text{round}}(z)]z \, dz = \frac{(r - 1)r^{-p}}{4 \ln r} \left(1 + \frac{1}{r}\right)$$

We thus see that the more rigorous analysis yields the same result as the approximate analysis in the case of chopping and a somewhat larger average error for rounding. In particular, for $r = 2$, the expected error of rounding is 3/4 (not 1/2, as the worst-case values and the approximate analysis indicate) that of chopping. These results are in good agreement with experimental results.

19.5 FORWARD ERROR ANALYSIS

Consider the simple computation $y = ax + b$ and its floating-point version:

$$y_{fp} = (a_{fp} \times_{fp} x_{fp}) +_{fp} b_{fp}$$

Assuming that $y_{fp} = (1 + \eta)y$ and given the relative errors in the input operands a_{fp}, b_{fp}, and x_{fp} can we establish any useful bound on the magnitude of the relative error η in the computation result? The answer is that we cannot establish a bound on η in general, but we may be able to do it with specific constraints on the input operand ranges. The reason for the impossibility of error-bounding in general is that if the two numbers $a_{fp} \times_{fp} x_{fp}$ and b_{fp} are comparable in magnitude but different in sign, loss of significance may occur in the final addition, making the result quite sensitive to even small errors in the inputs. Example 19.2 of Section 19.1 illustrates this point.

Estimating or bounding η, the relative error in the computation result, is known as "forward error analysis": that is, finding out how far y_{fp} can be from $ax + b$, or at least from $a_{fp}x_{fp} + b_{fp}$, in the worst case. In the remainder of this section, we briefly review four methods for forward error analysis.

a. Automatic error analysis

For an arithmetic-intensive computation whose accuracy is suspect, one might run selected test cases with higher precision and observe the differences between the new, more precise, results and the original ones. If the computation under study is single precision, for example, one might use double-precision arithmetic, or execute on a multiprecision software package in lieu of double precision. If test cases are selected carefully and the differences resulting from automatic error analysis turn out to be insignificant, the computation is probably safe, although nothing can be guaranteed.

b. Significance arithmetic

Roughly speaking, *significance arithmetic* is the same as unnormalized floating-point arithmetic, although there are some fine distinctions [Ashe59], [Metr63]. By not normalizing the intermediate computation results, except as needed to correct a significand spill, we at least get a warning when precision is lost. For example, the result of the unnormalized decimal addition

$$(.1234 \times 10^5) +_{fp} (.0000 \times 10^{10}) = .0000 \times 10^{10}$$

tells us that precision has been lost. Had we normalized the second intermediate result to true zero, we would have arrived at the misleading answer $.1234 \times 10^5$. The former answer gives us a much better feel for the potential errors.

Note that if 0.0000×10^{10} is a rounded intermediate decimal result, its infinitely precise version can be any value in $[-0.5 \times 10^6, 0.5 \times 10^6]$. Thus, the true magnitude of the second operand can be several times larger than that of the first operand. Normalization would hide this information.

c. Noisy-mode computation

In noisy-mode computation, (pseudo)random digits, rather than 0s, are inserted during left shifts that are performed for normalization of floating-point results. Noisy-mode computation can be either performed with special hardware support or programmed; in the latter case, significant software overhead is involved.

If several runs of the computation in noisy mode produce comparable results, loss of significance is probably not serious enough to cause problems. This is true because in various runs, different digits will be inserted during each normalization postshift. Getting comparable results from these runs is an indication that the computation is more or less insensitive to the random digits, and thus to the original digits that were lost as a result of cancellation or alignment right shifts.

d. Interval arithmetic

One can represent real values by intervals: an interval $[x_{lo}, x_{hi}]$ representing the real value x means that $x_{lo} \leq x \leq x_{hi}$. So, x_{lo} and x_{hi} are lower and upper bounds on the true value of x. To find $z = x/y$, say, we compute

$$[z_{lo}, z_{hi}] = [x_{lo}/_{\nabla fp} \, y_{hi}, x_{hi}/_{\triangle fp} \, y_{lo}] \quad \text{assuming } x_{lo}, x_{hi}, y_{lo}, y_{hi} > 0$$

with downward-directed rounding used in the first division ($/_{\nabla fp}$), and upward-directed rounding in the second one ($/_{\triangle fp}$), to ensure that the interval $[z_{lo}, z_{hi}]$ truly bounds the value of z.

Interval arithmetic [Moor66], [Alef83] is one the earliest methods for the automatic tracking of computational errors. It is quite intuitive, efficient, and theoretically appealing. Unfortunately, however, the intervals obtained in the course of long computations tend to widen until, after many steps, they become so wide as to be virtually worthless. Note that the span, $z_{hi} - z_{lo}$, of an interval is an indicator of the precision in the final result. So, an interval such as $[.8365 \times 10^{-3}, .2093 \times 10^{-2}]$ tells us little about the correct result.

It is sometimes possible to reformulate a computation to make the resulting output intervals narrower. Multiple computations also may help. If, using two different computation schemes (e.g., different formulas, as in Examples 19.3 and 19.4 at the end of Section 19.2) and find the intervals containing the result to be $[u_{lo}, u_{hi}]$ and $[v_{lo}, v_{hi}]$, we can use the potentially narrower interval

$$[w_{lo}, w_{hi}] = [max(u_{lo}, v_{lo}), min(u_{hi}, v_{hi})]$$

for continuing the computation or for output. We revisit interval arithmetic in Section 20.5 in connection with certifiable arithmetic computations.

19.6 BACKWARD ERROR ANALYSIS

In the absence of a general formula to bound the relative error $\eta = (y_{fp} - y)/y$ of the computation $y_{fp} = (a_{fp} \times_{fp} x_{fp}) +_{fp} b_{fp}$, alternative methods of error analysis may be sought. Backward error analysis replaces the original question

How much does the result y_{fp} deviate from the correct result y?

with another question:

What changes in the inputs would produce the same deviation in the result?

In other words, if the exact identity $y_{fp} = a_{alt}x_{alt} + b_{alt}$ holds for alternate input parameter values a_{alt}, b_{alt}, and x_{alt}, we want to find out how far a_{alt}, b_{alt}, and x_{alt} can be from a_{fp}, b_{fp}, and x_{fp}. Thus, computation errors are, in effect, converted or compared to additional input errors.

We can easily accomplish this goal for our example computation $y = (a \times x) + b$:

$$y_{fp} = (a_{fp} \times_{fp} x_{fp}) +_{fp} b_{fp}$$
$$= (1+\mu)\left[(a_{fp} \times_{fp} x_{fp}) + b_{fp}\right] \quad \text{with } |\mu| < r^{-p+1} = r \times ulp$$
$$= (1+\mu)\left[(1+\nu)a_{fp}x_{fp} + b_{fp}\right] \quad \text{with } |\nu| < r^{-p+1} = r \times ulp$$
$$= (1+\mu)a_{fp}(1+\nu)x_{fp} + (1+\mu)b_{fp}$$
$$= (1+\mu)(1+\sigma)a(1+\nu)(1+\delta)x + (1+\mu)(1+\gamma)b$$
$$\approx (1+\sigma+\mu)a(1+\delta+\nu)x + (1+\gamma+\mu)b$$

So the approximate solution of the original problem is viewed as the exact solution of a problem close to the original one (i.e., with each input having an additional relative error of μ or ν). According to the preceding analysis, we can assure the user that the effect of arithmetic errors on the result y_{fp} is no more severe than that of $r \times ulp$ additional error in each of the inputs a, b, and x. If the inputs are not precise to this level anyway, then arithmetic errors should not be a concern.

More generally, we do the computation $y_{fp} = f_{fp}(x_{fp}^{(1)}, x_{fp}^{(2)}, \cdots, x_{fp}^{(n)})$, where the subscripts "fp" indicate approximate operands and computation. Instead of trying to characterize the difference between y (the exact result) and y_{fp} (the result obtained), we try to characterize the difference between $x_{fp}^{(i)}$ and $x_{alt}^{(i)}$ such that the identity $y_{fp} = f(x_{alt}^{(1)}, x_{alt}^{(2)}, \cdots, x_{alt}^{(n)})$ holds exactly, with f being the exact computation. When it is applicable, this method is very powerful and useful.

PROBLEMS

19.1   Representation errors In Section 19.1, the maximum relative representation error was related to ulp using the assumption $1/r \le s < 1$. Repeat the analysis, this time assuming $1 \le s < r$ (as in IEEE floating-point standard format, e.g.). Explain your results.

19.2   Variations in rounding

a.   Show that in FLP(r, p, A) with even r, choosing round-to-nearest-even for $r/2$ odd, and round-to-nearest-odd for $r/2$ even, can reduce the errors. *Hint:* Successively round the decimal fraction 4.4445, each time removing one digit [Knut81].

b.   What about FLP(r, p, A) with an odd radix r?

19.3   Addition errors with guard digits

a.   Prove Theorem 19.1, given near the end of Section 19.1.

b.   Is the error derived in Example 19.1 of Section 19.1 consistent with Theorem 19.1?

c.   Redo the computation of Example 19.2 in Section 19.1 with two guard digits.

d.   Is it beneficial to have more than one guard digit as far as the worst-case error in floating-point addition is concerned?

19.4   Errors with guard digits

a. Show that in FLP(r, p, chop) with no guard digit, the relative error in addition or subtraction of exactly represented numbers can be as large as $r - 1$.

b. Show that if $x - y$ is computed with one guard digit and $y/2 \leq x \leq 2y$, the result is exact.

c. Modify Example 19.2 of Section 19.1 such that the relative arithmetic error is as close as possible to the bound given in the corollary to Theorem 19.1.

19.5   Optimal exponent base in a floating-point system   Consider two floating-point systems, FLP($r = 2^a$, p, A) and FLP($r = 2^b$, q, A), comparable ranges, and the same total number w of bits.

a. Derive a relationship between a, b, p, and q. *Hint:* Assume that x and y bits are used for the exponent parts and use the identity $x + ap = y + bq = w - 1$.

b. Using the relationship of part a, show that FLP($r = 2$, p, A) provides the lowest worst-case relative representation error among all floating-point systems with comparable ranges and power-of-2 radices.

19.6   Laws of algebra   In Section 19.2, examples were given to show that the associative law of addition may be violated in floating-point arithmetic. Provide examples that show the violation of the other laws of algebra listed in Section 19.2.

19.7   Laws of algebra for inequalities

a. Show that with floating-point arithmetic, if $a < b$, then $a +_{\text{fp}} c \leq b +_{\text{fp}} c$ holds for all c; that is, adding the same value to both sides of a strict inequality cannot affect its direction but may change the strict "$<$" relationship to "$\leq$."

b. Show that if $a < b$ and $c < d$, then $a +_{\text{fp}} c \leq b +_{\text{fp}} d$.

c. Show that if $c > 0$ and $a < b$, then $a \times_{\text{fp}} c \leq b \times_{\text{fp}} c$.

19.8   Equivalent computations   Evaluating expressions of the form $(1+g)^n$, where $g << 1$, is quite common in financial calculations. For example, g might be the daily interest rate ($0.06/365 \approx 0.000\ 164\ 383\ 6$ with a 6% annual rate) for a savings account that compounds interest daily. In calculating $1 +_{\text{fp}} g$, many bits of g are lost as a result of the alignment right shift. This error is then amplified when the result is raised to a large power n. The preceding expression can be rewritten as $e^{n \ln(1+g)}$. Even if an accurate natural logarithm function LN is available such that LN(x) is within $ulp/2$ of $\ln x$, our problem is still not quite solved since LN($1 +_{\text{fp}} g$) may not be close to $\ln(1 + g)$. Show that, for $g << 1$, computing $\ln(1 + g)$ as g when $1 +_{\text{fp}} g = g$ and as $[g \times_{\text{fp}} \text{LN}(1 +_{\text{fp}} g)]/_{\text{fp}} [(1 +_{\text{fp}} g) -_{\text{fp}} 1]$ when $1 +_{\text{fp}} g \neq 1$ provides good relative error.

19.9   Equivalent computations   Assume that x and y are numbers in FLP(r, p, chop(g)), $g \geq 1$.

a. Show that the midpoint of the interval [x, y], obtained from $(x +_{\text{fp}} y)/_{\text{fp}} 2$ may not be within the interval but that $x +_{\text{fp}} ((y -_{\text{fp}} x)/_{\text{fp}} 2)$ always is.

b. Show that the relative error in the floating-point calculation $(x \times_{\text{fp}} x) -_{\text{fp}} (y \times_{\text{fp}} y)$ can be quite large but that $(x -_{\text{fp}} y) \times_{\text{fp}} (x +_{\text{fp}} y)$ yields good relative error.

c.   Assume that the library program SQRT has good relative error. Show that calculating $1 -_{fp}$ SQRT$(1 -_{fp} x)$ may lead to bad worst-case relative error but that $x/_{fp}[1 +$ SQRT$(1 -_{fp} x)]$ is safe.

19.10   Errors in radix conversion

a.   Show that when a binary single-precision IEEE floating-point number is converted to the closest eight-digit decimal number, the original binary number may not be uniquely recoverable from the resulting decimal version.

b.   Would nine decimal digits be adequate to remedy the problem stated in part a? Fully justify your answer.

19.11   Kahan's summation algorithm

a.   Apply Kahan's summation algorithm, presented at the end of Section 19.3, to the example computations in Section 19.2 showing that the associative law of addition does not hold in floating-point arithmetic. Explain the results obtained.

b.   Provide an intuitive justification for the use of the correction term c in Kahan's summation algorithm.

19.12   Distribution of significand values

a.   Verify that Fig. 19.1 does in fact represent a probability density function.

b.   Find the average value of a normalized binary significand x based on Fig. 19.1 and comment on the result.

19.13   Error distribution and expected errors

a.   Verify that $pdf_{chop}(z)$ and $pdf_{round}(z)$, introduced near the end of Section 19.4, do in fact represent probability density functions.

b.   Verify that the probability density functions of part a lead to the ARRE values derived near the end of Section 19.4.

c.   Provide an intuitive explanation for the expected error in rounding being somewhat more than half that of truncation.

19.14   Noisy-mode computation   Perform the computation $(a +_{fp} b) +_{fp} c$, where $a = .123\ 41 \times 10^5, b = -.123\ 40 \times 10^5$, and $c = .143\ 21 \times 10^1$ four times in noisy mode, using pseudorandom digits during normalization left shifts. Compare and discuss the results.

19.15   Interval arithmetic   You are given the decimal floating-point numbers $x = .100 \times 10^0$ and $y = -.555 \times 10^{-1}$.

a.   Use interval arithmetic to compute the mean of x and y via the arithmetic expression $(x +_{fp} y)/_{fp} 2$.

b.   Repeat part a, this time using the arithmetic expression $x +_{fp} [(y -_{fp} x)/_{fp} 2]$.

c.   Combine the results of parts a and b into a more precise resulting interval. Discuss the result.

d.   Repeat parts a, b, and c with the equivalent computations $(x \times_{fp} x) -_{fp} (y \times_{fp} y)$ and $(x -_{fp} y) \times_{fp} (x +_{fp} y)$.

e.   Repeat parts a, b, and c with the equivalent computations $1 -_{\text{fp}} \text{SQRT}(1 -_{\text{fp}} x)$ and $x /_{\text{fp}} [1 + \text{SQRT}(1 -_{\text{fp}} x)]$, assuming that the library program SQRT provides precisely rounded results.

19.16   **Backward error analysis**   An $(n-1)$th-degree polynomial in x, with the coefficient of the ith-degree term denoted as $c^{(i)}$, is evaluated with at least one guard digit by using Horner's rule (i.e., n computation steps, each involving a floating-point multiplication by x followed by a floating-point addition). Using backward error analysis, show that this procedure, has allowed us to compute a polynomial with coefficients $(1 + \eta^{(i)})c^{(i)}$, and find a bound for $\eta^{(i)}$. Then, show that if $c^{(i)} \geq 0$ for all i and $x > 0$, a useful bound can be placed on the relative error of the final result.

19.17   **Computational errors**

a.   Armed with what you have learned from this chapter, reexamine the sources of computation errors in Problem 1.1 of Chapter 1. Describe your findings using the terminology introduced in this chapter.

b.   Repeat part a for Problem 1.2.

c.   Repeat part a for Problem 1.3.

REFERENCES

[Alef83]   Alefeld, G., and J. Herzberger, *An Introduction to Interval Computations*, Academic Press, 1983.

[Ashe59]   Ashenhurst, R.L., and N. Metropolis, "Unnormalized Floating-Point Arithmetic," *J. ACM*, Vol. 6, pp. 415–428, March 1959.

[Cody73]   Cody, W.J., "Static and Dynamic Numerical Characteristics of Floating-Point Arithmetic," *IEEE Trans. Computers*, Vol. 22, No. 6, pp. 598–601, 1973.

[Gold91]   Goldberg, D., "What Every Computer Scientist Should Know About Floating-Point Arithmetic," *ACM Computing Surveys*, Vol. 23, No. 1, pp. 5–48, March 1991.

[Knut81]   Knuth, D.E., *The Art of Computer Programming*, 2nd ed., *Vol. 2: Seminumerical Algorithms*, Addison-Wesley, 1981.

[Kuck77]   Kuck, D.J., D.S. Parker, and A.H. Sameh, "Analysis of Rounding Methods in Floating-Point Arithmetic," *IEEE Trans. Computers*, Vol. 26, No. 7, pp. 643–650, 1977.

[McKe67]   McKeenan, W. M., "Representation Error for Real Numbers in Binary Computer Arithmetic," *IEEE Trans. Computers*, Vol. 16, pp. 682–683, 1967.

[Metr63]   Metropolis, N., and R.L. Ashenhurst, "Basic Operations in an Unnormalized Arithmetic System," *IEEE Trans. Electronic Computers*, Vol. 12, pp. 896–904, 1963.

[Moor66]   Moore, R., *Interval Analysis*, Prentice-Hall, 1966.

[Ster74]   Sterbenz, P.H., *Floating-Point Computation*, Prentice-Hall, 1974.

[Tsao74]   Tsao, N., "On the Distribution of Significant Digits and Roundoff Errors," *Commun. ACM*, Vol. 17, No. 5, pp. 269–271, 1974.

Chapter 20 | PRECISE AND CERTIFIABLE ARITHMETIC

In certain application contexts, where wrong answers might jeopardize operational safety, or even endanger human lives, all system functions must be certifiable. In the case of arithmetic, this means either doing exact calculations or the ability to put strict upper bounds on the errors (fail-safe mode) and/or on the probability of intolerable errors (probabilistic certification). In this chapter, we review methods for performing arithmetic operations with greater precision and/or with guaranteed error bounds. Chapter topics include:

20.1 HIGH PRECISION AND CERTIFIABILITY

Numerical computations performed with short or long floating-point formats are remarkably accurate in most cases. Errors resulting from the finiteness of representation and imprecise calculations (e.g., approximation or convergence schemes) are by now reasonably well understood and can be kept under control by algorithmic methods. In some situations, however, ordinary floating-point arithmetic is inadequate, either because it is not precise enough or because of our inability to establish useful bounds on the errors. In such cases, the results may well possess adequate precision but there is a "credibility-gap problem . . . [as] we don't know how much of the computer's answers to believe" [Knut81].

We will discuss three distinct approaches for coping with the aforementioned credibility gap:

1. Obtaining completely trustworthy results by performing arithmetic calculations exactly (Section 20.2). Of course, if this approach were always possible and cost-effective, we wouldn't need any of the following alternatives.
2. Making the arithmetic highly precise, in order to raise our confidence in the validity of the results. This pragmatic goal can be accomplished by multiprecision calculations (Section

328

20.3) or via a more flexible variable-precision arithmetic system (Section 20.4). The two approaches correspond to static and dynamic precision enhancement, respectively. Both methods make irrelevant results less likely but provide no guarantee, except in a probabilistic sense.

3. Performing ordinary or high-precision calculations, while keeping track of potential error accumulation (Section 20.5). Then, based on the worst-case suspected error in the result, we can either certify the result as carrying adequate precision or produce a warning that would prevent incorrect conclusions or actions that might have catastrophic consequences (fail-safe operation).

After studying the preceding approaches, we devote Section 20.6 to techniques that render precise and/or certifiable arithmetic more efficient.

Besides problems with precision, the finite range of machine arithmetic can also become problematic. Thus provisions for exact or highly precise arithmetic are often accompanied by methods for extending the range. A common way is via number representation systems in which the range can grow dynamically. Usually, numbers are represented in a single word. However, one or two bits are assigned special meanings and allow the number to extend into subsequent words. The price we pay for this flexibility is loss of the aforementioned bit(s) and more complex arithmetic algorithms, including the overhead of the special checks needed to establish whether the range must be extended.

Of course certifiability in computer arithmetic is concerned not only with precision, or lack thereof, but also spans algorithm and hardware verification as well as fault detection and tolerance. Modern digital systems tend to be extremely complex. Thus, unless full attention is paid to correctness issues during the design, there is little hope of catching all problems afterward. The already difficult verification process is exacerbated by complex interrelationships between advanced design features such as parallelism, pipelining, and power-saving mechanisms. The Pentium floating-point division flaw aptly illustrates this point. As for fault-induced errors, we deal with them in Chapter 27.

20.2 EXACT ARITHMETIC

The ultimate in error control is exact (error-free) arithmetic. This ideal has been pursued by many arithmetic designers and researchers, leading to proposals for using continued fractions, rational numbers, and p-adic representations, among others. In this section, we introduce a few of the proposed methods and briefly discuss their implementation aspects, advantages, and drawbacks.

a. Continued Fractions

Any unsigned rational number $x = p/q$ has a unique continued-fraction expansion

$$x = \frac{p}{q} = a_0 + \cfrac{1}{a_1 + \cfrac{1}{a_2 + \cfrac{1}{\ddots \cfrac{1}{a_{m-1} + \cfrac{1}{a_m}}}}}$$

with $a_0 \geq 0$, $a_m \geq 2$, and $a_i \geq 1$ for $1 \leq i \leq m - 1$. For example, 277/642 has the following continued-fraction representation:

$$\frac{277}{642} = 0 + \cfrac{1}{2 + \cfrac{1}{3 + \cfrac{1}{6 + \cfrac{1}{1 + \cfrac{1}{3 + 1/3}}}}} = [0/2/3/6/1/3/3]$$

Representation of $-277/642$ is obtained by simply attaching a sign bit or negating all the digits in the representation of $277/642$.

Note that the continued-fraction representation of x is obtained by writing $x = s^{(0)}$ as $\lfloor s^{(0)} \rfloor + 1/s^{(1)}$, and then repeating the process for representing each $s^{(i)}$ in turn (i.e., $s^{(1)} = \lfloor s^{(1)} \rfloor + 1/s^{(2)}, \dots$). Thus, for $s^{(0)} = 277/642$, we get $s^{(1)} = 642/277$, $s^{(2)} = 277/88$, $s^{(3)} = 88/13$, $s^{(4)} = 13/10$, $s^{(5)} = 10/3$, and $s^{(6)} = 3$.

Approximations for finite representation can be obtained by limiting the number of "digits" in the continued-fraction representation. For example, the following are successively better approximations to the exact value $x = [0/2/3/6/1/3/3] = 277/642$:

[0]	$= 0$
[0/2]	$= 1/2$
[0/2/3]	$= 3/7$
[0/2/3/6]	$= 19/44$
[0/2/3/6/1]	$= 22/51$
[0/2/3/6/1/3]	$= 85/197$

Vuillemin [Vuil90] has suggested that continued fractions be used in the following way for performing exact arithmetic. Each potentially infinite, continued fraction is represented by a finite number of digits, plus a *continuation*, which is, in effect, a procedure for obtaining the next digit as well as a new continuation. Notationally, we can write the digits as before (i.e., separated by /), following them with a semicolon and a description of the continuation.

When the representation is periodic, the continuation can simply be specified by a sequence of one or more digits. This is what we do in decimal arithmetic when we write 8/3 as $(2.66;6)_{\text{ten}}$ and 1/7 as $(0.1;428571)_{\text{ten}}$. When additional digits can be derived as a simple function of an index $i \geq 0$, the relevant expression is given. Here are some examples:

$$
\begin{aligned}
(1 + \sqrt{5})/2 &= [1/1/1/1/\cdots] = [; 1] \\
\sqrt{2} &= [1/2/2/2/\cdots] = [1; 2] \\
e &= [2/1/2/1/1/4/1/1/6/1/\cdots] = [2; 1/2i + 2/1] \\
\infty &= [1/0/1/0/1/0\cdots] = [; 1/0] = [; 2/0] = \cdots \\
\text{aN} &= [0/0/0/0/\cdots] = [; 0] \qquad \{\text{any number}\}
\end{aligned}
$$

Unfortunately, arithmetic operations on continued fractions are quite complicated. So, we will not pursue this representation further.

b. Fixed-Slash Number Systems

In a fixed-slash number system, a rational number is represented as the ratio of a pair of integers p and q, each with a fixed range. Representation of numbers as finite-precision rationals is related to the continued-fraction expansion discussed earlier in the sense that when a number is not exactly representable, the best continued-fraction approximation that fits is used as its "rounded" version. For example, suppose we want to represent the rational number 277/642 in a $2 + 2$ decimal fixed-slash number system (2 digits each for the numerator and the denominator). From the continued-fraction representation given earlier, we find the best approximation to be 22/51, which has a relative error slightly exceeding 2%.

A possible fixed-slash format for representing rational numbers consists of a sign bit, followed by an "inexact" flag, a k-bit numerator, and an m-bit denominator, for a total of $k+m+2$ bits (Fig. 20.1). The inexact flag is useful for denoting a value that has been rounded off because the precise result did not fit within the available format. Note that integers are a subclass of representable numbers (with $q = 1$). The representation of a rational number is normalized if $\gcd(p, q) = 1$. Special values can also be represented by appropriate conventions. Here is one way to do it:

Rational number	if $p > 0, q > 0$
± 0	if $p = 0, q$ odd
$\pm\infty$	if p odd, $q = 0$
NaN (not a number)	otherwise

When a number is not representable exactly, it is rounded to the closest representable value. On overflow (underflow), the number is rounded to $\pm\infty(\pm 0)$ and the inexact bit is set.

The following mathematical result, due to Dirichlet, shows that the space waste due to multiple representations such as $3/5 = 6/10 = 9/15 = \cdots$ is no more than one bit:

$$\lim_{n \to \infty} \frac{|\{p/q \mid 1 \le p, q \le n, \gcd(p, q) = 1\}|}{n^2} = \frac{6}{\pi^2} \approx 0.608$$

This result essentially says that for n sufficiently large, two randomly selected numbers in $[1, n]$ are relatively prime with probability greater than 0.6. Thus, more than half of the codes represent unique numbers and the waste is less than 1 bit.

Note that the additive (multiplicative) inverse of a number is easily obtained with fixed-slash representation by simply flipping the sign bit (switching p and q). Adding two fixed-slash numbers requires three integer multiplications and one addition, while multiplying them involves two multiplications. Subtraction (division) can be done as addition (multiplication) by first forming the additive (multiplicative) inverse of the subtrahend (divisor).

The results of these operations are exact, unless the numerator or denominator becomes too large. In such a case, we can avoid overflow through *normalization* if p and q have a common factor. The overhead implied by computing $\gcd(p, q)$ is often unacceptably high. Additionally, once the capacity of the number system for exact representation of the result has been exceeded,

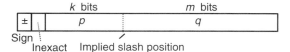

Fig. 20.1   Example fixed-slash number representation format.

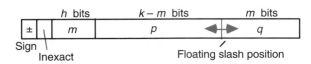

Fig. 20.2 Example floating-slash representation format.

the process of rounding the result to the nearest representable rational number is fairly complex. For these reasons, fixed-slash representations have not found widespread use.

c. Floating-Slash Number Systems

In a fixed-slash number system, a fixed number of bits is allocated to each of the numerator and denominator parts. These bits sometimes go to waste, as evident in the case of $q = 1$ for representing integers. A floating-slash format for representing rational numbers consists of a sign bit, followed by an "inexact" flag, an h-bit field (m) specifying the explicit slash position, and a k-bit field containing a $(k - m)$-bit numerator and the least significant m bits of an $(m + 1)$-bit denominator with a hidden MSB of 1. We obtain integers for $m = 0$. The set of numbers represented in such a floating-slash number system (Fig. 20.2) is:

$$\{\pm p/q \mid p, q \geq 1, \gcd(p, q) = 1, \lfloor \log_2 p \rfloor + \lfloor \log_2 q \rfloor \leq k - 2\}$$

Special codes for ± 0, $\pm \infty$, and NaN are also needed, as in fixed-slash representations. For the sake of simplicity, one can replace the preceding condition $\lfloor \log_2 p \rfloor + \lfloor \log_2 q \rfloor \leq k - 2$ with the approximate condition $pq \leq 2^k$. Again the following mathematical result, due to Dirichlet, shows that the space waste is no more than one bit:

$$\lim_{n \to \infty} \frac{|\{\pm p/q \mid pq \leq n, \gcd(p, q) = 1\}|}{|\{\pm p/q \mid pq \leq n, p, q \geq 1\}|} = \frac{6}{\pi^2} \approx 0.608$$

Floating-slash format removes some of the problems of fixed-slash representations, but arithmetic operations are complicated even further; hence, applications are limited.

20.3 MULTIPRECISION ARITHMETIC

One could in principle build a highly precise arithmetic unit, say operating on 1024-bit floating-point numbers instead of the standard 32- or 64-bit varieties. There are several obvious problems with this approach, including high cost, waste of time and hardware for computations that do not need such a high precision, and inability to adapt to special situations that call for even higher precision. Thus, floating-point hardware is provided for more commonly used 32- and 64-bit numbers.

When the range or precision of the number representation scheme supported by the hardware is inadequate for a given application, we are forced to represent numbers as multiword data structures and to perform arithmetic operations by means of software routines that manipulate these structures. Examples in the case of integer arithmetic can be found in cryptography, where large integers are used as keys for the encoding/decoding processes, and in mathematical research, where properties of large primes are investigated. Extended-precision floating-point numbers may be encountered in some scientific calculations, where highly precise results are required, or in error analysis efforts, where the numerical stability of algorithms must be verified by computing certain test cases with much higher precision.

Multiprecision arithmetic refers to the representation of numbers in multiple machine words. The number of words used to represent each integer or real number is chosen a priori; if the number of words can change dynamically, we have variable-precision arithmetic (see Section 20.4). In the case of integer values, the use of multiple words per number extends the range; for floating-point numbers, either the range or the precision parameter or both might be extended, depending on need. All these approaches are referred to as "multiprecision arithmetic," even though, strictly speaking, the term makes no sense for integers.

Multiprecision integer arithmetic is conceptually quite simple. An integer can be represented by a list of smaller integers, each of which fits within a single machine word (Fig. 20.3). These extended-precision integers are then viewed as radix-2^k numbers, where k is the word width. As an example, with 32-bit machine words, one can represent a quadruple-precision 2's-complement integer x by using the four unsigned words $x^{(3)}, x^{(2)}, x^{(1)}, x^{(0)}$, such that:

$$x = -x_{31}^{(3)} \, 2^{127} + 2^{96} \sum_{j=0}^{30} x_j^{(3)} \, 2^j + 2^{64} x^{(2)} + 2^{32} x^{(1)} + x^{(0)}$$

The radix in this example is 2^{32}. With this representation, radix-2^k digit-serial arithmetic algorithms can be applied to the multiprecision numbers in a straightforward manner to simulate 128-bit, 2's-complement arithmetic. To perform the addition $z = x + y$, for example, we begin by performing $z^{(0)} = x^{(0)} + y^{(0)}$, which leads to the carry-out $c^{(1)}$ being saved in the carry flag. Next, we perform the addition $z^{(1)} = x^{(1)} + y^{(1)} + c^{(1)}$. Virtually all processors provide a special instruction for adding with carry-in. The process can thus be repeated in a loop, with special overflow detection rules applied after the last iteration.

Multiplication can be performed by either implementing a shift/add algorithm directly or by using the machine's multiply instruction, if available. For further details, see [Knut81, Section 4.3, on multiple-precision arithmetic, pp. 250–301].

Performing complicated arithmetic computations on multiprecision numbers can be quite slow. For this reason, people sometimes prefer to perform such computations on highly parallel computers, thus speeding up the computation by concurrent operations on various words of the multiword numbers. Since each word of the resulting multiword numbers in general depends on all words of the operands, proper data distribution and occasional rearrangement may be required to minimize the communication overhead that otherwise might nullify much of the speed gain due to concurrency. Many standard parallel algorithms can be used directly in such arithmetic computations. For example, parallel prefix can be used for carry prediction (lookahead) and FFT for multiplication [Parh98]. Whether one uses a sequential or parallel computer for multiprecision arithmetic, the selection of the optimal algorithm depends strongly on the available hardware features and the width of numbers to be processed [Zura93].

Multiprecision floating-point arithmetic can be similarly programmed. When precision is to be extended but a wider range is not needed, a standard floating-point number can be used

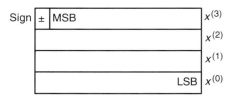

Fig. 20.3 Example quadruple-precision integer format.

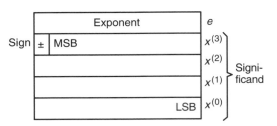

Fig. 20.4   Example quadruple-precision floating-point format.

to represent the sign, exponent, and part of the significand, with the remaining bits of the high-precision significand extending into one or more additional words. However, given that modern computers have plenty of register and storage space available, it is perhaps better to use a separate word for storing the exponent and one or more words for the extended-precision significand, thus eliminating the overhead for repeated packing and unpacking. The significand can be represented as an integer using the format of Fig. 20.3. The separate exponent, which is a 32-bit biased number, say, provides a very wide range that is adequate for all practical purposes. Figure 20.4 depicts the resulting format.

Arithmetic operations are performed by programming the required steps for the floating-point algorithms of Section 17.3, with details in Chapter 18. To perform addition, for example, the significand of the operand with the smaller exponent is shifted to the right by an amount equal to the difference of the two exponents, the aligned significands are added, and the resulting sum is normalized (Fig. 20.5). Floating-point multiplication and division are similarly performed.

As for rounding of the results, two approaches are possible. One is to simply chop any bit that is shifted out past the right end of the numbers, hoping that the extended precision will be adequate to compensate for any extra error. An alternative is to derive guard, round, and sticky bits from the bits that are shifted out (see Fig. 20.5) in the manner outlined in Section 18.3.

20.4 VARIABLE-PRECISION ARITHMETIC

As mentioned in Section 20.3, multiprecision arithmetic suffers both from inefficiency in the common case (i.e., when high precision is not needed) and from the inability to adapt to situations that might require even higher precision. Alternatively, a variable-precision floating-point capability can be implemented to operate on data of various widths under program control. Variable precision is useful not only for situations calling for high precision; it may be beneficial, as well, for improving performance when lower precision would do.

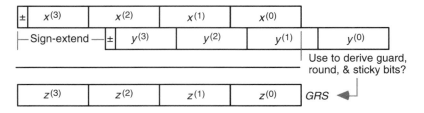

Fig. 20.5   Quadruple-precision significands aligned for the floating-point addition $z = x +_{\text{fp}} y$.

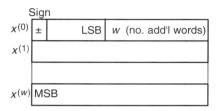

Fig. 20.6 Example variable-precision integer format.

Dispensing precision on demand in different stages of computations, or even at the level of individual arithmetic operations, has been an elusive goal in the field of computer arithmetic, except where bit- or digit-serial arithmetic is involved. For our discussion here, we consider variable precision with machine-word granularity. This is quite similar to multiprecision arithmetic, as discussed in Section 20.3, except that a "width" field must be added to all numbers that specifies how many words are used to represent the number. Also, if the operand widths are to be modifiable at run time, dynamic storage allocation and facilities for reclaiming space (garbage collection) are required.

To represent variable-precision (really variable-range) integers, we might use 1 or 2 bytes in the first 32-bit word to hold the width information, 1 bit for the sign, and the remaining part to hold the low-order 15 or 23 bits of the number. If the number is wider, additional words will be tacked on as needed to hold the higher-order bits (Fig. 20.6). Note that this convention, known as "little-endian," is opposite that of Fig. 20.4, which is referred to as "big-endian." Storing the low-order bits first leads to a slight simplification in variable-precision addition, since indexing for both operands and the result starts at 0.

Again to avoid packing and unpacking of values and to remove the need for special handling of the first chunk of the number, one might assign the number's width information to an entire word, which can then be directly loaded into a counter or register for processing.

A corresponding variable-precision floating-point format can be similarly devised. Figure 20.7 depicts one alternative. Here, the first word contains the number's sign, its width w, the exponent e, and designations for special operands. The significand then follows in w subsequent words. Again, we might want to put the exponent in a separate word, both to reduce the need for packing and unpacking and to provide greatly extended range.

From an implementation standpoint, addition becomes much simpler if the exponent base is taken to be 2^k instead of 2, since the former case would lead to shift amounts that are multiples of k bits (bit-level operations are avoided). This will, of course, have implications in terms of the available precision (see Section 17.1). The effect of shifting can then be taken into account by indexing rather than actual data movement. For example, if the alignment shift amount applied to the v-word operand y before adding it the u-word operand x to obtain the u-word sum z is h words, then referring to Fig. 20.8 and defining $g = v + h - u$, we can write the main part of the floating-point addition algorithm as the following three loops:

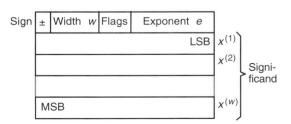

Fig. 20.7 Example variable-precision floating-point format.

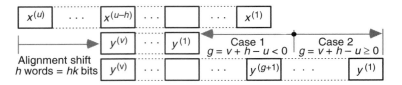

Fig. 20.8   Variable-precision floating-point addition.

for $i = 1$ to $-g$ do   {empty loop if $g \geq 0$}
$\quad c, z^{(i)} \leftarrow x^{(i)} + c$
endfor
for $i = \max(1, -g + 1)$ to $u - h$ do   {empty loop if $u \leq h$}
$\quad c, z^{(i)} \leftarrow x^{(i)} + y^{(g+i)} + c$
endfor
for $i = \max(1, u - h + 1)$ to u do   {empty loop if $h = 0$}
$\quad c, z^{(i)} \leftarrow x^{(i)} + c - \text{signbit}(y)$ {must sign-extend y}
endfor

In the complete algorithm, the loops must be preceded by various checks and initializations and followed by any normalization and rounding required.

20.5 ERROR BOUNDING VIA INTERVAL ARITHMETIC

Interval arithmetic was introduced at the end of Section 19.5 as an error analysis method. When computation with intervals yields a result $z = [z_{lo}, z_{hi}]$, the width of the interval $w = z_{hi} - z_{lo} \geq 0$ can be interpreted as the extent of uncertainty, and the midpoint $(z_{lo} + z_{hi})/2$ of the interval can be used as an approximate value for z with a worst-case error of about $w/2$. Even when a result interval is too wide to be practically useful, at least a fail-safe mode of operation can be ascertained.

The interval $[a, a]$ represents the real number a, while $[a, b]$, with $a > b$, can be viewed as representing the empty interval ϕ. Intervals can be combined and compared in a natural way. For example:

$$[x_{lo}, x_{hi}] \cap [y_{lo}, y_{hi}] = \big[max(x_{lo}, y_{lo}), min(x_{hi}, y_{hi}) \big]$$

$$[x_{lo}, x_{hi}] \cup [y_{lo}, y_{hi}] = \big[min(x_{lo}, y_{lo}), max(x_{hi}, y_{hi}) \big]$$

$$[x_{lo}, x_{hi}] \supseteq [y_{lo}, y_{hi}] \text{ iff } x_{lo} \leq y_{lo} \text{ and } x_{hi} \geq y_{hi}$$

$$[x_{lo}, x_{hi}] = [y_{lo}, y_{hi}] \text{ iff } x_{lo} = y_{lo} \text{ and } x_{hi} = y_{hi}$$

$$[x_{lo}, x_{hi}] < [y_{lo}, y_{hi}] \text{ iff } x_{hi} < y_{lo}$$

Interval arithmetic operations are quite intuitive and efficient. For example, the additive inverse $-x$ of an interval $x = [x_{lo}, x_{hi}]$ is derived as follows:

$$- [x_{lo}, x_{hi}] = [-x_{hi}, -x_{lo}]$$

The multiplicative inverse of an interval $x = [x_{lo}, x_{hi}]$ is derived as:

$$\frac{1}{[x_{lo}, x_{hi}]} = \left[\frac{1}{x_{hi}}, \frac{1}{x_{lo}}\right] \quad \text{provided } 0 \notin [x_{lo}, x_{hi}]$$

When $0 \in [x_{lo}, x_{hi}]$—that is, when x_{lo} and x_{hi} have unlike signs or are both 0s—the multiplicative inverse is undefined (alternatively, it can be said to be $[-\infty, +\infty]$). Note that with machine arithmetic, $1/x_{hi}$ must be computed with downward-directed rounding and $1/x_{lo}$ with upward-directed rounding.

In what follows, we assume that proper rounding is performed in each case and deal only with exact intervals for simplicity. Here are the four basic arithmetic operations on intervals:

$$[x_{lo}, x_{hi}] + [y_{lo}, y_{hi}] = [x_{lo} + y_{lo}, x_{hi} + y_{hi}]$$

$$[x_{lo}, x_{hi}] - [y_{lo}, y_{hi}] = [x_{lo} - y_{hi}, x_{hi} - y_{lo}]$$

$$[x_{lo}, x_{hi}] \times [y_{lo}, y_{hi}] = \big[min(x_{lo}y_{lo}, x_{lo}y_{hi}, x_{hi}y_{lo}, x_{hi}y_{hi}),$$

$$max(x_{lo}y_{lo}, x_{lo}y_{hi}, x_{hi}y_{lo}, x_{hi}y_{hi})\big]$$

$$[x_{lo}, x_{hi}] \, / \, [y_{lo}, y_{hi}] = [x_{lo}, x_{hi}] \times [1/y_{hi}, 1/y_{lo}]$$

Several interesting properties of intervals and interval arithmetic are explored in the end-of-chapter problems. In particular, we will see that multiplication is not as inefficient as the preceding definition might suggest.

From the viewpoint of arithmetic calculations, a very important property of interval arithmetic is stated in the following theorem.

THEOREM 20.1   If $f(x^{(1)}, x^{(2)}, \cdots, x^{(n)})$ is a rational expression in the interval variables $x^{(1)}, x^{(2)}, \cdots, x^{(n)}$, that is, f is a finite combination of $x^{(1)}, x^{(2)}, \cdots, x^{(n)}$ and a finite number of constant intervals by means of interval arithmetic operations, then $x^{(i)} \supset y^{(i)}$, $i = 1, 2, \cdots, n$, implies:

$$f(x^{(1)}, x^{(2)}, \cdots, x^{(n)}) \supset f(y^{(1)}, y^{(2)}, \cdots, y^{(n)})$$

Thus, arbitrarily narrow result intervals can be obtained by simply performing arithmetic with sufficiently high precision. In particular, we can show that with reasonable assumptions about machine arithmetic, the following theorem holds.

THEOREM 20.2   Consider the execution of an algorithm on real numbers by means of machine interval arithmetic with precision p in radix r [i.e., in FLP($r, p, \nabla|\Delta$)]. If the same algorithm is executed using the precision q, with $q > p$, the bounds for both absolute error and relative error are reduced by the factor r^{q-p}.

Note that the absolute or relative error itself may not be reduced by the same factor; the guaranteed reduction applies only to the upper bound.

Based on Theorem 20.2, one can devise a practical strategy for obtaining results with a desired bound on the absolute or relative error. For example, let $w_{\max}$ be the maximum width of a result interval when interval arithmetic is performed with p radix-r digits of precision and assume that the required bound on the absolute error is ε. If $w_{\max} \leq \varepsilon$, then we are done. Otherwise, interval calculations with the higher precision

$$q = p + \lceil \log_r w_{\max} - \log_r \varepsilon \rceil$$

is guaranteed to yield the desired accuracy.

20.6 ADAPTIVE AND LAZY ARITHMETIC

In some applications, arithmetic algorithms and/or hardware structures must adapt to changing conditions or requirements. For example, not all computations require the same precision, and using a 64-bit multiplier to multiply 8-bit numbers would be a waste of hardware resources, and perhaps even time. In this section, we briefly discuss some ideas for building adaptable arithmetic systems. An aspect of adaptability is fault tolerance, namely, the capacity for continued operation, perhaps at lower performance, acquired by reconfiguring around faulty elements. This latter type of adaptability is the subject of Chapter 27.

One way to provide adaptivity is via built-in multiprecision arithmetic capability. For example, facilities may be provided to allow the dynamic switching of a computation from single- to multiprecision according to the precision requirements for the results. Variable-precision capability can extend the preceding two-way adaptive scheme to an incremental or multiway scheme.

Interestingly, the opposite of multiprecision arithmetic, which we may call fractional precision arithmetic, is also of some interest. Whereas modern high-performance microprocessors have arithmetic capability for 32- or 64-bit numbers, many arithmetic-intensive applications, such as voice compression or image processing for multimedia, may deal with 8- or 16-bit data representing color or other audiovisual elements. Recent microprocessor designs have recognized the need for efficient handling of such fractional precision numbers through special hardware extensions. For example, Intel's MMX (multimedia extension) for the Pentium processor [Pele97] uses the microprocessor's eight floating-point registers to store 64-bit packed integer data (8×8, 4×16, 2×32, in signed/unsigned versions). Special add, multiply, multiply-add, and parallel compare instructions are made available that operate on these packed MMX data types.

An alternative approach to adaptive arithmetic is via multiple number representation formats that are distinguished by tagging. For example, in a simple two-way adaptive scheme, primary and secondary representation modes may be associated with each number type; the primary mode is more precise but offers limited range, while the secondary mode offers a wider range with less precision. Computation is then switched between the two representations based on need. In this way, overflow can be avoided or postponed. One proposal along these lines [Holm97] uses four-way tagging to distinguish between primary and secondary formats for exact and inexact values.

Lazy evaluation is a powerful paradigm that has been and is being used in many different contexts. For example, in evaluating composite conditionals such as

if *cond1* and *cond2* then *action*

the evaluation of *cond2* may be totally skipped if *cond1* evaluates to "false". More generally, lazy evaluation means postponing all computations or actions until they become irrelevant or unavoidable. In the context of computer hardware architecture, the opposite of lazy evaluation (viz., speculative or aggressive execution) has been applied extensively; however, lazy evaluation is found only in certain special-purpose systems with data- or demand-driven designs.

In the absence of hardware support for lazy arithmetic, all known implementations of this method rely on software. Schwarz [Schw89] describes a C++ library for arbitrary precision arithmetic that is based on representing results by a data value corresponding to the known bits and an expression that can be manipulated to obtain more bits when needed. A lazy rational arithmetic system [Mich97] uses a triple $\langle x_{lo}, x_{xct}, x_{hi} \rangle$ to represent each number, where x_{xct} is an exact rational value, or a pointer to a procedure for obtaining it, and $[x_{lo}, x_{hi}]$ represents an interval bounded by the floating-point values x_{lo} and x_{hi}. Computation normally proceeds with floating-point values using the rules of interval arithmetic. When this primary mode of computation runs into precision problems, and only then, exact computation is invoked.

Lazy arithmetic, as suggested above, comes with nontrivial representational and computational overheads. Thus far, the viability of lazy arithmetic, and its cost–performance implications, have been investigated only for certain geometric computations. Even within this limited application domain, some problems remain to be resolved [Mich97].

It is noteworthy that redundant number representations offer some advantages for lazy arithmetic. Since arithmetic on redundant numbers can be performed by means of MSD-first algorithms, it is possible to produce a small number of digits of the result by using correspondingly less computational effort. When precision problems are encountered, one can backtrack and obtain more digits of the results as needed.

PROBLEMS

20.1 Computing the *i*th Fibonacci number The sequence of Fibonacci numbers Fib(i), $i = 1, 2, 3, \cdots$, is defined recursively as Fib(1) = Fib(2) = 1 and Fib(i) = Fib($i - 1$) + Fib($i - 2$) for $i \geq 3$. One can show that Fib(i) = $(x^i - y^i)/\sqrt{5}$, where $x = (1 + \sqrt{5})/2$ and $y = (1 - \sqrt{5})/2$.

a. Devise an exact representation for numbers of the form $a + b\sqrt{5}$, where a and b are rational numbers.

b. Develop algorithms for addition, subtraction, multiplication, division, and exponentiation for the numbers in part a.

c. Use your representation and arithmetic algorithms to compute Fib(10) and Fib(64).

20.2 Converging interval representation The golden ratio $\phi = (1 + \sqrt{5})/2$ can be represented increasingly accurately by a sequence of intervals $x^{(j)} = [\text{Fib}(2j + 2)/\text{Fib}(2j + 1), \text{Fib}(2j + 1)/\text{Fib}(2j)]$ that get narrower as j increases. In the preceding description, Fib(i) is the ith Fibonacci number recursively defined as Fib(1) = Fib(2) = 1 and Fib(i) = Fib($i - 1$) + Fib($i - 2$) for $i \geq 3$.

a. Using exact rational arithmetic, obtain the first eight intervals in the sequence defined.

b. Repeat part a, this time using decimal arithmetic with six fractional digits. From the last result, find an approximation to ϕ with an associated error bound.

20.3 Approximating π with exact arithmetic Using exact rational arithmetic, find an interval that is guaranteed to contain the exact value of π based on the identity

$\pi/4 = \tan^{-1}(1/2) + \tan^{-1}(1/5) + \tan^{-1}(1/8)$ and the inequalities $x - x^3/3 + x^5/5 - x^7/7 < \tan^{-1} x < x - x^3/3 + x^5/5$.

20.4   Fixed-slash number systems

a. Discuss the factors that might affect the choice of the widths k and m in the fixed-slash format of Fig. 20.1. In what respects is $k = m$ a good choice?

b. Compute the number of different values that can be represented in a 15-bit signed, fixed-slash number system with 7-bit numerator and denominator parts, plus a sign bit (no inexact bit), and discuss its representation efficiency relative to a 15-bit, signed-magnitude, fixed-point binary system.

20.5   Floating-slash number systems   For the floating-slash number system shown in Fig. 20.2:

a. Obtain the parameters *max* and *min* (i.e., the largest representable magnitude and the smallest nonzero magnitude) as functions of h and k.

b. Calculate the maximum relative representation error for numbers in [*min*, *max*].

c. Obtain a lower bound on the total number of different values that can be represented as a function of h and k.

20.6   Continued-fraction number representation   In continued-fraction number representation, it is possible to use rounding, instead of the floor function, namely, $a_i = \text{round}(s^{(i)})$ rather than $a_i = \lfloor s^{(i)} \rfloor$, to obtain more accurate encodings with a given number of digits. Obtain 10-digit continued-fraction representations of $\sqrt{2}$, e, and π with the "rounding" rule and compare the results to the "floor" versions with respect to accuracy.

20.7   Exact representation of certain rationals   Consider rational numbers of the form $\pm 2^a 3^b 5^c$, represented in 16 bits by devoting 1 bit to the sign and 5 bits each to the 2's-complement representation of a, b, and c.

a. Obtain the parameters *max* and *min* (i.e., the largest representable magnitude and the smallest nonzero magnitude).

b. Calculate the maximum relative representation error for numbers in [*min*, *max*].

c. Find the number of different values represented and the representational efficiency of this number system.

d. Briefly discuss the feasibility of exact arithmetic operations on such numbers.

20.8   Multiprecision arithmetic

a. Provide the structure of an assembly-language program (similar to Fig. 9.3) to perform quadruple-precision integer arithmetic based on the format of Fig. 20.3

b. Repeat part a for floating-point arithmetic based on the format of Fig. 20.4.

20.9   Variable-precision arithmetic

a. Show that the three "for" loops in the program fragment given near the end of Section 20.4 do indeed process all the words of x and y properly.

b. Justify the inclusion of the term $-\text{signbit}(y)$ to effect sign extension for y.

c.   Modify the three loops for the case of a sum z that is to be of a specified width w, rather than of the same width u as the operand with the larger exponent.

20.10   Interval arithmetic Answer the following questions for interval arithmetic.

a.   Would interval arithmetic be of any use if machine arithmetic were exact? Discuss.

b.   How is the requirement $q = p + \lceil \log_r w_{max} - \log_r \varepsilon \rceil$ for extra bits of precision, given near the end of Section 20.5, derived from Theorem 20.2?

20.11   Archimedes' interval method To compute the number π, Archimedes used a sequence of increasing lower bounds, derived from the perimeters of inscribed polygons in a circle with unit diameter, and a sequence of decreasing upper bounds, based on circumscribing polygons.

a.   Use the method of Archimedes, with a pair of hexagons and exact calculations, to derive an interval that is guaranteed to contain π.

b.   Repeat part a, this time performing the arithmetic with four fractional decimal digits and proper rounding.

c.   Repeat part a with a pair of octagons.

d.   Repeat part b with a pair of octagons.

20.12   Distance between intervals The distance between two intervals $x = [x_{lo}, x_{hi}]$ and $y = [y_{lo}, y_{hi}]$ can be defined as $\delta(x, y) = max(|x_{lo} - y_{lo}|, |x_{hi} - y_{hi}|)$.

a.   Show that δ is a metric in that it satisfies the three conditions $\delta(x, y) \geq 0, \delta(x, y) = 0$ if and only if $x = y$, and $\delta(x, y) + \delta(y, z) \geq \delta(x, z)$ (the triangle inequality).

b.   Defining the absolute value $|x|$ of an interval x as $|[x_{lo}, x_{hi}]| = max(|x_{lo}|, |x_{hi}|)$, prove that $\delta[(x + y), (x + z)] = \delta(y, z)$ and $\delta(xy, xz) \leq |x| \delta(y, z)$.

20.13   Laws of algebra for intervals

a.   Show that the commutative laws of addition and multiplication hold for interval arithmetic; namely, $x + y = y + x$ and $xy = yx$ for intervals x and y.

b.   Show that the associative laws of addition and multiplication hold for interval arithmetic; namely, $x + (y + z) = (x + y) + z$ and $x(yz) = (xy)z$.

c.   Show that the distributive law $x(y + z) = xy + xz$ does not always hold.

d.   Show that subdistributivity holds; namely, $x(y + z)$ is contained in $xy + xz$.

20.14   Interval arithmetic operations

a.   Show that by testing the signs of x_{lo}, x_{hi}, y_{lo}, and y_{hi}, the formula for interval multiplication given in Section 20.5 can be broken down into nine cases, only one of which requires more than two multiplications.

b.   Discuss the square-rooting operation for intervals.

20.15   Multidimensional intervals A rectangle with sides parallel to the coordinate axes on the two-dimensional plane can be viewed as a two-dimensional interval. Relate two-dimensional intervals to arithmetic on complex numbers and derive the rules for complex interval arithmetic.

20.16   **Lazy arithmetic with intervals**   Consider a lazy arithmetic system with interval arithmetic and exact rational arithmetic as its primary and secondary (fallback) computation modes, respectively. Define rules for comparing numbers in the primary mode such that each comparison has three possible outcomes: "true," "false," and "unknown" (with the last outcome triggering exact computation to remove the ambiguity).

20.17   **Fixed-point iteration**   A *fixed point* of the function $f(x)$ is a value x_{fxpt} such that $x_{\text{fxpt}} = f(x_{\text{fxpt}})$. Geometrically, the fixed point x_{fxpt} corresponds to an intersection of the curve $y = f(x)$ with the line $y = x$. A fixed point of $f(x)$ can sometimes be obtained using the iterative formula $x^{(i+1)} = f(x^{(i)})$, with a suitably chosen initial value $x^{(0)}$.

    a.   The function $f(x) = 1 + x - x^2/a$ has two fixed points at $x = \pm\sqrt{a}$. Assuming $a = 2$ and $x^{(0)} = 3/2$, use exact rational arithmetic to find $x^{(4)}$.

    b.   Repeat part a using a calculator.

    c.   Repeat part a using interval arithmetic; round calculations to six fractional digits.

    d.   Compare the results of parts a, b, and c. Discuss.

REFERENCES

[Alef83]   Alefeld, G., and J. Herzberger, *An Introduction to Interval Computations*, Academic Press, 1983.

[Greg81]   Gregory, R.T., "Error-Free Computation with Rational Numbers," *BIT*, Vol. 21, pp. 194–202, 1981.

[Holm97]   Holmes, W.N., "Composite Arithmetic: Proposal for a New Standard," *IEEE Computer*, Vol. 30, No. 3, pp. 65–73, 1997.

[Knut81]   Knuth, D.E., *The Art of Computer Programming,* 2nd ed., *Vol. 2: Seminumerical Algorithms*, Addison-Wesley, 1981.

[Matu85]   Matula, D.W., and P. Kornerup, "Finite Precision Rational Arithmetic: Slash Number Systems," *IEEE Trans. Computers*, Vol. 34, No. 1, pp. 3–18, 1985.

[Mich97]   Michelucci, D., and J.-M. Moreau, "Lazy Arithmetic," *IEEE Trans. Computers*, Vol. 46, No. 9, pp. 961–975, 1997.

[Moor66]   Moore, R., *Interval Analysis*, Prentice-Hall, 1966.

[Parh98]   Parhami, B., *Introduction to Parallel Processing: Algorithms and Architectures*, Plenum Press, 1999.

[Pele97]   Peleg, A., S. Wilkie, and U. Weiser, "Intel MMX for Multimedia PCs," *Commun. ACM*, Vol. 40, No. 1, pp. 25–38, 1997.

[Schw89]   Schwarz, J., "Implementing Infinite Precision Arithmetic," *Proc. 9th Symp. Computer Arithmetic*, 1989, pp. 10–17.

[Vuil90]   Vuillemin, J., "Exact Real Computer Arithmetic with Continued Fractions," *IEEE Trans. Computers*, Vol. 39, No. 8, pp. 1087–1105, 1990.

[Zura93]   Zuras, D., "On Squaring and Multiplying Large Integers," *Proc. 11th Symp. Computer Arithmetic*, June 1993, pp. 260–271.

PART VI | FUNCTION EVALUATION

One way of computing functions such as $\sqrt{x}$, sin x, tanh x, ln x, and e^x is to evaluate their series expansions by means of addition, multiplication, and division operations. Another is through convergence computations of the type used for evaluating the functions z/d and $1/d$ in Chapter 16. In this part, we introduce several methods for evaluating elementary and other functions. We begin by examining the important operation of extracting the square root of a number, covering both digit-recurrence and convergence square-rooting methods. We then devote two chapters to CORDIC algorithms, other convergence methods, approximations, and merged arithmetic. We conclude by discussing versatile, and highly flexible, table-lookup schemes, which are assuming increasingly important roles as advances in VLSI technology lead to ever cheaper and denser memories. This part is composed of the following four chapters:

Chapter
21 | SQUARE-ROOTING METHODS

The function $\sqrt{z}$ is the most important elementary function. Since square-rooting is widely used in many applications, and hardware realization of square-rooting has quite a lot in common with division, the IEEE floating-point standard specifies square-rooting as a basic arithmetic operation alongside the usual four basic operations. This chapter is devoted to square-rooting methods, beginning with the pencil-and-paper algorithm and proceeding through shift/subtract, high-radix, and convergence versions. Chapter topics include:

21.1 THE PENCIL-AND-PAPER ALGORITHM

Unlike multiplication and division, for which the pencil-and-paper algorithms are widely taught and used, square-rooting by hand appears to have fallen prey to the five-dollar calculator. Since shift/subtract methods for computing $\sqrt{z}$, are derived directly from the ancient manual algorithm, we begin by describing the pencil-and-paper algorithm for square-rooting.

Our discussion of integer square-rooting algorithms uses the following notation:

z	Radicand	$z_{2k-1}z_{2k-2}\cdots z_1 z_0$
q	Square root	$q_{k-1}q_{k-2}\cdots q_1 q_0$
s	Remainder $(z - q^2)$	$s_k s_{k-1}s_{k-2}\cdots s_1 s_0$ $(k+1$ digits$)$

The expression $z - q^2$ for the remainder s is derived from the basic square-rooting equation $z = q^2 + s$. For integer values, the remainder satisfies $s \le 2q$, leading to the requirement for

$k + 1$ digits in the representation of s with a $2k$-digit radicand z and a k-digit root q. The reason for the requirement $s \leq 2q$ is that for $s \geq 2q + 1$, we have $z = q^2 + s \geq (q + 1)^2$ so q cannot be the correct square-root of z.

Consider the decimal square-rooting example depicted in Fig. 21.1. In this example, the five digits of the decimal number $(9\ 52\ 41)_{\text{ten}}$ are broken into groups of two digits starting at the right end. The number k of groups indicates the number of digits in the square root ($k = 3$ in this example).

The leftmost two-digit group (09) in the example of Fig. 21.1 indicates that the first root digit is 3. We subtract the square of 3 (really, the square of 300) from the 0th partial remainder z to find the 1st partial remainder 52. Next, we double the partial root 3 to get 6 and look for a digit q_1 such that $(6q_1)_{\text{ten}} \times q_1$ does not exceed the current partial remainder 52. Even 1 is too large for q_1, so $q_1 = 0$ is chosen. In the final iteration, we double the partial root 30 to get 60 and look for a digit q_0 such that $(60q_0)_{\text{ten}} \times q_0$ does not exceed the partial remainder 5241. This condition leads to the choice $q_0 = 8$, giving the results $q = (308)_{\text{ten}}$ for the root and $s = (377)_{\text{ten}}$ for the remainder.

The key to understanding the preceding algorithm is the process by which the next root digit is selected. If the partial root thus far is $q^{(i)}$, then attaching the next digit q_{k-i-1} to it will change its value to $10q^{(i)} + q_{k-i-1}$. The square of this latter number is $100(q^{(i)})^2 + 20q^{(i)}q_{k-i-1} + q_{k-i-1}^2$. Since the term $100(q^{(i)})^2 = (10q^{(i)})^2$ has been subtracted from the partial remainder in earlier steps, we need to subtract the last two terms, or $(10(2q^{(i)}) + q_{k-i-1}) \times q_{k-i-1}$, to obtain the new partial remainder. This is the reason for doubling the partial root and looking for a digit q_{k-i-1} to attach to the right end of the result, yielding $10(2q^{(i)}) + q_{k-i-1}$, such that this latter value times q_{k-i-1} does not exceed the partial remainder.

Figure 21.2 shows a binary example for the pencil-and-paper square-rooting algorithm. The root digits are in $\{0, 1\}$. In trying to determine the next root digit q_{k-i-1}, we note that the square of $2q^{(i)} + q_{k-i-1}$ is $4(q^{(i)})^2 + 4q^{(i)}q_{k-i-1} + q_{k-i-1}^2$. So, q_{k-i-1} must be selected such that $(4q^{(i)} + q_{k-i-1}) \times q_{k-i-1}$ does not exceed the partial remainder. For $q_{k-i-1} = 1$, this latter expression becomes $4q^{(i)} + 1$ (i.e., $q^{(i)}$ with 01 appended to its right end). Therefore, to determine whether the next root digit should be 1, we need to perform the trial subtraction of $q^{(i)}01$ from the partial remainder; q_{k-i-1} is 1 if the trial subtraction yields a positive result.

From the example in Fig. 21.2, we can abstract the dot notation representation of binary square-rooting (see Fig. 21.3). The radicand z and the root q are shown at the top. Each of the following four rows of dots corresponds to the product of the next root digit q_{k-i-1} and a number

$$
\begin{array}{ll}
q_2 \vdots q_1 \vdots q_0 & q \qquad\qquad\qquad\qquad\qquad\quad q^{(0)} = 0 \\[2pt]
\sqrt{9\vdots5\ 2\vdots4\ 1} \;=\; z & \qquad\qquad\quad q_2 = 3 \qquad q^{(1)} = 3 \\
\underline{9} \\
0\ 5\ 2 & 6q_1 \times q_1 \leq 52 \qquad q_1 = 0 \qquad q^{(2)} = 30 \\
\underline{0\ 0} \\
5\ 2\ 4\ 1 & 60q_0 \times q_0 \leq 5241 \quad q_0 = 8 \qquad q^{(3)} = 308 \\
\underline{4\ 8\ 6\ 4} \\
0\ 3\ 7\ 7 & s = (377)_{\text{ten}} \qquad\qquad\qquad q \;=\; (308)_{\text{ten}}
\end{array}
$$

Fig. 21.1   Using the pencil-and-paper algorithm to extract the square root of a decimal integer.

$$q_3 \quad q_2 \quad q_1 \quad q_0 \qquad\qquad q \qquad\qquad\qquad\qquad q^{(0)} = 0$$

$$\sqrt{0\ 1\ 1\ 1\ 0\ 1\ 1\ 0} \qquad z = (118)_{\text{ten}} \qquad q_3 = 1 \qquad q^{(1)} = 1$$

$$\underline{0\ 1}$$

$$0\ 0\ 1\ 1 \qquad\qquad \geq \underline{1}01? \qquad \text{No} \qquad q_2 = 0 \qquad q^{(2)} = 10$$

$$\underline{0\ 0\ 0}$$

$$0\ 1\ 1\ 0\ 1 \qquad\qquad \geq \underline{10}01? \qquad \text{Yes} \qquad q_1 = 1 \qquad q^{(3)} = 101$$

$$\underline{1\ 0\ 0\ 1}$$

$$0\ 1\ 0\ 0\ 1\ 0 \qquad\qquad \geq \underline{101}01? \qquad \text{No} \qquad q_0 = 0 \qquad q^{(4)} = 1010$$

$$\underline{0\ 0\ 0\ 0\ 0}$$

$$1\ 0\ 0\ 1\ 0 \qquad s = (18)_{\text{ten}} \qquad\qquad q = (1010)_{\text{two}} = (10)_{\text{ten}}$$

Fig. 21.2   Extracting the square root of a binary integer using the pencil-and-paper algorithm.

obtained by appending $0q_{k-i-1}$ to the right end of the partial root $q^{(i)}$. Thus, since the root digits are in $\{0, 1\}$, the problem of binary square-rooting reduces to subtracting a set of numbers, each being 0 or a shifted version of $(q^{(i)}01)_{\text{two}}$, from the radicand z.

The preceding discussion and Fig. 21.3 also apply to nonbinary square-rooting, except that with $r > 2$, both the selection of the next root digit q_{k-i-1} and the computation of the term $(2rq^{(i)} + q_{k-i-1}) \times q_{k-i-1}$ become more difficult. The rest of the process, however, remains substantially the same.

21.2 RESTORING SHIFT/SUBTRACT ALGORITHM

Like division, square-rooting can be formulated as a sequence of shift and subtract operations. The formulation is somewhat cleaner if we think in terms of fractional operands rather than integers. In fact, since in practice square-rooting is applied to floating-point numbers, we formulate our shift/subtract algorithms for a radicand in the range $1 \leq z < 4$ corresponding to the significand of a floating-point number in the IEEE standard format. Because the exponent must be halved in floating-point square-rooting, we decrement an odd exponent by 1 to make it even and shift the significand to the left by 1 bit; this accounts for the extended range assumed for z. The notation for our algorithm is thus as follows:

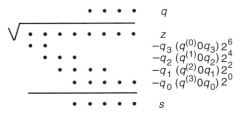

Fig. 21.3   Binary square-rooting in dot notation.

z	Radicand	$z_1 z_0 . z_{-1} z_{-2} \cdots z_{-l}$	$(1 \le z < 4)$
q	Square-root	$1 . q_{-1} q_{-2} \cdots q_{-l}$	$(1 \le q < 2)$
s	Scaled remainder	$s_1 s_0 . s_{-1} s_{-2} \cdots s_{-l}$	$(0 \le s < 4)$

With these assumptions, binary square-rooting is defined by the recurrence

$$s^{(j)} = 2s^{(j-1)} - q_{-j}(2q^{(j-1)} + 2^{-j}q_{-j}) \quad \text{with } s^{(0)} = z - 1, q^{(0)} = 1, s^{(l)} = s$$

where, for a binary quotient with digits in $\{0, 1\}$, the term subtracted from the shifted partial remainder $2s^{(j-1)}$ is $2q^{(j-1)} + 2^{-j}$ or 0. Here, $q^{(j)}$ stands for the root up to its $(-j)$th digit; thus $q = q^{(l)}$ is the desired square root.

Here is a general proof of the preceding square-rooting recurrence. First, we note that, by definition:

$$q^{(j)} = q^{(j-1)} + 2^{-j}q_{-j}$$

During square-rooting iterations, we strive to maintain the invariant:

$$s^{(j)} = z - [q^{(j)}]^2$$

In particular, $q^{(0)} = 1$ and $s^{(0)} = z - 1$. From the preceding invariant, we derive the requirement:

$$s^{(j-1)} - s^{(j)} = [q^{(j)}]^2 - [q^{(j-1)}]^2 = [q^{(j-1)} + 2^{-j}q_{-j}]^2 - [q^{(j-1)}]^2$$
$$= 2^{-j}q_{-j}[2q^{(j-1)} + 2^{-j}q_{-j}]$$

Multiplying both sides by 2^j and rearranging the terms, we get:

$$2^j s^{(j)} = 2(2^{j-1} s^{(j-1)}) - q_{-j}[2q^{(j-1)} + 2^{-j}q_{-j}]$$

Redefining the jth partial remainder to be $2^j s^{(j)}$ yields the desired recurrence. Note that after l iterations, the partial remainder $s^{(l)}$, which is in $[0, 4)$, represents the scaled remainder $s = 2^l(z - q^2)$.

To choose the next square-root digit q_{-j} from the set $\{0, 1\}$, we perform a trial subtraction of

$$2q^{(j-1)} + 2^{-j} = (1q_{-1}^{(j-1)} . q_{-2}^{(j-1)} \cdots q_{-j+1}^{(j-1)} 0\ 1)_{two}$$

from the shifted partial remainder $2s^{(j-1)}$. If the difference is negative, the shifted partial remainder is not modified and $q_{-j} = 0$. Otherwise, the difference becomes the new partial remainder and $q_{-j} = 1$.

The preceding algorithm, which is similar to restoring division, is quite naturally called "restoring square-rooting." An example of binary restoring square-rooting using the preceding recurrence is shown in Fig. 21.4, where we have provided three whole digits, plus the required six fractional digits, for representing the partial remainders. Two whole digits are required given that the partial remainders, as well as the radicand z, are in $[0, 4)$. The third whole digit is needed to accommodate the extra bit that results from shifting the partial remainder $s^{(j-1)}$ to the left to form $2s^{(j-1)}$. This bit also acts as the sign bit for the trial difference.

The hardware realization of restoring square-rooting is quite similar to restoring division. Figure 21.5 shows the required components and their connections, assuming that they will be used only for square-rooting. In practice, square-rooting hardware may be shared with division (and perhaps even multiplication). To allow such sharing of hardware, some changes are needed

```
=======================================
z                         0 1 . 1 1 0 1 1 0              (118/64)
=======================================
s(0) = z − 1              0 0 0 . 1 1 0 1 1 0    q_0 = 1    q^(0) = 1.
2s(0)                     0 0 1 . 1 0 1 1 0 0
−[2×(1.)+2^−1]                1 0 . 1
_____
s(1)                      1 1 1 . 0 0 1 1 0 0    q_−1 = 0   q^(1) = 1.0
s(1) = 2s(0)              0 0 1 . 1 0 1 1 0 0    Restore
2s(1)                     0 1 1 . 0 1 1 0 0 0
−[2×(1.0)+2^−2]               1 0 . 0 1
_____
s(2)                      0 0 1 . 0 0 1 0 0 0    q_−2 = 1   q^(2) = 1.01
2s(2)                     0 1 0 . 0 1 0 0 0 0
−[2×(1.01)+2^−3]              1 0 . 1 0 1
_____
s(3)                      1 1 1 . 1 0 1 0 0 0    q_−3 = 0   q^(3) = 1.010
s(3) = 2s(2)              0 1 0 . 0 1 0 0 0 0    Restore
2s(3)                     1 0 0 . 1 0 0 0 0 0
−[2×(1.010)+2^−4]             1 0 . 1 0 0 1
_____
s(4)                      0 0 1 . 1 1 1 1 0 0    q_−4 = 1   q^(4) = 1.0101
2s(4)                     0 1 1 . 1 1 1 0 0 0
−[2×(1.0101)+2^−5]            1 0 . 1 0 1 0 1
_____
s(5)                      0 0 1 . 0 0 1 1 1 0    q_−5 = 1   q^(5) = 1.01011
2s(5)                     0 1 0 . 0 1 1 1 0 0
−[2×(1.01011)+2^−6]           1 0 . 1 0 1 1 0 1
_____
s(6)                      1 1 1 . 1 0 1 1 1 1    q_−6 = 0   q^(6) = 1.010110
s(6) = 2s(5)              0 1 0 . 0 1 1 1 0 0    Restore     (156/64)
s  (true remainder)           0 . 0 0 0 0 1 0 0 1 1 1 0 0   (156/64^2)
q                             1 . 0 1 0 1 1 0             (86/64)
=======================================
```

Fig. 21.4 Example of sequential binary square-rooting by means of the restoring algorithm.

to maximize common parts. Any component or extension that is specific to one of the operations may then be incorporated into the unit's control logic. It is instructive to compare the design in Fig. 21.5 to that of restoring binary divider in Fig. 13.5.

In fractional square-rooting, the remainder is usually of no interest. To properly round the square root, we can produce an extra digit q_{-l-1} and use its value to decide whether to truncate ($q_{-l-1} = 0$) or to round up ($q_{-l-1} = 1$). The midway case, (i.e., $q_{-l-1} = 1$ with only 0s to its right), is impossible (why?), so we don't even have to test the remainder for 0.

For the Example of Fig. 21.4, an extra iteration produces $q_{-7} = 1$. So the root must be rounded up to $q = (1.010111)_{\text{two}} = 87/64$. To check that the rounded-up value is closer to the actual root than the truncated version, we note that:

$$118/64 = (87/64)^2 - 17/64^2$$

Thus, the rounded-up value yields a remainder with a smaller magnitude.

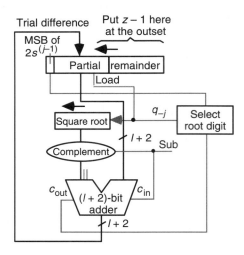

Trial difference   Put $z - 1$ here
                    at the outset

Fig. 21.5   Sequential shift/subtract restoring square-rooter.

21.3 BINARY NONRESTORING ALGORITHM

In a manner similar to binary division, one can formulate a binary nonrestoring square-rooting algorithm. Figure 21.6 shows the square-rooting example of Fig. 21.4 performed with the nonrestoring algorithm. As was the case for nonrestoring division, the square root must be corrected by subtracting *ulp* from it if the final remainder becomes negative. Remainder correction, however, is usually not needed, as discussed at the end of Section 21.2.

Performing an extra iteration in the binary square-rooting example of Fig. 21.6 yields $q_{-7} = $ ‑1 and $q = (1.1\text{‑}1\ 1\text{‑}1\ 1\ 1\text{‑}1)_{\text{two}} = (1.0101101)_{\text{two}}$. This indicates that the root must be rounded up to $q = (1.010111)_{\text{two}}$.

In nonrestoring square-rooting, root digits are chosen from the set $\{\text{‑}1, 1\}$ and the resulting BSD root is converted, on the fly, to binary format. The case $q_{-j} = 1$, corresponding to a nonnegative partial remainder, is handled as in the restoring algorithm; that is, it leads to the subtraction of

$$q_{-j}[2q^{(j-1)} + 2^{-j}q_{-j}] = 2q^{(j-1)} + 2^{-j}$$

from the partial remainder. For $q_{-j} = \text{‑}1$, we must subtract

$$q_{-j}[2q^{(j-1)} + 2^{-j}q_{-j}] = -[2q^{(j-1)} - 2^{-j}]$$

which is equivalent to adding $2q^{(j-1)} - 2^{-j}$ (see Fig. 21.6).

From the standpoint of hardware implementation, computing the term $2q^{(j-1)} - 2^{-j}$ is problematic. Recall that $2q^{(j-1)} + 2^{-j} = 2[q^{(j-1)} + 2^{-j-1}]$ is formed by simply appending 01 to the right end of $q^{(j-1)}$ and shifting.

The following scheme allows us to form $2q^{(j-1)} - 2^{-j}$ just as easily. Suppose that we keep $q^{(j-1)}$ and $q^{(j-1)} - 2^{-j+1}$ in registers Q (partial root) and Q* (diminished partial root), respectively. Then:

```
====================================
z                 0 1.1 1 0 1 1 0              (118/64)
====================================
s(0) = z − 1      0 0 0.1 1 0 1 1 0    q0 = 1     q(0) = 1.
2s(0)             0 0 1.1 0 1 1 0 0    q−1 = 1    q(1) = 1.1
−[2×(1.)+2−1]         1 0.1
────────────────────────────────────
s(1)              1 1 1.0 0 1 1 0 0    q−2 = ⁻1   q(2) = 1.01
2s(1)             1 1 0.0 1 1 0 0 0
+[2×(1.1)−2−2]        1 0.1 1
────────────────────────────────────
s(2)              0 0 1.0 0 1 0 0 0    q−3 = 1    q(3) = 1.011
2s(2)             0 1 0.0 1 0 0 0 0
−[2×(1.01)+2−3]       1 0.1 0 1
────────────────────────────────────
s(3)              1 1 1.1 0 1 0 0 0    q−4 = ⁻1   q(4) = 1.0101
2s(3)             1 1 1.0 1 0 0 0 0
+[2×(1.011)−2−4]      1 0.1 0 1 1
────────────────────────────────────
s(4)              0 0 1.1 1 1 1 0 0    q−5 = 1    q(5) = 1.01011
2s(4)             0 1 1.1 1 1 0 0 0
−[2×(1.0101)+2−5]     1 0.1 0 1 0 1
────────────────────────────────────
s(5)              0 0 1.0 0 1 1 1 0    q−6 = 1    q(6) = 1.010111
2s(5)             0 1 0.0 1 1 1 0 0
−[2×(1.01011)+2−6]    1 0.1 0 1 1 0 1
────────────────────────────────────
s(6)              1 1 1.1 0 1 1 1 1    Negative;    (−17/64)
+[2×(1.01011)+2−6]    1 0.1 0 1 1 0 1    Correct
────────────────────────────────────
s(6) (corrected)  0 1 0.0 1 1 1 0 0                 (156/64)
s (true remainder)      0.0 0 0 0 1 0 0 1 1 1 0 0   (156/64²)
q (signed-digit)        1.1 ⁻1 1 ⁻1 1 1             (87/64)
q (binary)              1.0 1 0 1 1 1               (87/64)
q (corrected binary)    1.0 1 0 1 1 0               (86/64)
====================================
```

Fig. 21.6 Example of sequential binary square-rooting by means of the nonrestoring algorithm.

$$q_{-j} = 1 \quad \text{Subtract} \quad 2q^{(j-1)} + 2^{-j} \quad \text{formed by shifting Q 01}$$
$$q_{-j} = {}^{-}1 \quad \text{Add} \quad 2q^{(j-1)} - 2^{-j} \quad \text{formed by shifting Q*11}$$

The updating rules for Q and Q* registers are also easily derived:

$$q_{-j} = 1 \quad \Rightarrow \quad Q := Q\,1 \quad Q^* := Q\,0$$
$$q_{-j} = {}^{-}1 \quad \Rightarrow \quad Q := Q^*1 \quad Q^* := Q^*0$$

The preceding can be easily extended to a square-rooting algorithm in which leading 0s or 1s in the partial remainder are detected and skipped (shifted over) while producing 0s as root digits.

The resulting algorithm is quite similar to SRT division and needs the following additional updating rule for Q and Q* registers:

$$q_{-j} = 0 \quad \Rightarrow \quad Q = Q0 \quad Q^* = Q^*1$$

As in the carry-save version of SRT division with quotient digit set $[-1, 1]$, discussed in Section 14.3, we can keep the partial remainder in stored-carry form and choose the next root digit by inspecting a few most significant bits of the sum and carry components. The preceding modifications in the algorithm, and the corresponding hardware realizations, are left to the reader.

21.4 HIGH-RADIX SQUARE-ROOTING

Square-rooting can be performed in higher radices using techniques that are quite similar to those of high-radix division. The basic recurrence for fractional radix-r square-rooting is:

$$s^{(j)} = rs^{(j-1)} - q_{-j}(2q^{(j-1)} + r^{-j}q_{-j})$$

As in the case of radix-2 nonrestoring algorithm in Section 21.3, we can use two registers Q and Q^* to hold $q^{(j-1)}$ and $q^{(j-1)} - r^{-j+1}$, respectively, suitably updating them in each step.

For example, with $r = 4$ and the root digit set $[-2, 2]$, Q^* will hold $q^{(j-1)} - 4^{-j+1} = q^{(j-1)} - 2^{-2j+2}$. Then, it is easy to see that one of the following values must be subtracted from or added to the shifted partial remainder $rs^{(j-1)}$:

$q_{-j} = 2$	Subtract	$4q^{(j-1)} + 2^{-2j+2}$	formed by double-shifting	Q 010
$q_{-j} = 1$	Subtract	$2q^{(j-1)} + 2^{-2j}$	formed by shifting	Q 001
$q_{-j} = \text{-}1$	Add	$2q^{(j-1)} - 2^{-2j}$	formed by shifting	Q^* 111
$q_{-j} = \text{-}2$	Add	$4q^{(j-1)} - 2^{-2j+2}$	formed by double-shifting	Q^* 110

For ANSI/IEEE standard floating-point numbers, a radicand in the range $[1, 4)$ yields a root in $[1, 2)$. As a radix-4 number with the digit set $[-2, 2]$, the root will have a single whole digit. This is more than adequate to represent the root that is in $[1, 2)$. In fact, the first root digit can be restricted to $[0, 2]$, though not to $[0, 1]$, which at first thought might appear to be adequate (why not?).

The updating rules for Q and Q^* registers are again easily derived:

$$q_{-j} = \phantom{\text{-}}2 \quad \Rightarrow \quad Q := Q\ 10 \quad Q^* := Q\ 01$$
$$q_{-j} = \phantom{\text{-}}1 \quad \Rightarrow \quad Q := Q\ 01 \quad Q^* := Q\ 00$$
$$q_{-j} = \phantom{\text{-}}0 \quad \Rightarrow \quad Q := Q\ 00 \quad Q^* := Q^*\ 11$$
$$q_{-j} = \text{-}1 \quad \Rightarrow \quad Q := Q^*\ 11 \quad Q^* := Q^*\ 10$$
$$q_{-j} = \text{-}2 \quad \Rightarrow \quad Q := Q^*\ 10 \quad Q^* := Q^*\ 01$$

In this way, the root is obtained in standard binary form without a need for a final conversion step (conversion takes place on the fly).

As in division, root digit selection can be based on examining a few bits of the partial remainder and of the partial root. Since only a few high-order bits are needed to estimate the next root digit, s can be kept in carry-save form to speed up the iterations. One extra bit of each component of s (sum and carry) must then be examined for root digit estimation.

In fact, with proper care, the same lookup table can be used for quotient digit selection in division and root digit selection in square-rooting. To see how, let us compare the recurrences for radix-4 division and square-rooting:

Division: $\qquad s^{(j)} = 4s^{(j-1)} - q_{-j}\, d$

Square-rooting: $\quad s^{(j)} = 4s^{(j-1)} - q_{-j}(2q^{(j-1)} + 4^{-j}q_{-j})$

To keep the magnitudes of the partial remainders for division and square-rooting comparable, thus allowing the use of the same tables, we can perform radix-4 square-rooting using the digit set {-1, -1/2, 0, 1/2, 1}. A radix-4 number with the latter digit set can be converted to a radix-4 number with the digit set $[-2, 2]$, or directly to binary, with no extra computation (how?). For details of the resulting square-rooting scheme, see [Omon94, pp. 387–389].

21.5 SQUARE-ROOTING BY CONVERGENCE

In Section 16.3, we used the Newton–Raphson method for computing the reciprocal of the divisor d, thus allowing division to be performed by means of multiplications with more rapid convergence. To use the Newton–Raphson method for computing $\sqrt{z}$, we choose $f(x) = x^2 - z$ which has a root at $x = \sqrt{z}$. Recall that the Newton–Raphson iteration is:

$$x^{(i+1)} = x^{(i)} - \frac{f(x^{(i)})}{f'(x^{(i)})}$$

Thus, the function $f(x) = x^2 - z$ leads to the following convergence scheme for square-rooting:

$$x^{(i+1)} = 0.5(x^{(i)} + z/x^{(i)})$$

Each iteration involves a division, an addition, and a single-bit shift. As was the case for reciprocation, it is easy to prove quadratic convergence of x to $\sqrt{z}$. Let $\delta_i = \sqrt{z} - x^{(i)}$. Then:

$$\delta_{i+1} = \sqrt{z} - x^{(i+1)} = \sqrt{z} - \frac{x^{(i)} + z/x^{(i)}}{2}$$

$$= \frac{-(\sqrt{z} - x^{(i)})^2}{2x^{(i)}} = \frac{-\delta_i^2}{2x^{(i)}}$$

Since δ_{i+1} is always negative, the recurrence converges to $\sqrt{z}$ from above. Let z be in the range $1 \leq z < 4$ (as in square-rooting with IEEE floating-point format). Then, beginning with the initial estimate $x^{(0)} = 2$, the value of $x^{(i)}$ will always remain in the range $1 \leq x^{(i)} < 2$. This means that $|\delta_{i+1}| \leq 0.5\delta_i^2$.

An initial table-lookup step can be used to obtain a better starting estimate for $\sqrt{z}$. For example, if the initial estimate is accurate to within 2^{-8}, then three iterations would be sufficient to increase the accuracy of the root to 64 bits.

■ **Example 21.1** Suppose we want to compute the square root of $z = (2.4)_{\text{ten}}$ and the initial table lookup provides the starting value $x^{(0)} = 1.5$, accurate to 10^{-1}. Then, we will go through the following steps to find the result to eight decimal positions (accurate to 10^{-8}):

$x^{(0)}$ (read out from table) = 1.5   Accurate to 10^{-1}

$x^{(1)} = 0.5(x^{(0)} + 2.4/x^{(0)}) = 1.550\,000\,000$ Accurate to 10^{-2}

$x^{(2)} = 0.5(x^{(1)} + 2.4/x^{(1)}) = 1.549\,193\,548$ Accurate to 10^{-4}

$x^{(3)} = 0.5(x^{(2)} + 2.4/x^{(2)}) = 1.549\,193\,338$ Accurate to 10^{-8}

Instead of referring to a table to get an estimate of $\sqrt{z}$, one can use an approximating function that is easy to compute. In the case of fractional square-rooting, that is, with z in [0.5, 1), the approximation $(1 + z)/2$ provides a good starting value without requiring any arithmetic. The error is 0 at $z = 1$ and reaches its maximum value of $0.75 - \sqrt{0.5} \approx 0.0429$, or about 6.07%, at $z = 0.5$.

For integer operands, a starting approximation with the same maximum error of 6.07% can be found as follows [Hash90]. Assume that the most significant 1 in the binary representation of an integer-valued radicand z is in position $2m - 1$ (if the most significant 1 is not in an odd position, simply double z and multiply the resulting square root by $1/\sqrt{2} \approx 0.707\,107$). Then, we have $z = 2^{2m-1} + z^{\text{rest}}$, with $0 \le z^{\text{rest}} < 2^{2m-1}$. We claim that the starting approximation

$$x^{(0)} = 2^{m-1} + 2^{-(m+1)} z = (3 \times 2^{m-2}) + 2^{-(m+1)} z^{\text{rest}}$$

which can be obtained from z by counting the leading zeros and shifting, has a maximum relative error of 6.07%. The difference between $(x^{(0)})^2$ and z is:

$$\Delta = (x^{(0)})^2 - z$$

$$= (9 \times 2^{2m-4}) + \frac{3z^{\text{rest}}}{4} + 2^{-2(m+1)}(z^{\text{rest}})^2 - (2^{2m-1} + z^{\text{rest}})$$

$$= 2^{2m-4} - \frac{z^{\text{rest}}}{4} + 2^{-2(m+1)}(z^{\text{rest}})^2$$

$$= 2^{2m-4} - \frac{z^{\text{rest}}(1 - 2^{-2m}\,z^{\text{rest}})}{4}$$

Since the derivative of Δ with respect to z^{rest} is uniformly negative, we only need to check the two extremes to find the worst-case error. At the upper extreme (i.e., for $z^{\text{rest}} \approx 2^{2m-1}$), we have $\Delta \approx 0$. At the lower extreme of $z^{\text{rest}} = 0$, we find $\Delta = 2^{2m-4}$. For this latter case, $x^{(0)}/\sqrt{z} = 3/\sqrt{8} \approx 1.0607$.

Schwarz and Flynn [Schw96] propose a general hardware approximation method and illustrate its applicability to the square-root function. Their method consists of generating a number of Boolean terms (bits or "dots") such that when these terms are added by the same hardware that is used for multiplication, the result is a good starting approximation for the desired function. In the case of square-rooting, they show that adding about 1000 gates of complexity to a 53-bit multiplier allows for the generation of a 16-bit approximation to the square root, which can then be refined in only two iterations.

The preceding convergence method involves a division in each iteration. Since division is a relatively slow operation, especially if a dedicated hardware divider is not available, division-free variants of the method have been suggested. One such variant relies on the availability of a circuit or table to compute the approximate reciprocal of a number. We can rewrite the square-root recurrence as follows:

$$x^{(i+1)} = x^{(i)} + 0.5(1/x^{(i)})(z - (x^{(i)})^2)$$

Let $\gamma(x^{(i)})$ be an approximation to $1/x^{(i)}$ obtained by a simple circuit or read out from a table. Then, each iteration requires a table lookup, a one-bit shift, two multiplications, and two additions. If multiplication is much more than twice as fast as division, this variant may be more efficient. However, note that because of the approximation used in lieu of the exact value of the reciprocal $1/x^{(i)}$, the convergence rate will be less than quadratic and a larger number of iterations will be needed in general.

Since we know that the reciprocal function can also be computed by Newton–Raphson iteration, one can use the preceding recurrence, but with the reciprocal itself computed iteratively, effectively interlacing the two iterative computations. Using the function $f(y) = 1/y - x$ to compute the reciprocal of x, we find the following combination of recurrences:

$$x^{(i+1)} = 0.5(x^{(i)} + zy^{(i)})$$
$$y^{(i+1)} = y^{(i)}(2 - x^{(i)}y^{(i)})$$

The two multiplications, of z and $x^{(i)}$ by $y^{(i)}$ can be pipelined for improved speed, as discussed in Section 16.5 for convergence division. The convergence rate of this algorithm is less than quadratic but better than linear.

■ **Example 21.2** Suppose we want to compute the square root of $z = (1.4)_{ten}$. Beginning with $x^{(0)} = y^{(0)} = 1.0$, we find the following results:

$$
\begin{aligned}
x^{(0)} &= & 1.0 \\
y^{(0)} &= & 1.0 \\
x^{(1)} &= 0.5(x^{(0)} + 1.4y^{(0)}) &= 1.200\,000\,000 \\
y^{(1)} &= y^{(0)}(2 - x^{(0)}y^{(0)}) &= 1.000\,000\,000 \\
x^{(2)} &= 0.5(x^{(1)} + 1.4y^{(1)}) &= 1.300\,000\,000 \\
y^{(2)} &= y^{(1)}(2 - x^{(1)}y^{(1)}) &= 0.800\,000\,000 \\
x^{(3)} &= 0.5(x^{(2)} + 1.4y^{(2)}) &= 1.210\,000\,000 \\
y^{(3)} &= y^{(2)}(2 - x^{(2)}y^{(2)}) &= 0.768\,000\,000 \\
x^{(4)} &= 0.5(x^{(3)} + 1.4y^{(3)}) &= 1.142\,600\,000 \\
y^{(4)} &= y^{(3)}(2 - x^{(3)}y^{(3)}) &= 0.822\,312\,960 \\
x^{(5)} &= 0.5(x^{(4)} + 1.4y^{(4)}) &= 1.146\,919\,072 \\
y^{(5)} &= y^{(4)}(2 - x^{(4)}y^{(4)}) &= 0.872\,001\,394 \\
x^{(6)} &= 0.5(x^{(5)} + 1.4y^{(5)}) &= 1.183\,860\,512 \approx \sqrt{1.4}
\end{aligned}
$$

A final variant, that has found wider application in high-performance processors, is based on computing the reciprocal of $\sqrt{z}$ and then multiplying the result by z to obtain $\sqrt{z}$. We can use the function $f(x) = 1/x^2 - z$ that has a root at $x = 1/\sqrt{z}$ for this purpose. Since $f'(x) = -2/x^3$, we get the recurrence:

$$x^{(i+1)} = 0.5x^{(i)}(3 - z(x^{(i)})^2)$$

Each iteration now requires three multiplications and one addition, but quadratic convergence leads to only a few iterations with a suitably accurate initial estimate.

The Cray-2 supercomputer uses this last method [Cray89]. An initial estimate $x^{(0)}$ for $1/\sqrt{z}$ is plugged into the equation to obtain a more accurate estimate $x^{(1)}$. In this first iteration, $1.5x^{(0)}$ and $0.5(x^{(0)})^3$ are read out from a table to reduce the number of operations to only one multiplication and one addition. Since $x^{(1)}$ is accurate to within half the machine precision, a second iteration to find $x^{(2)}$, followed by a multiplication by z, completes the process.

■ **Example 21.3** Suppose we want to obtain the square root of $z = (.5678)_{ten}$ and the initial table lookup provides the starting value $x^{(0)} = 1.3$ for $1/\sqrt{z}$. We can then to find a fairly accurate result by performing only two iterations, plus a final multiplicatin by z.

$$
\begin{aligned}
x^{(0)} \text{ (read out from table)} &= 1.3 \\
x^{(1)} = 0.5x^{(0)}(3 - 0.5678(x^{(0)})^2) &= 1.326\ 271\ 700 \\
x^{(2)} = 0.5x^{(1)}(3 - 0.5678(x^{(1)})^2) &= 1.327\ 095\ 128 \\
\sqrt{z} \approx z \times x^{(2)} &= 0.753\ 524\ 613
\end{aligned}
$$

21.6 PARALLEL HARDWARE SQUARE-ROOTERS

As stated in Section 21.2 in connection with the restoring square-rooter depicted in Fig. 21.5, and again at the end of Section 21.4, the hardware realization of digit-recurrence square-rooting algorithms (binary or high-radix) is quite similar to that of digit-recurrence division. Thus, it is feasible to modify divide or multiply/divide units (Fig. 15.9) to also compute the square-root function. An extensive discussion of design issues is available elsewhere [Zura87]. Similar observations apply to convergence methods that perform various combinations of multiplications, additions, and shifting in each iteration.

It is also possible to derive a restoring or nonrestoring array square-rooter directly from the dot notation representation of Fig. 21.3 in a manner similar to the derivation of the array dividers of Section 15.5 from the dot notation representation of division in Figure 13.1. Fig. 21.7 depicts a possible design for an 8-bit fractional square-rooter based on the nonrestoring algorithm. The design uses controlled add/subtract cells to perform the required subtraction/addition prescribed by the nonrestoring square-rooting algorithm depending on the sign of the preceding partial remainder.

The reader should be able to understand the operation of the array square-rooter of Fig. 21.7 based on our discussion of nonrestoring square-rooting in Section 21.3, and by comparison to the nonrestoring array divider in Fig. 15.8. The design of a restoring array square-rooter is left as an exercise.

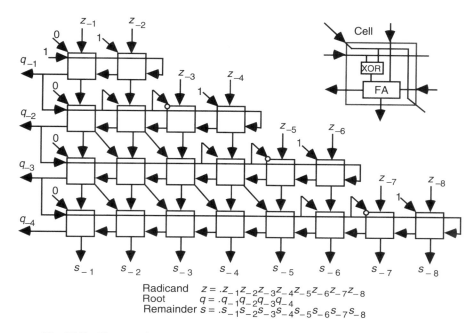

Fig. 21.7   Nonrestoring array square-rooter built of controlled add/subtract cells.

21.1   **Decimal square-rooting**   Using the pencil-and-paper square-rooting algorithm:

    a.   Compute the four-digit integer square root of the decimal number $(12\ 34\ 56\ 78)_{ten}$.

    b.   Compute the square root of the decimal fraction $(.4321)_{ten}$ with four fractional digits.

    c.   Repeat part b, this time obtaining the result rounded to 4 fractional digits.

21.2   **Integer square-rooting**   Compute the 8-bit square root of the unsigned radicand $z = (1011\ 0001\ 0111\ 1010)_{two}$.

    a.   Use the restoring radix-2 algorithm.

    b.   Use the nonrestoring radix-2 algorithm.

    c.   Convert the number to radix 4 and compute the square root in radix 4, using the pencil-and-paper method.

21.3   **Fractional square-rooting**   Compute the 8-bit square root of the unsigned fractional radicand $z = (.0111\ 1100)_{two}$.

    a.   Use the restoring radix-2 algorithm, with the result rounded to 8 bits.

    b.   Repeat part a with the nonrestoring radix-2 algorithm.

    c.   Convert the number to radix 4 and compute the square root in radix 4, using the pencil-and-paper method.

21.4   **Programmed square-rooting**   Write an assembly-language program similar to the division program in Fig. 13.4 for computing the square root of a $2k$-bit binary integer using the restoring shift/subtract algorithm.

21.5   **Combinational square-rooter**   A fully combinational multiplier circuit computing $p = ax$ can be used as a squarer by connecting both its inputs to x, leading to the output $p = x^2$. A fully combinational divider circuit computes $q = z/d$. If we feed back the quotient output q to the divisor input d, can we expect to get $q = \sqrt{z}$ at the output? Discuss.

21.6   **Restoring square-rooter**   For the restoring square-rooter in Fig. 21.5:

   a.   Explain the initial placement of $z - 1$ in the partial remainder register.

   b.   Explain the two unlabeled input bits on the left side of the adder (dotted lines).

   c.   Explain the alignment of the two inputs to the adder (i.e., Which bits of the partial remainder register are added to the complement of the partial square root?).

   d.   Provide a complete logic design for the root digit selection block.

21.7   **Nonrestoring square-rooter**   Consider the hardware implementation of a nonrestoring square-rooter.

   a.   Draw a block diagram similar to Fig. 21.5 for the hardware, assuming that the partial remainder is kept is standard binary form.

   b.   Repeat part a for a nonrestoring square-rooter that keeps the partial remainder in stored-carry form.

   c.   Provide a complete logic design for the root digit selection block in part b.

21.8   **High-radix integer square-rooting**   Compute the 8-bit square root of the following 16-bit unsigned binary numbers using the radix-4 square-rooting algorithm of Section 21.4. Do not worry about the process of selecting a root digit in $[-2, 2]$; that is, use a trial-and-error approach.

   a.   0011 0001 0111 1010

   b.   0111 0001 0111 1010

   c.   1011 0001 0111 1010

21.9   **High-radix fractional square-rooting**   Given the radicand $z = 0.0111\ 1100$, compute the square root $q = 0.q_{-1}q_{-2} \cdots q_{-8}$ and remainder $s = 0.0000\ 000r_{-8} \cdots r_{-16}$ using:

   a.   The radix-2 restoring algorithm.

   b.   The radix-4 algorithm with root digit set $[-2, 2]$. *Hint:* Preshifting is required to make the root representable with the given digit set.

21.10   **High-radix square-rooting**   Consider the radix-4 square-rooting algorithm discussed in Section 21.4

   a.   Develop a p–q plot (similar to the p–d plot in high-radix division) for this algorithm and discuss the root digit selection process.

b. Draw a block diagram of the hardware required to execute the radix-4 square-rooting algorithm. In particular, show the complete logical design of the elements needed to update the registers Q and Q*.

c. Derive the add/subtract rules and the updating process for Q and Q* in radix-8 square-rooting with the root digit set $[-4, 4]$.

d. Briefly discuss the cost-effectiveness of the radix-8 square-rooter of part c compared to the simpler radix-4 implementation.

21.11 Rounding of the square root

a. Prove that rounding of a fractional square root (see the end of Section 21.2) can be done by generating an extra digit of the result and that the equivalent of the "sticky bit" is not required (i.e., the midway case never arises).

b. Show that as an alternative to the extra iteration, the rounding decision can be based on whether $s^{(l)} \leq q$ (truncate) or $s^{(l)} > q$ (round up).

21.12 Approximating the square-root function Show that $(1+z)/2$ is a good approximation to $\sqrt{z}$ in the extended range $0.5 \leq z < 2$ (in Section 21.5, we dealt with the range $0.5 \leq z < 1$). Demonstrate that the approximation is still easy to obtain and analyze its worst-case error. Is the extended range of any help in computing the square root of a floating-point number?

21.13 Approximating the square-root function

a. Formulate and prove a theorem similar to Theorem 16.1 (concerning the initial multiplicative factor in convergence division) that relates the accuracy of the square root approximation to the required table size [Parh99].

b. Identify any special case that might allow smaller tables.

21.14 Convergence square-rooting Discuss the practicality of the following method for convergence square-rooting. Initially, the square root of a radicand in $[1, 4)$ is known to be in $[1, 2)$. The interval holding the square root is iteratively refined by a binary search process: the midpoint $m = (l + u)/2$ of the current interval $[l, u)$ is squared and the result compared to the radicand to decide if the search must be restricted to $[l, m)$ or to $[m, u)$ in the next iteration.

21.15 Convergence square-rooting

a. Derive a convergence scheme for square-rooting using the Newton–Raphson method and the function $f(x) = z/x^2 - 1$.

b. Show that with $x^{(0)} = y^{(0)} = 1$, the pair of iterative formulas $x^{(i+1)} = x^{(i)} + y^{(i)}z$ and $y^{(i+1)} = x^{(i)} + y^{(i)}$ converges to $x^{(m)}/y^{(m)} = \sqrt{z}$.

21.16 Square-rooting by convergence Consider square-rooting by convergence when the radicand z is in the range $[1, 4)$, intermediate computations are to be performed with 60 bits of precision after the radix point, and a lookup table is used to provide an initial estimate for the square root that is accurate to within $\pm 2^{-8}$. Identify the best approach by determining the required table size and analyzing the convergence methods described in Section 21.5. Assume that hardware add, multiply, and divide times are 1, 3, and 8 units, respectively, and that shifting and control overheads can be ignored.

21.17 Array square-rooter

a. In the nonrestoring square-rooter of Fig. 21.7, explain the roles of all inputs connected to a constant 0 or 1, the connections from horizontally broadcast signals to the diagonal inputs of some cells, and the wraparound connections of the cells located at the right edge.

b. Present the design of a restoring array square-rooter for radix-2 radicands.

c. Compare the design of part b to the nonrestoring square-rooter of Fig. 21.7 with regard to speed and cost.

d. Design a 4-bit array squarer with a cell layout similar to that in Fig. 21.7, so that the operand enters from the left side and the square emerges from the bottom.

e. Based on the design of part d, build an array that can compute the square or square-root function depending on the status of a control signal.

REFERENCES

[Agra79]   Agrawal, D.P., "High-Speed Arithmetic Arrays," *IEEE Trans. Computers*, Vol. 28, No. 3, pp. 215–224, 1979.

[Cimi90]   Ciminiera, L., and P. Montuschi, "Higher Radix Square Rooting," *IEEE Trans. Computers*, Vol. 39, No. 10, pp. 1220–1231, 1990.

[Cray89]   Cray Research, "Cray-2 Computer System Functional Description Manual," Cray Research, Chippewa Falls, WI, 1989.

[Erce94]   Ercegovac, M.D., and T. Lang, *Division and Square Root: Digit-Recurrence Algorithms and Implementations*, Kluwer, 1994.

[Hash90]   Hashemian, R., "Square Rooting Algorithms for Integer and Floating-Point Numbers," *IEEE Trans. Computers*, Vol. 39, No. 8, pp. 1025–1029, 1990.

[Maje85]   Majerski, S., "Square-Root Algorithms for High-Speed Digital Circuits," *IEEE Trans. Computers*, Vol. 34, No. 8, pp. 1016–1024, 1985.

[Maji71]   Majithia, J.C., "Cellular Array for Extraction of Squares and Square Roots of Binary Numbers," *IEEE Trans. Computers*, Vol. 20, No. 12, pp. 1617–1618, 1971.

[Mont90]   Montuschi, P., and M. Mezzalama, "Survey of Square-Rooting Algorithms," *Proc. IEE: Pt. E*, Vol. 137, pp. 31–40, 1990.

[Omon94]   Omondi, A.R., *Computer Arithmetic Systems: Algorithms, Architecture and Implementation*, Prentice-Hall, 1994.

[Parh99]   Parhami, B., "Analysis of the Lookup Table Size for Square-Rooting," *Proc. 33rd Asilomar Conf. Signals, Systems, and Computers*, pp. 1327–1330, October 1999.

[Schw96]   Schwarz, E.M., and M.J. Flynn, "Hardware Starting Approximation Method and Its Application to the Square Root Operation," *IEEE Trans. Computers*, Vol. 45, No. 12, pp. 1356–1369, 1996.

[Zura87]   Zurawski, J.H.P., and J.B. Gosling, "Design of a High-Speed Square Root, Multiply, and Divide Unit," *IEEE Trans. Computers*, Vol. 36, No. 1, pp. 13–23, 1987.

Chapter 22 | THE CORDIC ALGORITHMS

In this chapter, we learn an elegant convergence method for evaluating trigonometric and many other functions of interest. We will see that, somewhat surprisingly, all these functions can be evaluated with delays and hardware costs that are only slightly higher than those of division or square-rooting. The simple form of CORDIC is based on the observation that if a unit-length vector with end point at $(x, y) = (1, 0)$ is rotated by an angle z, its new end point will be at $(x, y) = (\cos z, \sin z)$. Thus, $\cos z$ and $\sin z$ can be computed by finding the coordinates of the new end point of the vector after rotation by z. Chapter topics include:

22.1 ROTATIONS AND PSEUDOROTATIONS

Consider the vector $OE^{(i)}$ in Fig. 22.1, having one end point at the origin O and the other at $E^{(i)}$ with coordinates $(x^{(i)}, y^{(i)})$. If $OE^{(i)}$ is rotated about the origin by an angle $\alpha^{(i)}$, as shown in Fig. 22.1, the new end point $E^{(i+1)}$ will have coordinates $(x^{(i+1)}, y^{(i+1)})$ satisfying:

$$
\begin{aligned}
x^{(i+1)} &= x^{(i)} \cos \alpha^{(i)} - y^{(i)} \sin \alpha^{(i)} \\
&= \frac{x^{(i)} - y^{(i)} \tan \alpha^{(i)}}{(1 + \tan^2 \alpha^{(i)})^{1/2}} \\
y^{(i+1)} &= y^{(i)} \cos \alpha^{(i)} + x^{(i)} \sin \alpha^{(i)} \qquad \text{[Real rotation]} \\
&= \frac{y^{(i)} + x^{(i)} \tan \alpha^{(i)}}{(1 + \tan^2 \alpha^{(i)})^{1/2}}
\end{aligned}
$$

$$z^{(i+1)} = z^{(i)} - \alpha_i$$

where the variable z allows us to keep track of the total rotation over several steps. More specifically, $z^{(i)}$ can be viewed as the residual rotation still to be performed; thus $z^{(i+1)}$ is the updated version of $z^{(i)}$ after rotation by $\alpha^{(i)}$. If $z^{(0)}$ is the initial rotation goal and if the $\alpha^{(i)}$ angles are selected at each step such that $z^{(m)}$ tends to 0, the end point $E^{(m)}$ with coordinates $(x^{(m)}, y^{(m)})$ will be the end point of the vector after it has been rotated by the angle $z^{(0)}$.

In the CORDIC computation method, which derives its name from the coordinate rotations digital computer designed in the late 1950s, rotation steps are replaced by pseudorotations as depicted in Fig. 22.1. Whereas a real rotation does not change the length $R^{(i)}$ of the vector, a pseudorotation step increases its length to:

$$R^{(i+1)} = R^{(i)}(1 + \tan^2 \alpha^{(i)})^{1/2}$$

The coordinates of the new end point $E'^{(i+1)}$ after pseudorotation are derived by multiplying the coordinates of $E^{(i+1)}$ by the expansion factor $(1 + \tan^2 \alpha^{(i)})^{1/2}$. The pseudorotation by the angle $\alpha^{(i)}$ is thus characterized by the equations:

$$
\begin{aligned}
x^{(i+1)} &= x^{(i)} - y^{(i)} \tan \alpha^{(i)} \\
y^{(i+1)} &= y^{(i)} + x^{(i)} \tan \alpha^{(i)} \qquad \text{[Pseudorotation]} \\
z^{(i+1)} &= z^{(i)} - \alpha^{(i)}
\end{aligned}
$$

Assuming $x^{(0)} = x$, $y^{(0)} = y$, and $z^{(0)} = z$, after m real rotations by the angles $\alpha^{(1)}, \alpha^{(2)}, \ldots, \alpha^{(m)}$, we have:

$$
\begin{aligned}
x^{(m)} &= x \, \cos\left(\sum \alpha^{(i)}\right) - y \, \sin\left(\sum \alpha^{(i)}\right) \\
y^{(m)} &= y \, \cos\left(\sum \alpha^{(i)}\right) + x \, \sin\left(\sum \alpha^{(i)}\right) \\
z^{(m)} &= z - \left(\sum \alpha^{(i)}\right)
\end{aligned}
$$

After m pseudorotations by the angles $\alpha^{(1)}, \alpha^{(2)}, \ldots, \alpha^{(m)}$, with $x^{(0)} = x$, $y^{(0)} = y$, and $z^{(0)} = z$, we have:

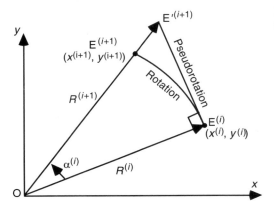

Fig. 22.1   A pseudorotation step in CORDIC.

$$x^{(m)} = \left(x \, \cos\left(\sum \alpha^{(i)}\right) - y \, \sin\left(\sum \alpha^{(i)}\right)\right) \prod (1 + \tan^2 \, \alpha^{(i)})^{1/2}$$

$$= K \left(x \, \cos\left(\sum \alpha^{(i)}\right) - y \, \sin\left(\sum \alpha^{(i)}\right)\right)$$

$$x^{(m)} = \left(y \, \cos\left(\sum \alpha^{(i)}\right) + x \, \sin\left(\sum \alpha^{(i)}\right)\right) \prod (1 + \tan^2 \, \alpha^{(i)})^{1/2} \qquad [*]$$

$$= K \left(y \, \cos\left(\sum \alpha^{(i)}\right) + x \, \sin\left(\sum \alpha^{(i)}\right)\right)$$

$$z^{(m)} = z - \left(\sum \alpha^{(i)}\right)$$

The expansion factor $K = \prod (1 + \tan^2 \, \alpha^{(i)})^{1/2}$ depends on the rotation angles $\alpha^{(1)}$, $\alpha^{(2)}, \ldots, \alpha^{(m)}$. However, if we always rotate by the same angles, with positive or negative signs, then K is a constant that can be precomputed. In this case, using the simpler pseudorotations instead of true rotations has the effect of expanding the vector coordinates and length by a known constant.

22.2 BASIC CORDIC ITERATIONS

To simplify each pseudorotation, pick $\alpha^{(i)}$ such that $\tan \alpha^{(i)} = d_i 2^{-i}$, $d_i \in \{-1, 1\}$. Then:

$$x^{(i+1)} = x^{(i)} - d_i y^{(i)} 2^{-i}$$
$$y^{(i+1)} = y^{(i)} + d_i x^{(i)} 2^{-i} \qquad \text{[CORDIC iteration]}$$
$$z^{(i+1)} = z^{(i)} - d_i \, \tan^{-1} \, 2^{-i}$$

The computation of $x^{(i+1)}$ or $y^{(i+1)}$ requires an i-bit right shift and an add/subtract. If the function $\tan^{-1} \, 2^{-i}$ is precomputed and stored in a table (see Table 22.1) for different values of i, a single add/subtract suffices to compute $z^{(i+1)}$. Each CORDIC iteration thus involves two shifts, a table lookup, and three additions.

If we always pseudorotate by the same set of angles (with + or − signs), then the expansion factor K is a constant that can be precomputed. For example, to pseudorotate by 30 degrees, we can pseudorotate by the following sequence of angles that add up to $\approx 30°$.

$$30.0 \approx 45.0 - 26.6 + 14.0 - 7.1 + 3.6 + 1.8 - 0.9 + 0.4 - 0.2 + 0.1$$
$$= 30.1$$

In effect, what actually happens in CORDIC is that z is initialized to $30°$ and then, in each step, the sign of the next rotation angle is selected to try to change the sign of z; that is, we choose $d_i = \text{sign}(z^{(i)})$, where the sign function is defined to be -1 or 1 depending on whether the argument is negative or nonnegative. This is reminiscent of nonrestoring division.

Table 22.2 shows the process of selecting the signs of the rotation angles for a desired rotation of $+30°$. Figure 22.2 depicts the first few steps in the process of forcing z to 0.

TABLE 22.1
Approximate value of the function $e^{(i)} = \tan^{-1} 2^{-i}$,
in degrees, for $0 \le i \le 9$

i	$e^{(i)}$
0	45.0
1	26.6
2	14.0
3	7.1
4	3.6
5	1.8
6	0.9
7	0.4
8	0.2
9	0.1

In CORDIC terminology, the preceding selection rule for d_i, which makes z converge to 0, is known as "rotation mode." We rewrite the CORDIC iterations as follows, where $e^{(i)} = \tan^{-1} 2^{-i}$:

$$x^{(i+1)} = x^{(i)} - d_i(2^{-i}y^{(i)})$$
$$y^{(i+1)} = y^{(i)} + d_i(2^{-i}x^{(i)})$$
$$z^{(i+1)} = z^{(i)} - d_i e^{(i)}$$

After m iterations in rotation mode, when $z^{(m)}$ is sufficiently close to 0, we have $\sum \alpha^{(i)} = z$, and the CORDIC equations [*] become:

TABLE 22.2
Choosing the signs of the rotation
angles to force z to 0

i	$z^{(i)}$	$-$	$\alpha^{(i)}$	$=$	$z^{(i+1)}$
0	+30.0	−	45.0	=	−15.0
1	−15.0	+	26.6	=	+11.6
2	+11.6	−	14.0	=	−2.4
3	−2.4	+	7.1	=	+4.7
4	+4.7	−	3.6	=	+1.1
5	+1.1	−	1.8	=	−0.7
6	−0.7	+	0.9	=	+0.2
7	+0.2	−	0.4	=	−0.2
8	−0.2	+	0.2	=	+0.0
9	+0.0	−	0.1	=	−0.1

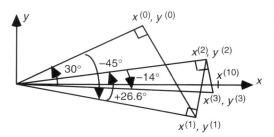

Fig. 22.2   The first three of 10 pseudorotations leading from $(x^{(0)}, y^{(0)})$ to $(x^{(10)}, 0)$ in rotating by $+30°$.

$$x^{(m)} = K(x \cos z - y \sin z)$$
$$y^{(m)} = K(y \cos z + x \sin z) \qquad \text{[Rotation mode]}$$
$$z^{(m)} = 0$$

Rule: Choose $d_i \in \{-1, 1\}$ such that $z \to 0$.

The constant K in the preceding equations is $K = 1.646\ 760\ 258\ 121 \cdots$. Thus, to compute $\cos z$ and $\sin z$, one can start with $x = 1/K = 0.607\ 252\ 935 \cdots$ and $y = 0$. Then, as $z^{(m)}$ tends to 0 with CORDIC iterations in rotation mode, $x^{(m)}$ and $y^{(m)}$ converge to $\cos z$ and $\sin z$, respectively. Once $\sin z$ and $\cos z$ are known, $\tan z$ can be obtained through division if necessary.

For k bits of precision in the resulting trigonometric functions, k CORDIC iterations are needed. The reason is that for large i, we have $\tan^{-1} 2^{-i} \approx 2^{-i}$. Hence, for $i > k$, the change in z will be less than *ulp*.

In rotation mode, convergence of z to 0 is possible because each angle in Table 22.1 is more than half the previous angle or, equivalently, each angle is less than the sum of all the angles following it. The domain of convergence is $-99.7° \le z \le 99.7°$, where $99.7°$ is the sum of all the angles in Table 22.1. Fortunately, this range includes angles from $-90°$ to $+90°$, or $[-\pi/2, \pi/2]$ in radians. For outside the preceding range, we can use trigonometric identities to convert the problem to one that is within the domain of convergence:

$$\cos(z \pm 2j\pi) = \cos z \qquad \sin(z \pm 2j\pi) = \sin z$$
$$\cos(z - \pi) = -\cos z \qquad \sin(z - \pi) = -\sin z$$

Note that these transformations become particularly convenient if angles are represented and manipulated in multiples of π radians, so that $z = 0.2$ really means $z = 0.2\pi$ radian or $36°$. The domain of convergence then includes $[-1/2, 1/2]$, with numbers outside this domain converted to numbers within the domain quite easily.

In a second way of utilizing CORDIC iterations, known as "vectoring mode," we make y tend to zero by choosing $d_i = -\text{sign}(x^{(i)} y^{(i)})$. After m iterations in vectoring mode we have $\tan(\sum \alpha^{(i)}) = -y/x$. This means that:

$$x^{(m)} = K \left[x \cos \left(\sum \alpha^{(i)} \right) - y \sin \left(\sum \alpha^{(i)} \right) \right]$$
$$= \frac{K \left(x - y \tan \left(\sum \alpha^{(i)} \right) \right)}{\left[1 + \tan^2 \left(\sum \alpha^{(i)} \right) \right]^{1/2}}$$

$$= \frac{K(x + y^2/x)}{(1 + y^2/x^2)^{1/2}}$$

$$= K(x^2 + y^2)^{1/2}$$

The CORDIC equations [*] thus become:

$$x^{(m)} = K(x^2 + y^2)^{1/2}$$

$$y^{(m)} = 0 \qquad\qquad\qquad\qquad \text{[Vectoring mode]}$$

$$z^{(m)} = z + \tan^{-1}(y/x)$$

Rule: Choose $d_i \in \{-1, 1\}$ such that $y \to 0$.

One can compute $\tan^{-1} y$ in vectoring mode by starting with $x = 1$ and $z = 0$. This computation always converges. However, one can take advantage of the identity

$$\tan^{-1}(1/y) = \pi/2 - \tan^{-1} y$$

to limit the range of fixed-point numbers that are encountered. We will see later, in Section 22.5, that the CORDIC method also allows the computation of other inverse trigonometric functions.

22.3 CORDIC HARDWARE

A straightforward hardware implementation for CORDIC arithmetic is shown in Fig. 22.3. It requires three registers for x, y, and z, a lookup table to store the values of $e^{(i)} = \tan^{-1} 2^{-i}$, and two shifters to supply the terms $2^{-i}x$ and $2^{-i}y$ to the adder/subtractor units. The d_i factor (-1 or 1) is accommodated by selecting the (shifted) operand or its complement.

Of course, a single adder and one shifter can be shared by the three computations if a reduction in speed by a factor of about 3 is acceptable. In the extreme, CORDIC iterations can be implemented in firmware (microprogram) or even software using the ALU and general-purpose registers of a standard microprocessor. In this case, the lookup table supplying the terms $e^{(i)}$ can be stored in the control ROM or in main memory.

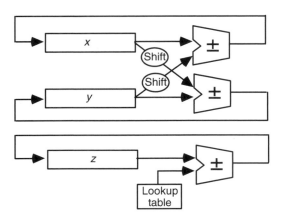

Fig. 22.3 Hardware elements needed for the CORDIC method.

Where high speed is not required and minimizing the hardware cost is important (as in calculators), the adders in Fig. 22.3 can be bit-serial. Then with k-bit operands, $O(k^2)$ clock cycles would be required to complete the k CORDIC iterations. This is acceptable for handheld calculators, since even a delay of tens of thousands of clock cycles constitutes a small fraction of a second and thus is hardly noticeable to a human user. Intermediate between the fully parallel and fully bit-serial realizations are a wide array of digit-serial (say decimal or radix-16) implementations that provide trade-offs of speed versus cost.

22.4 GENERALIZED CORDIC

The basic CORDIC method of Section 22.2 can be generalized to provide a more powerful tool for function evaluation. Generalized CORDIC is defined as follows:

$$
\begin{aligned}
x^{(i+1)} &= x^{(i)} - \mu d_i y^{(i)} 2^{-i} \\
y^{(i+1)} &= y^{(i)} + d_i x^{(i)} 2^{-i} \qquad \text{[Generalized CORDIC iteration]} \\
z^{(i+1)} &= z^{(i)} - d_i e^{(i)}
\end{aligned}
$$

Note that the only difference with basic CORDIC is the introduction of the parameter μ in the equation for x and redefinition of $e^{(i)}$. The parameter μ can assume one of three values:

$$
\begin{array}{llll}
\mu = & 1 & \text{Circular rotations (basic CORDIC)} & e = \tan^{-1} 2^{-i} \\
\mu = & 0 & \text{Linear rotations} & e^{(i)} = 2^{-i} \\
\mu = & -1 & \text{Hyperbolic rotations} & e^{(i)} = \tanh^{-1} 2^{-i}
\end{array}
$$

Figure 22.4 illustrates the three types of rotation in generalized CORDIC.

For the circular case with $\mu = 1$, we introduced pseudorotations that led to expansion of the vector length by a factor $(1 + \tan^2 \alpha^{(i)})^{1/2} = 1/\cos \alpha^{(i)}$ in each step, and by $K = 1.646\,760$ $258\,121 \cdots$ overall, where the vector length is the familiar $R^{(i)} = \sqrt{x^2 + y^2}$. With reference to Fig. 22.4, the rotation angle AOB can be defined in terms of the area of the sector AOB as follows:

$$
\text{angle AOB} = \frac{2(\text{area AOB})}{(\text{OU})^2}
$$

The following equations, repeated here for ready comparison, characterize the results of circular CORDIC rotations:

$$
\begin{aligned}
x^{(m)} &= K(x \cos z - y \sin z) \\
y^{(m)} &= K(y \cos z + x \sin z) \qquad \text{[Circular rotation mode]} \\
z^{(m)} &= 0
\end{aligned}
$$

Rule: Choose $d_i \in \{-1, 1\}$ such that $z \to 0$.

$$x^{(m)} = K(x^2 + y^2)^{1/2}$$
$$y^{(m)} = 0 \qquad\qquad \text{[Circular vectoring mode]}$$
$$z^{(m)} = z + \tan^{-1}(y/x)$$
Rule: Choose $d_i \in \{-1, 1\}$ such that $y \to 0$.

In linear rotations corresponding to $\mu = 0$, the end point of the vector is kept on the line $x = x^{(0)}$ and the vector "length" is defined by $R^{(i)} = x^{(i)}$. Hence, the length of the vector is always its true length OV and the scaling factor is 1 (our pseudorotations are true linear rotations in this case). The following equations characterize the results of linear CORDIC rotations:

$$x^{(m)} = x$$
$$y^{(m)} = y + xz \qquad\qquad \text{[Linear rotation mode]}$$
$$z^{(m)} = 0$$
Rule: Choose $d_i \in \{-1, 1\}$ such that $z \to 0$.

$$x^{(m)} = x$$
$$y^{(m)} = 0 \qquad\qquad \text{[Linear vectoring mode]}$$
$$z^{(m)} = z + y/x$$
Rule: Choose $d_i \in \{-1, 1\}$ such that $y \to 0$.

Hence, linear CORDIC rotations can be used to perform multiplication (rotation mode, $y = 0$), multiply-add (rotation mode), division (vectoring mode, $z = 0$), or divide-add (vectoring mode).

In hyperbolic rotations corresponding to $\mu = -1$, the rotation "angle" EOF can be defined in terms of the area of the hyperbolic sector EOF as follows:

$$\text{angle EOF} = \frac{2(\text{area EOF})}{(OW)^2}$$

The vector "length" is defined as $R^{(i)} = \sqrt{x^2 - y^2}$, with the length expansion due to pseudorotation being $(1 - \tanh^2 \alpha^{(i)})^{1/2} = 1/\cosh \alpha^{(i)}$. Because $\cosh \alpha^{(i)} > 1$, the vector length actually shrinks, leading to an overall shrinkage factor $K' = 0.828\ 159\ 360\ 960\ 2 \cdots$ after all the iterations. The following equations characterize the results of hyperbolic CORDIC rotations:

$$x^{(m)} = K'(x \cosh z + y \sinh z)$$
$$y^{(m)} = K(y \cosh z + x \sinh z) \qquad\qquad \text{[Hyperbolic rotation mode]}$$
$$z^{(m)} = 0$$
Rule: $d_i \in \{-1, 1\}$ such that $z \to 0$.

$$x^{(m)} = K(x^2 - y^2)^{1/2}$$
$$y^{(m)} = 0 \qquad\qquad \text{[Hyperbolic vectoring mode]}$$
$$z^{(m)} = z + \tanh^{-1}(y/x)$$
Rule: $d_i \in \{-1, 1\}$ such that $y \to 0$.

Hence, hyperbolic CORDIC rotations can be used to compute the hyperbolic sine and cosine functions (rotation mode, $x = 1/K'$, $y = 0$) or the $\tanh^{-1}$ function (vectoring mode, $x = 1$, $z = 0$). Other functions can be computed indirectly, as we shall see shortly.

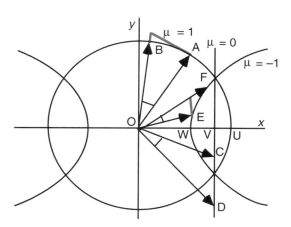

Fig. 22.4 Circular, linear, and hyperbolic CORDIC.

Convergence of circular CORDIC iterations was discussed in Section 22.2. Linear CORDIC iterations trivially converge for suitably restricted values of z (rotation mode) or y (vectoring mode). For hyperbolic CORDIC iterations, ensuring convergence is a bit more tricky, since whereas $\tan^{-1}(2^{-(i+1)}) \geq 0.5 \tan^{-1}(2^{-i})$, the corresponding relation for tanh, namely, $\tanh^{-1}(2^{-(i+1)}) \geq 0.5 \tanh^{-1}(2^{-i})$, does not hold in general.

A relatively simple cure is to repeat steps $i = 4, 13, 40, 121, \ldots, j, 3j + 1, \ldots$ to ensure convergence (each term is 1 more than 3 times the preceding term). In other words, the iterations corresponding to the foregoing values of i are executed twice. The effect of these repetitions on performance is minimal because in practice we always stop for $m < 121$. These repeated steps have already been taken into account in computing the shrinkage constant K' given earlier. With these provisions, convergence in computing hyperbolic sine and cosine functions is guaranteed for $|z| < 1.13$ and in the case of the $\tanh^{-1}$ function, for $|y| < 0.81$.

The preceding convergence domains are more than adequate to compute the cosh, sinh, and $\tanh^{-1}$ functions over the entire range of arguments using the following identities that hold for $|z| < \ln 2 \approx 0.69$:

$$\cosh(q \ln 2 + z) = 2^{q-1}[\cosh z + \sinh z + 2^{-2q}(\cosh z - \sinh z)]$$
$$\sinh(q \ln 2 + z) = 2^{q-1}[\cosh z + \sinh z - 2^{-2q}(\cosh z - \sinh z)]$$
$$\tanh^{-1}(1 - 2^{-e}s) = \tanh^{-1}\left(\frac{2 - s - 2^{-e}s}{2 + s - 2^{-e}s}\right) + \frac{e \ln 2}{2}$$

22.5 USING THE CORDIC METHOD

We have already seen that the generalized CORDIC method can directly compute sin, cos, $\tan^{-1}$, sinh, cosh, $\tanh^{-1}$, as well as multiplication and division functions. To use CORDIC iterations for computing these functions, it is necessary to check that the arguments are within the domain of convergence and to convert the problem, if necessary, to one for which the iterations are guaranteed to converge.

Of course, somewhat more complex functions such as $\tan^{-1}(y/x)$, $y + xz$, $(x^2 + y^2)^{1/2}$, $(x^2 - y^2)^{1/2}$, and $e^z = \sinh z + \cosh z$, can also be directly computed with suitable initializations. We will see shortly that some special cases of the above, such as $(1 + w^2)^{1/2}$ and $(1 - w^2)^{1/2}$, are quite useful in computing other functions.

Many other functions are computable by suitable pre- or postprocessing steps or by multiple passes through the CORDIC hardware. Figure 22.5 provides a summary of CORDIC for ease of reference and also contains formulas for computing some of these other functions. For example, the tan function can be computed by first computing sin and cos and then performing a division, perhaps through another set of (linear) CORDIC iterations. Similarly, the tanh function can be computed through dividing sinh by cosh.

Computing the natural logarithm function, $\ln w$, involves precomputing $y = w - 1$ and $x = w + 1$ via two additions and then using the identity:

$$\ln\ w = 2\ \tanh^{-1}\left|\frac{w - 1}{w + 1}\right|$$

Logarithms in other bases (such as 2 or 10) can be obtained from the natural logarithm through multiplication by constant factors. Thus, all such logarithms can be computed quite easily by suitably modifying the constant 2 in the preceding equation.

Exponentiation can be done through CORDIC iterations by noting that

$$w^t = e^{t\ \ln\ w}$$

with the natural logarithm, multiplication, and the exponential function all computable through CORDIC iterations.

The following procedures for computing the functions $\sin^{-1}$, $\cos^{-1}$, $\sinh^{-1}$, $\cosh^{-1}$, and for square-rooting are also listed in Fig. 22.5:

$$
\begin{aligned}
\cos^{-1} w &= \tan^{-1}(y/w) &&\text{for } y = \sqrt{1 - w^2}\\
\sin^{-1} w &= \tan^{-1}(w/x) &&\text{for } x = \sqrt{1 - w^2}\\
\cosh^{-1} w &= \ln(w + x) &&\text{for } x = \sqrt{1 - w^2}\\
\sinh^{-1} w &= \ln(w + x) &&\text{for } x = \sqrt{1 + w^2}\\
\sqrt{w} &= \sqrt{x^2 - y^2} &&\text{for } x = w + 1/4 \text{ and } y = w - 1/4
\end{aligned}
$$

Modified forms of CORDIC have been suggested for computing still other functions or for computing some of the aforementioned functions more efficiently. Some of these are explored in the end-of-chapter problems.

From the preceding discussion, we see that a CORDIC computation unit can evaluate virtually all functions of common interest and is, in a sense, a universally efficient hardware implementation for evaluating these functions.

The number or iterations in CORDIC is fixed, to ensure that K and K' remain constants. In other words, if at some point during the computation in rotation (vectoring) mode z (y) becomes 0, we cannot stop the computation, except of course for the linear version with $\mu = 0$. Thus, it appears that we always need k iterations for k digits of precision. Recall that basic sequential multiplication and division algorithms, discussed in Chapters 11 and 16, also involve k shift/add iterations. Each iteration of CORDIC requires three shift/adds. Nevertheless, it is quite remarkable that a large number of useful, and seemingly complicated, functions can be

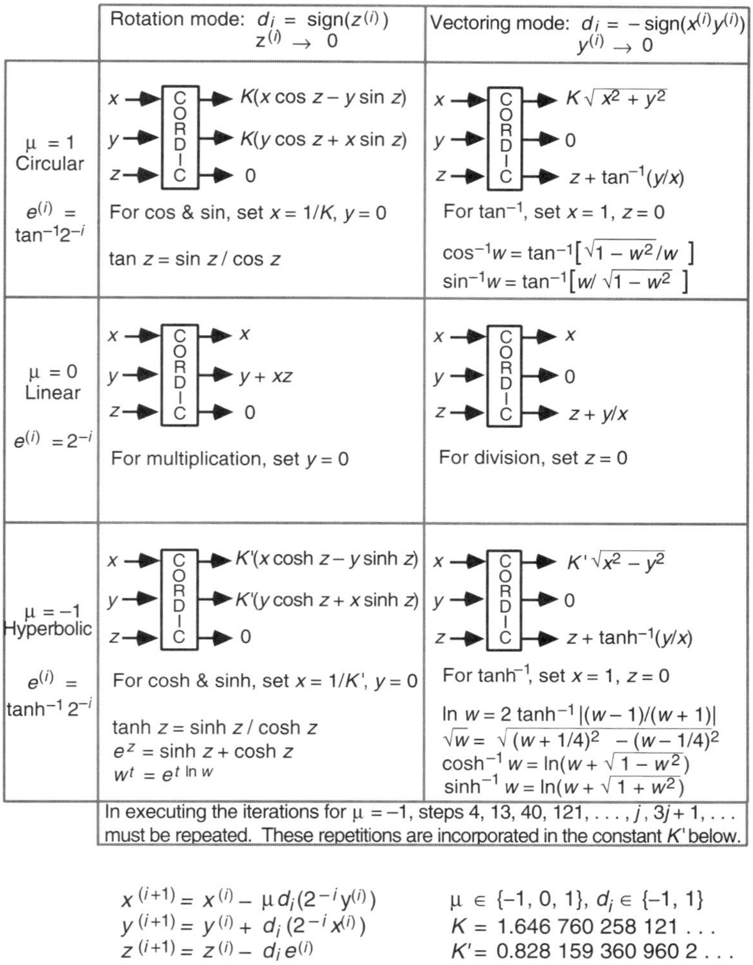

	Rotation mode: $d_i = \text{sign}(z^{(i)})$ $z^{(i)} \to 0$	Vectoring mode: $d_i = -\text{sign}(x^{(i)}y^{(i)})$ $y^{(i)} \to 0$
$\mu = 1$ Circular $e^{(i)} = \tan^{-1}2^{-i}$	$K(x \cos z - y \sin z)$ $K(y \cos z + x \sin z)$ 0 For cos & sin, set $x = 1/K$, $y = 0$ $\tan z = \sin z / \cos z$	$K\sqrt{x^2 + y^2}$ 0 $z + \tan^{-1}(y/x)$ For $\tan^{-1}$, set $x = 1$, $z = 0$ $\cos^{-1}w = \tan^{-1}[\sqrt{1 - w^2}/w\,]$ $\sin^{-1}w = \tan^{-1}[w/\sqrt{1 - w^2}\,]$
$\mu = 0$ Linear $e^{(i)} = 2^{-i}$	x $y + xz$ 0 For multiplication, set $y = 0$	x 0 $z + y/x$ For division, set $z = 0$
$\mu = -1$ Hyperbolic $e^{(i)} = \tanh^{-1}2^{-i}$	$K'(x \cosh z - y \sinh z)$ $K'(y \cosh z + x \sinh z)$ 0 For cosh & sinh, set $x = 1/K'$, $y = 0$ $\tanh z = \sinh z / \cosh z$ $e^z = \sinh z + \cosh z$ $w^t = e^{t \ln w}$	$K'\sqrt{x^2 - y^2}$ 0 $z + \tanh^{-1}(y/x)$ For $\tanh^{-1}$, set $x = 1$, $z = 0$ $\ln w = 2 \tanh^{-1}|(w - 1)/(w + 1)|$ $\sqrt{w} = \sqrt{(w + 1/4)^2 - (w - 1/4)^2}$ $\cosh^{-1}w = \ln(w + \sqrt{1 - w^2})$ $\sinh^{-1}w = \ln(w + \sqrt{1 + w^2})$

In executing the iterations for $\mu = -1$, steps 4, 13, 40, 121, ..., j, $3j + 1$, ... must be repeated. These repetitions are incorporated in the constant K' below.

$$x^{(i+1)} = x^{(i)} - \mu\, d_i(2^{-i}y^{(i)})$$
$$y^{(i+1)} = y^{(i)} + d_i\,(2^{-i}x^{(i)})$$
$$z^{(i+1)} = z^{(i)} - d_i\,e^{(i)}$$

$\mu \in \{-1, 0, 1\}$, $d_i \in \{-1, 1\}$
$K = 1.646\ 760\ 258\ 121 \ldots$
$K' = 0.828\ 159\ 360\ 960\ 2 \ldots$

Fig. 22.5 Summary of generalized CORDIC algorithms.

computed through CORDIC with a latency that is essentially comparable to that of sequential multiplication or division.

Note that it is possible to terminate the CORDIC algorithm with $\mu \neq 0$ before k iterations, or to skip some rotations, by keeping track of the expansion factor via the recurrence:

$$(K^{(i+1)})^2 = (K^{(i)})^2(1 \pm 2^{-2i})$$

Thus, by using an additional shift/add in each iteration to update the square of the expansion factor, we can free ourselves from the requirement that every rotation angle be used once and only once (or exactly twice in some iterations of the hyperbolic pseudorotations). At the end, after m iterations, we may have to divide the results by the square root of the $(K^{(m)})^2$ value thus obtained. Given the additional variable to be updated and the final adjustment steps involving square-rooting and division, these modifications are usually not worthwhile and *constant-factor* CORDIC is almost always preferred to the *variable-factor* version above.

Several speedup methods have been suggested to reduce the number of iterations in constant-factor CORDIC to less than k. One idea for circular CORDIC (in rotation mode) is to do $k/2$ iterations as usual and then combine the remaining $k/2$ iterations into a single step, involving multiplication, by means of the following:

$$x^{(k/2+1)} = x^{(k/2)} - y^{(k/2)}z^{(k/2)}$$
$$y^{(k/2+1)} = y^{(k/2)} + x^{(k/2)}z^{(k/2)}$$
$$z^{(k/2+1)} = z^{(k/2)} - z^{(k/2)} = 0$$

This is possible because for very small values of z, we have $\tan^{-1} z \approx z \approx \tan z$. The expansion factor K presents no problem because for $e^{(i)} < 2^{-k/2}$, the contribution of the ignored terms that would have been multiplied by K is provably less than *ulp*. In other words, the same expansion factor K can be used with $k/2$ or more iterations.

Like high-radix multiplication and division algorithms, CORDIC can be extended to higher radices. For example, in a radix-4 CORDIC algorithm, d_i assumes values in $\{-2, -1, 1, 2\}$ (perhaps with 0 also included in the set) rather than in $\{-1, 1\}$. The hardware required for the radix-4 version of CORDIC is quite similar to Fig. 22.3, except that 2-to-1 multiplexers are inserted after the shifters and the lookup table to allow the operand or twice the operand to be supplied to the corresponding adder/subtractor. The contents of the lookup table will of course be different for the radix-4 version. The number of iterations in radix-4 CORDIC will be half that of the radix-2 algorithm.

Such high-radix algorithms are best understood in terms of additive and multiplicative normalization methods discussed in Chapter 23.

22.6 AN ALGEBRAIC FORMULATION

Let us accept that the following iterations, with initial values $u^{(0)} = u$ and $v^{(0)} = v$, lead to the computation of the exponential function $v^{(m)} = ve^u$ when $u^{(m)}$ is made to converge to 0 (we will prove this in Section 23.3).

$$u^{(i+1)} = u^{(i)} - \ln c^{(i)}$$
$$v^{(i+1)} = v^{(i)}c^{(i)}$$

Since $\cos z + j \sin z = e^{jz}$, where $j = \sqrt{-1}$, we can compute both $\cos z$ and $\sin z$ by means of the iterations above if we start with $v^{(0)} = 1$ and $u^{(0)} = jz$ and use complex arithmetic. Consider now the identity

$$a + jb = \sqrt{a^2 + b^2}\, e^{j\theta} = \sqrt{a^2 + b^2}\, (\cos \theta + j \sin \theta)$$

where $\theta = \tan^{-1}(b/a)$ and suppose that we choose

$$c^{(i)} = \frac{1 + j\, d_i 2^{-i}}{\sqrt{1 + 2^{-2i}}}$$

with $d_i \in \{-1, 1\}$. Defining $g^{(i)} = \tan^{-1}(d_i 2^{-i})$, the complex number $c^{(i)}$ can be written in the form:

$$c^{(i)} = \frac{\sqrt{1 + 2^{-2i}}(\cos g^{(i)} + j \sin g^{(i)})}{\sqrt{1 + 2^{-2i}}} = \exp(j g^{(i)})$$

This leads to:

$$\ln c(i) = j g^{(i)} = j \tan^{-1}(d_i 2^{-i})$$

To make the multiplication needed for computing $v^{(i+1)}$ simpler, we can replace our second recurrence by:

$$v^{(i+1)} = v^{(i)} c^{(i)} \sqrt{1 + 2^{-2i}} = v^{(i)}(1 + j d_i 2^{-i})$$

The effect of multiplying the right-hand side by $\sqrt{1 + 2^{-2i}}$ will change $v^{(m)} = v^{(0)} e^{jz}$ to:

$$v^{(m)} = v^{(0)} e^{jz} \prod_{i=1}^{m-1} \sqrt{1 + 2^{-2i}}$$

Thus, we can still get $v^{(m)} = e^{jz}$ by setting $v^{(0)} = 1/(\prod_{i=1}^{m-1} \sqrt{1 + 2^{-2i}})$ instead of $v^{(0)} = 1$. Note that in the terminology of circular CORDIC, the term $\prod_{i=1}^{m-1} \sqrt{1 + 2^{-2i}}$ is the expansion factor K and the complex multiplication

$$v^{(i+1)} = v^{(i)}(1 + j d_i 2^{-i}) = (x^{(i)} + j y^{(i)})(1 + j d_i 2^{-i})$$

is performed by computing the real and imaginary parts separately:

$$x^{(i+1)} = x^{(i)} - d_i y^{(i)} 2^{-i}$$
$$y^{(i+1)} = y^{(i)} + d_i x^{(i)} 2^{-i}$$

Note also that since the variable u is initialized to the imaginary number jz and then only imaginary values $j g^{(i)}$ are subtracted from it until it converges to 0, we can ignore the factor j and use real computation on the real variable $z^{(i)} = -j u^{(i)}$, which is initialized to $z^{(0)} = z$, instead. This completes our algebraic derivation of the circular CORDIC method.

PROBLEMS

22.1   Circular CORDIC arithmetic example

    a.   Use the CORDIC method to compute sin 45° and cos 45°. Perform all arithmetic in decimal with at least six significant digits and show all intermediate steps. Note the absolute and relative errors by comparing the results to exact values.

    b.   Since sin 45° = cos 45°, explain any difference in the accuracy of the two results.

    c.   Repeat part a for $\tan^{-1} 1$.

22.2   Circular CORDIC arithmetic example

    a.   Use the CORDIC method to compute sin 30° and cos 30°. Perform all arithmetic in decimal with at least six significant digits and show all intermediate steps. Note the absolute and relative errors by comparing the results to exact values.

b. Calculate tan 30° from the results of part a and discuss its error.

c. Repeat part a for $\tan^{-1} 0.41421$.

22.3 **Generalized CORDIC arithmetic example** Use (generalized) CORDIC iterations, along with appropriate pre- and postprocessing steps, to compute the following. Use decimal arithmetic with at least six digits.

a. sinh 1 and cosh 1

b. $e^{0.5}$

c. $\tanh^{-1} 0.9$

d. $\sqrt{2}$

e. ln 2

f. $2^{1/3}$

22.4 **Generalized CORDIC arithmetic in binary** Use generalized CORDIC iterations, along with appropriate pre- and postprocessing steps, to compute the following. Use binary arithmetic with 8 bits after the radix point in all computations.

a. ln(1.1011 0001)

b. exp(.1011 0001)

c. $\sqrt{.1011\ 0001}$

d. $\sqrt[3]{.1011\ 0001}$

22.5 **Multiplication/Division via CORDIC** The generalized CORDIC iterations with $\mu = 0$ leave x unchanged and modify y and z as follows: $y^{(i+1)} = y^{(i)} \pm 2^{-i}x^{(i)}$, $z^{(i+1)} = z^{(i)} - (\pm 2^{-i})$.

a. Show how these iterations can be used to do multiplication and compare the procedure to basic (one-bit-at-a-time) sequential multiplication in terms of speed and implementation cost.

b. Repeat part a for division.

22.6 **CORDIC preprocessing** Assume that angles are represented and manipulated in multiples of π radians, as suggested near the end of Section 22.2.

a. Given an angle z' in fixed-point format, with k whole and l fractional digits, the computation of $\sin z'$ can be converted to the computation of $\pm \sin z$ or $\pm \cos z$, where z is in $[-1/2, 1/2]$. Show the details of the conversion process leading from z' to z.

b. Repeat part a for cos z.

c. Repeat part a when the input z is in 32-bit IEEE standard floating-point format.

22.7 **Composite CORDIC algorithms** Determine which of the functions listed in Section 22.5 requires the largest number of CORDIC iterations if it is to be evaluated solely by a CORDIC computation unit and no other hardware element.

22.8 **Truncated CORDIC iterations** Verify that the difference between the CORDIC scale factors for m and $m/2$ iterations [i.e., $K = K^{(m)} = \prod_{i=0}^{m}(1 + 2^{-2i})^{1/2}$ and $K^{(m/2)} =$

$\prod_{i=0}^{m/2}(1 + 2^{-2i})^{1/2}]$ is less than 2^{-m}, thus justifying the truncated version of CORDIC discussed in Section 22.5.

22.9 Scaling in CORDIC If in some step of the (generalized) CORDIC algorithm we multiply both x and y by a common factor, the algorithm will still converge but the result(s) would be larger than original values by the same factor. Such *scaling* steps can be inserted at will, provided the product of all scaling factors is maintained and used at the end to adjust the final results. In the special case that the product of all scaling factors is a power of 2, the final adjustment consists of a shifting operation. How can one use scaling steps to make $(K^{(m)})^2$, normally in $[1, K^2]$ for variable-factor CORDIC, converge to 4?

22.10 Circular CORDIC constant Show that the circular CORDIC constant K need not be recomputed for each word length k and that it can be derived by simply truncating a highly precise version to k bits. In other words, the first k bits of $K^{(k)}$ will not change if we compute it by multiplying more than k "expansion" terms to obtain $K^{(m)}$ for some $m > k$ [Vach87].

22.11 Composite CORDIC algorithms

  a. What would the final results be if the three output lines from the CORDIC computation box at the top left corner of Fig. 22.5 were directly connected to the three input lines of the box to its right?

  b. Repeat part a for the two linear CORDIC boxes of Fig. 22.5.

  c. Repeat part a for the two hyperbolic CORDIC boxes of Fig. 22.5.

22.12 Convergence of hyperbolic CORDIC To ensure the convergence of the hyperbolic version of CORDIC, certain steps must be performed twice. Consider the analogy of having to pay someone a sum z of money using bills and coins in the following denominations: $50, $20, $10, $5, $2, $1, $0.50, $0.25, $0.10, $0.05, and $0.01. The sum must be paid to within $0.01 (i.e., an error of $0.01 in either direction is acceptable). Every denomination must be used. For example, a $5 bill must be used, either in the form of payment or by way of refund.

  a. Prove or disprove that the goal can always be accomplished for $z \le \$100$ by giving or receiving each denomination exactly once and a few of them exactly twice.

  b. Add a minimum number of new denominations to the given list so that convergence is guaranteed with each denomination used exactly once.

22.13 Algebraic formulation of CORDIC An algebraic formulation of circular CORDIC iterations was presented in Section 22.6. Construct a similar formulation for the hyperbolic version of CORDIC.

22.14 Computing tan and cot via CORDIC The function $\tan z$ or $\cot z$, for $0 \le z < \pi/4$, can be computed by first using circular CORDIC iterations to find $\sin z$ and $\cos z$ and then performing a division. However, if we do not need $\sin z$ or $\cos z$ and are interested only in $\tan z$ or $\cot z$, we can use variable-factor CORDIC with no need to keep track of the expansion factor [Omon94].

  a. Use this method to compute $\tan 30°$.

  b. Use this method to compute $\cot 15°$.

    c. Estimate the worst-case absolute error in tan z if we stop after k iterations.

    d. Estimate the worst-case error in cot z if we stop after k iterations, and show that it can be quite large for $z \approx 0$.

22.15 **Redundant CORDIC algorithms** The values of x, y, and z in CORDIC computations can be represented in redundant form to speed up each iteration through carry-free addition. A problem that must be overcome is that the sign of a redundant value cannot be determined without full carry-propagation in the worst case. It has been suggested [Taka91] that an estimate of the sign be obtained by looking at a few bits of the redundant form, with the scale factor kept constant by (1) performing two rotations for every angle (possibly in opposite directions), and (2) inserting corrective iterations in some steps, the frequency of which is dependent on the accuracy of the sign estimation.

    a. Study the two methods and describe their implementation requirements.

    b. Compare the two methods with respect to speed and implementation cost.

22.16 **High-radix CORDIC algorithms** Study the issues involved in high-radix CORDIC algorithms and the differences between such algorithms with variable scale factor, constant scale factor, and constant scale factor that is forced to be a power of 2 [Lee92].

22.17 **Direct CORDIC method for inverse sine and cosine** The CORDIC equations [*] become $x^{(m)} = K \cos \theta$, $y^{(m)} = K \sin \theta$, and $z^{(m)} = -\theta$, where $\theta = -\sum \alpha^{(i)}$, if we start with $x = 1$, $y = 0$, and $z = 0$. To compute $\cos^{-1} u$, we pick the rotation directions (the digits d_i in $\{-1, 1\}$) such that x converges to Ku. Then, z will converge to $-\cos^{-1} u$. One way to make x converge to Ku is to compare $x^{(i)}$ to $K^{(i)}u$ at each step. If $x^{(i)} \geq K^{(i)}u$, we subtract from it; otherwise we add to it. The problem with this approach is that $K^{(i)}$ cannot be easily computed. However, if we perform each CORDIC pseudorotation exactly twice, the factor K will be replaced by K^2. Now, x must be compared to $(K^{(i)})^2 u$, a value that can be easily calculated in each step by using the recurrence $t^{(i+1)} = t^{(i)} + 2^{-2i} t^{(i)}$, with $t^{(0)} = u$ [Maze93].

    a. Supply the details of the algorithm for computing $\cos^{-1} u$, including the selection rule for d_i.

    b. Repeat part a for $\sin^{-1} u$.

    c. How do the methods of parts a and b compare to the methods shown in Fig. 22.5 for computing the $\sin^{-1}$ and $\cos^{-1}$ functions?

    d. Show that the iterations above can also lead to the computation of $\sqrt{1 - u^2}$.

    e. Show how a similar modification to generalized CORDIC iterations can be used for computing the $\sinh^{-1}$, $\cosh^{-1}$, and $\sqrt{1 + u^2}$ functions.

    f. Show that the use of double iterations extends the domain of convergence and that it leads to the need for extra iterations (how many?).

REFERENCES

[Dupr93] Duprat, J., and J.-M. Muller, "The CORDIC Algorithm: New Results for Fast VLSI Implementation," *IEEE Trans. Computers*, Vol. 42, No. 2, pp. 168–178, 1993.

[Lee92]   Lee, J.-A., and T. Lang, "Constant-Factor Redundant CORDIC for Angle Calculation and Rotation," *IEEE Trans. Computers*, Vol. 41, No. 8, pp. 1016–1025, 1992.

[Maze93]   Mazenc, C., X. Merrheim, and J.-M. Muller, "Computing Functions $\cos^{-1}$ and $\sin^{-1}$ Using CORDIC," *IEEE Trans. Computers*, Vol. 42, No. 1, pp. 118–122, 1993.

[Omon94]   Omondi, A.R., *Computer Arithmetic Systems: Algorithms, Architecture and Implementations*, Prentice Hall, 1994.

[Phat98]   Phatak, D.S., "Double Step Branching CORDIC: A New Algorithm for Fast Sine and Cosine Generation," *IEEE Trans. Computers*, Vol. 47, pp. 587–603, May 1998.

[Taka91]   Takagi, N., T. Asada, and S. Yajima, "Redundant CORDIC Methods with a Constant Scale Factor for Sine and Cosine Computations," *IEEE Trans. Computers*, Vol. 40, No. 9, pp. 989–995, 1991.

[Vach87]   Vachss, R., "The CORDIC Magnification Function," *IEEE Micro*, Vol. 7, No. 5, pp. 83–84, October 1987.

[Vold59]   Volder, J.E., "The CORDIC Trigonometric Computing Technique," *IRE Trans. Electronic Computers*, Vol. 8, pp. 330–334, September 1959.

[Walt71]   Walther, J.S., "A Unified Algorithm for Elementary Functions," *Proc. Spring Joint Computer Conf.*, 1971, pp. 379–385.

Chapter
23
VARIATIONS IN FUNCTION EVALUATION

The CORDIC method of Chapter 22 can be used to compute virtually all elementary functions of common interest. Now we turn to other schemes for evaluating some of the same functions. These alternate schemes may have advantages with certain implementation methods or technologies or may provide higher performance, given the availability of particular arithmetic operations as building blocks. In addition, we introduce the notion of merged arithmetic, a technique that allows us to optimize arithmetic computations at the level of bit manipulations as opposed to the word-level arithmetic found in CORDIC and other iterative methods. Chapter topics include:

23.1 ADDITIVE/MULTIPLICATIVE NORMALIZATION

We begin by introducing some terminology that is commonly used for characterizing iterative function evaluation methods. Recall from Section 16.1 that a general convergence method is characterized by two or three recurrences of the form:

$$u^{(i+1)} = f(u^{(i)}, v^{(i)}) \qquad u^{(i+1)} = f(u^{(i)}, v^{(i)}, w^{(i)})$$
$$v^{(i+1)} = g(u^{(i)}, v^{(i)}) \qquad v^{(i+1)} = g(u^{(i)}, v^{(i)}, w^{(i)})$$
$$w^{(i+1)} = h(u^{(i)}, v^{(i)}, w^{(i)})$$

Beginning with the initial values $u^{(0)}$, $v^{(0)}$, and perhaps $w^{(0)}$, we iterate such that one value, say u, converges to a constant; v and/or w then converge to the desired function(s). The iterations are performed a preset number of times based on the required precision, or a stopping rule may be applied to determine when the precision of the result is adequate.

Making u converge to a constant is sometimes referred to as "normalization." If u is normalized by adding a term to it in each iteration, the convergence method is said to be based on *additive normalization*. If a single multiplication is needed per iteration to normalize u, then we have a *multiplicative normalization* method. These two special classes of convergence methods are important in view of the availability of cost-effective fast adders and multipliers.

Of course, since multipliers are slower and more costly than adders, we try to avoid multiplicative normalization when additive normalization will do. However, multiplicative methods often offer faster convergence, thus making up for the slower steps by requiring fewer of them. Furthermore, when the multiplicative terms are of the form 1 ± 2^a, multiplication reduces to shift and add/subtract

$$u(1 \pm 2^a) = u \pm 2^a u$$

thus making multiplicative convergence just as fast as the additive schemes. Hence, both additive and multiplicative convergence are useful in practice.

The CORDIC computation algorithms of Chapter 22 use additive normalization. The rate of convergence for CORDIC is roughly one bit or digit per iteration. Thus, CORDIC is quite similar to digit-recurrence algorithms for division and square-rooting in terms of computation speed. Convergence division and reciprocation, discussed in Chapter 16, offer examples of multiplicative normalization. The rate of convergence is much higher for this class (e.g., quadratic). Trade-offs are often possible between the complexity of each iteration and the number of iterations. Redundant and high-radix CORDIC algorithms, mentioned in Section 22.5, provide good examples of such trade-offs.

In the next three sections, we examine convergence methods based on additive or multiplicative normalization for logarithm evaluation, exponentiation, and square-rooting. Similar convergence methods exist for evaluating many other functions of interest (e.g., reciprocals, cube roots, and trigonometric functions, both circular and hyperbolic).

23.2 COMPUTING LOGARITHMS

The logarithm function and its inverse (exponentiation) are important for many applications and, thus, various methods have been suggested for their evaluation. For example, these functions are needed for converting numbers to and from logarithmic number systems (Section 17.6). We begin by discussing a method for computing $\ln x$. The following equations define a convergence method based on multiplicative normalization in which multiplications are done by shift/add:

$$x^{(i+1)} = x^{(i)}c^{(i)} = x^{(i)}(1 + d_i 2^{-i}) \quad d_i \in \{-1, 0, 1\}$$
$$y^{(i+1)} = y^{(i)} - \ln c^{(i)} = y^{(i)} - \ln(1 + d_i 2^{-i})$$

where $\ln(1 + d_i 2^{-i})$ is read out from a table. Beginning with $x^{(0)} = x$ and $y^{(0)} = y$ and choosing the d_i digits such that $x^{(m)}$ converges to 1, we have, after m steps:

$$x^{(m)} = x \prod c^{(i)} \approx 1 \quad \Rightarrow \quad \prod c^{(i)} \approx 1/x$$
$$y^{(m)} = y - \sum \ln c^{(i)} = y - \ln \prod c^{(i)} \approx y + \ln x$$

So starting with $y = 0$ leads to the computation of $\ln x$. The domain of convergence for this algorithm is easily obtained:

$$\frac{1}{\prod(1 + 2^{-i})} \le x \le \frac{1}{\prod(1 - 2^{-i})} \quad \text{or} \quad 0.21 \le x \le 3.45$$

We need k iterations to obtain $\ln x$ with k bits of precision. The reason is that for large i, we have $\ln(1 \pm 2^{-i}) \approx \pm 2^{-i}$. Thus, the kth iteration changes the value of y by at most ulp and subsequent iterations have even smaller effects.

Clearly, the preceding method can be used directly for x in $[1, 2)$. Any value x outside $[1, 2)$ can be written as $x = 2^q s$, with $1 \le s < 2$. Then:

$$\begin{aligned} \ln x &= \ln(2^q s) = q \ \ln 2 + \ln s \\ &= 0.693\ 147\ 180\ q + \ln s \end{aligned}$$

The logarithm function in other bases can be computed just as easily. For example, base-2 logarithms are computed as follows:

$$\begin{aligned} \log_2 x &= \log_2(2^q s) = q + \log_2 s \\ &= q + \log_2 e \times \ln s = q + 1.442\ 695\ 041\ \ln s \end{aligned}$$

A radix-4 version of this algorithm can be easily developed. For this purpose, we begin with general, radix-r version of the preceding recurrences for x and y

$$\begin{aligned} x^{(i+1)} &= x^{(i)} b^{(i)} = x^{(i)}(1 + d_i r^{-i}) & d_i \in [-a, a] \\ y^{(i+1)} &= y^{(i)} - \ln b^{(i)} = y^{(i)} - \ln(1 + d_i r^{-i}) \end{aligned}$$

where $\ln(1 + d_i r^{-i})$ is read out from a table.

In practice, it is easier to deal with scaled values $u^{(i)} = r^i(x^{(i)} - 1)$. This scaled value must then be made to converge to 0, using comparisons of the magnitude of $u^{(i)}$ with a few constants to determine the next choice for d_i. The scaled versions of the radix-r recurrences are:

$$\begin{aligned} u^{(i+1)} &= r(u^{(i)} + d_i + d_i u^{(i)} r^{-i}) & d_i \in [-a, a] \\ y^{(i+1)} &= y^{(i)} - \ln(1 + d_i r^{-i}) \end{aligned}$$

The following selection rules apply to $d_i \in [-2, 2]$ for the radix-4 version of this algorithm

$$d_i = \begin{cases} 2 & \text{if } u \le -13/8 \\ 1 & \text{if } -13/8 < u \le -5/8 \\ 0 & \text{if } -5/8 < u < 5/8 \\ -1 & \text{if } 5/8 \le u < 13/8 \\ -2 & \text{if } u \ge 13/8 \end{cases}$$

provided u and y are initialized to $4(\delta x - 1)$ and $- \ln \delta$, respectively, with $\delta = 2$ if $1/2 \le x < 5/8$ and $\delta = 1$ if $5/8 \le x < 1$. For justification of the preceding rules, see [Omon94 pp. 410–412].

We next describe a clever method [Lo87] that requires the availability of a fast multiplier (actually a fast squarer would do). To compute base-2 logarithms, let $y = \log_2 x$ be a fractional number represented in binary as $(.y_{-1} y_{-2} \cdots y_{-l})_{\text{two}}$. Hence:

$$x = 2^y = 2^{(.y_{-1}y_{-2}y_{-3}\cdots y_{-l})_{\text{two}}}$$

$$x^2 = 2^{2y} = 2^{(y_{-1}.y_{-2}y_{-3}\cdots y_{-l})_{\text{two}}} \quad \Rightarrow \quad y_{-1} = 1 \text{ iff } x^2 \geq 2$$

Thus, computing x^2 and comparing the result to 2 allows us to determine the most significant bit y_{-1} of y. If $y_{-1} = 1$, then dividing both sides of the preceding equation by 2 yields:

$$\frac{x^2}{2} = \frac{2^{(1.y_{-2}y_{-3}\cdots y_{-l})_{\text{two}}}}{2} = 2^{(.y_{-2}y_{-3}\cdots y_{-l})_{\text{two}}}$$

Subsequent bits of y can be determined in a similar way. The complete procedure for computing $\log_2 x$ for $1 \leq x < 2$ is thus:

$$\begin{aligned}
&\text{for } i = 1 \text{ to } l \text{ do} \\
&\quad x := x^2 \\
&\quad \text{if } x \geq 2 \\
&\quad \text{then } y_{-i} = 1; \; x := x/2 \\
&\quad \text{else } y_{-i} = 0 \\
&\quad \text{endif} \\
&\text{endfor}
\end{aligned}$$

A hardware realization for the preceding algorithm is shown in Fig. 23.1.

Generalization to base-b logarithms is straightforward if one notes that $y = \log_b x$ implies:

$$x = b^y = b^{(.y_{-1}y_{-2}y_{-3}\cdots y_{-l})_{\text{two}}}$$

$$x^2 = b^{2y} = b^{(y_{-1}.y_{-2}y_{-3}\cdots y_{-l})_{\text{two}}} \quad \Rightarrow \quad y_{-1} = 1 \text{ iff } x^2 \geq b$$

Hence, the comparison with 2 in the base-2 version is replaced by a comparison with b for computing base-b logarithms. If $y_{-1} = 1$, then dividing both sides of the preceding equation by b allows us to iterate as before. However, since both comparison to b and division by b are in general more complicated, the method is of direct interest only for bases that are powers of 2. Note that logarithms in other bases are easily computed by scaling base-2 logarithms.

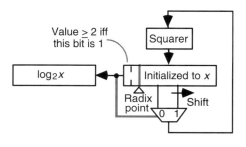

Fig. 23.1 Hardware elements needed for computing $\log_2 x$.

23.3 EXPONENTIATION

We begin by presenting a convergence method based on additive normalization for computing the exponential function e^x:

$$x^{(i+1)} = x^{(i)} - \ln c^{(i)} = x^{(i)} - \ln(1 + d_i 2^{-i})$$
$$y^{(i+1)} = y^{(i)} c^{(i)} = y^{(i)}(1 + d_i 2^{-i}) \quad d_i \in \{-1, 0, 1\}$$

As before, $\ln(1 + d_i 2^{-i})$ is read out from a table. If we choose the d_i digits such that x converges to 0, we have after m steps:

$$x^{(m)} = x - \sum \ln c^{(i)} \approx 0 \quad \Rightarrow \quad \sum \ln c^{(i)} \approx x$$
$$y^{(m)} = y \prod c^{(i)} = y\, e^{\ln \Pi c^{(i)}} = y\, e^{\Sigma \ln c^{(i)}} \approx y\, e^x$$

The domain of convergence for this algorithm is easily obtained:

$$\sum \ln(1 - 2^{-i}) \leq x \leq \sum \ln(1 + 2^{-i}) \quad \text{or} \quad -1.24 \leq x \leq 1.56$$

The algorithm requires k iterations to provide the result with k bits of precision. This is true because in the kth iteration, $\ln(1 \pm 2^{-k}) \approx \pm 2^{-k}$ is subtracted from x. The effect of all subsequent changes would be less than ulp. Half the k iterations can be eliminated by noting that for $\varepsilon^2 < ulp$, we have:

$$\ln(1 + \varepsilon) = \varepsilon - \varepsilon^2/2 + \varepsilon^3/3 - \cdots \approx \varepsilon$$

So when $x^{(j)} = 0.00 \cdots 00xx \cdots xx$, with $k/2$ leading zeros, we have $\ln(1 + x^{(j)}) \approx x^{(j)}$, allowing us to perform the computation step

$$x^{(j+1)} = x^{(j)} - x^{(j)} = 0$$
$$y^{(j+1)} = y^{(j)}(1 + x^{(j)})$$

to terminate the algorithm. This termination process replaces the remaining iterations with a single (true) multiplication.

Clearly, the preceding method can be used directly for x in $(-1, 1)$. Any value x outside $(-1, 1)$ can be written as $2^q s$, for $-1 < s < 1$ and some integer q. Then, the following equality, where squaring or square-rooting is done $|q|$ times, will hold:

$$e^x = (e^s)^{2^q} = ((\cdots (e^s)^2 \cdots)^2)^2 \quad \text{if } q \geq 0$$
$$= \sqrt{\sqrt{\cdots \sqrt{e^s}}} \quad \text{if } q < 0$$

A more efficient method is as follows. Rewrite x as $x\,(\log_2 e)(\ln 2)$ and let $x(\log_2 e) = h + f$, with h an integer and f a fraction. Then:

$$e^x = e^{(x \log_2 e)\ln 2} = e^{(h+f)\ln 2}$$
$$= e^{h \ln 2} e^{f \ln 2} = 2^h\, e^{f \ln 2}$$

Hence, one can premultiply x by $\log_2 e = 1.442\ 695\ 041 \cdots$ to obtain h and f, multiply f by $\ln 2 = 0.693\ 147\ 180 \cdots$ to get $u = f \ln 2$, and then compute $2^h e^u$ by using the exponential algorithm followed by shifts (or exponent adjustment).

A radix-4 version of the algorithm for computing e^x can be easily developed. Again, begin with the general radix-r version of the recurrences for x and y:

$$x^{(i+1)} = x^{(i)} - \ln c^{(i)} = x^{(i)} - \ln(1 + d_i r^{-i})$$
$$y^{(i+1)} = y^{(i)} c^{(i)} = y^{(i)} (1 + d_i r^{-i}) \qquad d_i \in [-a, a]$$

where $\ln(1 + d_i r^{-i})$ is read out from a table. As for the radix-4 natural logarithm function, we convert the two recurrences to include scaled values $u^{(i)} = r^i x^{(i)}$, comparing the magnitude of $u^{(i)}$ with a few constants to determine the next choice for d_i. Scaled versions of the radix-r recurrences for the exponential function are:

$$u^{(i+1)} = r(u^{(i)} - r^i \ln(1 + d_i r^{-i}))$$
$$y^{(i+1)} = y^{(i)} + d_i r^{-i} y^{(i)} \qquad d_i \in [-a, a]$$

Assuming $d_i \in [-2, 2]$, selection rules for the radix-4 version of this algorithm are:

$$d_i = \begin{cases} 2 & \text{if } u \le -11/8 \\ 1 & \text{if } -11/8 < u \le -3/8 \\ 0 & \text{if } -3/8 < u < 3/8 \\ -1 & \text{if } 3/8 \le u < 11/8 \\ -2 & \text{if } u \ge 11/8 \end{cases}$$

provided u and y are initialized to $4(x - \delta)$ and e^δ, respectively, with $\delta = -1/2$ if $x < -1/4$, $\delta = 0$ if $-1/4 \le x < 1/4$, and $\delta = 1/2$ if $x \ge 1/4$. For justification of the preceding rules, see [Omon94, pp. 413–415].

The general exponentiation function x^y can be computed by noting that:

$$x^y = (e^{\ln x})^y = e^{y \ln x}$$

Thus, general exponentiation can be performed by combining the logarithm and exponential functions, separated by a single multiplication.

When y is a positive integer, exponentiation can be done by repeated multiplication. In particular, when y is a constant, the methods used are reminiscent of multiplication by constants as discussed in Section 9.5. This method will lead to better accuracy, since in the preceding approach, the errors in evaluating the logarithm and exponential functions add up.

As an example, we can compute x^{25} using the identity

$$x^{25} = ((((x)^2 x)^2)^2)^2 x$$

which implies four squarings and two multiplications. Noting that

$$25 = (1\ 1\ 0\ 0\ 1)_{\text{two}}$$

leads us to a general procedure. To raise x to the power y, where y is a positive integer, initialize the partial result to 1. Scan the binary representation of y starting with its most significant bit. If the current bit is 1, multiply the partial result by x; if the current bit is 0, do not change the partial result. In either case, square the partial result before the next step (if any).

Methods similar to those used to obtain more efficient routines for multiplication by certain constants are applicable here. For example, to compute x^{15}, the preceding method involves three squarings and three multiplications (four if the redundant multiplication by 1 is not avoided):

$$x^{15} = ((((x)^2)x)^2x)^2x$$

Applying Booth's recoding $15 = (1\ 1\ 1\ 1)_{\text{two}} = (1\ 0\ 0\ 0\ \text{-}1)_{\text{two}}$ leads to the computation of x^{15} using three squarings and one division. Taking advantage of the factorization $15 = 3 \times 5$ leads to three squarings and two multiplications, provided the value of x^3 can be stored in a temporary register:

$$w = x^3 = (x)^2x \quad \text{and} \quad x^{15} = \big(((w)^2)^2\big)w$$

For $y = dq + s$, we can write:

$$w = x^y = x^s(x^d)^q$$

Thus, if we compute x^d in an extra register z and initialize w to x^s, the problem is converted to computing z^q. Details of this divide-and-conquer scheme are given elsewhere [Walt98].

23.4 DIVISION AND SQUARE-ROOTING, AGAIN

In Chapter 16, we examined a convergence method based on multiplicative normalization for computing the quotient $q = z/d$. The digit-recurrence division schemes of Chapters 13–15, are essentially additive normalization methods, where the partial remainder s is made to converge to 0 as q converges z/d. CORDIC division also falls in the additive normalization category. At this point, it is instructive to examine a broader formulation of division via additive normalization.

Let z and d be the dividend and divisor, respectively. Then, the following recurrences compute the quotient $q = z/d$ and the remainder s:

$$s^{(i+1)} = s^{(i)} - \gamma^{(i)} \times d \qquad \text{Set } s^{(0)} = z \text{ and make } s^{(m)} \text{ converge to 0}$$
$$q^{(i+1)} = q^{(i)} + \gamma^{(i)} \qquad\qquad \text{Set } q^{(0)} = 0 \text{ and find } q = q^{(m)}$$

The preceding formulation is quite general and can be tailored to form a wide array of useful, and not so useful, division schemes. For example, given integer operands z and d, we can choose $\gamma^{(i)}$ to be $+1$ or -1, depending on whether z and d have identical or opposing signs. The resulting algorithm, which is often assigned as an exercise to help novice programmers master the notion of loop, is too slow for general use. However, if z is in a very limited range, say $0 \le z < 2d$ as in addition modulo d, this is the algorithm of choice.

Since $s^{(i)}$ becomes successively smaller as it converges to 0, a scaled version of the recurrences, where $s^{(i)}$ now stands for $s^{(i)}r^i$ and $q^{(i)}$ for $q^{(i)}r^i$, is often used. Assuming fractional dividend z and divisor $d (0 \le z, d < 1)$ we have:

$$s^{(i+1)} = rs^{(i)} - \gamma^{(i)} \times d \qquad \text{Set } s^{(0)} = z \text{ and keep } s^{(i)} \text{ bounded}$$
$$q^{(i+1)} = rq^{(i)} + \gamma^{(i)} \qquad\qquad \text{Set } q^{(0)} = 0 \text{ and find } q^* = q^{(m)}r^{-m}$$

Note, in particular, that in this general version of the division recurrence based on additive normalization, the term $\gamma^{(i)}$ does not have to be a quotient "digit"; rather, it can be any estimate for

$$r(r^{i-m}q - q^{(i)}) = r(r^i q^* - q^{(i)})$$

where $r^{-m}q$ is the true quotient q^*. If $\gamma^{(i)}$ is indeed the quotient digit q_{-i-1}, then the addition required to compute $rq^{(i)} + \gamma^{(i)}$ is simplified (it turns into concatenation). See [Erce94] for a thorough treatment of digit-recurrence algorithms for division and square-rooting.

As in the case of division, we have already seen three approaches to square-rooting. One approach, based on digit-recurrence (division-like) algorithms, was discussed in Section 21.2 (radix 2, restoring), Section 21.3 (radix 2, nonrestoring), and Section 21.4 (high radix). The second approach using convergence methods, including those based on Newton–Raphson iteration, was covered in Section 21.5. The third approach, based on CORDIC, was introduced in Section 22.5. Here, we will see still other convergence algorithms for square-rooting based on additive and multiplicative normalization.

An algorithm based on multiplicative normalization can be developed by noting that if z is multiplied by a sequence of values $(c^{(i)})^2$, chosen such that the product converges to 1, then z multiplied by the $c^{(i)}$ values converges to $\sqrt{z}$, since:

$$z \prod (c^{(i)})^2 \approx 1 \quad \Rightarrow \quad \prod c^{(i)} \approx 1/\sqrt{z} \quad \Rightarrow \quad z \prod c^{(i)} \approx \sqrt{z}$$

So, one can initialize $x^{(0)}$ and $y^{(0)}$ to z and use the following iterations:

$$x^{(i+1)} = x^{(i)}(1 + d_i 2^{-i})^2 = x^{(i)}(1 + 2d_i 2^{-i} + d_i^2\, 2^{-2i})$$
$$y^{(i+1)} = y^{(i)}(1 + d_i 2^{-i})$$

Devising rules for selecting d_i from the set $\{-1, 0, 1\}$ completes the algorithm. Basically, $d_i = 1$ is selected for $x^{(i)} < 1 - \varepsilon$ and $d_i = -1$ is selected for $x^{(i)} > 1 + \varepsilon$, where $\varepsilon = \alpha 2^{-i}$ is suitably picked to guarantee convergence. To avoid different comparison constants in different steps, $x^{(i)}$ is replaced by its scaled form $u^{(i)} = 2^i(x^{(i)} - 1)$, leading to the iterations:

$$u^{(i+1)} = 2(u^{(i)} + 2d_i) + 2^{-i+1}(2d_i u^{(i)} + d_i^2) + 2^{-2i+1}d_i^2 u^{(i)}$$
$$y^{(i+1)} = y^{(i)}(1 + d_i 2^{-i})$$

Then, selection of d_i in each step will be based on uniform comparisons with $\pm \alpha$. The radix-4 version of this square-rooting algorithm, with d_i in $[-2, 2]$, or equivalently in $\{-1, -1/2, 0, 1/2, 1\}$, has also been proposed and analyzed. The radix-4 algorithm requires comparison constants $\pm \alpha$ and $\pm \beta$. For details of the radix-2 and radix-4 algorithms, including the choice of the comparison constants, the reader is referred to [Omon94, pp. 380–385].

Similarly, an algorithm based on additive normalization uses the property that if a sequence of values $c^{(i)}$ can be obtained with $z - (\sum c^{(i)})^2$ converging to 0, then $\sqrt{z}$ is approximated by $\sum c^{(i)}$. Letting $c^{(i)} = -d_i 2^{-i}$ with d_i in $\{-1, 0, 1\}$, we derive:

$$x^{(i+1)} = z - (y^{(i+1)})^2 = z - (y^{(i)} + c^{(i)})^2$$
$$= x^{(i)} + 2d_i y^{(i)} 2^{-i} - d_i^2 2^{-2i}$$
$$y^{(i+1)} = y^{(i)} + c^{(i)} = y^{(i)} - d_i 2^{-i}$$

Initial values for this algorithm are $x^{(0)} = z$ and $y^{(0)} = 0$. The choice of the d_i digit in $\{-1, 0, 1\}$ must ensure that $|x|$ is reduced in every step. Comparison with the constants $\pm \alpha 2^{-i}$ is one way to ensure convergence. As usual, to make the comparison constants the same for all steps, we rewrite $x^{(i)}$ as $2^{-i} u^{(i)}$, leading to:

$$u^{(i+1)} = 2(u^{(i)} + 2d_i y^{(i)} - d_i^2 2^{-i})$$

$$y^{(i+1)} = y^{(i)} - d_i 2^{-i}$$

Selection of the digit d_i in each step is then based on uniform comparison with $\pm \alpha$. Again, speed can be gained by using the radix-4 version of this algorithm, with d_i in $[-2, 2]$, or equivalently in $\{-1, -1/2, 0, 1/2, 1\}$. For details of both the radix-2 and the radix-4 algorithms, including a discussion of their convergence and choice of the required comparison constants, see [Omon94, pp. 385–389].

23.5 USE OF APPROXIMATING FUNCTIONS

The problem of evaluating a given function f can be converted to that of evaluating a different function g that approximates f, perhaps with a small number of pre- and postprocessing operations to bring the operands within appropriate ranges for g, to scale the results, or to minimize the effects of computational errors.

Since polynomial evaluation involves only additions and multiplications, the use of approximating polynomials can lead to efficient computations when a fast multiplier is available. Polynomial approximations can be obtained based on various schemes (e.g., Taylor–Maclaurin series expansion).

The Taylor series expansion of $f(x)$ about $x = a$ is

$$f(x) = \sum_{j=0}^{\infty} f^{(j)}(a) \frac{(x-a)^j}{j!}$$

The error that results from omitting all terms of degree greater than m is:

$$f^{(m+1)}(a + \mu(x - a)) \frac{(x-a)^{m+1}}{(m+1)!} \qquad 0 < \mu < 1$$

Setting $a = 0$ yields the Maclaurin–series expansion

$$f(x) = \sum_{j=0}^{\infty} f^{(j)}(0) \frac{x^j}{j!}$$

and its corresponding error bound:

$$f^{(m+1)}(\mu x) \frac{x^{m+1}}{(m+1)!} \qquad 0 < \mu < 1$$

Table 23.1 shows approximating polynomials, obtained from Taylor–Maclaurin series expansions, for some functions of interest. Others can be easily derived or looked up in standard mathematical handbooks.

The particular polynomial chosen affects the number of terms to be included for a given precision and thus the computational complexity. For example, if $\ln x$ is to be computed where x is fairly close to 1, the polynomial given in Table 23.1 in terms of $y = 1 - x$, which is the Maclaurin series expansion of $\ln(1 - y)$, converges rapidly and constitutes a good approximating function for $\ln x$. However, if $x \approx 2$, say, we have $y \approx -1$. A very large number of terms must be included to get $\ln x$ with about 32 bits of precision. In this latter case, the expansion in terms of $z = (x - 1)/(x + 1)$, which is derived from the Maclaurin series for $\ln[(1 + z)/(1 - z)]$, is much more efficient, since $z = (x - 1)/(x + 1) \approx 1/3$.

Evaluating an mth-degree polynomial may appear to be quite difficult. However, we can use Horner's method

$$f(y) = c^{(m)} y^m + c^{(m-1)} y^{m-1} + \cdots + c^{(1)} y + c^{(0)}$$
$$= ((c^{(m)} y + c^{(m-1)}) y + \cdots + c^{(1)}) y + c^{(0)}$$

to efficiently evaluate an mth-degree polynomial by means of m multiply-add steps. The coefficients $c^{(i)}$ for some of the approximating polynomials in Table 23.1 are relatively simple functions of i that can be stored in tables or computed on the fly [e.g., $1/(2i + 1)$ for $\ln x$ or $\tanh^{-1} x$]. For other polynomials, the coefficients are more complicated but can be incrementally evaluated based on previously computed values: for example, $c^{(i)} = c^{(i-1)}/[2i(2i + 1)]$ for $\sin x$ or $\sinh x$.

A divide-and-conquer strategy, similar to that used for synthesizing larger multipliers from smaller ones (see Section 12.1), can be used for general function evaluation. Let x in $[0, 4)$ be the $(l + 2)$-bit significand of a floating-point number or its shifted version. Divide x into two chunks x_H and x_L (the high and low parts):

TABLE 23.1
Polynomial approximations for some useful functions

Function	Polynomial approximation	Conditions
$1/x$	$1 + y + y^2 + y^3 + \cdots + y^i + \cdots$	$0 < x < 2$ and $y = 1 - x$
$\sqrt{x}$	$1 - \frac{1}{2}y - \frac{1}{2\times4}y^2 - \frac{1\times3}{2\times4\times6}y^3 - \cdots - \frac{1\times3\times5\times\cdots\times(2i-3)}{2\times4\times6\times\cdots\times2i}y^i - \cdots$	$y = 1 - x$
e^x	$1 + \frac{1}{1!}x + \frac{1}{2!}x^2 + \frac{1}{3!}x^3 + \cdots + \frac{1}{i!}x^i + \cdots$	
$\ln x$	$-y - \frac{1}{2}y^2 - \frac{1}{3}y^3 - \frac{1}{4}y^4 - \cdots - \frac{1}{i}y^i - \cdots$	$0 < x \le 2$ and $y = 1 - x$
$\ln x$	$2\left(z + \frac{1}{3}z^3 + \frac{1}{5}z^5 + \cdots + \frac{1}{2i+1}z^{2i+1} + \cdots\right)$	$x > 0$ and $z = (x - 1)/(x + 1)$
$\sin x$	$x - \frac{1}{3!}x^3 + \frac{1}{5!}x^5 - \frac{1}{7!}x^7 + \cdots + (-1)^i\frac{1}{(2i+1)!}x^{2i+1} + \cdots$	
$\cos x$	$1 - \frac{1}{2!}x^2 + \frac{1}{4!}x^4 - \frac{1}{6!}x^6 + \cdots + (-1)^i\frac{1}{(2i)!}x^{2i} + \cdots$	
$\tan^{-1} x$	$x - \frac{1}{3}x^3 + \frac{1}{5}x^5 - \frac{1}{7}x^7 + \cdots + (-1)^i\frac{1}{2i+1}x^{2i+1} + \cdots$	$-1 < x < 1$
$\sinh x$	$x + \frac{1}{3!}x^3 + \frac{1}{5!}x^5 + \frac{1}{7!}x^7 + \cdots + \frac{1}{(2i+1)!}x^{2i+1} + \cdots$	
$\cosh x$	$1 + \frac{1}{2!}x^2 + \frac{1}{4!}x^4 + \frac{1}{6!}x^6 + \cdots + \frac{1}{(2i)!}x^{2i} + \cdots$	
$\tanh^{-1} x$	$x + \frac{1}{3}x^3 + \frac{1}{5}x^5 + \frac{1}{7}x^7 + \cdots + \frac{1}{2i+1}x^{2i+1} + \cdots$	$-1 < x < 1$

$$x = x_H + 2^{-t}x_L \qquad 0 \le x_H < 4 \qquad 0 \le x_L < 1$$
$$t + 2 \text{ bits} \qquad l - t \text{ bits}$$

The Taylor series expansion of $f(x)$ about $x = x_H$ is

$$f(x) = \sum_{j=0}^{\infty} f^{(j)}(x_H) \frac{(2^{-t}x_L)^j}{j!}$$

where $f^{(j)}(x)$ is the jth derivative of $f(x)$, with the 0th derivative being $f(x)$ itself. If one takes just the first two terms, a linear approximation is obtained

$$f(x) \approx f(x_H) + 2^{-t}x_L f'(x_H)$$

In practice, only a few terms are needed, since as j becomes large, $2^{-jt}/j!$ rapidly diminishes in magnitude. If t is not too large, the evaluation of f and/or f' (as well as subsequent derivatives of f, if needed) can be done by table lookup. Examples of such table-based methods are presented in Chapter 24.

Functions can be approximated in many other ways (e.g., by the ratio of two polynomials with suitably chosen coefficients). For example, it has been suggested that good results can be obtained for many elementary functions if we approximate them using the ratio of two fifth-degree polynomials [Kore90]:

$$f(x) \approx \frac{a^{(5)}x^5 + a^{(4)}x^4 + a^{(3)}x^3 + a^{(2)}x^2 + a^{(1)}x + a^{(0)}}{b^{(5)}x^5 + b^{(4)}x^4 + b^{(3)}x^3 + b^{(2)}x^2 + b^{(1)}x + b^{(0)}}$$

When Horner's method for evaluating the numerator and the denominator is used, such a "rational approximation" needs 10 multiplications, 10 additions, and 1 division.

23.6 MERGED ARITHMETIC

The methods we have discussed thus far are based on building-block operations such as addition, multiplication, and shifting. When very high performance is needed, it is sometimes desirable, or even necessary, to build hardware structures to compute the function of interest directly without breaking it down into conventional operations. This "merged arithmetic" approach [Swar80] always leads to higher speed and often implies lower component count and power consumption as well. The drawback of starting from scratch is that designing, implementing, and testing of the corresponding algorithms and hardware structures may become difficult and thus more costly.

We have already seen several examples of merged arithmetic in the construction of additive multiply modules of Section 12.2 and combined multiply-add units of Section 12.6. In particular, Figs. 12.4 and 12.19 show how the required composite operations are synthesized at the bit level rather than through the use of standard word-level arithmetic building blocks.

Here, we illustrate the power of merged arithmetic through an additional example. Suppose that the inner product of two three-element vectors must be computed and the result added to an initial value. The computation, written as

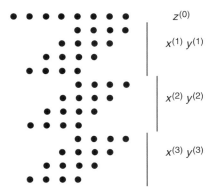

$z^{(0)}$

$x^{(1)} y^{(1)}$

$x^{(2)} y^{(2)}$

$x^{(3)} y^{(3)}$

Fig. 23.2   Merged arithmetic computation of an inner product followed by accumulation.

		1	4	7	10	13	10	7	4	16 FAs
		2	4	6	8	8	6	4	2	10 FAs + 1 HA
		3	4	4	6	6	3	3	1	9 FAs
1	2	3	4	4	3	2	1	1		4 FAs + 1 HA
1	3	2	3	3	2	1	1	1		3 FAs + 2 HAs
2	2	2	2	2	1	1	1	1		5-bit CPA

Fig. 23.3   Tabular representation of the dot matrix for inner-product computation and its reduction.

$$z = z^{(0)} + x^{(1)} y^{(1)} + x^{(2)} y^{(2)} + x^{(3)} y^{(3)}$$

involves three multiplications and three additions if broken down into conventional word-level operations. However, one can also compute the result directly as a function of the seven operands ($8k$ Boolean variables for k-bit vector elements and a $2k$-bit $z^{(0)}$), provided the partial results $x^{(1)} y^{(1)}$, $x^{(2)} y^{(2)}$, and $x^{(3)} y^{(3)}$ are not needed for other purposes.

Figure 23.2 shows the computation in dot notation if $x^{(i)}$ and $y^{(i)}$ are 4-bit unsigned numbers and $z^{(0)}$ is an 8-bit unsigned number. This matrix of partial products, or dots, can be reduced using the methods discussed for the design of tree multipliers (e.g., by using the Wallace or the Dadda method). Figure 23.3 is a tabular representation of the reduction process for our example. The numbers in the first row are obtained by counting the number of dots in each column of Fig. 23.2. Subsequent rows are obtained by Wallace's reduction method.

The critical path of the resulting merged arithmetic circuit goes through one 2-input AND gate, 5 full adders, and a 5-bit carry-propagate adder: the cost is 48 AND gates, 46 FAs, 4 HAs, and a 5-bit adder—considerably less than the corresponding parameters if three separate 4×4 multipliers were implemented and their results added to the 8-bit input $z^{(0)}$.

PROBLEMS

23.1   **Alternate view of convergence algorithms**   Given a function $z = f(x)$, a convergence algorithm for evaluating $c = f(a)$ can be constructed based on the following observations. Suppose we introduce an additional variable y and a convergence function $F(x, y)$ with the following three properties: (1) there is a known initiation value $y = b$ such that $F(a, b) = f(a)$; (2) a given pair of values $(x^{(i)}, y^{(i)})$ can be conveniently transformed to the new pair $(x^{(i+1)}, y^{(i+1)})$ such that $F(x^{(i)}, y^{(i)}) = F(x^{(i+1)}, y^{(i+1)})$; that is, the value of F is invariant under the transformation; and (3) there exists a constant d, such that $F(d, y) = y$ for all y. Thus, if we make x converge to d, y will converge to $c = f(a)$, given the invariance of $F(x, y)$ under the transformation [Chen72].

a. Provide a geometric interpretation of the process above in the three-dimensional xyz space. *Hint:* Use the $x = a$, $y = b$, and $z = c$ planes.

b. Show that the convergence function $F(x, y) = y/\sqrt{x}$ can be used to compute $f(x) = \sqrt{x}$ and derive the needed transformations $x^{(i+1)} = \varphi(x^{(i)}, y^{(i)})$ and $y^{(i+1)} = \psi(x^{(i)}, y^{(i)})$.

c. Repeat part b for $F(x, y) = y + \ln x$ and $f(x) = \ln x$.

d. Repeat part b for $F(x, y) = ye^x$ and $f(x) = e^x$.

e. Derive $F(x, y)$ and its associated transformation rules for computing the reciprocal function $f(x) = 1/x$.

23.2   Computing natural logarithms

a. Compute $\ln 2$ with 8 bits of precision using the radix-2 convergence algorithm based on multiplicative normalization given at the beginning of Section 23.2.

b. Repeat part a using a radix-4 version of the algorithm.

c. Repeat part a using the method based on squaring discussed near the end of Section 23.2. *Hint:* $\ln 2 = 1/\log_2 e$.

d. Compare the results of parts a–c and discuss.

23.3   Computing base-2 logarithms Compute the base-2 logarithm of $x = (1.0110\ 1101)_{\text{two}}$ with 8 bits of precision using:

a. Radix-2 convergence algorithm based on multiplicative normalization given at the beginning of Section 23.2.

b. Radix-4 version of the algorithm of part a.

c. The method based on squaring discussed near the end of Section 23.2.

23.4   Computing base-2 logarithms Here is an alternate method for computing $\log_2 x$ [Kost91]. A temporary variable y is initialized to x. For decreasing values of an index i, each time y is compared to 2^{2^i}. If y is greater than 2^{2^i}, the next digit of the logarithm is 1, and y is multiplied by 2^{-2^i}. Otherwise, the next digit is 0 and nothing is done.

a. Show that the algorithm is correct as described.

b. Use the algorithm to compute the base-2 logarithm of $x = (1.0110\ 1101)_{\text{two}}$.

c. Compare this new algorithm to radix-2 and radix-4 convergence methods, and to the method based on squaring (Section 23.2), with respect to speed and cost.

d. Can you generalize the algorithm to base-2^a logarithms? What about generalization to an arbitrary base b?

23.5   Computing the exponential function Compute $e^{0.5}$ with 8 bits of precision using:

a. Radix-2 convergence algorithm based on additive normalization given at the beginning of Section 23.3.

b. Radix-4 version of the algorithm of part a.

c. A convergence algorithm for square-rooting that you choose at will.

d. Compare the results of parts a–c and discuss.

23.6 **Exponentiation** Assuming that shift-and-add takes 1 time unit, multiplication 3 time units, and division 8 time units:

a. Devise an efficient algorithm for computing x^{30} using the method discussed near the end of Section 23.3.

b. Use the algorithm of part a to compute 0.99^{30}, with all intermediate values and results carrying eight fractional digits in radix 10.

c. Use the convergence algorithm of Section 23.3 to compute 0.99^{30}.

d. Compare the accuracy of the results and the computational complexity for the algorithms of parts b and c. Discuss.

23.7 **Modular exponentiation** Modular exponentiation—namely, the computation of x^y mod m, where x, y, and m are k-bit integers, k is potentially very large, and m is a prime number—plays an important role in some public-key cryptography.

a. Show how x^y mod m can be computed using k-bit arithmetic operations.

b. Show how the algorithm can be speeded up if Booth's recoding is used on y.

c. Can radix-4 modified Booth's recoding of the exponent lead to further speedup?

23.8 **Logarithmic multiplication/division** Discuss the feasibility of performing multiplication or division by computing the natural logarithms of the operands, performing an add/subtract operation, and finally computing the exponential function.

23.9 **Convergence division and reciprocation**

a. Consider the problem of computing $q = z/d$, where $1 \le z, d < 2$ and $1/2 < q < 2$, using a strategy similar to the binary search algorithm. The midpoint of $[0.5, 2]$ (viz., 1.25) is taken as an initial estimate for q. Multiplication and comparison then allow us to refine the interval containing q to $[0.5, 1.25]$ or $[1.25, 2]$. This refinement process continues until the interval is as narrow as the desired precision for q. Compare the preceding convergence method to other convergence division algorithms and discuss.

b. Devise an algorithm similar to that in part a for computing $1/d$ that uses interpolation for identifying the next point, instead of always taking the midpoint of the interval.

23.10 **Computing the generalized square-root function** Show that the following convergence computation scheme can lead to the computation of the generalized square-root function $\sqrt{x + y^2}$, provided $d_i = \text{sign}(x^{(i)} y^{(i)})$.

$$x^{(i+1)} = x^{(i)} - 2d_i 2^{-i} y^{(i)} - d_i^2 2^{-2i}$$

$$y^{(i+1)} = y^{(i)} + d_i 2^{-i}$$

23.11 Convergence algorithm for square-rooting In discussing the radix-4 convergence algorithm for square-rooting near the end of Section 23.4, we stated that the root digit set can be $[-2, 2]$ or $\{-1, -1/2, 0, 1/2, 1\}$. Discuss possible advantages of the latter digit set over the former and devise an algorithm for converting such a radix-4 number to standard binary.

23.12 Approximating functions

a. The polynomial approximation for $\tan^{-1} x$ given in Section 23.5 (Table 23.1) is valid only for $x^2 < 1$. Show how this approximation can be used within an algorithm to evaluate $\tan^{-1} x$ for all x. *Hint:* For $x^2 > 1$, $y = 1/x$ satisfies $y^2 < 1$.

b. When $|x|$ is close to 1, the preceding approximation converges slowly. How can one speed up the computation via the application of suitable pre- and postprocessing steps? *Hint:* $\tan(2x) = 2 \tan x/(1 - \tan^2 x)$.

c. Repeat part b for the function $\tanh^{-1} x$.

23.13 Approximating functions Derive approximating functions for $\sin^{-1} x$, $\cos^{-1} x$, $\sinh^{-1} x$, $\cosh^{-1} x$ based on Taylor–Maclaurin series expansions and compare the effort required for their evaluation with those based on indirect methods such as $\sin^{-1} x = \tan^{-1}(x/\sqrt{1 - x^2})$.

23.14 Approximating functions For each of the functions $f(x)$ below, use the approximating polynomial given in Table 23.1 and a convergence computation method of your choice to compute $f(0.75)$ to four decimal digits of precision. Compare the computational efforts expended and the results obtained. Discuss.

a. $1/x$

b. $\sqrt{x}$

c. e^x

d. $\ln x$

e. $\sin x$

f. $\tan^{-1} x$

g. $\sinh x$

23.15 Merged arithmetic operations Consider the computation $s = vw + xy + z$, where v, w, x, and y are k-bit integers and z is a $2k$-bit integer (all numbers are in 2's-complement format).

a. Prove that s can be represented correctly using $2k + 1$ bits.

b. Assuming $k = 4$, draw the partial products matrix for the entire computation in dot notation; 16 dots for each of the two multiplications and 8 dots for z, plus additional dots as required to take care of signed multiplication using the (modified) Baugh–Wooley method of Fig. 11.8d.

c. Use Wallace's method to reduce the matrix of dots in part b to only two rows.

d. Use Dadda's method to reduce the matrix of dots in part b to only two rows.

e. Derive the lengths of the final carry-propagate adders required in parts c and d.

> **f.** Compare the design of part c, with regard to delay and cost, to a design based on two 4×4 multipliers (separately designed using the Baugh–Wooley and Wallace methods), a single level of carry-save addition, and a final fast adder.
>
> **g.** Repeat part f, replacing Wallace's method with Dadda's method.
>
> **h.** Summarize the delay–cost comparisons of parts f and g in a table and discuss.
>
> **i.** Simplify the circuit of part d if it is to perform the computation $s = v^2 + x^2 + z$.

23.16 Merged arithmetic/logic operations Arithmetic operations can sometimes be merged with nonarithmetic functions to derive speed benefits. One example is merging the addition required for computing a cache memory address with the address decoding function in the cache [Lync98].

> **a.** Consider a small example of two 4-bit unsigned values added to find a 4-bit memory address and design the merged adder/decoder circuit.
>
> **b.** Compare the delay and cost of the design in part a to the respective parameters of a design with separate adder and decoder. Discuss.

REFERENCES

[Chen72] Chen, T.C., "Automatic Computation of Exponentials, Logarithms, Ratios and Square Roots," *IBM J. Research and Development*, Vol. 16, pp. 380–388, 1972.

[Erce73] Ercegovac, M.D., "Radix-16 Evaluation of Certain Elementary Functions," *IEEE Trans. Computers*, Vol. 22, No. 6, pp. 561–566, 1973.

[Erce94] Ercegovac, M.D., and T. Lang, *Division and Square Root: Digit-Recurrence Algorithms and Implementations*, Kluwer, 1994.

[Kore90] Koren, I., and O. Zinaty, "Evaluating Elementary Functions in a Numerical Coprocessor Based on Rational Approximations," *IEEE Trans. Computers*, Vol. 39, No. 8, pp. 1030–1037, 1990.

[Kost91] Kostopoulos, D.K., "An Algorithm for the Computation of Binary Logarithms," *IEEE Trans. Computers*, Vol. 40, No. 11, pp. 1267–1270, 1991.

[Lo87]   Lo, H.-Y., and J.-L. Chen, "A Hardwired Generalized Algorithm for Generating the Logarithm Base-k by Iteration," *IEEE Trans. Computers*, Vol. 36, No. 11, pp. 1363–1367, 1987.

[Lync98] Lynch, W.L., G. Lauterbach, and J.I. Chamdani, "Low Load Latency Through Sum-Addressed Memory," *Proc. Int. Symp. Computer Architecture*, 1998, pp. 369–379.

[Omon94] Omondi, A.R., *Computer Arithmetic Systems: Algorithms, Architecture, and Implementations*, Prentice-Hall, 1994.

[Swar80] Swartzlander, E.E., Jr., "Merged Arithmetic," *IEEE Trans. Computers*, Vol. 29, No. 10, pp. 946–950, 1980.

[Tang91] Tang, P.K.P., "Table Lookup Algorithms for Elementary Functions and Their Error Analysis," *Proc. 10th Symp. Computer Arithmetic*, 1991, pp. 232–236.

[Walt98] Walter, C. D., "Exponentiation Using Division Chains," *IEEE Trans. Computers*, Vol. 47, No. 7, pp. 757–765, 1998.

Chapter 24 | ARITHMETIC BY TABLE LOOKUP

In earlier chapters we saw how table lookup can be used as an aid in arithmetic computations. Examples include quotient digit selection in high-radix division, speedup of iterative division or reciprocation through an initial table-lookup step, and using tables to store constants of interest in CORDIC. In this chapter, we deal with the use of table lookup as a primary computational mechanism rather than in a supporting role.

24.1 DIRECT AND INDIRECT TABLE LOOKUP

Computation by table lookup is attractive because memory is much denser than random logic in VLSI realizations. Multimegabit lookup tables are already practical in some applications; even larger tables should become practical in the near future as memory densities continue to improve. The use of tables reduces the costs of hardware development (design, validation, testing), provides more flexibility for last-minute design changes, and reduces the number of different building blocks or modules required for arithmetic system design.

Tables stored in read-only memories (especially if individual entries or blocks of data are encoded in error-detecting or error-correcting codes) are more robust than combinational logic circuits, thus leading to improved reliability. With read/write memory and reconfigurable peripheral logic, the same building block can be used for evaluating many different functions by simply loading appropriate values in the table(s). This feature facilitates maintenance and repair.

Given an m-variable function $f(x_{m-1}, x_{m-2}, \cdots, x_1, x_0)$, the *direct table-lookup* evaluation of f requires the construction of a $2^u \times v$ table that holds for each combination of input values (needing a total of u bits to represent), the desired v-bit result. The u-bit string obtained from concatenating the input values is then used as an address into the table, with the v-bit value read out from the table directly forwarded to the output. Such an arrangement is quite flexible

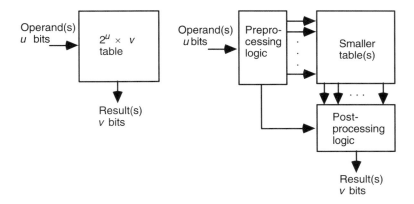

Fig. 24.1   Direct table lookup versus table-lookup with pre- and post-processing.

but unfortunately not very practical in most cases. For unary (single-variable) functions such as $1/x$, $\ln x$, or x^2, the table size remains manageable when the input operand is up to 12–16 bits; table size of 4K–16K words. Binary functions, such as xy, $x \bmod y$, or x^y, can be realized with table lookup only if the operands are very short (8 bits or less, say). For $m > 2$, the exponential growth of the table size becomes totally intolerable.

One solution to the exponential growth of the table size is to apply preprocessing steps to the operands and postprocessing steps to the value(s) read out from the table(s), leading to *indirect table lookup*. If both the pre- and postprocessing elements are simple and fast, this hybrid scheme (Fig. 24.1) may be more cost-effective than either the pure table-lookup approach or the pure logic circuit implementation based on the algorithms discussed in earlier chapters. In a multitable scheme, the tables can be physically separate (with identical or different contents) or realized by multiple accesses to the same table. We explore some such hybrid schemes in the rest of this chapter.

As stated earlier, in contrast to the applications discussed already, in which small tables were used for quotient digit selection, initial approximations, or storage of a few precomputed constants, our focus in this chapter is on the use of tables as primary computational mechanisms.

In reality, the boundary between the two uses of tables (in supporting or primary role) is quite fuzzy. We can visualize the pure logic and pure tabular approaches as extreme points in a continuum of hybrid solutions. In earlier discussions, we started with the goal of designing logic circuits for particular arithmetic computations and ended up using tables to facilitate or speed up certain computational steps. Here, we begin with the goal of a tabular implementation and finish by using peripheral logic circuits to reduce the table size, thus making the approach practical. Some of the intermediate solutions can be derived starting at either end point.

24.2 BINARY-TO-UNARY REDUCTION

One approach to reducing the table size is to evaluate a desired binary function by means of an auxiliary unary function. The unary function requires a smaller table (2^k vs. 2^{2k} entries, say), but its output obviously is not what we are after. However, pre- and postprocessing steps allow us to use the unary function table to compute our binary function. In this section, we review two well-known examples of this method.

We discussed an example of this approach in connection with logarithmic number systems in Section 18.6 To add the sign-and-logarithm numbers (Sx, Lx) and (Sy, Ly), representing $\pm x$ and $\pm y$ with $x \geq y \geq 0$, we need to compute the sign Sz of the result $\pm z$ and its logarithm $Lz = \log z = \log(x \pm y)$. The base of the logarithm is immaterial for this discussion, so we leave it unspecified. The computation of Lz can be transformed to finding the sum of Lx and a unary function of $\Delta = Ly - Lx$ using the following equality

$$
\begin{aligned}
Lz &= \log(x \pm y) = \log[x(1 \pm y/x)] \\
&= \log x + \log(1 \pm y/x) \\
&= Lx + \log(1 \pm \log^{-1} \Delta)
\end{aligned}
$$

where $\log^{-1} \Delta$ denotes the inverse logarithm function; that is, b^Δ if the base of the logarithm is b.

The required preprocessing steps involve identifying the input $\pm x$ with the larger logarithm (and thus the larger magnitude), determining the sign Sz of the result, and computing $\Delta = Ly - Lx$. Postprocessing consists of adding Lx to the value read out from the table. If the preprocessing, table access, and postprocessing steps are done by distinct hardware elements, a pipelined implementation may be possible for which the cycle time is dictated by the table access time. So, with many additions performed in sequence, the preceding scheme can be as fast as a pure tabular realization and thus considerably more cost-effective.

Our second example concerns multiplication by table lookup. Again, direct table lookup is infeasible in most practical cases. The following identity allows us to convert the problem to the evaluation of a unary function (in this case, squaring):

$$
xy = \frac{1}{4}[(x + y)^2 - (x - y)^2]
$$

The preprocessing steps consist of computing $x + y$ and $x - y$. Then, after two table lookups yielding $(x + y)^2$ and $(x - y)^2$, a subtraction and a 2-bit shift complete the computation. Again, pipelining can be used to reduce the time overhead of the peripheral logic. Several optimizations are possible for the preceding hybrid solution. For example, if a lower speed is acceptable, one squaring table can be used and consulted twice for finding $(x + y)^2$ and $(x - y)^2$. This would allow us to share the adder/subtractor hardware as well.

In either case, the following observation leads to hardware simplifications. Let x and y be k-bit 2's-complement integers (the same considerations apply to any fixed-point format). Then, $x + y$ and $x - y$ are $(k + 1)$-bit values, and a straightforward application of the preceding method would need one or two tables of size $2^{k+1} \times 2k$ (sign bit is not needed for table entries, since they are all positive). Closer scrutiny, however, reveals that $x + y$ and $x - y$ are both even or odd. Thus, the least significant two bits of $(x + y)^2$ and $(x - y)^2$ are identical (both are 00 or 01). Hence, these two bits always cancel each other out, with the resulting 0s shifted out in the final division by 4, and need not be stored in the tables. This feature reduces the required table size to $2^{k+1} \times (2k - 2)$ and eliminates the 2-bit shift.

The aforementioned reduction in table size is relatively insignificant, but it is achieved at no cost (in fact it improves the speed by eliminating the final shift step). A more significant factor-of-2 reduction in table size can be achieved with some peripheral overhead. Let ε denote the least significant bit of $x + y$ and $x - y$, where $\varepsilon \in \{0, 1\}$. Then:

$$\frac{x+y}{2} = \left\lfloor \frac{x+y}{2} \right\rfloor + \frac{\varepsilon}{2}$$

$$\frac{x-y}{2} = \left\lfloor \frac{x-y}{2} \right\rfloor + \frac{\varepsilon}{2}$$

Then, we can write:

$$\frac{1}{4}[(x+y)^2 - (x-y)^2] = \left(\left\lfloor \frac{x+y}{2} \right\rfloor + \frac{\varepsilon}{2} \right)^2 - \left(\left\lfloor \frac{x-y}{2} \right\rfloor + \frac{\varepsilon}{2} \right)^2$$

$$= \left\lfloor \frac{x+y}{2} \right\rfloor^2 - \left\lfloor \frac{x-y}{2} \right\rfloor^2 + \varepsilon y$$

Based on the preceding equality, upon computing $x + y$ and $x - y$, we can drop the least significant bit of each result, consult squaring tables of size $2^k \times (2k - 1)$, and then perform a three-operand addition, with the third operand being 0 or y depending on the dropped bit ε being 0 or 1. The postprocessing hardware then requires a carry-save adder (to reduce the three values to two) followed by a carry-propagate adder.

To use a single adder and one squaring table to evaluate the preceding three-operand sum, we simply initialize the result to εy and then overlap the first addition $\lfloor (x + y)/2 \rfloor^2 + \varepsilon y$ with the second table access, thus essentially hiding the delay of the extra addition resulting from the introduction of the new εy term.

The preceding is an excellent example of the trade-offs that frequently exist between table size and cost/delay of the required peripheral logic circuits in hybrid implementations using a mix of lookup tables and custom logic.

When the product xy is to be rounded to a k-bit number (as for fractional operands), the entries of the squaring table(s) can be shortened to k bits (again no sign is needed). The extra bit guarantees that the total error remains below *ulp*.

An additional optimization may be applicable to some unary function tables. Assume that a v-bit result is to be computed based on a k-bit operand. Let w bits of the result ($w < v$) depend only on l bits of the operand ($l < k$). Then a split-table approach can be used, with one table of size $2^l w$ providing w bits of the result and another of size $2^k (v - w)$ supplying the remaining $v - w$ bits. The total table size is reduced to $2^k v - (2^k - 2^l)w$, with the fraction of table size saved being:

$$\frac{(2^k - 2^l)w}{2^k v} = \frac{(1 - 2^{k-l})w}{v}$$

Application of this last optimization to squaring leads to additional savings in the table size for multiplication via squaring [Vinn95].

24.3 BIT-SERIAL AND DISTRIBUTED ARITHMETIC

The many advantages of bit-serial arithmetic were discussed in Section 12.3 in connection with bit-serial multipliers. Here, we discuss two examples of tabular implementation of bit-serial arithmetic that are used for entirely different reasons.

The first example is found in the processors of a massively parallel computer: the Connection Machine CM-2 of Thinking Machines Corporation. Even though CM-2 is no longer in production, its approach to bit-serial computation is quite interesting and potentially useful. CM-2 can have up to 64K processors, each one so simple that 16 processors fit on single IC chip. The processors are bit-serial because otherwise their parallel I/O and memory access requirements could not be satisfied within the pin limitations of a single chip. The design philosophy of CM-2 is that using a large number of slow, inexpensive processors is a cost-effective alternative to a small number of very fast, expensive processors. This is sometimes referred to as the "army of ants" approach to high-performance computing.

The ALU in a CM-2 processor receives three single-bit inputs and produces two single-bit outputs. For addition (e.g.), the three inputs can be the operand bits and the incoming carry, with the two outputs corresponding to the sum bit and the outgoing carry. To provide complete flexibility in programming other computations, CM-2 designers decided that the user should be able to specify each output of the ALU to be any arbitrary logic function of the three input bits. There are $2^{2^3} = 256$ such logic functions, leading to the requirement for an 8-bit op code. The remaining problem is how to encode the 256 functions within an 8-bit op code. The answer is strikingly simple: each of the 256 functions is completely characterized by its 8-bit truth table. So we can simply use the truth table for each function as the op code. Figure 24.2 shows the resulting ALU, which is nothing but two 8-to-1 multiplexers!

In the CM-2 ALU, two of the bit streams, say a and b, come from a 64K-bit memory and are read out in consecutive clock cycles. The third input, c, comes from a 4-bit "flags" register. Thus $16 + 16 + 2$ bits are required to specify the addresses of these operands. The f output is stored as a flag bit (2-bit address) and the g output replaces the a memory operand in a third clock cycle. Three more bits are used to specify a flag bit and a value (0 or 1) to conditionalize the operation, thus allowing some processors to selectively ignore the common instruction broadcast to all processors, but this aspect of the processor's design is not relevant to our discussion here.

To perform integer addition with the CM-2 ALU shown in Fig. 24.2, the a and b operands will correspond to the two numbers to be added, and c will be a flag bit that is used to hold the carry from one bit position into the next. The f function op code will be "00010111" (majority or $ab + bc + ca$) and the g function op code will be "01010101" (three-input XOR). A k-bit addition requires $3k$ clock cycles and is thus quite slow. But up to 64K additions can be performed in parallel. As for floating-point arithmetic, bit-serial computation (which was used in CM-1) is too slow. So, designers of CM-2 provided floating-point accelerator chips that are shared by 32 processors.

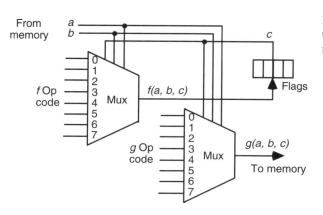

Fig. 24.2 Bit-serial ALU with two tables implemented as multiplexers.

Programming bit-serial arithmetic operations is a tedious and error-prone task. However, it is an easy matter to build useful "macros" that are made available to machine-language programmers of CM-2 and other bit-serial machines. These programmers then do not need to worry about coding the details of bit-serial arithmetic for such routine computations as integer addition, integer multiplication, or their floating-point counterparts. The use of bit-level instructions will then be required only for special operations or for hand-optimization of critical operations in the inner loops of computation-intensive algorithms.

Our second example concerns the implementation of a digital filter, but the method is applicable to computing any linear function of several variables. Consider a second-order digital filter characterized by the equation

$$y^{(i)} = a^{(0)}x^{(i)} + a^{(1)}x^{(i-1)} + a^{(2)}x^{(i-2)} - b^{(1)}y^{(i-1)} - b^{(2)}y^{(i-2)}$$

where the $a^{(j)}$s and $b^{(j)}$s are constants, $x^{(i)}$ is the filter input at time step i, and $y^{(i)}$ is the filter output at time step i. Such a filter is useful in itself and may also be a component in a more complex filter.

Expanding the equation for $y^{(i)}$ in terms of the individual bits of the 2's-complement operands $x = (x_0.x_{-1}x_{-2}\cdots x_{-l})_{\text{two}}$ and $y = (y_0.y_{-1}y_{-2}\cdots y_{-l})_{\text{two}}$, we get:

$$y^{(i)} = a^{(0)}\left(-x_0^{(i)} + \sum_{j=-l}^{-1} 2^j x_j^{(i)}\right) + a^{(1)}\left(-x_0^{(i-1)} + \sum_{j=-l}^{-1} 2^j x_j^{(i-1)}\right)$$

$$+ a^{(2)}\left(-x_0^{(i-2)} + \sum_{j=-l}^{-1} 2^j x_j^{(i-2)}\right) - b^{(1)}\left(-y_0^{(i-1)} + \sum_{j=-l}^{-1} 2^j y_j^{(i-1)}\right)$$

$$- b^{(2)}\left(-y_0^{(i-2)} + \sum_{j=-l}^{-1} 2^j y_j^{(i-2)}\right)$$

Define $f(s, t, u, v, w) = a^{(0)}s + a^{(1)}t + a^{(2)}u - b^{(1)}v - b^{(2)}w$, where $s, t, u, v,$ and w are single-bit variables. If the coefficients are m-bit constants, then each of the 32 possible values for f is representable in $m + 3$ bits, as it is the sum of five m-bit operands. These 32 values can be precomputed and stored in a $32 \times (m + 3)$-bit table.

Using the function f, we can rewrite the expression for $y^{(i)}$ as follows:

$$y^{(i)} = \sum_{j=-l}^{-1} 2^j f\left(x_j^{(i)}, x_j^{(i-1)}, x_j^{(i-2)}, y_j^{(i-1)}, y_j^{(i-2)}\right)$$

$$- f\left(x_0^{(i)}, x_0^{(i-1)}, x_0^{(i-2)}, y_0^{(i-1)}, y_0^{(i-2)}\right)$$

Figure 24.3 shows a hardware unit for computing this last expression with bit-serial input and output. The value of $y^{(i)}$ is accumulated in the s register as $y^{(i-1)}$ is output from the output shift register. At the end of the cycle, the result in the s register is loaded into the output shift register, s is reset to 0, and a new accumulation cycle begins. The output bit $y_j^{(i-1)}$ is supplied to the ROM as an address bit. A second shift register at the output side supplies the corresponding bit $y_j^{(i-2)}$ of the preceding output. At the input side, $x^{(i)}$ is processed on the fly, and two shift registers are used to supply the corresponding bits of the two preceding inputs, $x^{(i-1)}$ and $x^{(i-2)}$, to the 32-entry table.

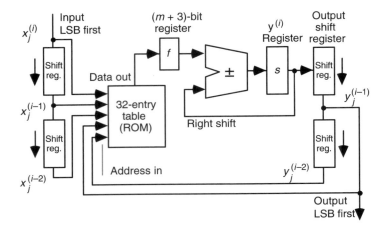

Fig. 24.3   Bit-serial tabular realization of a second-order filter.

Structures similar to that shown in Fig. 24.3 are useful for computing many other functions. For example, if $(x + y + z) \bmod m$ is to be computed for integer-valued operands x, y, z and a modulus m, then the residues of 2^i, 2×2^i, and 3×2^i can be stored in a table for different values of i. The bits x_i, y_i, z_i, and the index i are used to derive an address from which the value of $2^i(x_i + y_i + z_i) \bmod m$ is read out and added to the modulo-m running total.

24.4 INTERPOLATING MEMORY

If the value of a function $f(x)$ is known for $x = x_{\text{lo}}$ and $x = x_{\text{hi}}$, where $x_{\text{lo}} < x_{\text{hi}}$, the function's value for x in the interval $[x_{\text{lo}}, x_{\text{hi}}]$ can be computed from $f(x_{\text{lo}})$ and $f(x_{\text{hi}})$ by interpolation. The simplest method is linear interpolation where $f(x)$ for x in $[x_{\text{lo}}, x_{\text{hi}}]$ is computed as follows:

$$f(x) = f(x_{\text{lo}}) + \frac{(x - x_{\text{lo}})[f(x_{\text{hi}}) - f(x_{\text{lo}})]}{x_{\text{hi}} - x_{\text{lo}}}$$

On the surface, evaluating this expression requires four additions, one multiplication, and one division. However, by choosing the end points x_{lo} and x_{hi} to be consecutive multiples of a power of 2, the division and two of the additions can be reduced to trivial operations.

For example, suppose that $\log_2 x$ is to be evaluated for x in $[1, 2)$. Since $f(x_{\text{lo}}) = \log_2 1 = 0$ and $f(x_{\text{hi}}) = \log_2 2 = 1$, the linear interpolation formula becomes:

$$\log_2 x \approx x - 1 = \text{the fractional part of } x$$

The error in this extremely simple approximation is $\varepsilon = \log_2 x - x + 1$, which assumes its maximum absolute value of 0.086 071 for $x = \log_2 e = 1.442\ 695$ and maximum relative value of 0.061 476 for $x = e/2 = 1.359\ 141$. Errors this large are obviously unacceptable for useful computations, but before proceeding to make the approach more practical, let us note an improvement in the preceding linear interpolation scheme.

Instead of approximating the function $f(x)$ with a straight line between the two end points of $f(x)$ at x_{lo} and x_{hi}, one can use another straight line that minimizes the absolute or relative error in the worst case. Figure 24.4 depicts this strategy, along with the hardware structure needed for its realization. We now have errors at the two end points as well as elsewhere within the interval (x_{lo}, x_{hi}), but the maximum error has been reduced.

Applying the preceding strategy to computing $\log_2 x$ for x in $[1, 2)$, we can easily derive the following straight-line approximation $a + b(x - 1) = a + b\Delta x$ for minimizing the absolute error (to 0.043 036 for $x = 1.0$, 1.442 695, or 2.0):

$$\log_2 x \approx \frac{\ln 2 - \ln(\ln 2) - 1}{2 \ln 2} + (x - 1) = 0.043\ 036 + \Delta x$$

This is better than our first try (half the error), but still too coarse an approximation to be useful. The derivation of a straight line that minimizes the relative error in the worst case is similar but does not lead to closed-form results for a and b.

It appears that a single straight line won't do for the entire interval of interest and we need to apply the interpolation method in narrower intervals to obtain acceptable results. This observation leads to an "interpolating memory" [Noet89] that begins with table lookup to retrieve the coefficients $a^{(i)}$ and $b^{(i)}$ of the approximating straight line $a^{(i)} + b^{(i)}\Delta x$, given the index i of the subinterval containing x, and then uses one multiplication and one addition to complete the computation (Fig. 24.5). Note that since Δx begins with two 0s, it would be more efficient to use $4\Delta x$, which is representable with two fewer bits. The table entries $b^{(i)}$ must then be divided by 4 to keep the products the same.

Clearly, second-degree or higher-order interpolation can be used, an approach that involves more computation but yields correspondingly better approximations. For example, with second-degree interpolation, the coefficients $a^{(i)}$, $b^{(i)}$, and $c^{(i)}$ are read out from tables and the expression $a^{(i)} + b^{(i)}\Delta x + c^{(i)} \Delta x^2$ is evaluated using three multipliers and a three-operand adder. The multiplication (squaring) to obtain Δx^2 can be overlapped with table access to obtain better performance. Third- or higher-degree interpolation is also possible but often less cost-effective than simpler linear or quadratic schemes using narrower intervals.

If the number of subintervals is 2^h then the subinterval containing x can be determined by looking at the h most significant bits of x, with the offset Δx simply derived from the remaining bits of x. Since it is more efficient to deal with $2^h \Delta x$, which has h fewer bits than Δx, the tables must contain $a^{(i)}$, $b^{(i)}/2^h$, $c^{(i)}/2^{2h}$, etc.

Let us now apply the method of Fig. 24.5 with four subintervals to compute $\log_2 x$ for x in $[1, 2)$. The four subintervals are $[1.00, 1.25)$, $[1.25, 1.50)$, $[1.50, 1.75)$, and $[1.75, 2.00)$.

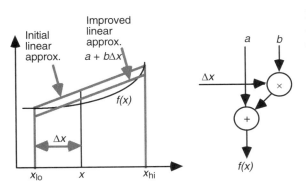

Fig. 24.4 Linear interpolation for computing $f(x)$ and its hardware realization.

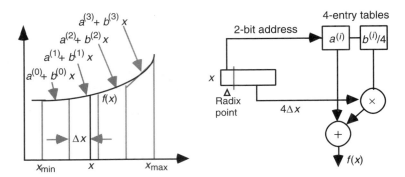

Fig. 24.5   Linear interpolation for computing $f(x)$ using four subintervals.

Table 24.1 lists the parameters of the best linear approximation, along with its worst-case error, for each subinterval.

We see from Table 24.1 that the maximum error is now much less than for simple linear interpolation. We can improve the quality of approximation even further by using more intervals (larger tables) or superlinear interpolation (more tables and peripheral arithmetic computations). The optimal choice will be different for each problem and must be determined by careful analysis based on a reasonably realistic cost model.

24.5 TRADE-OFFS IN COST, SPEED, AND ACCURACY

As noted in Section 24.4, trade-offs exist between table size and complexity/delay of peripheral circuits for a given precision. Generally, the higher the order of interpolation (more peripheral circuits or longer delay with hardware sharing), the smaller the number of subintervals needed to guarantee a given precision for the results (smaller tables). However, it is seldom cost-effective to go beyond second-degree interpolation.

As an example of such trade-offs, Fig. 24.6 shows the maximum absolute error in an interpolating memory unit computing $\log_2 x$ for various numbers h of address bits using mth-degree interpolation, with $m = 1, 2$, or 3. With these parameters, the total number of table entries is $(m + 1)2^h$.

Figure 24.6 can be used in two ways to implement an appropriate interpolating memory unit for evaluating $\log_2 x$. First, if the table size is limited by component availability or chip area to a

TABLE 24.1
Approximating $\log_2 x$ for x in $[1, 2)$ using linear interpolation within 4 subintervals

i	x_{lo}	x_{hi}	$a^{(i)}$	$b^{(i)}/4$	Maximum error
0	1.00	1.25	0.004 487	0.321 928	±0.004 487
1	1.25	1.50	0.324 924	0.263 034	±0.002 996
2	1.50	1.75	0.587 105	0.222 392	±0.002 142
3	1.75	2.00	0.808 962	0.192 645	±0.001 607

total of 256 words, say, then 7 address bits can be used with linear, and 6 bits with either second- or third-degree interpolation. This leads to worst-case absolute errors of about 10^{-5}, 10^{-7}, and 10^{-10}, respectively. Of course if the table size is limited by chip area, then it is unlikely that the second- or third-order schemes can be implemented, since they require multiple adders and multipliers. So, we have an accuracy/speed trade-off to consider.

If a maximum tolerable error of 10^{-6}, say, is given, then Fig. 24.6 tells us that we can use linear interpolation with 9 address bits (two 512-entry tables), second-degree interpolation with 5 address bits (three 32-entry tables), or third-degree interpolation with 3 address bits (four 8-entry tables). Since 32-entry tables are already small enough, little is gained from using third-degree interpolation, which requires significantly more complex and slower peripheral logic.

Except for slight upward or downward shifting of the curves, the shapes of error curves for other functions of interest are quite similar to the ones for $\log_2 x$ shown in Fig. 24.6. In most cases, the number of address bits required for a given precision is within ± 1 of that needed for the $\log_2$ functions. This makes it practical to build a general-purpose interpolating memory unit that can be customized for various functions of interest by plugging in ROMs with appropriate contents or by dynamically loading its RAM tables.

24.6 PIECEWISE LOOKUP TABLES

Several practical methods for function evaluation are based on table lookup using fragments of the operands. These methods essentially fall between the two extremes of direct table lookup and the bit-serial methods discussed in Section 24.3. Here, we review two such methods as representative examples.

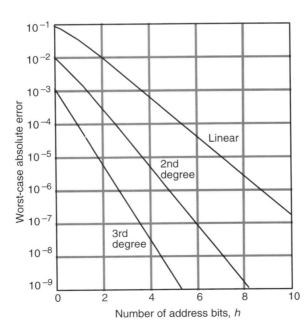

Fig. 24.6 Maximum absolute error in computing $\log_2 x$ as a function of number h of address bits for the tables with linear, quadratic (second-degree), and cubic (third-degree) interpolations [Noet89].

The first method deals with evaluating elementary functions in single-precision IEEE floating-point format. We ignore the sign and exponent in this brief discussion. For details of how the exponent affects the evaluation process, see [Wong95].

Let us divide the 26-bit significand x (with 2 whole and 24 fractional bits) into four sections:

$$x = t + \lambda u + \lambda^2 v + \lambda^3 w = t + 2^{-6}u + 2^{-12}v + 2^{-18}w$$

Each of the components u, v, and w is a 6-bit fraction in $[0, 1)$ and t, with up to 8 bits depending on the function being evaluated, is in $[0, 4)$. The Taylor polynomial for $f(x)$ is:

$$f(x) = \sum_{i=0}^{\infty} f^{(i)}(t + \lambda u) \frac{(\lambda^2 v + \lambda^3 w)^i}{i!}$$

The value of $f(x)$ can be approximated by ignoring terms smaller than $\lambda^5 = 2^{-30}$. Using the Taylor polynomial, one can obtain the following approximation to $f(x)$ which is accurate to $O(\lambda^5)$:

$$f(x) \approx f(t + \lambda u) + \frac{\lambda}{2} [f(t + \lambda u + \lambda v) - f(t + \lambda u - \lambda v)]$$

$$+ \frac{\lambda^2}{2} [f(t + \lambda u + \lambda w) - f(t + \lambda u - \lambda w)] + \lambda^4 \left[\frac{v^2}{2} f^{(2)}(t) - \frac{v^3}{6} f^{(3)}(t) \right]$$

The tedious analysis needed to derive the preceding formula, and its associated error bound, is not presented here. With this method, computing $f(x)$ reduces to:

1. Deriving the four 14-bit values $t + \lambda u + \lambda v, t + \lambda u - \lambda v, t + \lambda u + \lambda w$, and $t + \lambda u - \lambda w$ using four additions ($t + \lambda u$ needs no computation).
2. Reading the five values of f from a single table or from parallel tables (for higher speed).
3. Reading the value of the last term $\lambda^4[(v^2/2) f^{(2)}(t) - (v^3/6) f^{(3)}(t)]$, which is a function of t and v, from a different table.
4. Performing a six-operand addition.

Analytical evaluation has shown that the error in the preceding computation is guaranteed to be less than the upper bound $ulp/2 = 2^{-24}$. In fact, exhaustive search with all possible 24-bit operands has revealed that the results are accurate to anywhere from 27.3 to 33.3 bits for elementary functions of interest [Wong95].

Our second example of piecewise lookup tables is for modular reduction, that is, finding the d-bit residue modulo p of a given b-bit number z in the range $[0, m)$, where $b = \lceil \log_2 m \rceil$ and $d = \lceil \log_2 p \rceil$. Dividing z into two segments with $b - g$ and g bits, we write:

$$z = 2^g \lfloor z/2^g \rfloor + z \bmod 2^g = 2^g z_{[b-1,g]} + z_{[g-1,0]}$$

For $g \geq d$, the preceding equation leads to a two-table method. The most significant $b - g$ bits, $z_{[b-1,g]}$, index a table with $v_{\mathrm{H}} = \lceil m/2^g \rceil$ words to obtain a d-bit residue. The least significant g bits of z, namely, $z_{[g-1,0]}$, index a v_L-word table ($v_L = 2^g$) to obtain another d-bit residue. These residues are then added and the final d-bit residue is obtained by the standard method of trial subtraction followed by selection, as shown in Fig. 24.7. The total table size, in bits, is

$$B_{\mathrm{divide}} = d(v_{\mathrm{H}} + v_{\mathrm{L}}) = d(\lceil m/2^g \rceil + 2^g)$$

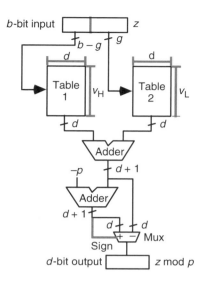

Fig. 24.7 Two-table modular reduction scheme based on the divide-and-conquer approach.

which is minimized if we choose $g = \lfloor \lceil \log_2 m \rceil / 2 \rfloor = \lfloor b/2 \rfloor$. Note that the lower adder and the multiplexer can be replaced by a $2^{d+1} \times d$ table. Alternatively, both adders and the multiplexer in Fig. 24.7 can be replaced by a $2^{2d} \times d$ table.

For example, with $p = 13$, $m = 2^{16}$, $d = 4$, and $b = 16$, the aforementioned optimization leads to tables of total size of 2048 bits—a factor of 128 improvement over direct table lookup.

An alternate two-phase (successive refinement) approach is depicted in Fig. 24.8. First, several high-order bits of z in $[0, m)$ are used to determine what negative multiple of p should be added to z to yield a d^*-bit result z^* in the range $[0, m^*)$, where $p < m^* < m$, $z \bmod p = z^* \bmod p$, and $d^* = \lceil \log_2 m^* \rceil$. Then, the simpler computation $z^* \bmod p$ is performed by direct table lookup.

The most significant $b - h$ bits of z, namely, $z_{[b-1,h]}$, are used to access a v-word table ($v = \lceil m/2^h \rceil$) to obtain a d^*-bit value. This value is the least significant d^* bits of a negative multiple of p such that when it is added to z, the result z^* is guaranteed to satisfy $0 \le z^* \le m^*$. A second m^*-word table is used to obtain the d-bit final result $z^* \bmod p$. The total table size, in bits, is:

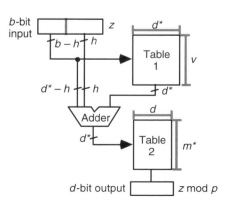

Fig. 24.8 Two-table modular reduction based on successive refinement.

$$B_{\text{refine}} = d^*v + dm^* = d^*\lceil m/2^h \rceil + dm^*$$

In the special case of $m^* < 2p$, the second table can be eliminated and replaced by a subtractor and a multiplexer if desired, thus leading to a single-table scheme.

We see that the total table size is dependent on the parameter m^*. One can prove that the total table size B_{refine} is minimized if d^* is chosen to minimize the objective function $f(d^*) = d^*\lceil m/2^{d^*-1} \rceil + (d \times 2^{d^*-1})$ and m^* is chosen to be $m^* = 2^{d^*-1} + p$. For our earlier example with $p = 13$, $m = 2^{16}$, $d = 4$, $b = 16$, the optimal values for d^* and m^* are 9 and 269, respectively, leading to a total table size of 3380 bits. The resulting tables in this case are larger than for the divide-and-conquer scheme in Fig. 24.7, but the simplicity of the peripheral circuitry (only a single adder besides the tables) can make up for the larger tables.

Modular reduction finds applications in converting numbers from binary or decimal representation to RNS [Parh93a], [Parh94] and in certain error-coding schemes that are based on residues. Details of the preceding methods, including proofs of the results used here, can be found elsewhere [Parh94a], [Parh97].

PROBLEMS

24.1   Squaring by table lookup Show that if the integers x and y are identical in their least significant h bits, their squares will be identical in $h + 1$ bits. Use this result to propose a split-table method (as discussed at the end of Section 24.2) for squaring and estimate the extent of savings in the total table size [Vinn95].

24.2   Squaring by table lookup Consider the following scheme for squaring a k-bit integer x by using much smaller squaring tables. Divide x into two equal-width parts x_H and x_L. Then use the identity $(2^{k/2}x_H + x_L)^2 = 2^k x_H^2 + 2^{k/2+1}x_H x_L + x_L^2$ and perform the multiplication $x_H x_L$ through squaring. Supply the details of the preceding table-lookup scheme for squaring and discuss its speed and cost compared to other methods based on table lookup.

24.3   Squaring by table lookup In Section 24.2 we saw that the table size for squaring can be reduced by a factor of about 2 if the least significant bit ε of $x + y$ and $x - y$ is handled in a specific way. Consider γ and δ, the second LSB of $x + y$ and $x - y$, respectively. Would more complex pre- and postprocessing steps allow us to ignore these bits in table lookup, thus reducing the table size by another factor of 2? Investigate this question, and comment on the cost-effectiveness of the resulting scheme.

24.4   Binary-to-unary reduction method

    a. Use the binary-to-unary reduction approach of Section 24.2 to devise a method for computing $x\,e^y$ via table lookup with pre- and/or postprocessing elements.

    b. Repeat part a for the function x^y.

24.5   Bit-serial second-order filter Consider the bit-serial second-order filter shown in Fig. 24.3.

    a. Show the modifications required in the design to allow radix-4 (2-bits-at-a-time) operation.

b.   Show the modifications required in the design to allow the partially accumulated result, now held in register s, to be kept in carry-save form, so that the main adder is replaced by a faster carry-save adder.

c.   Compare the suggested modifications of parts a and b with respect to improved speed and added cost.

24.6   **Bit-serial arithmetic with table lookup**   Show how the second-order filter computation depicted in Fig. 24.3 can be programmed on the CM-2 arithmetic unit shown in Fig. 24.2. Assume that the filter coefficients are known at compile time and that all numbers are to be represented as 2's-complement fixed-point numbers with 1 whole (sign) bit and an l-bit fractional part.

24.7   **Programmable second-order filter**   A *programmable filter* is one for which the coefficients $a^{(i)}$ and $b^{(i)}$ can change.

a.   How should the filter design in Fig. 24.3 be modified if the coefficients are to be dynamically selectable from among eight sets of values that are known at design time?

b.   How should the design be modified if the coefficients are to be dynamically adjustable at run time?

24.8   **Function evaluation by table lookup**   Base-2 logarithm of 16-bit unsigned fractions is to be computed at the input interface of a logarithmic number system processor in which the logarithm is represented as a 12-bit, fixed-point, 2's-complement number with 5 whole (including the sign position) and 7 fractional bits. Using a single table of size $2^{16} \times 12$ bits is impractical. Suggest a method that can use smaller tables (say, up to 10K bits in all) and is also quite fast compared to convergence schemes. Analyze your method with respect to representation error and hardware requirements.

24.9   **Interpolating memory for computing $\sin x$**   Let angles be represented as 8-bit unsigned fractions x in units of π radians; for example, $(.1000\ 0000)_{two}$ represents the angle $\pi/2$. Consider the following "interpolating memory" scheme for computing $\sin x$. Two four-word memories are used to store 10-bit, 2's-complement fractions $a^{(i)}$ and $b^{(i)}/4$, $0 \leq i \leq 3$. The function $\sin x$ is then computed by using the linear interpolation formula $\sin x \approx a^{(i)} + b^{(i)}\Delta x$, where $i = (x_{-1}x_{-2})_{two}$ is the interval index and $4\ \Delta x = (0.x_{-3}x_{-4}x_{-5}x_{-6}x_{-7}x_{-8})_{two}$ is the scaled offset.

a.   Determine the contents of the two tables to minimize the maximum absolute error in computing $\sin x$ for $0 \leq x \leq 1$.

b.   Compute the maximum absolute and relative errors implied by your tables.

c.   Compare these errors and the implementation cost of your scheme to those of a straight table-lookup scheme, where x is used to access a 256×8 table, and discuss.

24.10   **Interpolating memory**

a.   Construct a table similar to Table 24.1 corresponding to the tabular evaluation of the function e^x for x in $[1, 2)$. Compare the absolute and relative errors for this function to those in Table 24.1 and discuss.

b.   Repeat part a for the function $1/x$, with x in $[1, 2)$.

c.   Repeat part a for the function $\sqrt{x}$, where x in $[1, 4)$.

24.11 Accuracy of interpolating memory

a. Extend the linear interpolation part of Fig. 24.6 for h up to 16 bits. Show your analysis in full and present the resulting data in tabular as well as graphic form.

b. Repeat part a for linear interpolation applied to the function $\sin x$.

c. Repeat part a for linear interpolation applied to the function e^x.

d. Discuss and compare the observed trends in parts a, b, and c.

24.12 Piecewise table lookup For the piecewise table-lookup method of function evaluation, presented at the beginning of Section 24.6, discuss how the exponent and sign are handled [Wong95].

24.13 Modular reduction with a single table In the description of Fig. 24.7, it was mentioned that for $g \geq d$, two tables are required. For $g < d$, Table 2 of Fig. 24.7 can be eliminated. Derive conditions under which such a single-table realization leads to a smaller total table size.

24.14 Modular reduction by two-step refinement In the two-table modular reduction method shown in Fig. 24.8, it is possible to modify the contents of Table 1 (without increasing its size) in such a way that the d^*-bit adder can be replaced by an h-bit adder plus some extra logic. Show how this can be accomplished and discuss the speed and cost implications of the modified design.

24.15 Modular reduction using tables only Consider tabular reduction by multilevel table lookup using no component other than tables. Figures 24.7 and 24.8 can both be converted to such pure tabular realizations by replacing the adders with tables. Note that other simplifications might occur once the adders have been removed.

a. Derive the total table size for the pure tabular version of Fig. 24.7.

b. Derive the total table size for the pure tabular version of Fig. 24.8.

c. Compare the results of parts a and b and discuss.

24.16 Multilevel modular reduction

a. Generalize the two-level table-lookup scheme of Fig. 24.7 to more than two tables in level 1 followed by a single table, and no other component, in level 2. Discuss how the optimal number of tables in level 1 can be determined.

b. Show how the scheme of part a can be extended to three or more levels.

c. Is the scheme of Fig. 24.8 generalizable to more than two levels?

24.17 Reduced tables for RNS multiplication

a. By relating the mod-p product of $p - x$ and $p - y$ to $xy \bmod p$, show that the size of a mod-p multiplication table can be reduced by a factor of about 4 [Parh93b].

b. Show that an additional twofold reduction in table size is possible because of the commutativity of modular multiplication, namely, $xy \bmod p = yx \bmod p$. Explain how the reduced table is addressed.

REFERENCES

[Ferg91]   Ferguson, W.E., Jr., and T. Brightman, "Accurate and Monotone Approximations of Some Transcendental Functions," *Proc. 10th Symp. Computer Arithmetic*, pp. 237–244, 1991.

[Ling90]   Ling, H., "An Approach to Implementing Multiplication with Small Tables," *IEEE Trans. Computers*, Vol. 39, No. 5, pp. 717–718, 1990.

[Noet89]   Noetzel, A.S., "An Interpolating Memory Unit for Function Evaluation: Analysis and Design," *IEEE Trans. Computers*, Vol. 38, No. 3, pp. 377–384, 1989.

[Parh93a]   Parhami, B., "Optimal Table-Lookup Schemes for Binary-to-Residue and Residue-to-Binary Conversions," *Proc. 27th Asilomar Conf. Signals, Systems, and Computers*, Vol. 1, pp. 812–816, November 1993.

[Parh93b]   Parhami, B., and H.-F. Lai, "Alternate Memory Compression Schemes for Modular Multiplication," *IEEE Trans. Signal Processing*, Vol. 41, pp. 1378–1385, March 1993.

[Parh94a]   Parhami, B., "Analysis of Tabular Methods for Modular Reduction," *Proc. 28th Asilomar Conf. Signals, Systems, and Computers*, October/November 1994, pp. 526–530.

[Parh94b]   Parhami, B., and C.Y. Hung, "Optimal Table Lookup Schemes for VLSI Implementation of Input/Output Conversions and Other Residue Number Operations," *VLSI Signal Processing VII* (Proceedings of an IEEE workshop), October 1994, pp. 470–481.

[Parh97]   Parhami, B., "Modular Reduction by Multi-Level Table Lookup," *Proc. 40th Midwest Symp. Circuits and Systems*, August 1997, Vol. 1, pp. 381–384.

[Tang91]   Tang, P.T.P., "Table-Lookup Algorithms for Elementary Functions and Their Error Analysis," *Proc. Symp. Computer Arithmetic*, 1991, pp. 232–236.

[Vinn95]   Vinnakota, B., "Implementing Multiplication with Split Read-Only Memory," *IEEE Trans. Computers*, Vol. 44, No. 11, pp. 1352-1356, 1995.

[Wong95]   Wong, W.F., and E. Goto, "Fast Evaluation of the Elementary Functions in Single Precision," *IEEE Trans. Computers*, Vol. 44, No. 3, pp. 453–457, 1995.

PART VII

IMPLEMENTATION TOPICS

We have thus far ignored several important topics that bear on the usefulness and overall quality of computer arithmetic units. In some contexts—say, when we want the hardware to support two floating-point arithmetic operations per cycle on the average and do not mind that the result of each operation becomes available after many cycles—throughput might be more important than latency. Pipelining is the mechanism used to achieve high throughput while keeping the cost and size of the circuits in check. In other contexts, the size or power requirements of the arithmetic circuits are of primary concern. Finally, in critical applications, or in harsh operating environments, tolerance to permanent and transient hardware faults might be required. These topics, along with historical perspectives, case studies, and a look at the impact of emerging technologies, form the following four chapters of this part.

Chapter 25 | HIGH-THROUGHPUT ARITHMETIC

With very few exceptions, our discussions to this point have focused on methods of speeding up arithmetic computations by reducing the input-to-output latency, defined as the time interval between the application of inputs and the availability of outputs. When two equal-cost implementations were possible, we always chose the one offering a smaller latency. Once we look beyond individual operations, however, latency ceases to be the only indicator of performance. In pipelined mode of operation, arithmetic operations may have higher latencies owing to pipelining overhead. However, one hardware unit can perform multiple overlapped operations at once. This *concurrency* often more than makes up for the higher latency. Chapter topics include:

25.1 Pipelining of Arithmetic Functions
25.2 Clock Rate and Throughput
25.3 The Earle Latch
25.4 Parallel and Digit-Serial Pipelines
25.5 On-Line or Digit-Pipelined Arithmetic
25.6 Systolic Arithmetic Units

25.1 PIPELINING OF ARITHMETIC FUNCTIONS

The key figure of merit for a pipelined implementation is its computational *throughput*, defined as the number of operations that can be performed per unit time. The inverse of throughput, the *pipelining period*, is the time interval between the application of successive input data sets for proper overlapped computation. Of course, latency is still important for two reasons:

1. There may be an occasional need to perform single operations that are not immediately followed by others of the same type.
2. Data dependencies or conditional execution (*pipeline hazards*) may force us to insert *bubbles* into the pipeline or to *drain* it altogether.

413

However, in pipelined arithmetic, latency assumes a secondary role. We will see later in this chapter that at times, a pipelined implementation may improve the latency of a multistep arithmetic computation while also reducing its hardware cost. In such a case, pipelining is obviously the preferred method, offering the best of all worlds.

Figure 25.1 shows the structure of a σ-stage arithmetic pipeline. Before considering a number of practical issues in the design of arithmetic pipelines, it is instructive to study the trade-offs between throughput, latency, and implementation cost.

Consider an arithmetic function unit whose initial cost is g (in number of logic gates, say) and has a latency of t. Our analysis will be based on a number of simplifying assumptions:

1. The pipelining time overhead per stage is τ (latching time delay).
2. The pipelining cost overhead per stage is γ (latching cost).
3. The function can be divided into σ stages of equal latency for any σ.

Then, the latency T, throughput R, and cost G of the pipelined implementation are:

$$\text{Latency} \qquad T = t + \sigma\tau$$

$$\text{Throughput} \qquad R = \frac{1}{T/\sigma} = \frac{1}{t/\sigma + \tau}$$

$$\text{Cost} \qquad G = g + \sigma\gamma$$

We see that, theoretically, throughput approaches its maximum possible value of $1/\tau$ when σ becomes very large. In practice, however, it does not pay to reduce t/σ below a certain threshold; typically four logic gate levels. Even then, one seldom divides the logic into four-level slices blindly; rather, one looks for natural boundaries at which interstage signals (and thus latching costs) will be minimized, even though this may lead to additional stage delay. But let us assume, for the sake of simplifying our analysis, that pipeline stage delay is uniformly equal to four gate delays (4δ). Then, $\sigma = t/(4\delta)$ and:

$$\text{Latency} \qquad T = t\left(1 + \frac{\tau}{4\delta}\right)$$

$$\text{Throughput} \qquad R = \frac{1}{T/\sigma} = \frac{1}{4\delta + \tau}$$

$$\text{Cost} \qquad G = g\left(1 + \frac{t\gamma}{4g\delta}\right)$$

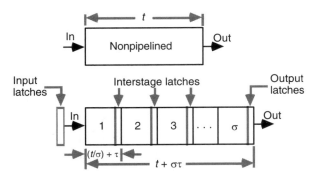

Fig. 25.1   An arithmetic function unit and its σ-stage pipelined version.

The preceding equalities give us an idea of the overhead in latency, $\tau/(4\delta)$, and implementation cost, $t\gamma/(4g\delta)$, to maximize the computational throughput within practical limits.

If throughput is not the single most important factor, one might try to maximize a composite figure of merit. For example, throughput per unit cost may be taken as representing cost-effectiveness:

$$E = \frac{R}{G} = \frac{\sigma}{(t + \sigma\tau)(g + \sigma\gamma)}$$

To maximize E, we compute $dE/d\sigma$:

$$\frac{dE}{d\sigma} = \frac{tg - \sigma^2\tau\gamma}{(t + \sigma\tau)^2(g + \sigma\gamma)^2}$$

Equating $dE/d\sigma$ with 0 yields:

$$\sigma^{\text{opt}} = \left(\frac{t}{\tau}\frac{g}{\gamma}\right)^{1/2}$$

Our simplified analysis thus suggests that the optimal number of pipeline stages for maximal cost-effectiveness is directly related to the latency and cost of the original function and inversely related to pipelining delay and cost overheads: it pays to have many pipeline stages if the function to be implemented is very slow or highly complex, but few pipeline stages are in order if the time and/or cost overhead of pipelining is too high. All in all, not a surprising result!

As an example, with $t = 40\delta$, $g = 500$ gates, $\tau = 4\delta$, and $\gamma = 50$ gates, we obtain $\sigma^{\text{opt}} = 10$ stages. The result of pipelining is that both cost and latency increase by a factor of 2 and throughput improves by a factor of 5. Of course when pipeline hazards are factored in, the optimal number of stages will be much smaller.

25.2 CLOCK RATE AND THROUGHPUT

Consider a σ-stage pipeline and let the worst-case pipeline stage delay be t_{stage}. Suppose one set of inputs is applied to the pipeline at time t_1. At time $t_1 + t_{\text{stage}} + \tau$, the results of this set are safely stored in output latches for the stage. Applying the next set of inputs at time t_2 satisfying $t_2 \geq t_1 + t_{\text{stage}} + \tau$ is enough to ensure proper pipeline operation. With the preceding condition, one set of inputs can be applied to the pipeline every $t_{\text{stage}} + \tau$ time units:

$$\text{Clock period} = \Delta t = t_2 - t_1 \geq t_{\text{stage}} + \tau$$

Pipeline throughput is simply the inverse of the clock period:

$$\text{Throughput} = \frac{1}{\text{clock period}} \leq \frac{1}{t_{\text{stage}} + \tau}$$

The preceding analysis assumes that a single clock signal is distributed to all circuit elements and that all latches are clocked at precisely the same time. In reality, we have some uncontrolled or random *clock skew* that may cause the clock signal to arrive at point B before or after its arrival at point A. With proper design of the clock distribution network, we can place an upper bound $\pm\varepsilon$ on the amount of uncontrolled clock skew at the input and output latches of a pipeline stage. Then, the clock period is lower-bounded as follows:

$$\text{Clock period} = \Delta t = t_2 - t_1 \geq t_{stage} + \tau + 2\varepsilon$$

The term 2ε is included because we must assume the worst case when input latches are clocked later and the output latches earlier than planned, reducing the time that is available for stage computation by 2ε. We thus see that uncontrolled clock skew degrades the throughput that would otherwise be achievable.

For a more detailed examination of pipelining, we note that the stage delay t_{stage} is really not a constant but varies from t_{min} to t_{max}, say; t_{min} corresponds to fast paths through the logic (fewer gates or faster gates on the path) and t_{max} to slow paths. Suppose that one set of inputs is applied at time t_1. At time $t_1 + t_{max} + \tau$, the results of this set are safely stored in output latches for the stage. Assuming that the next set of inputs are applied at time t_2, we must have

$$t_2 + t_{min} \geq t_1 + t_{max} + \tau$$

if the signals for the second set of inputs are not to get intermixed with those of the preceding inputs. This places a lower bound on the clock period:

$$\text{Clock period} = \Delta t = t_2 - t_1 \geq t_{max} - t_{min} + \tau$$

The preceding inequality suggests that we can approach the maximum possible throughput of $1/\tau$ without necessarily requiring very small stage delay. All that is required is to have a very small delay variance $t_{max} - t_{min}$.

Using the delay through a pipeline segment as a kind of temporary storage, thus allowing "waves" of unlatched data to travel through the pipeline, is known as *wave pipelining* [Flyn95]. The concept of wave pipelining is depicted in Fig. 25.2, with the wave fronts showing the spatial distribution of fast and slow signals at a given instant. Figure 25.3, an alternate representation of wave pipelining, shows why it is acceptable for the transient regions of consecutive input sets to overlap in time (horizontally) as long as they are separated in space (vertically). Note that conventional pipelining provides separation in both time and space.

The preceding discussion reveals two distinct strategies for increasing the throughput of a pipelined function unit: (1) the traditional method of reducing t_{max}, and (2) the counterintuitive method of increasing t_{min} so that it is as close to t_{max} as possible. In the latter method, reducing

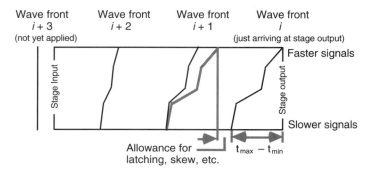

Fig. 25.2 Wave pipelining allows multiple computational wave fronts to coexist in a single pipeline stage.

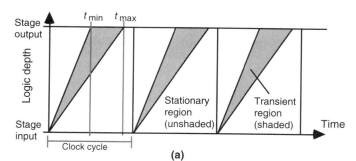

Fig. 25.3 An alternate view of the throughput advantage of wave pipelining (b) over ordinary pipelining (a) using a time–space representation.

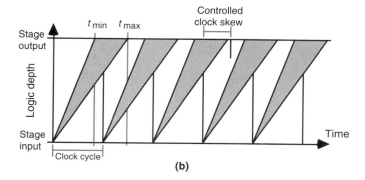

t_{max} is beneficial only to the extent that such reduction softens the performance penalty of pipeline hazards.

Suppose, for the moment, that $t_{max} - t_{min} = 0$. Then, the clock period can be taken to be $\Delta t \geq \tau$ and the throughput becomes $1/\Delta t \leq 1/\tau$. Since a new input enters the pipeline stage every Δt time units and the stage latency is $t_{max} + \tau$, the clock application at the output latch must be skewed by $(t_{max} + \tau) \bmod \Delta t$ to ensure proper sampling of the results. For example, if $t_{max} + \tau = 12$ ns and $\Delta t = 5$ ns, then a clock skew of $+2$ ns is required at the stage output latches relative to the input latches. This *controlled clock skew* is a necessary part of wave pipelining.

More generally, $t_{max} - t_{min}$ is nonzero and perhaps different for the various pipeline stages. Then, the clock period Δt is lower-bounded as follows:

$$\Delta t \geq \max_{1 \leq i \leq \sigma} \left(t_{max}^{(i)} - t_{min}^{(i)} + \tau \right)$$

and the controlled clock skew at the output of stage i will be:

$$S^{(i)} = \sum_{j=1}^{i} \left(t_{max}^{(j)} + \tau \right) \bmod \Delta t$$

We still need to worry about uncontrolled or random clock skew. With the amount of uncontrolled skew upper-bounded by $\pm\varepsilon$, we must have:

$$\text{Clock period} = \Delta t = t_2 - t_1 \geq t_{max} - t_{min} + \tau + 4\varepsilon$$

We include the term 4ε because at input, the clocking of the first set of inputs may lag by ε, while that of the second set leads by ε (a net difference of 2ε). In the worst case, the same difference of 2ε may exist at the output, but in the opposite direction. We thus see that uncontrolled clock skew has a larger effect on the performance of wave pipelining than on standard pipelining, especially in relative terms (ε is now a larger fraction of the clock period).

25.3 THE EARLE LATCH

The Earle latch, named after its inventor, J. G. Earle, is a storage element whose output z follows the data input d whenever the clock input C becomes 1. The input data is thus sampled and held in the latch as the clock goes from 1 to 0. Once the input has been sampled, the latch is insensitive to further changes in d as long as the clock C remains at 0. Earle designed the latch of Fig. 25.4 specifically for latching carry-save adders.

Earlier, we derived constraints on the minimum clock period Δt or maximum clock rate $1/\Delta t$. The clock period Δt has two parts: the duration of the clock being high, C_{high}, and duration of the clock being low, C_{low}.

$$\Delta t = C_{\text{high}} + C_{\text{low}}$$

Now, consider a pipeline stage that is preceded and followed by Earle latches. The duration of the clock being high in each period, C_{high}, must satisfy the inequalities

$$3\delta_{\max} - \delta_{\min} + S_{\max}(C\uparrow, \bar{C}\downarrow) \leq C_{\text{high}} \leq 2\delta_{\min} + t_{\min}$$

where $\delta_{\max}$ and $\delta_{\min}$ are maximum and minimum gate delays and $S_{\max}(C\uparrow, \bar{C}\downarrow) \geq 0$ is the maximum skew between C going high and $\bar{C}$ going low at the latch input. The right-hand inequality, constraining the maximum width of the clock pulse, simply asserts that the clock must go low before the fastest signals from the next input data set can affect the input z of the Earle latch at the end of the stage. The left-hand inequality asserts that the clock pulse must be wide enough to ensure that valid data is stored in the output latch and to avoid logic hazard, should the 0-to-1 transition of C slightly lead the 1-to-0 transition of $\bar{C}$ at the latch inputs.

The constraints given in the preceding paragraph must be augmented with additional terms to account for clock skew between pipeline segments and to ensure that logic hazards do not lead to the latching of erroneous data. For a more detailed discussion, see [Flyn82, pp. 221–222].

An attractive property of the Earle latch is that it can be merged with the two-level AND-OR logic that precedes it. For example, to latch

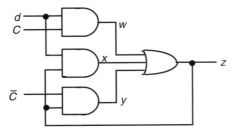

Fig. 25.4 Two-level AND-OR realization of the Earl latch.

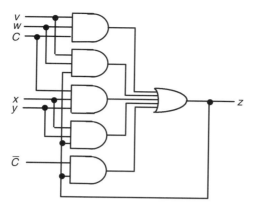

Fig. 25.5 Two-level AND-OR latched realization of the function $z = vw + xy$.

$$d = vw + xy$$

coming from a two-level AND-OR circuit, we substitute for d in the equation for the Earle latch

$$z = dC + dz + \overline{C}z$$

to get the following combined (logic and latch) circuit implementing $z = vw + xy$:

$$z = (vw + xy)C + (vw + xy)z + \overline{C}z$$
$$= vwC + xyC + vwz + xyz + \overline{C}z$$

The resulting two-level AND-OR circuit is shown in Fig. 25.5.

25.4 PARALLEL AND DIGIT-SERIAL PIPELINES

Consider the computation:

$$z = \left[\frac{(a + b)cd}{e - f}\right]^{1/2}$$

To compute z, we need to perform two additions, two multiplications, a division, and a square-root extraction, in the order prescribed by the flow graph shown in Fig. 25.6a. Assuming that multiplication, division, and square-rooting take roughly the same amount of time and that addition is much faster, a timing diagram for the computation can be drawn as shown in Fig. 25.6b. In deriving this timing diagram, it is assumed that enough hardware components are available to do the computation with maximum possible parallelism. This implies the availability of one adder and perhaps a shared multiply/divide/square-root unit.

If the preceding computation is to be performed repeatedly, a pipelined implementation might be contemplated. By using a separate function unit for each node in the flow graph of Fig. 25.6a and inserting latches between consecutive operations, the throughput can be increased

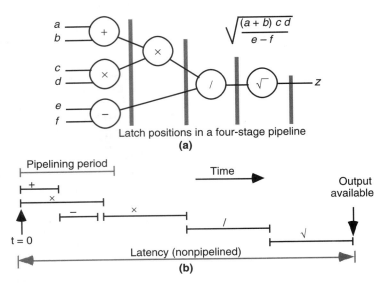

Latch positions in a four-stage pipeline
(a)

(b)

Fig. 25.6   (a) Flow graph representation of an arithmetic expression and (b) timing diagram for its evaluation with digit-parallel computation.

by roughly a factor of 4. However, the requirement for separate multiply, divide, and square-root units would cause the implementation cost to become quite high.

How would one go about doing this computation bit-serially? Bit-serial addition, with the inputs supplied from the least significant end, is easy. We also know how to design an LSB-first, bit-serial multiplier (Section 12.3). With LSB-first, bit-serial computation, as soon as the LSBs of $a + b$ and $c \times d$ are produced, a second bit-serial multiplier can begin the computation of $(a + b) \times (cd)$. This bit-level pipelining is attractive because each additional function unit on the critical path adds very little to the overall latency.

Unfortunately, however, both division and square-rooting are MSB-first operations. So, we cannot begin the division operation in Fig. 25.6 until the results of $(a + b) \times (cd)$ and $e - f$ are available in full. Even then, the division operation cannot be performed in an MSB-first, bit-serial fashion since the MSB of the quotient q in general depends on all the bits of dividend and divisor. To see this, consider the decimal division example 0.1234/0.2469. After inspecting the most significant digits of the two operands, we cannot tell what the MSD of the quotient should be, since

$$\frac{0.1\text{xxx}}{0.2\text{xxx}}$$

can be as large as $0.1999/0.2000 \approx 0.9995$ or as small as $0.1000/0.2999 \approx 0.3334$ (the MSD of the quotient can thus assume any value in [3, 9]). After seeing the second digit of each operand, the ambiguity is still not resolved, since

$$\frac{0.12\text{xx}}{0.24\text{xx}}$$

can be as large as $0.1299/0.2400 \approx 0.5413$ or as small as $0.1200/0.2499 \approx 0.4802$. The next pair of digits further restricts the quotient value to the interval from $0.1239/0.2460 \approx 0.5037$ to

0.1230/0.2469 ≈ 0.4982 but does not resolve the ambiguity in the MSD of q. Only after seeing all digits of both operands are we able to decide that $q_{-1} = 4$.

To summarize the preceding discussion, with standard number representations, pipelined bit-serial or digit-serial arithmetic is feasible only for computations involving additions and multiplications. These operations are done in LSB-first order, with the output from one block immediately fed to the next block. Division and square-rooting force us to assemble the entire operand(s) and then use one of the algorithms discussed earlier in the book.

If we are allowed to produce the output in a redundant format, quotient/root digits can be produced after only a few bits of each operand have been seen, since the precision required for selecting the next quotient digit is limited. This is essentially because a redundant representation allows us to recover from an underestimated or overestimated quotient or root digit. However, the fundamental difference between LSB-first addition and multiplication and MSB-first division and square-rooting remains and renders a bit-serial approach unattractive.

25.5 ON-LINE OR DIGIT-PIPELINED ARITHMETIC

Redundant number representation can be used to solve the problems discussed at the end of Section 25.4. With redundant numbers, not only can we perform division and square-rooting digit-serially, but we can also convert addition and multiplication to MSD-first operations, thus allowing for smooth flow of data in a pipelined digit-serial fashion [Erce84], [Erce88].

Figure 25.7 contrasts the timing of the digit-parallel computation scheme (Fig. 25.6) to that of a digit-pipelined scheme. Operations now take somewhat longer to complete (though not much longer, since the larger number of cycles required is partially offset by the higher clock rate allowed for the simpler incremental computation steps). However, the various computation steps are almost completely overlapped, leading to smaller overall latency despite the simpler hardware. The reason for varying operation latencies, defined as the time interval between receiving the ith input digits and producing the ith output digit, will become clear later.

Again, if the computation is to be performed repeatedly, the pattern shown in the digit-pipelined part of Fig. 25.7 can be repeated in time (with a small gap for resetting of the storage elements). Thus, the second computation in Fig. 25.7 can begin as soon as all the digits of the current inputs have been used up.

All that remains is to show that arithmetic operations can be performed in a digit-serial MSD-first fashion, producing the stream of output digits with a small, fixed latency in each case. Binary signed-digit operands, using the digit set $[-1, 1]$ in radix 2, result in the simplest digit-pipelined arithmetic hardware. A higher radix r, with its correspondingly larger digit set, leads to greater circuit complexity, as well as higher pin count, but may improve the performance, given the smaller number of cycles required to supply the inputs. An improvement in performance is uncertain because the more complicated circuit will likely dictate a lower clock rate, thus nullifying some or all of the gain due to reduced cycle count. In practice, $r > 16$ is seldom cost-effective.

Floating-point numbers present additional problems in that the exponents must arrive first and the significands must be processed according to the result of the exponent preprocessing. However, the adjustments needed are straightforward and do not affect the fundamental notions being emphasized here.

Addition is the simplest operation. We already know that in carry-free addition, the $(-i)$th result digit is a function of the $(-i)$th and $(-i-1)$th operand digits. Thus, upon receiving the two

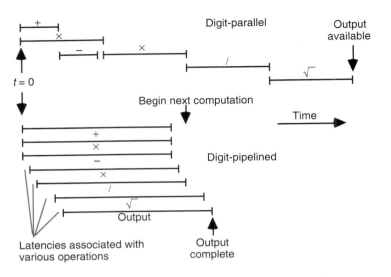

Fig. 25.7   Digit-parallel versus digit-pipelined computation.

most significant digits of the two operands, we have all the information that we need to produce the MSD of the sum/difference.

Figure 25.8 shows a digit-serial MSD-first implementation of carry-free addition. The circuit shown in Fig. 25.8 essentially corresponds to a diagonal slice of Fig. 3.2b and imposes a latency of 1 clock cycle between its input and output.

When carry-free addition is inapplicable (as is the case for binary signed-digit inputs, e.g.), a limited-carry addition algorithm must be implemented. For example, using a diagonal slice of Fig. 3.11a, we obtain the design shown in Fig. 25.9 for digit-pipelined limited-carry addition with a latency of 2 clock cycles.

Multiplication can also be done with a delay of 1 or 2 clock cycles, depending on whether the chosen representation supports carry-free addition. Figure 25.10 depicts the process. In the ith cycle, $i - 1$ digits of the operands a and x have already been received and are available in internal registers; call these $a_{[-1,-i+1]}$ and $x_{[-1,-i+1]}$. Also an accumulated partial product $p^{(i-1)}$ (true sum of the processed terms, minus the digits that have already been output) is available. When a_{-i} and x_{-i} are received, the three terms $x_{-i}a_{[-1,-i+1]}$ (two-digit horizontal value in Fig. 25.10),

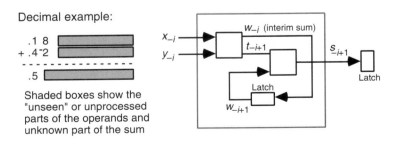

Fig. 25.8   Digit-pipelined MSD-first carry-free addition.

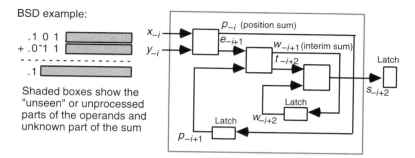

BSD example:

```
  .1 0 1  ▓▓▓▓▓▓
+ .0⁻1 1  ▓▓▓▓▓▓
- - - - - - - - - -
  .1      ▓▓▓▓▓▓
```

Shaded boxes show the
"unseen" or unprocessed
parts of the operands and
unknown part of the sum

Fig. 25.9   Digit-pipelined MSD-first limited-carry addition.

$a_{-i}x_{[-1,-i+1]}$ (two-digit diagonal value in Fig. 25.10), and $a_{-i}x_{-i}$ (circled term in Fig. 25.10) are computed and combined with the left-shifted $p^{(i-1)}$ to produce an interim partial product by a fast carry-free (limited-carry) addition process. The most significant digit of this result is the next output digit and is thus discarded before the next step. The remaining digits form $p^{(i)}$.

Figure 25.11 depicts a possible hardware realization for digit-pipelined multiplication of BSD fractions. The partial multiplicand $a_{[-1,-i+1]}$ and partial multiplier $x_{[-1,-i+1]}$ are held in registers and the incoming digits a_{-i} and x_{-i} are used to select the appropriate multiples of the two for combining with the product residual $p^{(i-1)}$. This three-operand carry-free addition yields an output digit and a new product residual $p^{(i)}$ to be used for the next step. Note that if the digit-pipelined multiplier is implemented based on Fig. 25.10, then a_{-i} and x_{-i} must be inserted into the appropriate position in their respective registers. Alternatively, each of the digits a_{-i} and x_{-i} may be inserted into the LSD of its respective register, with p_{-i+2} extracted from the appropriate position of the three-operand sum.

Digit-pipelined division is more complicated and involves a delay of 3–4 cycles. Intuitively, the reason for the higher delay in division is seen to lie in the uncertainties in the dividend and divisor, which affect the result in opposite directions. The division example of Table 25.1 shows that with $r = 4$ and digit set $[-2, 2]$, the first quotient digit q_{-1} may remain ambiguous until the fourth digit in the dividend and divisor have appeared. Note that with the given digit set, only fractions in the range $(-2/3, 2/3)$ are representable (we have assumed that overflow is impossible and that the quotient is indeed a fraction).

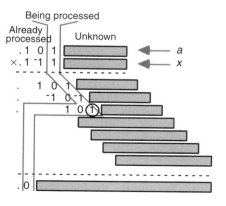

Fig. 25.10   Digit-pipelined MSD-first multiplication process.

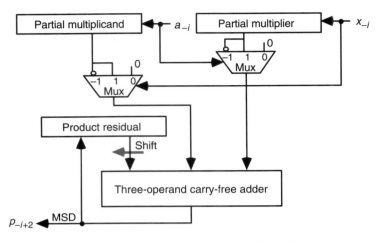

Fig. 25.11   Digit-pipelined MSD-first BSD multiplier.

Note that the example in Table 25.1 shows only that the worst-case delay with this particular representation is at least 3 cycles. One can in fact prove that 3 cycles of delay always is sufficient, provided the number representation system used supports carry-free addition. If limited-carry addition is called for, 4 cycles of delay is necessary and sufficient.

The algorithm for digit-pipelined division and its hardware implementation are similar to those of multiplication. A residual is maintained which is in effect the result of subtracting the product of the known digits of the quotient q and the known digits of the divisor d from the dividend z. With each new digit of q that becomes known, the product of that digit and the partial divisor, as well as the product of the new digit of d and the partial quotient, must be subtracted from the residual. A few bits of the residual, and of the divisor d, may then be used to estimate the next quotient digit.

Square-rooting can be done with a delay of 1–2 cycles, depending on the number representation system used. The first square-rooting example in Table 25.2 shows that, with $r = 10$ and digit set $[-6, 6]$, the first root digit q_{-1} may remain ambiguous until the second digit in the radicand has appeared. The second example, with $r = 2$ and digit set $[-1, 1]$, shows that 2 cycles of delay may be needed in some cases. Again the algorithm and required hardware for digit-pipelined square-rooting are similar to those for digit-pipelined multiplication and division.

TABLE 25.1
Example of digit-pipelined division showing the requirement for 3 cycles of delay before quotient digits can be output (radix = 4, digit set = $[-2, 2]$)

Cycle	Dividend	Divisor	q Range	q_{-1} Range
1	$(.0\cdots)_{four}$	$(.1\cdots)_{four}$	$(-2/3, 2/3)$	$[-2, 2]$
2	$(.0\,0\cdots)_{four}$	$(.1^-2\cdots)_{four}$	$(-2/4, 2/4)$	$[-2, 2]$
3	$(.0\,0\,1\cdots)_{four}$	$(.1^-2^-2\cdots)_{four}$	$(1/16,\ 5/16)$	$[0,\ 1]$
4	$(.0\,0\,1\,0\cdots)_{four}$	$(.1^-2^-2^-2\cdots)_{four}$	$(10/64,\ 14/64)$	1

TABLE 25.2

Examples of digit-pipelined square-root computation showing the requirement for 1–2 cycles of delay before root digits can be output (radix = 10, digit set = [−6, 6], and radix = 2, digit set = [−1, 1])

Cycle	Radicand	q Range	q_{-1} Range
1	$(.3\cdots)_{ten}$	$(\sqrt{7/30}, \sqrt{11/30})$	[5, 6]
2	$(.3\ 4\cdots)_{ten}$	$(\sqrt{1/3}, \sqrt{26/75})$	6
1	$(.0\cdots)_{two}$	$(0, \sqrt{1/2})$	[0, 1]
2	$(.0\ 1\cdots)_{two}$	$(0, \sqrt{1/2})$	[0, 1]
3	$(.0\ 1\ 1\cdots)_{two}$	$(1/2, \sqrt{1/2})$	1

25.6 SYSTOLIC ARITHMETIC UNITS

In our discussion of the design of semisystolic and systolic bit-serial unsigned or 2's-complement multipliers (Section 12.3), we noted that the systolic design paradigm allows us to implement certain functions of interest as regular arrays of simple cells (ideally, all identical) with intercell signals carried by short, local wires. To be more precise, we must add to the requirements above the following: no unlatched signal can be allowed to propagate across multiple cells (for otherwise a ripple-carry adder would qualify as a systolic design).

The term "systolic arrays" [Kung82] was coined to characterize cellular circuits in which data elements, entering at the boundaries, advance from cell to cell, are transformed in an incremental fashion, and eventually exit the array, with the lock-step data movement across the array likened to the rhythmic pumping of blood in the veins. As VLSI circuits become faster and denser, we can no longer ignore the contribution of signal propagation delay on long wires to the latency of various computational circuits. In fact, propagation delay, as opposed to switching or gate delays, is now the main source of latency in modern VLSI design. Thus, any high-performance design requires great attention to minimizing wire length, and in the extreme, adherence to systolic design principles.

Fortunately, we already have all the tools needed to design high-performance systolic arithmetic circuits. In what follows, we present two examples.

An array multiplier can be transformed into a bit-parallel systolic multiplier through the application of pipelining methods discussed earlier in this chapter. Referring to the pipelined 5×5 array multiplier in Fig. 11.17, we note that it requires the bits a_i and x_j to be broadcast within the cells of the same column and row, respectively. Now, if a_i is supplied to the cell at the top row and is then passed from cell to cell in the same column on successive clock ticks, the operation of each cell will be delayed by one time step with respect to the cell immediately above it. If the timing of the elements is adjusted, through insertion of latches where needed, such that all other inputs to the cell experience the same added delay, the function realized by the circuit will be unaffected. This type of transformation is known as *systolic retiming*. Of course, additional delays must be inserted on the p outputs if all bits of the product are to become available at once. A similar modification to remove the broadcasting of the x_j signals completes the design.

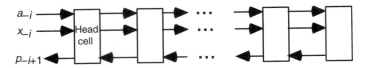

Fig. 25.12   High-level design of a systolic radix-4, digit-pipelined multiplier.

Similarly, a digit-pipelined multiplier can be designed in systolic form to maximize the clock rate and thus the computation speed. Since in the design shown in Fig. 25.11, a_{-i} and x_{-i} are effectively broadcast to a set of 2-to-1 multiplexers, long wires and large fan-outs are involved. Since, however, not all the digits of $x_{-i}a_{[-1,-i+1]}$ and $a_{-i}x_{[-1,-i+1]}$ are needed right away, we can convert the design into a cellular array (Fig. 25.12) in which only the most significant digits of $x_{-i}a_{[-1,-i+1]}$ and $a_{-i}x_{[-1,-i+1]}$ are immediately formed at the head cell, with a_{-i} and x_{-i} passed on to the right on the next clock tick to allow the formation of other digits in subsequent clock cycles and passing of the results to the left when they are needed. Supplying the details of this systolic design is left as an exercise.

PROBLEMS

25.1   Maximizing a pipeline's throughput   The assertion in Section 25.1 that the throughput of a pipeline is the inverse of its clock period (which is the sum of the stage delay and latching overhead) is based on the implicit assumption that the pipeline will be utilized continuously for a long period of time. Let ϕ be the probability that a computation is dependent on the preceding computation so that it cannot be initiated until the results of its predecessor have emerged from the pipeline. For each such computation encountered, the pipeline will go unused for $\sigma - 1$ cycles, where σ is the number of stages. Derive the optimal number of pipeline stages to maximize the effective throughput of a pipeline under these conditions.

25.2   Clock rate and pipeline throughput   A four-stage pipeline has stage delays of 17, 15, 19, and 14 ns and a fixed per-stage latching overhead of 2 ns. The parameter ϕ, defined as the fraction of operations that cannot enter the pipeline before the preceding operation has been completed, is 0.2.

    a.   What clock cycle time maximizes throughput if stages cannot be further subdivided? Assume that there is no uncontrolled clock skew.

    b.   Compare the throughput of part a to the throughput without pipelining.

    c.   What is the total latency through the pipeline with the cycle time of part a?

    d.   What clock cycle time maximizes the throughput with arbitrary subdivisions allowed within stages? Latches at the natural boundaries above are not to be removed, but additional latches can be inserted wherever they would be beneficial.

    e.   What is the total latency through the pipeline with the assumptions of part d?

    f.   Repeat parts a–e, this time assuming an uncontrolled skew of ± 1 ns in the arrival of each clock pulse.

    g.   The use of a more elaborate clock distribution network, doubling the clock wiring area (cost) from 20% to 40% of g, can virtually eliminate the uncontrolled clock skew of part f. Would you use the alternate network? Explain.

25.3 **Optimal pipelining** In the analysis of optimal pipelining in Section 25.1, we assumed that pipelining time and cost overhead per stage are constants. These are simplifying assumptions: in fact, the effects of clock skew intensify for longer, more complex stages and latching overhead increases if the function is sliced indiscriminately at a large number of points. Discuss the optimal number of pipeline stages with each of the following modifications to our original simplifying assumptions.

    a. Clock skew increases linearly with stage delay, so that the time or clocking overhead per stage is $\tau + t\alpha/\sigma$.

    b. Cost overhead per stage, which grows if the logic function is cut at points other then natural subfunction boundaries, is modeled as a linear function $\gamma + \beta\sigma$ of the number of stages.

    c. Both modifications given in parts a and b are in effect.

25.4 **Wave pipelining** A four-stage pipeline has maximum stage delays of 14, 12, 16, 11 ns, minimum stage delays of 7, 9, 10, 5 ns, and a fixed per-stage overhead of 3 ns. The parameter ϕ defined as the fraction of operations that cannot enter the pipeline before the preceding operation has been completed, is 0.2.

    a. With no controlled clock skew allowed, what are the minimum cycle time and the resulting latency?

    b. If we allow controlled clock skew, what are the minimum cycle time, clock skews required at the end of each of the four stages, and the overall latency?

    c. Repeat parts a and b, this time assuming an uncontrolled skew of ± 1 ns in the arrival of each clock pulse.

25.5 **Earle latch logic hazard** The Earle latch shown in Fig. 25.4 has a logic hazard.

    a. Show the hazard on a Karnaugh map and determine when it leads to failure.

    b. Propose a modified latch without a hazard and discuss its practicality.

25.6 **Latched full adders**

    a. Present the complete design of a binary full adder with its sum and carry computations merged with Earle latches.

    b. Derive the latching cost overhead with respect to an unlatched FA and an FA followed by separate Earle latches.

25.7 **Evaluating a pipelined array multiplier** For the pipelined array multiplier design of Fig. 11.17, assume that FA delay is 8 ns and latching overhead is 3 ns.

    a. Find the throughput of the design as shown in Fig. 11.17.

    b. Modify the design of Fig. 11.17 to have latches following every 2 FAs and repeat part a.

    c. Modify the design to have latches following every 3 FAs and repeat part a.

    d. Compare the cost-effectiveness of the designs of parts a–c and discuss.

    e. The design of Fig. 11.17 can be modified so that the lower part uses HAs instead of FAs. Show how the modification should be done and discuss its implications on optimal pipelining. Assume that HA delay is 4 ns.

25.8 **Pipelined ripple-carry adders** In designing a deeply pipelined adder, the ripple-carry design provides a good starting point. Study the variations in pipelined ripple-carry adders and their cost–performance implications [Dadd96].

25.9 **Optimally pipelined adders** In a particular application, 80% of all additions result from operations on long vectors and can thus be performed with full pipeline utilization, leading to a throughput of one addition per clock cycle. The remaining 20% are individual additions for which the total latency of the pipelined adder determines the execution rate. Considering each adder type discussed in Chapters 5–7, derive an optimally pipelined design for the preceding application so that the average addition time is minimized. Is there any adder type that cannot be effectively pipelined? Discuss.

25.10 **Pipelined multioperand adders** Show that pipelined implementation of a multioperand adder with binary inputs is possible so that the clock period is dictated by the latency of one full-adder [Yeh96].

25.11 **Digit-pipelined incrementer/decrementer** To compute the expression $(x - 1)/(x + 1)$ in digit-pipelined fashion, we need to use an incrementer and a decrementer that feed a divider. Assume the use of BSD numbers.

   a. Present the design of a combined digit-pipelined incrementer/decrementer unit.

   b. Compare your design to a digit-pipelined BSD adder and discuss.

25.12 **Digit-pipelined multiplier** The multiplier design shown is Fig. 25.11 is incomplete in two respects. First, it does not show how the term $a_{-i}x_{-i}$ is accommodated. Second, it does not specify the alignment of the operands in the three-operand addition or even the width of the adder.

   a. Complete the design of Fig. 25.11 by taking care of the problems just identified.

   b. Specify additions and modifications to the design for radix-4 multiplication using the digit set $[-2, 2]$.

25.13 **Digit-pipelined voting circuits** An n-input majority voter produces an output that is equal to a majority of its n inputs, if such a majority exists; otherwise it produces an error signal. A median (mean) voter outputs the median (numerical average) of its n inputs.

   a. Show how a three-input digit-serial mean voter can be designed if the inputs are presented in BSD form. What is the latency of your design?

   b. Under what conditions can a bit-serial mean voter, with standard binary inputs, be designed and what would be its latency?

   c. Discuss whether, and if so, how a digit-serial majority or median voter with BSD inputs can be implemented.

   d. Repeat part c with standard binary inputs.

25.14 **Systolic digit-pipelined multiplier** Design a systolic radix-4 digit-pipelined multiplier structured as in Fig. 25.12 based on the ideas presented in Section 25.6.

25.15   Systolic array multiplier

  a.   Based on the discussions in Section 25.6, convert the pipelined array multiplier design of Fig. 11.17 into a fully pipelined systolic array multiplier.

  b.   Repeat part a, this time assuming that propagation across two cells is acceptable.

25.16   Delays in on-line arithmetic That digit-pipelined addition can be performed with one or two cycles of delay between input arrival and output production is a direct result of the theories of carry-free and limited-carry addition developed in Chapter 3.

  a.   With reference to Fig. 25.10 for digit-pipelined multiplication of BSD numbers, show that two cycles of delay is adequate.

  b.   Show that digit-pipelined multiplication can be performed with 2–3 cycles of delay.

  c.   What would be the delay of a digit-pipelined multiply-add unit?

  d.   Show that digit-pipelined square-rooting can be performed with 1–2 cycles of delay.

  e.   Show that digit-pipelined division can be performed with 3–4 cycles of delay.

REFERENCES

[Burl98]   Burleson, W.P., M. Ciesielski, F. Klass, and W. Liu, "Wave Pipelining: A Tutorial and Research Survey," *IEEE Trans. Very Large Scale Integrated Systems*, Vol. 6, No. 3, pp. 464–474, September 1998.

[Dadd96]   Dadda, L., and V. Piuri, "Pipelined Adders," *IEEE Trans. Computers*, Vol. 45, No. 3, pp. 348–356, 1996.

[Davi97]   Davidovic, G., J. Ciric, J. Ristic-Djurovic, V. Milutinovic, and M. Flynn, "A Comparative Study of Adders: Wave Pipelining vs. Classical Design," *IEEE Computer Architecture Technical Committee Newsletter*, June 1997, pp. 64–71.

[Erce84]   Ercegovac, M.D., "On-Line Arithmetic: An Overview," *Real-Time Signal Processing VII*, SPIE Vol. 495, pp. 86–92, 1984.

[Erce88]   Ercegovac, M.D., and T. Lang, "On-Line Arithmetic: A Design Methodology and Applications," *VLSI Signal Processing III* (Proceedings of an IEEE workshop), 1988, pp. 252–263.

[Flyn82]   Flynn, M.J., and S. Waser, *Introduction to Arithmetic for Digital Systems Designers*, Holt, Rinehart, & Winston, 1982.

[Flyn95]   Flynn, M.J., *Computer Architecture: Pipelined and Parallel Processor Design*, Jones and Bartlett, 1995.

[Frie94]   Friedman, G., and J.H. Mulligan, Jr., "Pipelining and Clocking of High Performance Synchronous Digital Systems," in *VLSI Signal Processing Technology*, M.A. Bayoumi and E.E. Swartzlander, Jr., (eds.), Kluwer, 1994, pp. 97–133.

[Irwi87]   Irwin, M.J., and R.M. Owens, "Digit-Pipelined Arithmetic as Illustrated by the Paste-Up System: A Tutorial," *IEEE Computer*, Vol. 20, No. 4, pp. 61–73, 1987.

[Kung82]   Kung, H.T., "Why Systolic Architectures?" *IEEE Computer*, Vol. 15, No. 1, pp. 37–46, 1982.

[Yeh96]   Yeh, C.-H., and B. Parhami, "Efficient Pipelined Multi-Operand Adders with High Throughput and Low Latency: Design and Applications," *Proc. 30th Asilomar Conf. Signals, Systems, and Computers*, November 1996, pp. 894–898.

Chapter 26 | LOW-POWER ARITHMETIC

Classical computer arithmetic focuses on latency and hardware complexity as the primary parameters to be optimized or traded off against each other. We saw in Chapter 25 that throughput is also important and may be considered in design trade-offs. Recently, power consumption has emerged as a key factor for two reasons: limited availability of power in small portable or embedded systems and limited capacity to dispose of the heat generated by fast, power-hungry circuits. In this chapter, we review low-power design concepts that pertain to the algorithm or logic design level; as opposed to circuit-level methods, which are outside the scope of this book. Chapter topics include:

26.1. The Need for Low-Power Design
26.2. Sources of Power Consumption
26.3. Reduction of Power Waste
26.4. Reduction of Activity
26.5. Transformations and Tradeoffs
26.6. Some Emerging Methods

26.1 THE NEED FOR LOW-POWER DESIGN

In modern digital systems, factors other then speed and cost are becoming increasingly important. For example, portable or wearable computers are severely constrained in weight, volume, and power consumption. Whereas weight and volume might seem to be strongly correlated with circuit complexity or cost, factors external to the circuits themselves often dominate the system's weight and volume. For example, packaging, power supply, and cooling provisions might exhibit variations over different technologies that dwarf the contribution of the circuit elements to weight and volume. In power consumption, too, logic and arithmetic circuits might be responsible for only a small fraction of the total power. Nevertheless, it is important to minimize power wastage and to apply power saving methods wherever possible.

In portable and wearable electronic devices, power is at a premium. Nickel–cadmium batteries offer around 40–50 watt-hours of energy per kilogram of weight [Raba96], requiring the total power consumption to be limited to 3–5 W to make a day's worth of operation feasible between recharges, given a practical battery weight of under 1 kg. Power management becomes even more daunting if we focus on personal communication/computation devices with a battery weight of 0.1 kg or less. Newer battery technologies improve the situation only marginally.

This limited power must be budgeted for computation, storage (primary and secondary), video display, and communication, making the share available for computation relatively small. The power consumption of modern microprocessors grows almost linearly with the product of die area and clock frequency and today stands at a few tens of watts in high-performance designs. This is 1–2 orders of magnitude higher than what is required to achieve the aforementioned goal of 3–5 W total power. Roughly speaking, such processors offer 10–20 MFLOPS of performance for each watt of power dissipated.

The preceding discussion leads to the somewhat surprising conclusion that reducing power consumption is also important for high-performance uniprocessor and parallel systems that do not need to be portable or battery-operated. The reason is that higher power dissipation requires the use of more complex cooling techniques, which are costly to build, operate, and maintain. In addition, digital electronic circuits tend to become much less reliable at high operating temperatures; hence we have another incentive for low-power design.

While improvements in technology will steadily increase the battery capacity in portable systems, it is a virtual certainty that increases in die area and clock speed will outpace the improvements in power supplies. Larger circuit area and higher speed are direct results of greater demand for functionality as well as increasing emphasis on computation-intensive applications (e.g., in multimedia), which also require the storage, searching, and analyzing of vast amounts of data.

Thus, low-power design methods, which are quite important now, will likely rise in significance in the coming years as portable digital systems and high-end supercomputers become more prevalent.

Figure 26.1 shows the power consumption trend for each MIPS (million instructions per second) of computational performance in DSP chips [Raba98]. We note that despite higher overall power consumption, there has been a tenfold decrease in power consumption per MIPS every 5 years. This reduction is due to a combination of improved power management methods

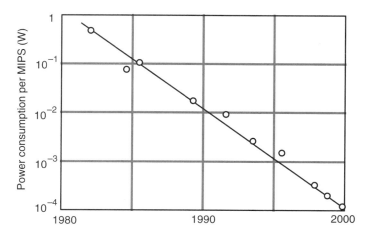

Fig. 26.1   Power consumption trend in DSPs [Raba98].

and lower supply voltages. The 1999–2000 estimates in Fig. 26.1 are for supply voltage of 1–2 V, with 0.5-V DSPs anticipated by the year 2005.

26.2 SOURCES OF POWER CONSUMPTION

To design low-power arithmetic circuits, one must understand the sources of power dissipation and the relationship of power consumption to other important system parameters. Some circuit technologies, such as TTL, are quite unsuitable for low-power designs in view of their relatively high average power consumption. The inherently low-power CMOS technology, on the other hand, can be readily adapted to even more stringent power consumption goals. We will limit our discussion to CMOS, which is currently the predominant implementation technology for both low-cost and high-performance systems.

Besides average power consumption, which is limited by the power budgeted for each subsystem or activity, the peak power consumption is also important in view of its impact on power distribution and signal integrity [Raba96]. Typically, low-power design aims at reducing both the average and peak power.

Power dissipation in CMOS digital circuits is classified as static or dynamic. Static power dissipation occurs, for example, as a result of leakage currents through MOS transistors that form imperfect switches. Excluding certain CMOS families (such as ratioed CMOS logic also known as pseudo-NMOS) that are not used in low-power designs, the aforementioned and other sources of static power dissipation are typically responsible for less than 10% of total power.

Dynamic power dissipation in a CMOS device arises from its transient switching behavior. A small part of such dynamic power dissipation is due to brief short circuits when both the NMOS and PMOS devices between the supply voltage and ground are momentarily turned on. This part of dynamic power dissipation can be kept under control by circuit design techniques and by regulating the signal rise and fall times. This leaves us the dynamic dissipation due to charging and discharging of parasitic capacitance to contend with.

Switching from ground to the supply voltage V, and back to ground, dissipates a power equal to CV^2, where C is the capacitance. Thus, the average power consumption in CMOS can be characterized by the equation

$$P_{avg} \approx \alpha f C V^2$$

where f is the data rate (clock frequency) and α, known as "activity," is the average number of 0-to-1 transitions per clock cycle.

As a numerical example, consider the power consumption of a 32-bit off-chip bus operating at 5 V and 100 MHz, driving a capacitance of 30 pF per bit. If random values were placed on the bus in every cycle, we would have $\alpha = 0.5$. To account for data correlation and idle bus cycles, let us assume $\alpha = 0.2$. Then:

$$P_{avg} \approx \alpha f C V^2 = 0.2 \times 10^8 (32 \times 30 \times 10^{-12}) 5^2 = 0.48 \text{ W}$$

Based on the equation for dynamic power dissipation in CMOS digital circuits, once the data rate f has been fixed, there are but three ways to reduce the power requirements:

1. Using a lower supply voltage V.
2. Reducing the parasitic capacitance C.
3. Lowering the switching activity α.

An alternative to all of the above is to avoid power dissipation altogether, perhaps through circuit augmentation and redesign, such that the normally dissipated energy is conserved for later reuse [Atha96]. However, this latter technique, known as adiabatic switching/charging, is still in its infancy and faces many obstacles before practical applications can be planned.

Given that power dissipation increases quadratically with the supply voltage, reduction of V is a highly effective method for low-power design. A great deal of effort has been expended in recent years on the development of low-voltage technologies and design methods. Unfortunately, however, whereas the transition from 5 V to the present 3.3 V was achieved simply and with little degradation in performance, lower supply voltages come with moderate to serious speed penalties and also present problems with regard to compatibility with peripheral off-the-shelf components. Some of the resulting performance degradation can be mitigated by architectural methods such as increased pipeline depth or parallelism, in effect trading silicon area for lower power. Such methods should make supply voltages at or slightly above 1 V feasible in the near future. Beyond that, however, reduction of V becomes even more difficult.

Parasitic capacitance in CMOS can be reduced by using fewer and smaller devices as well as sparser and shorter interconnects. Of course both device-size reduction and interconnect localization have nontrivial performance implications. Smaller devices, with their lower drive currents, tend to be slower. Similarly, high-speed designs often imply a certain amount of nonlocal wires. For example, a ripple-carry adder has a relatively small number of devices and only short local wires, which lead to lower capacitance. However, the resulting capacitance reduction is usually not significant enough for us to altogether avoid the faster carry-lookahead designs with their attendant long, nonlocal interconnects. This interplay between capacitance and speed, combined with the performance effects of lower supply voltage, make the low-power design process a challenging global optimization problem (see Section 26.5).

The preceding points, along with methods for reducing the activity α, as discussed in Section 26.4, lead to several paradigms that are recurring themes in low-power design [Raba96]:

Avoiding waste. Glitching, or signals going through multiple transitions before settling at their final values, clocking modules when they are idle, and use of programmable (rather than dedicated) hardware constitute examples of waste that can be avoided.

Performance vs. power. Slower circuits use less power, so low-power circuits are often designed to barely meet performance requirements.

Area (cost) vs. power. Parallel processing and pipelining, with their attendant area overheads, can be applied to achieve desired performance levels at lower supply voltage and, thus, lower power.

Exploiting locality. Partitioning the design to exploit data locality improves both speed and power consumption.

Minimizing signal transitions. Careful encoding of data and state information, along with optimizations in the order and type of data manipulations, can reduce the average number of signal transitions per clock cycle and thus lead to lower power consumption. This is where number representations and arithmetic algorithms play key roles.

Dynamic adaptation. Changing the operating environment based on the input characteristics, selective precomputation of logic values before they are actually needed, and lazy evaluation (not computing values until absolutely necessary) all affect the power requirements.

These and other methods of saving power are being actively pursued within the research community. The following sections discuss specific examples of these methods in the context of arithmetic circuits.

26.3 REDUCTION OF POWER WASTE

The most obvious method of lowering the power consumption is to reduce the number or complexity of arithmetic operations performed. Two multiplications consume more power than one, and shifting plus addition requires less power than multiplication. Thus, computing from the expression $a(b + c)$ is better than using $ab + ac$. Similarly, $16a - a$ is preferable to $15a$.

Of course, the preceding examples represent optimizations that should be done regardless of whether power consumption is an issue. In other cases, however, operator reduction implies a sacrifice in speed, thus making the trade-off less clear-cut, especially if the lost speed is to be recovered by using a higher clock rate and/or supply voltage.

Multiplication of complex numbers provides a good example. Consider the following complex multiplication:

$$(a + bj)(c + dj) = (ac - bd) + (ad + bc)j$$

which requires four multiplications and two additions if implemented directly. The following equivalent formulation, however, includes only three multiplications, since $c(a + b)$, which appears in both the real and imaginary parts, needs to be computed only once:

$$(a + bj)(c + dj) = [c(a + b) - b(c + d)] + [c(a + b) - a(c - d)]j$$

The resulting circuit will have a critical path that is longer than that of the first design by at least one adder delay. This method becomes more attractive if $c + dj$ is a constant that must be multiplied by a given sequence of complex values $a^{(i)} + b^{(i)}j$. In this case, $c + d$ and $c - d$ are computed only once, leading to three multiplications and three additions per complex step thereafter.

When an arithmetic system consists of several functional units, or subcircuits, some of which remain unused for extended periods, it is advantageous to disable or turn off those units through clock gating (Fig. 26.2). The elimination of unnecessary clock activities inside the gated functional unit saves power, provided the gating signal itself changes at a much lower rate than the clock. Of course, the generation of the gating signals implies some overhead in terms of both cost and power consumption in the control logic. There may also be a speed penalty in view of a slight increase in the critical path for some signals.

A technique related to clock gating is guarded evaluation (Fig. 26.3). If the output of a function unit (FU) is relevant only if a particular select signal is high, that same select signal can be used to control a set of latches (or blocking gates) at the input to the unit. When the select signal is high, the latches become transparent; otherwise, the earlier inputs to the function unit are preserved, to suppress any activity in the unit.

A major source of wasted power in arithmetic and other digital circuits is glitching. Glitching occurs as a result of delay imbalances in signal propagation paths that lead to spurious transitions.

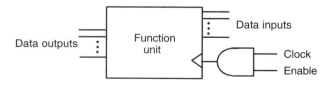

Fig. 26.2   Saving power through clock gating.

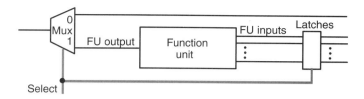

Fig. 26.3   Saving power via guarded evaluation.

Consider, for example, the full-adder cell in position i of a ripple-carry adder (Fig. 26.4). Suppose that c_i, p_i, and s_i are initially set to 0s and that both c_i and p_i are to change to 1 for a new set of inputs. The change in p_i takes effect almost immediately, whereas the 0-to-1 transition of c_i may occur after a long propagation delay. Therefore, s_i becomes 1 and is then switched back to 0. This redundant switching to 1 and then back to 0 wastes power.

Glitching can be eliminated, or substantially reduced, through delay balancing. Consider, for example, the array multiplier of Fig. 26.5. In this multiplier, each cell has four inputs, rather than three for a standard full adder, because one input to the FA is internally computed as the logical AND of the upper-horizontal and vertical inputs. The diagonal output is the sum and the lower-horizontal output is the carry.

Tracing the signal propagation paths in Fig. 26.5, we find that the lower-horizontal carry input and the diagonal sum input into the cell at the intersection of row x_i and column a_j and both experience a critical path delay of $2i + j$ cells, whereas the other input signals arrive with virtually no delay from the primary inputs. This difference can cause significant glitching. To reduce the power waste due to this glitching, one can insert delays along the paths of the vertical and horizontal broadcast inputs, a_i and x_j. Placing 1 and 2 units of delay within each cell on the horizontal and vertical broadcast lines, respectively, balances all the signal paths. Of course, the latency of the array multiplier will increase as a result of this delay balancing.

Similar methods of delay balancing can be applied to fast tree multipliers. However, deriving the delay-balanced design is somewhat harder for the latter in view of their irregular structures leading to signal paths with varying delays. Some delay balancing methods for such multipliers

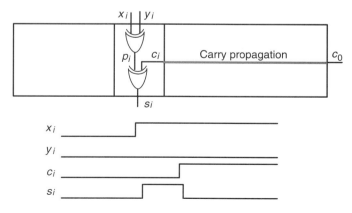

Fig. 26.4   Example of glitching in a ripple-carry adder.

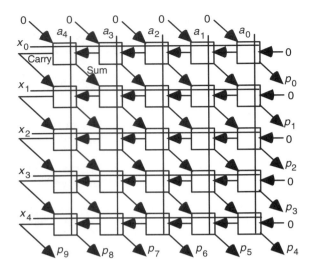

Fig. 26.5   An array multiplier with gated FA cells.

are given in [Saku95], where it is concluded that a power saving of more than 1/3 is feasible. Delay balancing methods for tree multipliers were studied even before their implications for power consumption became important. For example, we saw in Section 11.2, that balanced-tree multipliers were developed to facilitate the synthesis of partial product reduction trees from identical bit slices.

Pipelining also helps with glitch reduction and thus can lead to power savings. In a pipelined implementation, the logic depth within each pipeline segment can be made fairly small, leading to reduced opportunities for glitching. Existence of nodes that are deep, on the other hand, virtually guarantees that glitching will occur, both because of variations in signal path lengths and as a result of the deeper circuit nodes being within the cone of influence of a larger number of primary inputs. The effects of pipelining are further discussed in Sections 26.5 and 26.6.

26.4 REDUCTION OF ACTIVITY

Reduction of the activity α can be accomplished by a variety of methods. An examination of the effects of various information encoding schemes makes a good starting point. Consider, for example, the effect of 2's-complement encoding of numbers versus signed-magnitude encoding during negation or sign change. A signed-magnitude number is negated by simply flipping its sign bit, which involves minimal activity. For a 2's-complement number, on the other hand, many bits will change on the average, thus creating a great deal of activity. This does not mean, however, that signed-magnitude number representation is always better from the standpoint of power consumption. The more complex addition/subtraction process for such numbers may nullify some or all of this gain.

As another example of the effect of information encoding on power consumption, consider the design of a counter. Standard binary encoding of the count implies an average of about two transitions, or bit inversions, per cycle. Counting according to a Gray code, in which the representation of the next higher or lower number always differs from the current one in exactly one bit, reduces the activity by a factor of 2. This advantage exists in unidirectional counting as well as in up/down counting. One can generalize from this and examine energy-efficient state encoding schemes for sequential machines. If the states of a sequential machine are encoded such that states frequently visited in successive transitions have adjacent codes, the activity will be reduced.

The encoding scheme used might have an effect on power consumption in the implementation of high-radix or redundant arithmetic, as well. Each high-radix or redundant digit is typically encoded in multiple bits. We saw in Section 3.4, for example, that the particular encoding used to represent the BSD digit set $[-1, 1]$ has significant speed and cost implications. Power consumption might also be factored in when selecting the encoding. Very little can be said in general about power-efficient encodings. Distribution and correlation of data have significant effects on the optimal choice.

Generally speaking, shared, as opposed to dedicated, processing elements and data paths tend to increase the activity and should be avoided in low-power design if possible. If a wire or bus carries a positively correlated data stream on successive cycles, then switching activity is likely to be small (e.g., the high-order bits of numbers do not change in every cycle). If the same wire or bus carries elements from two independent data streams on alternate cycles, there will be significant switching activity, as each bit will change with probability 1/2 in every cycle.

Reordering of operations sometimes helps reduce the activity. For example, in adding a list of n numbers, separating them into two groups of positive and negative values, adding each group separately, and then adding the results together is likely to lead to reduced activity. Interestingly, this strategy also minimizes the effect of round-off errors, so it is doubly beneficial.

A method known as precomputation can sometimes help reduce the activity. Suppose we want to evaluate a function f of n variables such that the value of f can often be determined from a small number m of the n variables. Then the scheme depicted in Fig. 26.6 can be used to reduce the switching activity within the main computation circuit. In this scheme, a smaller "prediction" circuit detects the special cases in which the value of f actually depends on the remaining $n - m$ variables, and only then allows these values to be loaded into the input registers. Of course, since the precomputation circuit is added to the critical path, this scheme does involve a speed penalty in addition to the obvious cost overhead.

A variant of the precomputation scheme is to decompose a complicated computation into two or more simpler computations based on the value of one or more input variables. For

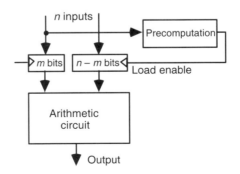

Fig. 26.6   Reduction of activity by precomputation.

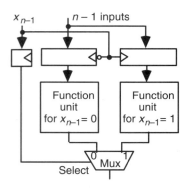

Fig. 26.7   Reduction of activity via Shannon expansion.

example, using the Shannon expansion of a function around the input variable x_{n-1} leads to the implementation shown in Fig. 26.7. Here, the input register is duplicated for $n-1$ of the n variables and the value of x_{n-1} is used to load the input data into one or the other register. The obvious overhead in terms of registers is unavoidable in this scheme. The overhead in the computation portion of the circuit can be minimized by proper selection of the expansion variable(s).

26.5 TRANSFORMATIONS AND TRADE-OFFS

Many power-saving schemes require that some other aspect of the arithmetic circuit, such as its speed or simplicity, be sacrificed. In this section, we look at some trade-offs of this nature.

Replacing the commonly used single-edge-triggered flip-flops (that load data at the rising or falling edge of the clock signal) by double-edge-triggered flip-flops would allow a factor-of-2 reduction in the clock frequency. Since clock distribution constitutes a major source of power consumption in synchronous systems, this transformation can lead to savings in power at the cost of more complex flip-flops. Flip-flops can also be designed to be self-gating, so that if the input of the flip-flop is identical to its output, the switching of its internal clock signal is suppressed to save power. Again, a self-gating flip-flop is more complex that a standard one.

Parallelism and pipelining are complementary methods of increasing the throughput of an arithmetic circuit. A two-way parallel circuit or a two-stage pipelined circuit can potentially increase the throughput by a factor of 2. Both methods can also be used to reduce the power consumption.

Consider an arithmetic circuit, such as a multiplier, that is required to operate at the frequency f; that is, it must perform f operations per second. A standard design, operating at voltage V, is shown in Fig. 26.8a. The power dissipation of this design is proportional to fCV^2, as discussed in Section 26.2, where C is the effective capacitance. If we duplicate the circuit and use each copy to operate on alternating input values, as shown in Fig. 26.8b, then the required operating frequency of each copy becomes $f/2$. This increases the effective capacitance of the overall circuit to $2.2C$, say, but allows the slower copies to use a lower voltage of $0.6V$, say. The net

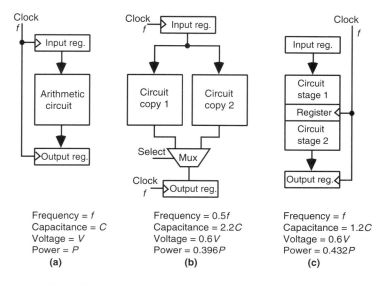

Fig. 26.8   Reduction of power via parallelism or pipelining.

effect is that the power is reduced from P to $(0.5 \times 2.2 \times 0.6^2)P = 0.396P$ while maintaining the original performance.

An alternative power reduction architecture with pipelining is shown in Fig. 26.8c. Here, the computation is sliced into two stages, each only half as deep as the original circuit. Thus, voltage can again be reduced from V to $0.6V$, say. The hardware overhead of pipelining increases the capacitance to $1.2C$, say, while the operating frequency f remains the same. The net effect is that power is reduced from P to $(1 \times 1.2 \times 0.6^2)P = 0.432P$ while maintaining the original performance in terms of throughput.

The possibility of using parallelism or pipelining to save power is not always easily perceived. Consider, for example, the recursive computation

$$y^{(i)} = ax^{(i)} + by^{(i-1)}$$

where the coefficients a and b are constants. For this first-order, infinite impulse response (IIR) filter, the circuit implementation shown in Fig. 26.9 immediately suggests itself. The operating frequency of this circuit is dictated by the latency of a multiply-add operation.

The method that allows us to apply parallelism to this computation is known as loop unrolling. In this method, we essentially compute the two outputs $y^{(i)}$ and $y^{(i+1)}$ simultaneously using the equations:

$$y^{(i)} = ax^{(i)} + by^{(i-1)}$$
$$y^{(i+1)} = ax^{(i+1)} + abx^{(i)} + b^2 y^{(i-1)}$$

The preceding equations lead to the implementation shown in Fig. 26.10 which, just like the parallel scheme of Fig. 26.8, can operate at a lower frequency, and thus at a lower voltage, without affecting the throughput. The new operating frequency will be somewhat lower than $f/2$

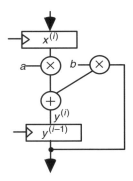

Fig. 26.9   Direct realization of a first-order IIR filter.

because the three-operand adder in Fig. 26.10 is slower than a two-operand adder. However, the difference between the operating frequency and $f/2$ will be negligible if the three-operand adder is implemented by a carry-save adder followed by a standard two-operand adder.

Retiming, or redistribution of delay elements (registers) in a design, is another method that may be used to reduce the power consumption. Note that retiming can also be used for throughput enhancement, as discussed in connection with the design of systolic arithmetic function units in Section 25.6. As an example of power implications of retiming, consider a fourth-order, finite impulse response (FIR) filter characterized by the following equation:

$$y^{(i)} = ax^{(i)} + bx^{(i-1)} + cx^{(i-2)} + dx^{(i-3)}$$

Figure 26.11 shows a straightforward realization of the filter. The frequency at which the filter can operate, and thus the supply voltage, is dictated by the latency of one multiplication and three additions. The number of addition levels can be reduced to two by using a two-level

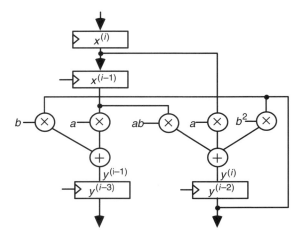

Fig. 26.10   Realization of a first-order IIR filter, unrolled once.

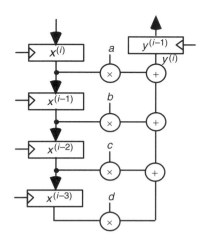

Fig. 26.11   Possible realization of a fourth-order FIR filter.

binary tree of adders, but the resulting design is less regular and more difficult to expand in a modular fashion.

An alternative design, depicted in Fig. 26.12, moves the registers to the right side of the circuit, thereby making the stage latency equal to that of one multiplication and one addition. The registers now hold:

$$
\begin{aligned}
u^{(i-1)} &= dx^{(i-1)} \\
v^{(i-1)} &= cx^{(i-1)} + dx^{(i-2)} \\
w^{(i-1)} &= bx^{(i-1)} + cx^{(i-2)} + dx^{(i-3)} \\
y^{(i-1)} &= ax^{(i-1)} + bx^{(i-2)} + cx^{(i-3)} + dx^{(i-4)}
\end{aligned}
$$

This alternate computation scheme allows a higher operating frequency at a given supply voltage or, alternatively, a lower supply voltage for a desired throughput. The effect of this transformation on the capacitance is difficult to predict and will depend on the detailed design and layout of the arithmetic elements.

26.6 SOME EMERGING METHODS

Asynchronous digital circuits have been studied for many years. Despite advantages in speed, distributed (localized) control, and built-in capability for pipelining, such circuits are not yet widely used. The only exceptions are found in bus handshaking protocols, interrupt handling mechanisms, and the design of certain classes of high-performance, special-purpose systems (wave front arrays). Localized connections and elimination of the clock distribution network may give asynchronous circuits an edge in power consumption. This, along with improvements in the asynchronous circuit design methodologies and reduced overhead may bring such circuits to the forefront in the design of general-purpose digital systems. However, before this happens, design/synthesis tools and testing methods must be improved.

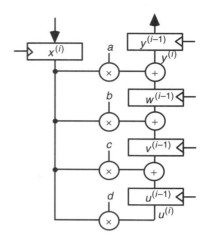

Fig. 26.12   Realization of the retimed fourth-order FIR filter.

In asynchronous circuits, timing information is embedded in, or travels along with, the data signals. Each function unit is activated when its input data becomes available and in turn notifies the next unit in the chain when its results are ready (Fig. 26.13). In the bundled data protocol, a "data ready" or "request" signal is added to a bundle of data lines to inform the receiver, which then uses an "acknowledge" line to release the sending module. In the two-rail protocol, each signal is individually encoded in a self-timed format using two wires. The latter approach essentially doubles the number of wires that go from module to module, but has the advantage of being completely insensitive to delay.

The best form of asynchronous design from the viewpoint of low power uses dual-rail data encoding with transition signaling: two wires are used for each signal, with a transition on one wire indicating that a 0 has arrived and a transition on the other designating the arrival of a 1. Level-sensitive signaling is also possible, but because the signal must return to 0 after each transaction, power consumption is higher.

Wave pipelining, discussed in Section 25.2, affects the power requirements for two reasons. One reason is that the careful balancing of delays within each stage, which is required for maximum performance, also tends to reduce glitching. A second, more important, reason is that in a wave-pipelined system, the same throughput can be achieved at a lower clock frequency. Like asynchronous circuit design, wave pipelining is not yet widely used. However, as problems with this method are better understood and automatic synthesis tools are developed, application of wave pipelining may become commonplace in the design of high-performance digital systems, with or without power considerations.

Clearly, the reduction of dynamic power dissipation in CMOS circuits, which was the focus of our discussions in this chapter, is not the only relevant criterion in dealing with low-power designs. Efforts in this area must deal with a spectrum of methods ranging from the architecture to the individual wires and transistors. Availability of more data on the power requirements of various arithmetic circuits and design styles [Call96] will help in this regard. Similarly, the development of better low-power synthesis and power estimation tools, which will allow the designers to experiment with various designs and fine-tune their parameters, will no doubt lead to greater applicability of these methods. For tutorial material on low-power design, see [Kuro99], [Beni01]. Power consumption issues in general-purpose and high-performance microprocessors are treated in [Mudg01], [Gonz96].

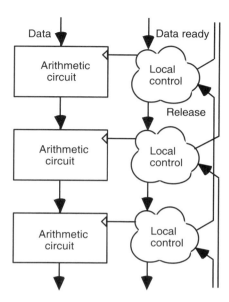

Fig. 26.13 Part of an asynchronous chain of computations.

26.1 Clock-related power dissipation Estimate the power dissipation associated with clock distribution in a 250 MHz processor chip operating at 3.3 V if the die dimensions are 1 cm × 1.3 cm, the length of the 1-μm-wide clock distribution network is roughly four times the die's perimeter, and the parasitic capacitance of the metal layer is 1 nF/mm^2. How will the power dissipation be affected if the chip's technology is scaled down by a factor of 1.4 in all dimensions, assuming that the supply voltage and frequency remain the same? *Hint:* Capacitance of a wire is directly proportional to its area and inversely proportional to the thickness of insulation.

26.2 Power implications of other optimizations Many of the methods considered in earlier chapters for increasing the operation speed or reducing the hardware cost have implications for power consumption. Furthermore, reduction in power consumption is not always in conflict with other optimizations.

   a.   Provide an example of a speed enhancement method that also reduces power.

   b.   Describe a speed enhancement method that substantially increases power.

   c.   Provide an example of a cost-saving method that also leads to reduced power.

   d.   Describe a cost reduction method that substantially increases power.

26.3 Saving power by operator reduction Consider the complex-number multiplication scheme discussed at the beginning of Section 26.3.

   a.   Can a similar method be applied to synthesizing a $2k \times 2k$ multiplier from $k \times k$ multipliers? Discuss.

b. What about rotating a series of vectors by the constant angle θ using the familiar transformations $X = x \sin \theta + y \cos \theta$ and $Y = x \cos \theta - y \sin \theta$?

26.4 Saving power by operation reordering

a. The expression $u + 2^{-8}v + 2^{-10}w$, with the fixed-point fractional operands u, v, and w, is to be evaluated using two adders. What is the best order of evaluation from the standpoint of minimizing signal transitions? Does the best order depend on whether the numbers are signed?

b. Generalize the result of part a to the addition of n fractions, where the magnitude of the ith fraction is known to be in $[0, 2^{-m_i})$.

26.5 Saving power by reduction and reordering Rearrange the accompanying computation to reduce the power requirements. If more than one rearrangement is possible, compare them with respect to operation complexity (power), latency, and cost.

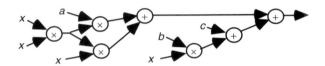

26.6 Saving power via delay balancing The array multiplier of Fig. 26.5 is different from the one shown in Fig. 11.13 and in some ways inferior to it. Compare the two designs with respect to worst-case delay and glitching, before and after the application of delay balancing.

26.7 Reduction of activity by bus-invert encoding Bus-invert encoding is a scheme whereby a single wire is added to a bus to designate polarity: a polarity of 0 indicates that the desired data is on the bus, whereas a polarity of 1 means that the complement of the desired data is being transmitted.

a. Draw a complete block diagram of this scheme, including all units needed on the sender and receiver sides.

b. Discuss the power-saving implications of this method. Then, using reasonable assumptions about the data, try to quantify the extent of savings achieved.

26.8 Saving power via precomputation

a. Apply the precomputation scheme of Fig. 26.6 to the design of a 32-bit integer comparator that determines whether $x > y$. Assume 2's-complement inputs and use the sign bit plus 2 magnitude bits for the precomputation. *Hint:* Invert the sign bits and compare as unsigned integers.

b. Repeat part a, this time assuming signed-magnitude inputs.

26.9 Power implications of pipelining

a. Suppose that in the design of Fig. 26.10, the three-operand adder is to be implemented by means of a pair of two-operand adders. The critical path of the circuit will then become longer than that in the original circuit before unrolling. Show how circuit throughput can be maintained or improved by conversion into a two-stage pipeline.

b. Repeat part a for an implementation of the IIR filter of Fig. 26.9 that uses two steps of unrolling.

26.10 Parallelism and pipelining

a. Choose three convergence computation methods from among those discussed in Chapters 16, 21, and 23. Discuss opportunities that might exist for power savings in these computations through parallelism and/or pipelining.

b. Compare convergence and digit-recurrence methods with regard to their power requirements.

26.11 Arithmetic by table lookup In Chapter 24, we saw that table-lookup methods can be highly cost-effective for certain arithmetic computations.

a. What are the power consumption implications of arithmetic by table lookup?

b. Can you think of any power-saving method for use with tabular implementations?

26.12 A circuit technique for power reduction In CMOS circuit implementation of symmetric functions, such as AND, OR, or XOR, the logically equivalent input nodes may differ in their physical characteristics. For example, the inputs of a four-input AND gate may have different capacitances.

a. How is this observation relevant to the design of low-power arithmetic circuits?

b. Describe an application context for which this property may be used to reduce power. *Hint:* Look at the filter implementations of Section 26.5.

26.13 Power considerations in fast counters Consider the power consumption aspects of the fast counter designs of Section 5.5. Compare the designs with each other and with standard counters and discuss.

26.14 Bit-serial versus parallel arithmetic Study the power efficiency aspects of bit-serial, digit-serial, and bit-parallel arithmetic. What would be a good composite figure of merit incorporating speed, cost, and power?

26.15 Power implications of arithmetic methods Based on what you have learned in this chapter, identify power consumption implications, if any, of the following design choices. Justify your answers.

a. Multiplication with and without Booth's recoding.

b. Floating-point versus logarithmic number representation.

c. Restoring versus nonrestoring division or square-rooting.

26.16 Low-power division Contrast convergence and digit-recurrence division methods from the viewpoint of power consumption, and discuss power reduction strategies that might be applicable in each case. Begin by studying the approach taken in [Nann99].

REFERENCES

[Atha96] Athas, W.C., "Energy-Recovery CMOS," in *Low-Power Design Methodologies*, J.M. Rabaey and M. Pedram (eds.), Kluwer, 1996, pp. 65–100.

[Beni01] Benini, L., G. De Micheli, and E. Macii, "Designing Low-Power Circuits: Practical Recipes," *IEEE Circuits and Systems*, Vol. 1, No. 1, pp. 6–25, First Quarter 2001.

[Call96] Callaway, T.K., and E.E. Swartzlander, Jr., "Low Power Arithmetic Components," in *Low-Power Design Methodologies*, J.M. Rabaey and M. Pedram (eds.), Kluwer, 1996, pp. 161–200.

[Chan95] Chandrakasan, A.P., and R.W. Broderson, *Low Power Digital CMOS Design*, Kluwer, 1995.

[Gonz96] Gonzalez, R. and M. Horowitz, "Energy Dissipation in General-Purpose Microprocessors," *IEEE J. Solid-State Circuits*, pp. 1277–1284, 1996.

[Kuro99] Kuroda, T. and T. Sakurai, "Low Power CMOS VLSI Design," Chap. 24 in *Digital Signal Processing for Multimedia Systems*, ed. by K.K. Parhi and T. Nishitani, Marcel Dekker, 1999, pp. 693–739.

[Mudg01] Mudge, T., "Power: A First-Class Architectural Design Constraint," *IEEE Computer*, Vol. 34, No. 4, pp. 52–58, April 2001.

[Nann99] Nannarelli, A., and T. Lang, "Low-Power Divider," *IEEE Trans. Computers,* Vol. 48, No. 1, pp. 2–14, 1999.

[Parh96] Parhi, K.K., and F. Catthoor, "Design of High-Performance DSP Systems," in *Emerging Technologies: Designing Low-Power Digital Systems*, R.K. Cavin III and W. Liu, eds., IEEE Press, pp. 447–507.

[Raba96] Rabaey, J.M., M. Pedram, and P.E. Landman, "Introduction," in *Low-Power Design Methodologies*, J.M. Rabaey and M. Pedram (eds.), Kluwer, 1996, pp. 1–18.

[Raba98] Rabaey, J.M. (ed.), "VLSI Design and Implementation Fuels the Signal Processing Revolution," *IEEE Signal Processing*, Vol. 15, No. 1, pp. 22–37, 1998.

[Saku95] Sakuta, T., W. Lee, and P. Balsara, "Delay Balanced Multipliers for Low Power/Low Voltage DSP Core," *Digest IEEE Symp. Low-Power Electronics*, 1995, pp. 36–37.

[Yeap98] Yeap, G., *Practical Low Power Digital VLSI Design*, Kluwer, 1998.

Chapter
27 | FAULT-TOLERANT ARITHMETIC

Modern digital components are remarkably robust, but with a great many of them put together in a complex arithmetic system, things can and do go wrong. In data communication, a per-bit error probability of around 10^{-10} is considered quite good. However, at a rate of many millions of arithmetic operations per second, such an error probability in computations can lead to several bit-errors per second. While coding techniques are routinely applied to protect against errors in data transmission or storage, the same cannot be said about computations performed in an arithmetic circuit. In this chapter, we examine key methods that can be used to improve the robustness and reliability of arithmetic systems. Chapter topics include:

- **27.1** Faults, Errors, and Error Codes
- **27.2** Arithmetic Error-Detecting Codes
- **27.3** Arithmetic Error-Correcting Codes
- **27.4** Self-Checking Function Units
- **27.5** Algorithm-Based Fault Tolerance
- **27.6** Fault-Tolerant RNS Arithmetic

27.1 FAULTS, ERRORS, AND ERROR CODES

So far, we have assumed that arithmetic and logic elements always behave as expected: an AND gate always outputs the logical AND of its inputs, a table entry maintains its correct initial value, and a wire remains permanently connected. Even though modern integrated circuits are extremely reliable, faults (deviations from specified or correct functional behavior) do occur in the course of lengthy computations, especially in systems that operate under harsh environmental conditions, deal with extreme/unpredictable loads, or are used during long missions. The output of an AND gate may become permanently "stuck on 1," thus yielding an incorrect output when at least one input is 0. Or cross talk or external interference may cause the AND gate to suffer a "transient fault" in which its output becomes incorrect for only a few clock cycles. A table entry may become corrupt as a result of manufacturing imperfections in the memory cells or

447

logic faults in the read/write circuitry. Because of overheating, a VLSI manufacturing defect, or a combination of both, a wire may break or short-circuit to another wire.

Ensuring correct functioning of digital systems in the presence of (permanent and transient) faults is the subject of the *fault-tolerant computing* discipline, also known as *reliable* (*dependable*) *computing* [Parh94]. In this chapter, we review some ideas in fault-tolerant computing that are particularly relevant to the computation of arithmetic functions.

Methods of detecting or correcting data errors have their origins in the field of communications. Early communications channels were highly unreliable and extremely noisy. So signals sent from one end were often distorted or changed by the time they reached the receiving end. The remedy, thought up by communications engineers, was to encode the data in redundant formats known as "codes" or "error codes." Examples of coding methods include adding a parity bit (an example of a single-error-detecting or SED code), checksums, and Hamming single-error-correcting, double-error-detecting (SEC/DED) code. Today, error-detecting and error-correcting codes are still used extensively in communications, for even though the reliability of these systems and noise reduction/shielding methods have improved enormously, so have the data rates and data transmission volumes, making the error probability nonnegligible.

Codes originally developed for communications can be used to protect against storage errors. When the early integrated-circuit memories proved to be less reliable than the then-common magnetic core technology, IC designers were quick to incorporate SEC/DED codes into their designs.

The data processing cycle in a system whose storage and memory-to-processor data transfers are protected by an error code can be represented as in Fig. 27.1. In this scheme, which is routinely applied to modern digital systems, the data manipulation part is unprotected. Decoding/encoding is necessary because common codes are not closed under arithmetic operations. For example, the sum of two even-parity numbers does not necessarily have even parity. As another example, when we change an element within a list that is protected by a checksum, we must compute a new checksum that replaces the old one.

One way to protect the arithmetic computation against fault-induced errors is to use duplication with comparison of the two results (for single fault/error detection) or triplication with 2-out-of-3 voting on the three results (for single fault masking or error correction). Figure 27.2 shows possible ways for implementing such duplication and triplication schemes.

In Fig. 27.2a, the decoding logic is duplicated along with the ALU, to ensure that a single fault in the decoder does not go undetected. The encoder, on the other hand, remains a critical element whose failure will lead to undetected errors. However, since the output of the encoder is redundant (coded), it is possible to design the encoding circuitry in a way that ensures the production of a non-codeword at its output if anything goes wrong. Such a design, referred to as *self-checking*, leads to error detection by the checker associated with the memory subsystem or later when the erroneous stored value is used as an input to the ALU. Assuming the use of a self-checking encoder, the duplicated design in Fig. 27.2a can detect any error resulting from a fault that is totally confined within one of the blocks shown in the diagram. This includes the "compare" block whose failure may produce a *false alarm*. An undetected mismatch would require at least two faults in separate blocks.

The design with triplicated ALU in Fig. 27.2b is similar. Here, the voter is a critical element and must be designed with care. Self-checking design cannot be applied to the voter (as used here), since its output is nonredundant. However, by combining the voting and encoding functions, one may be able to design an efficient self-checking voter-encoder. This *three-channel* computation strategy can be generalized to n channels to permit the tolerance of more faults. However, the cost overhead of a higher degree of replication becomes prohibitive.

Since the preceding replication schemes involve significant hardware overheads, one might attempt to apply coding methods for fault detection or fault tolerance within the ALU. The

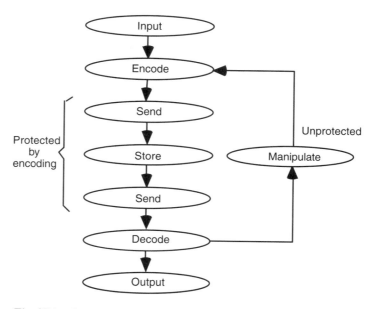

Fig. 27.1 A common way of applying information coding techniques.

first issue we encounter in trying to use this approach is that single, double, burst, and other error types commonly dealt with in communications do not provide useful characterizations for arithmetic. Whereas a spike due to noise may affect a single bit (random error) or a small number of consecutive bits (burst error), a single erroneous carry signal within an adder (caused, e.g., by a faulty gate in the carry logic) may produce an arbitrary number of bit inversions in the output. Figure 27.3 provides an example.

We see in the example of Fig. 27.3 that a single fault in the adder has caused 12 of the sum bits to be inverted. In coding theory parlance, we say that the *Hamming distance* between the correct and incorrect results is 12 or that the error has a *Hamming weight* (number of 1s in the XOR of the two values) of 12.

Error detection and correction capabilities of codes can be related to the minimum Hamming distance between *codewords* as exemplified by the following:

Single-error-detecting (SED)	Min. Hamming distance $= 2$
Single-error-correcting (SEC)	Min. Hamming distance $= 3$
SEC/DED	Min. Hamming distance $= 4$

For example, in the case of SED codes, any single-bit inversion in a codeword is guaranteed not to change it to another codeword, thus leading to error detection. For SEC, a single-bit inversion leads to an invalid word that is closer (in terms of Hamming distance) to the original correct codeword than to any other valid codeword, thus allowing for error correction.

From the addition example in Fig. 27.3, we see that even if some "single-error-detecting code" were closed under addition, it would be incapable of detecting the erroneous result in this case. We note, however, that in our example, the erroneous sum differs from the correct sum by 2^4. Since in computer arithmetic we deal with numbers as opposed to arbitrary bit strings, it is

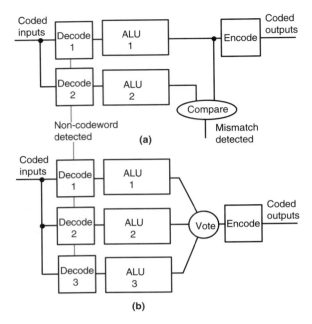

Fig. 27.2   Arithmetic fault detection or fault tolerance (masking) with replicated units.

the numerical difference between the erroneous and correct values that is of interest to us, not the number of bits in which they differ.

Accordingly, we define the *arithmetic weight* of an error as the minimum number of signed powers of 2 that must be added to the correct value to produce the erroneous result (or vice versa). Here are two examples:

Correct result	0111 1111 1111 0100	1101 1111 1111 0100
Erroneous result	1000 0000 0000 0100	0110 0000 0000 0100
Difference (error)	$16 = 2^4$	$-32752 = -2^{15} + 2^4$
Error, in minimum-weight BSD form	0000 0000 0001 0000	$^-$1000 0000 0001 0000
Arithmetic weight of the error	1	2
Type of error	Single, positive	Double, negative

Hence, the errors in the preceding examples can be viewed as "single" and "double" errors in the arithmetic sense. Special *arithmetic error codes* have been developed that are capable of detecting or correcting errors that are characterized by their arithmetic, rather than Hamming, weights. We review some such codes in Sections 27.2 and 27.3.

Note that a minimum-weight BSD representation of a k-bit error magnitude has at most $\lceil (k + 1)/2 \rceil$ nonzero digits and can always be written in *canonic BSD* form without any consecutive nonzero digits. The canonic form of a BSD number, which is unique, is intimately related to the notion of arithmetic error weight.

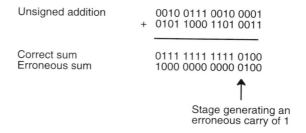

Fig. 27.3   How a single carry error can produce an arbitrary number of bit-errors (inversions) in the sum.

27.2 ARITHMETIC ERROR-DETECTING CODES

Arithmetic error-detecting codes:

1. Are characterized in terms of the arithmetic weights of detectable errors.
2. Allow us to perform arithmetic operations on coded operands directly.

The importance of the first property was discussed at the end of Section 27.1. The second property is crucial because it allows us to protect arithmetic computations against circuit faults with much lower hardware redundancy (overhead) than full duplication or triplication.

In this section, we discuss two classes of arithmetic error-detecting codes: product codes and residue codes. In both cases we will assume unsigned integer operands. Extension of the concepts to signed integers and arbitrary fixed-point numbers is straightforward. Codes for floating-point numbers tend to be more complicated and have received limited attention from arithmetic and fault tolerance researchers.

a. Product codes

In a *product code*, also known as *AN code*, a number N is represented as the product AN, where the check modulus A is a constant. Verifying the validity of an AN-coded operand requires checking its divisibility by A. For odd A, all weight-1 arithmetic errors (including all single-bit errors) are detected. Arithmetic errors of weight 2 and higher may not be detectable. For example, the error $32736 = 2^{15} - 2^5$ is not detectable with $A = 3, 11$, or 31, since the error magnitude is divisible by each of these check moduli.

Encoding/decoding of numbers with product codes requires multiplication/division by A. We will see shortly that performing arithmetic operations with product-coded operands also requires multiplication and division by A. Thus, for these codes to be practically viable, multiplication and division by the check modulus A should be simple. We are thus led to the class of *low-cost product codes* with check moduli of the form $A = 2^a - 1$.

Multiplication by $A = 2^a - 1$ is simple because it requires a shift and a subtract. In particular, if the computation is performed a bits at a time (i.e., digit-serially in radix 2^a), then one needs only an a-bit adder, an a-bit register to store the previous radix-2^a digit, and a flip-flop for storing the carry. Division by $A = 2^a - 1$ is similarly simple if done a bits at a time. Given $y = (2^a - 1)x$, we find x by computing $2^a x - y$. The first term in this expression is unknown, but we know that it ends in a zeros. This is all that we need to compute the least significant a bits of x based on the knowledge of y. These computed bits of x form the next a bits of $2^a x$, allowing us to find the next a bits of x, etc.

Since $A = 2^a - 1$ is odd, low-cost product codes can detect any weight-1 arithmetic error. Some weight-2 and higher-weight errors may go undetected, but the fraction of such errors becomes smaller with an increase in A. Unidirectional errors, in which all erroneous bits are 0-to-1 or 1-to-0 inversions (but not both), form an important class of errors in VLSI implementations. For unidirectional errors, the error magnitude is the sum of several powers of 2 with the same signs.

THEOREM 27.1   Any unidirectional error with arithmetic weight not exceeding $a - 1$ is detectable by a low-cost product code that uses the check modulus $A = 2^a - 1$.

For example, the low-cost product code with $A = 15$ can detect any weight-2 or weight-3 unidirectional arithmetic error in addition to all weight-1 errors. The following are examples of weight-2 and weight-3 unidirectional errors that are detectable because the resulting error magnitude is not a multiple of 15:

$$8 + 4 = 12$$
$$128 + 4 = 132$$
$$16 + 4 + 2 = 22$$
$$256 + 16 + 2 = 274$$

Product codes are examples of nonseparate, or nonseparable, codes in which the original data and the redundant information for checking are intermixed. In other words, the original number N is not immediately apparent from inspecting its encoded version AN but must be obtained through decoding (in this case, division by the check modulus A).

Arithmetic operations on product-coded operands are quite simple. Addition or subtraction is done directly, since:

$$Ax \pm Ay = A(x \pm y)$$

Direct multiplication results in:

$$Aa \times Ax = A^2 ax$$

So the result must be corrected through division by A. For division, if $z = qd + s$, with q being the quotient and s the remainder, we have:

$$Az = q(Ad) + As$$

So, direct division yields the quotient q along with the remainder As. The remainder is thus obtained in encoded form, but the resulting quotient q must be encoded via multiplication by A. Because q is obtained in nonredundant form, an error occurring in its computation will go undetected. To keep the data protected against errors in the course of the division process, one can premultiply the dividend Az by A and then divide A^2z by Ad as usual. The problem with this approach is that the division leads to a quotient q^* and remainder s^* satisfying

$$A^2z = q^*(Ad) + s^*$$

which may be different from the expected results Aq and A^2s (the latter needing correction through division by A). Since q^* can be larger than Aq by up to $A - 1$ units, the quotient and remainder obtained from normal division may need correction. However, this again raises the possibility of undetected errors in the handling of the unprotected value q^*, which is not necessarily a multiple of A.

A possible solution to the preceding problem, when one is doing the division a bits at a time for $A = 2^a - 1$, is to adjust the last radix-2^a digit of q^* in such a way that the adjusted quotient q^{**} becomes a multiple of A. This can be done rather easily by keeping a modulo-A checksum of the previous quotient digits. One can prove that suitably choosing the last radix-2^a digit of q^{**} in $[-2^a + 2, 1]$ is sufficient to correct the problem. A subtraction is then needed to convert q^{**} to standard binary representation. Details can be found elsewhere [Aviz73].

Square-rooting leads to a problem similar to that encountered in division. Suppose that we multiply the radicand Az by A and then use a standard square-rooting algorithm to compute:

$$\lfloor\sqrt{A^2x}\rfloor = \lfloor A\sqrt{x}\rfloor$$

Since the preceding result is in general different from the correct result $A\lfloor\sqrt{x}\rfloor$, there is a need for correction. Again, the computed value $\lfloor A\sqrt{x}\rfloor$ can exceed the correct root $A\lfloor\sqrt{x}\rfloor$ by up to $A - 1$ units. So, the same correction procedure suggested for division is applicable here as well.

b. Residue codes

In a *residue code*, an operand N is represented by a pair of numbers $(N, C(N))$, where $C(N) = N$ mod A is the check part. The check modulus A is a constant. Residue codes are examples of *separate* or *separable* codes in which the data and check parts are not intermixed, thus making decoding trivial. Encoding a number N requires the computation of $C(N) = N$ mod A, which is attached to N to form its encoded representation $(N, C(N))$.

As in the case of product codes, we can define the class of *low-cost residue codes*, with $A = 2^a - 1$, for which the encoding computation N mod A is simple: it requires that a-bit segments of N be added modulo $2^a - 1$ (using an a-bit adder with end-around carry). This can be done digit-serially by using a single adder or in parallel by using a binary tree of a-bit 1's-complement adders.

Arithmetic operations on residue-coded operands are quite simple, especially if a low-cost check modulus $A = 2^a - 1$ is used. Addition or subtraction is done by operating on the data parts and check parts separately. That is:

$$(x, C(x)) \pm (y, C(y)) = (x \pm y, (C(x) \pm C(y)) \bmod A)$$

Hence, as shown in Fig. 27.4, an arithmetic unit for residue-coded operands has a main adder for adding/subtracting the data parts and a small modulo-A adder to add/subtract the residue checks. To detect faults within the arithmetic unit, the output of this small modular adder (check processor) is compared to the residue of the output from the main adder.

Multiplication of residue-coded operands is equally simple, since:

$$(a, C(a)) \times (x, C(x)) = (a \times x, (C(a) \times C(x)) \bmod A)$$

So, again, the structure shown in Fig. 27.4 is applicable. This method of checking the multiplication operation is essentially what we do when we verify the correctness of our pencil-and-paper multiplication result by casting out nines.

Just as in RNS, division and square-rooting are complicated with residue-coded operands. For these operations, the small residue check processor cannot operate independently from the main processor and must interact with it to compute the check part of the result. Details are beyond the scope of this chapter.

As in product codes, choosing any odd value for A guarantees the detection of all weight-1 arithmetic errors with residue codes. However, residue codes are less capable than product codes for detecting multiple unidirectional errors. For example, we saw earlier that the $15N$ code can detect all weight-2 and weight-3 unidirectional arithmetic errors. The residue code with $A = 15$ cannot detect the weight-2 error resulting from 0-to-1 inversion of the least significant bit of the data as well as the least significant bit of the residue. This error goes undetected because it adds 1 to the data as well as to the residue, making the result a valid codeword.

To correct the preceding problem, *inverse residue codes* have been proposed for which the check part represents $A - (N \bmod A)$ rather than $N \bmod A$. In the special case of $A = 2^a - 1$, the check bits constitute the bitwise complement of $N \bmod A$. Unidirectional errors now affect the data and check parts in opposite directions, making their detection more likely. By noting that attachment of the a-bit inverse residue $C'(N) = A - (N \bmod A)$ to the least significant end of a k-bit number N makes the resulting $(k + a)$-bit number a multiple of $A = 2^a - 1$, the following result is easily proven.

THEOREM 27.2   Any unidirectional error with arithmetic weight not exceeding $a - 1$ is detectable by a low-cost inverse residue code that uses the check modulus $A = 2^a - 1$.

The added cost or overhead of an error-detecting code has two components:

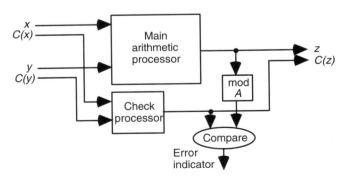

Fig. 27.4   Arithmetic processor with residue checking.

The increased word width for coded operands adds to the cost of registers, memory, and data links.

Checked arithmetic or wider operands make the ALU more complex.

With respect to the first component of cost, product, residue, and inverse residue codes are similar. For example, the low-cost versions of these codes with the check modulus $A = 2^a - 1$ all require a additional bits to represent the coded operands. With regard to arithmetic, residue and inverse residue codes are simpler than product codes for addition and multiplication and more complex for division.

It is interesting to note that the residue-class codes are the only possible separable codes for checking an adder [Pete58]. Also, it has been proven that bitwise logical operations such as AND, OR, and XOR, cannot be checked by any coding scheme with less than 100% redundancy; that is, the best we can do for error detection in logical operations is duplication and comparison [Pete59].

27.3 ARITHMETIC ERROR-CORRECTING CODES

We illustrate the main ideas relating to arithmetic error-correcting codes by way of examples from the class of *biresidue codes*. A biresidue code represents a number N as the triple (N, $C(N)$, $D(N)$), where the check components $C(N) = N \bmod A$ and $D(N) = N \bmod B$ are residues with respect to the check moduli A and B. If the original number requires k bits for its binary representation, its biresidue-coded representation would need $k + \lceil \log_2 A \rceil + \lceil \log_2 B \rceil$ bits.

Encoding for the class of biresidue codes is similar to that of single-residue codes, except that two residues must be computed. Addition and multiplication of biresidue-coded operands can be performed by an arithmetic processor similar to that shown in Fig. 27.4, but with two check processors. Since the two residues can be computed and checked in parallel, no speed is lost.

Consider errors that affect the number N or only one of the residues, say $C(N)$. Such errors can be corrected as follows.

Error in C(N). In this case, $C(N)$ will fail the residue check, while $D(N)$ passes its check; $C(N)$ can then be corrected by recomputing $N \bmod A$.

Error in N. Unless the error magnitude happens to be a multiple of A and/or B (thus being either totally undetectable or else indistinguishable from a residue error), both residue checks will fail, thus pointing to N as the erroneous component. To correct such errors, the differences between $N_{\text{wrong}} \bmod A$ ($N_{\text{wrong}} \bmod B$) and $C(N)$ ($D(N)$) must be noted. The two differences, $[(N_{\text{wrong}} \bmod A) - C(N)] \bmod A$ and $[(N_{\text{wrong}} \bmod B) - D(N)] \bmod B$, constitute an *error syndrome*. The error is then correctable if the syndromes for different errors are distinct.

Consider, as an example, a biresidue code with the low-cost check moduli $A = 7$ and $B = 15$. Table 27.1 shows that any weight-1 arithmetic error E with $|E| \leq 2048$ leads to a unique error syndrome, thus allowing us to correct it by subtracting the associated error value from N_{wrong}. For $|E| \geq 4096$, the syndromes assume the same values as for $E/4096$. Hence, weight-1 error correction is guaranteed only for a 12-bit data part. Since the two residues require a total of 7 bits for their representations, the redundancy for this biresidue code is $7/12 \approx 58\%$.

TABLE 27.1
Error syndrome s for weight-1 arithmetic errors in the (7, 15) biresidue code

Positive Error	Error syndrome		Negative error	Error syndrome	
	mod 7	mod 15		mod 7	mod 15
1	1	1	−1	6	14
2	2	2	−2	5	13
4	4	4	−4	3	11
8	1	8	−8	6	7
16	2	1	−16	5	14
32	4	2	−32	3	13
64	1	4	−64	6	11
128	2	8	−128	5	7
256	4	1	−256	3	14
512	1	2	−512	6	13
1024	2	4	−1024	5	11
2048	4	8	−2048	3	7
4096	1	1	−4096	6	14
8192	2	2	−8192	5	13
16384	4	4	−16384	3	11
32768	1	8	−32768	6	7

A product code with the check modulus $A \times B = 7 \times 15 = 105$ would similarly allow us to correct weight-1 errors via checking the divisibility of the codeword by 7 and 15 and noting the remainders. This is much less efficient, however, since the total word width must be limited to 12 bits for full error coverage. The largest representable number is thus $4095/105 = 39$. This is equivalent to about 5.3 bits of data, leading to a redundancy of 127%.

In general, a biresidue code with relatively prime low-cost check moduli $A = 2^a - 1$ and $B = 2^b - 1$ can support a data part of ab bits for weight-1 error correction with a representational redundancy of $(a+b)/(ab) = 1/a + 1/b$. Thus, with a choice of suitably large values for a and b, the redundancy can be kept low.

Based on our discussion of arithmetic error-detecting and error-correcting codes, we conclude that such codes are effective not only for protecting against fault-induced errors during arithmetic computations but also for dealing with storage and transmission errors. Using a single code throughout the system obviates the need for frequent encoding and decoding, and minimizes the chance of data corruption during the handling of unencoded data.

27.4 SELF-CHECKING FUNCTION UNITS

A self-checking function unit can be designed with or without encoded inputs and outputs. For example, if in Fig. 27.4, $x \bmod A$ and $y \bmod A$ are computed internally, as opposed to being supplied as inputs, a self-checking arithmetic unit with unencoded input/output is obtained.

The theory of self-checking logic design is quite well developed and can be used to implement highly reliable, or at least fail-safe, arithmetic units. The idea is to design the required logic circuits in such a way that any fault, from a prescribed set of faults which we wish to protect against, either does not affect the correctness of the outputs (is *masked*) or else leads to a non-codeword output (is made *observable*). In the latter case, the invalid result is either detected immediately by a code checker attached to the unit's output or else is propagated downstream by the next self-checking module that is required to produce a non-codeword output for any non-codeword input it receives (somewhat similar to computation with NaNs in floating-point arithmetic).

An important issue in the design of such self-checking units is the ability to build self-checking code checkers that are guaranteed not to validate a non-codeword despite internal faults. For example, a self-checking checker for an inverse residue code $(N, C'(N))$ might be designed as follows. First, $N \bmod A$ is computed. If the input is a valid codeword, this computed value must be the bitwise complement of $C'(N)$. We can view the process of verifying that $x_{b-1} \cdots x_1 x_0$ is the bitwise complement of $y_{b-1} \cdots y_1 y_0$ as that of ensuring that the signal pairs (x_i, y_i) are all (1, 0) or (0, 1). This amounts to computing the logical AND of a set of Boolean values that are represented using the following 2-bit encoding:

$$1 \quad \text{encoded as} \quad (1, 0) \text{ or } (0, 1)$$
$$0 \quad \text{encoded as} \quad (0, 0) \text{ or } (1, 1)$$

Note that the code checker produces two outputs that carry (1, 0) or (0, 1) if the input is correct and (0, 0) or (1, 1) if it is not. It is an easy matter to design the required AND circuit such that no single gate or line fault leads to a (1, 0) or (0, 1) output for a non-codeword input. For example, one can build an AND tree from the two-input AND circuit shown in Fig. 27.5. Note that any code checker that has only one output line cannot be self-checking, since a single stuck-at fault on its output line can produce a misleading result.

Fault detection can also be achieved by *result checking*. This is similar to what, in the field of software fault tolerance, is known as *acceptance testing*. An acceptance test is a (hopefully simple) verification process. For example, the correct functioning of a square-rooter can be verified by squaring each obtained root and comparing the result to the original radicand. If we assume that any error in the squaring process is independent from, and thus unlikely to compensate for, errors in the square-rooting process, a result that passes the verification test is correct with very high probability.

Acceptance tests do not have to be perfect. A test with *imperfect coverage* (e.g., comparing residues) may not detect each fault immediately after it occurs, but over time will signal a

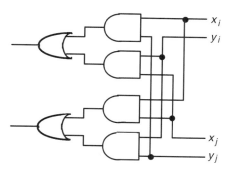

Fig. 27.5 Two-input AND circuit, with 2-bit inputs (x_i, y_i) and (x_j, y_j), for use in a self-checking code checker.

malfunctioning unit with high probability. On the other hand, if we assume that faults are permanent and occur very rarely, then periodic, as opposed to concurrent or on-line, verification might be adequate for fault detection. Such periodic checks might involve computing with several random operands and verifying the correctness of the results to make it less likely for compensating errors to render the fault undetectable [Blum96].

27.5 ALGORITHM-BASED FAULT TOLERANCE

So far, our focus has been on methods that allow us to detect and/or correct errors at the level of individual basic arithmetic operations such as addition and multiplication. An alternative strategy is to accept that arithmetic operations may yield incorrect results and build the mechanisms for detecting or correcting errors at the data structure or application level.

As an example of this approach, consider the multiplication of matrices X and Y yielding the result matrix P. The checksum of a list of numbers (a vector) is simply the algebraic sum of all the numbers modulo some check constant A. For any $m \times n$ matrix M, we define the row-checksum matrix M_r as an $m \times (n+1)$ matrix that is identical to M in its columns 0 through $n-1$ and has as its nth column the respective row checksums. Similarly, the column-checksum matrix M_c is an $(m+1) \times n$ matrix that is identical to M in its rows 0 through $m-1$ and has as its mth row the respective column checksums. The full-checksum matrix M_f is defined as the $(m+1) \times (n+1)$ matrix $(M_r)_c$: that is, the column-checksum matrix of the row-checksum matrix of M. Figure 27.6 shows a 3×3 matrix with its row, column, and full checksum matrices, where the checksums are computed modulo $A = 8$.

The following result allows us to detect and/or correct computation errors in matrix multiplication.

THEOREM 27.3   For matrices X, Y, and P satisfying $P = X \times Y$, we have $P_f = X_c \times Y_r$.

According to Theorem 27.3, we can perform standard matrix multiplication on the encoded matrices X_c and Y_r, and then compare the values in the last column and row of the product matrix to checksums that are computed based on the remaining elements to detect any error that may have occurred. If matrix elements are floating-point numbers, the equalities will hold

$$
M = \begin{bmatrix} 2 & 1 & 6 \\ 5 & 3 & 4 \\ 3 & 2 & 7 \end{bmatrix} \qquad
M_r = \begin{bmatrix} 2 & 1 & 6 & 1 \\ 5 & 3 & 4 & 4 \\ 3 & 2 & 7 & 4 \end{bmatrix}
$$

$$
M_c = \begin{bmatrix} 2 & 1 & 6 \\ 5 & 3 & 4 \\ 3 & 2 & 7 \\ 2 & 6 & 1 \end{bmatrix} \qquad
M_f = \begin{bmatrix} 2 & 1 & 6 & 1 \\ 5 & 3 & 4 & 4 \\ 3 & 2 & 7 & 4 \\ 2 & 6 & 1 & 1 \end{bmatrix}
$$

Fig. 27.6   A 3×3 matrix M with its row, column, and full checksum matrices M_r, M_c, and M_f.

approximately, leading to difficulties in selecting a suitable threshold for considering values equal. Some methods to resolve this problem are given in [Dutt96].

The full-checksum matrix M_f is an example of a *robust data structure* for which the following properties of error detection and correction hold.

THEOREM 27.4   In a full-checksum matrix, any single erroneous element can be corrected and any three erroneous elements can be detected.

Thus, for highly localized fault-induced errors (e.g., arising from a very brief transient fault in a hardware multiplier affecting no more than three elements of the product matrix), the preceding scheme allows for error correction or detection. Detection of more extensive errors, though not guaranteed, is quite likely; it would indeed be improbable for several errors to be compensatory in such a way that they escape detection by any of the checksums.

Designing such robust data structures with given capabilities of error detection and/or correction, such that they also lend themselves to direct manipulation by suitably modified arithmetic algorithms, is still an art. However, steady progress is being made in this area. For a review of algorithm-based fault tolerance methods, see [Vija97].

27.6 FAULT-TOLERANT RNS ARITHMETIC

Redundant encodings can be used with any number representation scheme to detect or correct errors. Residue number systems, in particular, allow very elegant and effective error detection and correction schemes through the use of redundant residues corresponding to extra moduli.

Suppose we choose the set of moduli in an RNS in such a way that one residue is redundant (i.e., if we remove any one modulus, the remaining moduli are adequate for the desired dynamic range). Then, any error that is confined to a single residue will be detectable, since such an error would make the affected residue inconsistent with the others. If this scheme is to work, the redundant modulus obviously must be the largest one (say m). The error detection scheme is thus as follows. Use all other residues to compute the residue of the number mod m. This is done by a process known as *base extension* for which many algorithms exist. Then compare the computed mod-m residue with the mod-m residue in the number representation to detect a possible error.

The beauty of this method is that arithmetic algorithms are totally unaffected; error detection is made possible by simply extending the dynamic range of the RNS. The base extension operation needed for error detection is frequently provided in an RNS processor for other reasons—for example, as a building block for synthesizing different RNS operations. In such a case, no additional hardware, beyond that required to handle the extra residue, is needed for error detection. In fact, it is possible to disable the error-checking capabilities and use the extended dynamic range offered by all the moduli when performing less critical computations.

Providing multiple redundant residues can lead to the detection of more errors and/or correction of certain error classes [Etze80] in a manner similar to the error-correction property of biresidue and multiresidue codes of Section 27.3. Again, the only new elements that are needed are the checking algorithms and the corresponding hardware structures. The arithmetic algorithms do not change.

As an example, consider adding the two redundant moduli 13 and 11 to the RNS with the four moduli 8, 7, 5, 3 (dynamic range = 840). In the resulting 6-modulus redundant RNS, the number 25 is represented as (12, 3, 1, 4, 0, 1). Now suppose that the mod-7 residue is corrupted and the number becomes (12, 3, 1, 6, 0, 1). Using base extension, we compute the two redundant residues from the other four residues; that is, we transform $(-, -, 1, 6, 0, 1)$ to $(5, 1, 1, 6, 0, 1)$. The difference between the first two components of the original corrupted number and the reconstructed number is $(+7, +2)$, which is the error syndrome that points to a particular residue in need of correction. We see that the error correction scheme here is quite similar to that shown in Table 27.1 for a biresidue code.

27.1   Voting on integer results One way to design the voter shown in Fig. 27.2 is to use a three-input majority circuit (identical in function to the carry-out of a full adder) and do serial bitwise voting on the outputs of the three ALUs. Assume that the ALU outputs are 8-bit unsigned integers.

a. Show that serial bitwise voting produces the correct voting result, given at most one faulty ALU.

b. What would the output of the bit-serial voter be if its inputs are 15, 19, and 38?

c. Present the design a bit-serial voter that can indicate the absence of majority agreement, should a situation similar to the one in part b arise.

27.2   Approximate voting Suppose that the three-input voter shown in Fig. 27.2 is to interpret its 32-bit unsigned inputs as fractional values that may contain small computational errors (possibly a different amount for each input).

a. Provide a suitable definition of majority agreement in this case.

b. Can a bit-serial voter, producing its output on the fly, be designed in accordance with the definition of part a?

c. Design a bit-serial median voter that outputs the middle value among its three imprecise inputs.

d. Under what conditions is the output of a median voter the same as that of a majority voter?

27.3   Design of comparators For the two-channel redundant arrangement of Fig. 27.2, discuss the design of bit-serial comparators for integer (exact) and fractional (approximate) results.

27.4   Arithmetic weight

a. Prove that any minimal-weight binary signed-digit (BSD) representation of a k-bit binary number has at most $\lceil (k+1)/2 \rceil$ nonzero digits and can always be written in *canonic BSD* form without any consecutive nonzero digits.

b. Show that the arithmetic weight of a binary number x is the same as the Hamming distance between the binary representations of x and $3x$.

27.5   Low-cost product codes

a. Prove Theorem 27.1 characterizing the unidirectional error-detecting power of low-cost product codes.

b. What fraction of random double-bit errors are detectable by a low-cost product code with $A = 2^a - 1$?

c. Can moduli of the form $A = 2^a + 1$ be included in low-cost product codes?

27.6   Low-cost residue codes

a. Prove Theorem 27.2, which characterizes the unidirectional error-detecting power of low-cost inverse residue codes.

b. What fraction of random double-bit errors is detectable by a low-cost residue code with the check modulus $A = 2^a - 1$?

c. Repeat part b for low-cost inverse residue codes.

d. Show how the computation of the modulo-$(2^a - 1)$ residue of a number can be speeded up by using a tree of carry-save adders rather than a tree of a-bit adders with end-around carries.

e. Apply your method of part d to the computation of the mod-15 residue of a 32-bit number and compare the result with respect to speed and cost to the alternative approach.

f. Suggest an efficient method for computing the modulo-17 residue of a 32-bit number and generalize it to the computation of mod-$(2^a + 1)$ residues.

27.7   Division with product-coded operands
Show that if q and s are the quotient and remainder in dividing z by d (i.e., $z = qd + s$) and $A = 2^a - 1$, then in dividing $A^2 z$ by Ad, the obtained quotient q^{**} can always be made equal to Aq by choosing the last radix-2^a digit of q^{**} in $[-2^a + 2, 1]$.

27.8   Low-cost biresidue codes

a. Characterize the error correction capability of a (7, 3) low-cost biresidue code.

b. If only error detection is required, how much more effective is the (7, 3) biresidue code compared to a single-residue code with the check modulus 7? Would you say that the additional redundancy due to the second check modulus 3 is worth its cost?

c. Propose a low-cost biresidue code that is capable of correcting all weight-1 arithmetic errors in data elements that are 32 bits wide.

27.9   Self-checking checkers

a. Verify that the AND circuit of Fig. 27.5 is an optimal implementation of the desired functionality. Note that the specification of the design has "coupled don't-cares": that is, one output of the AND circuit can be 0 or 1 provided that the other one is (not) equal to it.

b. Verify that the AND circuit of Fig. 27.5 is self-testing in the sense that both output combinations (0, 1) and (1, 0) appear during normal operation when there is no input error. Note that if a self-checking checker produces only the output (1, 0), say, during normal operation, some output stuck-at faults may go undetected.

c. Use the AND circuit of Fig. 27.5 to construct a self-checking circuit to check the validity of a 10-bit integer that has been encoded in the low-cost product code with the check modulus $A = 3$.

d. Design the OR-circuit and NOT-circuit (inverter) counterparts to the AND circuit of Fig. 27.5. Discuss whether these additional circuits could be useful in practice.

27.10 Self-checking function unit Present the complete design a self-checking additive multiply module (AMM) using the low-cost product code with $A = 3$. The two additive and two multiplicative inputs, originally 4-bit unsigned numbers, are presented in 6-bit encoded form, and the encoded output is 10 bits wide. Analyze the speed and cost overhead of your self-checking design.

27.11 Self-checking arithmetic circuits Consider the design of self-checking arithmetic circuits using two-rail encoding of the signals: 0 represented as (0, 1) and 1 as (1, 0), with (0, 0) and (1, 1) signaling an error.

a. Design a two-rail self-checking full-adder cell. *Hint:* Think of how two-rail AND, OR, and NOT elements might be built.

b. Using the design of an array multiplier as an example, compare the two-rail self-checking design approach to circuit duplication with comparison. Discuss.

27.12 Algorithm-based fault tolerance

a. Verify that the product of the matrices M_c and M_r of Fig. 27.6 yields the full checksum matrix $(M^2)_f$ if the additions corresponding to the checksum elements are performed modulo 8.

b. Prove Theorem 27.3 in general.

c. Construct an example showing that the presence of four erroneous elements in the full checksum matrix M_f can go undetected. Then, prove Theorem 27.4.

27.13 Algorithm-based fault tolerance Formulate an algorithm-based fault tolerance scheme for multiplying a matrix by a vector and discuss its error detection and correction characteristics.

27.14 Redundant RNS representations For the redundant RNS example presented at the end of Section 27.6 (original moduli 8, 7, 5, 3; redundant moduli 13, 11):

a. What is the redundancy with binary-encoded residues? How do you define the redundancy?

b. Construct a syndrome table similar to Table 27.1 for single-residue error correction.

c. Show that all double-residue errors are detectable.

d. Explain whether, and if so, how, one can detect double-residue errors and correct single-residue errors at the same time.

27.15 Redundant RNS representations

a. Prove or disprove: In an RNS having a range approximately equal to that of k-bit numbers, any single-residue error can be detected with $O(\log k)$ bits of redundancy.

b. Repeat part a for single-residue error correction.

27.16 BSD adder with parity checking Show how a binary signed-digit adder can be designed to always produce an output word with even parity. Discuss the fault tolerance capabilities of the resulting adder. *Hint*: If one of the three digit values in $[-1, 1]$ is assigned two 2-bit codes with odd and even parities, it is possible to encode pairs of output digits so that the resulting 4 bits have even parity [Thor97].

REFERENCES

[Aviz72]   Avizienis, A., "Arithmetic Error Codes: Cost and Effectiveness Studies for Application in Digital System Design," *IEEE Trans. Computers*, Vol. 20, No. 11, pp. 1322–1331, 1971.

[Aviz73]   Avizienis, A., "Algorithms for Error-Coded Operands," *IEEE Trans. Computers*, Vol. 22, No. 6, pp. 567–572, 1973.

[Blum96]   Blum, M., and H. Wasserman, "Reflections on the Pentium Division Bug," *IEEE Trans. Computers*, Vol. 45, No. 4, pp. 385–393, 1996.

[Dutt96]   Dutt, S., and F.T. Assaad, "Mantissa-Preserving Operations and Robust Algorithm-Based Fault Tolerance for Matrix Computations," *IEEE Trans. Computers*, Vol. 45, No. 4, pp. 408–424, 1996.

[Etze80]   Etzel, M.H., and W.K. Jenkins, "Redundant Residue Number Systems for Error Detection and Correction in Digital Filters," *IEEE Trans. Acoustics, Speech, and Signal Processing*, Vol. 28, No. 5, pp. 538–545, October 1980.

[Huan84]   Huang, K.H., and J.A. Abraham, "Algorithm-Based Fault Tolerance for Matrix Operations," *IEEE Trans. Computers*, Vol. 33, No. 6, pp. 518–528, 1984.

[Parh78]   Parhami, B., and A. Avizienis, "Detection of Storage Errors in Mass Memories Using Arithmetic Error Codes," *IEEE Trans. Computers*, Vol. 27, pp. 302–308, April 1978.

[Parh94]   Parhami, B., "A Multi-Level View of Dependable Computing," *Computers and Electrical Engineering*, Vol. 20, No. 4, pp. 347–368, 1994.

[Pete58]   Peterson, W.W., "On Checking an Adder," *IBM J. Research and Development*, Vol. 2, No. 2, pp. 166–168, April 1958.

[Pete59]   Peterson, W.W., and M.O. Rabin, "On Codes for Checking Logical Operations," *IBM J. Research and Development*, Vol. 3, No. 2, pp. 163–168, April 1959.

[Rao74]   Rao, T.R.N., *Error Codes for Arithmetic Processors*, Academic Press, 1974.

[Thor97]   Thornton, M.A., "Signed Binary Addition Circuitry with Inherent Even Parity Output," *IEEE Trans. Computers*, Vol. 46, No. 7, pp. 811–816, 1997.

[Vija97]   Vijay, M. and R. Mittal, "Algorithm-Based Fault Tolerance: A Review," *Microprocessors and Microsystems*, Vol. 21, pp. 151–161, 1997.

Chapter
28 PAST, PRESENT, AND FUTURE

In this last chapter, we present a few interesting and diverse case studies that show the applications of some of the algorithms and implementation techniques studied thus far in the context of computational requirements, technological constraints, and overall design goals. We also take a look backward and forward, both to provide some historical perspective and to gauge the current trends and future directions of computer arithmetic. Chapter topics include:

28.1 Historical Perspective
28.2 An Early High-Performance Machine
28.3 A Modern Vector Supercomputer
28.4 Digital Signal Processors
28.5 A Widely Used Microprocessor
28.6 Trends and Future Outlook

28.1 HISTORICAL PERSPECTIVE

The history of computer arithmetic is intertwined with that of digital computers. Much of this history can be traced through a collection of key papers [Swar90] in the field, some of which are not easily accessible in the original form. Certain ideas used in computer arithmetic have their origins in the age of mechanical calculators. In fact Charles Babbage is said to have been aware of ideas such as carry-skip addition, carry-save addition, and restoring division [Omon94].

In the 1940s, machine arithmetic was a crucial element in efforts to prove the feasibility of computing with stored-program electronic devices. Hardware mechanisms for addition, use of complement representation to facilitate subtraction, and implementation of multiplication and division through shift/add algorithms were developed and fine-tuned early on. A seminal report in the initial development of stored-program electronic digital computers by A. W. Burkes, H. H. Goldstein, and J. von Neumann [Burk46] contained interesting ideas on arithmetic algorithms and their hardware realizations, including choice of number representation radix, distribution of carry-propagation chains, fast multiplication via carry-save addition, and restoring division. The state of computer arithmetic circa 1950 is evident from an overview paper by R. F. Shaw [Shaw50].

Early stored-program digital computers were primarily number-crunching machines with limited storage and I/O capabilities. Thus, the bulk of design effort was necessarily expended on cost-effective realization of the instruction sequencing and arithmetic/logic functions. The 1950s brought about many important advances in computer arithmetic. With the questions of feasibility already settled, the focus now shifted to algorithmic speedup methods and cost-effective hardware realizations. By the end of the decade, virtually all important fast adder designs had already been published or were in the final phases of development. Similarly, the notions of residue arithmetic, SRT division, and CORDIC algorithms were all proposed and implemented in the 1950s. An overview paper by O.L. MacSorley [MacS61] contains a snapshot of the state of the art circa 1960.

Computer arithmetic advances continued in the 1960s with the introduction of tree multipliers, array multipliers, high-radix dividers, convergence division, redundant signed-digit arithmetic, and implementation of floating-point arithmetic operations in hardware or firmware (in microprogram). A by-product of microprogrammed control, which became prevalent for flexibility and economy of hardware implementations, was that greater arithmetic functionality could be incorporated into even the smallest processors by means of using standardized word widths across a whole range of machines with different computing powers.

Some of the most innovative ideas originated from the design of early supercomputers in the 1960s, when the demand for high performance, along with the still high cost of hardware, led designers to novel solutions that made high-speed machine arithmetic quite cost-effective. Striking examples of design ingenuity can be found in the arithmetic units of the IBM System/360 Model 91 [Ande67] and CDC 6600 [Thor70]. Other digital systems of the pre-IC era no doubt contained interesting design ideas, but the IBM and CDC systems were extensively documented in the open technical literature, making them excellent case studies. It is quite regrettable that today's designs are not described in the technical literature with the same degree of openness and detail. We briefly discuss the design of the floating-point execution unit of IBM System/360 Model 91 in Section 28.2. From this case study, we can deduce that the state of computer arithmetic was quite advanced in the mid-1960s.

As applications of computers expanded in scope and significance, faster algorithms and more compact implementations were sought to keep up with the demand for higher performance and lower cost. The 1970s are distinguished by the advent of microprocessors and vector supercomputers. Early LSI chips were quite limited in the number of transistors or logic gates they could accommodate; thus microprogrammed implementation was a natural choice for single-chip processors, which were not yet expected to offer high performance. At the high end of performance spectrum, pipelining methods were perfected to allow the throughput of arithmetic units to keep up with computational demand in vector supercomputers. In Section 28.3, we study the design of one such vector supercomputer, the Cray X-MP/Model 24.

Widespread application of VLSI circuits in the 1980s triggered a reconsideration of virtually all arithmetic designs in light of interconnection cost and pin limitations. For example, carry-lookahead adders, which appeared to be ill-suited to VLSI implementation, were shown to be efficiently realizable after suitable modifications. Similar ideas were applied to more efficient VLSI implementation of tree and array multipliers. Additionally, bit-serial and on-line arithmetic were advanced to deal with severe pin limitations in VLSI packages. This phase of the development of computer arithmetic was also guided by the demand to perform arithmetic-intensive signal processing functions using low-cost and/or high-performance embedded hardware. Examples of fixed- and floating-point processors for digital signal processing applications are provided in Section 28.4.

During the 1990s, computer arithmetic continued to mature. Despite the lack of any break-through design concept, both theoretical development and refinement of the designs continued at a rapid pace. The increasing demand for performance resulted in fine-tuning of arithmetic algorithms to take advantage of particular features of implementation technologies. Thus, we witnessed the emergence of a wide array of hybrid designs that combined features from one or more pure designs into a highly optimized arithmetic structure. Other trends included increasing use of table lookup and tight integration of arithmetic unit and other parts of the processor for maximum performance. As clock speeds reached and surpassed 100, 200, 300, 400, and 500 MHz in rapid succession, everything had to be (deeply) pipelined to ensure the smooth flow of data through the system. A modern example of such methods in the design of Intel's Pentium Pro (P6) microprocessor is discussed in Section 28.5.

28.2 AN EARLY HIGH-PERFORMANCE MACHINE

In this section, we review key design features of the floating-point arithmetic hardware of IBM System/360 Model 91, a supercomputer of the mid-1960s, which brought forth numerous architectural innovations. The technical paper on which this description is based [Ande67] is considered one of the key publications in the history of computer arithmetic. For an insightful retrospective on the Model 91, see [Flyn98].

The IBM System/360 Model 91 had two concurrently operating floating-point execution units (Fig. 28.1), each with a two-stage pipelined adder and a 12×56 pipelined multiplier, to meet the ambitious design goal of executing one floating-point instruction per 20-ns clock cycle on the average. The unit could handle 32-bit or 64-bit floating-point numbers with sign, 7-bit excess-64 base-16 exponent, and 24-bit or 56-bit normalized significand in [1/16, 1). Floating-point operands were supplied to the execution units from a number of buffers or registers. Within the execution units, a number of "reservation stations" (RS), each holding two operands, allowed effective utilization of hardware by ensuring that the next set of operands always was available when an arithmetic circuit was ready to accept it.

The Model 91 floating-point adder consisted of standard blocks such as exponent adder, preshifter, postshifter, and exponent adjuster, in addition to a 56-bit fraction adder. The fraction adder had a three-level carry-lookahead design with 4-bit groups and 8-bit sections. Thus, there were two groups per section and seven sections in the adder. Many clever design methods were used to speed up and simplify the adder. For example, the adder was designed to produce both the true sum and its 2's complement, one of which was then selected as the adder's output. This feature served to reduce the length of the adder's critical path; only the operand that was not preshifted could be complemented. This could force the computation of $y - x$ instead of the desired $x - y$, thus necessitating output complementation. As a result of various optimization and speedup techniques, a floating-add arithmetic operation could be executed in 2 clock cycles (or one add per cycle per floating-point unit with pipelining).

The Model 91 floating-point multiplier could multiply a 56-bit multiplicand by a 12-bit multiplier in one pass through its hardware tree of CSA adders, keeping the partial product in carry-save form, to be subsequently combined with the results from other 12-bit segments of the multiplier. Radix-4 Booth's recoding was used to form six multiples of the multiplicand to be added (thus, actually 13 bits of the multiplier were required in each step in view of the 1-bit overlap). The six multiples were reduced to two in a three-level CSA tree. Another two CSA levels were used to combine these two values with the shifted carry-save partial product from earlier steps. Pipelining allowed 12 multiplier bits to be processed in each clock cycle. The floating-point multiply took 6 clock cycles, or 120 ns, overall.

Floating-point division was performed by the Newton–Raphson convergence method using the hardware multiplier and a small amount of extra logic. An initial table lookup provided an approximate reciprocal of the divisor that led to 7 bits of convergence with a 12-bit multiplier. Three more steps of such short multiplications (requiring a single pass through the CSA tree) increased the convergence to 14, 23, and 28 bits. A final half-multiply, needing three passes through the CSA tree, completed the process. The pair of multiplications was pipelined in each step, with the result that floating-point divide took only 18 clock cycles. Early versions of the Model 91 floating-point unit sometimes yielded an incorrect least significant bit for the quotient. This problem, which had been due to inadequate analysis of the division convergence process, was corrected in subsequent versions.

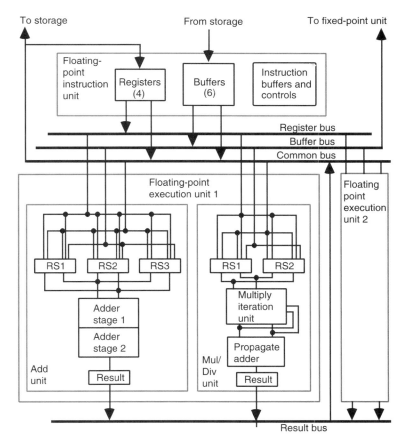

Fig. 28.1   Overall structure of the IBM System/360 Model 91 floating-point execution unit.

28.3 A MODERN VECTOR SUPERCOMPUTER

Modern supercomputers come in two varieties: vector multiprocessors consisting of a small number of powerful vector processors, and parallel computers using a moderate to very large ensemble of simpler processors.

Moderately parallel computers typically use off-the-shelf, high-performance microprocessors as their basic building blocks, while some massively parallel computers are based on very simple custom processors, perhaps with multiple processors on a single microchip. Since we discuss arithmetic in a modern microprocessor in Section 28.5, and since we have already covered an example of arithmetic in the simple bit-serial processors of the CM-2 massively parallel computer (Section 24.3), here we focus on the design of the Cray X-MP/Model 24 processor as an example of the former category [Robb89]. This machine has been superseded by the Y-MP, C-90, and various other Cray supercomputers, but it offers a good example for discussing the principles of high-performance vector processing, with the associated highly pipelined implementation of arithmetic operations and pipeline chaining.

The Cray X-MP/Model 24 consists of two identical CPUs sharing a main memory and an I/O subsystem. Most instructions can begin execution in a single 9.5-ns machine cycle and are capable of producing results on every machine cycle, given suitably long vector computations and appropriate data layout in memory to avoid memory bank conflicts. Each CPU has an address section, a scalar section, and a vector section, each with its own registers and functional units.

The address section is the simplest of the three sections. It uses an integer multiplier and an adder (four- and two-stage pipeline, respectively) for operating on, and computing, 24-bit memory addresses.

The scalar section has functional units for addition (three-stage pipeline), weight/parity/leading-0s determination (three- or four-stage), shifting (two-stage), and logical operations (one-stage). With very few exceptions, all arithmetic and logical operations deal with 64-bit integer or floating-point operands. Floating-point numbers have a sign bit, 15 exponent bits, and 48 significand bits (including an explicit 1 after the radix point).

The vector section is perhaps the most interesting and elaborate part of the processor, and we focus on it in the remainder of this section. Figure 28.2 is a block diagram of the Cray X-MP's vector section. There are eight sets of 64-element vector registers that are used to supply operands to, and accept results from, the functional units. These allow the required vectors or vector segments to be prefetched, and the vector results stored back in memory, concurrently with arithmetic/logic operations on other vectors or vector segments. In fact, intermediate computation results do not need to be stored in a register before further processing. A method known as *pipeline chaining* allows the output of one pipeline (e.g., multiplier) to be forwarded to another (say, adder) if a vector computation such as $(A[i] \times B[i]) + C[i]$ is to be performed.

Vector computations need 3 clock cycles for their *setup*, which includes preparing the appropriate functional units and establishing paths from/to source and destination registers to them. At the end of a vector computation, 3 more clock cycles are needed for *shutdown* before the results in the destination vector register can be used in other operations. This type of pipelining overhead, which becomes insignificant when one is dealing with long vectors, is the main reason for vector machines having a "break-even" vector length (i.e., a length beyond which vector arithmetic is faster than scalar arithmetic performed in a program loop).

Once a vector computation has been set up, a pair of elements enters the first stage of the pipeline on every clock cycle and the partial results for the preceding pairs move one stage forward in the pipeline. Figure 28.2 lists the number σ of pipeline stages for various operations.

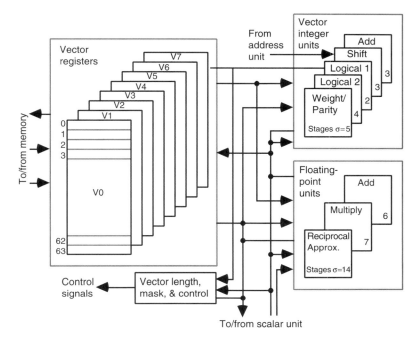

Fig. 28.2   The vector section of one of the processors in the Cray X-MP/Model 24 supercomputer.

The output of a σ-stage pipelined unit becomes available for chaining after $\sigma + 5$ clock cycles. Such a unit needs $\lambda + \sigma + 5$ clock cycles to operate on a λ-element vector. However, the functional unit is freed for the next vector operation after $\lambda + 4$ cycles.

28.4 DIGITAL SIGNAL PROCESSORS

Many digital signal processing (DSP) applications are arithmetic-intensive and cost-sensitive, thus requiring innovative solutions for cost-effective implementation. A digital signal processor (also abbreviated as DSP), can be a special-purpose or a general-purpose unit. Special-purpose DSPs have been designed in a variety of ways, using conventional or unconventional (RNS, logarithmic) number representations. It is impossible to review all these approaches here [Sode86], [Jull94]. We thus focus on the design of typical general-purpose DSP chips.

General-purpose DSPs are available as standard components from several microchip manufacturers. They come in two varieties: fixed point and floating point. Integer DSP chips are simpler and thus both faster and less expensive. They are used whenever the application deals with numerical values in limited and well-defined ranges so that scaling can be done with acceptable overhead (e.g., in simple voice processing). The payoff then is faster processing or higher accuracy. When the range of numerical values is highly variable or unpredictable, or the data rate is too high to allow the use of lengthy scaling computations, built-in floating-point arithmetic capability becomes mandatory (e.g., in multimedia workstations).

Motorola's DSP56002 chip is a 24-bit fixed-point DSP [ElSh96]. It deals with 24-bit and 48-bit signed fractions and internally uses a 56-bit format consisting of 9 whole bits, including the sign, and 47 fractional bits. As shown in Fig. 28.3, there are four 24-bit input registers that can also be used as two 48-bit registers. Similarly, the two 56-bit accumulator registers can be viewed as four 24-bit and two 8-bit registers. Arithmetic/logic operations are performed on up to three operands, with the 56-bit result always stored in an accumulator. Example instructions include the following:

$$
\begin{array}{lll}
\text{ADD} & \text{A, B} & \{A + B \rightarrow B\} \\
\text{SUB} & \text{X, A} & \{A - X \rightarrow A\} \\
\text{MPY} & \pm\text{X1, X0, B} & \{\pm X1 \times X0 \rightarrow B\} \\
\text{MAC} & \pm \text{Y1, X1, A} & \{A \pm (Y1 \times X1) \rightarrow A\} \\
\text{AND} & \text{X1, A} & \{A \text{ AND } X1 \rightarrow A\}
\end{array}
$$

The ALU can round the least significant half (A0 or B0) into the most significant half (A1 or B1) of each accumulator. So, for example, an MPY or MAC instruction can be executed with or without rounding, leading to a 24- or 48-bit result in an accumulator.

The 56-bit shifter can shift left or right by 1 bit or pass the data through unshifted. The two data shifters, associated with the A and B accumulators, take 56-bit inputs and produce 24-bit

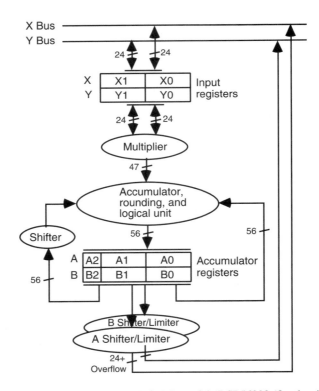

Fig. 28.3   Block diagram of the data ALU in Motorola's DSP56002 (fixed-point) processor.

outputs, each with an "overflow" bit. One-bit left or right shift is possible for scaling purposes. The data limiter causes the largest value of the same sign to be output when the (shifted) 56-bit data is not representable in 24 bits.

There are also a variety of data movement, bit manipulation, and flow control instructions, as in any other processor. Details of the instruction set and programming considerations for Motorola's DSP56002 processor, along with example applications in filter implementation and fast Fourier transform, have been published [ElSh96].

As an example of a floating-point DSP chip, we briefly review Motorola's DSP96002, which has many features of a 32-bit general-purpose processor along with enhancement for DSP applications [Sohi88]. Multiple DSP96002 chips can share a bus and communicate directly with each other in a parallel configuration with very high performance.

DSP96002 implements the IEEE single-precision (32-bit) and single-extended-precision $(1 + 11 + 32 = 44$ bits, no hidden bit) floating-point arithmetic. An internal 96-bit format (sign, 20 bits of special tags, 11-bit exponent, 64-bit significand) is used to minimize error accumulation.

The data ALU (Fig. 28.4), so named to distinguish it from address computation units, supports IEEE floating-point arithmetic in a single instruction cycle or 2 clock cycles. The full instruction actually takes 3 instruction (or 6 clock) cycles to finish but is executed in a three-stage (fetch, decode, execute) pipeline that can accept a new instruction in every cycle.

The floating-point add/subtract unit calculates both the sum and the difference of its two inputs, with one or both results stored in the register file in the same cycle. The add/subtract unit is also used for integer arithmetic, a variety of data type conversions, and multibit shift operations (taking advantage of its barrel shifter). The floating-point multiply unit contains a 32×32 hardware multiplier, thus supporting both 32-bit signed/unsigned integer multiplication and single-extended-precision floating-point multiplication (with 32-bit significands) in one cycle. A full 64-bit product is produced.

Finally, the special function unit implements division, square-rooting, and logical operations. Division and square-rooting require multiple instructions, beginning with a special instruction to generate a reciprocal (root) seed and continuing with a convergence computation.

DSP96002 accepts, and properly handles, denormalized numbers, but requires one additional machine cycle to process each denormalized source operand or denormalized result. A

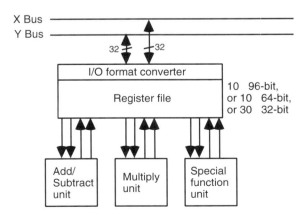

Fig. 28.4   Block diagram of the data ALU in Motorola's DSP96002 (floating-point) processor.

"flush-to-zero" underflow mode can be optionally selected to force denormalized numbers to 0, thus avoiding the possible extra cycles and making the execution timing completely data-independent.

28.5 A WIDELY USED MICROPROCESSOR

Older microprocessors contained an ALU for integer arithmetic within the basic CPU chip and an optional floating-point coprocessor on a separate chip. Recently, increasing VLSI circuit density has led to the trend of integrating both units on a single microchip, while still leaving enough space for large on-chip cache memories for data and instructions.

As an example, we describe a member of the Intel's Pentium family of microprocessors: the Intel Pentium Pro, also known as Intel P6. The primary design goal for the Intel P6 was to achieve the highest possible performance, while keeping the external appearances compatible with the Pentium and using the same mass-production technology [Shan98]. Intel's Pentium II is essentially a Pentium Pro, complemented with a set of multimedia instructions.

The Intel P6 has a 32-bit architecture, internally using a 64-bit data bus, 36-bit addresses, and an 80-bit floating-point format (sign, 15-bit exponent field, 64-bit significand). In the terminology of modern microprocessors, P6 is superscalar and superpipelined: superscalar because it can execute multiple independent instructions concurrently in its many functional units, as opposed to the Cray machine of Section 28.3, which has concurrent execution only for vector operations; superpipelined because its instruction execution pipeline with 14^+ stages is very deep. The design of the Intel P6, which was initially based on a 150- to 200-MHz clock, has 21M transistors, roughly a quarter of which are for the CPU and the rest for the on-chip cache memory. The Intel P6 is also capable of glueless multiprocessing with up to four processors.

Figure 28.5 shows parts of the CPU that are relevant to our discussion. Since high performance in the Intel P6 is gained by out-of-order and speculative instruction execution, a key component in the design is a reservation station that is essentially a hardware-level scheduler of micro-operations. Each instruction is converted to one or more micro-operations, which are then executed in arbitrary order whenever their required operands are available.

The result of a micro-operation is sent to both the reservation station and a special unit called the reorder buffer. This latter unit is responsible for making sure that program execution remains consistent by committing the results of micro-operations to the machine's "retirement" registers only after all pieces of an instruction have terminated and the instruction's "turn" to execute has arrived within the sequential program flow. Thus, if an interrupt occurs, all operations that are in progress can be discarded without causing inconsistency in the machine's state. There is a full crossbar between all five ports of the reservation station so that any returning result can be forwarded directly to any other unit for the next clock cycle.

Fetching, decoding, and setting up the components of an instruction in the reservation station takes 8 clock cycles and is performed as an eight-stage pipelined operation. The retirement process, mentioned above, takes 3 clock cycles and is also pipelined. Sandwiched between the preceding two pipelines is a variable-length pipeline for instruction execution. For this middle part of instruction execution, the reservation station needs 2 cycles to ascertain that the operands are available and to schedule the micro-operation on an appropriate unit. The operation itself takes one cycle for register-to-register integer add and longer for more complex functions. Because of the multiplicity of functional units with different latencies, out-of-order and speculative execution (e.g., branch prediction) are crucial to high performance.

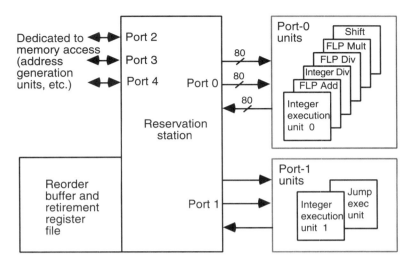

Fig. 28.5   Key parts of the CPU in the Intel Pentium Pro (P6) microprocessor.

In a sense, the deep pipelining of instruction execution in the Intel P6 makes the performance less sensitive to the arithmetic algorithms and circuits. Indeed, the bulk of hardware in the P6 is devoted to the management of pipelining and out-of-order instruction execution rather than to arithmetic circuits.

28.6 TRENDS AND FUTURE OUTLOOK

Arithmetic designs are evolving as a result of changes in the underlying technology. The move from small-scale integration through medium- and large-scale integration to VLSI has gradually shifted the emphasis from reducing the number of gates and gate levels in arithmetic circuits to considering the overall design in terms of both computational elements and interconnections. Increasing densities have also led to concerns about adequate input/output bandwidth, clock and power distribution, heat dissipation, and testability. Design challenges will no doubt continue to emerge as we deal with even newer technologies and application requirements (fully distributed micropipelines, subnanosecond arithmetic, low-power design, the quest for petaFLOPS, etc.).

Today, designs for arithmetic circuits are developed not by analyzing an elegant algorithm and optimizing its various parameters, but rather by getting down to the level of transistors and wires. This explains the proliferation of hybrid designs that use two or more distinct paradigms (e.g., fast adders using Manchester carry chains along with carry-lookahead and carry-select structures) to obtain the best designs for given cost–performance requirements.

Concurrent with developments in the VLSI technology, changing application characteristics have dictated a shift of focus in computer arithmetic from high-speed or high-throughput designs in mainframe computers to low-cost and low-power designs for embedded and mobile applications. These have in turn led to renewed interest in bit- and digit-serial arithmetic as mechanisms to reduce the VLSI area and to improve packageability and testability. High-performance designs requiring lookahead and speculative execution are expensive and often at odds with the goal of reducing power consumption to extend the battery life and/or simplify heat dissipation. Many challenging problems are being addressed in these areas.

The desirability of synchronous versus asynchronous design is also being reexamined. Thus far, synchronous circuits have prevailed in view of their ease of design, tractability of analysis, and predictability of performance. A secondary, but still important, drawback of asynchronous design is the overhead in time and area for the required handshaking circuits that regulate the flow of data between circuit segments. However, the higher speeds and packaging densities of modern digital circuits are stretching the limits of our ability to distribute the clock signal to all the required points [Frie99]. Also, signal propagation delays over long wires are forcing the designers to modularize the design (e.g., via systolic arrays), thus in some cases introducing an overhead that is comparable to that of handshaking for asynchronous operation. Novel design paradigms and improved tools for the synthesis and analysis of asynchronous systems are slowly changing the balance in favor of the latter [Hauc95]. For example, low-level pipelining methods (micropipelines), perhaps extending all the way down to the logic gate level, are thought to hold promise for the arithmetic circuits of the future.

Fundamentally new technologies and design paradigms may alter the way in which we view or design arithmetic circuits. Just as the availability of cheap, high-density memories brought table-lookup methods to the forefront, certain computational elements being developed in connection with artificial neural networks may revolutionize our approach to arithmetic algorithms. As an example, imagine the deep changes that would ensue if an artificial neuron capable of summing several weighted inputs and comparing the result to a fixed threshold could be built from a few transistors. Such a cell would be considerably more powerful than a switch or standard logic gate, thus leading to new designs for arithmetic functions [Vass96]. As a second example, researchers in the field of optical computing, eager to take full advantage of parallel operations made possible by the absence of pin limitations, have paid significant attention to redundant number representations. Yet another example is found in the field of multivalued logic, which has an inherent bias toward high-radix arithmetic.

On the theoretical front, studies in arithmetic complexity [Pipp87] have been instrumental in broadening our understanding of algorithmic speedup methods. Any n-variable Boolean function that is actually dependent on all n variables (say, the most significant output bit of an $n/2 \times n/2$ unsigned multiplier) requires a gate count or circuit complexity of at least $\Omega(n)$ and a delay or circuit depth of $\Omega(\log n)$. On the other hand, any Boolean function can be realized by a size-$(2^n - 1)$, depth-n, complete binary tree of 2-to-1 multiplexers by using the Shannon expansion

$$f(x_1, x_2, \cdots, x_n) = x_1 \, f(1, x_2, \cdots, x_n) + \overline{x}_1 \, f(0, x_2, \cdots, x_n)$$

for each variable in turn. Key questions in arithmetic complexity thus deal with the determination of where in the wide spectrum of $\Omega(n)$ to $O(2^n)$ circuit complexity, and $\Omega(\log n)$ to $O(n)$ circuit depth, practical implementations of the various arithmetic functions may lie, and what can be achieved in terms of cost (delay) if we restrict the design, say, to having logarithmic delay (linear, or polynomial, cost).

For example, we know in the case of addition/subtraction that the bounds $O(n)$ on cost and $O(\log n)$ on delay are achievable simultaneously by means of certain carry-lookahead adder designs, say. For multiplication, we can achieve $O(\log n)$ delay with $O(n \log n \log \log n)$ cost in theory, though practical designs for small word widths have logarithmic delay with $O(n^2)$ cost. Logarithmic-depth circuits for division are now known, but they are much more complex than logarithmic-depth multipliers. Note that a logarithmic-depth multiplier is capable of performing division in $O(\log^2 n)$ time when a convergence method is used.

Many innovations have appeared in computer arithmetic since the early days of electronic computers [Burk46]. The emergence of new technologies and the unwavering quest for higher performance are bound to create new challenges in the coming years. These will include completely new challenges, as well as novel or transformed versions of the ones discussed in the preceding paragraphs. Computer arithmetic designers, who helped make digital computers into indispensable tools in the five decades since the introduction of the stored-program concept, will thus have a significant role to play in making them even more useful and ubiquitous as the second half-century of digital computing unfolds.

PROBLEMS

28.1   Historical perspective Using the discussion in Section 28.1 as a basis, and consulting additional references as needed, draw a time line that shows significant events in the development of digital computer arithmetic. On your time line, identify what you consider to be the three most significant ideas or events related to the topics discussed in each of the Parts I to IV of this book. Briefly justify your choices. Include floating-point numbers and arithmetic in your discussion (i.e., floating-point representation in Part I, floating-point addition in Part II, etc.).

28.2   Arithmetic before electronic digital computers

    a.   Study the implementation of arithmetic operations on mechanical calculators and other machines that preceded electronic computers. Prepare a report (including a time line) discussing the developments of key ideas and various implementations.

    b.   Repeat part a for electronic analog computers. Compare the ideas and methods to those of digital arithmetic and discuss.

28.3   IBM System/360 Model 91

    a.   Based on the description in Section 28.2 and what you learned about convergence division in Chapter 16, determine the size of the lookup table providing the initial approximation to the divisor reciprocal in the IBM System/360 Model 91.

    b.   Estimate, using back-of-the-envelope calculations, the MFLOPS computational power of the IBM System/360 Model 91. Assume complete overlap between instruction preparation and execution. Use an instruction mix of 60% add, 30% multiply, and 10% divide.

    c.   Study the integer arithmetic capabilities of the IBM System/360 Model 91.

28.4   The CDC 6600 computer Prepare a description of the arithmetic capabilities of CDC 6600 in a manner similar to the discussion of the IBM System/360 Model 91 in Section 28.2. Stress similarities and key differences between the two systems.

28.5   Cray X-MP/Model 24 A polynomial $f(x)$ of degree $n - 1$ (n coefficients, stored in a vector register) is to be evaluated using Horner's rule for n different values of x (available in a second vector register). The n results are to be left in a third vector register. Estimate the number of cycles needed for this computation on the CRAY X-MP/Model 24 with pipeline chaining. What is the machine's MFLOPS rating for this computation?

28.6   Floating-point representation formats The IBM System 360 Model 91 did not use the IEEE standard floating-point format because its design preceded the standard. Until recently, Cray machines did not use the standard either, mainly for performance and program compatibility reasons. Compare these two nonstandard floating-point formats to the IEEE standard format and discuss difficulties that might arise in porting programs among the three floating-point implementations.

28.7 Digital filtering on a fixed-point DSP

a. A median filter operates on a black-and-white digital image and replaces each pixel value (representing the gray level) with the median of nine values in the pixel itself and in the eight horizontally, vertically, and diagonally adjacent pixels. Estimate the number of cycles for median filtering of a 1024×1024 image using the Motorola DSP56002 fixed-point signal processor, assuming that control is completely overlapped with computation.

b. Repeat part a for a mean filter.

28.8 Polynomial evaluation on a floating-point DSP A degree-$(n - 1)$ polynomial $f(x)$ is to be evaluated using Horner's rule for n values of x. Using reasonable assumptions as needed, estimate the execution time of this problem on the Motorola DSP96002 floating-point signal processor. Discuss the cost-effectiveness of this solution compared to a vector supercomputer applied to the same problem.

28.9 A high-performance DSP Recent DSP products announced by Texas Instruments and other suppliers have much greater computational capabilities than those studied in Section 28.4. Pick one such system and describe its arithmetic capabilities and performance relative to the corresponding DSP chip (fixed- or floating-point) described in Section 28.4.

28.10 Higher than peak performance The peak MFLOPS performance of a processor is usually determined based on the speed of floating-point addition. For example, if one floating-point addition can be initiated in every 5-ns clock cycle, the peak performance is considered to be 200 MFLOPS.

a. Show that the Motorola DSP96002 floating-point signal processor can exceed its peak performance for certain problems.

b. Show that a similar effect is possible when arithmetic is performed bit-serially.

28.11 CISC versus RISC microprocessors The Intel Pentium Pro (P6) microprocessor is an example of the class of complex instruction set computers (CISCs). Most modern microprocessors belong to the complementary class of reduced instruction set computers (RISCs). Choose one example of this latter class and contrast it to the Intel P6 with regard to the implementation of arithmetic functions The MIPS R10000 is a particularly good example and has been described in some detail in [Yeag96].

28.12 The Alpha microprocessor The Alpha microprocessor of Digital Equipment Corporation (now part of Compaq) is among the fastest processors available today. Study arithmetic in Alpha and compare it to the Intel P6.

28.13 Role of arithmetic in microprocessor performance Pick a microprocessor with which you are most familiar and/or have ready access to the relevant technical information. Estimate the percentage of instruction cycle time taken up by arithmetic operations. Include in this figure arithmetic operations performed for address calculations and other bookkeeping tasks. When arithmetic is fully overlapped with nonarithmetic functions, divide the time equally between the two.

28.14 Multiprecision arithmetic on microprocessors We would like to design a set of routines for operating on multiprecision unsigned integers that are represented by variable-length vectors. The 0th element of the vector is the length of the number in k-bit words (e.g., 3 means that the number is $3k$ bits long and is represented in three k-bit chunks following the 0th vector element, MSB first).

    a. Express the length of the numbers resulting from addition, multiplication, and division of two numbers, having the length field values of m and n, respectively.

    b. Design an algorithm for performing multiprecision add from the most significant end. One way to do this is to store temporary sum digits and then go back and correct them if a carry is produced that affects them. Write the algorithm in such a way that only final sum digit values are written. *Hint:* The value of a digit can be finalized when the next position sum is not $2^k - 1$. So, you need only keep a count of how many such positions appear in a row.

    c. Compare the performance of two microprocessors of your choosing in running the multiprecision addition algorithm of part b.

    d. It is sometimes necessary to multiply or divide a multiprecision number by a regular (single-precision) number. Provide complete algorithms for this purpose.

    e. Repeat part c for the computations defined in part d.

28.15 Synchronous versus asynchronous design Study synchronous and asynchronous adder designs with regard to speed, hardware implementation cost, and power requirement [Kinn96].

28.16 Neuronlike hardware elements Consider the availability of a very simple neuronlike element with three binary inputs and one binary output. During the manufacturing of the element, each input can be given an arbitrary integer weight in [1, 3] and the element can be given an arbitrary threshold in [1, 9]. The output will be 1 if the weighted sum of the inputs equals or exceeds the threshold. Synthesize a single-bit full adder using these elements.

REFERENCES

[Ande67] Anderson, S.F., J.G. Earle, R.E. Goldschmidt, and D.M. Powers, "The IBM System/360 Model 91: Floating-Point Execution Unit," *IBM J. Research and Development*, Vol. 11, No. 1, pp. 34–53, 1967.

[Burk46] Burkes, A.W., H.H. Goldstine, and J. von Neumann, "Preliminary Discussion of the Logical Design of an Electronic Computing Instrument," Institute for Advanced Study Report, Princeton, NJ, 1946.

[ElSh96] El-Sharkawy, M., *Digital Signal Processing Applications with Motorola's DSP56002 Processor*, Prentice-Hall, 1996.

[Flyn98] Flynn, M. J., "Computer Engineering 30 Years After the IBM Model 91," *IEEE Computer*, Vol. 31, No. 4, pp. 27–31, 1998.

[Frie99] Friedman, E.G., "Clock Distribution in Synchronous Systems," in *Wiley Encyclopedia of Electrical and Electronics Engineering*, Vol. 3, pp. 474–497, 1999.

[Hauc95] Hauck, S., "Asynchronous Design Methodologies," *Proc. IEEE*, Vol. 83, No. 1, pp. 67–93, 1995.

[Jull94] Jullien, G.A., "High Performance Arithmetic for DSP Systems," in *VLSI Signal Processing Technology*, ed. by M.A. Bayoumi and E.E. Swartzlander, Jr. (eds.), Kluwer, 1994, pp. 59–96.

[Kinn96] Kinniment, D.J., "An Evaluation of Asynchronous Addition," *IEEE Trans. Very Large Scale Integration Systems*, Vol. 4, No. 1, pp. 137–140, March 1996.

[Lind96] Linder, D.H., and J.C. Harden, "Phased Logic: Supporting the Synchronous Design Paradigm with Delay-Insensitive Circuitry," *IEEE Trans. Computers*, Vol. 45, No. 9, pp. 1031–1044, 1996.

[MacS61] MacSorley, O.L., "High-Speed Arithmetic in Binary Computers," *IRE Proc.*, Vol. 49, pp. 67–91, 1961. Reprinted in [Swar90], Vol. 1, pp. 14–38.

[Omon94] Omondi, A.R., *Computer Arithmetic Systems: Algorithms, Architecture and Implementation*, Prentice-Hall, 1994.

[Pipp87] Pippenger, N., "The Complexity of Computations by Networks," *IBM J. Research and Development*, Vol. 31, No. 2, pp. 235–243, March 1987.

[Robb89] Robbins, K.A., and S. Robbins, *The Cray X-MP/Model 24: A Case Study in Pipelined Architecture and Vector Processing*, Springer-Verlag, 1989.

[Shan98] Shanley, T., *Pentium Pro and Pentium II System Architecture*, 2nd ed., MindShare, 1998.

[Shaw50] Shaw, R.F., "Arithmetic Operations in a Binary Computer," *Rev. Scientific Instruments*, Vol. 21, pp. 687–693, 1950. Reprinted in [Swar90], Vol. 1, pp. 7–13.

[Sode86] Soderstrand, M.A., W.K. Jenkins, G.A. Jullien, and F.J. Taylor (eds.), *Residue Number System Arithmetic*, IEEE Press, 1986.

[Sohi88] Sohie, G.R.L., and K.L. Kloker, "A Digital Signal Processor with IEEE Floating-Point Arithmetic," *IEEE Micro*, Vol. 8, No. 6, pp. 49–67, December 1988.

[Swar90] Swartzlander, E.E., Jr., *Computer Arithmetic*, Vols. 1 and 2, IEEE Computer Society Press, 1990.

[Thor70] Thornton, J.E., *Design of a Computer: The Control Data 6600*, Scott, Foresman, & Co., 1970.

[Vass96] Vassiliadis, S., S. Cotofana, and K. Bertels, "2-1 Addition and Related Arithmetic Operations with Threshold Logic," *IEEE Trans. Computers*, Vol. 45, No. 9, pp. 1062–1067, 1996.

[Yeag96] Yeager, K.C., "The MIPS R10000 Superscalar Microprocessor," *IEEE Micro*, Vol. 16, No. 2, pp. 28–40, April 1996.

INDEX